A Historical Guide to World Slavery

A Historical Guide
to
World Slavery

Edited by

Seymour Drescher and Stanley L. Engerman

OXFORD UNIVERSITY PRESS

New York   1998   Oxford

OXFORD UNIVERSITY PRESS

Oxford   New York
Athens   Auckland   Bangkok   Bogotá   Bombay
Buenos Aires   Calcutta   Cape Town   Dar es Salaam
Delhi   Florence   Hong Kong   Istanbul   Karachi
Kuala Lumpur   Madras   Madrid   Melbourne
Mexico City   Nairobi   Paris   Singapore
Taipei   Tokyo   Toronto   Warsaw

and associated companies in
Berlin   Ibadan

Published by Oxford University Press, Inc.,
198 Madison Avenue, New York, New York 10016

Oxford is a registered trademark of Oxford University Press

Library of Congress Cataloging-in-Publication Data
A historical guide to world slavery / edited by Seymour Drescher
and Stanley L. Engerman
p.   cm.
Includes bibliographical references and index.
1. Slavery—History.   2. Slavery—Cross-cultural studies.
3. Antislavery movement—History.   I. Drescher, Seymour.
II. Engerman, Stanley L.
HT861.H59   1998   306.3'62—dc21   97-47659 CIP
ISBN 0-19-512091-4

Printing (last digit): 9 8 7 6 5 4 3 2 1

Printed in the United States of America
on acid-free paper

Contents

Preface

NO ONE FAMILIAR WITH THE RECENT PUBLIC DISCUSSIONS, COMMEMORATIONS, and educational debates concerning slavery would be surprised at the late Moses I. Finley's observation that "the volume and polemical ferocity of work on the history of slavery are striking features of contemporary historiography" (*Ancient Slavery and Modern Ideology*, 1980, p. 11). During the past thirty years there has been a virtual explosion of empirical research and theoretical discussion of slavery and its abolition. The scholarship of slavery has, however, moved beyond narrow polemical disputes as historians and social scientists have increasingly brought the subject into a worldwide and cross-cultural focus. Slavery and related forms of dependence and subordination were found in human societies throughout the world; as a result, systematic studies of slavery on every continent and ocean archipelago are a part of current historiography, and scholars now routinely incorporate into their analyses empirical findings and theoretical constructs from times and places distant from their areas of study. The rapid expansion of information about particular regions and systems, as well as the acknowledged utility of a comparative frame of reference, provide the rationale for this historical guide.

For those seeking to find their way through this burgeoning field of scholarship, the articles that make up this volume will provide both an accessible overview of the complexities of the subject and an excellent point of departure for further inquiry. Our conceptual organization throughout the subsequent pages addresses the dual concern for global geographic and generic topical coverage. Following the introductory essay by David Brion Davis, the contributors focus on regional approaches and perspectives, as well as the structures, processes, institutions, and concepts that have gained acceptance as distinguishing features of contemporary historiography. Particular emphasis is given to those regions in which slavery predominated either as a social formation or in the organization of production. The range of topics covered includes many whose original designations, such as the "Middle Passage," would have been quite familiar to those who lived at the height of their operation, but whose nature and dynamics are placed in new contexts by current scholarship. Other subjects would have been beyond the imagination, much less the articulation, of contemporary observers. The primary objective of the contributors is thus to explore patterns of relationships and production, or to elucidate long-term changes and cumulative effects. This focus reflects our wish to emphasize the impact of mass cumulative social processes and unintended consequences rather than individual events or persons.

With the assistance of our editorial advisers, we have selected those scholars we believe to be the best qualified to write about particular topics, and have made no attempt to impose a uniformity of analysis or interpretation. That there may be some differing views among the assembled authors should not be surprising; the historiography of slavery and abolition consists not only of regional and topical discussions but of shifting interpretations. Certain scholarly paradigms have changed dramatically during the past thirty years, often without the awareness of the educated public. A number of extended entries are devoted to those aspects of the historiography of slavery, the slave trade, and abolition that have been particularly dynamic and innovative. The volume's scope and focus thus attempt to faithfully reflect the scholarly attention accorded to major subjects and issues in the field, and to offer sufficient references and resources so that the interested reader may quickly discover the state of the topic in question, from classic interpretations and basic documents to the latest important works. Suggestions for further reading are intended to complement the annual summary bibliography published in each December issue of the journal *Slavery and Abolition,* many of which have been further compiled in Joseph C. Miller's *Slavery and Slaving in World History: A Bibliography, 1900–1991* (1993).

The editors wish to acknowledge the efforts of the many contributors to this volume. Without their enthusiastic participation our imagined global community of scholarship would have been impossible to achieve. Foremost among them are the members of our advisory committee: Frederick Cooper, David Eltis, Ruth Mazo Karras, Colin Palmer, and Anthony Reid. Lesa A. Gresh and Patricia A. Zogran offered indispensable coordination with the contributors and kept the operation moving through its various phases. We are also indebted to three graduate students at the History Department of the University of Pittsburgh—Marguerite Brown, Erik Zissu, and Molly Abraham—for their talents as research assistants and copyeditors as well as their word processing skills. Special thanks are also due to Garland Publishing for suggesting the project to us, and to David Brion Davis for suggesting us to them. In the final preparation of this volume we benefited from the considerable expertise of Claude Conyers, Mark Mones, and Jeffrey Edelstein of the Scholarly and Professional Reference Department of Oxford University Press.

—Seymour Drescher and Stanley L. Engerman
October 1997

Introduction:
The Problem of Slavery

DAVID BRION DAVIS

AS EVEN ARISTOTLE ACKNOWLEDGED, CHATTEL SLAVERY IS DIFFERENT FROM other varieties of servitude. More than thirteen centuries before Aristotle, the Hammurabi Code in Babylonia defined a concept of chattel slavery that served as a way of classifying the lowliest and most dependent workers in society. Among the salient features of this legal and philosophical status was the fact that once they were owned, slaves could be sold or inherited; the same features would reappear through the ages in scores of cultures.

In the ancient Near East, as in Asia, Europe, Africa, and the preconquest Americas, various forms of slavery and servitude almost certainly emerged long before they were systematized by laws or legal codes. Such laws and codes, however, encouraged the wielders of power to make the actual condition of servitude conform as much as possible to a model of hereditary dishonor and powerlessness— much as wielders of power promoted the opposite ideal model of hereditary kingship.

As historians have carefully examined specific slave systems, they have often expressed surprise over the privileges and even freedom enjoyed by certain individual slaves. In ancient Babylonia and Rome, as in the medieval Islamic world and sub-Saharan Africa, slaves served as soldiers, business agents, and high administrators. In seventeenth-century Virginia, a slave named Francis Payne harvested enough tobacco to buy his owner two white indentured servants and then purchase freedom for himself, his wife, and his children; Payne later married a white woman and sued a white planter. In the interior of Britain's Cape Colony in southwestern Africa, black slave herdsmen in the 1820s were allowed to tend herds of livestock in regions so remote that they would travel many weeks without supervision or even sighting a white figure of authority.

In the 1850s, an American slave named Simon Gray served as the captain of a flatboat on the Mississippi River, supervising and paying wages to a crew that included white men. Entrusted with large sums of money for business purposes, Gray carried firearms, drew a regular salary, rented a house where his family lived in privacy, and took a vacation to Hot Springs, Arkansas, when his health declined. Some decades earlier, a South Carolina slave named April Ellison won his freedom after learning how to build and repair cotton gins. After changing his first name to William, buying the freedom of his wife and daughter, and winning a legal suit against a white man who had failed to pay a debt, Ellison became a wealthy planter and owner of sixty-three slaves, a statistic that placed him by 1860 among the upper 3 percent of the slave holders in South Carolina.

Such highly exceptional examples point to the often-forgotten fact that, regardless of law or theory, a slave's actual status or condition could vary along a broad spectrum of rights, powers, and protections that would include, as suggested by Moses Finley (1964, pp. 247–248), claims to property or power over things; power over one's own or others' labor and movement; power to punish or be exempt from punishment; privileges or liabilities within the judicial process; rights and privileges associated with the family; privileges of social mobility; and privileges and duties in religious, political, and military spheres.

Although most slaves in human history no doubt gravitated toward the bottom of such a scale, the spectrum of slave conditions clearly overlaps a larger spectrum that includes all varieties of oppression and powerlessness. Thus some forms of contract labor, though technically free, would score lower on the larger spectrum than many systems of conventional bondage. One thinks, for example, of the Chinese "coolies" who were transported in the mid-nineteenth century across the Pacific to the coast of Peru, where they died in appalling numbers from the lethal effects of mining and shoveling seabird excrement for the world's fertilizer market.

The same point applies to much convict labor, which as "involuntary servitude" is specifically legitimated by the Thirteenth Amendment of the U.S. Constitution as an exception to its national abolition of slavery. If the twentieth century witnessed the slow eradication of most chattel slavery in Africa, Asia, and the Mideast, it also set new records for cruelty and atrocity as tens of millions of men, women, and children were subjected to state servitude by Nazi Germany, the Soviet Union, communist China, and smaller totalitarian nations. Even in the southern United States, for instance at the notorious Parchman Farm in Mississippi, those sentenced to prison—mostly African Americans, and many of them convicted unjustly or for very minor crimes—were subjected to chain gangs and other forms of penal servitude that approximated the Soviet and Chinese gulags. In contrast to traditional chattel slaves, who usually represented a valuable investment, these political or ethnic prisoners were by definition expendable. As late as the 1990s, testimony from former political prisoners in China has proved once again how torture, constant surveillance, and a near-starvation diet can transform human behavior. Students of slavery should at least be aware that strong-minded men and women admit that in the Chinese camps they fawningly tried to ingratiate themselves with guards, stole food from one another, informed on friends, and finally became convinced that it was their own fault that they were dying from starvation.

The difficulties of appraising or ranking slave systems have been underscored by Orlando Patterson's great comparative study, *Slavery and Social Death*. In some primitive societies, such as the Tupinamba of Brazil, slaves were spared from heavy labor but were destined to be eaten, like sacrificial animals, following a ceremonial killing. Some societies that achieved high rates of manumission by allowing slaves to purchase their freedom were extraordinarily brutal and oppressive in other ways, such as sanctioning torture and mass executions. We learn that impressive-sounding laws to protect slaves were seldom enforced. As Jean Bodin pointed out in the sixteenth century, only an absolutist state could override the antithetical or competitive authority of slaveholders. Yet this principle of slave holder autonomy could also mean that slaveholders might strongly encourage slave marriages and slave families, as in the nineteenth-century U.S. South, even though such marriages had no legal standing.

While Patterson has been especially interested in premodern slavery and in the social and psychological functions of "natal alienation" and "generalized dishonor," we should remember that the central *quality* of most forms of slavery has been defined by the nature of the work performed. For example, the slave might have been cutting sugar cane or sweating in the boiler room of a sugar mill in the tropical West Indies, or serving as a sex object in a Persian harem, or wearing fine linens and driving rich white people in a coach in Virginia, or performing as an acrobat, dancer, soldier, doctor, or bureaucrat in Rome.

Nevertheless, when we think of highly privileged slaves—the wealthy farm agent in Babylon, the Greek poet or teacher in Rome, the black silversmith, musician, or boat captain in the American South—we must also remember another crucial point. Being slaves, they could at any moment be stripped of their privileges and property. They could be quickly sold, whipped, or sometimes even killed at the whim of an owner. All slave systems shared this radical uncertainty and unpredictability. Even the Mamluk army officer or powerful eunuch who issued orders in the sultan's name could not summon the aid of a supportive family, clan, or lineage. Whatever rights or privileges a slave might have gained could be taken in a flash, leaving an isolated man or woman as naked as a beast at an auction. This vulnerability, this sense of being removed from the increments and coherence of historical time, may be the essence of dehumanization.

Although historians have long recognized dehumanization as a central aspect of slavery, they have failed to explore the *bestializing* aspects of dehumanization, despite the significant clue Aristotle provided when he called the ox "the poor man's slave." Drawing on the historically ubiquitous comparisons of slaves with domestic animals, Karl Jacoby has argued convincingly that the domestication of sheep, goats, pigs, cattle, horses, and other animals during the Neolithic Revolution served as a model for enslaving humans. Whether used for food, clothing, transport, or heavy labor, these social animals underwent an evolutionary process of neoteny, or progressive "juvenilization." That is, they became more submissive than their wild counterparts, less fearful of strangers, and less aggressive (signified morphologically by a shortening of the jawbone and a decrease in size of the teeth).

Far from being fortuitous, these changes in anatomy and behavior were closely geared to human needs, especially in farming. To control such beasts, humans devised collars, chains, prods, whips, and branding irons. They also castrated males and subjected animals to specific breeding patterns. More positive incentives arose from a kind of paternalism as humans replaced the dominant animal that had exercised some control over the membership and movements of a social group. And as Jacoby astutely observes, the same means of control were eventually applied to human captives. The objectives of well-planned raids to steal the stock and grain wealth a community had saved from a year of labor might also involve some indiscriminate raping and the kidnapping of a few dozen workers.

No doubt the archetypal slave, as Gerda Lerner has maintained, was a woman. In patriarchal societies, women were treated like domesticated or pet-like animals in order to ensure their dependency and appearance of inferiority. Women not only worked in the fields but also reproduced, augmenting the size and wealth of tribes and lineages. In the Hebrew Bible, as in Homer and other early sources, male captives were typically killed on the spot; otherwise they might have escaped or risen in revolt. Women, one gathers, were customarily raped and then enslaved as concubines. With the rise of great urban and agricultural states, however, the need for servants and labor for public works coincided with improved techniques for controlling male prisoners, whose inability to understand their captors' language might have made them seem more like animals than men. As the laws governing chattel property evolved in the earliest civilizations, it was almost universally agreed that a slave, like an animal, could be bought, sold, traded, leased, mortgaged, bequeathed, presented as a gift, pledged for a debt, included in a dowry, or seized in a bankruptcy. These vulnerabilities applied even to the most privileged slaves in Babylonia and other ancient civilizations; for the Western world they were eventually codified in Roman law.

Despite the long attempts to equate human captives with domestic animals— the first African slaves shipped to Lisbon in the mid-1400s were stripped naked and marketed and priced exactly like livestock—slaves were fortunately never held long enough in distinctive, endogamous groups to undergo evolutionary neoteny. Looking back at history from the perspective of modern science, we can be confident that no group of slaves remained genetically distinct over the immense period of time required for significant hereditary change. Nonetheless, neoteny was clearly the goal of many slaveholders, despite their lack of any scientific understanding of how domestication had changed the nature and behavior of tame animals.

In ancient Mesopotamia slaves were not only named and branded as if they were domestic animals, but were actually priced according to their equivalent in cows, horses, pigs, and chickens. And as Orlando Patterson has pointed out, the key to the "Sambo" stereotype of the typical slave, "an ideological imperative of all systems of slavery," is the total absence of "any hint of 'manhood.'" Patterson quotes the famous description by the historian Stanley Elkins (1959, p. 82): "Sambo, the typical plantation slave, was docile but irresponsible, loyal but lazy, humble but chronically given to lying and stealing; his behavior was full of infantile silliness and his talk inflated with childish exaggeration. His relationship with his master was one of utter dependence and childlike attachment: it was indeed this childlike quality that was the very key to his being."

What needs to be added is that this stereotype describes precisely what a human male slave would be like if slaves had been subjected to neoteny, the same process that domesticated tame animals. While ancient Greeks identified similar slavelike traits with "barbarians," and the stereotype was much later associated with so-called Slavs—the root of the word *slave* in Western European languages—it was only in the fifteenth century, when slavery increasingly became linked with various peoples from sub-Saharan Africa, that the slave stereotype began to acquire racist connotations. As slavery in the Western world became more and more limited to black Africans, this arbitrarily defined "race" took on all the qualities, in the eyes of many white people, of the infantilized and animalized slave.

Because humans have always had a remarkable ability to imagine states of perfection, they also succeeded at an early stage in imagining a perfect form of subordination. Plato compared the slave to the human body, the master to the body's rational soul. Slaves incarnated the irrationality and chaos of the material universe, as distinct from the masterlike Demiurge. There was thus a cosmic justification behind Aristotle's dictum that "from the hour of their birth, some men are marked out for subjection, others for rule." Aristotle's ideal of the natural slave, which would help shape virtually all subsequent pro-slavery thought, also in effect pictured what a human being would be like if "tamed" and disciplined by neoteny.

Aristotle began by stressing the parallel between slaves and domesticated beasts:

> Tame animals are naturally better than wild animals, yet for all tame animals there is an advantage in being under human control, as this secures their survival. And as regards the relationship between male and female, the former is naturally superior, the latter inferior, the male rules and the female is subject. By analogy, the same must necessarily apply to mankind as a whole. Therefore all men who differ from one another by as much as the soul differs from the body or a man from a wild beast (and

that is the state of those who work by using their bodies, and for whom that is the best they can do)—these people are slaves by nature, and it is better for them to be subject to this kind of control, as it is better for the other creatures I have mentioned.

Aristotle then proceeded to distinguish the natural slave as having a different body and soul:

For a man who is able to belong to another person is by nature a slave (for that is why he belongs to someone else), as is a man who participates in reason only in far as to realize that it exists, but not so far as to have it himself—other animals do not recognize reason, but follow their passions. The way we use slaves isn't very different: assistance regarding the necessities of life is provided by both groups, by slaves and by domestic animals. Nature must therefore have intended to make the bodies of free men and of slaves different also; slaves' bodies strong for the services they have to do, men upright and not much use for that kind of work, but instead useful for community life.

Aristotle did recognize that on occasion "slaves can have the bodies of free men, free men only the souls and not the bodies of free men." Even more troubling was the fact that some people "of the most respected family" sometimes became slaves "simply because they happened to be captured and sold." Yet such instances of injustice could not weaken Aristotle's concluding conviction that "it is clear that certain people who are free and certain people who are slaves by nature, and it is both to their advantage, and just, for them to be slaves."

This tactic of animalization may well be universal; enslavement is simply its most extreme and institutionalized manifestation. Yet, as Aristotle noted, the slave was not totally dehumanized or seen as only an animal or *nothing but* an animal. Various Greek philosophers, especially the Cynics and Stoics, saw a fundamental contradiction in trying to reduce any human being to such a petlike or animal status. "It would be absurd," Diogenes of Sinope reportedly said, when his own slave had run away, "if Manes [the slave] can live without Diogenes, but Diogenes cannot get on without Manes." When pirates captured Diogenes and took him to a slave market in Crete, he pointed to a spectator wearing rich purple robes, and said, "Sell me to this man; he needs a master." Externally, according to the Stoics, the servant might be the instrument of his master's will, but internally, in his own self-consciousness, he remained a free soul.

In other words, the master's identity depended on having a slave who recognized him as master, and this in turn required an independent consciousness. Contrary to Aristotle and in contrast to the relationship between a man and pet dog, the roles of master and slave could be reversed: Diogenes could become the slave and Manes, who even as a slave might have had a freer soul and been less enslaved to his passions, could become the master.

This is the basic "problem of slavery," which arises from the irreducible humanness of the slave. Although slaves were supposed be treated in many respects like dogs, horses, or oxen, as reflected in all the laws that defined slaves as chattel, the same laws recognized that throughout history slaves have run away, outwitted their masters, rebelled, murdered, raped, stolen, divulged plots for insurrection, and helped protect the state from external danger. No masters or lawmakers, whether in ancient Rome, medieval Tuscany, or seventeenth-century Brazil, could forget that the obsequious servant might also be a "domestic enemy" bent on theft, poisoning, or arson. Throughout history it has been said that slaves, if occasionally as loyal and faithful as good dogs, were for the most part lazy, irresponsible, cunning, rebellious, untrustworthy, and sexually promiscuous. This central contradiction was underscored in Roman law (the Code of Justinian), which ruled that slavery was the single *institution* contrary to the law of nature but sanctioned by law of nations. That is to say, slavery would not be permitted in an ideal world of perfect justice, but it was simply a fact of life that symbolized the compromises that must be made in the sinful world of reality. This was the official view of Christian churches from the late Roman Empire to the eighteenth century.

The *institution* of slavery, then, has always given rise to conflict, fear, and accommodation. The settlement of the New World magnified these liabilities, because the slaves now came from an alien and unfamiliar culture; they often outnumbered their European rulers; and many colonial settlements were vulnerable to military attack or close to wilderness areas that offered easy refuge. Accordingly, the introduction of black slavery to the Americas brought spasmodic cries of warning, anxiety, and racial repugnance; however, the grandiose visions of New World wealth—once the Spanish had plundered the Aztecs and Incas— seemed always to require slave labor. Largely because many experiments at enslaving Indians failed, African slaves became an intrinsic part of the American experience.

From the Spanish and Portuguese to the English, Dutch, and French, colonizers turned to the purchase of slaves in Africa as the cheapest and most expedient labor supply to meet the immediate demands of mining and tropical agriculture. The institution took on a variety of forms as a result of European cultural differences, the character of the work performed, and a host of other variables. Anglo-American slavery was not unique in animalizing human beings, or in defining the bondsman as chattel property endowed with elements of human personality. In the mid-eighteenth century, when black slaves could be found in all regions from French Canada to Chile, there was nothing unprecedented about New World chattel slavery, even the enslavement of one ethnic group by another. What was unprecedented by the 1760s and early 1770s was the emergence of a widespread conviction that New World slavery symbolized all the forces that threatened the true destiny of the human race.

This eruption of anti-slavery thought cannot be explained by economic interest. The Atlantic slave system, far from being in decay, had never appeared so prosperous, so secure, or so full of promise. The first groups to denounce the principle of slavery, and all that it implied, were the perfectionist and millennialist Christian sects who sought to live their lives free from sin. In essence, their ideal involved a form of mutual love and recognition that precluded treating men as objects or animals, even as objects with souls. The sectarian groups that emerged in the English civil wars of the mid-seventeenth century looked for a form of authentic service, or selflessness, that could not be used as a lever for exploitation. Because they strove to realize a mode of interpersonal life that was the precise antithesis of chattel slavery, they threatened the existing social order and were either annihilated or reduced to spiritualistic withdrawal.

The notable exception was the Society of Friends, which early found the means of compromise and thus of survival. The Quakers not only contained and stabilized their quest for a purified life but also institutionalized methods for bearing witness to their faith. In other words, the Quakers achieved a dynamic balance between the impulse to perfection and the "reality principle." They also acquired considerable economic and political power, and they were the only sect to become deeply involved with the Atlantic slave system. By the early eighteenth century there were Quaker planters in the West Indies and Quaker slave merchants in London, Philadelphia, and Newport, Rhode Island. Partly because of the Friends' testimony against war, slaveholding occasioned moral tensions that were less common among other denominations. For social critics within the sect, the wealthy masters and slave-trading merchants presented a flagrant symbol of worldly compromise and an ideal target for attack. For a variety of reasons, the Seven Years' War (1756–1763) brought a spiritual crisis for the Society of Friends, resulting in much soul-searching, attempts at self-purification, and a final commitment to disengage themselves collectively from the Atlantic slave system.

The Quakers' growing anguish coincided with other reformist developments in Western culture, particularly the culture of British Protestantism. First, the rise of secular social philosophy necessitated a redefinition of the place of human bondage in the rational order of being. Because John Locke celebrated the importance of natural liberty, he had to place slavery outside the social compact, which was designed to protect man's inalienable rights. Locke thus imagined slavery as "the state of War continued, between a lawful Conqueror, and a Captive." Even by the 1730s, such arguments were beginning to appear absurd to a generation of English and French writers who had learned from Locke and others to take an irreverent view of past authority and to subject all questions to the test of reason. It was Montesquieu, more than any other thinker, who put the subject of black slavery on the agenda of the European Enlightenment. He weighed the institution against the general laws or principles that promoted human happiness, and he encouraged the imaginative experiment of a reversal of roles between masters and slaves in a world turned upside down. By the 1760s, the anti-slavery arguments of Montesquieu and Francis Hutcheson were being repeated, developed, and propagated by the intellectuals of the enlightened world. John Locke, the great enemy of all absolute and arbitrary power, was the last major philosopher to seek a justification for absolute and perpetual slavery.

A second and closely related transformation was the popularization of an ethic of benevolence, personified in the "man of feeling." The insistence on humanity's inner goodness, identified with the power of sympathy, became part of a gradual secularizing tendency in British Protestantism. Ultimately this liberal spirit led in two directions, described respectively by the titles of Adam Smith's two books: *The Theory of Moral Sentiments* and *The Wealth of Nations*. Smith's theories of sympathetic benevolence and individual enterprise both condemned slavery as an intolerable obstacle to human progress. The man of sensibility needed to objectify his virtue by relieving the sufferings of innocent victims. The economic man required a social order that allowed and morally vindicated the free play of individual self-interest. By definition, the slave was both innocent and a victim, because he could not be held responsible for his own condition. The African's enslavement, unlike the legitimate restraints of society, seemed wholly undeserved. He represented innocent nature and hence corresponded, psychologically, to the natural and spontaneous impulses of the man of feeling. Accordingly, the key to progress lay in the controlled emancipation of innocent nature as found both in the objective slave and in the subjective affections of the reformer. The slave would be lifted to a level of independent action and social obligation. The reformer would be assured of the beneficence of his own self-interest by merging himself in a transcendent cause. These results, at least, were the expectation of the philanthropists who increasingly transformed the quest for salvation *from* a sinful world into a mission to cleanse the world of sin.

By the eve of the American Revolution there was a remarkable convergence of cultural and intellectual developments that at once undercut traditional rationalizations for slavery and offered new modes of sensibility for identifying with its victims. Thus the African's cultural difference acquired a positive image at the hands of eighteenth-century primitivists and evangelical Christians, such as John Wesley, who searched through travel accounts and descriptions of exotic lands for examples of humanity's inherent virtue and creativity. In some ways the "noble savage" was little more than a literary convention that conflated the Iroquois and South Sea Islander with sable Venuses and tear-bedewed daughters of "injur'd Afric." The convention did, however, modify Europe's arrogant ethnocentrism and provide for at least a momentary ambivalence toward the human costs of modern civilization. It also tended to counteract the many fears and prejudices that had long cut the African off from the normal mechanisms of sympathy and identification. Ultimately, literary primitivism was no match for the pseudoscientific racism that drew on the Enlightenment and reduced the African to a "link" or even separate species between man and the ape. But for many Europeans, as diverse as John Wesley and the Abbé Raynal, the African was not a human animal but an innocent child of nature whose enslavement in America betrayed the very notion of the New World as a land of natural innocence and new hope for mankind. By the early 1770s, such writers portrayed the black slave as a man of natural virtue and sensitivity who was at once oppressed by the worst vices of civilization and yet capable of receiving its greatest benefits.

This complex change in moral vision was a precondition for anti-slavery movements and for the eventual abolition of New World slavery from 1777, when Vermont's constitution outlawed the institution, to 1888, when in a state of almost revolutionary turmoil Brazil finally freed its one-half million remaining slaves. The emergence of religious and secular anti-slavery arguments, however, in no way guaranteed such an outcome. If Washington, Jefferson, Madison, and other slaveholding Founders could view human bondage as an embarrassing and even dangerous social evil, they also respected the rights of private property and expressed profound fear of the consequences of any general and unrestricted act of emancipation. The U.S. Constitution was designed to protect the rights and security of slaveholders, and from 1792 to 1845 the American political system encouraged and rewarded the expansion of slavery into nine new states.

As the American slave system became increasingly profitable, the moral doubts of the Revolutionary generation gave way in the South to strong religious, economic, and racial arguments that defended slavery as a "positive good." Historians are still sharply divided over the fundamental reasons and motives for slave emancipation, which ultimately required an imposition of power even in the regions that were spared a Haitian Revolution or an American Civil War. Yet regardless of the final importance of contending interests, it was the inherent contradiction of chattel slavery—the impossible effort to bestialize human beings—that provided substance for a revolution in moral perception, a recognition that slaves could become masters or masters slaves, and that we are therefore not required to resign ourselves to the world that has always been.

BIBLIOGRAPHY

Davis, David Brion. *Slavery and Human Progress.* New York and Oxford: Oxford University Press, 1984.

Elkins, Stanley M. *Slavery: A Problem in American Institutional and Intellectual Life.* Chicago: University of Chicago Press, 1959.

Finley, Moses I. "Between Slavery and Freedom." *Comparative Studies in Society and History* 6 (1964): 233–242.

Jacoby, Karl. "Slaves by Nature? Domestic Animals and Human Slaves." *Slavery and Abolition* 15 (1994): 89–97.

Lerner, Gerda. *The Creation of Patriarchy.* New York and Oxford: Oxford University Press, 1986.

Patterson, Orlando. *Slavery and Social Death.* Cambridge, Mass.: Harvard University Press, 1982.

Wiedemann, Thomas. *Greek and Roman Slavery.* Baltimore: Johns Hopkins University Press, 1981.

Contributors

GEORGE REID ANDREWS is Professor of History and UCIS Research Professor at the University of Pittsburgh. He is the author of *The Afro-Argentines of Buenos Aires, 1800–1900* (1980) and *Blacks & Whites in São Paulo, Brazil, 1888–1988* (1991), and is working on a comparative history of Afro-Latin America.

RALPH A. AUSTEN is Professor of African History and Co-Chair of the Committee on African and African-American Studies at the University of Chicago. He has written extensively on the Islamic slave trade out of Africa and is the author of *African Economic History: Internal Development and External Dependency* (1987).

STEPHEN P. BENSCH is Associate Professor of History at Swarthmore College and the author of *Barcelona and Its Rulers, 1096–1291* (1995).

LAIRD W. BERGAD teaches Latin American and Caribbean history at Lehman College and at the Graduate and University Center of the City University of New York. His most recent book (written with Fe Iglesias García and María del Carmen Barcia) is *The Cuban Slave Market 1790–1880* (1995).

ROBIN BLACKBURN is editor of *New Left Review* and was a Fellow at the Woodrow Wilson Center in Washington, D.C., in 1993–1994. He is the author of *The Making of New World Slavery* (1988), a study of the formation of the slave systems of the Americas.

PETER BLANCHARD is Professor of History at the University of Toronto. He is the author of *Slavery & Abolition in Early Republican Peru* (1992) and editor of *Markham in Peru: The Travels of Clements R. Markham, 1852–1853* (1991), and is presently conducting research on slaves who fought in the independence wars in Spanish South America.

O. NIGEL BOLLAND, Professor of Sociology at Colgate University, has published extensively on the colonial society of Belize and on the transition from slave to wage labor in the Caribbean. He is the author of *On the March: Labor Rebellions in the British Caribbean, 1934–39* (1995).

KEITH BRADLEY is Professor of Classics at the University of Victoria; his publications include *Slaves and Masters in the Roman Empire* (1985) and *Slavery and Society at Rome* (1994).

ROSEMARY BRANA-SHUTE is Associate Professor of History at the College of Charleston and co-editor (with Gary Brana-Shute) of *Crime and Punishment in the Caribbean* (1980).

BRIDGET BRERETON is Professor of History at the University of the West Indies. She has written and edited several books and numerous articles on the history of Trinidad and Tobago and on the post-emancipation Caribbean.

JANE TURNER CENSER is Associate Professor of History at George Mason University and the author of *North Carolina Planters and Their Children, 1800–1860* (1984).

RAYMOND L. COHN, Professor of Economics at Illinois State University, has written several articles on mortality in the trans-Atlantic slave trade and on other oceanic voyages.

ROBERT EDGAR CONRAD, formerly of the University of Illinois and the Free University of Berlin, is the author of several books on Brazilian slavery, including *The Destruction of Brazilian Slavery 1850–1880* (1972; 2d ed., 1993), *Children of God's Fire: A Documentary History of Black Slavery in Brazil* (1983; reissued 1994), and *World of Sorrow: The African Slave Trade to Brazil* (1986).

MICHAEL J. CRATON is Professor Emeritus of History at the University of Waterloo. He is the author of *Sinews of Empire: A Short History of British Slavery* (1974), *Searching for the Invisible Man: Slaves and Plantation Life in Jamaica* (1978), and *Testing the Chains: Resistance to Slavery in the British West Indies* (1983), and co-author (with Gail Saunders) of *Islands in the Stream* (1992, 1996), a two-volume social history of the Bahamas.

DAVID BRION DAVIS is Sterling Professor of History at Yale University and the author of the Pulitzer Prize-winning *The Problem of Slavery in Western Culture* (1966; reissued 1988), as well as *Slavery and Human Progress* (1984) and *From Homicide to Slavery: Studies in American Culture* (1986).

ALEJANDRO DE LA FUENTE is Assistant Professor of History at the University of South Florida.

MARTINA DEUCHLER is Professor of Korean Studies at the University of London and teaches Korean history at the School of Oriental and African Studies.

CHARLES B. DEW is W. Van Clark Third Century Professor of Social Sciences and Director of the Francis C. Oakley Center for the Humanities and Social Sciences at Williams College. His books include *Ironmaker to the Confederacy: Joseph R. Anderson and the Tredeger Iron Works* (1966) and *Bond of Iron: Master and Slave at Buffalo Forge* (1994).

PATRICK S. DOWD is a Ph.D. candidate at the University of Pittsburgh. His dissertation focuses on the development of German anthropology during the period 1870–1914.

SEYMOUR DRESCHER is University Professor of History and Professor of Sociology at the University of Pittsburgh and a past Secretary of the Woodrow Wilson Center for Scholars in Washington, D.C. He is the author of *Econocide: British Slavery in the Era of Abolition* (1977) and *Capitalism and Antislavery: British Mobilization in Comparative Perspective* (1986). Co-edited volumes include *Anti-Slavery, Religion, and Reform* (with Christine Bolt, 1980) and *The Meaning of Freedom: Economics, Politics, and Culture after Slavery* (with Frank McGlynn, 1992).

CHRISTINA DUREAU, an anthropologist who works on the historical ethnography of the western Solomon Islands and Fiji and a former Postdoctoral Fellow in the Research School of Pacific and Asian Studies at Australian National University, is currently Lecturer in Social Anthropology at the University of Auckland.

DAVID ELTIS is Professor of History at Queen's University (Kingston), a Research Fellow of the Du Bois Institute at Harvard University, and a Research Associate at the University of Hull. He obtained his Ph.D. in History from the University of Rochester in 1979 and is the author of *Economic Growth and the Ending of the Transatlantic Slave Trade* (1987).

PIETER EMMER is Professor of the History of the Expansion of Europe at Leiden University. He has written on the history of the slave trade and on slavery and the migration of indentured laborers from Asia to the Caribbean. Among his publications are the edited volumes *Colonialism and Migration: Indentured Labor Before and After Slavery* (1986) and (with Magnus Mörner) *European Expansion and Migration* (1992).

STANLEY L. ENGERMAN is John H. Munro Professor of Economics and Professor of History at the University of Rochester and co-author (with Robert W. Fogel) of *Time on the Cross: The Economics of American Negro Slavery* (winner of the Bancroft Prize in American History; 1974, rev. ed., 1989).

JANET J. EWALD is Associate Professor of History at Duke University. A specialist in African history, she is researching port and maritime labor in the western Indian Ocean and has published a book and a number of articles about Sudanese history, slavery, and the slave trade.

DAVID FEENY is Professor of Economics and Clinical Epidemiology and Biostatistics at McMaster University and the author of *The Political Economy of Productivity: Thai Agricultural Development, 1880–1975* (1982).

CAROLYN FICK is Associate Professor of History at Concordia University, Montreal, where she teaches Caribbean and Latin American history. Her publications include *The Making of Haiti: The Saint Domingue Revolution from Below* (1991); in addition to this work, she is pursuing a social history research project on slavery, slave emancipation, and the slave family on the West Indian island of Saint-Barthélemy in the nineteenth century.

ROBERT P. FORBES is a Lecturer in History at Yale University, where he received his Ph.D. in 1994. He is currently revising his dissertation (entitled "Slavery and the Meaning of America, 1819–1833") for publication.

DAVID W. GALENSON is Professor of Economics at the University of Chicago; his publications include *White Servitude in Colonial America: An Economic Analysis* (1981) and *Traders, Planters, and Slaves: Market Behavior in Early English America* (1985).

DAVID GEGGUS, Professor of History at the University of Florida, is the author of *Slavery, War, and Revolution: The British Occupation of Saint Domingue 1793–1798* (1982) and co-editor (with Barry Gaspar) of *A Turbulent Time: The French Revolution and the Greater Caribbean* (1997).

LAURENCE GLASCO is Associate Professor of History and Director of the Program for the Study of Race and Ethnicity in World Perspective at the University of Pittsburgh. His publications include articles in *Diaspora* and the *Journal of Afro-Latin American Studies and Literature*. He is currently working on a history of African-Americans in Pittsburgh and a comparative study of race relations in Cuba and the United States.

WILLIAM A. GREEN is John E. Brooks Professor of the Humanities at Holy Cross College. He is the author of *British Slave Emancipation: The Sugar Colonies and the Great Experiment 1830–1865* (1976) and *History, Historians, and the Dynamics of Change* (1993), as well as numerous articles on the history of the British Empire and modern Western historiography.

FARLEY GRUBB, Professor of Economics at the University of Delaware, is the author of *Runaway Servants, Convicts, and Apprentices Advertised in the Pennsylvania Gazette, 1728–1796* (1992).

RICHARD HELLIE is Professor of History at the University of Chicago. His publications include *Enserfment and Military Change in Muscovy* (1971), *Slavery in Russia, 1450–1725* (1982), and the forthcoming volume *Economy and Material Culture of Russia, 1600–1725*.

GAD HEUMAN is a Senior Lecturer in History at the University of Warwick. Co-editor of the journal *Slavery and Abolition*, his publications include *Between Black and White: Race, Politics, and Free Coloreds in Jamaica, 1792–1865* (1981) and *"The Killing Time": The Morant Bay Rebellion in Jamaica* (1994), as well as edited volumes on slave resistance and on labor.

BARRY HIGMAN, Professor of History at the Research School of Social Sciences, Australian National University, is the author of *Slave Population and Economy in Jamaica, 1807–1834* (1979) and *Slave Populations of the British Caribbean, 1807–1834* (1984).

STEVEN L. HOCH, a specialist on nineteenth-century Russian serfdom, is Professor of History at the University of Iowa and the author of *Serfdom and Social Control in Russia: Petrovskoe, A Village in Tambov* (1986).

JAN S. HOGENDORN is Grossman Professor of Economics at Colby College. He is the author of *Economic Development* (1992), the co-author of *The Shell Money of the Slave Trade* with Marion Johnson (1986) and *Slow Death for Slavery: The Course of Abolition in Northern Nigeria, 1897–1936* with Paul E. Lovejoy (1993), and co-editor (with Henry A. Gemery) of *The Uncommon Market: Essays in the History of the Atlantic Slave Trade* (1979).

LARRY E. HUDSON, JR., is Associate Professor of History at the University of Rochester. He is the author of *"To Have and to Hold": Slave Work and Family Life in Antebellum South Carolina* (1997) and editor of *Working Toward Freedom: Slave Society and Domestic Economy in the American South* (1994).

JOHN O. HUNWICK is Professor of Religion and Professor of African History at Northwestern University. He is the author of *Sharia in Songhay* (1985) and *Arabic Literature in Africa*, volume 2, *The Writings of Central Sudanic Africa* (1996) and editor of *Religion and National Integration in Africa* (1992).

JOSEPH INIKORI, an economic historian who specializes in international trade and economic development, is Professor of History and a member of the Frederick Douglass Institute for African and African-American Studies at the University of Rochester. He is the editor of *Forced Migration* (1982) and co-editor (with Stanley L. Engerman) of *The Atlantic Slave Trade* (1992).

EPHRAIM ISAAC is Director of the Institute of Semitic Studies, a Fellow of Butler College at Princeton University, and a Fellow of the Dead Sea Scrolls Foundation. His publications include *The Book of Enoch* (1983) and *An Ethiopic History of Joseph* (1990).

BERNARD S. JACKSON is Queen Victoria Professor of Law at the University of Liverpool and has taught Jewish law at Harvard and Oxford Universities. He is the author of *Theft in Early Jewish Law* (1972), *Essays in Jewish and Comparative Legal History* (1975), and *Wisdom-Laws* (1996) and served as the founding editor of *The Jewish Law Annual* from 1978 to 1996.

NORRECE T. JONES is Associate Professor of History at Virginia Commonwealth University and author of *Born a Child of Freedom, Yet a Slave* (1990).

RUTH MAZO KARRAS, Associate Professor of History at Temple University, is the author of *Slavery and Society in Medieval Scandinavia* (1988), as well as several works on gender and sexuality in medieval Europe.

HERBERT S. KLEIN is Professor of History at Columbia University; his books include *Slavery in the Americas* (1969), *The Middle Passage* (1978), and *African Slavery in Latin America and the Caribbean* (1986).

MARTIN A. KLEIN is Professor of History at the University of Toronto. He is the editor of *Breaking the Chains: Slavery, Bondage, and Emancipation in Modern Africa and Asia* (1993) and the author of *Slavery and French Colonial Rule in West Africa: Senegal, Guinea, and Mali, 1848–1860* (1998).

FRANKLIN W. KNIGHT is Leonard and Helen R. Stulman Professor of History and former Director of the Latin American Studies Program at The Johns Hopkins University. His publications include *Slave Society in Cuba During the Nineteenth Century* (1970) and *The Caribbean: The Genesis of a Fragmented Nationalism* (1978; 2nd edition 1990). He has co-edited *The Modern Caribbean* with Colin A. Palmer (1989) and *Atlantic Port Cities: Economy, Culture, and Society in the Atlantic World, 1650–1983* with Peggy K. Liss (1991).

DHARMA KUMAR, formerly Professor of Economic History at the Delhi School of Economics, is Senior Fellow at the

Nehru Museum and Library at the University of Delhi and editor of the two-volume *Cambridge Economic History of India* (1981, 1983).

CARL H. LANDÉ, a specialist on Southeast Asian politics, is Professor of Political Sciences and East Asian Studies at the University of Kansas.

DOUGLAS LIBBY is Associate Professor of History at the Universidade Federal de Minas Gerais, Belo Horizonte, Brazil. He has written books and articles on slave labor in mining and other industrial activities, as well as on slave demography in Brazil.

PAUL E. LOVEJOY, Professor of History at York University, is a Fellow of the Royal Society of Canada and a Vice-President of the Social Sciences and Humanities Research Council of Canada. He has written and edited numerous books on African economic and social history.

MURDO J. MACLEOD, Graduate Research Professor of Latin American History at the University of Florida, has taught at the Universities of Pittsburgh and Arizona. Author of two books and more than fifty articles, he is currently researching Native American accommodation and resistance in colonial Central America.

ELIAS MANDALA is Associate Professor of History at the University of Rochester and the author of *Work and Control in a Peasant Economy: A History of the Lower Tchiri Valley in Malawi, 1859–1960* (1990).

PATRICK MANNING is Professor of History and African-American Studies at Northeastern University, where he directs the World History Center. Author of *Slavery and African Life: Occidental, Oriental, and African Slave Trades* (1990) and other studies on the demographic and social history of slavery, he also writes on the economic and social history of francophone Africa and the interpretation of world history.

FRANK MCGLYNN is Associate Professor of Anthropology at the University of Pittsburgh. His research focuses on the Caribbean, comparative slavery, ethnohistory, and comparative racisms; co-edited publications include *Anthropological Approaches to Political Behavior* with Arthur Tuden (1991) and *The Meaning of Freedom: Economics, Politics, and Culture After Slavery* with Seymour Drescher (1992).

JOHN R. MCKIVIGAN is Associate Professor of History at West Virginia University, author of *The War Against Proslavery Religion* (1984), and co-editor (with John W. Blassingame) of the Frederick Douglass Papers.

CLAUDE MEILLASSOUX is Directeur Honoraire de Recherche at the Centre Nationale de la Recherche Scientifique in Paris. Author of *The Anthropology of Slavery: The Womb of Iron and Gold* (1991), his present areas of study include Africa, slavery, child labor, and military societies.

SUZANNE MIERS, Professor of History Emerita at Ohio University, is the author of *Britain and the Ending of the Slave Trade* (1975) and co-editor of *Slavery in Africa: Historical and Anthropological Perspectives* with Igor Kopytoff (1977), *The End of Slavery in Africa* with Richard Roberts (1988), and *Women and Chinese Patriarchy* with Maria Jaschok (1994). She is currently working on a book on Britain and the suppression of slavery since 1890.

PHILIP MORGAN is Professor of History at the College of William and Mary and editor of the *William and Mary Quarterly*.

THOMAS D. MORRIS is Professor of History at Portland State University. His publications include *Free Men All: The Personal Liberty Laws of the North, 1780–1861* (1974) and *Southern Slavery and the Law, 1619–1860* (1996).

PATRICIA A. MULVEY is Professor of History at Bluefield State College; her publications include several articles on slave confraternities in colonial Brazil.

David Murray is Professor of History at the University of Guelph and the author of *Odious Commerce: Britain, Spain, and the Abolition of the Cuban Slave Trade* (1980).

MICHAEL NARAGON received his Ph.D. from the University of Pittsburgh. He specializes in urban politics, African-American history, and the South. His publications include "Communities in Motion: Drapetomania, Work, and the Development of African-American Slave Cultures," which appeared in the December 1994 issue of *Slavery and Abolition*.

JAMES OAKES, Professor of History and Director of the American Studies Program at Northwestern University, is the author of *The Ruling Race: A History of American Slaveholders* (1980) and *Slavery and Freedom: An Interpretation of the Old South* (1990).

COLIN A. PALMER, Distinguished Professor of History at the Graduate School and Research Center of the City University of New York, is the author of *Human Cargoes: The British Slave Trade to Spanish America, 1700–1739* (1981).

ROBERT L. PAQUETTE, Publius Virgilius Rogers Professor of History at Hamilton College, is the author of *Sugar Is Made with Blood* (1988) and co-editor (with Stanley L. Engerman) of *The Lesser Antilles in the Age of European Expansion* (1996).

UTSA PATNAIK is Professor at the Centre for Economic Studies and Planning at Jawaharlal Nehru University. She received her Master's degree from the Delhi School of Economics and her D.Phil. from Somerville College, Oxford University, in 1972. Co-editor (with Manjari Dingwaney) of *Chains of Servitude: Bondage and Slavery in India* (1985), her main research interests include problems of comparative economic history and economic development (with particular reference to agrarian relations).

DONALD A. PETESCH is Associate Professor of English at the University of Pittsburgh and the author of *A Spy in the Enemy's Country: The Emergence of Modern Black Literature* (1989), as well as articles on black literature and on William Faulkner.

WILLIAM D. PHILLIPS, JR., is Professor of History at the University of Minnesota. He is the author of *Enrique IV and the Crisis of Fifteenth-Century Castile* (1978), *Slavery from Roman Times to the Early Transatlantic Trade* (1985), and *Historía de la Esclavitud en España* (1989) and co-author (with Carla Rahn Phillips) of *The Worlds of Christopher Columbus* (1992) and *Spain's Golden Fleece: Wool Production and the Wool Trade from the Middle Ages to the Nineteenth Century* (1997).

RICHARD PRICE is Dittman Professor of American Studies and Professor of Anthropology and History at the College of William and Mary. His most recent book, written with Sally Price, is *Enigma Variations* (1995).

DAVID RICHARDSON, Reader in Economic History at the University of Hull, is the editor of the four-volume *Bristol, Africa, and the Eighteenth-Century Slave Trade to America* (1986–1996) and the author of numerous articles on the Atlantic slave trade (with a particular focus on its volume).

ROSS SAMSON is Director of the Cruithne Press, an editor of the *Journal of European Archaeology*, and an assistant editor of both the *Journal of Theoretical Archaeology* and the *Scottish Archaeological Review*. His research focuses on early medieval social and economic history.

JAMES SANDERS is a Ph.D. candidate at the University of Pittsburgh; his research focuses on peasants and slaves in nineteenth-century Columbia.

FRANCISCO A. SCARANO, Professor of History at the University of Wisconsin, is the author of *Sugar and Slavery in Puerto Rico: The Plantation Economy of Ponce, 1800–1850* (1984).

CHRISTOPHER SCHMIDT-NOWARA, a lecturer in History at Stanford University, received his Ph.D. from the University of Michigan in 1995. His dissertation focused on elite antislavery mobilization in Spain, Cuba, and Puerto Rico.

STUART B. SCHWARTZ is George Burton Adams Professor of History at Yale University. He has conducted extensive research on Brazilian slavery and is the author of *Sugar Plantations in the Formation of Brazilian Society* (1986) and *Slaves, Peasants, and Rebels: Reconsidering Brazilian Slavery* (1992).

PAMELA SCULLY is Assistant Professor of History at Kenyon College and the author of *Liberating the Family: Gender and British Slave Emancipation in the Rural Western Cape, South Africa, 1823–1853* (1998).

JOHN SEKORA is Professor of English and Dean of Graduate Studies at North Carolina Central University. Author of *Luxury: The Concept in Western Thought, Eden to Smollett* (1978), *The Art of Slave Narrative* (1983), *Frederick Douglass* (1996), and thirty articles on African-American literature, he is currently writing a genre study of slave narratives and editing *The Frederick Douglass Encyclopedia*.

VERENE A. SHEPHERD is a Senior Lecturer in History at the University of the West Indies and secretary-treasurer of the Association of Caribbean Historians. Author of *Transients to Settlers: The Experience of Indians in Jamaica 1845–1950* (1994), she has co-edited *Caribbean Slave Society and Economy* (1991) and *Caribbean Freedom* (1993), both with Hilary Beckles, as well as *Engendering History: Caribbean Women in Historical Perspective* with Barbara Bailey and Bridget Brereton (1995).

RALPH SHLOMOWITZ completed his Ph.D. at the University of Chicago and is a Reader in Economic History at the Flinders University of South Australia. Co-author (with Lance Brennan and John McDonald) of *Mortality and Migration in the Modern World* (1996), his current research concerns the anthropometric history of Indians under British rule.

JAMES SMALLS is Assistant Professor of Art History at Rutgers University. He teaches and has published in such areas as African-American art and nineteenth-century French art, and is most interested in those aspects of visual culture in which elements of race, sexuality, and gender converge.

AUDREY SMEDLEY is Professor of Anthropology at Virginia Commonwealth University. Her recent book, *Race in North America: Origin and Evolution of a Worldview* (1993) won an Outstanding Book Award from the Gustavus Myers Center.

JEAN R. SODERLUND, Professor of History at Lehigh University, is the author of *Quakers & Slavery: A Divided Spirit* (1985) and co-author (with Gary B. Nash) of *Freedom by Degrees: Emancipation in Pennsylvania and Its Aftermath* (1991).

RICHARD H. STECKEL is Professor of Economics and Anthropology at Ohio State University. He is the author of *The Economics of U.S. Slave and Southern White Fertility* (1985), as well as numerous articles on health, nutrition, fertility, and living standards.

SEAN STILWELL is a Ph.D. candidate in African History at York University.

ALLEN STOUFFER is Professor of History at St. Francis Xavier University. Author of *The Light of Nature and the Law of God: Antislavery in Ontario, 1833–1877* (1992), he is currently researching nineteenth-century African-Canadian associational activity.

IAN B. STRAKER is Director of Placement and Field Education Administration at Union Theological Seminary. He completed his Ph.D. in American Religious History at Princeton University in 1996 and has taught at Wesleyan University.

HOWARD TEMPERLEY is Professor of History at the University of East Anglia; his most recent book is *White Dreams, Black Africa: The Antislavery Expedition to the River Niger 1841–1842* (1991).

JOHN K. THORNTON, author of *Africa and Africans in the Making of the Atlantic World, 1400–1680* (1992), is Professor of History at Millersville University of Pennsylvania.

ALVIN O. THOMPSON is Associate Professor of History at the University of the West Indies (Cave Hill Campus) and specializes in African and Caribbean History. He is the author of *Colonialism and Underdevelopment in Guyana, 1580–1803* (1987) and *The Haunting Past: Politics, Economics, and Race in Caribbean Life* (1997).

DALE TOMICH is Associate Professor of Sociology at the State University of New York at Binghamton. He is currently engaged in a study of slavery in Cuba, Brazil, and the U.S. South and its role in the nineteenth-century world economy; his publications include *Slavery in the Circuit of Sugar: Martinique and the World Economy, 1830–1848* (1990).

MICHAEL TWADDLE is Reader in Commonwealth Studies at London University and has lectured at Makerere University in Uganda. His most recent publication (co-edited with Holger Bernt Hansen) is *Religion and Politics in East Africa: The Period Since Independence* (1995).

JAMES WALVIN is Professor of History at the University of York, co-editor of the journal *Slavery and Abolition*, and has written extensively on the history of British slavery and modern British social history.

JAMES F. WARREN, author of *Ah Ku and Karayuki-san: Prostitution in Singapore, 1870–1940* (1993), is Professor of Southeast Asian Modern History at Murdoch University.

ALAN WATSON, Ernest P. Rogers Professor of Law Research Fellow at the University of Georgia, is the author of numerous books on Roman and comparative law, *Roman Slave Law* (1987), *Slave Laws in the Americas* (1990), and *The Spirit of Roman Law* (1995) among them.

JAMES L. WATSON is Fairbank Professor of Chinese Society and Professor of Anthropology at Harvard University. A specialist on southern Chinese ethnography, he is editor of *Asian and African Systems of Slavery* (1980).

ELLEN M. WIMBERG received her Ph.D. in Soviet History from the University of Pittsburgh in 1996 and has taught at Thomas More College, Northern Kentucky University, and St. Xavier High School.

GAVIN WRIGHT is William Robertson Coe Professor of American Economic History at Stanford University and has written extensively on the economic history of the U.S. South, before and after the American Civil War. His publications include *Old South, New South: Revolutions in the Southern Economy Since the Civil War* (1986).

CHING-HWANG YEN is Reader in History at the University of Adelaide, a former Professor of History at the University of Hong Kong, and author of several books on modern Chinese and overseas Chinese history.

A Historical Guide to World Slavery

ABOLITION AND ANTI-SLAVERY. [*This entry comprises seven articles that discuss the premises and practices of abolition and anti-slavery in major regions around the world from the eighteenth century to the twentieth:*

> Africa
> India
> Southeast Asia
> Britain
> Continental Europe
> Latin America
> United States

For particular discussion of the role Christianity played in the abolition and anti-slavery movement in North America, see Christian Perspectives on Slavery.]

Africa

Just as slavery in Africa was multifaceted, so was the freeing of the slaves under colonial rule during the nineteenth and early twentieth centuries. Abolition covered a period of many years and followed divergent patterns in different geographical areas, even in various territories of the same colonial power. The process generally involved one or a combination of the following patterns: slaves stayed with their owners, with the two groups developing new definitions of dependency; slaves left their owners but remained in the general vicinity; or slaves removed to a distance from the owners. In the first pattern slaves might be closely integrated with their masters' families, while in the last, all ties would probably be broken.

This article is limited to sub-Saharan Africa exclusive of the area of European settlement in southern Africa. (In the British colonies there, slavery was abolished in 1833, contributing to the Great Trek of the Boers away from British au-

thority.) The discussion also excludes the pawning and pledging of people, which, though distinct from chattel slavery, bore some relationship to it. Finally, it does not touch on the topic of royal or court slaves, who could sometimes reach positions of considerable authority or technical expertise (for example, musketeer corps in several precolonial armies), and whose status was little changed in some areas well into the colonial period or even after independence. Even with these limitations, the subject area is vast. Slavery existed very widely, with slaves working in farming, herding, craft activities, transport, government, and the military. In addition, female slaves were valued for their sexual attributes and the production of children.

Before the colonial period, no organized indigenous opposition to slavery arose, even though manumission of individual slaves by owners (especially in Muslim areas), self-ransom, and gradual incorporation into owners' families were common practices. The abolition movement in Africa was instead associated with the colonial administrations and fortified by the public outcry against slavery in metropolitan countries. Nonetheless, these colonial administrations had to be careful. Aggressive anti-slavery activity ran the risk of alienating powerful indigenous elites, whose cooperation immensely simplified the colonial task of governance. Moreover, an immediate eradication of slavery might have devastating economic consequences—or so reasoned many colonial officials.

Early abolition in the small British West African territories (1833) was limited to European slaveholders. Administrators there feared the results of attempting to alienate the human property of African masters. This fear contributed to a British move toward the protectorate form of govern-

French engraving of a meeting between English naval officers and Africans about the abolition of the African slave trade, c.1815; Bibliothèque Nationale, Paris.

ment, with slavery allowed to continue inside the bounds of the protectorates.

As the British acquired more territory later in the nineteenth century, their standard strategy toward emancipation became "abolition of the legal status of slavery," an idea taken from action in British India in 1843. Under legal-status abolition, slavery held no lawful standing in the courts. Another British standard practice was to prohibit slave-dealing and to declare children born after a given date to be free. Ordinarily, owners were not compensated for any loss, nor were special measures taken to assist freed slaves. Legal-status abolition was first adopted for a large African territory in 1874, following the annexation of the Gold Coast protectorate. Slave-dealing was attacked haphaz-

ardly at first, but by 1914 large-scale dealing was a thing of the past except in some non-British colonial territories, especially in Mauritania, where it never ended entirely, and in the independent states of Ethiopia and Liberia. Slaveholding itself was not usually abolished by the British until much later—for example, in 1936 in Northern Nigeria.

France legally abolished slavery in its colonies in 1848, but the laws were winked at for many years. Many slaves who fled to French territory were expelled, and much territory was "disannexed" and made into protectorates, where attention to the slavery issue could be minimal. Italy outlawed slavery in its Somaliland colony in 1903 and 1904, and the Belgian Congo did so in 1910.

Portugal took weak action, in spite of a strong law nominally abolishing slavery in 1878. Slavery in surreptitious forms, such as contracted labor, survived for many years, even after a second abolition law of 1910. Euphemistic terms such as *libertos* did not conceal the survival of slavelike status in Portuguese colonies.

East Africa was a special case, with a commercialized Arab state centered on Zanzibar, a large legal export slave trade to the Middle East and an illegal one to French and Portuguese territory, and plantations manned by slaves producing cash crops for export. Following exposure of these practices by the missionary David Livingstone, treaties with Zanzibar considerably reduced the external slave trade by the 1880s, although the internal slave economy stayed intact. Legal-status abolition in Zanzibar and Pemba (its island territory to the north, where most slaves worked on clove plantations) took place in 1897. There, as was typical elsewhere, concubines were not freed; atypically, owners received some compensation for their losses.

In general, the colonial powers were motivated to abolish slavery by the influence of abolitionist forces at home and by a strong moral antipathy to the practice on the part of at least some colonial administrators. Many punitive expeditions and episodes of territorial acquisition were justified on the ground that slave-raiding had to be put down. These same governments, however, did not compel a comprehensive end to slavery, owing both to their reluctance to risk the economic disruption they believed would flow from abolition and to their knowledge that the widespread practice of concubinage—and indeed the hegemony of men over women—would be jeopardized by abolition. Colonial reluctance to abolish slavery was also fortified by an initial belief, held by at least some officials in most parts of Africa, that indigenous slavery was more benign than its New World counterpart. This notion contained some truth. In Africa slaves more frequently worked alongside masters, had more autonomy in their daily lives, endured less discipline, and might more likely expect eventual manumission or incorporation into a family lineage. In spite of much scholarly attention to lineage slavery, however, it is probable that its relative benevolence applied to only a minority of Africa's total slave population. In any case, even where conditions were more benign, slavery was a harsh system. Colonial administrators, then, found themselves caught between the moral position against slavery at home and their need to gain and retain indigenous support among local elites, and to guard against upsetting the social and economic structure.

The longstanding reluctance of the colonial powers to support the abolition of slavery itself led slaves in many areas to vote with their feet by running away. This phenomenon was especially prevalent in French West Africa, Italian Somaliland, and British Northern Nigeria in the first decade of the twentieth century. Where did these slaves go? Some slaves who left their masters found employment as soldiers, police, porters, and construction workers (especially in railway-building) in the service of the European colonial powers. Some fled to other masters and political leaders. Many apparently reached their ancestral home areas, though too little is known about these returns. Others joined religious settlements: freed slaves joined the Murids of Senegal and the Islamic brotherhoods in Somaliland; religious radicals established large settlements such as Satiru in Northern Nigeria and across the colonial frontier in French Niger; and along the Kenya coast numerous slaves fled to mission stations. Still others formed villages of their own. Presumably, those who fled included the people who had received the worst treatment and those more inclined toward risk-taking.

Although precise data are not available and even broad numerical estimates can be doubtful, in most areas the great majority of slaves probably stayed either with or near their masters. What factors tended to keep slaves from leaving masters? Inability to acquire land was a major consideration in many areas, especially in economically advanced, densely populated areas such as Zanzibar. Even where land was available, an inability to provide for oneself immediately could restrict departures. Where poll taxes were collected, masters might pay for former slaves who remained in place, whereas those who decamped might encounter difficulties in paying the tax. It was sometimes difficult to include all family members in an escape. There was significant risk of recapture, at least in the earlier period of colonial rule. Harsh vagrancy laws made life more difficult for a runaway. Distant kin in the former home area might be unwilling to accept a returnee. Finally, slave women faced additional difficulties. Not only did they find it burdensome to leave because of their children but, being thought of as "wives," they were expected by both indigenous public opinion and colonial authorities simply to stay in place. Female slaves thus had to deal not only with the prejudice facing them in their own social relations, but also with the intolerance of colonial officials, who often preferred to ignore the widespread subjugation of females. (It should be noted that the colonial papers of the period are replete with references to slaves when really what is meant is "male slaves.") Women trying to flee alone were frequently in an untenable position.

When the colonial governments dealt with slavery, institutional changes were sometimes adopted that differed little from the indigenous practices. The "contract labor" of the Portuguese territory, Spanish Fernando Po, and British Zanzibar and Pemba is a case in point. So is Governor Frederic Lugard's systematizing of *murgu* arrangements in Northern Nigeria, whereby slaves had to participate in their self-ransom with payments, often monthly over a period of several years. Islamic courts treated *murgu* issues and engaged in the return of escaped slaves on many occasions, even though provincial courts were prohibited from doing so under the concept of legal-status abolition. *Murgu* also served to provide owners with a measure of compensation. By contrast, Southern Nigeria ended slavery quite early, declaring all slaves

free in 1901. That freedom, however, was illusory until about the time of World War I, because a "Native House Rule Ordinance," with accompanying apprenticeship measures and vagrancy laws, kept the "freed" slaves from leaving the "houses," which were an important feature of the territory's economy at that time. Former slaves by statute became members of masters' households and subject to their virtually complete authority.

When slaves remained *in situ* or close by their former masters, their new ties with them could range from familiar or even familial to rather distant. Often the institution of slavery became one of mutual obligation and dependence on both sides. Labor and allegiance were offered by the former slaves in exchange for economic and political support from the former masters, in reinterpretations of the old servile status that could be more or less significant. In areas where improved transportation and world demand for commodities led to an expansion of cash cropping, ex-slaves often shared in the growth of income from exports. It is plausible that even ex-slaves who were heavily dependent on their former masters experienced improvement in their treatment because of the increasing ability of people to find work elsewhere as the colonial period advanced. There is much evidence that abolition affected such social features as household labor routines, marriage patterns, the development of patron-client relations in trade, credit, tenancy, and the like, although systematic research on such topics is generally sparse.

The eventual breakdown of slavery had political and economic roots that went well beyond colonial legal efforts to abolish it gradually. As colonial states grew more powerful, for example, the opposition of local authorities and slave-owners did not have to be feared as much as before. Colonial pacification, which encouraged local and regional trade, and the later transport improvements, which led to agricultural and mineral cash exports, increased the demand for labor and thereby the opportunity for ex-slaves to find work. The spread of poll taxes requiring cash income for payment was a factor in the realignment of production toward cash activities. Nonetheless, in parts of some territories, such as Mauritania and Bechuanaland, the colonial authorities were so weak that they simply allowed slavery to continue.

In general, the attitude of colonial officials toward slavery hardened noticeably as their power increased and as their need for alliances with local elites lessened. Despite this tendency, however, the many survivals of slavery and of some slave-trading evident even after World War I led the League of Nations to become involved in the issue. The resulting Slavery Convention of 1926 required the signatory powers to suppress all forms of slavery. Only thereafter was the legal status of slavery at last abolished in Sierra Leone (1927) and Bechuanaland (1936). In the latter year involuntary slavery itself, as distinct from its legal status, was finally abolished in Northern Nigeria and by the Italians in newly conquered Ethiopia, where slave-trading had only recently been brought under a measure of control by the Ethiopian authorities. During those years a Liberian form of quasi-slavery, contract labor supplied to Spain's colony of Fernando Po, was finally curbed.

Unfortunately for some Africans, complete abolition of slavery had yet to be accomplished in the 1990s. Reports of slavery still emanated from parts of the continent, with Mauritania and southern Sudan two prominent cases. For women, continued concubinage and male domination meant that some remained among the unfree at the end of the twentieth century.

[*See also* Africa, *overview article and article on* East Africa; Manumission; *and* Slave Trade, *article on* Trans-Saharan Trade.]

BIBLIOGRAPHY

Cooper, Frederick. *Plantation Slavery on the East Coast of Africa*. New Haven: Yale University Press, 1977.

Klein, Martin A., ed. *Breaking the Chains: Slavery, Bondage and Emancipation in Africa and Asia*. Madison: University of Wisconsin Press, 1993.

Lovejoy, Paul E. *Transformations in Slavery: A History of Slavery in Africa*. Cambridge: Cambridge University Press, 1983.

Lovejoy, Paul E., and Jan S. Hogendorn. *Slow Death for Slavery: The Course of Abolition in Northern Nigeria, 1897–1936*. Cambridge: Cambridge University Press, 1993.

Miers, Suzanne. *Britain and the Ending of the Slave Trade*. London: Longmans, 1975.

Miers, Suzanne, and Richard Roberts, eds. *The End of Slavery in Africa*. Madison: University of Wisconsin Press, 1988. See especially chapter 1, an essay of the same title by the editors.

Miers, Suzanne, and Igor Kopytoff, eds. *Slavery in Africa: Historical and Anthropological Perspectives*. Madison: University of Wisconsin Press, 1977.

Morton, Fred. *Children of Ham: Freed Slaves and Fugitive Slaves on the Kenya Coast, 1873 to 1907*. Boulder, Colo.: Westview, 1990.

—JAN S. HOGENDORN

India

Agitations by abolitionists in England in the nineteenth century resulted in extensive official inquiries into the extent of slavery in India. These revealed that slaves were bought and sold, and exported and imported, but this slave traffic was much less significant than the revelation that over much of the country, agricultural laborers lived in a state of bondage. These laborers generally belonged to the lowest castes. The caste system itself imposed severe disabilities; by virtue of their birth, members of the low castes often could not change employers but might be bought and sold by them.

The British found several different systems of bondage in operation in India, and the extent and forms of bondage varied from locality to locality. Apart from the bondage implicit in the caste system, various forms of bondage, from chattel slavery to debt peonage, were recognized in both the classical Hindu and Muslim legal systems, as well as in the customary laws of each district. These legal and customary forms did not necessarily correspond to either classical or New World slavery; they must be seen in their Indian context. Moreover, the conditions of domestic slaves differed from those of agricultural laborers. Women could be purchased for sexual services as well as for field or domestic labor, and the purchased woman's child might belong to her master. For this reason, the prices of bonded males and females frequently diverged. Children could be sold into slavery, especially during famines; prisoners of war could be enslaved; and bondage of varying terms could be imposed as a punishment by a ruler.

Indian languages have various words for "slave," although the full meaning of the word depended on its context. A slave or bondsman could in theory belong to any caste, with the possible exception of brahmans. Similarly, members even of the lower castes were not necessarily bonded. Caste and civil states were thus not completely congruent, but in practice they were closely linked. Members of the upper castes were much less likely to become *dāsas* (roughly "slaves") than the lower castes, and in many parts of India agricultural laborers were drawn largely from certain very low castes. Similar caste systems were found outside India, for instance in Nepal. The tribal population of India was very large, and some tribes practiced slavery, although anthropologists have argued that a tribal "slave" was in fact better off than a nominally "free" untouchable in a village in the plains.

Knowledge of conditions before the British arrived is very limited, although it is known that there were great regional variations. Local customs governed practice more than formal legal texts, and these customs varied greatly. The colonial period was marked by greater efficiency in enforcement, and the official records are much better than for previous regimes, but even so, there are huge gaps in our knowledge of actual conditions. At first the British followed their predecessors and not only recognized but supported caste divisions. For instance, early nineteenth-century officials often returned "runaway slaves" to their former masters. Such official policies in matters of land revenue, debt bondage, forced labor, and related issues were reversed later in the nineteenth century, and official support was tacitly withdrawn from the masters.

The British also attempted to attack slavery by law. In response to the English abolition move-

ment, the government of India passed Act V of 1843. This did not abolish slavery but withdrew all official support from it. Courts no longer enforced rights arising out of the alleged possession of slaves. The changes in the law undoubtedly improved the conditions of, for example, chattel slaves, but the greater part of bondage was embedded in the caste system, and the withdrawal of official support for the masters' alleged rights over laborers had little effect in the short run.

Changes in the form and degree of bondage, especially in the countryside, were uncertain and slow. It seems likely, too, that changes in the law or in official policies played a far smaller part in freeing slaves, debt peons, and bonded laborers in general than did urbanization, ideological changes and political organization, and emigration. Running away from one's employer to a public works job, a city, or abroad was the best escape. Between 1846 and 1932 about twenty-eight million Indians emigrated, mainly to work in the tropics.

There can be no doubt that thousands of laborers escaped from bondage and that the conditions of others improved during the colonial period. Both processes, however, were slow because economic growth and urbanization was slower in India than in many other parts of the developing world.

Both processes accelerated after Indian independence in 1947, despite relatively slow economic growth, rapid population growth, and low emigration. (Information on Pakistan and Bangladesh is not readily available). Nonetheless, debt bondage was still prevalent in India at the end of the twentieth century, even in some new industries. Children remained particularly prone to becoming bonded laborers. Despite these undeniable facts, though, enormous strides have been taken.

The pace of change has been uneven. Change has been particularly striking in the state of Kerala, where in some areas the lowest castes were virtually slaves at the beginning of the nineteenth century. They were bought, sold and mortgaged, and could even be killed by their masters. Kerala is not the richest part of India, but it enjoys a high level of education; in addition, missionaries of various religions and political parties have been very active there. As a result, today the lower castes in Kerala can go where they will.

[*See also* Asia, *article on* South Asia; *and* Slave Trade, *article on* Asia and Oceania.]

BIBLIOGRAPHY

Breman, Jan. *Patronage and Exploitation: Changing Agrarian Relations in South Gujarat, India*. Translated by Wil van Gulik. Berkeley: University of California Press, 1974.

Kumar, Dharma. *Land and Caste in South India*. New Delhi: Manohar, 1992.

Moffat, Michael. *An Untouchable Community in South India: Structure and Consensus*. Princeton: Princeton University Press, 1979.

Prakash, Gyan. *Bonded Histories: Genealogies of Labour Servitude in Colonial India*. Cambridge: Cambridge University Press, 1990.

—DHARMA KUMAR

Southeast Asia

During the nineteenth century the region of Southeast Asia underwent fundamental social and economic changes. Prominent among the trends was a decline of corvée and slavery and the rise of human self-ownership. Concomitantly, more elaborate property rights in land developed. Change occurred in an increasingly monetized and commercialized economy in which both domestic and international trade and migration became relatively more important.

Economic change was accompanied by major changes in political and administrative structure. Many countries were or would become colonies of Western powers (Spain, the Netherlands, Great Britain, France, and later the United States) during this period; there were also important changes in the degree of centralization and governmental control, especially under colonial rule. In the one Southeast Asian country that maintained its independence, Thailand, major domestic political change included the rise of the power of the central government, and within that government, a

rise in the power of the monarch. These changes were associated with a decline in warfare among neighboring states.

Generalizations on Human-Property Rights. The literature of economic history on preindustrial Europe and the Americas provides important generalizations about the origins and evolution of property rights in humans. First, property rights in humans are associated with land-abundant, labor-scarce economies (Domar, 1970; Engerman, 1992). Labor scarcity creates rents and makes labor relatively valuable. Property rights in humans provide a mechanism for elites to appropriate part of the high value of human labor. Furthermore, in circumstances of abundant land and scarce labor, labor markets typically are thin: little labor is supplied to the market, and employers cannot rely on being able to hire or retain workers, providing additional incentives to create and maintain human-property rights. Second, political rather than strictly economic factors are critical to an understanding of the motives for the abolition of various forms of slavery.

Generalizations based on experience in Europe and the Americas are largely but not entirely consistent with evidence from other settings. Corvée and slavery were found in Southeast Asian economies characterized by an abundance of land and scarcity of labor. Their abolition was largely influenced by political rather than strictly economic motives.

Change in property rights in Southeast Asia took place in the context of a rapidly changing economy. The expansion of intra-Asian trade and development of world markets for a number of products resulted in changes in relative commodity prices that generally favored the producers of primary products. The changes in relative commodity prices in turn induced changes in relative factor prices that in general favored land prices with respect to real wages. Domestic and international political trends reinforced the incentives for changing property rights created by the economic change and were further reinforced by an international moral climate that disapproved of slavery.

Economic Change in Southeast Asia. Conditions at the onset of the nineteenth century varied considerably within Southeast Asia. Some economies had long participated in world trade; other economies remained predominantly subsistence-oriented, but in most, international trade was already important. Reductions in the costs of communication and transportation favored the development of trade in bulky, low-value commodities, in contrast to the earlier reliance on scarce, high-value commodities such as spices and certain forest products. In exchange, imports of manufactured goods such as textiles increased rapidly. In general, the volume of international trade expanded considerably over the first half of the nineteenth century and even more vigorously in the latter half.

Nature of Property Rights in Humans around 1800. The control of manpower has long been viewed as the key to power in Southeast Asian societies. For instance, in the early nineteenth century Thai society could be divided into five categories: the monarch, members of the royal family, the nobility, commoners, and slaves. Officials or nobles, the *nai*, were directly responsible for the control of commoners, the *phrai*. The *nai-phrai* system was based on personal ties and was not a territorially based system of government. In addition, there were two fundamental categories of slaves in Thai society, war captives and debt slaves. Slaves were the traditional booty of war in mainland Southeast Asia; typically prisoners of war were settled as whole communities on lands far from their point of capture. Thai debt slavery might be better understood as servitude or indenture in the European context. In an economy with an abundance of land and usufruct property rights in land, people served as collateral on loans.

Broadly similar forms of property rights in man existed in other countries of Southeast Asia. Many regimes relied on property rights in humans to restrict movements of labor and to enforce settlement patterns in the interest of the elite. In general, as warfare became less endemic and colonial rule more effective, the prisoner-of-war category of slavery declined.

Evolution of Property Rights in Humans. Changes in the system of corvée and slavery must be understood within the context of major concomitant trends, including the commercialization of the economy and the decline of warfare among neighboring states. The growing importance of trade in the economy broadened and deepened both product and factor markets. Increasing links with India and southern China underwrote the immigration of large numbers of traders and workers, who often migrated to Southeast Asia under some form of formal or informal contract of indentured labor. Growing commercialization meant that money payments could increasingly be substituted for in-kind payments of services for corvée obligations. The development of an enlarged labor market meant that the government could turn reliably to wage workers for major public-works projects rather than relying on corvée laborers, who in general had little incentive to perform tasks conscientiously. The substitution of Chinese coolies for corvée labor on public works was common in Thailand, the Philippines, and Indonesia.

Political and administrative change also contributed importantly to the trend away from human-property rights. As colonial administrations became more powerful, they created territorial forms of administration. Officials became responsible for the administration of geographically defined regions rather than defined groups of people. This trend was also evident in Thailand, where King Chulalongkorn patterned many of his administrative changes, especially those of 1892, after the colonial system of administration in British India.

Parallel with the gradual dismantling of corvée was the abolition of slavery. Changes aimed at making Thai slavery more humane were forthcoming in the reign of King Mongkut (1851–1868). In order to combat the growth of slavery due to gambling debts, Mongkut issued an edict in 1868 that required that a wife consent before she or her children could be sold into slavery. Mongkut found it morally objectionable that under the old law "a woman is like a buffalo, a man a human being" (Chatthip and Suthy, 1977, p. 57). Major changes came in the next reign when King Chulalongkorn moved to abolish slavery gradually by decreeing that for slaves born after October 1868, the price of the child slave would decline according to a prescribed schedule, until by age twenty-one the slave would be freed. By 1915 slavery legally ceased in Thailand.

King Chulalongkorn adopted a gradual path of abolition. He was aware of the difficulties experienced in Russia and the United States when human-property rights were abolished abruptly. The scheduled decreases in the legal prices of slaves served to accomplish the goal of abolition without generating a fiscal burden on the government to compensate former owners. Gradualism also blunted the opposition of slave-owners, many of whom were members of powerful bureaucratic families or of the royal family. The removal of manpower from the control of bureaucratic officials was in fact one of Chulalongkorn's motives.

Humanitarian motives were also clearly evident. Moral judgments and authority were used by the monarchs in the arguments for and legitimization of the abolition of slavery. Moreover, the political motives for abolition of slavery in Thailand were not entirely domestically generated. The abolition of slavery was clearly required if Thailand were to regain sovereignty and abrogate extraterritoriality provisions in treaties signed with Western powers.

Similar patterns of gradual abolition of slavery and corvée were seen in the European colonies. The moral arguments against slavery there were often reinforced by the spread of cosmopolitan religions such as Islam and Christianity that disapproved of slavery. Political pressure in Europe resulted in the abolition of slave-trading by Great Britain in 1807, France in 1815, and the Netherlands in 1818. The abolition of slavery itself in the colonies was more gradual, with formal legislation to end slavery coming in the Dutch East Indies in 1860, in Cambodia in 1877 and 1884, in Malaya in 1915, and in Burma in 1926.

Conclusions. Domestic and international political motives rather than economic incentives appear to have played the direct role in accounting for the dismantling of human-property rights in Southeast Asia in the nineteenth century. Corvée was not discontinued because officials were no longer interested in extracting surplus from commoners, and slavery was not abolished because it became unprofitable. The role of economic forces was indirect. Economic change created the product and factor markets that made corvée and slavery less attractive. The erosion of these arrangements helped to fuel the movements of labor on which further expansion of the commercial economy depended.

The rise of self-ownership for humans was part of a fundamental change in the nature of societies in Southeast Asia. Economic change favored the creation of property rights in land, territorially based public administration, and the development of a reliable wage labor market. Political change favored the deliberate creation of modern colonial regimes, or of a nation-state in the case of Thailand. Trends in human-property rights reflected the growing influences of international political and economic forces, including the normative judgment that slavery and bondage were immoral, and an ideological position that only a society of freemen would have the incentive to work hard and prosper. In the nineteenth century in the Western democracies voters expressing their distaste for human-property rights were able to alter government policy on slavery both at home and in colonial dependencies. The result of both the domestic and international political struggles was the redistribution of the control of labor services from traditional and colonial elites to commoners.

[See also Asia, *article on* Southeast Asia; *and* Property.]

BIBLIOGRAPHY

Domar, Evsey D. "The Causes of Slavery or Serfdom: A Hypothesis." *Journal of Economic History* 30 (Mar. 1970): 18–32.

Engerman, Stanley L. "Coerced and Free Labor: Property Rights and the Development of the Labor Force." *Explorations in Economic History* 29 (1992): 1–29.

Feeny, David. "The Demise of Corvée and Slavery in Thailand, 1782–1913." In Klein, 1993.

Klein, Martin A., ed. *Breaking the Chains: Slavery, Bondage, and Emancipation in Africa and Asia*. Madison: University of Wisconsin Press, 1993.

Nartsupha, Chatthip, and Suthy Prasartset, eds. *Socio-Economic Institutions and Cultural Change in Siam, 1851–1910: A Documentary Survey*. Singapore: Institute of Southeast Asian Studies, 1977.

Reid, Anthony, ed. *Slavery, Bondage and Dependency in Southeast Asia*. St Lucia: University of Queensland Press, 1983.

Watson, James L., ed. *Asian and African Systems of Slavery*. Oxford: Basil Blackwell, 1980.

—DAVID FEENY

Britain

The conversion of Britain from a slave power into the world's leading opponent of slavery is one of the most striking transformations of modern history. Occurring at a time when Britain's position both as a slave trader and as an employer of slaves was at its zenith, it cannot, like most such historical transformations, be accounted for as a consequence either of war or of economic interest. Although historians continue to debate its underlying causes, there is little disagreement concerning the manner in which it occurred or its important contribution to ending both the trade and chattel slavery generally.

Until the last quarter of the eighteenth century the British, like other colonizing powers, took slavery largely for granted. It was in any case an institution that affected few directly, being almost entirely confined to the colonies. There were several thousand blacks in Britain, some of whom were treated as slaves, and occasionally these were bought and sold, but slavery in Britain lacked the legal status it possessed in the colonies. A key decision in this regard was the ruling by Lord Chief Justice, Baron Mansfield in 1772 that James Somerset, a former Virginian slave, could not be forcibly returned to bondage in America. Although Mansfield's ruling did not immediately prevent blacks from being treated as slaves, it showed that slavery was unsupported by English law, destroying whatever claims to legitimacy it had once possessed.

Meanwhile, popular attitudes were changing. One important factor in bringing this about was the spread of Enlightenment ideas regarding natural rights and political liberty. Another was the growing conviction in Nonconformist and evangelical circles that slavery was contrary to the teaching of the Gospels. How could practices of the kind reported from the colonies, still less the horrors of the slave trade, be reconciled with the injunction to love one's neighbor? The more the British thought about slavery—as they were encouraged to do by the rise of evangelical nonconformity and the political debates occasioned by the American War of Independence—the less morally defensible it appeared.

To disapprove of an institution, however, was one thing; actively to seek its overthrow was quite another. Here the contribution of the Quakers was crucial. During the 1770s the Society of Friends purged its own membership first of those involved in the slave trade and then of slave-owners. In 1783, responding to a request from Philadelphia Quakers, the London Meeting for Sufferings established what was effectively the first British anti-slavery society. In defense of their own sectarian interests Quakers had become adept at using a broad range of techniques designed to bring pressure to bear on Parliament; they now proceeded to use these in promoting the anti-slavery cause.

The major breakthroughs, however, came in 1787 with the creation of the Society for the Abolition of the Slave Trade (1787–1807), which broadened the base of operation by bringing non-Quakers into the movement, and with the launching in 1787 and 1788 of the first campaign for the mass petitioning of Parliament. Among the new recruits were William Wilberforce, who became the movement's principal parliamentary spokesman, and Thomas Clarkson. Clarkson's role was to gather information and mobilize support throughout the country by establishing local organizations. In this respect the work already done by the Quakers proved useful. Not only did the Quakers' system of weekly, monthly, and quarterly meetings provide a ready-made structure on which to build a network of provincial auxiliaries, but it was they who provided the movement with much of its funding.

Not even Clarkson, however, was prepared for the massive response to the petition campaign of 1787–1786. Manchester alone produced almost eleven thousand signatures, representing some two-thirds of the city's adult male population (it not being thought appropriate at that time for women to subscribe). In Sheffield two thousand signed, and in York, one thousand eight hundred. Other major towns as well as many smaller places also contributed. In all, about one hundred petitions were submitted containing perhaps sixty thousand names. Impressive as this was as a first attempt, it was dwarfed by subsequent campaigns, culminating in the great emancipation effort of 1833 with its five thousand petitions and almost one and one-half million signers. On the basis of the numbers alone it might be concluded that abolitionism rated ahead of parliamentary reform and religious liberalization as the most broadly based reform movement of the period.

Realizing that it would be impolitic to attack both the slave trade and slave-owning at the same

Brigantine H.M.S. Acorn Captures the Slaver Gabriel; painting, Thomas Dutton, nineteenth century; National Maritime Museum, Greenwich.

time, the movement's leaders had from the start resolved to concentrate on the former as the more vulnerable. A number of shocking accounts, together with Clarkson's revelations regarding the high death rate among white sailors engaged in the traffic, also played into the abolitionists' hands. Parliament was impressed by the display of public feeling, and for a moment in 1792 it looked as if the abolitionists might carry the day; conceivably they would have done so but for the alarm occasioned by events across the Channel and the subsequent war with France.

Nevertheless, there was little doubt that it was the abolitionists who henceforth occupied the moral high ground. The slaving interests were reduced to emphasizing the impolicy of interfering with traditional practices and institutions, as exemplified by the way French attempts at reform had given rise to the slave revolt in Haiti. Even so, between 1792 and 1804 British abolitionism remained virtually in abeyance.

Matters changed with the French defeat at Trafalgar and the acquisition of new colonies in the Caribbean. The prospect of these being stocked with slaves, thereby challenging the position of the older colonies, divided the West Indian interest by persuading some of its members of the need to restrict the slave trade. In 1806 Parliament agreed to abolish the traffic to the newly conquered territories. Because these were the only areas where demand remained buoyant, the traders were left with little to fight for, and in 1807 a comprehensive measure abolishing the trade to foreign and imperial possessions was triumphantly approved by large majorities in both the Lords and the Commons.

Many had supposed that the ending of the slave trade would lead eventually to the abolition of slavery, on the grounds that owners would need to conserve labor and that free workers, having more incentive, would be more productive than slaves. This proved not to be the case. Meanwhile, the Society for the Abolition of the Slave Trade had been replaced by the African Institution (1807–1827), a body concerned principally with persuading other nations to emulate the British by renouncing the slave trade and by encouraging Africans to engage in other forms of commerce. Here, too, the results were disappointing. The French, having given up the trade during the Napoleonic wars, regarded it as only fair that they should be allowed time to restock their possessions. Others, exploiting the economic opportunities created, hastened to fill the vacuum occasioned by Britain's withdrawal.

Most immediately aggravating, however, was the West Indian planters' determination not only to retain slavery but also to resist all efforts to improve the treatment of their slaves. Abolitionists responded by establishing a new organization, the Society for the Amelioration and Gradual Abolition of Slavery (1823–1839), more generally known as the Anti-Slavery Society. As its full title indicates, the initial aim of this body was to reform rather than abolish. That certainly was the intention of its principal parliamentary spokesman, Thomas Fowell Buxton, who had taken over leadership of the movement from Wilberforce. Once again Clarkson found himself touring the country organizing support. Confronted with the planters' intransigence, however, abolitionists became increasingly frustrated, with the result that a breakaway group, the Agency Committee (1831–1834), began demanding nothing less than immediate and unconditional emancipation.

The final stages of the campaign against colonial slavery coincided with the rising excitement over the Great Reform Bill of 1832. It was a time of great liberal fervor. The Agency Committee employed a team of professional lecturers to organize petitions and persuade local electors to obtain pledges from parliamentary candidates. But although the reformed Commons was prepared to end slavery, there was no hope of getting such a bill through the Lords without compensation for the slaveholders and a transitional period of apprenticeship designed to allow both slaves and owners to adjust to their new circumstances.

These were onerous conditions. The Emancipation Act of 1833 provided that as of 1 August 1834 slavery would cease throughout Britain's colonies. In return for their freedom, however, the slaves would be required to devote three-quarters of their time to the service of their former owners in return for food and clothing, the remaining quarter being set aside for them to work on their own plots. This apprenticeship system was to be supervised by salaried magistrates sent out from Britain and was to last, in the case of fieldhands, until 1840. For their part of the bargain, the planters received compensation of twenty million pounds, an enormous sum by the standards of the day, roughly equivalent to half the nation's annual budget. Considering that this had ultimately to be funded by taxpayers, and that the price of colonial sugar

underwent a sharp rise following the eventual shift to free labor, the cost of emancipation to ordinary Britons was not inconsiderable.

Until the eve of the Emancipation Act, the British anti-slavery movement had shown remarkable solidarity. At its center stood the metropolitan committee, which, in consultation with its parliamentary spokesman, was responsible for formulating policy. Around the periphery were the provincial bodies, some large and active, others little more than church congregations but nevertheless capable of being moved to action. Not surprisingly, many of these were puzzled by the appearance of a second metropolitan organization in the form of the Agency Committee (later Society). During the 1832–1833 campaign the two

British anti-slavery meeting at Exeter Hall, London; engraving from
The Illustrated London News, nineteenth century.

bodies worked closely together, with the result that only those belonging to their inner groups were aware of the differences separating them. In the aftermath of victory, however, these were no longer concealed. Many in the Agency camp expressed their belief that Buxton and the Anti-Slavery Society had been precipitous in accepting the government's conditions and that a further effort at arousing the public would have secured the freedmen better terms.

These divisions acquired an edge of bitterness in the course of the subsequent campaign for the overthrow of apprenticeship. The Anti-Slavery Society, having agreed to apprenticeship, was prepared to let matters take their course. Joseph Sturge, a Birmingham Quaker who had emerged as a leader of the Agency faction, was not. Having visited the West Indies to observe matters for himself, he established a new body, the Central Negro Emancipation Committee (1837–1840), which set about impressing Parliament with yet another display of public indignation. Eventually, finding the apprenticeship system cumbersome and reluctant to incur further public oppression, Parliament refused to act, although the effort appears to have been partly instrumental in persuading the planters to end apprenticeship in 1838, two years earlier than originally planned.

Having now achieved all its original goals, the British movement became ever more divided. The government's main concern was to secure the suppression of the remaining Atlantic slave trade by concluding treaties with foreign nations and deploying naval power. In this it received little popular support and was actively opposed by the movement's Quakers, on the grounds that the use of force was contrary to their pacifist principles. Meanwhile, Buxton, with the backing of many groups who were now willing to associate themselves with what they saw as a victorious movement, had established the African Civilization Society (1839–1843) with the intention of cutting off the trade at root by establishing model settlements in Africa. He succeeded in persuading the

Whig administration to back the scheme, but the resulting Niger Expedition (1841–1842) was a fiasco. Sturge's Quaker-dominated British and Foreign Anti-Slavery Society, also founded in 1839, placed its faith in the influence of Christian benevolence and sought to turn the triumph of the British movement into a worldwide moral crusade. Not surprisingly, it soon discovered that other countries did not welcome British interference in their internal affairs. The society's attempt to stop the importation of foreign (and thus slave-grown) sugar into Britain proved unsuccessful and alienated free-traders and others on whose support abolitionists had counted.

By the 1850s the public had grown tired of supporting organizations it saw as faction-ridden and given to supporting dubious causes. The economic consequences of emancipation had proved disappointing, and few could understand the ideological differences among the various American abolitionist groups, whose members had begun appearing on British lecture circuits. Nevertheless, the country remained firmly committed to anti-slavery principles, as was evident from unwearying British efforts to suppress the Atlantic slave trade and the frequent invocation of these efforts in justification of other British actions around the world.

The British anti-slavery movement has continued to intrigue historians, not least because of the apparent lack of self-interest on the part of its principal supporters. This is so contrary to conventional views of political behavior that it has given rise to scholarly controversy. Yet in spite of the exercise of much ingenuity, no one has succeeded in showing that those who campaigned for the ending of the slave trade and then for the freeing of the slaves stood to gain personally in any tangible way, or that these measures were other than economically costly to the country. In due course Britain's anti-slavery achievements came to be viewed with pride as expressing the nation's commitment to humane and liberal principles. Occasionally these principles were invoked in defense of British expansionism, as in the scramble for Africa, but that was a later development and hardly explains why they were adopted in the first place. Although chattel slavery has virtually disappeared at the end of the twentieth century, other forms of bondage continue to arouse British concern, as exemplified by the efforts of the London-based Anti-Slavery International in the 1990s.

[*See also* Apprenticeship; *and* Emancipation in the Americas.]

BIBLIOGRAPHY

Blackburn, Robin. *The Overthrow of Colonial Slavery, 1776–1848*. London: Verso, 1988.
Drescher, Seymour. *Capitalism and Antislavery: British Mobilization in Comparative Perspective*. London: Macmillan, 1986.
Drescher, Seymour. *Econocide: British Slavery in the Era of Abolition*. Pittsburgh: University of Pittsburgh Press, 1977.
Temperley, Howard. *British Antislavery, 1833–1870*. London: Longmans, 1972.
Wilson, Ellen Gibson. *Thomas Clarkson: A Biography*. London: Macmillan, 1989.

—HOWARD TEMPERLEY

Continental Europe

The problem of abolition concerned the nations of continental Europe from the French Revolution until well into the twentieth century. The primary objectives of continental anti-slavery were the abolition of the slave trade between Africa and the Americas and the abolition of slavery in the Caribbean colonies. Beginning in the 1880s, European governments turned their attention to ending slavery and the slave trade in Africa, although the origins of those initiatives lay in the early to mid-nineteenth century.

Abolition of the slave trade was often the first step in the dismantling of Caribbean slavery. Without a steady supply of new slaves, colonial slave-owners realized that emancipation was inevitable, but they fought to delay that outcome for as long as possible.

Great Britain was most active in enforcing the abolition of the Atlantic slave trade through treaties with European and African powers and through direct naval pressure. Sweden, Denmark, and the Netherlands ceased to participate in the slave trade after the Napoleonic Wars. France, however, revived its slave trade during the Restoration and only effectively abolished the trade after 1830 with the consolidation of the July Monarchy. The Spanish and Portuguese were the most recalcitrant slave-traders. Portugal had lost its American slave colonies with the independence of Brazil in 1822, but Portuguese and Spanish traders continued to transport slaves from the western coast of Africa to Brazil and Cuba. British pressure, both military and diplomatic, finally brought the trans-Atlantic slave trade to an end through treaties signed with Brazil in 1850 and with Spain in 1867.

In the Caribbean, France abolished colonial slavery in 1794, reinstated it in 1802 (except in Saint Domingue, which in 1804 became the sovereign nation of Haiti), and definitively abolished it in 1848, when abolition took place in the French African colonies as well. Sweden abolished slavery in its Caribbean possessions in 1847, Denmark in 1848, and the Netherlands in 1863. Spain was the last European nation to abolish Caribbean slavery, in Puerto Rico in 1873 and in Cuba in 1886.

Unlike the influential abolitionist movement in Great Britain, continental anti-slavery associations such as the French Amis des Noirs (established in 1788) played little role in the destruction of Caribbean slavery. Generally, metropolitan governments and colonial slave-owners dictated the timing of emancipation. As Seymour Drescher has argued, continental anti-slavery associations, unlike their North American and British counterparts, were narrowly elite organizations that sought to work within and through the government rather than resort to mass extra-parliamentary pressure to bring about abolition.

Dutch anti-slavery and abolition is illustrative. The Dutch government generally catered to the interests of planters in Suriname, the largest Dutch Caribbean colony. Efforts in the Netherlands to produce a significant anti-slavery movement, often encouraged by British anti-slavery associations, generally failed. The associations that did form were narrow, short-lived organizations of political and religious leaders who worked peacefully within the parliament rather than seeking to place popular pressure on the government. The Dutch government enacted final abolition in 1863 after more than a decade of negotiation with colonial slave-owners.

Abolition in the French and Spanish Caribbean colonies were exceptions to this pattern, though only at particular moments. In those cases revolution from below, in both the colonies and the metropolis, radicalized the abolition process. The destruction of slavery in Saint Domingue (Haiti) was the most dramatic example. In August 1793 the French Jacobin commissioner Léger Felicité

Masthead of *La Campana de Gracia*, Barcelona, 22 December 1872, with the legend "We are all brothers!"

Oprobi etern per los que en plé sigle XIX. se atrevelxen á defensar la esclavitut.

Sonthonax declared the abolition of slavery in Saint Domingue. He acted in part in recognition of the slave rebellion that had torn Saint Domingue since 1791. He also sought to mobilize the slave population in defense of French sovereignty against British and Spanish invasions, as well as out of republican principles. Several months later, in February 1794, the Jacobin-controlled National Convention in France supported his move by enacting abolition in all French colonies. The Jacobins too acted out of mixed motives. On the one hand, they condemned slavery as one more inhumane, irrational element of the old regime; on the other. they sought to preserve French hegemony in the Caribbean colonies by allying themselves with insurgent slaves against rival European powers.

The alliance between colonial slaves and metropolitan revolutionaries between 1793 and 1802 (when Bonaparte reinstated colonial slavery) represented the highest point of continental anti-slavery radicalism. That nexus between colonial and metropolitan revolution would reoccur in Spain and its Antillean colonies, Cuba and Puerto Rico, between 1868 and 1874. When slaves and slave-owners in eastern Cuba rebelled against Spanish rule in 1868, Spain's revolutionary regimes, especially the First Republic (February 1873–January 1874), sought to reconstruct Spanish hegemony in the Antilles by abolishing slavery. Counter-revolution headed by metropolitan and colonial conservatives cut off the metropolitan initiatives, though not before the Republic abolished Puerto Rican slavery in March 1873. The restored Bourbon monarchy reinstated colonial policies dictated by the interests of the large slave-owners of western Cuba, who, despite the continuation of the eastern rebellion until 1880, defended slavery until final abolition in 1886.

European efforts in Africa were intimately tied to the imperial rivalries of the late nineteenth century during the "scramble for Africa." By that time Protestant and Catholic missionaries were the driving forces in influencing European public opinion. At the conferences of Berlin (1884–1885) and Brussels (1889–1890) the European powers, in part to legitimate the partitioning of Africa, agreed in principle to abolish slavery and the slave trade. However, European antislavery policies in Africa were deeply fractured; policies were often formulated to meet the approval of metropolitan publics but practiced differently within Africa. Suppression varied greatly in timing and effectiveness, and slavery persisted in some parts of Africa into the late twentieth century.

Robin Blackburn's discussion of "revolutionary emancipationism" points toward further research into the destruction of slavery in the colonies of continental Europe. Popular insurgencies in the colonies and the metropolis, rather than well-orchestrated abolitionist movements as in Great Britain, were fundamental in challenging the interests of slave-owners and metropolitan governments. In Europe and the European colonies revolution was the necessary condition for powerful attacks on slavery. Nevertheless, the spectacle of revolution should not blind us to the daily conflicts, especially between masters and slaves, that helped bring slavery to an end.

[*See also* Caribbean Region; Emancipation in the Americas; *and* Revolts.]

BIBLIOGRAPHY

Blackburn, Robin. *The Overthrow of Colonial Slavery, 1776–1848*. London: Verso, 1988.

Bolt, Christine, and Seymour Drescher, eds. *Antislavery, Religion, and Reform: Essays in Memory of Roger Anstey*. Folkestone: William Dawson & Sons, 1980.

James, C. L. R. *The Black Jacobins: Toussaint L'Ouverture and the San Domingo Revolution*. 2d rev. ed. New York: Vintage Books, 1963.

Knight, Franklin. *The Caribbean: The Genesis of a Fragmented Nationalism*. 2d ed. New York and Oxford: Oxford University Press, 1990.

Miers, Suzanne, and Richard Roberts, eds. *The End of Slavery in Africa*. Madison: University of Wisconsin Press, 1988.

Oostindie, Gert, ed. *Fifty Years Later: Antislavery, Capitalism and Modernity in the Dutch Orbit*. Pittsburgh: University of Pittsburgh Press, 1996.

—CHRISTOPHER SCHMIDT-NOWARA

Latin America

On 13 May 1888 Princess Isabel, daughter of the emperor of Brazil, signed the "Golden Law," abolishing slavery in Brazil and bringing an end to an institution that had existed in Latin America since the Age of Discovery. Her actions capped a lengthy process: the roots of abolition can be traced back to the beginnings of the institution in Spanish and Portuguese America and to the ways it evolved over the generations.

The process of abolition in Latin America had been a long one, but the critical factors that ultimately destroyed the system emerged in the late eighteenth and early nineteenth centuries. The length of the process, the various anti-slavery pressures, and the unique features of the several countries, along with the varying anti-slavery pressures, produced differing abolition experiences as well as divergent explanations of the events. Historians who subscribed to the Tannenbaum-Freyre thesis—that Latin American slavery was less harsh than its United States counterpart—contended that emancipation in Latin America was relatively straightforward, with little conflict. Later works challenged the picture of a milder slave system but shared the view of a nonconfrontational abolition process, describing Latin American slavery as having died "of old age" and abolition as having been a "non-event." Others have disagreed, arguing that while Latin American emancipation may not have been as apocalyptic as the U.S. example, it was a wide-ranging and momentous struggle against powerful pro-slavery forces.

Academics have challenged one another over the nature of Latin American abolition as well as its principal cause, but on the whole they agree that a combination of external and internal factors were involved. Among the former were the changes wrought by the eighteenth-century Enlightenment, the rise of liberalism, and the "Age of Revolution" that gave birth to the crusade against the slave trade. Spearheaded by Great Britain, this effort was joined by other European nations, the United States, and the Latin American states following their independence, and it eventually ended the trade in African slaves. Equally significant was the slave revolution in Saint Domingue (1791–1804), which secured independence for Haiti and freedom for the country's slaves. It awakened slaveholders in neighboring countries to the possibility of a similar crisis and gave their slaves a model to follow.

A third external factor was the spread of industrial capitalism. Some historians have seen a cause-and-effect relationship between capitalism's rise and the decline of Latin American slavery, arguing that the acceptance of the former with its expensive technology, forward-looking elites, and free and efficient wage labor force was incompatible with the survival of the latter. Whether responding to capitalism's impact or not, Latin America's employers required an alternative supply of new workers. Local populations of Indians, mestizos, mulattoes, and free blacks proved a rich source of labor, as did people on foreign shores: in China coolies were contracted for Peru and Cuba, and in Portugal and Italy workers for Brazil were hired. The consequences were a reduction in the number of slaves, an increasing acceptance of wage labor, and a broadening inquiry into the status and future of slavery.

Internal pressures produced similar results. Economic factors—such as the weak export sector that affected much of post-independence Latin America and the rise in the cost of slaves, particularly in Cuba and Brazil—helped to reduce the number of slaves, slaveholders, and those who could afford slaves. Political factors also contributed to slavery's demise. In general, the turmoil of the independence period and subsequent decades fractured local elites, leaving them too weak to cope effectively with anti-slavery pressures. Political developments played a vital role in some countries; thus in Venezuela, a liberal government in 1854 implemented an abolition decree to prevent restive conservatives from recruiting slaves

for another of the internecine struggles that plagued that country's early republican years. That same year in Peru, a rebellious ex-president issued a similar decree to win slave support away from the president, applying the decree nationwide after overthrowing the government. In Cuba rebels offered freedom to slaves who joined their cause during a ten-year independence war, prompting the Spanish government to issue the anti-slavery Moret Law in 1870. In Paraguay abolition was a byproduct of the War of the Triple Alliance (1864–1870), being implemented by occupying Brazilian forces.

While recognizing these and other pressures, recent works have tended to focus on the social factors in slavery's demise. Demographic shifts were crucial. The contraction of the slave population in much of Latin America—owing to mortality, the end of the slave trade, manumission, and low reproductive rates—rendered the system uneconomic and incapable of supplying an adequate labor force. By the early 1820s Chile had at most 4,000 slaves, Mexico about 3,000, and Bolivia 4,700. From the 1820s to the 1850s Colombia's slave population fell from 54,000 to 20,000, Peru's from 50,000 to 25,000, and Venezuela's from 55,000 to 12,000.

Abolitionists constituted another social force. Though few in number and limited in effectiveness, they kept the issues associated with slavery alive, fulminating against its immorality and barbarism in newspapers, pamphlets, books, and public rallies. In Brazil, where the most influential abolitionist movement emerged behind the leadership of Joaquim Nabuco, they became increasingly militant during the 1880s as Brazil remained the hemisphere's last slaveholding nation. Abolitionists urged slaves to flee, armed them, and helped them to confront both their owners and the authorities.

The most effective social actors in the anti-slavery process were the slaves themselves. Slave resistance from nonviolent acts to open rebellion. Slaves stole, worked unproductively, and engaged in sabotage, cultivating reputations that reduced their saleability and value. A less confrontational but equally subversive stratagem was simply to marry; marriage secured the protection of the Roman Catholic church, which opposed the separation of families, and thus inhibited the sale and movement of slaves. Another common avenue open to slaves was the purchase of their own freedom, reducing the numbers left in bondage. They also resorted to self-destructive acts, committing suicide and aborting fetuses. Desperate slaves attacked and sometimes killed their exploiters. More frequently they ran away, joining the bands of fugitives, highwaymen, and guerrillas who threatened the social and political stability of many countries. Runaways established communities as they had in the past, although less frequently in remote areas as many found safe havens on neighboring plantations or in the black barrios of urban centers, blending easily into the expanding populations of free blacks and mulattoes.

With various ways open to them to resist and secure their freedom, few slaves turned to rebellion. Although conspiracies and plots abounded, only rarely did they graduate to open revolt. But instances did occur—for example, in 1825 and 1843 in Matanzas, in 1835 in Bahia where Muslim slaves rose, and in 1851 in Peru's Chicama Valley. None was successful in ending slavery or even freeing the participants, and in some cases they provoked vicious repression. Nevertheless, such revolts directed attention to the violence and the potential for violence that underlay these slaveholding societies.

The pressures and threats gradually convinced governments, slaveholders, and their supporters that slavery had to go. The operative word here is *gradually,* for the process was ponderously slow. Support for slavery remained strong throughout much of Latin America as slaves continued to be a valuable commodity and owners demanded compensation. At the same time, the anti-slavery elements were divided and weak. Consequently, the struggle was prolonged, and only when various

pressures came together was an irresistible anti-slavery force created.

Laws abolishing slavery were promulgated in Latin America between 1823 and 1888. Despite earlier calls for abolition, the first concrete steps were taken during the wars of independence. Leaders such as Simón Bolívar of Venezuela and José Artigas of Uruguay saw the contradiction in fighting for national liberation while a sector of the population remained in chains. Practical considerations also moved them; Bolívar, for example, wanted to attract slaves into his army, and in 1816 he promised the president of Haiti to abolish slavery in all the lands he freed in return for much-needed supplies. Similarly, the realities of the liberators' often desperate situation prevented them from decreeing immediate and complete emancipation. Nonetheless, anti-slavery legislation was introduced everywhere during the independence period. Laws ended the slave trade and freed all children born subsequently to slave women (under "free womb" laws), thereby halting the reproduction of slaves. Slaves were permitted to change owners, whipping was restricted, and manumission funds were established to free slaves. With independence secured, three of the new nations where slavery was no longer of any consequence abolished the institution completely: Chile in 1823, the United Provinces of Central America in 1824, and Mexico in 1829.

Elsewhere, however, slavery survived the independence wars and in some places even reasserted itself. Emancipation decrees in Bolivia and Colombia were revoked. The slave trade continued, especially to Cuba and Brazil; half a million slaves were imported to Brazil after 1831. Newborn children of slaves found their period of apprenticeship extended, and manumission funds were starved. Politically and economically weak, the governments of the new states were unprepared or unable to challenge the slaveholders.

During this hiatus the anti-slavery pressures continued to grow, producing within a generation a new wave of abolition decrees. Uruguay, with

Liberation of the Slaves by Simón Bolívar; watercolor, Cancino, nineteenth
century; Museum of the Twentieth of July, Bogotá.

only three hundred slaves, led the way in 1842, followed by Bolivia and Colombia (1851), Ecuador
(1852), Argentina (1853), Venezuela (1854), and
Peru (1855). The situation of the Spanish Caribbean islands was complicated by their colonial status and the resistance of the Spanish government
to emancipation. This was the last region to end
the slave trade, succumbing finally to American
and British pressure in the 1860s. The Moret Law of
1870 freed both aged slaves and the newborn children of slaves, prompting Puerto Rico to liberate its
remaining slaves over the next three years. Cuba,
with a much larger and more valuable slave popu-

lation, continued to hold out, but it eventually
freed its last slaves in 1886.

Brazil remained alone. The anti-slavery struggle
there proved to be the longest and most intense in
Latin America. With one and one-half million
slaves in 1820, constituting more than 40 percent
of the population, the Brazilian government
fended off demands to end the slave trade until
1851 and did not pass a free womb law until 1871.
But even these mortal blows failed to hasten slavery's end, and as the government continued to vac-
illate, the anti-slavery pressures mounted. Abolitionists fired up their campaign; northeastern

sugar-planters, satisfied with wage labor, divorced themselves from the slavery cause; states and cities began to declare themselves free areas; a growing urban bourgeoisie favoring a free market system joined the abolitionists; and slaves in the coffee-producing south turned to violence. Under attack and facing the threat of social conflict, Brazil's slaveholders had little choice but to accept the princess regent's decision in 1888, thereby ending an institution that had played a vital role in Latin America's development for almost four hundred years.

[See also Brazil; Caribbean Region; Central America; Emancipation in the Americas; and South America.]

BIBLIOGRAPHY

Blanchard, Peter. Slavery and Abolition in Early Republican Peru. Wilmington, Del.: Scholarly Resources, 1992.

Conrad, Robert. The Destruction of Barzilian Slavery, 1856–1888. Berkeley: University of California Press, 1972.

Klein, Herbert S. African Slavery in Latin America and the Caribbean. New York and Oxford: Oxford University Press, 1986.

Scott, Rebecca J. Slave Emancipation in Cuba: The Transition to Free Labor, 1860–1899. Princeton: Princeton University Press, 1985.

—PETER BLANCHARD

United States

Although slavery had proven problematic to justify since ancient times, a compelling and effective critique of the institution emerged only in the eighteenth century, sparked in part by the glaring contradiction between unprecedented liberty and absolute servitude that characterized North American society. Nonetheless, the anti-slavery movement in the United States, though dynamic and influential, failed to bring an end to slavery without resort to war.

The religious origins of much North American settlement by Europeans provided fertile soil for early anti-slavery arguments, such as the petition of the Germantown Quakers of 1688, or Samuel Sewell's The Selling of Joseph in 1701, although such views probably constitute an anti-slavery "tradition" only in retrospect. More typical early American tracts on behalf of slaves, such as Morgan Godwyn's The Negro's & Indian's Advocate (1680), rarely challenged the legality of slavery, instead stressing the humanity and spiritual equality of slaves.

This view posed no paradox in rigidly hierarchical Old World society. The unusual economic conditions of North America, however—land was cheap and labor expensive, an inversion of the European pattern—weakened this hierarchical structure, elevating the position of workers and undermining slavery in the Northern colonies. By contrast, in the staple-growing colonies of the South this high land-to-labor ratio provided a strong incentive for planters to rely on slavery, because the cost of free labor under the harsh conditions of plantation agriculture proved prohibitive. Moreover, a large enslaved African labor force helped to depress the economic power of non-slaveholding whites while bolstering the status of the slaveholding elite. Thus slavery had become an inextricable element of Southern colonial society by the first part of the eighteenth century, if not earlier.

Enlightenment philosophers such as Locke and Montesquieu elaborated a doctrine of natural liberty and equality based significantly on an idealized interpretation of New World conditions. "In the beginning," Locke wrote, "all the world was America." As slavery took deeper root, America came less and less to resemble this Arcadian portrait. Nevertheless, these idealistic principles gained ground throughout the colonies, particularly as transmitted through the influential Scottish Common-Sense school of philosophy.

From the late 1750s, the increasingly forceful Quaker anti-slavery movement fortified the abstract Scottish critique of slavery with a morally compelling example of practical action. Although the powerful anti-slavery witnesses of John Woolman and Anthony Benezet had little immediate impact in America (outside of Quaker circles), they profoundly influenced such figures as Abbé Raynal and England's John Wesley, whose *Thoughts upon Slavery* (1774) gave a strong anti-slavery direction to American Methodism. In the year 1774 the American colonies also closed the slave trade, an early harbinger of independence. Revolutionary rhetoric that excoriated political slavery and exalted freedom as more valuable than life exposed American patriots to charges of hypocrisy—Samuel Johnson asked, "How is it that we hear the loudest *yelps* for liberty among the drivers of negroes?"—but they also undermined traditional justifications of slavery. Before the revolution, most Americans had regarded slavery as an unpleasant but unavoidable aspect of human experience; after it, many questioned its legitimacy.

In the North and the middle states, where the hold of slavery was weak, it was abolished by explicit constitutional prohibition, judicial interpretation, or legislated gradual emancipation. Pennsylvania's gradual emancipation act of 1780 was probably the first abolition enacted by a legislative body. Four years later the Continental Congress failed by one vote to bar slavery from all western territories; in 1787, however, it prohibited it in the Northwest Territory.

The federal constitution has often been seen as slowing, if not halting, this anti-slavery momentum. Although its framers cautiously refrained from mentioning the word *slavery*, several articles—including a fugitive slave clause, a twenty-year prohibition on banning the slave trade, and the counting of three-fifths of a state's slave population for purposes of apportioning congressional representation—explicitly strengthened slavery; others, including the so-called "great compromise," which secured an equality of states in the Senate, ultimately benefited the slave states, whose populations were growing at a much slower rate than those in the North and West. By authorizing the closure of the slave trade in 1808, however, many delegates reasonably (but wrongly) believed that they had put slavery on the road to extinction.

Yet by binding free and slave states together, the constitution established a national responsibility for slavery and provided mechanisms, in principle at least, for the central state to contain if not to abolish it.

In practice, opponents of slavery found the door to federal anti-slavery action barred by a solid Southern front, arrayed against a divided North. Anti-slavery activity thus tended to be informal and small in scale, with efforts by private individuals and associations on one hand, and on the other direct action by slaves themselves, including escape, revolt, and rebellion. Manumissions by upper-South slaveholders peaked in the early 1790s, as did the labors of elite-dominated early anti-slavery societies. The successful revolutionary war for independence of Haitian slaves (1791–1804) chilled many white Americans' ardor for emancipation measure while inspiring a firestorm of slave revolts, including Gabriel's in Richmond (1800) and an 1811 uprising in Louisiana that may have involved as many as ten thousand slaves.

Fear of slave revolt, concerns about the "africanization" of America, and the desire of upper-South slaveholders to increase the value of their property may have been as important as anti-slavery sentiment in Congress's prompt closure of American involvement in the African slave trade in 1807. A principal goal of reformers became the removal of blacks, not just of slavery. In 1816 an uncomfortable alliance of moderate emancipationists and slaveholders interested principally in strengthening slavery founded the American Colonization Society to relocate freed blacks to Liberia in West Africa. By ceaselessly stressing the hostile racial climate for blacks in the United States, colonizationists ultimately aggravated the racism for which they claimed removal to Africa was the only answer. Free blacks, however, overwhelmingly rejected the option of exile, choosing instead to wage the battle against slavery and racism in their native land on the principles of liberty embodied in America's revolutionary heritage. This determination at once sharpened the moral challenge of anti-slavery and raised its political cost.

Nonetheless, it would be wrong to underestimate anti-slavery sentiment in the United States, even if it rarely stemmed from sympathy for blacks. In 1819, when the proposed admission of Missouri as a slave state threatened the extension of slavery across the continent, an unprecedented upsurge of Northern public opinion demanded its rejection. Although Congress, after a bruising two-year battle, finally admitted Missouri, opponents barred slavery from the Louisiana Territory north of latitude 36°30′, in effect restricting its expansion to Arkansas. Thus the Missouri fight proved at best a Pyrrhic victory for slaveholders and set the stage for future vicious territorial struggles.

Among those Southerners convinced by the Missouri debate that the North would not aid the South in the event of a slave revolt was Denmark Vesey, a free black Charlestonian who in 1822 organized a large-scale conspiracy to seize that city. Disclosed at the last moment, Vesey's plot sent the South into a paroxysm of fear and repression. Proslavery South Carolinians passed laws mandating that black crewmen (perhaps one-fifth of the entire merchant marine) be jailed while their ships anchored in the state's harbors. This measure, which damaged the state's commerce and put it at odds with the Constitution and international treaties, underscored the vital role of free blacks in the slavery controversy—both as anti-slavery activists and as living contradictions of the emerging doctrine that identified Africans as *prima facie* slaves. This "racialization" of slavery made it clear to free blacks, who numbered almost a quarter of a million in 1820, that their fortunes were inextricably tied to those of slaves.

No one felt this charge more keenly than David Walker, a black Boston clothes-dealer, whose militant appeal, *To the Colored Citizens of the World* (1829), urged slaves and free blacks to rise up together to throw off the yoke of servitude. Walker's jeremiad crystallized the disillusionment and despair of African Americans at the outset of Andrew Jackson's administration, in the face of hardening discrimination and abuse and the apparent indifference of white America to the sin of slavery.

Walker's early death in 1830 was believed by many to have been murder.

Walker's prophecy of bloody divine retribution against slaveholders seemed confirmed in August 1831, when a religiously inspired slave, Nat Turner, led a party of slaves in rural Virginia in an assault that left sixty whites dead. Ironically, an unprecedented era of interracial action against slavery was just commencing. William Lloyd Garrison, a crusading young journalist strongly influenced by free blacks in Boston and Baltimore, declared war on slavery and colonization in the first issue of his newspaper, the *Liberator*, 1 January 1831. Around the same time many young evangelicals who had been converted in the fervor of the Second Great Awakening, such as Theodore Dwight Weld, became convinced that slavery constituted the nation's greatest obstacle to moral progress and dedicated their lives to its abolition.

If *anti-slavery* is broadly defined as the view that slavery is wrong in principle, a majority of Americans in the antebellum era would have so described themselves, including many slaveholders and proslavery leaders who regarded slavery as a necessary evil. Those defining themselves as abolitionists, by contrast, rejected gradualism and colonization and denounced slaveholding itself, not merely slavery, as sin, and slaveholders as sinners. Though inspired by Britain's successful anti-slavery campaign, American abolitionists faced obstacles not shared by their British counterparts, including a decentralized federal political system and a far more powerful slaveholding class. Additionally, American abolitionists appeared less disposed to compromise on tactical matters than were their British counterparts. The Americans' drive for immediate emancipation, in the light of the obstacles they faced, often seemed more a religious crusade than a practical political program.

An additional obstacle to emancipation faced in the United States but not in Britain was the presence of more than two million slaves within the nation. To their credit, abolitionists from the first faced this fact squarely, arguing that the only just

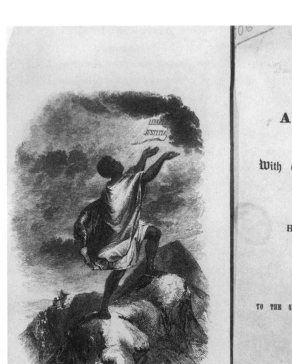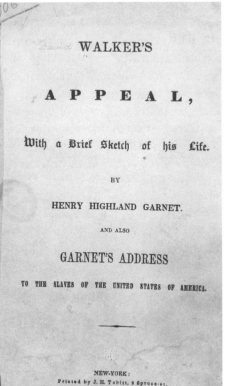

WALKER'S

A P P E A L,

With a Brief Sketch of his Life.

BY

HENRY HIGHLAND GARNET.

AND ALSO

GARNET'S ADDRESS

TO THE SLAVES OF THE UNITED STATES OF AMERICA.

NEW-YORK:
Printed by J. H. Tobitt, 9 Spruce-st.
1848.

Title page and frontispiece of an 1848 edition of *Walker's Appeal*,
originally published as *Citizens of the World* (1829).

and practical approach to emancipation was the acceptance of freed people into the body politic. The shift of the debate from opposition to slavery, which had widespread popular support, to "the overthrow of prejudice" called for by the American Anti-Slavery Society, pleased some pro-slavery politicians. Among the latter was editor Duff Green, who breathed a sigh of relief when such radical views gained influence within the anti-slavery camp: "When it began to fall into the hands of the religious fanatics," Green reflected later, "we thought nothing of it."

The abolitionist movement in the early 1830s was a loose confederation of activists organized around three centers: Boston, where Garrison led an organization including Samuel E. Sewall, Samuel J. May, Lydia Maria Child, Maria Chap-man, and James Lenox Remond; Cincinnati, where Theodore J. Weld, James G. Birney, Amos A. Phelps, Henry B. Stanton, and Elizur Wright were prominent; and New York, which included among its leadership William Jay, Joshua Leavitt, and Lewis Tappan, a businessman and philanthropist whose funds helped all three branches. The American Anti-Slavery Society was founded in Philadelphia on 4 December 1833. More influential nationally was the "agency system" pioneered by Weld, which applied the techniques of revivalism to abolition. Using methods developed to promote sabbatarianism and temperance, abolitionists adopted a two-pronged approach that employed moral arguments to persuade individual slaveholders to change their hearts and free their slaves, while seeking to extricate the federal government from the sin of slavery. (In practice, this meant attempting to ban it from the District of Columbia, since the question of slavery in the territories did not re-open until the Mexican-American War of 1846–1848.) Between 1833 and 1835 the number of local anti-slavery societies grew exponentially.

Abolitionists soon faced stiff, even violent resistance. As long as the debate could be framed as a referendum on slavery itself, a clear majority of Americans opposed it; thus defenders of the institution successfully employed the tactic of changing the subject to debates over British influence, states' rights, the sanctity of property, and above all, supposed African inferiority. After 1834 slavery activists routinely confronted hecklers and mobs comprised of "gentlemen of property and standing"—colonizationists, politicians, merchants, industrialists, and clergymen—along with working-class recruits. In October 1835 such a "broadcloth mob" came close to lynching Garrison. The peak of anti-abolitionist violence occurred during the presidential campaign of 1836, when supporters of the Northern presidential candidates Martin Van Buren and Daniel Webster orchestrated such incidents to reassure Southern voters of the North's "soundness" on slavery. In the North such violence was primarily symbolic (although the newspaperman Elijah Lovejoy was shot by a pro-slavery mob in Alton, Illinois, in 1837); but in the South persons suspected of abolitionism were horsewhipped and even hanged.

Since mob discipline precluded lecturing in the South, in 1835 abolitionists launched a postal campaign designed to flood the region with anti-slavery pamphlets. In response, inflamed Southerners demanded Northern legislation to criminalize such mailings, and the U.S. postmaster general prohibited his subordinates from transporting them. Anti-slavery activists then instituted petition drives calling for federal curbs on slavery, especially in the District of Columbia and the territories. In 1836 Southern legislators demanded that Congress refuse to accept all such petitions; a compromise gag rule, in effect until 1844, tabled anti-slavery petitions and prohibited their debate. This apparent infringement of constitutional rights, along with other efforts to check free discussion of slavery, won to the anti-slavery cause many Northern moderates who had not previously considered it relevant to their concerns.

As the anti-slavery constituency broadened, however, the abolitionist movement grew increasingly divided on matters of religion, the role of women, and most importantly, the value of expedient compromise and political action. The split stemmed partly from the Garrisonian wing's increasing antinomianism and rejection of all government, and partly from the opportunism of the "political" abolitionists, who in 1839 founded the Liberty Party, running James G. Birney for president the following year. Political abolitionists sought to capitalize on Northern voters' increasing resentment of Southern domination of national affairs. As this anti-Southern sentiment spread, support for anti-slavery broadened but grew more diffuse and limited in its goals. Nonetheless, the prospect that political action could topple slavery seemed to abolitionist leaders (such as Frederick Douglass, who broke with Garrison at this time) both a noble enough goal and a more practical one than the immediate reformation of society, root and branch.

No event more clearly symbolized both this new Northern assertiveness and the doubtfulness of its anti-slavery commitment than the nomination in 1848 of Martin Van Buren, the erstwhile "Northern man with Southern principles," as the candidate of the Free Soil party, which was dedicated to the exclusion of new slave states. By this time opposition to slavery—or more properly, to its extension—had attracted sufficient Northern support to threaten the entire structure of party politics. Southerners, their political backs to the wall, stoked the fires of abolitionist sentiment by mounting ever greater demands for the protection of slavery.

Ironically, then, the South's hardening resolve to defend slavery by focusing attention on the in-

Engraving from an 1822 anti-slavery tract depicting a woman and
child being kidnapped and taken into slavery.

stitution itself proved more effective than abolitionist critiques in mobilizing a mass anti-slavery
constituency in the North. The draconian Fugitive
Slave Act of 1850, which in effect stripped free
blacks of the protection of law and required whites
to assist slave-catchers, was a case in point. Although the act affected few whites directly, Harriet
Beecher Stowe's novel *Uncle Tom's Cabin* (1852)
dramatically brought home its human cost to hundreds of thousands of readers and drove a chink in
the wall of white prejudice. The Kansas-Nebraska
Act (1854), which revoked the Missouri Compromise—the "sacred compact" of antebellum politics—put freedom and slavery on an equal level. Its
passage helped to launch the Republican Party, a
diverse coalition encompassing racist free-soilers
and staunch abolitionists. Although critical of the
party's tepid stand on slavery, even Garrison recognized its creation as the beginning of the end.

After Kansas-Nebraska the anti-slavery constituency expanded dramatically, and abolitionists embraced a new militancy. In several states
whites and blacks together violently resisted enforcement of the Fugitive Slave Act. Northern industrialists formed the New England Emigrant Aid
Company to promote anti-slavery immigration to
Kansas, arming settlers with Sharp's rifles, known
as "Beecher's Bibles," to defend against pro-slavery
"border ruffians." In 1856 Republicans endorsed
John C. Frémont for president on an explicitly
anti-slavery platform, although fears of Southern
secession caused conservative Northerners to back
the Democrat James Buchanan. Many soon la-
mented the latter choice when the Supreme
Court's Dred Scott decision (1857) ruled territorial slavery restriction unconstitutional, in effect
proscribing political anti-slavery activity. John
Brown's quixotic raid against slavery at Harper's

Ferry (1859) foreshadowed the alternative. Though widely condemned, Brown's eloquence and courage while awaiting execution made him an emblem of resistance to the slave powers.

Although Abraham Lincoln's election in 1860 owed much to his reputation as an anti-slavery moderate, his steadfast refusal to compromise on issues that he believed would have given a national imprimatur to slavery, such as its extension to the territories, guaranteed a civil war in which emancipation became a military necessity. Abolitionists, free blacks, and above all escaped slaves who fled to the Union ranks, transformed a war against secession into a war against slavery. Lincoln's Emancipation Proclamation freed all Confederate slaves on 1 January 1863; the Thirteenth Amendment to the U.S. Constitution formally outlawed slavery on 18 December 1865.

[*See also* Abolition and Anti-slavery Literature; Indentured Servitude; Law, *article on* United States Law; *and* United States.]

BIBLIOGRAPHY

Barnes, Gilbert Hobbs. *The Antislavery Impulse, 1830–1844.* New York: Harbinger, 1964.

Davis, David Brion. *The Problem of Slavery in the Age of Revolution, 1770–1823.* Ithaca, N.Y.: Cornell University Press, 1975.

Kraditor, Aileen S. *Means and Ends in American Abolitionism: Garrison and His Critics on Strategy and Tactics, 1834–1850.* New York: Pantheon, 1969.

Quarles, Benjamin. *Black Abolitionists.* New York: Oxford University Press, 1969.

Stewart, James Brewer. *Holy Warriors: The Abolitionists and American Slavery.* New York: Hill and Wang, 1976.

—ROBERT P. FORBES

AFRICA. [*To survey the impact of slavery and slaving in pre- and postcolonial Africa, this entry comprises five articles, a general overview followed by four regional surveys that trace these practices in major parts of the continent in the postcolonial era:*

    An Overview
    West Africa
    Central Africa
    East Africa
    Southern Africa

For discussion of slavery in North Africa, see Mediterranean *and* Law, *article on* Islamic Law. *For discussion of the experiences of African slaves in the New World, see* Anti-Slavery Literature, *article on* African-American Perspectives.]

An Overview

Most historians studying Africa agree that many if not all precolonial African societies had systems of slavery. There is substantial disagreement, however, about the significance of this universality and the degree to which slavery in Africa was comparable to slavery in other parts of the world, most notably Europe and the Americas. In some views African slavery was "mild" and amounted to little more than providing families with additional members, while others have tended to view African slavery as being more or less analogous to the slavery of Europe, America, and the Mediterranean world. A second debate concerns what the historian Paul Lovejoy called the "transformation hypothesis," which posits that African participation in the Atlantic slave trade (and to a lesser degree the Indian Ocean trade) caused an originally mild and patriarchal system of slavery of limited extent to become harsher and more widespread over time.

The definitions of *slave* and *slavery* , as well as slavery's social, political, and economic context, have been worked out in the history of Europe and the Mediterranean world. For this reason, much work on comparative slavery has been required to translate these terms into different cultural and legal systems. This requires great care in making definitions and in attempting to get at the root of the most important issues in human interactions.

This general problem is particularly acute for the African case, because the development of slavery in Africa is intimately connected with the development of slavery in Europe (to some degree), and particularly in the Americas. Thus the study of African slavery is not entirely independent of the study of European and Euro-American slavery, and this has created problems for debate as long as slavery has been discussed. At the same time, however, African institutional frameworks were substantially different from those of Europe, colonial America, or the Mediterranean.

In its European setting, slavery has generally been viewed in a legal sense and in an economic sense. In the legal sense, the slave has become the subject of a master rather than the subject of a state. The master takes over the rule-generating and enforcing functions of the state as well as being the court of last appeal for slaves. Debates about the legality of slavery have typically focused on the degree to which such extrastatal jurisdiction could be exercised and to what degree the role of the state as final arbitrator of justice could countenance the existence of an exempt sphere of private justice.

In the economic sense, slavery has been seen in the types of labor slaves perform, in their terms and conditions of labor, and in the degree to which slavery has been a predominant form of labor. Historians influenced by Marxism have often written in this regard of a "slave mode of production" and of distinctions between "household" or "patriarchal" slavery, and the slave mode of production.

For many years all discussions of slavery have involved a moral dimension as well as one of comparative history. Morally, slavery has been seen either as an institution that deprives slaves of their natural political rights (working from the legal angle), or as one that exposes them to harsh conditions of labor and deprives them of rights of contract (the economic approach). Thus slavery and slave systems have been judged as liberal or as harsh depending on the degree of deprivation of rights and the conditions of labor.

The geographical land mass defined as Africa can be divided in a social and legal context into two parts: one part, which includes the northern littoral of the Mediterranean, the Nile Valley, and

Ethiopia, forms part of a larger complex that includes the Arabian Peninsula and the Middle East as well as much of the Mediterranean world. Since its institutional base is closer to that of the Euro-Mediterranean world than to that of the rest of the African continent, it is best to leave it for discussion elsewhere. This article, then, will focus on the remaining bulk of the African continent.

In confronting the issue of slavery in Africa we must resolve two basic issues. The first is linguistic: how should the myriad of words in various African languages that might refer to dependency in either a legal or economic sense be translated, and which ones should be rendered as "slavery?" The second issue is institutional: how should specific institutions named by the words in question be seen in their larger institutional (and linguistic) contexts? The degree to which the linguistic and institutional definitions of African societies lack exact congruence with those of the Western world creates problems in making comparisons.

Solutions to these problems are compounded by the very uneven nature of modern historians' understanding of life in much of Africa in precolonial times. Many African societies left no written historical records of their own. Records of others are frequently in languages other than their indigenous ones. The most detailed descriptions of African societies were often written by foreigners whose knowledge was faulty, especially on fine points of legal theory, and whose judgments were biased by their interests as missionaries, slave-traders, or spokespersons for abolitionist causes. For many other African societies, the only information available comes from orally transmitted memories and traditions recorded in the twentieth century, after slavery had been abolished or when legal systems were being altered by colonial legislation.

Given this scanty evidence and its ambiguous nature, historians are unlikely to be able to answer conclusively many important empirical questions. Not surprisingly, the lack of scholarly consensus on many issues derives as much from varying interpretation of the records themselves as from theoretical debate about their meaning and significance.

For precolonial Africa, our best information comes from the Muslim regions of the western Sudan (from modern Senegal to Sudan, north of the tropical rain forest), where local literacy combined with some travelers' accounts (especially since the fifteenth century); from the Atlantic coastal regions of West Africa, with large numbers of foreign travelers' accounts; and finally from coastal Central Africa, where both local literacy and travelers' accounts provide data.

Fundamental to understanding the role of slaves in any society is an understanding of the way in which economic and legal status were defined in that society as a whole. One of the distinguishing features of the precolonial African legal systems was the absence of private ownership of land. African legal systems granted individuals the right to cultivate uncultivated land, and they protected the crops or buildings on such land from use by others; but they did not allow lands to be rented, sold, or transmitted through inheritance, although other rights pertaining to cultivation might be passed down.

Because of this feature, African legal and constitutional systems were fundamentally different from those of Europe or Asia, where land could be owned and revenue derived from the rent of land provided the most widespread form of reproducing wealth. Ownership of land in Europe and Asia was the primary means of allowing individuals wealth. Its relative independence from state control helped to check state power and underwrote various types of noble status.

In Africa the same function of providing for private wealth was performed by various institutions of dependency, including slavery and certain types of marriage and pawnship. These dependents could provide labor or service, the fruits of which would supply the income of their patron. Thus whereas a wealthy European bought or acquired land to ensure a secure, steady, long-term, and transmissible income, a wealthy African might acquire dependents to ensure the same result.

The effect of this legal situation was that there was a wide range of personal dependency statuses, having varying rights and political powers and used in a variety of ways to generate wealth for the patron. Many of these dependents fit more or less into a European-oriented definition of a slave: they might be subject to the law of a master and not the state, and rights to their dependency might be transferable by assignment, inheritance, or sale. In these circumstances many people were found in one or another state of dependency, making the institution widespread and the marketing of slaves commonplace. It also meant, however, that from both a legal and economic viewpoint, slavery was a complex institution.

For example, dependents who might be described as slaves could be field-workers, domestic workers, soldiers, or even administrators. This wide range in status and variable amount of power complicates attempts to describe African slavery as harsh, or the political situation of slaves as rightless and powerless. In some of these institutions of dependency, the condition was not permanent, or it was not transmissible by heredity, or the second dependent generation had a different legal status than the first.

Similarly, as dependent workers slaves could be found in many varied statuses and could possess varied rights, as reflected in multiple terminologies for slaves. Some people who were classed as slaves could not be sold or were attached to particular villages; others were integrated into families, sometimes as junior members and at other times as full members.

The situation in the sixteenth- and seventeenth-century kingdom of Ndongo in Central Africa can illustrate these difficulties. Ndongo is described in contemporary documents, some written by inhabitants of the kingdom; there are texts in Kimbundu, the language of the state. There are suggestions that Ndongo was in some ways typical of many other African states.

Late-sixteenth-century sources describe two types of slaves: those who were born in slavery and attached to lands, typically settled in villages, called *kijiko* (singular, plural *ijiko*), who were not vulnerable to resale; and those more recently captured or purchased, who were vulnerable to resale and movement and were called *mubika* (singular, plural *abika*). The Kimbudu Roman Catholic catechism (1642) shows that the word *mubika* was also used generically for "slave," and that its root was related to law and the power of the state. Hence one can surmise that the legal idea of the transfer of the power of the state to the master was implied in these terms.

In addition to these dependents, on whom the basic economy of Ndongo depended, there were others who had more political functions but who were often still referred to as "slaves" (Portuguese, *escravos*) in Portuguese-language documents written by Ndongo rulers like Queen Njinga (r. 1624–1663). Among them were dependent soldiers, some settled in villages but liable for military call-up (*kilamba*; plural, *ilamba*) and some who were officials of the state. Traditions recorded in the seventeenth century suggested that some of the royal slaves had the power collectively to ensure the election of rulers. Another group described as slaves were the Imbangala, military groups who often functioned independently of the state and who recruited their members through capture, while promoting leadership from within through election.

We can learn more about slavery in the regions of the western Sudan (modern Senegal, Gambia, Guinea, and Mali) from sixteenth- and seventeenth-century local histories. These reveal the presence of villages of people who were owned by the state and whose revenue could be transferred to others. A local term, *zanj*, derived from one of the various Arabic terms for Africans, was used to described such groups, who seem to have enjoyed some rights to stability of residence. In addition, there were rice plantations worked by slaves and managed by slave overseers who enjoyed considerable power and wealth. The army was led by officers who were sometimes referred to as "slaves" in the Arabic of the texts. Askia Muhammed, who came from this slave officer corps, seized power in a coup d'état in 1492 and founded a dynasty.

The development of slave armies led by slave generals in the Senegambian region after 1700 shows the possibilities of this element of slavery. Many of the states in the region of modern Senegal and Gambia came to be controlled by military officers of slave origin, often known by the pejorative nickname *ceddo*. Although the *ceddo* did not exercise power directly as rulers, they played an important role in the politics of the region, owning and selling slaves in their own right as well as serving the interests of their masters.

Although such sources allow us to plumb the range of legal definitions that might be encompassed by the term *slave*, other questions of interest are not to be answered. For example, we know very little about labor regimes, in Ndongo or elsewhere in Africa, even though the spotty evidence suggests that they ranged from closely supervised gang work in mines and occasionally on agricultural establishments, through the provision of forced labor by an otherwise self-producing and self-reproducing group, to a regime indistinguishable from that of free cultivators. For those dependents taken into domestic, political, or military service, the idea of labor regime as it is used in Marxian-influenced discussions of mode of production is probably inappropriate.

Similarly, it is impossible to make quantitative assessments of the percentage of slaves among the population for any period save the immediate precolonial one, which can be extrapolated from the first censuses conducted by the conquering governments in the late nineteenth and early twentieth centuries. These data, as well as impressionistic data from travelers at earlier times, suggest that the number of people in various forms of dependency was quite high. Because of this, it is difficult to say for certain how and in what direction slave status, labor regime, or numbers may have changed. However, the mobility of slaves may well have caused concentrations of slaves to develop in areas where there was considerable private economic enterprise, and to decline where these enterprises failed or where the initiative was taken up through state auspices or by collective groups. Such processes may lead to the appearance of a great increase in slavery in some areas and to the impression that slavery was spreading or intensifying.

An example of the role of slaves in economically advancing regions can be found in the Gold Coast (modern Ghana), where European commerce established in the late fifteenth century stimulated the coastal communities. Wealthy commoners invested the profits of commercial activities in the purchase of slaves, developing quasi-independent communities by the seventeenth and eighteenth centuries. Sometimes the communities became the base for political activities—sometimes even the formation of new states. Some scholars even posit that much of the development of the earliest states in the forest regions of the Gold Coast area originally derived from colonizing activities of these wealthy commoners, connected either to a northward export of gold to the western Sudan, or southward to the European factors on the coast.

Slavery undoubtedly increased in areas where civil strife or disturbed conditions led to protracted warfare or a breakdown of civil order. Such conditions necessarily led to greater use of private labor forces and encouraged the development of slave-based military and administrative systems. In the eighteenth-century Kingdom of Kongo, where a longstanding civil war between rival factions of the ruling family had caused the partition of the country and a decline in local law and order, gangs of bandits inhabited many areas, exporting their captives through merchant networks, even as the rival rulers built up their own following by acquiring slaves or increased their revenue by selling them.

To the degree that Atlantic commerce either stimulated private enterprise or encouraged warfare and disorder, it might have led to an increase in the domestic use of slaves as well as in their export, although obviously the causes, both immediate and deep-seated, of warfare, political collapse, and economic growth are controversial among specialists. Some argue that the development of external trades directed either at the Atlantic Ocean or the Indian Ocean coast were primarily responsible for both political and economic change, while others argue that politics was independent of these external influences.

Although African slavery may have been influenced in its development by the Atlantic economy, the end of the external slave trade did not end or lessen slavery in Africa. Indeed, recent research suggests that the economy of nineteenth-century Africa was deeply dependent on the use of slaves, and that it is likely that the use and sale of slaves expanded dramatically during that time. The earliest colonial censuses, for example, found a significant percentage of the population enslaved. More impressionistic data confirm that the new economic activity spurred by world commercial patterns following the Industrial Revolution gave African entrepreneurs especially many more opportunities to use slaves for private development than ever before.

During the colonial period there were moves to abolish African slavery. Colonial powers jointly decided to make abolition of slavery one of their goals, but its extirpation proved difficult. In many colonies legal supports for slavery were abolished by changing definitions while retaining the essence of the dependency relations. In some instances. the introduction of property law on European lines allowed tenancy relationships to develop in lieu of slavery, especially in areas where there was substantial European settlement, such as South Africa, the Rhodesias (modern Zambia and Zimbabwe), Kenya, and Angola. In many areas, however, the abolition of slavery was not accompanied by such legal changes, and in these cases slavery often took on informal, extralegal characteristics.

[*See also* Abolition and Anti-Slavery, *article on* Africa; Historiography, *article on* Africa; *and* Slave Trade, *articles on* Brazil and the United States, Trans-Atlantic Trade, *and* Trans-Saharan Trade.]

BIBLIOGRAPHY

Lovejoy, Paul. *Transformations in Slavery: A History of Slavery in Africa*. Cambridge: Cambridge University Press, 1983.

Miers, Suzanne, and Igor Kopytoff, eds. *Slavery in Africa: Historical and Anthropological Perspectives*. Madison: University of Wisconsin Press, 1977.

Miers, Suzanne, and Richard Roberts, eds. *The End of Slavery in Africa*. Madison: University of Wisconsin Press, 1988.

Thornton, John. *Africa and Africans in the Making of the Atlantic World, 1400–1680*. Cambridge: Cambridge University Press, 1992.

—JOHN K. THORNTON

West Africa

West Africa was integrated into the world economy as a supplier of slaves first for the Mediterranean and the Middle East and later for the trans-Atlantic trade. No region of the world has been so intensively slaved over such a long period of time, and in few has slavery had such a vital impact on the development of state and society.

Slave systems within West Africa tended to conform to one of two types. The older, well described by Suzanne Miers and Igor Kopytoff, is a very integrative form of slavery common in smaller-scale kinship-based societies. In it slaves made up a low percentage of the population; they lived in the master's compound, worked alongside his family, and often ate with them. Children of slaves were initiated with those of the free and raised in the master's culture. Slave status was rapidly ameliorated, sometimes disappearing within a single generation. Some aspects of the integrative system persist in more exploitative, market-oriented societies. In Asante, slave status disappeared after three gen-

erations. Elsewhere the distinction between captives and slaves "born in the house" persisted primarily in a ban on the sale of the latter.

More intensive exploitation resulted both from political centralization and from the increasing importance of the market. In the more intensive form of slavery there were often slave majorities, sometimes as high as 75 percent. Most slaves lived separately from their masters and worked in groups. The master did not eat with or work alongside his slaves; instead, he supervised them. Manumission was limited and work was carefully regulated. These systems can be referred to as slave modes of production because slavery was the dominant form of labor.

There were also privileged slaves. Some argue that these people were not slaves, but in fact their privileges were rooted in their dependence. They had no kinship ties and were therefore totally dependent on their masters. The largest privileged category was the warriors, who made up the core of the more powerful armies. Military commanders, administrators, diplomats, and servants were often recruited from among the slave warriors. Slaves also worked in commercial enterprises and could become important traders. Slave concubines could become favored partners, and if they gave birth to sons, they could benefit from a son's success.

Slavery probably existed long before the rise of Ghana early in the first millennium. Climate change led to a struggle for control of scarce resources at least as far back as the first millennium BCE and created the conditions for conflict and state formation and thus for enslavement. We know little about the first states in the western and central Sudan, but there is evidence that by the seventh century, there was a slave trade into and across the Sahara. These slaves were obtained by kidnapping and slave-raiding. The possession of horses and iron weapons made it possible for raiding parties from the savannah states to raid farther south. The absence of barriers to movement meant that armed horsemen could dominate large areas. Conversion of Sudanic princes to Islam provided a justification for enslavement, though one based on a faulty reading of Muḥammad's teachings. According to the Qur'ān, a person could be enslaved only in a *jihād* (war against unbelievers); few wars and no slave raids met that requirement.

Large numbers of slaves were also used within the Sudanic empires. The Arab traveler Ibn Battutah referred to slaves working as soldiers, servants, porters, and concubines in fourteenth-century Mali. They were also traded and given as presents. In sixteenth-century Songhai there were numerous slaves at court and in slave villages who helped feed court and army. Within these empires specialized merchant communities used profits to buy slaves, who were used to produce commodities.

Walter Rodney has questioned whether the term *slave* should be used to describe servile groups on the upper Guinea coast, but he and most other writers agree that some form of slavery existed on many parts of the coast. In Senegal, for example, rulers raided for slaves, who could be either sold or put to work growing food for the court. Farther down the coast, the early Portuguese explorers found slave systems, although the number of slaves available for sale was limited. With the exception of Benin, states were small and had few newly enslaved persons they wanted to trade. During the fifteenth and sixteenth centuries the Portuguese sold slaves on the Gold Coast in exchange for gold.

For West Africa to become a massive supplier of slaves for the New World, two changes were necessary. First, its states had to develop marketing networks capable of channeling surplus slaves from the interior into coastal barracoons. Fueled by European demand, African slave-traders did this during the sixteenth and seventeenth centuries. Sec-

Drawing depicting the layout of a European slave-trading center in West Africa, c.1746.

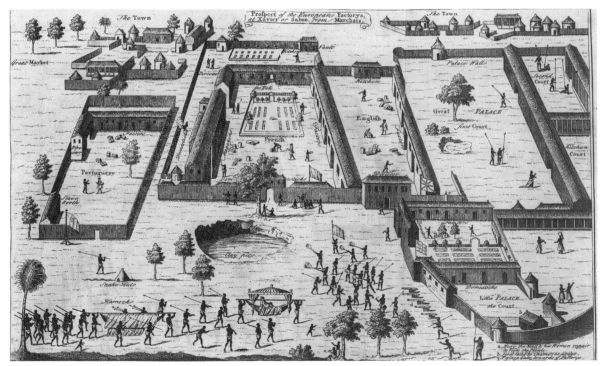

ond, it was necessary to develop military structures capable of enslaving large numbers of people. Slaves were "produced" in a variety of ways: some were kidnapped; some were enslaved as a result of unpaid debts or criminal penalties; the majority, however, came as a result of war and raiding. Wars were fought for many reasons, but in any war the victorious army took large numbers of prisoners. Raiding focused on areas where population was dense or where raiders would face little resistance. Raiders would surround a village, often before sunrise, and attack it, taking as many prisoners as they could control. Slave-raiding shaped patterns of settlement as vulnerable peoples often retreated to safer areas, seeking easily defended sites in hilly regions and building walled towns in the savanna.

The sharpest increase in slave exports came in the middle of the seventeenth century, when the development of sugar plantations in the West Indies stimulated the demand for slaves and led to higher prices. During the same period Europeans began selling guns to Africans, which facilitated the work of slaving. The result was the emergence of a series of powerful slave-producing states in the hinterland. In western Nigeria, Oyo, a savanna state with a powerful cavalry, expanded from the middle of the seventeenth century. Tributary to Oyo but quite powerful in its own right, Dahomey developed a small but efficient slave-producing army in the early eighteenth century. In the forest zone of Ghana, Asante became dominant after destroying its major rival in 1702. Farther east the Bambara state of Segou was created in about 1712. Finally, later in the century the Futa Jallon in central Guinea emerged from a bitter half-century civil war between Muslims and followers of traditional religion, which ended only in 1776.

These slaving states had a number of features in common. All made war regularly; Oyo and Dahomey sent their armies into the field every dry season. Others relied heavily on raiding into neighboring areas. Most had forces of warriors recruited from slaves. Asante depended largely on tribute from the three to five million people it ruled, many of whom owed a certain number of slaves every year. Religious conflict, and later raiding and trade, provided the Futa Jallon with slaves for sale. In Segou mounted slave warriors operated over a large area.

There has been a heated debate over the demographic effects of the slave trade. It is probable that more than seven million West Africans were exported in the Atlantic trade, constituting about 60 percent of that trade. If we include the trans-Saharan trade, between eight and nine million were exported from West Africa over four centuries. The greatest impact of the trade, however, was not from the number exported, but in the number who died as a result of warfare and disease. People resisted slave-raiders and died or were wounded in the effort. Those who fled often returned to burned-out villages where they had difficulty sustaining themselves. The captives also experienced high mortality. They were first marketed and then walked down to the coast. Poorly clothed and ill-fed, many died on the way or became ill. They were then held in barracoons at the coast until some European trader bought them. Paul Lovejoy suggests that one-quarter to one-third of those reaching the coast could not be sold to European traders. We cannot estimate how many lives were lost overall, but it was certainly several times the number shipped out.

One byproduct of a slave-producing economy was that slaves were increasingly used within Africa. Invariably both those who enslaved people and those who traded in them decided to keep some of the slaves they handled, preferring slaves to more consumer goods. Those kept were used as concubines, wives, soldiers, cultivators, and laborers. It is probable that as many of the newly enslaved were kept within Africa as were exported. This can be deduced from the juxtaposition of two aspects of West African slaving. First, the majority of those enslaved were women and children, largely because men resisted and were often killed or wounded in raids. At the same time, almost twice as many men as women were exported.

African purchasers preferred women and children. Children were easier to acculturate. Women were sought as concubines, as rewards to soldiers and male slaves, because they could do a wide variety of tasks, and because they were less likely to resist or flee. The evolution of African slave systems is a subject that needs further study.

Political centralization and economic accumulation meant that West Africa was increasingly dominated by wealthy and powerful men, each surrounded by kin, slaves, pawns, and clients. Merchants and warriors differed in their values but were tightly linked by their interests. The warriors sold their captives to merchants, who provided them with weapons and consumer goods, but the two groups used slaves in different ways. Merchants saw slaves as an investment and were interested in profit. Military elites used female booty as a reward for service. Slave wives probably did much of the farming for the warriors. The state also sought young males to be trained as soldiers and farmers to feed court and army. Merchants put slaves to work producing goods for sale. Slaves grew grain, raised cotton, wove cloth, and worked leather. By the nineteenth century, Juula and Hausa towns were generally surrounded by a ring of intensively worked slave plantations, and many were also major centres of craft production. Slave labor was also important in the desertside towns, where Saharan nomads arrived annually to exchange salt and animals for grain and cloth. By the late nineteenth century a slave producing grain and cloth could cover his purchase price in three to five years. There was also a constant flow of slaves into the Sahara, where they worked as miners, cultivators, and herders.

The growth of a slave economy within West Africa meant that African slave producers were able to adapt relatively easily to the end of the Atlantic trade. Beginning with Denmark in 1803, the European powers abolished first the slave trade and then slavery. The key action was Britain's abolition of the slave trade in 1807 and of slaveholding in 1833. Some areas had difficulty. Asante had a brief crisis because slaves flowed in faster than Asante could dispose of them. The end of the Atlantic trade also fueled the Yoruba civil wars, which continued intermittently until 1893. However, slaving activities continued. In part this was to feed an illegal slave trade, which remained important for half a century despite British abolition and the efforts of the British Navy. More important was the increasing demand for agricultural produce by both industrial Europe and Saharan nomads. The most important exports to Europe were palm oil and peanut oil, used for lubrication and the manufacture of soap. The eighteenth and nineteenth centuries also saw a series of Muslim *jihāds*. Although some of these movements originated as reactions of industrious Muslim peasants to the demands of predatory slave-trading states, the new Muslim states almost all ended up using slave labor in a more rigorous way. One effect was that slave prices dropped only briefly after Atlantic markets were closed.

West African slavers not only remained active but even became more effective with the importation of new weapons from Europe. Most important were breech-loading rifles, which were more accurate, had greater range, and could be loaded more rapidly. It was thus easier for small armed bands to dominate large populations. By the end of the nineteenth century the Sokoto Caliphate in northern Nigeria had about two and a half million slaves, and French West Africa had more than two million. The last quarter of the century was probably the bloodiest period in West Africa's history as new contenders for power sought to overturn older states. West Africa was so much oriented to a slave economy that these new contenders could often get the money they needed for guns only by selling slaves.

With increasing accumulations of slaves, domestic models of slavery gave way to the plantation or slave village. Slave labor was more systematically exploited for profit, and thus more strictly controlled. Few African slaves worked the dawn-to-dusk routine of the American slave. The work cycle was dependent on climate and the nature of agriculture. The newly enslaved worked full-time for and were fed by their masters. Once the slave was integrated in the society, he or she received a plot of land. In grain-growing areas integrated slaves generally worked about five days a week from sunrise to early afternoon on the master's lands. Usually such male slaves were given female partners. Evenings and the two other days, they worked their own lands. In the more market-oriented societies the hours of labor were extended either by adding a sixth day or by a longer workday. With time a slave ménage could be freed of direct control and allowed to work for themselves in exchange for a fixed annual payment. Male slaves owed approximately what it took to feed a healthy male for a year; women generally owed one-half that. In slave villages work was supervised by a slave chief or a member of the master's family. During the dry season slaves had many other tasks. They repaired houses and rebuilt fences. In many societies, they produced cloth; the women spun and the men wove. In merchant families male slaves might work as porters on the caravans that left shortly after harvest.

Law and custom afforded the slaves some protection. Those born in the house were not supposed to be sold. It is not clear how often this was violated, but it could probably be done only during famine years or when the slave's behavior so alienated other slaves that they approved sale. Within Muslim communities, slave women who bore children for their masters were freed after the master's death. This was probably the most common form of manumission, but Islam also recommended manumission of all a dying person's slaves as a pious act. Faithful retainers were often the beneficiaries of this practice.

In theory, slaves did not marry, but they did cohabit. The difference was that they had none of the rights that spouses had to each other's services or to their children. They could neither bequeath nor inherit: in theory, the slave owned nothing. In practice, masters were forced to recognize the slave's personality. This meant allowing the slave a full family life. Children could, however, be taken from their parents when they were old enough to work, and either put to work in the master's house or given as servants to his children. This meant that slave society was more atomized than that of the freeborn. In spite of this, slaves lived in family units. The surplus of female slaves made it possible for almost all male slaves to have spouses and for some to have two. Domesticity was probably a key factor tying slaves into their new societies. When slaves fled their masters, they often left in family units; when parents fled alone, they often tried to recover their children.

The abolition of slavery by European powers had little effect on African slaves. European colonies were very small and reluctant to shelter fugitive slaves because it threatened their relations with African states. In 1848, when the French abolished slavery, slaves living on the islands of St. Louis and Goree were freed, but the French soon began expelling runaway slaves as vagabonds, often by arrangement with their owners. The British also worked out extradition arrangements with slave-owning neighboring polities. When colonial rule extended beyond coastal bases, both powers used the device of a protectorate to avoid enforcing their own anti-slavery legislation. Gradually these systems were changed. In the 1850s an abolitionist governor began giving sanctuary in the Gold Coast; in Senegal during the 1870s, a determined prosecuting attorney brought charges against slave-owners and freed their slaves within the colony. Slavery was abolished in the Gold Coast in 1874, though even there an effort was made to limit enforcement. The armies that conquered Africa for Europe were largely made up of slaves, often purchased for the army and often rewarded with slave prisoners.

When the conquest was completed at the turn of the century, the colonial powers acted. Even though the colonies depended heavily on slave-owning collaborators, slavery was seen in the metropolis as immoral, and emancipation was afterward offered as one of the goals of colonization. The colonial regime generally chose a variant of what can be called the Indian formula, under which colonial states refused to enforce the control of the masters over the slaves. In 1905 French West Africa prohibited any transactions in persons; it did not actually abolish slavery, but a refusal to enforce the rights of masters led to between one-half and three-quarters of a million slaves returning to earlier homes. In Northern Nigeria too there was large-scale flight, but Governor Frederic Lugard feared economic and social disruption. He proclaimed the freedom of children born after 1901 and made provision for older slaves to purchase their freedom, but he reinforced control of masters over the bulk of their slaves. In Sierra Leone, once the beacon in the anti-slavery struggle, slave-trading was abolished in 1896, but slavery itself was not prohibited until 1926, after a League of Nations inquiry on slavery.

The struggles to control the labor of former slaves in West Africa have been poorly studied. The majority of slaves remained where they were. In most areas they were able to establish control over both family and work life. Where masters established control over land, the former slaves became a dependent class of sharecroppers and rural workers. Where the former slaves were able to get access to land, they became an independent and often successful peasantry.

[See also Abolition and Anti-Slavery, article on Africa; and Historiography, article on African Slavery.]

BIBLIOGRAPHY

Curtin, Philip D. The Atlantic Slave Trade: A Census. Madison: University of Wisconsin Press, 1969.

Lovejoy, Paul E. Transformations in Slavery: A History of Slavery in Africa. Cambridge: Cambridge University Press, 1983.

Manning, Patrick. Slavery and African Life: Occidental, Oriental, and African Slave Traders. Cambridge: Cambridge University Press, 1990.

Meillassoux, Claude. The Anthropology of Slavery: The Womb of Iron and Gold. Translated by Alide Dasnois. Chicago: University of Chicago Press, 1991.

Miers, Suzanne, and Igor Kopytoff, eds. Slavery in Africa: Historical and Anthropological Perspectives. Madison: University of Wisconsin Press, 1977.

Robertson, Claire, and Martin A. Klein, eds. Women and Slavery in Africa. Madison: University of Wisconsin Press, 1983.

Rodney, Walter. West Africa and the Atlantic Slave-Trade. Dar es Salaam: Historical Society of Tanzania, 1967.

—MARTIN A. KLEIN

Central Africa

We know very little about slavery in the region that today comprises the central African states of Malawi, Zambia, and Zimbabwe. There is no book-length study dealing with the subject in any of these countries; the most extensive treatment is Marcia Wright's biographical account of six ex-slaves. The literature on the institution in nineteenth-century Malawi and Zambia includes a few published articles, observations in general historical surveys, and dissertations. Even sparser is our knowledge about slavery in nineteenth-century Zimbabwe; this article derives its information on Zimbabwe from Albino Pacheco's report of his journey from Tete to Zumbo in 1861. Some general works, such as David Beach's The Shona and Zimbabwe, 900–1850 (1980), do not even mention the institution. Hoyini Bhila's Trade and Politics in a Shona Kingdom (1982) has only a single reference, and this is to the slave trade rather than slavery. It appears that slavery was not an important institution in many communities of precolonial Zimbabwe, and much of Zimbabwe may have been little affected by the slave trade. Present-day Malawi and Zambia have figured in discussions of slavery mainly because of their involvement in the so-called "Arab" slave trade that became the staple target of British anti-slavery propaganda in the late nineteenth century.

One significant exception to this overall pattern was Bulozi in what is today northwestern Zambia. Bulozi may have attracted the attention of other observers besides the abolitionists because slavery was a major institution in this kingdom, which came into being in the eighteenth century. As among the Bemba, slavery in Bulozi relied on and buttressed a well-developed state system. The rulers used both impressment and raiding to recruit slaves from within and outside the kingdom. Sometimes housed in their own separate villages, the slaves formed a distinct and identifiable social class. The situation of such slaves was in many respects different from slaves in the kin-ordered communities that made up much of nineteenth-century central Africa. In the latter societies people obtained slaves by purchasing them with cattle, salt, hoes, grain, or other goods. Intervillage warfare and kidnapping were also used to recruit slaves. Finally, chiefs and other village notables relied on the legal system to get slaves. It was common to accept slaves as payment of debts or fines. Indeed, as Albino Pacheco remarked in 1861, the people of Dande and Katayama, in what is today eastern Zimbabwe, did not sell or buy one another as slaves; they bought foreigners beyond their borders. The only citizens of these two states who became slaves in their respective communities were those condemned by the poison ordeal. Slave populations in such communities were necessarily small, in sharp contrast to the situation in Bulozi; there, according to some estimates, slaves made up one-quarter to one-third of the entire population in the late nineteenth century.

Regardless of the methods they employed, most people acquired slaves for use as laborers. It was a shortage of labor among the people of Dande and Chidima that made them buy slaves at Nsenga and from the Maravis for employment in their fields. Similarly, a childless Mang'anja bachelor risked starvation in 1861 by selling his maize in order to buy a slave woman to perform the duties of a wife. The slaves of the kings of Bulozi worked as cooks, messengers, hunters, and cattle-herders, in addition to the daily routines associated with farming. Slavery was in all these societies principally a system of labor mobilization. As workers in the fields and in the home, slaves toiled side by side with their owners in communities where age and sex were the primary factors in the social division of labor.

Although technically equivalent to their masters as units of agricultural and household labor, slaves were a socially deprived class. It was their lot to do the most onerous tasks. Among the Ila, slaves were responsible for driving cattle to the floodplains during the dry season, building and repairing shelters and cattle fences, and herding and milking the cattle. Slaves were also among the first to experience famine in times of food shortage; in this regard they were similar to the young, pawns, and bondsmen. What set these dependents off from slaves was that the latter never gained control over their time, whatever their age or the time they spent in a particular community. In becoming a slave among the peoples of Central Africa one transferred one's rights over one's labor and products to others, although who the others were differed from society to society and from one context to another within the same society. In most communities people used slaves as members of individual households, and slaves typically worked for a certain individual; this "private" use did not, however, exclude collective responsibility over slaves. In their different ways, the peoples of Central Africa did not consider slaves as privately owned pieces of property. It was as servants of the powerful Lozi state that most people acquired, kept, and employed slaves in Bulozi. The kings, members of the royal family, and their senior councilors were ultimately dependent on state machinery for the slaves' existence as a class of permanently dispossessed persons. Lozi commoners, while they did not benefit from the slave system directly, had a stake in it because it protected them from some of the labor demands of the ruling class. In the less-stratified communities, kinship provided the framework for both incorporating and excluding slaves from the local community. Kinship remained central to a system of control that in some societies, like the

Mang'anja of Malawi, promoted the view of slaves as nonhuman beings.

By defining slaves as nonhuman beings the Mang'anja placed them in the same category as social juniors. This radical definition disqualified most slaves from participation in the community's public rituals as well as key branches of nonagricultural production, especially the salt and iron industries. The "labor of enslaved men" was not, as Claude Meillassoux has surmised for the Sahelo-Sudanic region, "devoted to the production of mercantile goods for exchange." As nonhuman beings, slaves were equal to, but not the producers of, mercantile goods that were exchanged in the local and regional systems of economic transactions. Normal rules of inheritance did not apply to slaves, either. Thus, although the Ila allowed some of their slaves to own certain forms of property—including other slaves—slaves could not inherit the property of the kinship group to which they were supposed to belong. Like social juniors, slaves could be used but could not actively participate in the reproduction of the lineage. Tension was the trademark of a slave's life.

The denial of the slave's humanity formed only one dimension of the system of control. A contradictory aspect required the recognition of the slave as a human being who might, at the very least, resist oppression. Masters acknowledged this reality by, among other things, providing their slaves with spouses. This was not always an easy obligation to fulfill. For one thing, in many communities there were not enough slaves for masters to establish purely slave marriages. They had to marry their slaves to free persons, which brought into sharp relief the anomalies of the institution. In addition, the availability of slaves as reproducers, especially in kin-ordered communities, created opportunities for some individuals to establish social relationships outside the existing framework of kinship. Men and women—including some slaves—could use their slave spouses to form their own autonomous family groupings. The materialization of such a possibility depended on the economy, in particular on the way it intersected with the prevailing rules of filiation, descent, and inheritance.

Such rules varied widely in Central Africa, although one can isolate three main systems for the purposes of illustration. Two of these were unilineal, requiring individuals to trace their descent and to inherit property from either the mother's (matrilineal) or the father's (patrilineal) line. The Bemba and Mang'anja were matrilineal, whereas the inhabitants of Chidima and Dande in northeastern Zimbabwe were patrilineal. The Ila of Zambia represent a third system. They followed either the mother's or the father's lines, depending on the issue at hand. Their system was more flexible than the first two. Nonetheless, all three regimes were similar in one respect: they all imposed limitations on the ambitious individual's taking advantage of a marriage to a slave, while offering the opportunity to do so as well.

Among the Mang'anja, where every husband was a dependent to his wife and her kin, a married male slave posed no threat to anyone. Only criminals and the incorrigibly lazy were denied wives; the main factor limiting a slave-owner's generosity to his men was the paucity of nubile women. Owners without female slaves normally married their male slaves to their sisters' daughters, which underlined the view of slaves as the common property of the lineage segment.

An entirely different reality faced male slaves in a patrilineal setting. The overriding concern here was that a determined male slave might convert his dependent nuclear family into an important lineage segment that could compete with his master's. Only trusted slaves were given wives; marriage was a favor that crowned years of faithful service to a reliable master. There must have been many who died unmarried, and it was probably such a population of discontented bachelors that formed the basis of the common perception of male slaves as a more difficult category to absorb at the family level. Female slaves everywhere found it easy to get spouses.

Three factors explain the ease with which female slaves secured husbands. First, female slaves in a patrilineal context shared with free women the distinct handicap that they could not become recognized heads of households. Their marriage to free men could accomplish only one purpose—to strengthen the man's economic and social position—although the marriage gave a man no advantage he did not already have as a husband of free women. The situation was more complex among the Mang'anja, who, like the Ila, never resolved the tension in the equation of woman and slave. Free men married slave wives for two distinct reasons. Some saw nothing in the women but slaves. Marrying a slave in this type of society not only increased the husband's power, as in patrilineal communities; it transformed the very nature of that power.

Photograph of a captured slave in the Belgian Congo, date unknown; Musée de l'Homme, Paris.

Husbands could exercise full control over, and add to their kin group, the children of slave wives—something they could not do with the offspring of free Mang'anja women. The prospect of having children without maternal kin made marriage to slave women a very attractive proposition for many men.

The slave wives' position as slaves was the basis for both these kinds of preference. A third was based on their womanhood. Ila and Mang'anja owners preferred keeping married female slaves because unmarried older women were difficult to control. As she grew older, an unmarried female slave in these societies became more a woman and less a slave. She could, like free elderly women, own property, including other slaves. She could emulate the example of free Ila female slave-owners who hired men to impregnate their slaves. Elderly female slaves could, in other words, establish their own lineage segments, much as married male slaves threatened to do in a patrilineal setting. Slave-owners never trusted these women. The Ila closely monitored their movements; the Mang'anja had a whole list of derogatory terms to refer to them, and they sought to prevent their multiplication by encouraging female slaves to marry soon after reaching puberty. Young slaves of either sex created fewer headaches for their masters. Owners found them easier to handle and generally treated them well, and masters only reluctantly sold such pliable workers to slave-traders.

Malawi and eastern Zambia effectively entered the modern slave-trading era at the beginning of the nineteenth century, when, besides supplying the old Persian Gulf markets, they started sending captives to Zanzibar, the Mascarene Islands, and some parts of the Caribbean. Western Zambia, including Bulozi, may have done so earlier as an extension of the Angola-Congo network, although it was not until the middle of the century that Bulozi began to deal with slave-traders from the East Coast. Only Zimbabwe appears to have been left unscathed by the Indian Ocean traffic that raged in other parts of the region up to the end of the century. Large parts of Malawi and Zambia entered the twentieth century with their economies and political systems seriously distorted by that trade.

The trade's impact on indigenous slavery was not uniform. It weakened some forms in response to broader societal pressures. Extreme violence characterized the entire era of the slave trade in much of this region. Raiding for captives created chaos and famines that tore many communities apart, undermining their social and economic basis and thus also weakening the original institution of slavery. British imperialists did not have to fight against slavery in these communities. The slave regime of the Mang'anja barely survived the devastating, slave-trade-induced famines of the 1860s; it was virtually extinct by the time the British took control of the region in the 1890s. Thus, except for a few places (notably Bulozi), in much of Malawi and Zambia British anti-slavery campaigns had two related targets: the slave trade and the new system of slavery.

This new slave system developed with the rise of new states and fueled considerable slave-trading activity within the region. Some of these polities, like those of the Ngoni and the Kololo in Malawi, had only benefited from the chaos created by the Indian Ocean traffic; but many others, like those of Msiri and Tippu Tip, had emerged out of the slave-trading activities of their creators. As empire-builders and as slave-owners, the rulers of the new states became the archenemies of British imperialists. As elsewhere in Africa, colonial legislative activity always required a changed economic environment to become an effective weapon against slavery. Even in Bulozi, where the British did not face open opposition, the edict of 1906 killed slavery only as part of a wage labor policy and, in particular, of a fiscal policy that required slave-owners to pay taxes for their slaves. Many slave-owners did not have money and had to let their slaves go.

[See also Abolition and Anti-Slavery, article on Africa; and Slave Trade, article on Trans-Saharan Trade.]

BIBLIOGRAPHY

Hermitte, Eugene. "An Economic History of Barotseland, 1800–1940." Diss., Northwestern University, 1974.

Mandala, Elias. *Work and Control in a Peasant Economy: A History of the Lower Tchiri Valley in Malawi, 1859–1960.* Madison: University of Wisconsin Press, 1990.

Meillassoux, Claude. "The Role of Slavery in the Economic and Social History of Sahelo-Sudanic Africa." In *Forced Migration: The Impact of the Export Slave Trade on African Societies*, edited by Joseph Inikori. New York: Africana, 1982.

Pacheco, Albino. "The Diary of Albino Manuel Pacheco: A Voyage from Tete to Zumbo," in *The Shona and the Portuguese, 1575–1890*, vol. 2, edited by David Beach and H. DeNoronha. Harare: University of Zimbabwe, 1980.

Prins, Gwyn. *The Hidden Hippopotamus: Reappraisal in African History: The Early Colonial Experience in Western Zambia.* Cambridge: Cambridge University Press, 1980.

Roberts, Andrew. *A History of the Bemba: Political Growth and Change in North-eastern Zambia before 1900.* Madison: University of Wisconsin Press, 1973.

Tuden, Arthur. "Slavery and Stratification among the Ila of Central Africa." In *Social Stratification in Africa.*, edited by Arthur Tuden and Leonard Plotnicov. New York: Free Press, 1970.

Wright, Marcia. *Strategies of Slaves and Women: Life-Stories from East/Central Africa.* New York: Lilian Barber Press, 1993.

—ELIAS MANDALA

East Africa

In no other part of Africa, and at no other time, did slavery and the slave trade expand as rapidly as in nineteenth-century East Africa. More slaves than ever before left East Africa for the Mediterranean basin and Asia; many even reached the Americas. Slave-raiding and slave-trading penetrated deep into the interior, until East African raiding and trading frontiers merged with those of Central and southern Africa. Most of the people who fell into the hands of traders, however, did not leave East Africa. As slavery spread through the area, its nature changed. Men and women who had lived as servile dependents, somewhat as junior kin, found themselves vulnerable to becoming human commodities. Masters put slaves to work in new ways; production based on slave labor developed. Slave soldiers bolstered the power of upstart leaders, while older kingdoms and chiefdoms collapsed. The developing competitive commercial systems, to which slavery belonged, sometimes produced tensions leading to uprisings, but these rebellions seldom challenged slavery itself. Slavery within East Africa disappeared only when slaves took advantage of changing economic and political conditions, mainly in the early twentieth century, to find their own freedom—although often an equivocal freedom.

These transformations affected three regions of East Africa. This article focuses on the region consisting of the Indian Ocean coast from the mouth of the Zambezi River to the Horn of Africa, including its hinterland and the island of Madagascar. The coast and hinterland in turn can be divided into three areas: the south, where an Afro-Portuguese diaspora spread inland; the center, origin of Swahili commerce and culture; and the north, dominated by Somali herders and townsmen. Also deserving mention are the two northern extremities of East Africa—the upper Nile Valley, or Sudan, and the Ethiopian highlands.

Before the late eighteenth century East Africa exported relatively few slaves. Although evidence is impressionistic at best, available sources suggest generally low exports, interrupted by sporadic bursts when wars produced a spate of captives or a sudden demand stimulated the export market. The southern and central coast, for example, sent probably fewer than two thousand slaves annually across the Indian Ocean. Ports on the Red Sea and Gulf of Aden dispatched perhaps an average of three thousand five hundred slaves annually. Three thousand slaves, mainly from Ethiopia and the Sudan, crossed the Sahara to Egypt every year.

Although relatively few East Africans entered the export trade before the nineteenth century, some found themselves in a servile state in East Africa. Involuntary servitude ranged from conditions of chattel slavery to forms of dependency resembling those of junior kin, clients, or even wives. Africans experienced chattel slavery most

frequently in areas integrated into long-distance trade networks: the coastal littoral and Zambezi Valley, the banks of the upper Nile, and Ethiopia. There merchants who traded slaves also often put them to work in their households and enterprises. Rulers not only gained revenues from the export trade in slaves; they also used slaves in their armies, administrations, and households. In the upper Nile Valley, northern and central coast, and parts of Ethiopia, Islam provided an ideological and legal base for slavery.

Between about 1600 and 1800 Africans experienced both ends of the spectrum of servility—from dependency to chattel slavery—in the Zambezi Valley, where Afro-Portuguese gold and ivory traders established estates. Estate residents included both free Africans and slaves, on whom the estate-holder based his power. Most of the male slaves formed an army; some served as administrators, porters, or trading agents. Some slave women mined gold and copper. Owners could sell these slaves and their children, who inherited slave status. The free Africans, who produced the estate's food, themselves controlled the labor of servile men and women; the status of these dependents, however, neared that of junior kin. Seldom sold, they eventually became members of their master's lineage, and servile status did not last more than one generation.

Exports of slaves from East Africa gradually increased in the middle and late eighteenth century, before rising rapidly after 1800 and then declining around 1880. The southern and central coast experienced the sharpest increase. Although scholars disagree on the volume of the trade, one estimate suggests that slave exports increased by more than tenfold from their levels before the late eighteenth century: between about 1820 and 1880, between 20,000 and 30,000 slaves left the central and southern coast annually. The Red Sea and Gulf of Aden trade increased less precipitously, probably to a peak of around 5,500 slaves annually between 1831 and 1885. Between 1820 and 1877 Egypt's yearly imports almost doubled, to about 5,900. Although it is possible to make only a rough estimate, at least 1,700,000 and perhaps as many as 2,400,000 East African slaves traveled on the Red Sea, Gulf of Aden, Indian Ocean, and trans-Saharan routes. Southwest Asia, especially Arabia and the Persian Gulf, imported at the very least 800,000 slaves, while perhaps another 400,000 went to Egypt. Brazil and Cuba imported at least 385,000 East Africans, while perhaps another 200,000 found themselves laboring in plantations in Mauritius and Réunion. A few East African slaves traveled to India.

The nineteenth-century transformation of the slave trade and slavery in East Africa occurred in the dual context of African, Arab, and European empire-building and market expansion. With the exception of the decentralized Portuguese regime in Mozambique, European political rule arrived only in the late nineteenth or early twentieth centuries. Earlier empire-building involved the expansion of the Egyptian, Ethiopian, Omani, and Merina (Madagascar) states. Sometimes raiding for slaves themselves, these empires also allowed merchants to enrich themselves. Decades before Western political imperialism, European demands for slaves in the late eighteenth century, followed by a voracious appetite for ivory beginning in the 1820s, stimulated the slave trade in particular and commerce in general. Able to sell ivory at high prices and buy European imports cheaply, armed hunters and traders moved into the interior, where they trafficked in slaves as well as tusks. A general commercial revival in the entire western Indian Ocean basin also created demand for slaves to fill labor bottlenecks in transport, construction, and various services. Merchants often invested their commercial profits in slaves or goods produced by slaves.

Stretching from the port of Kilwa southward to the mouth of the Zambezi and including Madagascar, the southern part of the coast first felt external demands for slaves. Beginning around 1730 and accelerating later in the century, the burgeoning plantation economy of Mauritius and Réunion im-

ported slaves from this region, including captives shipped under the fiction of contract labor. In the late eighteenth century the Atlantic slave trade reached the southern coast. French plantations in the Antilles first imported East African slaves. With the suppression of the Atlantic trade after 1807, Cuba and Brazil increasingly sought slaves from the southern coast of East Africa. In both the export and regional slave trades Madagascar played a pivotal role. Raids on the frontiers of the Merina Empire produced captives, some of whom were exported. In addition, the Merina imported slaves from the coast to work in various state enterprises.

The Afro-Portuguese estates of the Zambezi collapsed under the new export markets for slaves. Responding to Brazilian and Cuban demand, estate-holders turned from exporting gold and ivory to exporting slaves. When trading and raiding could not supply enough slaves, the estateholders sold their own slaves as well as the free Africans on their estates. An insecure populace fled. Depleted by population loss and afflicted by violence, estates disintegrated. The end of the estates, however, did not bring about the end of slavery. New polities arose, using slaves in armies and elephant-hunting bands.

The central coast became the focus for the slave and ivory trade when the Omani state, based in southwestern Arabia, established hegemony over the Swahili coast in the early nineteenth century. Primarily a commercial empire, the sultanate itself did not raid for slaves. Rather, the Omanis attracted Indian capital to the coast and backed the authority of slave-owners. The center of Omani power in Africa, the offshore island of Zanzibar, became the most important entrepôt on the entire coast. Traders from other ports, especially Kilwa in the south, arrived with ivory and slaves. At the height of the slave trade, between 1859 and 1872, from fifteen to twenty thousand slaves entered Zanzibar annually; more than half continued their journeys to other parts of the coast, Arabia, or the Persian Gulf.

Partly to service the trade itself, slaves filled

Zanzibar. They formed the majority—perhaps two-thirds to three-quarters—of the island's population. Urban slaves worked as crews of lightering boats, deckhands, and porters. They processed and packed trade goods. Slave men served as unskilled workers, artisans and trade agents; both men and women performed domestic services and carried water.

Slaves also supported a form of production new to the eastern coast—the plantation. Export agriculture attracted merchant investment, especially when European anti-slave measures temporarily disrupted slave exports. Merchants kept their slaves on Zanzibar, by the 1830s putting them to work on clove plantations. From Zanzibar clove plantations spread to the nearby island of Pemba. Mainland entrepreneurs established plantations growing sugar and other export crops, as well as grain with which to feed the workers and merchants of the Indian Ocean trade.

The cities and ships of the Indian Ocean trade also imported food from the Somali coast in the north. Responding to this market, as well as to the availability of slaves from the Swahili coast, Somali entrepreneurs used slave labor to open lands along the Shabelle River to agriculture, farming an array of new crops. Somali urban slaves worked as their counterparts did in Zanzibar; they also wove cloth from cotton grown by agricultural slaves. Between 1800 and 1890, probably fifty thousand slaves entered southern Somalia.

The nineteenth-century coastal demand for slaves reached deep into the interior. The hinterland of the southern port of Kilwa supplied Zanzibar with most of its slaves until the 1870s. From the southern coast, trade routes quickly extended into the interior, eventually reaching as far west as the eastern part of the Zaire River basin in Central Africa and south into the Zimbabwe highlands in southern Africa. After 1873, when British pressure suppressed the maritime slave trade between Kilwa and Zanzibar, the source of coastal slaves shifted to the central interior, including the lands immediately behind the coast. In both central and south-ern hinterlands men from the interior engaged in trade, as did a variety of coastal and Asian merchants—Swahili, Afro-Portuguese, Omani, and Baluchi. In exchange for slaves and ivory, traders supplied beads, iron, alcohol, guns, and cloth.

The demands of the coast triggered changes in the political, economic, and social lives of Africans living in the interior. With the general rise in commercial activity, dependent people became acceptable as currency in local exchanges, especially for debt payment. Dependent girls and women entered households where the most fortunate of them found permanent homes or were ransomed back to their own families. Less fortunate girls and women were exchanged repeatedly, eventually becoming commodities in the hands of traders. Enslaved boys and men often labored in commercial enterprises or in armed bands under leaders who derived their power from alliances with traders and command of slave soldiers. This new style of political leadership challenged and often destroyed older forms of political organization.

In both coast and interior, slaves struggled to build collective lives in families and communities. Some slaves established their own communities after running away from their masters; maroon settlements sprang up in the hinterland of the Swahili coast, as well as south of the Shabelle Valley in Somali territory. Other slaves did not separate themselves from the communities of their masters, but rather struggled to become more full-fledged community members. Women slaves sometimes moved closer to full membership by bearing the children of their masters. For men in towns and trade enterprises, community membership meant sharing more fully in public commercial and religious life. Plantation slaves tried to gain access to land. Everywhere slaves sought to exert authority over their own families and often to control other dependents, who might themselves be slaves.

Opposing the claims of slaves to community membership, Swahili masters used not only their political and economic resources but also ideology. The rhetoric of paternalism and Islam allowed masters to depict slaves as dependent, uncultured, and thus unworthy of full membership in the community. Slaves used the same language in their struggles to belong. Evoking the paternalism of their masters, reciprocity between masters and slaves, and the shared practice of Islam, slaves laid claim to community membership.

Tensions over slavery and community membership grew particularly acute in the central Swahili coastal towns. By the 1870s some masters began to coalesce into a class, increasingly engaged in exporting crops and looking to the Omani state to defend their rights over land and slave labor. The masters subjected the slaves on sugar plantations to particularly severe control, preventing them from forming families and replenishing their ranks with slaves purchased in the market. Moreover, caravans and trade enterprises employed free men from upcountry and slaves who sought to participate in both the commerce and the Islamic rituals of the towns. Finally, in some places along the coast Swahili traders and landowners found themselves challenged by the newly emerging upper class with its links to the Omani state. These tensions erupted into a wave of rebellions along the coast in the 1880s, just as colonial powers arrived.

In the northeastern and northwestern extremities of East Africa, state violence, more than an external demand for slaves, triggered the nineteenth-century increase in slave-raiding and slave-trading. Government raiding in the Sudan and Ethiopia produced plentiful—and thus cheap—supplies of slaves, encouraging masters to put slaves to work in new ways. The internal demand for slaves thus acquired a momentum of its own, stimulating continued raiding and trading.

In the upper Nile Valley, slavery and the slave trade expanded when a violent conquest regime interacted with merchant capital. In 1820 troops under orders of the Ottoman viceroy of Egypt invaded the Sudan and established rule over the land around and below the confluence of the two Niles. During much of its first two decades of rule the chronically underfinanced regime supported itself partly through plunder. Massive annual government raids captured slaves; the state also accepted slaves as tribute, as well as giving slaves to soldiers in lieu of their wages. Traders traveled in the wake of government raids, buying up captives cheaply and sending them to local and export markets.

The Egyptian conquest regime triggered cycles of raiding, trading, and exploitation that continued even when large-scale government slave raids ended after 1845. Local raiders, especially cattle-herders, captured slaves partly to sell to traders for cash or goods with which they could pay tribute. When slave prices fell as the export trade to Egypt declined after 1840, Sudanese masters put slaves to work in new ways. By mid-century, for the first time slaves labored on rainland agriculture. They also worked in the ivory trade, which expanded along the White Nile and its tributaries after 1850. Moving beyond government control, merchants commanded slave soldiers and laborers in armed camps that served as bases for raiding and trading. By the 1880s these violent bands pushed the slave-raiding and slave-trading frontier to the marches of the Ethiopian highlands in the southeast and to the watershed of the Zaire Basin in the southwest.

The growing power of merchants contributed to a crisis that culminated in a militant Muslim reform movement. Most acutely on the southern frontiers, but also in the central Sudan, factions led by traders fought with each other. Merchants parlayed their command of cash and armed men into government offices, injecting commercial competition into state politics. Sudanese Muslims turned to a religious leader, the Mahdi, who promised to unify and purify their society. Attracting some of his most important officers from the slave-raiding frontier, the Mahdi led a revolution that expelled the conquest regime and established a militant theocracy. The Mahdi's followers did not seek to end slavery but rather to direct its violence away from the Muslim community. Slavery in the upper Nile Valley ended only slowly under the joint rule of Britain and Egypt, whose forces defeated the Islamic regime in 1898.

In Ethiopia the imperial state did not succumb to the violence it sponsored on its frontiers. For centuries the frontiers had supported the central state, both by providing export goods, including slaves, and by serving as an outlet for dissident or ambitious men. Slave-raiding on the frontiers increased during a period of imperial decentralization in the mid-eighteenth century. Wars among small frontier states produced many captives; at least one frontier state raided with the specific aim of capturing slaves. In the mid-nineteenth century, the policies, if not the public pronouncements, of a consolidating and expanding empire further stimulated raiding and trading. Local rulers who remained in power gave slaves as tribute. In other areas imperial governors commanded garrisons of soldiers who raided slaves, carrying them back to the north as booty.

Slave-raiding stimulated wider exploitation of slave labor in Ethiopia. In the first half of the century, internal markets absorbed about half of the slaves captured on the frontiers. Elite households quickly purchased more slaves. But with increasing numbers and declining prices of captives, even smallholders and relatively poor peasants began to put slaves to work in households and fields. Slaves also worked in local industry, producing cloth and leather goods.

As in the rest of East Africa, slavery slowly ended in twentieth-century Ethiopia; unlike the other regions, however, emancipation began under an independent African regime. Changes in the political economies of both the central state and the slave-raiding frontier gradually ended slavery. In the 1920s and early 1930s Emperor Haile Selassie and his followers undertook the first steps of emancipation as part of their struggle to create a centralized state and reduce the power of provincial elites. Ending slavery undermined the economic base of both the northern, land-owning oligarchy and the southern military and merchant elites. At the same time, the supply of slaves from the frontiers decreased as merchants in the south turned increasingly to commodity production. For their part, military officers no longer raided extensively but instead sought to settle local people on their estates as tenants and laborers. The example of Ethiopia thus suggests that slavery slowly ended in East Africa not simply because of the policies of European regimes, but because of more general changes in East African political economies.

[See also Slave Trade, article on Trans-Saharan Trade.]

BIBLIOGRAPHY

Clarence-Smith, William Gervase, ed. *The Economics of the Indian Ocean Slave Trade in the Nineteenth Century.* London: Frank Cass, 1989.

Cooper, Frederick. *Plantation Slavery on the East Coast of Africa.* New Haven: Yale University Press, 1977.

Ewald, Janet J. *Soldiers, Traders, and Slaves: State Formation and Economic Transformation in the Greater Nile Valley, 1700–1885.* Madison: University of Wisconsin Press, 1990.

Isaacman, Allen F. *Mozambique: The Africanization of a European Institution: The Zambezi Prazos, 1750–1902.* Madison: University of Wisconsin Press, 1972.

Miers, Suzanne, and Richard Roberts, eds. *The End of Slavery in Africa.* Madison: University of Wisconsin Press, 1988.

Wright, Marcia. *Strategies of Slaves and Women: Life-stories from East/Central Africa.* New York: Lilian Barber Press, 1993.

—JANET J. EWALD

Southern Africa

Great regional diversity characterized slavery in southern Africa. In the western districts of the Cape Colony, a slave society under European domination emerged in the late seventeenth century. In other parts of southern Africa domestic slavery appeared mainly in the nineteenth century, and most societies with slaves depended on a number of other dependent labor and social relations.

One characteristic distinguishing slavery in the western Cape was that the slave population was overwhelmingly male. In most other slave societies in southern Africa, women predominated in the slave population. These differences arose in part because of the different gender ideologies of these cultures. European colonizers believed that men were better fit for agricultural and pastoral work, while in many indigenous African societies female slaves tended to be more valued because women were the primary agricultural workers. The nature of the slave trade at different times also affected gender ratios. For example, until the ending of the trans-Atlantic slave trade in the mid-nineteenth century, the demand for men in the slave markets of the Americas left women the main source of labor for domestic slavery in southern Africa.

Despite this diversity, the enslavement of children was common to all areas. Settlers in the western Cape indentured ex-slaves' children and illegally captured children from the interior. In the north, Dutch-speaking settlers also participated in raids to enslave African children.

In contrast to other areas of southern Africa, slavery in the western region of the Cape Colony and the area around the Zambezi River in Mozambique dated to the seventeenth century. Slavery was introduced to the Cape Colony in 1658 by the Dutch East India Company (VOC), which ruled the Cape from 1652 to the late eighteenth century. Established as a supply station for VOC ships, the Cape soon became a colony of white settlers who depended on the labor of others to work their farms. The VOC imported slaves, because the company forbade the enslavement of indigenous people in its possessions. Slaves originally came from the VOC charter area, especially the Dutch East Indies. By the eighteenth century the supply of slaves increasingly came from Africa, especially from present-day Angola and Mozambique.

As in the U.S. South, slavery was widely distributed among the settler population, although most settlers owned fewer than eight slaves per household. When the British took over the Cape permanently in 1806, however, most British settlers, who arrived predominantly in the 1820s, were forbidden to own slaves. Thus Dutch-speaking settlers constituted the vast majority of slaveholders; however, some English speakers as well as free blacks owned slaves. Slaves in Cape Town enjoyed greater freedom than their rural peers; they sometimes lived in houses separate from their owners and engaged in wage work. In addition, urban slaves had more opportunities to practice formal religion. The Cape Town slave population was marked by its adherence to Islam and came to form what is now known as the Malay community. In contrast, the influence of Islam in the rural areas was more limited. Farmers also forbade their slaves conversion to Christianity because of a fear that this would lead to their manumission.

Areas of present-day Mozambique on the southeast coast of Africa also had a long acquaintance with slavery, owing in part to European influence. From the early seventeenth century the Portuguese crown gave out large feudal estates, called *prazos*, to settlers in an attempt to facilitate the extension

Portraits of slaves from Mozambique, nineteenth century.

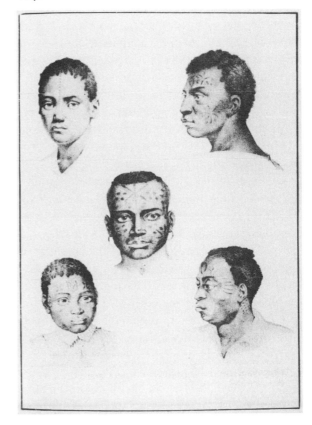

of colonial rule. The *prazeros* (estateholders) depended both on the tribute of subject local people called *colonos* and on the labor and services of slaves. By 1806 the *prazeros* owned about fifty thousand slaves. The estates formed the base for a wide-ranging trade in ivory and gold, and increasingly from the early nineteenth century, in slaves. Slave armies, or *achikunda,* in the service of the *prazeros* were responsible for seizing of captives in the interior for sale at the port of Quelimane. But as Leroy Vail and Landeg White discuss, beginning in 1807, when the demand for slaves increased as a result of the ending of the British slave trade, the *prazeros* turned to the populations of their own estates to furnish slaves for the Brazilian and Indian Ocean markets.

Since the 1980s the historiography of slavery in southern Africa has undergone great transformation. Early works on Cape slavery, such as that of Victor De Kock, portrayed Cape slavery as mild in comparison to other slave societies of the Atlantic world. More recently, historians such as Robert Ross and Nigel Worden have argued that slavery in the western Cape was marked by considerable brutality and by the absence of a thriving slave culture owing to the heterogeneity of the slave population and to the hostile geography of the region. Clifton Crais and Susan Newton-King also stressed the role of violence in slavery on the colonial frontier. Others proposed that a familial ethos better characterized slavery at the Cape, and they argued that slave culture flourished in both the urban areas and the rural districts of the western Cape. Researchers also found evidence that Afrikaans, the creole language derived from Dutch that became the language of many settlers and also the language of the apartheid era in South Africa, had its origins primarily in slave society of the western Cape. Studies in the 1990s began to consider the relationship between gender and slavery at the Cape.

Historians of slavery in South Africa have tended to apply the term *slave* only to persons formally enslaved. Khoisan and people of mixed Khoi and white descent who found themselves trapped in relations of servitude through indenture contracts, a system that dated back to at least 1775, have been termed "dependent laborers." Scholarship appearing in the 1990s argued, however, that indenture merely concealed the enslavement of indigenous people. These authors suggested that *slavery* is a more accurate term to denote the lives of people who experienced bonded labor from early childhood. Scholarship also began to focus attention on the ways in which European settlers contributed to slave-raiding and the extension of slavery into the interior of present South Africa. Historians have shown, for example, that from the mid to late nineteenth century settlers throughout the northern regions, particularly from the northern South African Republic, engaged in a lucrative and ongoing trade in both ivory and slaves. They traded with the Gaza Nguni of southern Mozambique and the BaTwana of northern Botswana as well as raiding local societies. Slaves were used on the farms of settlers who participated in raiding and in a slave trade that extended down to the Cape Colony.

For much of the nineteenth century in southern Africa, the rise of a trade in slaves and the growth of domestic slavery went hand in hand. In the 1820s and 1830s new predatory states emerged concurrently with the increasing demand for slaves in the Indian Ocean and Brazil. In these states, age regiments (societies of young men) traditionally plundered neighboring people for cattle for trade in lieu of ivory, but the early 1800s witnessed a spread of slave-raiding throughout southern Africa. This resulted in part from the chaos caused by the expansion of white settlers into the South African interior, as well as from the rise of the Zulu state in the present-day South African province of KwaZulu Natal. That state, in conquering the Ndwandwe alliance, caused great disruption throughout southern Africa. Offshoots of the Ndwandwe moved as far north as Malawi and into southern Mozambique, where the Gaza Nguni polity under Shoshangane became sufficiently strong by the 1830s to demand tribute from local estateholders.

Much of the historiographical debate on slavery in southern Africa, as in other parts of Africa, has centered on how to conceptualize indigenous slavery and how to distinguish it from a host of other dependent labor relations. Most indigenous societies in southern Africa that practiced slavery or contained some slaves up to the early years of the twentieth century should not be termed slave societies, because they did not depend on slave labor to survive. Rather, slavery existed in the context of multiple forms of forced or coerced labor. This was very similar to the situation on the colonial frontier of the eastern Cape. Formal slavery akin to the western Cape version was imported by Dutch-speaking settlers to the eastern Cape in the late eighteenth and early nineteenth centuries. While settlers exploited slave labor, they also relied on the labor and skills of free indigenous Khoisan people.

Because many indigenous societies that practiced slavery in southern Africa incorporated slave men and women into the slaveholding kin group through marriage or some other form of assimilation, historians have struggled with the applicability of the term *slavery* for these societies. In the Sena society of the lower Zambezi, *akaporo,* or slaves, occupied a position akin to adopted dependency. A child was incorporated by taking the clan name of the patron, and slaves were permitted to marry into the slaveholding family. Debate continues over patterns and practices of indigenous slavery, for example, as to the nature and timeline of slavery in the northern Kalahari desert state of the BaTswana. Scholars agree that this state, which developed from the early 1800s, instituted at least one form of dependency over indigenous BaSarwa or Bushmen societies, but some contend that this institution, *botlhanka,* was a condition more akin to serfdom than to slavery. Recently it has been argued that *botlhanka* was indeed a form of indigenous slavery that dated back to the early eighteenth century, but that it became increasingly entrenched in the mid-nineteenth century. Owing to demands from the Cape settler markets, the Ba-Sarwa were increasingly coerced by the BaTswana

to hunt for ivory as well as to supply goods as a form of tribute.

Debates have also arisen with regard to the practice of slavery on the eastern coast among Nguni societies. Traditionally, historians have argued that the Nguni did not practice slavery themselves but only engaged in slave-raiding. The Gaza Nguni, however, used domestic slave labor as early as the 1850s as the importance of the slave trade in the economies of southeastern Africa declined. Male slaves were taken from the Chopi and Amatonga, whom the Gaza saw as "outsiders." In the 1870s the labor of slave women and children became crucial because it allowed men to leave the homesteads to travel to the mines and farms of South Africa. It further allowed Nguni women to engaged primarily in child care and reproduction rather than agriculture. Slavery brought the Gaza Nguni into capitalist relations in South Africa.

In Mozambique the Portuguese colonial government abolished slavery and *akaporo* in the early twentieth century, although some forms of slavery survived abolition. Formal Cape slavery ended earlier because it fell under the terms that abolished slavery in the British West Indies. Cape slavery was ameliorated in the 1820s, replaced by a six-year apprenticeship system in 1834, and finally ended in 1838. Nonetheless, conditions akin to slavery were long part of the tradition of rural labor relations in South Africa, and a trade in people was documented near the Mozambican border as late as the 1990s.

[*See also* Gender and Slavery; *and* Historiography, *article on* African Slavery.]

BIBLIOGRAPHY

De Kock, Victor. *Those in Bondage.* London: George Allen and Unwin, 1950.

Eldredge, Elizabeth, and Fred Morton, eds. *Slavery in South Africa: Captive Labor on the Dutch Frontier.* Boulder, Colo.: Westview Press, 1994.

Harries, Patrick. "Slavery, Social Incorporation and Surplus Extraction: The Nature of Free and Unfree Labor in South-East Africa." *Journal of African History* 22 (1981): 309–330.

Isaacman, Allen. *Mozambique: The Africanization of a European Institution: The Zambezi Prazos, 1750–1902*. Madison: University of Wisconsin Press, 1972.

Scully, Pamela. *Liberating the Family: Gender and British Slave Emancipation in the Rural Western Cape, South Africa, 1823–1853*. Portsmouth: Heinemann, 1998.

Shell, Robert C.-H. *Children of Bondage: A Social History of the Slave Society at the Cape of Good Hope, 1652–1838*. Hanover, N.H.: University Press of New England, 1994.

Vail, Leroy, and Landeg White. *Capitalism and Colonialism in Mozambique: A Study of the Quelimane District*. Minneapolis: University of Minnesota Press, 1980.

Worden, Nigel. *Slavery in Dutch South Africa*. Cambridge: Cambridge University Press, 1985.

—PAMELA SCULLY

ANTI-SLAVERY LITERATURE.

[*This entry comprises two articles. The first is an overview of the major figures and currents of thought associated with anti-slavery literature in North America during the eighteenth and nineteenth centuries. The second is an expanded discussion of African-American perspectives from the eighteenth century to the present day.*]

An Overview

"This makes an ill report in all those countries of Europe, where they hear off, that ye Quakers doe here handel men as they handel there ye cattle," declared a petition of Germantown, Pennsylvania Friends and Mennonites in 1688. Despite this early protest, however, anti-slavery literature was slow to appear in the American colonies. Winthrop Jordan identifies only fifteen examples before 1750, almost all of them by Quakers. The earliest Quaker statements—the 1688 Germantown Friends' protest, George Keith's 1693 pamphlet, and Robert Pikes's brief 1698 paper—grounded their objections to slavery on biblical injunctions and precepts, as in the Germantown appeal to the Golden Rule and Keith's declaration that Christ had died to bring "Liberty both inward and outward." It was the Puritan Samuel Sewall, in *The Selling of Joseph* (1700), who first refuted the pro-slavery arguments

that would continue to be cited to justify slavery for the next 160 years: that blacks were under the curse of slavery as the posterity of Ham; that masters were bringing the Gospel to the heathens; that slaves were the lawful captives of African wars; and that slavery was biblically sanctioned.

Quaker thought proved to be an excellent seedbed for democratic sentiment, which would flower in the nineteenth century in abolitionist theory and practice. Central to Quaker thought was the concept of equality before God; "*Christ dyed for all*," wrote George Fox in 1676. The doctrines of the brotherhood of man and the inner light led Quakers to think egalitarian thoughts, and some even to defy manmade fugitive slave laws. The two major Quaker voices of the eighteenth century, John Woolman and Anthony Benezet, forcefully stated the major religious arguments against slavery, but their influence derived in large part from the fact that they had also absorbed the Enlightenment ideas that would soon help to fuel the American Revolution. For both—as for John Locke, the intellectual father of the revolution—it was the social environment, not the slave's innate nature, that determined his condition. The only innate aspect Woolman recognized was race, but race was significant only because "Black Colour" and "Slavery" were "twisted into our Minds" because of "the Force of long Custom." As early as 1762 Benezet's *Pamphlet on Negroes in Africa* was marshalling evidence from a wide variety of travelers to demonstrate that Africans, when undisturbed by the slave trade, were sociable, civil, peaceable, industrious peoples, living in well-established towns and villages. The language of the Enlightenment mixed with that of the Bible in the introductory paragraphs of Benezet's *Caution and Warning*: "Many thousands of our fellow-creatures, as free as ourselves by nature, and equally with us the subjects of Christ's redeeming grace, are yearly brought into inextricable and barbarous bondage."

Benezet's *An Account of Guinea* (1771) made an abolitionist of the Englishman Thomas Clarkson; it also profoundly influenced John Wesley and

Granville Sharp. This influence was part of a trans-Atlantic commerce in anti-slavery literature and ideas in the form of books, pamphlets, correspondence, and reciprocal visits between America and England. Harriet Beecher Stowe's visit to England in 1853 is only one example. From it she brought back an anti-slavery petition containing more than one-half million names, along with a gold brooch containing a lock of Thomas Clarkson's hair, presented to her by his wife.

Writer after writer in the Revolutionary period—influenced by Quaker thought and the 1740 Great Awakening—blended the religious arguments of the Golden Rule, the brotherhood of man, and Christ's redeeming grace with secular arguments for "natural rights" and the determining impress of the environment. Many of the founders of the United States made anti-slavery statements. It would have been inconsistent to have demanded freedom from England and to have denied that same freedom to slaves, argued abolitionists on streetcorners, in debating societies, and in taverns. The Declaration of Independence was cited as a major anti-slavery document. Anti-slavery ardor cooled, however, in the period from 1787 to 1830, signaled by the Constitution's slavery provisions, and reflecting the influence of several factors: the slave revolt in Saint Domingue; hostility toward freed blacks and the specter of racial amalgamation; the growing importance of property, including slaves; and the growing economic ties between Southern planters and Northern shippers, traders, bankers, and industrialists. Gradualism and moderation triumphed, epitomized by the growth and respectability (except among freed black leaders) of the American Colonization Society, which urged that ex-slaves be returned to Africa. The period after 1830 witnessed a proliferation of anti-slavery literature, based on earlier biblical and natural-rights arguments but reflecting a considerably heightened militancy, as well as the organization of formal institutional structures such as anti-slavery societies and political parties, and the development of a general anti-slavery culture.

Gradualism and moderation were supplanted around 1830 by an increasingly passionate and uncompromising anti-slavery literature. Two figures signaled this shift—David Walker and William Lloyd Garrison. Walker's *Appeal to the Colored Citizens of the World* was published in 1829 and went through three printings. In language that often drew its prophetic condemnation from the Bible, Walker called for the establishment of a self-governing black nation, and for the destruction, if necessary, of the blacks' and slaves' oppressors. He ended by contrasting the abominable actions of slaveholders with both the militant language of the Declaration of Independence and the righteous language of prayer.

Garrison was a masterful rhetorician. He declared in the first issue of the *Liberator*, 1 January 1831:

> I *will be* as harsh as truth, and as uncompromising as justice. On this subject [slavery] I do not wish to think, or speak, or write with moderation. No! No! Tell a man whose house is on fire to give a moderate alarm; tell him to moderately rescue his wife from the hands of a ravisher; tell the mother to gradually extricate her babe from the fire into which it has fallen—but urge me not to use moderation in a cause like the present. I am in earnest—I will not equivocate—I will not excuse—I will not retreat a single inch—AND I WILL BE HEARD. The apathy of the people is enough to make every statue leap from its pedestal, and to hasten the resurrection of the dead.

Garrison's language and views were cited by some Southerners as the inspiration for Nat Turner's insurrection. To such claims Garrison responded in his second issue, "Ye patriotic hypocrites! ye panegyrists of Frenchmen, Greeks, and Poles! ye fustian declaimers for liberty! . . . they deserve no more censure than the Greeks in destroying the Turks, or the Poles in exterminating the Russians, or our fathers in slaughtering the British." Influenced by black opposition, Garrison condemned both the motives and the intent of the respected American

Masthead of *The Liberator*, William Lloyd Garrison's abolitionist
newspaper, designed by D. C. Johnston, c.1830s.

Colonization Society and championed abolition, or "immediate emancipation" (or "immediatism"), rejecting gradualism. Over a thirty-five-year period in which he never missed a single weekly issue, Garrison continued to vilify the hypocritical Bible-and-Declaration-of-Independence-quoting man-stealers in language that was often poetic, damningly rational, and dipped in fire.

The *Liberator* was one of more than a dozen black and white anti-slavery journals. Most were short-lived; all were in debt. At the time in 1860 that Frederick Douglass suspended publication of his journal (begun in 1847 as the *North Star* and re-named *Frederick Douglass' Paper* in 1850), he had invested twelve thousand dollars of his own money. The *Liberator* was two thousand dollars in debt by the third year of publication, and its sub-scribers—three-quarters of them from the free black population in the North—never exceeded three thousand. The numbers, however, under-state both the influence and the cultural impor-tance of these periodicals. Copies regularly passed from hand to hand, so that actual numbers of readers are impossible to estimate. As oppositional journalism, the periodicals provided a forum for black representation through nationwide news about both significant and ordinary blacks that de-fied the crude stereotypes of the popular press. They served as a vehicle to knit together a commu-nity of like-minded persons. Their pages carried notices of a wide range of public activities, along

with advertisements for anti-slavery publications, for accommodations for blacks, and for many other goods and services.

The journals were part of an anti-slavery culture that came into being during the nineteenth cen-tury. It included regional and national anti-slavery societies and women's auxiliaries (although some organizations admitted women from the begin-ning), meetings and conventions, and temperance, mutual-aid, and self-improvement societies. At the more informal level there were bazaars, annual cel-ebrations (for example, to celebrate abolition of slavery in the West Indies), anti-slavery fairs (in-cluding children's fairs), food-purchasing groups, exhibitions of dioramas of slave scenes, and lec-tures of all sorts—and of course, discussions with like-minded friends.

Slave narratives, the autobiographical accounts of former slaves, were a major form of anti-slavery literature and a significant weapon in the political struggle. They helped to explain to Northern whites what slavery was really like. The environ-ment of the nonslave states was itself rather harsh. It included indentured and bound servants; sailors, servants, and wives were often whipped; industri-alization was transforming rural America and cre-ating crowded, wretched cities; the apprenticeship system in the crafts was giving way to twelve- or sixteen-hour working days in mills and factories; economic fluctuations caused unemployment, hunger, and homelessness; the white workingman feared the competition of freed blacks; and the newly arrived immigrant could be puzzled by the need for antislavery agitation in his new land of opportunity. In such a world slave narratives were a window onto the slave states and the much more frightening and inhumane condition of the enslaved.

This was necessary at a time when travel and communication were limited, and when Southern ideology pictured slavery as a largely beneficent institution. In the antebellum decade, the Southern social commentator George Fitzhugh asserted that "the negro slaves of the South are the happiest, and, in some sense, the freest people in the world." Graphic representations on the popular minstrel stage and in Currier and Ives prints pictured a plantation world of happy, comic "darkies." The Southern plantation novels of the 1820s and 1830s by such writers as George Tucker, William Gilmore Simms, James Kirke Paulding, John Pendleton Kennedy, and Nathaniel Beverly Tucker portrayed a world where everyone on the plantation, white and black, was part of an extended patriarchal family, governed by a sense of mutual obligation. In these novels—which borrowed from both the Old Testament's depictions of patriarchy and the medieval culture of chivalry as viewed through the novels of Sir Walter Scott—the black members typically accorded their white "kin" love, loyalty, and faithfulness.

Slave narratives provided first-person accounts that challenged Southern ideology, picturing a world where human beings were treated as things—a world of casual brutalities, separation of families, sexual license (even incest), denial of literacy, and restriction of religious practice and distortion of the biblical message. In structure slave narratives resembled earlier conversion narratives, bondage to man replacing bondage to sin; the slave's recognition of his or her overwhelming desire to be free recalled the sinner's moment of conversion. (In a significant parallel, abolitionists, many of whom were trained in the revivalist tradition, viewed slavery as a sin, and the recognition

of this sinfulness as equivalent to conversion.) William L. Andrews lists more than one hundred self-written slave narratives in the period from 1760 to 1865. Frederick Law Olmsted stated, "Most Northerners got their impression of slavery from having read slave narratives." Among the most popular were the narratives of Olaudah Equiano (or Gustavus Vassa), Charles Ball, Moses Roper, James Mars, Josiah Henson (often cited as a source for *Uncle Tom's Cabin*), Solomon Northup, William Wells Brown, and Frederick Douglass.

Contrast and paradox are basic to slave narratives. Ideals derived from the Bible and from democratic and revolutionary rhetoric are contrasted

Newspaper advertisement offering a reward for the return of a runaway slave, from the *American Beacon*, Norfolk, Virginia, 4 July 1835.

$100 REWARD

WILL be given for the apprehension and delivery of my Servant Girl, HARRIET. She is a light mulatto; 21 years of age, about 5 feet 4 inches high, of a thick and corpulent habit, having on her head a thick covering of black hair that curls naturally, but which can be easily combed straight. She speaks easily and fluently, and has an agreeable carriage and address. Being a good seamstress, she has been accustomed to dress well, has a variety of very fine clothes, made in the prevailing fashion, and will probably appear, if abroad, tricked out in gay and fashionable finery. As this girl absconded from the plantation of my son without any known cause or provocation, it is probable she designs to transport herself to the North.

The above reward, with all reasonable charges, will be given for apprehending her, or securing her in any prison or jail within the U. States.

All persons are hereby forewarned against harboring or entertaining her, or being in any way instrumental in her escape, under the most rigorous penalties of the law.

JAMES NORCOM.

Edenton, N. C. June 30   TT&2w

with self-serving greed and brutal authoritarianism. Men and women are defined as chattel, but also—in slave sermons and slave catechisms—enjoined to act as morally responsible creatures. White clerics urged slaves to obey their masters as they would God, because the master had been placed there in God's stead. Faithfulness was lauded as the prime virtue of men and women who could be listed on a bill of sale as under "Slaves and Stock."

Narrative of the Life of Frederick Douglass (1845), the most popular antebellum slave narrative, reflects these contrasts while presenting a self whose nobility (a favorite nineteenth-century quality), dignity, perseverance, heroism, and dedication to such ideals as liberty, self-understanding, literacy and knowledge, truth, and hard work contrast with the callousness, brutality, duplicity, and hypocrisy of the system. In a Romantic period he was a Romantic hero. Douglass helped to put flesh on abstract abolitionist concepts. And, importantly, he required his reader to reimagine certain accepted universals. He demonstrated that a slave could be treated in commerce as an animal; that the idealized, patriarchal Southern familly was a self-serving myth ("The opinion was also whispered that my master was my father"); and that religious ideals dissolved in the alembic of slavery ("Of all slaveholders I have ever met religious slaveholders are the worst"). In a tradition that began as early as Roger Williams's *A Key into the Language of America* (1643), in which Williams asked the reader to rethink such terms as *civilized* and *savage* (finding the Indian, contrary to Puritan views, to manifest ideal qualities), Douglass probed for the reality underlying words: "I can see no reason, but the most deceitful one, for calling the religion of this land Christianity. I look upon it as the climax of all misnomers, the boldest of all frauds, and the grossest of all libels." Douglass declared that after a fight with his overseer, "I now resolved that, however long I might remain a slave in form, the day had passed forever when I could be a slave in fact."

Recent feminist criticism has argued that the Douglass model accords well with both male literary biases and national Romantic myths that privilege the single, heroic male figure while virtually ignoring the female experience. Indeed, Douglass's 1845 narrative had little to say regarding female slaves and the important roles of his grandmother, his mother, and his wife Anna Murray. For insight into women's experience under slavery the critics turn to Jean Fagan Yellin's 1987 edition of Harriet A. Jacobs's *Incidents in the Life of a Slave Girl* (1861), a groundbreaking female slave narrative. Jacobs declared, "Slavery is terrible for men; but it is far more terrible for women." She pointed out how inapplicable to the slave woman's condition were white, middle-class standards of purity. In contrast to the world of the white women of the North, whom she is addressing, beauty ill became a female slave: "If God has bestowed beauty upon her, it will prove her greatest curse." By the time Jacobs had reached fifteen, "My master began to whisper foul words in my ears." To resist her master, she permitted herself to be seduced by a white neighbor and bore him two children. As a mother she had to fear for the fate of her children, especially her little girl. Jacobs described a network of men and, especially, women (including the white wife of a slaveowner), who helped her to escape her master and to hide in an attic for seven years, able to watch her children but unable to touch them.

Like Douglass, Jacobs was highly sensitive to the ideological uses of language, revealing the reality behind such words as the iconic, romanticized *home* ("I am glad that missionaries go out to the dark corners of the earth; but I ask them not to overlook the dark corners at home"); the chivalric *gentlemen* and *Christian* ("The master who did these things was highly educated, and styled a perfect gentleman. He also boasted the name and standing of a Christian, though Satan never had a truer follower"); and Southern *civilization* ("Cruelty is contagious in uncivilized communites"). Her free black lover becomes, in her telling, the true gentleman; whereas her master, attempting to seduce her, cries out, "I would cherish you. I would make a lady of you." Jacobs's stress on freedom and a home—critics writing from the experience of male narrative writers had stressed freedom and literacy—helps to broaden our understanding of the gendered complexity of slavery.

Douglass's career bears witness to another, peculiarly nineteenth-century type of anti-slavery literature, public speeches, which were often reprinted in anti-slavery newspapers or in later books or collections of essays. His style, like that of Emerson's essays, bears the stamp of the public lectern, especially in Douglass's use of figurative language, wit and paradox, and short sentences. James A. Collins, who believed the public was "itching" to hear a slave speak, recruited Douglass as speaker for the American Anti-Slavery Society. Other fugitive slaves who reached the public both on the stage and through the pages of their narratives included Henry Bibb, William Wells Brown, Josiah Henson, Ellen and William Craft, Anthony Burns, and Henry "Box" Brown. White speakers who delivered significant anti-slavery orations included Wendell Phillips, Angelina Grimké, Charles Sumner, and Henry David Thoreau. Charlotte Forten noted in her journal in 1855, "It is *some* encouragement that nearly all the finest orators now are antislavery."

In the battle of the books fought by the proponents and opponents in the antebellum period, the critical voices of foreign visitors were often very effective, as in the earliest writings of Tom Paine, and the accounts of Harriet Martineau, Alexis de Tocqueville, Frances Trollope, and Frances Anne Kemble. Theodore Dwight Weld's *American Slavery As It Is* (1839), a self-indicting compilation of documents from Southern sources, sold more than one hundred thousand copies in its first year of publication; Frederick Law Olmsted's three volumes recounted fourteen months spent journeying through the Southern states from 1852 to 1854. Such journalistic works were invaluable sources of information for the minds and hearts of nineteenth-century Northern readers.

It was Harriet Beecher Stowe's *Uncle Tom's Cabin* that most profoundly appealed to the hearts, but also to the minds, of Northern readers. The humanity and goodness of her black characters, caught in the travails of an inhumane system, appealed to their hearts. She appealed to their minds through a complex process of literary alchemy: her principle black characters—Uncle Tom, Eliza, and George Harris—possessed the virtues generally ascribed to whites (courage, honor, fidelity, hard work, piety, and love), marred only by the accidental fact of their blackness. By possessing these virtues and thus exhibiting a white semblance (a similarity insisted on by authorial interjections, along with George Harris's egalitarian arguments and St. Clare's environmental arguments), Stowe's black characters implicitly qualified for the equality and freedom contained within the eighteenth-century view of "natural rights."

At the same time, these virtues are so magnified in the character of Uncle Tom that he becomes a black Christ who is ready to die for the redemption of others and for the protection of Cassy, but also ready to die in the knowledge (as Frederick Douglass after his fight with Covey) that his soul was unconquered. The good that Tom represents is pitted both against the abstract system of slavery and against its horrifying representative Simon Legree. Tom's sufferings and struggles are lent resonance by Stowe's firm grounding in biblical language and ideas.

Thus Stowe's book embodied the major biblical and "natural rights" arguments that had inspired anti-slavery literature since the eighteenth century. It is perhaps only fitting that Lincoln, who is said to have addressed Stowe as "the little lady who started this big war," might be regarded as having delivered the ultimate in anti-slavery literature: the Emancipation Proclamation of 1 January 1863. Joan D. Hedrick in her biography (1994) of Stowe describes her going with others to the Boston Music Hall to await telegraphed word of the proclamation. The crowd "chanted 'Harriet Beecher Stowe, Harriet Beecher Stowe!'" until she "stood up and, with tears in her eyes, silently acknowledged the tribute."

[*See also* Abolition and Anti-Slavery, *articles on* Britain *and* United States; *and* Gender and Slavery.]

BIBLIOGRAPHY

Andrews, William L. *To Tell a Free Story: The First Century of Afro-American Autobiography, 1760–1865*. Urbana: University of Illinois Press, 1986.

Bruns, Roger, ed. *Am I Not a Man and a Brother: The Antislavery Crusade of Revolutionary America 1688–1788*. New York: Chelsea House, 1977.

Davis, David Brion. *The Problem of Slavery in Western Culture*. Ithaca, N.Y.: Cornell University Press, 1966.

Hedrick, Joan D. *Harriet Beecher Stowe: A Life*. New York and Oxford: Oxford University Press, 1994.

Jordan, Winthrop D. *White Over Black: American Attitudes toward the Negro 1550–1812*. Chapel Hill: University of North Carolina Press, 1968.

Quarles, Benjamin. *Black Abolitionists*. New York: Oxford University Press, 1969.

Rose, Willie Lee. *A Documentary History of Slavery in North America*. New York: Oxford University Press, 1976.

—DONALD A. PETESCH

African-American Literature

During the 1790s Richard Allen was probably the most prominent African American in the United States. Preacher, spokesman, and founder of the African Methodist Episcopal Church, he was in the public eye throughout his adult life, but he was known to relatively few people outside his audiences. The journal by which he is known today was private and was not published until long after his death. Only two generations later, in contrast, Frederick Douglass became known to hundreds of thousands in the 1840s through the trans-Atlantic anti-slavery press and his own speeches and writings. Douglass sometimes addressed more people in a month, it is estimated, than Allen did in his lifetime. The change during the intervening years was largely the work of anti-slavery forces, both black and white, who permanently transformed the literary as well as moral character of America.

In the late eighteenth century, no African-American newspaper yet existed; by 1860, at least eighteen had been established. Earlier no abolitionist groups had been active; by the mid-1850s, thirty major organizations were at work, with fifty more satellite groups giving support in New England, New York, Pennsylvania, Ohio, Indiana, and Illinois, extending into Canada, the West, and California. The abolitionists and their British allies usually had presses and periodicals hungry for material. Abolitionist writing changed from a provincial focus to assume a national or even international character. Nonetheless, the spoken anti-slavery word often preceded the written; it was an age of oratory and journalism, of memorable speeches eagerly recorded by the newspapers and then reproduced by significant organs of the movement on two continents.

Much of the work distinctive of the age appeared in newspapers. Black and white, they sought to cultivate every possible contributor, argument, occasion, and form. They printed news, poetry, debate, drama, letters, speeches, histories, biographies, autobiographies, and travel accounts. They recorded the stories of the nonliterate by dictation; the gifted they cultivated as agents, writers, lecturers, and correspondents. The assumption that the word would make people not only free but also strong had many consequences, important in a nation where one in seven of the population was African-American, but only one in seventy was a free black. It was the first great age of social and historical studies of black America by black Americans. Personal histories abound, as do histories of communities, churches, families, leaders, soldiers, and innovators. It was the initial age for the novel, short story, drama, and travel book, and the start of the large-scale collection of songs and spirituals, proverbs and folktales.

African-American newspapers were founded throughout the middle of the nineteenth century. The earliest was the work of the indefatigable Samuel Cornish, who with John Russwurm established *Freedom's Journal* in New York City in 1827. With its demise Cornish returned with *Rights of All* in 1829, the *Weekly Advocate* in 1837, and most influential of all, the *Colored American* (published 1837–1841); all were published in New York City. William Whipper, a businessman, skilled essayist, and leader of the Moral Reform Society, edited the *National Reformer* in Philadelphia (1838–1839). The *Mirror of Liberty* (1838–1840) was the more radical effort of David Ruggles. In Pittsburgh the talented Martin R. Delany published the *Mystery* (1843–1847), then assisted Douglass in Rochester with the *Northern Star* from 1847 to 1849. Delany, who had earned an M.D. from Harvard, was in his full life a journalist, physician, lecturer, explorer, ethnologist, army officer, civil servant, trial judge, novelist, and organizer of emigration projects. Only Douglass himself could approach such a range of activity.

Although united against slavery, abolitionists employed differing strategies to combat it. Open rebellion was the most direct means, with the examples of Toussaint Louverture, Gabriel Prosser, and Denmark Vesey near at hand. Until *The Confessions of Nat Turner* was published in 1831, however, no rebel had left a literary testament. Two years earlier, the most widely circulated work before the 1840s, David Walker's famous *Appeal*, had warned that peace and slavery could not coexist. In the 1830s David Ruggles continued the militant tradition in lectures and articles, as Henry Highland Garnet did in the succeeding decade. A former slave who ministered to a Presbyterian congregation in Troy, New York, Garnet delivered a fervent "Address to the Slaves of the United States of America" at a convention in 1843; it was published five years later with Walker's *Appeal* as a demand for political action. The convention movement, an innovation of the age, was a significant training ground for the education and self-expression of many.

Few abolitionists promoted rebellion, but many advocated escape. Because the rigors of bondage were growing as rapidly as the spirit of abolition, the rate of flight increased dramatically, and so did tales of flight. Besides being exciting tales of adven-

Photograph of Frederick Douglass (seated to the left of the speaker's table) at an outdoor abolitionist meeting in Cazenovia, New York, 1850.

ture, the fugitive slave narratives were vivid descriptions of the mechanisms of the "peculiar institution" from across the South, told from within, a point of view unfamiliar to most Northern readers. The most popular literary form of the antebellum years, they became the springboards for professional careers. About two dozen fugitives got their start as agents, lecturers, and writers by recounting their personal histories. Douglass gained his reputation as orator and conscience of the nation by retailing his life story, later turning it into two masterpieces of the genre. His *Narrative* (1845) is a small gem, surpassed only by *My Bondage and My Freedom* ten years later.

As Douglass was launching his independent literary career as editor and publisher, William Wells Brown was developing into a literary pioneer, striking out into fiction, drama, history, biography, and travel literature. After publishing his narrative (1847) and a book of anti-slavery songs (1848) in Boston, he traveled to England, where he produced *Three Years in Europe*, an important travel book, in 1852, and a year later the earliest African-American novel, *Clotel, or The President's Daughter*. He followed these with the earliest published African-American play, *The Escape; or, A Leap for Freedom* (1858), another memoir, more travel writing, and four histories. *Clotel*, which appeared one year after *Uncle Tom's Cabin*, established the power of fiction in the movement. Douglass published a short novel, *The Heroic Slave*, in the 1853 annual *Autographs for Freedom*. Frances Watkins Harper's short story "The Two Offers" appeared in the *Anglo-African*, which also serialized Delany's unfinished novel, *Blake; or, The Huts of America* (1859). The year 1859 also saw publication of the earliest novel by an African-American woman, Harriet E. Wilson's *Our Nig; or, Sketches from the Life of a Free Black*.

Fulfilling its declared ambition "to tell a free story," Harriet Jacobs's *Incidents in the Life of A Slave Girl* was published in 1861 under the pen name Linda Brent. One of the very few slave narratives by a woman and one of the last to be published separately before Emancipation, it attempted to enfold Northern white women readers within the threads of its design, as early as its opening sentence, "Reader, be assured this narrative is no fiction." Its subject was the taboo one of the sexual exploitation of slave women by their owners. Its style was crafted understatement, and its method of release ingenious: Jacobs left clues that she had fled north but actually hid in the tiny garret of her grandmother's house, remaining there for seven years to watch the growth of her children.

Because of a low rate of escape, heavy responsibility for children once free, and a lack of encouragement from abolitionist sponsors, few fugitive women published their stories as books or pamphlets. Instead, they joined free women in the growing Women's Club movement; their writing is found more readily in periodicals and anti-slavery annuals. Important free speakers and writers included Sojourner Truth, Sarah P. Remond, Maria Stewart, Frances Watkins Harper, Mary Ann Shadd Cary, and Margretta and Sarah Forten. Narratives by men, in contrast, appeared with increasing frequency after 1840. Notable examples were Moses Roper (1839), Lunsford Lane (1842), Moses Grandy (1844), Lewis and Milton Clarke (1845, 1846), Henry Bibb (1849), James W. C. Pennington (1849), Josiah Henson (1849), Henry "Box" Brown (1849), Solomon Northup (1853), Samuel Ringgold Ward (1855), John Brown (1855), William and Ellen Craft (1860), and Jacob D. Green (1864).

When Lincoln was grappling with issues of slavery and emancipation in the summer of 1862, he called the Library of Congress for a copy of *A Key to Uncle Tom's Cabin*, a later volume citing Stowe's sources in the anti-slavery papers and narratives. It includes references to several studies of black American life. Going beyond the content of periodicals, volumes were appearing that traced the social, cultural, and historical conditions of African Americans. The learned scholar James McCune Smith from 1837 contributed dozens of essays to the black press, containing what would later be termed social and political analysis. Smith had earned an M.D. from the University of Glasgow and brought an international and evolutionary perspective to political questions. James W. C. Pennington, a Presbyterian minister and holder of a doctorate from the University of Heidelberg, wrote *A Text Book on the Origin and History . . . of the Colored People* (1841) and *The Past and Present Condition, and the Destiny of the Colored Race* (1848). Martin Delany produced the most scholarly account of free blacks before the Civil War, *The Condition, Elevation, Emigration and Destiny of the Colored People of the United States, Politically Considered* (1852), followed two years later by a pamphlet distilling his findings. His next project was to study the practicability of various emigration schemes. Others writing political and historical commentary included William C. Nell, William G. Allen, Lewis H. Putnam, and John B. Meachum. The accomplished prose stylist Alexander Crummell offered a nationalist vision of an Africa cleansed of her despoilers in *The Relations and Duties of Free Colored Men in America to Africa* (1861). Some of his best writing was collected in *The Future of Africa* (1862).

An age of crisis, the anti-slavery period was intense and fertile in its interests. Its accents have echoed in african-American writing when similar conditions have recurred—the 1890s, 1920s, or 1960s. When asked why the abolitionist press seemed to be thriving, Samuel Ringgold Ward replied, "Any Negro living well is an anti-slavery fighter." This is an explanation too for the richness and diversity of the age, as well as its great influence on American literature.

"From the *Narrative* and the many other accounts of runaways published in Douglass's day, right down to Toni Morrison's *Beloved* in ours, there has been no escape from the slave in American letters," wrote William S. McFeely, biographer of Frederick Douglass, reminding us that slavery has remained close to the consciousness of Americans, white and black, ever since. Among popular writers since the mid-nineteenth century it has been an uninterrupted fount of inspiration; *Uncle Tom's Cabin*, *Gone with the Wind*, and *Roots* are merely the most spectacular results. It has inspired overarching theories for social scientists and grand themes for creative writers, from Herman Melville and Mark Twain to William Faulkner and Toni Morrison. The lessons of Twain's *Huckleberry Finn* are translated in Faulkner's *Absalom, Absalom* and deepened in Morrison's *Song of Solomon* and *Beloved*. As a subject slavery is far from exhausted, perhaps because it is worse than anything anyone can say about it.

At least four reasons can be suggested for the preoccupation of American writers with slavery. From her earliest decades America was engaged with tales of bondage; the African-American slave narratives were simply the major form of those tales in the first half of the nineteenth century. During that period the literature of slavery was important to practically all writers in the nation. Fol-

lowing the Civil War, they remained absorbed in the issues raised by slavery, usually in attempts to understand better the struggles of their own day. Finally, several twentieth-century historians have seen a national literature mixed or creolized from its inception, with white writers borrowing freely from a large store of black images, themes, and language. The case is put by Shelley Fisher Fishkin:

A shift in paradigm is in order. Understanding African-American tradition is essential if one wants to understand *mainstream* American literary history. And understanding mainstream literary history is important if one wants to understand African-American writing in the twentieth century. We can no longer deny the mixed literary bloodlines on both sides. (1993, p. 143)

In order to comprehend the national destiny, Americans have often turned to stories of confinement, challenge, and redemption. In 1697 Cotton Mather described such a pattern in *Humiliations Follow'd with Deliverances*, an instance of the most successful literary form in early colonial America, the captivity narrative. These were stories of valiant white colonists morally tested during confinement by Indian tribes, then transmuting that harrowing experience into physical and spiritual salvation. With the Bible and *Pilgrim's Progress*, such tales were the best-selling American books of the first century of European settlement, establishing a pattern so familiar that writers employed it in explaining the causes of the War of Independence, asserting the colonies' need to break their bondage to Great Britain. Like the captured settlers, the colonies were held in thrall by a distant, uncaring foe; withstanding that foe developed strength and nationhood—not simply a courageous people but also a just one.

Captives were not only as good as other Christians; they might be even better. That lesson became especially pointed during the anti-slavery era, the period of nearly two generations when the most prominent captives in the nation were African-American slaves like Douglass, William

Wells Brown, James W. C. Pennington, and Sojourner Truth. Not only were they internationally known for their efforts on behalf of abolition; they were also among the best-selling authors of the age. They were indeed paragons of bondage. Earlier European captives could fuel their faith by drawing on memories of a time before their capture by Indians; thus Mary Rowlandson had an identity, a history, and a family to recall, and an existence prior to and independent of bondage from which to draw hope and virtue. Only the slave, in a pure condition, was without solace, respite, termination, or sight of a better or alternative world. If adversity tested one's virtue, then slavery was the supreme trial. Here were the naked soul at its most besieged, the solitary journey most uncharted, the source of evil most blatant, and the beauty of virtue most transparent.

For several decades the slave narratives set the tone for American political sensibility as well as literary sensitivity. Although unadorned, they were for contemporaries more eloquent in their authenticity than the measured rhetoric of senators. Dozens were published in the form of books, pamphlets, or broadsides; many more appeared in periodicals and as interviews with the Freedmen's Bureau. By Emancipation, slavery had replaced captivity as a central metaphor of American history that few writers could ignore.

They could, however, alter its meaning and its center of gravity. In a study of more than fifty autobiographies of former slaves published between the Civil War and the 1930s, William L. Andrews (1986) discerned a conception of the central experience of slavery different from that of antebellum accounts. For Douglass, the first great slave narrator writing in 1845, slavery was a tomb from which he had to be resurrected. For Booker T. Washington, who in many ways replaced Douglass as spokesperson and whose *Up from Slavery* (1901) remained in print throughout the century, slavery was a school: one learned and graduated from it. This more pragmatic postbellum view looked not so much at the facts of slavery as at how the memory of slavery could change white attitudes in the present.

Between Douglass and Washington more than a half-century passed, but the old and new versions of the female slave narrative were compressed into a much shorter period, the seven years between Harriet Jacobs's *Incidents in the Life of a Slave Girl* (1861) and Elizabeth Keckley's *Behind the Scenes* (1868). The two women had similar stories. Light-skinned and of about the same age, both were bedeviled by insistent white men and bore children by them. Leaving slavery at about the same age, they may have known each other while working in Washington, D.C., yet the books they chose to write were continents apart. *Incidents* is a powerful indictment of the institution of slavery, reflecting the influence of anti-slavery literature and plainly telling difficult truths about sexual exploitation. *Behind the Scenes,* in contrast, is no indictment; its main object of analysis is not slavery as an institution but success in the white world. A dressmaker to Mary Todd Lincoln, Keckley chose to relate stories of life in the White House. While Jacobs expressed frustrated maternal feelings, she emphasized satisfied entrepreneurial ambition. Rather than speedily escaping slavery, she purchased her freedom for twelve hundred dollars, a large price; rather than repudiating her own and all other slave-owners, she recounted a happy reunion with her former owners.

After the war, former slaves found publication much more difficult, unless their stories went beyond the experience of slavery, for instance to success in some area of white activity. For her account of achievement Keckley was rewarded with a contract from a large commercial publisher, one of the first offered to an African-American writer. The lesson was not lost on Washington, Josiah Henson, Elisha W. Green, and several other postbellum narrators; even Douglass's third autobiography (1881) chronicles at length his later successes. Narratives of this type were often written by persons who were young at Emancipation, did not escape, and were not brutalized; they expressed no grievance against the social system. They stressed economic success over political rights, and social reconciliation overall, perhaps to the extent of including, like Keckley, a reunion scene with former owners. A strong pattern was formed that persisted well into the twentieth century, as in Sammy Davis's *Yes, I Can* (1965).

While Washington was perfecting his brand of pragmatism, several novelists were posing alternative uses for the memories and metaphors of slavery. Protest fiction like Frances Ellen Watkins Harper's *Iola Leroy* (1892), Pauline Hopkins's *Contending Forces* (1900), and W. E. B. DuBois's *The Quest for the Silver Fleece* (1911) kept alive the passion ignited by the slave narrators. Two important works went further. Charles W. Chesnutt's *The Conjure Woman* (1899) was presented as a series of slave stories transcribed by a white entrepreneur, offering text and commentary that did not usually coincide: while black Uncle Julius recounted African-American folktales, the white businessman offered quaint redactions of Southern folk culture. Since neither Chesnutt nor his publisher identified the author as African-American, readers were faced with a modernist choice of two implied authors. Even more demanding was James Weldon Johnson's *The Autobiography of an Ex-Coloured Man* (1912), an anonymous novel convincingly presented as autobiography, not fiction. Among its many elements was a series of challenges to the certainties cherished by Booker T. Washington.

Direct challenges to Washington's revisionism came in many forms, from DuBois's recreations of slave life in *The Souls of Black Folk* (1903) to William Pickens's autobiography, *Bursting Bonds* (1923), with its title echoing Douglass, as well as his earlier *New Negro*, published in 1916, a year after Washington's death. In their work and that of the New Negroes of the Harlem Renaissance, the abolitionist and modern views of slavery were melded. It was as though Chesnutt and Johnson had held on to the central history of slavery long enough for contemporary visions of folklore, narration, and psychology to catch up and absorb it.

The bridge-building of the 1920s was not only timely but substantial. It prepared the way for a decade when many Americans—and not only intellectual leaders—would seek to recall the lessons of slavery. In spirit and specific goal, the Great Depression provided such an occasion, inspiring new histories, innovative fiction, and an extraordinary form of autobiography. The masterworks of Charles S. Johnson, St. Clair Drake, Zora Neale Hurston, Arna Bontemps, and Richard Wright illumined the era. Its signal achievement, however, may be the 2,194 narratives of slavery gathered between 1935 and 1939 by Works Progress Administration (WPA) and Fisk University researchers. The New Deal agency most helpful to black writers was the Federal Writers Project (FWP), established in 1935 as a subdivision of the WPA. It assisted several hundred black writers of varying degrees of talent, including masters like Johnson, Drake, Hurston, Bontemps, Wright, Sterling A. Brown, Claude McKay, Chester Himes, Ralph Ellison, Frank Yerby, William Attaway, Willard Motley, and Margaret Walker. In addition to compiling 378 regional books and pamphlets, WPA writers took the opportunity to interview survivors of slavery. The results were not fully published until nineteen volumes were brought together by George P. Rawick in 1972 (with later supplements). State volumes were released earlier, however, and the most serious and talented writers were given opportunities to continue their own creative projects. For the first time since Douglass, many writers were testifying that slavery was the focal issue of American history; for the first time ever, a few made the related claim that the antebellum narratives supply the basic pattern for almost all later African-American fiction and autobiography.

The generation of the depression cultivated a searching interest in unknown and relatively unreported history. As an archivist and librarian at Fisk, Bontemps did important work preserving and editing slave materials. Two of his three novels deal with slave revolts—*Black Thunder* (1936) with Gabriel's uprising in Virginia in 1800, and

Drums as Dusk (1939) with the Haitian revolution of 1791–1803. All Hurston's work of the time is imbued with folk culture, especially *Their Eyes Were Watching God* (1937) and her autobiographical volume, *Dust Tracks on the Road* (1942), which has resemblances to Jacobs and Keckley. Looking equally backward and forward is the rich, complex work of Richard Wright. *American Hunger*, the autobiography he sent his editors in the early 1940s, was divided into Southern and Northern testaments, the earlier published as *Black Boy* in 1945 and the latter under its original title posthumously in 1977. Part of *Black Boy* reproduced the trajectory of Douglass and other male narrators: radical individualism, freedom as literacy and creation, a systematic analysis of white hegemony, and Wright's attempt at the close to enter a community of like-minded souls. *American Hunger* recalled the second of Douglass's narratives, as its description of Wright's break with the Communist Party recalled Douglass's estrangement from the Garrisonians. Stories like "Big Boy Leaves Home" and "The Man Who Lived Underground" combined with the five novels mentioned to teach a younger generation the modern meaning of bondage and confinement.

As influential as Douglass, Wright brought to the slave narrative tradition a stark, naturalistic vision of the paradoxes that bound all Americans yet victimized only some. It offered bondage as a metaphor for writers concerned with racism within the law, such as Chester Himes, Piri Thomas, George Jackson, and Eldridge Cleaver; for writers engrossed in the deceptions of migration and urbanism, like William Attaway, Ann Petry, and John Oliver Killens; and for those concerned with the prison of gender, like Alice Walker. Most significant were three works that fulfilled the vision by transcending the technique. One of the most admired novels of the twentieth century, Ralph Ellison's *Invisible Man* (1952), blended an epic tale of myth, legend, and ritual with a fugitive's journey northward. The anonymous protagonist charted slavery ancient and modern; like Douglass, he found a home and sufficient light. If Ellison recreated Douglass's search for identity, John A. Williams rehearsed his quest for meaning in a remarkable novel, *The Man Who Cried I Am* (1967). Williams reenacted a smaller portion of African American history—mainly the 1950s and 1960s—but told the story with sardonic symbolism and a shifting frame of time and space; the protagonist, a successful writer and advisor to presidents, discovered that he has been enslaved by ignorance and deceit. Malcolm X (who appeared as a fictionalized character in Williams's novel) related a drama of mental enslavement and final redemption in his *Autobiography* (1965), written with Alex Haley.

The 1960s brought a renewed sense of black oppression and a flood of historical fiction about slavery; the more serious works included *The Confessions of Nat Turner* (1967) by William Styron, whose portrait of Turner was controversial without attempting to revive the sentimental plantation tradition. Margaret Walker's *Jubilee* (1966), the first such novel by an African-American woman since Hopkins's *Contending Forces* at the turn of the century, was notable for its scrupulous research and its focus on the lives of women under slavery; equally distinctive was its attempt to reconcile domestic themes and political radicalism. A male novelist, Ernest J. Gaines, dealt with a similar situation in the memorable heroine and narrator of *The Autobiography of Miss Jane Pittman* (1971). He sought to interweave the image of the female slave from the early narratives, a framing device akin to the WPA oral history, and changes in black consciousness since the civil rights movement. Another instance of "neo-slave narrative"—a term developed because so many were being written—was the novel *Dessa Rose* (1986) by Sherley Anne Williams, whose vibrant title character leads a revolt. Charles Johnson used slavery more as backdrop for character and incident than for historical reconstruction in *Oxherding Tale* (1982) and *Middle Passage* (1990). Ishmael Reed used it for his inimitable form of burlesque in *Flight to Canada* (1976).

As Reed dared to seek the absurd where most found only tragedy, so Toni Morrison uncovered new dimensions of significance in her novel *Beloved* (1987). Retold from the 1856 story of Margaret Garner and her infant daughter, the novel represented in several ways a culmination of the slave narrative, telling the truth as no nineteenth-century account could. Unlike the original narratives, which could bring retribution upon their authors, it had no need to deny, evade, or suppress anything. Its experimental format could elevate consciousness without evoking sentimentality, and it could do something neither Douglass nor Jacobs could do alone: tell the male and female tales together, in a carefully convergent way, related to each other. This brought to fruition the tradition of a communal story, antiphonally and communally told.

[*See also* Emancipation in the Americas; Slave Culture; *and* United States.]

BIBLIOGRAPHY

Andrews, William L. *To Tell a Free Story: The First Century of Afro-American Autobiography, 1760–1865.* Urbana: University of Illinois Press, 1986.

Bell, Bernard W. *The Afro-American Novel and Its Tradition.* Amherst: University of Massachusetts Press, 1987.

Fishkin, Shelley Fisher. *Was Huck Black? Mark Twain and African-American Voices.* New York and Oxford: Oxford University Press, 1993.

Loggins, Vernon. *The Negro Author: His Development in America to 1900.* Port Washington, N.Y.: Kennikat Press, 1964.

McDowell, Deborah E., and Arnold Rampersad, eds. *Slavery and the Literary Imagination.* Baltimore: Johns Hopkins University Press, 1989.

Sekora, John. *Frederick Douglass.* New York: Macmillan, 1996.

Shuffleton, Frank, ed. *A Mixed Race: Ethnicity in America.* New York: Oxford University Press, 1993.

Sundquist, Eric. *To Wake the Nations: Race in the Making of American Literature.* Cambridge, Mass.: Harvard University Press, 1993.

—JOHN SEKORA

APPRENTICESHIP. Apprenticeship provided for gradual transition between slavery and freedom in New World slave societies. Designed by ruling elements to mitigate the social and economic shocks of emancipation, apprenticeship enabled masters to retain the mandatory labor services of former slaves for a limited time under specific statutory terms. The system offered employers an opportunity to introduce new methods of labor management and to educate former slaves in the responsibilities of free citizenry. In most cases, they did neither. In all cases, slaves resisted apprenticeship.

Among major American slave societies, direct transition to freedom was achieved only in the French colonies and the United States. In the British West Indies (except Antigua and Bermuda), Hispanic America, and Brazil, varying modes of apprenticeship were adopted.

All British slaves were emancipated simultaneously in August 1834, and all freedmen above age six were compelled to serve a transitional apprenticeship. Domestic slaves were assigned an additional four years of mandatory labor; agricultural slaves, six. Apprentices worked forty-five hours per week for their former owners in exchange for legally specified allowances of food, clothing, lodging, and medical care. They were permitted to earn wages by working more than forty-five hours, and they could purchase the unexpired terms of their apprenticeship at prices determined by "impartial" appraisal. Children under age six were entrusted to the care of their mothers. A body of one hundred special magistrates was appointed by the crown to enforce apprenticeship laws, to participate in appraisement tribunals, and to arbitrate all manner of disputes between planters and apprentices. Although most planters took an exacting rather than conciliatory approach to their apprentices, working conditions generally improved during the apprenticeship years.

Two powerful forces were arrayed against the system: the apprentices themselves and their abolitionist allies. Abolitionists toured the colonies as watchdogs, publicizing the misdeeds of planters and the grievances of apprentices. Their national campaign against apprenticeship achieved the abolition of the system two years ahead of schedule. Britain's painful experience with apprenticeship discouraged French authorities from instituting a similar transitional process.

Gradualism took a different form in Ibero-America. At independence most Spanish-American republics adopted "free womb" laws liberating all newborn children of slave mothers. Such children, called *manumisos*, were subject to eighteen years of service (subsequently twenty-one years) to their mothers' masters. In Venezuela, a further four-year apprenticeship was added during which the apprentices were entitled by law to choose their own masters and to learn a trade. The privileges embodied in such laws were rarely realized, and *manumisos* everywhere lived very much as slaves. Slave numbers fell consistently; in 1851, for example, Colombia had only sixteen thousand slaves, compared with the fifty-four thousand recorded at independence. Complete abolition occurred in most of the Latin American states during the 1850s.

Cuba and Brazil were exceptions. During the Ten Years' War (1868–1878) the Cuban insurgents who opposed Spanish rule granted qualified freedom to slaves living under their jurisdiction. Spain retaliated with the Moret Law (1870), extending freedom to all Cuban slaves over age sixty and to all children born to slave women after 1868. Such children were apprenticed to their mothers' masters until they reached age twenty-two, receiving half-wages beginning at age eighteen.

The Treaty of Zanjón (1878) freed slaves who had fought on both sides of the war. Other slaves became rebellious, and the Spanish government, facing heavy pressure from abolitionists, ended slavery in 1880 and instituted an eight-year apprenticeship, the *patronato*. Spain's rationale paralleled that of the British five decades earlier: apprenticeship would ease social and economic shocks and permit instruction of ex-slaves in the responsibilities of freedom.

Under *patronato*, masters commanded their ex-slaves' labor. They represented them in legal sit-uations and exercised the right to corporal punishment. At the same time, masters assumed responsibility to educate as well as to feed and clothe the young, and they were forbidden to separate families. After 1884 one-quarter of the apprentices in Cuba were to be freed each year, the oldest going first, until 1888 when all apprentices would be free and *patronato* would cease.

The system ended two years early. In the first four years (1880–1884) sixty thousand *patrocinados* obtained full freedom through indemnification, through mutual agreement with masters, by judicial action against masters for nonfulfillment of obligations, and by other means. When a royal decree abolished *patronato* two years early, in 1886, there were only twenty-five thousand people still serving apprenticeships.

Brazil passed a "free womb" law in 1871, obligating masters to care for the children of slave women until they reached age eight. For their troubles masters were offered either indemnification from the state in thirty-year bonds or the right to use the labor of such children, called *ingenuos*, until they attained twenty-one years. Overwhelmingly, they chose the latter. *Ingenuos* lived in the manner of slaves. Few received public instruction; all were subject to corporal punishment; and, contrary to spirit of the law, their labor services were both rented and sold. The power of Brazilian abolitionism swelled in the 1880s. In May 1888, with internal tensions at the boiling point, the government decreed complete, immediate, and uncompensated emancipation for all slaves and *ingenuos*.

In no instance had apprenticeship achieved significant conciliation between masters and former slaves. The British experience was the most comprehensive, the most orderly, and the most fertile in generating institutional change, but its premature termination caught colonial authorities with the legal apparatus of a free society still incomplete. Cuban apprenticeship provided some measure of gradualism, albeit a chaotic one. "Free womb" laws did little to ease the burdens of child apprentices in Latin America. In all cases, the efforts of masters to prolong coerced labor through various modes of apprenticeship were broken by the intense opposition of former slaves and ardent abolitionists.

[*See also* Abolition and Anti-Slavery, *article on* Britain; Brazil; *and* Emancipation in the Americas.]

BIBLIOGRAPHY

Conrad, Robert. *The Destruction of Brazilian Slavery, 1850–1888.* Berkeley: University of California Press, 1972.

Fraginals, Manuel Moreno, Frank Moya Pons, and Stanley L. Engerman, eds. *Between Slavery and Free Labor: The Spanish-Speaking Caribbean in the Nineteenth Century.* Baltimore: Johns Hopkins University Press, 1985.

Green, William A. *British Slave Emancipation: The Sugar Colonies and the Great Experiment, 1830–1865.* Oxford: Clarendon Press, 1976.

Lombardi, John V. *The Decline and Abolition of Negro Slavery in Venezuela, 1820–1854.* Westport: Greenwood, 1971.

Scott, Rebecca J. *Slave Emancipation in Cuba: The Transition to Free Labor, 1860–1899.* Princeton: Princeton University Press, 1985.

—WILLIAM A. GREEN

ART AND ILLUSTRATION. Generally speaking, slavery and the slave trade have rarely been subject matter for art. Although many artists from different parts of the globe produced an image or two reflecting the practice of human enslavement, most avoided the topic altogether for political, ideological, or esthetic reasons. The visualization of slavery and the slave trade through art is an inherently political act that automatically positions an artist as either pro- or anti-slavery. The visual representation of slavery or the slave trade was for the most part instigated by and parallel in development with abolitionist movements.

With the increase in anti-slavery sentiment throughout Europe and the United States during the late eighteenth century and throughout most of the nineteenth, there developed a need for visual propaganda to support the cause. Thus most graphic representations were didactic, intended to stir sympathy and outrage in the viewer. Most were rendered during the eighteenth and nineteenth centuries in such forms as etchings, engravings, or other print media to accompany the text of abolitionist books, pamphlets, and political tracts. They periodically surfaced in such illustrated publications as *Harper's Weekly*, the *London Illustrated News*, *L'Illustration*, and *Le Tour du Monde*. Many of these images were fashioned anonymously and left unsigned. Because of the volatile political nature of slave-trade imagery and the reluctance of most art-lovers to patronize such work, far fewer paintings and sculptures were created representing slavery's brutalizing history.

The artists who chose slavery or the slave trade as subject material for art rarely experienced the institution at first hand. Most culled their visual information from second- and third-hand accounts based on writings by travelers, explorers, and missionaries, whose descriptive detail regarding the acquisition and treatment of slaves tended to be sensationally embellished.

The nature of slavery as a subject of graphic art, and the kind and number of images produced, depended on the quality and quantity of historic contact between the enslaver as member of a particular nation, and the enslaved. Owing to very early contacts between the Netherlands and parts of Africa, Dutch artists began representing black Africans in their works of art as early as the fourteenth century. However, in terms of direct representations of slavery and its abolition, the history of contact between England and Africa and between England and the United States was longer and much more extensive than was that between Africa and France, for example. As a result there exists more visual information on the slave trade from England and the United States than from continental Europe or from other parts of the Americas. In the United States and Britain artists tended to use narrative and genre formats for representations of slavery or the slave trade. Owing to these countries' more extensive contacts with Africans, there was in general a lesser tendency there to idealize or romanticize.

France's history of relations with the African

continent was less extensive but just as significant. Slavery within France was strictly forbidden by a decree dating back to the Middle Ages. Slaves who were imported into the country had to be registered with the government and acquired the status of either "servant" or free. These kinds of legal loopholes in the metropolis did not, however, prevent the brutalizing practice of slavery in France's distant Caribbean colonies. Because of this history, French artists tended to set slave imagery in a more subtle and exotic tradition designed to appeal to emotions guided by Enlightenment principles. French artists frequently made use of allegory and tended to apply erotic connotations, lavish coloration, highly contrived compositions, and atmospheric settings to the raw themes of slavery (Figure 3).

Artists from England were particularly prone to using graphic art an as effective teaching tool to showcase the horrors of slavery as an institution. Typically, moralistic and humanistic themes predominated. Scenes were often rendered to stir religious, moral, and emotional sentiment against the practice of human bondage and trade. They appealed especially to the Quakers in their abolitionist causes. In mid-eighteenth century England one result of the Industrial Revolution was the popularization of anti-slavery politics and the commercialization of abolitionist imagery. An entire popular visual culture evolved around the issues of slavery and abolition. Many anti-slavery medallions, medals, cameos, pins, and other trinkets were mass-produced and marketed to a large consumer public. One, a cameo seal by Josiah Wedgwood called *Am I Not a Man and a Brother?*, showing a kneeling and shackled slave, became the most popular and recognizable emblem of abolitionism in England as well as on the European continent.

African slavery was not the only form of slavery depicted by artists. In the United States, for example, the importation and involuntary enslavement of the Chinese (the so-called coolie trade) was represented by exploiting the same themes of brutality that had been used to show black enslave-

ment (Figure 6). In Europe white slavery—the capture and involuntary imprisonment of white women and eunuchs in harems of North Africa and the Near East—was a popular visual subject. Whereas black slavery was usually presented in unpolished graphic terms, images of white slavery formed part of a lavish exotic tradition in art called Orientalism, which tended to be both highly descriptive and intensely sensuous. As a popular genre of literary and visual art, Orientalism was practiced by artists of almost all European and European-American nations, especially in the latter part of the nineteenth century.

Whether presented in the raw and direct manner of American images of slavery and the slave trade, or in the more subtle and enigmatic portrayals of human bondage by the French, there are six general areas or themes on which artists based such depictions: blatant acts of cruelty such as flogging and other forms of torture (Figures 1, 2, and 6); scenes of capture and transport from Africa (Figures 3–5); activities aboard slave ships during the Middle Passage (Figures 6–9); slave resistance and fugitives (Figures 10–11); slave auctions and sales (Figures 12–13); and plantation labor or house servitude.

Because they were intended primarily as propaganda to stir anti-slavery sentiment, most graphic illustrations of slavery's practices were deliberately crafted to expose the horrors and cruelties of the institution. In England a diagrammatic representation of a slave ship, the *Brookes of Liverpool* (Figure 9), was published just one year after the founding of the British Abolitionist Society in 1788. The image shows how slave ships were loaded with human cargo for transport. It is an image of depersonalized humanity in which people are turned into objects of merchandise. The illustration was meant to have an emotional impact on those who saw it and to remind them of the horrors of the Middle Passage. Quakers hung it on the walls of their homes to inspire their benevolence and stir sympathy. The print was distributed to members of Parliament to urge political influence against the slave trade. It was also disseminated on the European continent, where shortly thereafter the French produced their own version.

Within a decade of the appearance of the *Brookes of Liverpool* print, the English artist William Blake produced a series of images to accompany John Gabriel Stedman's *Narrative of a Five Years' Expedition Against the Revolted Negroes of Surinam* (1796). One engraving from this text, *A Negro Hung Alive by the Ribs to a Gallows* (Figure 1), graphically

Figure 1. (right) *A Negro Hung Alive by the Ribs to a Gallows*; engraving, William Blake, from John Gabriel Stedman's *Narrative of a Five Years' Expedition against the Revolted Negroes of Surinam* (1796).

Figure 2. (below) *Châtiment des quatre piquets dans le colonies* (Punishment of Four Stakes in the Colonies); painting, Marcel Verdier, 1849; Menil Collection, Houston.

records the abominable tortures and cruel punishments inflicted on slaves. Even though the artist himself never witnessed such horrors, the stark graphic medium serves well to give the illusion of truthful documentation. Stedman's account of the slave uprising and reprisal in Suriname was very popular and was instrumental in swaying the reading public to supporting abolition.

J. M. W. Turner's *Slave Ship* (1840, Figure 8) makes direct reference to the slave trade and the

Figure 3. (opposite, top) *Slave Market on the West Coast of Africa*; painting, François-Aguste Biard, 1840; Wilberforce House, Hull City Museums Art Gallery and Archives.

Figure 4. (opposite, bottom) *The Slave Trade*; painting, George Morland, 1788; The British Museum.

Figure 5. (below) *Marché d'esclaves* (Slave Market); engraving for F. Chambon's *Le commerce de l'Amérique par Marseille* (1764).

Middle Passage in the medium of oil painting. It was inspired by the abolitionist Thomas Clarkson's *Cries of Africa* and by a poem by James Thomson describing the slave ship *Zong*, which sailed from West Africa in September 1781 with a cargo of 470 slaves bound for Jamaica. The ship had been caught in a typhoon, and the captain had ordered a large number of slaves thrown overboard so he could collect on the insurance. The abolitionists used the incident to promote their position. Even though British colonial slavery had been technically abolished in 1834, Turner used the event six years later as a means to keep the atrocities of slavery uppermost in the public mind. The work, shown in the Royal Academy of 1840, is essentially a Romantic exercise of pessimistic fascination with human and elemental violence. Turner was more interested in expressing an overall effect than in describing or making a political statement, but his painting underscores the horrors of the Middle Passage by displaying the body parts of slaves strewn in the ocean amid debris (note the shackled leg at right). Such powerful imagery had a lasting and chilling effect on those who had been either neutral to or ignorant of the slave-trading business.

The first visual image to give a full account of the slave-trade operation came from a French book on commerce (Figure 5, *Marché d'esclaves*, copper engraving for Chambon, *Le Commerce de l'Amérique par Marseille*, 1764). Like most illustrations of the slave trade produced in France during the eighteenth century, this one was designed to incite anti-slavery sentiment by subtly arousing the viewer's sensibility. Even though France was where the first graphic image pertaining to the slave trade was produced, England saw the earliest recorded painting of slave trading to be exhibited (Figure 4, George Morland, *The Slave Trade*, 1788). Characteristic of art from England on this subject is a moralizing tendency and the use of literary references to appeal to both the emotions and the intellect of a literate middle-class public.

The subversive potential of visual art to stir

thoughts of slave retaliation and to spark abolitionist fervor was of concern to many pro-slavers. Revolts on slave ships were depicted frequently in art. Although images such as these were intended to document and provoke abolitionist outrage at slave-trading, they were often too picturesque to have any real influence in ending the practice. In addition, the text with which such imagery was associated rarely condemned the institution outright.

More to the taste of those who supported slavery were depictions of slave auctions and scenes of fugitives (Figures 10–13). Ironically, these also formed two major programmatic abolitionist themes in the American visual representation of slavery and the slave trade. Their focused attention on traumatic events such as the heartless separation of families could be read as serious appeals to the abolitionist cause. Unlike the situation in Europe, there was less demand from American abolitionists for depictions of the horrors of slavery. Nonetheless, a healthy amount of imagery focusing on the physical brutality inflicted on slaves was

Figure 6.   (below) *Preserving the Peace*; illustration from *Harper's Weekly*, volume 29, June 1864.

Figure 7.   (opposite, top) *Nègres à fond de calle* (Negroes in the Ship's Hold); print by Johann Moritz Rugendas, 1827, for his *Voyage pittoresque dans le Brésil* (1827–1835); National Library of Jamaica.

Figure 8.   (opposite, bottom) *Slave Ship* (*Slavers Throwing Overboard the Dead and Dying, Typhoon Coming On*); painting, J. M. W. Turner, 1840; Museum of Fine Arts, Boston.

71

DESCRIPTION OF A SLAVE SHIP.

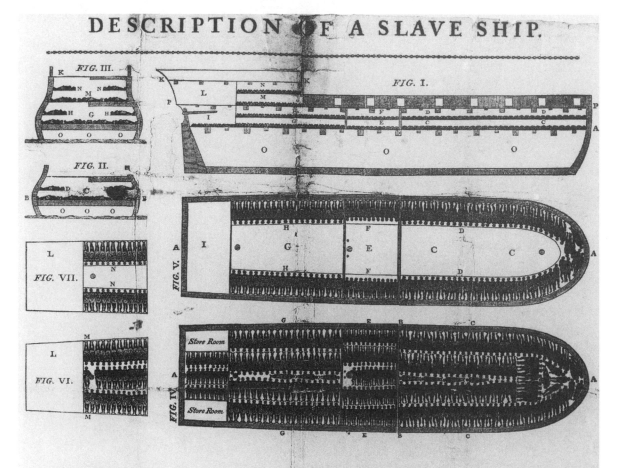

Figure 9. (opposite) *Brookes of Liverpool*; printed propaganda broadside of the London Abolition Society, 1789.

produced in print or graphic form in the United States during the nineteenth century. The most notable group of American images of slave brutalization were those destined to be included in Harriet Beecher Stowe's *Uncle Tom's Cabin* (1852). Stowe was herself an amateur artist and played a hand in selecting the illustrations for her immensely popular anti-slavery book. Artist Hammett Billings was hired to draw most of these illustrations; typically, they were based on second-hand written sources rather than on eyewitness accounts. Scenes included slave auctions and the breakup of families, floggings, the hunting down of runaways, and other displays of physical and psychological abuse endemic to slavery. Billings avoided caricature and presented most scenes in a matter-of-fact manner that served to make the abolitionist point even stronger. Both Stowe's book and its illustrations were popular and internationally influential. The British were particularly moved by them. Inspired by both the imagery and Stowe's text, the English artist Thomas Moran created *Slaves Escaping through the Swamp* (1862, Figure 10). Its focus on the damp expanse of swampland and the uniquely American practice of hunting slaves with bloodhounds made the picture a sensation in England. In a similar vein, Richard Ansdell created his dramatic *Hunted Slaves* (1861, Figure 11) exhibited at the Royal Academy. This image was highly regarded by public and critics alike and was widely reproduced in print form.

In 1827 Johann Moritz Rugendas executed a print titled *Nègres à fond de calle*, illustrative of the slave trade to Brazil (Figure 7). This image is unique because Rugendas was an eyewitness to the scene. The work serves as his memory of seeing the hold of a slave ship when he joined a scientific mission to the Brazilian interior financed by the Russian government. This was to be one of several prints serving as illustrations for his book *Voyage pittoresque dans le Brésil*, published between 1827 and 1835. Although Rugendas softened the horrors of the scene, the atmosphere is evocative of an overcrowded and fetid environment typical of slave ships. The work is intended to be informative rather than declamatory or emotive, but it is picturesque and translates the graphic horrors suggested by the *Brookes of Liverpool* and by Blake's horrific print into an accessible and memorable scene.

Whereas Rugendas's *Nègres à fond de calle* had been the first explicit image to show the slave trade in the French Salon, Auguste Biard's *Slave Market on the West Coast of Africa* (Figure 3) was the first large-scale oil painting on the subject to be exhibited in the Salon, where it appeared in 1835. At that time it received no critical attention, perhaps as a result of apathy toward overseas slavery in France in particular and on the European continent in general in the 1830s. Five years later, however, it was exhibited in the Royal Academy in London and caused a sensation. The work purports to function as a documentary print showing the practice of the selling of slaves by African chiefs to European traders. It was intended to implicate both white slave-traders and black Africans in the slave trade. However, it is ineffective as an abolitionist statement and is basically a series of sensationalized vignettes that work actually to glorify and romanticize slavery while simultaneously posturing as a serious anti-slavery manifesto. Such is the ambiguity of art that tackles themes of slavery, the slave trade, and abolition.

Even though most blatant acts of cruelty toward slaves were illustrated in the print rather than fine-art medium, there were some exceptions. For example, Marcel Verdier's *Châtiment des quatre piquets dans les colonies* (1843, but dated 1849; Figure 2) exposes the cruelties and evils of slavery. The *quatre piquets* was a form of punishment described in the abolitionist literature in which the stripped victim was pegged by the extremities to the ground and mercilessly whipped. The physical and psychologi-

cal suffering of the slaves and the cruel indifference of the slavemaster are emphasized. Other artists, such as the Puerto Rican painter Francisco Oller, witnessed and documented this and other forms of cruel punishment in the Antilles in extensive print series. Verdier's painting was briefly shown in the Salon of 1843 but was refused further exhibition out of fear that it might stir rebellious unrest among sympathetic onlookers. The work was exhibited subsequently in an alternate venue and later reproduced in *L'Illustration*. Again, the artist never witnessed such a scene at first hand but instead pieced together a series of sensationalized vignettes culled from written descriptions. The artist's changing the picture's apparent date from 1843 to 1849, one year after the abolition of slavery in the French colonies, was a politically strategic move intended to remove the stigma of French involvement in such activities. This kind of manipulation of slave imagery and the facts related to

Figure 10. (opposite, top) *Slaves Escaping through the Swamp*; painting, Thomas Moran, 1862; The Philbrook Museum of Art, Tulsa.

Figure 11. (opposite, bottom) *Hunted Slaves*; painting, Richard Ansdell, 1861; Walker Art Gallery, Liverpool.

Figure 12. (below) *After the Sale: Going South from Richmond*; painting, Eyre Crowe, 1853; Chicago Historical Society.

Figure 13. *Slave Auction;* painting, artist unknown, c. 1850s;
Carnegie Museum of Art, Pittsburgh.

it was common practice by artists of the eighteenth and nineteenth centuries. Verdier's act shows that the subject of slavery, whether treated directly or indirectly in art, before or after abolition, remained a politically explosive and emotionally charged subject for both artist and viewer.

[*See also* Anti-Slavery Literature, *overview article*; *and* Slave Trade, *article on* Trans-Atlantic Trade.]

BIBLIOGRAPHY

Boime, Albert. *The Art of Exclusion: Representing Blacks in the Nineteenth Century*. Washington: Smithsonian Institution Press, 1990.

Honour, Hugh. *The Image of the Black in Western Art*. Vol. 4, pts. 1 and 2. Cambridge, Mass.: Harvard University Press, 1989.

—JAMES SMALLS

ASIA. [*This entry comprises two articles: a general description of slavery and other forms of servitude in the Indian subcontinent, followed by a detailed discussion of these practices throughout Southeast Asia and its environs. For discussion of slavery in East Asia, see* China *and* Korea.]

South Asia

It is difficult, on the basis of the historical evidence, to distinguish clearly between slavery and other severe forms of servitude in the South Asian context. A high incidence of chattel slavery was confined to brief periods; whereas relations of servitude of varying severity, with the person and laboring capacity of the worker being under the absolute control of the master but falling short of chattel status, seem to have been very common both temporally and spatially. It has been argued that the evolution of the institution of caste entailed servile status and work burdens that weighed heavily on the laboring poor, who were assigned low caste and "outcaste" status in the hegemonic brahmanical hierarchical order. This obviated the large-scale use by landed proprietors of chattel slaves in production on the Greco-Roman model. It is useful to think of a continuum of relations of servitude ranging from chattel slavery at one extreme to milder forms at the other, where propertyless workers inherited low and outcaste status and were bound to the estates of higher caste landed proprietors.

It is also useful to draw a distinction between agrestic slavery and domestic slavery, the former referring to the systematic use of slave labor in primary-sector production and the latter to its use in household labor and personal services. In South Asia agrestic slavery for agricultural, forest, or mining production—where the extent of slave labor predominated over peasant or wage-paid labor—has been rather exceptional. It would be difficult to think of a historic period corresponding to a "slave mode of production"; the Mauryan society in North India (325–184 BCE) is arguably the closest approximation. By contrast, systems of agrestic bondage of the low-caste and outcaste propertyless groups to estates of landed proprietors have been common, and many authors have loosely referred to these relations as "slavery." These workers could be transferred to other proprietors along with the land but could not generally be individually bought and sold. Apart from this aspect, their persons were in absolute subjection to their masters, as is typical of slavery.

The historic origins of slavery and servitude in the Indian subcontinent lay proximately in the subjugation of the civilized Indus Valley people, and over the longer run in the exploitative integration of autochthonous forest-dwelling and other tribal communities into plough agriculture, by the invading pastoral Aryan peoples in North India from earliest Vedic times (c. 1750 BCE on). The initial references in the *Ṛgveda* to constant armed conflict between the pejoratively termed "dark-complexioned" and "noseless" *dāsa* and *dasyu* on the one hand and the Aryans on the other gives way in the later parts of the *Ṛgveda* to an equation of the term *dāsa* with "slave" (f., *dāsi*), indicating that those of the *dāsa* tribes not killed outright had been reduced to servile status. The Aryans, who had been little differentiated as long as they were confined to holding wealth only in cattle, increasingly now measured their personal wealth in both cattle and enslaved *dāsas*, and particularly *dāsis*, who like cattle could be freely transferred. The ruling chiefs of the Gangetic and sub-Himalayan kingdoms and republics held, either individually or in common, large numbers of *dāsas* and *dāsis* for performing household and personal services, and a retinue of *dāsis* accompanied newly married daughters to the spousal home. *Dāsis* were referred to by the particular service in which they specialized; thus *kumbha-dāsis* fetched water, *vihi-kottika dāsis* husked grain, while the *dhati-dāsis* provided wet-nurses. No restrictions are observed in the late Vedic and early Buddhist literature on commensality or connubiality with the *dāsa*. Hence by the Epic period (the *Rāmāyaṇa* and the *Mahābhārata*) the earlier marked, ethnic dimension of servile status appears to have been modified greatly through continuous miscegenation, in which those brahmans who ventured to settle in the forests played an important role; the principal epic heroes are referred to as dark-complexioned. Household *dāsis* were not protected from sexual exploitation by their masters, and this also contributed to ethnic mixing.

Nevertheless, the extensive use of *dāsa* and servile labor in production had to await the transition from seminomadic pastoralism to rural settlements based on the use of iron and on plow agriculture in the valley of the Ganges from around 800 BCE. It received further impetus from the "urban revolution" and the more complex class structures made possible by the production of a stable agricultural surplus. In this process of exploitative integration of local peoples into plow agriculture, the generic term *śūdra* emerged to designate, as a fourth and lowest caste (below the brahman, *kṣatriya* and *vaiśya*), all those whose labor was at the command of others. Because ample cultivable land was available, the use of others' labor necessarily took place on the basis of direct coercive relations and was legitimized through caste ranking. The term *dāsa-karmakara* was increasingly used to refer collectively to "slave-workers," while subject and servile status not amounting to slavery characterized the *śūdra* cultivators and artisans. A famous passage in the *Aitareya Brāhmana* refers to the *śūdra* as the "servant of another," bound to render labor and to be beaten. Personal servants and dependents of the well-to-do household were its *bhrtya*, literally "those who are supported" (a term still used with the same connotation today in the modern period, while the term *dāsa* has disappeared).

The patriarchal head of the landed or merchant household was assumed to have absolute power to dispose of the persons not only of his slaves but also of his children and wives. If he wished, he could give them as slaves to others or mortgage their services as slaves to others against loans. A distinction emerged between those who were born into slavery of slave parents and hence were slaves for life—no doubt the majority of the *dāsas* comprised this category—and those free persons who were temporarily reduced to the status of slaves of creditors owing to unpaid debt, or because the patriarch gave or mortgaged family members as slaves, or because persons rendered destitute by harvest failure or other causes were forced to offer themselves or their children as slaves in return for subsistence. In Kautilya's *Arthaśāstra* there is a detailed classification of the types of *dāsa* by their origin. Legal limitations on the abuse of the temporary *dāsa* are clearly specified, indicating a better position for them than for the hereditary slaves, who had no rights. If the patriarch had children by *dāsis* they were to be deemed free, as was the mother. To what extent these injunctions were actually followed is not clear, but some upward mobility seems to have been possible for this group.

During the *Arthaśāstra* period (the Mauryan Empire, 325–184 BCE) large landholdings appear to have predominated, with the *gahapati* or patriarchal householders cultivating them through the labor of the *dāsa-karmakara*. With the decline of the Mauryan state, the use of *dāsa* labor in agrestic production also declined, never reviving to the same extent. The Buddhist monasteries of Sri Lanka and of the Indian mainland, as well as the large Hindu temples in India, employed *dāsa* labor along with wage labor in cultivation and personal services; the slaves along with land had been donated by wealthy patrons. Runaway slaves were forbidden to enter the Buddhist order as monks and if caught could be branded. Both the Hindu and Buddhist scriptures enjoined their followers not to acquire wealth by engaging in the trade in slaves, but they did not abjure their employment.

In South India, the settlement of the fertile river valleys through land grants to brahmans and other high-caste groups from the sixth century CE on resulted in slave-based production. Here the slaves, again overwhelmingly of local tribal origin, were integrated exploitatively as particularly low and "untouchable" castes within the hegemonic system. They were usually transferable along with the landed estates of proprietors but were not sold individually. There was also cultivation by *śūdra* peasants. The commodity form of slave labor developed to a much greater extent in areas growing cash crops for export from earliest times, such as the Malabar coast. Purchase and sale of slaves persisted well into the eighteenth century in these regions, and the British East India Company's records show it buying slaves in Malabar.

Elsewhere in India, by the medieval period chattel slavery in agrestic production had virtually disappeared, although hereditary and debt-bonded labor remained. The overwhelming bulk of production was carried on by free peasants, and by servile peasants and workers of tribal origin who had been exploitatively integrated over the centuries as *śūdra*s and as untouchables into the caste system; these workers were socially and economically dominated by the high-caste landed proprietors but not reduced to chattel status. The chattel slaves of the past had probably been absorbed gradually into this larger group. The brahmanical religion rationalized this system through ideas of ritual ranking of purity and pollution, placing the artisans and the unskilled manual field-workers at the lowest level of caste, and treating those engaged in socially essential but unpleasant tasks—waste disposal, tanning, and disposal of the dead—as being outside the pale of the caste system itself. The process of tribal integration into the larger society was still visible in the late twentieth century as the few remaining pockets where tribal life continued were invaded by influences from the modern economy.

The medieval period saw the Turco-Mongol seizure of political power in North India and the importation of new types of slaves, following practices prevalent in Central Asia. They included the numerous slave-eunuchs guarding royal and aristocratic harems, skilled artisans and construction workers, and militarily trained and highly valued slaves from Central Asia who even established a ruling dynasty—the "slave dynasty" of the thir-

teenth-century Delhi Sultanate. Thus a qualitatively very different type of slavery was superimposed on the age-old servile relations involving the continuing customary subjugation of low-caste and outcaste groups to the proprietors of landed and mercantile wealth. Artisanal production received an impetus, with slave-manned workshops producing a range a goods for direct consumption by the Muslim ruling aristocracy. Domestic slavery also expanded greatly; many thousands of slaves were owned by the richest nobles, differentiated by levels of skill and training and varying in price. The expansion of this group was aided by the emulation of the ruling class lifestyle (including purdah and harem) by the local Hindu aristocracies, who were integrated into the new systems of revenue collection. The practice of manumission allowed some social mobility to the better-off elements of this new servile class. With the decline and eventual disintegration of the Mughal Empire and the similar decline of the ruling dynasties in the outlying provinces during the eighteenth century, the large bands of domestic and other types of slaves were scattered and absorbed into the larger, relatively freer civil society.

The colonial period, dating from the acquisition of the revenue-collecting right of Bengal by the British East India Company (1765), saw little initial attempt to modify the existing social relations. Indeed, in the last decades of the eighteenth century some company officials in South India insisted on the sale of agrestic slaves in order to realize revenue from landed proprietors who had defaulted on tax payment, even though such sale away from the land was not customary. There were also transactions in imported slaves for both personal and sexual services, regularly carried on by Europeans in the main port cities.

With the abolition of slavery in Britain's other dominions in 1833, the British Parliament and the East India Company's court of directors pressed for a similar act in India. The main economic impetus came from the new labor requirements of the developing plantation system both within India and

Sri Lanka, and in Britain's far-flung colonial possessions in the West Indies, Guyana, Mauritius (and later South Africa). Planter interests espoused labor mobility and migration through the indentured labor system: this required a weakening of traditional systems tying labor locally through the caste-based relations of servitude. The 1843 act "abolishing" slavery in India specified that contracts for the purchase and sale of persons were illegal; stringent new laws (the Workman's Breach of Contract Act, 1859, and section 200 of the Civil Procedure Code) strengthened the hands of employers holding persons in debt bondage and inducting them into the system of indentured migration.

[*See also* Abolition and Anti-Slavery, *article on* India; *and* Slave Trade, *article on* Asia and Oceania.]

BIBLIOGRAPHY

Bandyopadhyaya [Banerjee], N. C. *Economic Life and Progress in Ancient India*. Vol. 1. Calcutta: Hare Press, 1925.

Chanana, D. R. *Slavery in Ancient India*. New Delhi: People's Publishing House, 1960.

Ghoshal, U. N. *The Agrarian System in Ancient India*. Calcutta: University of Calcutta, 1930.

Habib, Irfan. "Social Distribution of Landed Property in Pre-British India: A Historical Survey." In *Essays in Indian History, in Honour of Cuthbert Colin Davies*, edited by Donovan Williams and E. Daniel Potts. New York: Asia Publishing House, 1973.

Kosambi, D. D. *An Introduction to the Study of Indian History*. 2d rev. ed. Bombay: Popular Prakashan, 1975.

Kosambi, D. D. *The Culture and Civilisation of Ancient India in Historical Outline*. Delhi: Vikas Publications, 1970.

Patnaik, U., and M. Dingwaney, eds. *Chains of Servitude: Bondage and Slavery in India*. Madras: Sangam Books, 1985.

Sharma, R. S. *Sudras in Ancient India*. Delhi: Motilal Banarsidass, 1958.

—Utsa Patnaik

Southeast Asia

Slavery and other forms of bondage and dependency in Southeast Asia (the region encompassing all the countries within a boundary defined by India, China, Australia, and New Guinea) was not as rigidly defined an institution as in the West, where it was historically synonymous with property and violent domination. Slavery in the former polities and societies of the modern states of Thailand (Siam), Myanmar (Burma), Malaysia, Indonesia, and the Philippines, as in other parts of Southeast Asia, was primarily but not exclusively a property relation. The term *slave* implies a spectrum of statuses of acquired persons, often forcefully transferred from one society to another. A distinction was drawn in these states and societies between chattel slaves—totally powerless persons in principle—and those laboring under conditions of bondage or dependence. Between these two extremes there was a continuum of status and privilege.

The first half of the twentieth century saw slavery in Southeast Asia examined from the perspectives of economics, anthropology, sociology, and history in the pioneering study of Herman J. Nieboer, *Slavery as an Industrial System: Ethnological Researches* (1910), and in Bruno Lasker's broad-ranging *Human Bondage in Southeast Asia* (1950). Not until the 1980s, however, did some of the more original and productive Asian specialists cast new light on the complexities of Southeast Asian social structure; they raised entirely new issues about slavery, bondage and dependency, and began utilizing a range of hitherto unknown source materials and new multidisciplinary frameworks. Among them James Watson, Anthony Reid, and James Warren particularly expanded knowledge of Southeast Asian forms of "slavery" and the evolution of social formations.

In an analytic introductory essay about Asian and African systems of slavery, Watson (1980) asserts that slavery, as a complex social institution, is difficult to define. Building on the comparative work of Nieboer and on Moses I. Finley's classic studies of slavery in ancient Greece, he argues that the treatment of human beings as property in Southeast Asia at all times is primary. Fundamental to Watson's guidelines for defining slavery cross-culturally as a property relationship is the importance of permanent coercive domination: all slaves, particularly women, were in the final analysis subject to the will of their owners. However, Watson does not confine himself to the property aspect of slavery in the narrow sense—the type best known from Athens and the Americas. Rather, the other defining criterion that emerges in his guidelines encompasses the marginal status of slaves, in which the person involved in forms of nonfree labor is an inseparable part of a community. He therefore stresses that the property aspect of slavery and the marginal status of slaves are critical to understanding the institution, irrespective of local variation and historical era, in Southeast Asia.

Slaves are acquired by purchase or capture; their labor is extracted through coercion; and as long as they remain slaves, they are never accepted into the kinship group of the master. Slavery is thus the institutionalization of these relationships between slave and owner. Reid, seeking new definitions of slavery and a conceptual framework for the study of the institution in Southeast Asia, has emphasized the importance of indigenous systems and values and the evolution of local societies. A historian, his lucid work has focused on the social-institutional complexities of slavery and the economic relationships inextricably bound up with it, in order to show what "slavery" meant in the Indianized kingdoms of Angkor and Pagan, in kinship-oriented "stateless societies," in Islamic sultanates, and in European colonial cities and outposts. Reid tackles the definition of slavery and gives guidelines by focusing on Southeast Asia as a cockpit of conflicting cultures, productive areas, and cultural-ecological zones, as well as an integral part of a far wider regional economy in which national boundaries are fairly recent.

The works of both Reid and Warren examine indigenous systems of slavery and Southeast Asian social structure and history in depth. Both historians argue that it is important to recognize, from the standpoint of local and social cultural reference, who was to be counted as a slave. They have decried the work of earlier metropolitan scholars who focused on slavery and Southeast Asian society in light of their own social and cultural preconceptions. Both historians are right in their contention that the very considerable range and variety of dependent personal statuses found in different Southeast Asian societies have too often been abstracted from their social-cultural contexts.

Not only is slavery in Southeast Asia different in important respects from Athenian and other Asian forms, but other diverse systems of dependency flourished alongside it in various parts of the region. In this regard Reid makes two important points. The first is that the labor system of Southeast Asia was based on the obligation to labor for a creditor, master, or lord. The second is that a form of bondage that must be recognized as slavery arose from within the broader basic pattern, assuming in certain circumstances and societies a major role in economic and political life. Reid rejects, however, conceptual schemes that posit a linear evolution of chattel slavery in Southeast Asia from communal servitude. He maintains that slavery becomes more clear-cut "at the interface between two cultures, when labor is being transferred from the relatively poor or weak to relatively rich or powerful societies" (Reid, 1983, p. 2). David J. Steinberg also argues that in eighteenth-century Southeast Asia, slavery was practiced in many forms—hereditary and nonhereditary, temporary and permanent. Thus Reid reasons that an acceptable synthesis of the history of slavery can be understood only in terms of Southeast Asian notions of hierarchy. Here as elsewhere he builds on the views of Watson, Warren, and Nieboer, who maintained that a slave was a "man [or woman] who is the property of another, politically and socially at a lower level than the mass of the people, and performing compulsory labor" (*Slavery as an Industrial System*, p. 5).

Of particular interest is Reid's spirited argument that "vertical bonding" shapes Southeast Asian social systems. He points to the centrality of hierarchical status, especially dyadic ties, as proof that individuals at each level of society required the others' assistance. He notes that the crucial features were the cooperative vertical bond and the element of choice and mutuality between two individuals, and therefore lineage (in a genealogical sense) was not the most important part of the social structure in the formulation of "statuses." The vertical bond forged between two persons was absolutely critical. The master provided protection and prosperity; and the bonded person filled a dependent role in the socioeconomic process that enabled the master as a free individual to acquire resources and engage in politics, war, and social life. In all Southeast Asian societies in which dependent labor was common, if a peasant was in economic difficulty or required support for a ritual obligation, she or he would seek assistance from another. If the debt was not repaid within a specified time, the bonded person often became obligated for life, along with her or his immediate dependents. In Southeast Asian societies where there was broad variation in forms of dependent labor, as Warren shows in nineteenth-century Sulu, not everyone possessed equal opportunities for advancement because custom or law often removed freedom of choice and action, either for a long time or life.

Reid maintains that throughout most of Southeast Asian history, labor was in large measure performed under varying conditions of bondage or dependence. Steinberg also demonstrates that, contrary to earlier impressions, debt bondage was far more common than chattel slavery in the eighteenth century, especially in Siam, Burma, and parts of the Islamic Malay world where the rural economy was becoming increasingly monetized. Reid concludes that the Southeast Asian institutions of dependent labor and bondage in many ways resembled cross-cultural counterparts in other societies in which slaves were recruited largely from the indigenous population, by virtue of birth into a dependent class or as a result of debt. He maintains that Southeast Asian institutions of dependence and bondage were far more "benign" than systems such as those established in the New World plantations or by the Ming-dynasty Chinese, where laborers, often foreigners of an alien race, were commonly sold as a commodity. Both Reid and Warren conclude that slaves and other dependent groups were not economic classes as such, since the statuses were often based on legal and kinship distinctions, but that the broad range of economic and social functions were embedded in the social relations of dependence of the various individuals and groups within particular Southeast Asian polities and societies.

Reid argues that various forms of bondage and dependence in Southeast Asia over the past eight centuries are indigenous developments that have their roots in vertical bonding and a regional sense of mutual obligation. The key to slavery, and to the evolution of Southeast Asian social systems generally, was control over the productive and reproductive powers of human beings (rather than over land as in Europe). In Southeast Asia land was not viewed as an index to power because it was abundant. The important issue was to whom a person was bonded, rather than any abstract legal notions of bondage.

Open and Closed Modes of Slavery. Southeast Asian slavery was marked by "closed" and "open" kinship systems. A closed system is oriented primarily toward retaining the labor of slaves by reinforcing their distinctiveness, as outsiders, from the dominant population. In Southeast Asia this pattern occurred primarily in wet-rice-growing, labor-intensive indianized kingdoms and kinship-oriented stateless societies, where commercial exchange and a money economy had made little impact. Open kinship systems, such as the Sulu Sultanate, acquired labor through capture or purchase of slaves and assimilated them as insiders into the dominant group. The most recently acquired slaves were those most clearly demarcated from other dependent groups and the wider society. Within the first generation, those individuals most likely to be incorporated in an open system were female slaves, because of the importance of their productive and reproductive activities, and children. The most striking examples of this pattern were the wealthy trade-based *kerajaan* (states) and entrepôts and a few labor-deficient areas in the region. In Southeast Asian societies where various forms of dependent labor were common, individuals did not emphasize the route taken to slavery unless this corresponded with the critically important legal-social distinction in both open and closed systems between being an insider or outsider.

Outsiders in closed systems—such as the classic indianized and Buddhist kingdoms of Angkor, Pagan, and Ayudha, and the stateless societies of tribes such as the Toba Batak and Toraja—were often powerless and totally rightless human beings. Frequently they were captives of common ethnic origins, criminals with shared experiences, or other outcasts. Cut off from their families and their roots, these slaves were legally nonpersons and deserving of death. They were deliberately set apart from the dominant kinship group, religious institutions, and the state, as well as from other dependent groups in the society. The not-so-subtle prejudice inherent in this kind of system should also emphasize the fact that physical features such as desirable color of skin, hair, and eyes remained prized commodities. Not everyone possessed equal opportunities for advancement in closed systems, because some ethnic groups possessed physical properties that made them more inferior than others in the eyes of the dominant society. Thus the barriers to deracinated slaves' entering the dominant group were formidable. Masters usually resisted creating a bond that could make future assimilation possible for such persons. The slave's sense of permanent, violent domination as an outsider and as a socially dead person was reflected in the Thai practice of branding war captives. Outsiders enslaved in closed Southeast Asian systems were usually natally alienated, dishonored human beings who, irrespective of location and era, were completely dependent on their masters.

In closed systems in kingdoms such as Angkor, Pagan, and Ayudha, and among stratified tribes such as the Toba Batak, Kenyah, and Toraja, ethnicity was not a critical integrating concept in the enslavement process. However, in open systems such as in Sulu, slavery and ethnicity had become mutually reinforcing. Slavery and dependent labor were not solely economic instruments that enabled the late eighteenth-century expansion of the Sulu state and domination of the regional trade network; slavery and ethnogenesis had virtually become the very basis of organized society in the sultanate.

Slave Supply and Use. Because the key to power in Southeast Asia lay in control over slaves, trade goods, and guns, it is not surprising that slavery in the region was bound up with warfare and raiding. Captives were a main source of booty and, not surprisingly, they were also one of the leading items of regional trade. The unprecedented international and regional trade demands and the rise of urbanism in Southeast Asia from the sixteenth century onward created the need for large-scale recruitment of dependent and forced labor. As the regional-local market grew, especially with China, port-polities like Melaka, Aceh, and Makasar, and metropolitan cities such as Batavia and Manila flourished, as did the demand to import slaves on a considerable scale. Driven by international market forces and their patrons' desire for wealth and power, predatory maritime groups met the demand for slaves in Southeast Asia. From the sixteenth to the nineteenth century the harsh exploits of these marauders were carried out on a vast regional scale; manning well-organized fleets of large, swift vessels, professional slave raiders like the Bugis, Butonese, Tobello, Iranun, and Balangingi jeopardized the maritime trade routes of Southeast Asia and dominated the capture and transport of slaves to markets at Batavia, Makasar, Bali, Nias, Singapore, and Sulu. The in-

Drawing of the *Gary*, a Balangingi slave-raiding vessel built for speed, maneuverability, and striking power.

ternal structure of these marauding communities was invariably based on dependence and clientage that subordinated slave raiders like the Iranun and Balangingi to the leading officials of a dominant state, such as the Sulu Sultanate. After the initial act of capture, these daring, fierce marauders often cooperated with local tribal chieftains, Chinese traders, and occasional Europeans who acted as middlemen, to meet the demand in major cities and smaller-scale communities for slaves. Slave-raiding also extended overland into the interiors of the large islands of Borneo, Sulawesi, and Luzon.

After capture and warfare, natural increase was a principal source of slaves in Southeast Asian soci-

eties, particularly in open systems during most eras. Little research has been devoted to the relative importance of productive and reproductive activities in the lives of Southeast Asian slaves. The reproductive powers of female slaves contributed greatly to their worth in societies like Sulu, Aceh, and Banjarmassin. Studies of Sulu and regional slave-raiding patterns provide evidence that Iranun and Balangingi chose females at random, but the number of separated spouses was still high, especially in the coastal areas of the Philippines and eastern Indonesia. Despite lack of information on the marital status of female slaves prior to capture or initial purchase, it is clear that many marriages were destroyed by the slave trade in Southeast Asia, and that many men were slaughtered in the course of the capture of their women.

Breeding and capture were principal modes of recruitment, but debt and fine obligations among Southeast Asians themselves also provided quite significant numbers of slaves for internal markets. Convictions for criminal offenses such as stealing and acts of sexual impropriety, particularly adultery, were punishable by heavy fines during most periods in Southeast Asia. Inability to pay or offer some form of security for the fine subjected offenders to bonded status. In addition to nonpayment of fines, debts were incurred by gambling and pawning in societies like Sulu and Siam in the nineteenth century. Not infrequently a Southeast Asian offered her or his services voluntarily for a fixed period of time in return for money or goods to meet the expenses of a wedding or a funeral, or to liquidate a debt. The concept of a "welfare syndrome" can also be used in explaining the Southeast Asian propensity for people selling themselves into slavery, especially in periods of acute distress such as wars, famines, and epidemics. Here "slavery" appears to have been an institution of bondage or dependent labor, designed to provide a form of social welfare in the absence of state institutions to a predominantly rural indigent population.

Debt bondage as an economic institution was most fully developed in Southeast Asia in the second half of the nineteenth century, as global trade and monetization affected local social systems and regional trade networks. At the same time, the very survival of slavery in different parts of Southeast Asia, as elsewhere in the world, was being called into question. The main slave-raiding zones in the South China Sea and the waters of eastern Indonesia attracted the intense naval pressure of Britain, Spain, and the Netherlands for more than a quarter-century; by the 1880s the number of slaves moving across the region had been reduced to a trickle. The abolition of slave traffic in Southeast Asia was a mortal blow to the economies of states like Perak and Sulu. When aristocratic Malays in Perak, Taosug in Sulu, and others could no longer

rely on slave raids to supply sufficient numbers of slaves for their needs, the amount of tribute ordinarily collected from dependents increased dramatically, and fines in the various legal codes became far higher. These traditional states recognized that with able-bodied replacements becoming scarce, that they derived their greatest advantage from extending various systems of bondage and dependent labor. The bonded could be given away as gifts, donations, tribute, or security for a loan; they could be sold and inherited. Forced sales into slavery and bondage to ensure survival rose in

Engraving of an Iranun slave raider, attired in cotton quilted red vest and armed with a spear (*kris*) and a *kampilan* (an Iranun sword decorated with human hair), nineteenth century.

the second half of the nineteenth century as the autonomy of traditional states and slave-raiding both declined under the combined pressure of modern colonial navies. Interesting in terms of social values and everyday life, anthropological investigations of the heritage of slaves from the late nineteenth century on conclude that their late-twentieth-century descendants still suffered the effects of centuries of bondage in parts of Southeast Asia.

Slaves in Southeast Asian societies were not defined solely in terms of their status as property. Their social status was also determined by factors often independent of their servility. In Southeast Asian states and cities slaves could have family roles as husband or wife; they could own property, including other slaves; and they often filled a variety of political and economic roles—as bureaucrats, farmers, warriors, concubines, or traders—by virtue of which they were entitled to certain rights and privileges accorded to other members of the dominant society. Slavery appears to have been an institution designed to provide labor and service to an expansive state's larger and more important military and economic elites; slaves were household servants, craftsmen, stewards to manage elite holdings while the owners were away on campaigns and commercial expeditions, and military retainers—soldiers, sailors, and translators—to accompany them to war and on their annual trading trips in the hinterlands and on the region's frontiers.

In slave-owning states like Aceh, Johor, and Sulu and mainland kingdoms such as Pagan and Ayudha, slaves were reported by travelers, traders, and emissaries to be engaged in every conceivable domestic function and in agricultural and industrial occupations. A genuine "slave mode of production" did not exist in most of these societies because most forms of dependence were at the level of the household rather than being centrally managed. Nevertheless, there are examples of large-scale operations and some notable exceptions such as Sulu, where by the beginning of the nineteenth

century slavery and slave-raiding were fundamental to the state. The Taosug aristocracy relied on both to supply goods for cross-cultural trade and to man the marauding fleets.

Manumission and Resistance. The basic difference between slavery in Southeast Asia and slavery as it was generally understood in the West was the variability of social distance that existed between slave and master. A master was often constrained to feed and clothe his slaves or give them sufficient opportunities to earn a living; otherwise his slaves might demand to be sold. It appears to have been a common practice in the Sulu Sultanate to allow a slave who desired to change masters to do so rather than risk the slave's desertion. Nevertheless, there are also statements of fugitive slaves from different societies and other accounts that present a much less benign view of the master-slave relationship in Southeast Asia. In principle, the master's ownership was usually absolute and her or his authority unbounded. A slave in Perak, Aceh, Ayudha, or Sulu could suffer physical hardship and be put to death by the master; she or he could be sold, bartered, or given away if it served the master's interests. Slaves who repeatedly tried to escape were occasionally put to death, but it was far more common for them to be disposed of to someone outside the culture and society. A master was likely to neglect or mistreat slaves or dependents who were remiss in their duties, but evidence reveals that Southeast Asian slaves, especially those with knowledge and skills, often had good relations with their masters and were not easily distinguished from free retainers.

Manumission was commonly practiced in slave-owning societies with open kinship systems throughout Southeast Asia, and freed slaves were merged into the dominant group, often assuming a new ethnicity and status. For slaves in Muslim Malay societies like Aceh, Johor, or Sulu, conversion or marriage, or both, were prerequisites to manumission. The fact that some ethnic groups—for example, the Bugis—took extreme pride in their cultural heritage slowed the process, since manumission implied going through a process of assimilation. Slaves could also purchase their freedom in precolonial states such as the Sulu Sultanate, and this was frequent among those who had an aptitude for trade. After manumission reciprocal obligations usually continued to bind the former master and slave, although on terms of patron and client. The likelihood of manumission depended on the slave's occupation. Slaves who provided immediate and indispensable services to their masters, serving in their households, business enterprises, or vessels, had better chances of manumission than those who did menial labor in the forests, fields, and fisheries.

For many slaves among the Taosug, Bugis, Malays, Kenyah, Chinese, and others, escape remained their central ambition. Flight was more likely among the newly enslaved and those who shared a sense of community that grew out of common ethnic origins, culture, and experiences. The potential for escape and uprising was always greater among males, particularly those who had been separated from their families, or those who clung to their faith, especially Christianity. Slaves often fled their masters after repeated beatings or broken promises, and small runaway communities appeared in the mountains of Luzon and at the margins of indianized kingdoms such as at Kuta in South Bali, as well as on the fringes of colonial outposts like Zamboanga and Menado.

A study by James Warren (1987) of slave desertions in the Sulu Archipelago, particularly Jolo, the seat of the sultanate, distinguishes between various forms of resistance. Coercive control was difficult to apply in the Sulu system, and one hundred to two hundred slaves fled annually to foreign vessels at Jolo, to the interior of Jolo, to other islands in the archipelago, or to a neighboring colonial garrison. In contrast to the uncertainties of escape to trading vessels, fugitives were assured protection on European warships.

Little is known about the fate of Southeast Asian slaves who actually managed to return to their villages and homes. Records concerning repatriation are rare for most parts of Southeast Asia. Undoubtedly some ex-slaves reached home to find some or all of the family deceased, spouses remarried, and outstanding debts and reciprocal obligations unfulfilled. Many who escaped were left to make a new life, the reality of which was harsher than the one they had fled from.

Future research should take account of both the extension of colonialism and shifts in the international economy that made the slave trade the heart of the political economy of particular states from the sixteenth to the nineteenth century. Not surprisingly, almost nothing is known about where the slaves came from in Southeast Asia, nor about how the trade of the late eighteenth and nineteenth centuries differed from that of earlier centuries. There are also few rounded portraits of life within the interstices of particular slave cultures. By contrast, the final decades of the nineteenth century offer an important field in which to study links between abolition and emancipation, the rise of peasant and plantation forms of monoculture, and forced and contract labor, as a dominant productive system in colonial Southeast Asia.

[*See also* Clientage; Law, *article on* Islamic Law; Occupational Mobility; *and* Slave Trade, *article on* Asia and Oceania.]

BIBLIOGRAPHY

Reid, Anthony, ed. *Slavery, Bondage and Dependency in Southeast Asia*. St Lucia: University of Queensland Press, 1983.

Reid, Anthony. *Southeast Asia in the Age of Commerce 1450–1680*. Vol. 1. New Haven: Yale University Press, 1988.

Steinberg, David J. *In Search of Southeast Asia: A Modern History*. North Sydney: Allen and Unwin, 1987.

Warren, James F. "The Sulu Zone 1768–1898." In *The Dynamics of External Trade, Slavery, and Ethnicity in the Transformation of a Southeast Asian Maritime State*. Singapore: Singapore University Press, 1981.

Warren, James F. *At the Edge of Southeast Asian History*. Quezon City: New Day Press, 1987.

Watson, James L., ed. *Asian and African Systems of Slavery*. Oxford: Basil Blackwell, 1980.

—JAMES F. WARREN

ASIENTO. First introduced in 1595, the *asiento* ("trading contract") was a monopoly contract awarded by Spain to individuals, joint stock companies, or nation-states to supply her colonies in the Americas with African slaves. The contract stipulated the number of slaves or, more accurately, *piezas de Indias* to be delivered annually for a fixed period of time, sometimes up to thirty years. The Spanish did not calculate slaves by individual head; a *pieza de India*, roughly an "Indian piece," was a prime or standard slave against whom others would be measured. Slaves who possessed physical disabilities or who were too old or too young constituted a fraction of a *pieza*.

Prior to 1595 the Spanish awarded licenses to individual traders to supply the colonies with slaves. These licenses determined the number of *piezas* to be delivered at particular ports. Several licenses could be awarded simultaneously. Many licensees failed to deliver their slave cargoes on time or neglected to fulfill the arrangement. The system was also bureaucratically cumbersome and inefficient, producing angry demands for change from dissatisfied colonists.

The monopoly contract or *asiento* system that replaced the licenses survived for almost two centuries, undergoing various vicissitudes of fortune. Prior to awarding the contracts the Spanish authorities invited bids from prospective traders. These entrepreneurs had to convince the authorities that they had the capacity to meet their obligations. The Spanish were particularly suspicious of entrepreneurs or nation-states whose primary interest was not the human commerce, but who wanted a pretext to engage in other forms of trade, such as in silver or manufactured goods. *Asiento* contracts normally restricted the recipients to the slave trade, but this was contravened in practice.

A Spaniard, Pedro Gómez Reynel, won the first *asiento* contract. It allowed him to deliver 4,250 *piezas* annually for nine years. For this privilege Reynel paid nine hundred thousand ducats. The contract permitted Reynel to employ Spanish or Portuguese agents and to sell his slaves in all the colonies except Tierra Firme (the Spanish Main) and Buenos Aires. The crown, however, retained the right to determine the destination of two thousand *piezas* annually. Although Reynel managed to discharge his obligations for a few years, the authorities accused him of smuggling and terminated the contract.

The crown awarded six *asientos* between 1595 and 1640, perhaps the most active period for this institution. In 1601 the Portuguese trader João Rodrigues Coutinho won the contract, obtaining terms similar to those Reynel had accepted. In fact, Portuguese traders won all of the *asiento* contracts for the next several decades. This pattern ended in 1640 when the union between the Spanish and Portuguese crowns was dissolved. Spain reverted to the licensing system, a decision that facilitated an increased penetration of her American empire by foreign interlopers, chiefly the ubiquitous Dutch traders.

The second phase of the *asiento* system began in 1662 when two Genoese traders, Domingo Grillo and Ambrosio Lomelin, won the contract; it proved to be abortive. Meanwhile, the Dutch continued their relentless assault on Spain's monopoly of trade with her colonies, with the connivance of the colonists. Spain awarded a few *asientos* after Grillo and Lomelin's failure, but none succeeded. Caught in the throes of the War of the League of Augsburg, a weakened Spain signed a new contract with the Portuguese Cacheu Company in 1696. The Portuguese crown played an active role in the negotiations, winning from the reluctant Spanish an agreement that permitted Portuguese citizens to trade with Spain's empire.

This agreement inaugurated a new phase in the history of the *asiento,* in which nation-states became officially involved in the contractual negotiations or tried to procure contracts for joint stock companies in which public funds were invested. In 1701 the French Guinea Company won the contract; the English later obtained it as part of the negotiations that led to the Treaty of Utrecht in 1713.

The English crown designated the South Sea Company to fulfill the terms of the agreement.

The *asiento* system saw its demise in the second half of the eighteenth century. Few if any of the awardees had met the terms of their contract, and it contributed to an undermining of Spain's commercial system. *Asentistas* (contracting traders) engaged in other forms of trade with the colonists, often with impunity. Starved for human chattel, the Spanish colonists welcomed interlopers, further weakening Spain's system of monopoly control. But the *asiento* system had also become anachronistic. The age of free trade was at hand, and in 1789 Spain bowed to the inevitable by issuing a decree opening its empire to foreign traders. The *asiento* was one of the casualties of this new policy. Seen entirely from the perspective of the colonists and of the metropolitan country, it had been a protracted failure.

[*See also* Slave Trade, *article on* Trans-Atlantic Trade.]

BIBLIOGRAPHY

Curtin, Philip D. *The Atlantic Slave Trade: A Census*. Madison: University of Wisconsin Press, 1969.

Palmer, Colin. *Human Cargoes: The British Slave Trade to Spanish America, 1700–1739*. Urbana: University of Illinois Press, 1981.

Postma, Johannes. *The Dutch in the Atlantic Slave Trade, 1600–1815*. Cambridge: Cambridge University Press, 1990.

Rawley, James A. *The Transatlantic Slave Trade: A History*. New York: W. W. Norton, 1981.

—COLIN PALMER

BIBLICAL LITERATURE. [*This entry comprises two articles: an overview of the principles and practice of slavery in biblical Israel, and a detailed discussion of the references to slavery and slaves in the Hebrew Scriptures.*]

An Overview

As elsewhere in the ancient world, "slavery" in biblical Israel encompassed a variety of statuses, depending primarily on its source. The principal distinction was between debt slavery of a member of the community, which was in principle of temporary duration, and capture of foreigners in war, which generated permanent slavery. The children of permanent slave women were also permanent slaves (*Ex.* 21.4), but Israelite slave women could be used for breeding only if accorded a status akin to that of a free wife (*Ex.* 21.7–11).

The biblical presentation of slavery is dominated by the cultural consciousness of the slavery of the Israelites themselves in Egypt (*Ex.* 1–12), before their liberation under Moses and the subsequent revelation of the law at Sinai. The first verse of the Ten Commandments reminds the children of Israel that God brought them out from the house of bondage, and the regulation of slavery—specifically, liberation from (debt) slavery—was placed at the beginning of the earliest collection of laws found in the Bible (the "Covenant Code" of *Ex.* 21–23).

Debt slavery could arise by self-sale of the debtor, either to the creditor directly, or—as is widely attested in the ancient Near East—to a "merchant," who paid off the creditor; or it could arise by the debtor's sale of a member of his family, both sons and daughters being mentioned in this context (*Jer.* 34.9–11, *Neh.* 5.2). In the ancient Near East the institution clearly applied also to wives (Laws of Eshnunna sec. 24, Laws of Hammurabi sec. 117). We know from the ancient Near East that the creditor could also take the initiative (Laws of Eshnunna sec. 22–24) by seizing the debtor and holding him pending payment, and this may be contemplated also in *Exodus* 21.2, in the mention of "acquiring" a Hebrew slave.

The Bible imposes a maximum period of six years (*Ex.* 21.2, *Dt.* 15.12) on such debt slavery. Persuading creditors to release debt slaves on the basis of the actual equivalence of their labor for the debt seems to have been a recurrent problem: the Laws of Hammurabi also impose a maximum period (here, three years, sec. 117); and the Bible and other documents of the ancient Near East mention debt amnesties proclaimed from time to time, especially near the beginning of a king's reign. *Deuteronomy* emphasizes the humanitarian aspect of seventh-year release, in requiring not only that it be "free" but also that the former master not send out the debt slave empty-handed and destitute.

In *Exodus* seventh-year release applies to the male Hebrew slave (the *eved ivri*) but is explicitly denied for the female Hebrew slave (the *amah*). *Deuteronomy,* however, speaks of temporary slavery for Hebrew women and insists that seventh-year release applies here too (*Dt.* 15.12). The author reconciled the apparent contradiction in the status of female Hebrew slaves by viewing the case of the *amah* as one where the permanency of slavery was the result of the voluntary act of the slave herself, as in *Exodus* 21.5–6.

The prophet Jeremiah complains that the Israelites failed to observe the law of automatic release of debt slaves after six years. It was necessary in the reign of King Zedekiah (early sixth century BCE) formally to reaffirm that this was an obligation owed by the people as a result of their covenant with God.

Exodus and *Deuteronomy* required the male debt slave on manumission to leave behind any children he had fathered in his master's household, but the law gave him the option to convert his status to permanent slavery if he wanted to remain with his family. In such a case, "His master shall bring him to God: he shall bring him to the door or the door-post, and his master shall pierce his ear with an awl, and the man shall be his slave for life" (*Ex.* 21.6). By contrast, release in the seventh year was automatic and was apparently marked by no formality. The author of the text in *Exodus*, it seems, wished to stress the difference in kind between the two different changes of status that were possible at the end of the sixth year: reversion of the debt slave to freedom was the norm; it was conversion of debt slavery into permanent slavery that was unusual and thus required due signification to the community through a special ceremony. The slave himself became marked: his change of status was so important that it was accompanied by a visible reminder.

By contrast with the *Exodus-Deuteronomy* tradition, the author of *Leviticus* 25 (generally regarded as a later, "priestly" source) objected to the very classification of Hebrew debt slaves as "slaves." Although the debtor could serve, according to *Leviticus* 25:40 "until the year of the Jubilee" (the fiftieth year according to a calendrically fixed cycle, and thus potentially longer than the maximum six years of *Exodus* and *Deuteronomy*), on release he took his children with him. *Leviticus* 25.44 contrasts the position of the Israelite debtor with foreign slaves bought from the surrounding nations: these were "property" and formed part of the master's estate (*Lv.* 25.44). The different statuses of the slave are reflected also in rules regarding injuries. Homicide of a slave made the master liable to blood vengeance (*Ex.* 21.20), but if the slave survived a day or two, there was no vengeance (*Ex.* 21.20). In the case of a debt slave, the master was required to liberate the slave if he inflicted on the slave certain non-fatal injuries, such as destruction of an eye or even knocking out a tooth (*Ex.* 21.26–27); the latter, at least, may be regarded as a statement of the ideal.

BIBLIOGRAPHY

Chirichigno, Gregory C. *Debt-Slavery in Israel and the Ancient Near East*. Sheffield: JSOT Press, 1993.
Daube, David. *The Exodus Pattern in the Bible*. London: Faber and Faber, 1963.
Lemche, Niels P. "The Hebrew Slave." *Vetus Testamentum* 25 (1975): 129–144.
Jackson, Bernard S. "Biblical Laws of Slavery: A Comparative Approach." In *Slavery and Other Forms of Unfree Labour*, edited by L. Archer. London: Routledge, 1988.
Matthews, V. H. "The Anthropology of Slavery in the Covenant Code." In *Theory and Method in Biblical and Cuneiform Law*, edited by B. M. Levinson. Sheffield: Sheffield Academic Press, 1994.
Phillips, Anthony. "The Laws of Slavery: Exodus 21:2–11," *Journal for the Study of the Old Testament* 30 (1984): 51–66.

—BERNARD S. JACKSON

Hebrew Scriptures

There are many references to slaves and slavery in the Hebrew Bible, called the Old Testament in Christian writings. The most important are *Exodus* 21.1–11, *Deuteronomy* 15.12–18, and *Leviticus* 25.12–18. Inasmuch as the Bible is the most exegeted work we have, there are innumerable commentaries on these passages in various kinds of secondary literature.

The most common term for *slave* in the Hebrew Bible is ʿbd for "male slave" and ʿmh for "female slave." The first, ʿbd, is derived from the verbal root ʿbd, meaning "to work" or "to serve." It is related to the same word in both Jewish Aramaic and Christian Aramaic (Syriac), meaning "to do, to make," from which in these languages the terms for "slave," "vassal," and "religious service or worship" are derived. The root gives rise to a rich variety of semantic references, including agricultural work, civil service, and divine liturgy.

In the sense of ordinary work the term refers to labor, tilling the land, or doing civil or military service (e.g., *Gn.* 2.5; 3.23; *Ex.* 5.18, 9; *Dt.* 5.13; *2 Sm.* 9.10; *Is.* 30.24; *Ez.* 29.18.) In the sense of divine service it refers to religious worship (*Ex.* 3.12; *Dt.* 7.16; *2 Kgs.* 19.35; *Jb.* 21.15; *Is.* 19.21). In the sense of slave labor the term signifies service to others or being subject to others, but it does not always imply powerlessness or the juristic concept of property (*Gn.* 29.15, 18, 25; *Ex.* 1.14, 21.2, 6; *Jgs.* 9.28, 38; *Jer.* 34.14; *Mal.* 3.17).

The nominal or substantive derived form ʿbd, "slave," like the verbal root origin, has many nuances, including "servant" (*Gn.* 9.25; *Ex.* 20.10, 21.2; *Lv.* 25.6; *Jb.* 31.13); "political dependent" or "subject," "military person or soldier," and "civil servant" (*Gn.* 26.15, 19; *Ex.* 7.28, 29; *1 Sm.* 17.8, 25.10, 29.3; *1 Kgs.* 11.26; *Is.* 36.9; *Nm.* 22.18); "religious devotees," "ministers," and "angels" (*Ex.* 14.31; *Jos.* 1.1, 2, 7; *Jb.* 1.8, 4.18; *1 Kgs.* 8.23; *Is.* 63.17; *Ez.* 28.25.)

The term equivalent to ʿbd for "female slave or servant" is ʿmh. It appears in the Hebrew Bible much less frequently than ʿabd and has much narrower range of meanings. In most cases it parallels only the uses of ʿabd for "servant" or "slave" (*Gn.* 21.10, 30.3; *2 Sm.* 6.20, 22). It does appear in few places in the form denoting "religious devotee" (*1 Sm.* 1). It does not refer to soldiers or officials. Where ʿmh distinctly differs from ʿbd, it means "concubine," a supplementary meaning applied to conjugal relations of a female servant with her master .

Further details about the uses of the term ʿbd and its innumerable other nuances, including its many other metaphorical uses, can be found elsewhere. We also do not treat here the many verbal derivatives of the term with numerous shades of meanings. However, it is enough to mention that the many uses of ʿbd in biblical Hebrew throw light on the concept, nature, and history of biblical slavery. At best it was a form of servitude, not chattel slavery. Slaves could be sold, bought, given as gift, or inherited; however, the claim expressed by Mendelsohn that "his father's name was never mentioned; he had no genealogy . . . [He is] a piece of property" (in Crim, p. 385) is an exaggeration taken out of context.

Moreover, there is no evidence of the kind we find in neighboring ancient Sumer, where the words *nita-kur*, "male of foreign country," or *munus-kur*, "female of foreign country," were used to denote slaves. No parallel expressions of that type exist in the Hebrew Bible. The closest such expression is ʿebri, "Hebrew," or ʿbd ebri, "Hebrew slave," which refers to the Israelites themselves. Scholars agree that the term "Hebrew" in the Hebrew Bible always stands for Israelite people; but some, not fully convincingly, tend to make *Exodus* 21.1–12, the law concerning Hebrew slaves, an exception. They suggest that "Hebrew" slaves, like the Canaanite slaves, were not themselves necessarily Israelites. They base this on the view that the term *Habiru/Hapiru*, found in certain ancient Semitic and Egyptian documents, might be equivalent to "displaced persons," "foreigners," or "refugees," of whom a small subgroup became "Israelites" after the Exodus and in premonarchic times. This is not a place to argue the validity of a term whose etymology and correct spelling is still a matter of some debate among scholars. However, biblical sources, including the passage referred to here, offer no definitive proof. Moreover, even the "Canaanites," the non-Israelite slaves, were ethnically akin to the Israelites.

Other terms in the Hebrew Bible that can mean "slave" or "servant" are the words *n'ar,* "boy"; *nfs,* "soul", "person"; and *mqnh ksf,* "acquired by money." These, however, appear less frequently.

Unlike Greece and Rome, ancient Israel was not a slave society, and the national economy did not depend on slave labor. Although statistics are lacking, the number of slaves in Israel, based on the few references to slaves and slave-owners, must have been very small. Even the rough estimate of 10 percent given by some scholars seems inflated.

The main sources of slaves in the biblical world appear to be native civil or foreign war captives and self-sale by destitute persons. When a town surrenders to the peaceful approach of the Israelites, "all the people present there shall serve you at forced labor." Should the town not respond to the peaceful approach, "but would join battle with you," the Israelites were to "take as your booty the women, the children, the livestock, and everything in the town—all the spoil" (*Dt.* 20.11–14). However, in biblical Israel war captives were subjected to slavery only when they were not redeemed by the state or by a spouse (*Nm.* 31.7ff; *Dt.* 20.10ff; *1 Kgs.* 20.39.)

No doubt this is a custom the Israelites inherited from their neighbors. According to the Middle Assyrian laws, intertribal and interstate wars produced captives of war who were reduced to slavery. Israelites or Hebrews themselves were victims of such slavery (*Ex.* 21.26). That enslavement of captives was a common practice in the ancient Near East is attested not only in the legal Code of Hammurabi (c. 1700 BCE) but also deduced from linguis-

tic evidence. The earliest words in Sumerian representing male and female slaves were literally translated as "male of a foreign country" and "female of a foreign country." According to scholarly opinion, this indicates that the first slaves in ancient Babylonia were captives of foreign war (Mendelsohn in Crim, p. 383).

The laws pertaining to self-sale had precedents in ancient Egypt (*Ex.* 21.5, 6; *Lv.* 25.39ff). During the great famine that struck Egypt and Canaan, Joseph stored food and grain, which the Egyptians bought with their money and livestock. When neither money nor livestock remained, the Egyptians came to Joseph and begged: "Let us not perish before your eyes, both we and our land. Take us and our land in exchange for bread, and we with our land will be serfs to Pharaoh" (*Gn.* 47.19). Voluntary servitude or serfdom was sometimes chosen over freedom in the face of extreme poverty: "If your kinsman under you continues in straits and must give himself over to you" (*Lv.* 25.39). Children, the father alone, or the entire family might be offered for sale. Occasionally self-sale into slavery occurred when a servant entitled to manumission chose to stay with the master. One reason for such a choice was the desire to remain united with a spouse or children who were to remain in the master's possession (*Ex* 21.5; *Dt.* 15.16). Some scholars think that a servant selected slavery over freedom because of inculcated loyalty, but such loyalty must have been exceptional. Other scholars think that continued economic security might be the real reason for such a decision (Mendelsohn in Crim, p. 384). A combination of these factors must at times have been the reason for choosing to remain a slave. It was obligatory to free self-sale slaves during a year of Jubilee.

It is apparent that in some conditions, slaves were a type of commodity or property bought and exchanged for tangible goods. Except in the case of extreme poverty, an Israelite was forbidden to enslave another Israelite (*Lv.* 25.42). However, the purchase of foreigners was permitted: "Such male and female slaves as you may have—it is from nations round about you that you may acquire male and female slaves. You may also buy them from among the children of aliens resident among you, or from their families that are among you, whom they begot in your land" (*Lv*. 25.43–45).

In this regard, the giving of slaves as a means of reparation or making of amends is mentioned twice in the Hebrew Bible. After King Abimelech of Gerar learns of the true identity of Sarah, not only does he release her, but he also sends gifts to her lawful husband Abraham: "Abimelech took sheep and oxen, *male and female slaves,* and gave them to Abraham; and he restored his wife Sarah to him" (*Gn*. 20.14–16).

There is no proof for the sale of minors into slavery, in spite of the use of the expression *n'ar* ("boy") for "slave." The bestowal of dowry for the marriage of girls should not be confused with such sale (*Ex*. 21.7ff; *Neh*. 5.1ff).

It is not clear whether debt bondage was common. The practice seems to have existed in the biblical world, as in the case heard before the prophet Elisha or the condemned noblemen of *Nehemiah* (*2 Kgs*. 4.1; *Neh*. 5.1–13; cf. *1 Sm*. 22.2). Nonetheless, biblical law strictly forbids taking interest, as well as the sale of a person for insolvency (*Ex*. 22.25; *Lv*. 25.35ff; *Dt*. 23.20f; *Ez*. 18.18ff; *Ps*. 15.5). Historians who suggest that there was a catastrophic increase in debt slavery subsequent to and mitigated by King Josiah's reforms read their own conjectures into biblical text.

That slavery could be a form of punishment for a crime is implied in the story of Joseph in Egypt. Joseph, himself a former slave sold to the Ishmaelites by his own brothers, pictures his youngest brother Benjamin as a thief, a crime punishable by imprisonment and servitude. Although some commentators differ as to whether Joseph was really pursuing revenge or simply testing his brothers, regardless of Joseph's true motivation for treating his brothers in such a manner, slavery is mentioned as a certain means of retaliation.

Finally, although enslaving kidnapped foreigners might have been known, it too is strictly forbid-

den in the Hebrew Bible. The law against it was so strong that it was punishable by death (*Ex*. 21.16; *Dt*. 24.7). Furthermore, there was a law against extradition of fugitive slaves: "You shall not give up to his master a slave who has escaped from his master to you; he shall dwell with you, in your midst, in the place which he shall choose within one of your towns, where it pleases him best; you shall not oppress him" (*Dt*. 23.15, 16). Such laws throw light on the Bible as a highly progressive document for its time.

In the Hebrew Bible, the Torah or the Five Books of Moses represent an ancient legal code. As biblical scholars have noted, the Hebrew Bible affirms the common humanity of the slave and establishes laws to delineate the limits of the master-slave relationship. Extensive descriptions regarding who can be a slave, how slaves should be treated, and the procedures for manumission are included in the biblical code.

Along with the many meanings of the terms for slaves and slavery and an examination of the sources of slavery, the legal status of slaves in the numerous references in the Hebrew Bible reveals various perspectives about slavery. In particular, points of legal status and references to the general treatment of slaves disclose that the slave worked along with the master and was treated as a family member.

Perhaps the most significant biblical law affirming the equal humanity of the slave is the law of capital punishment. Murder is murder, whether it is committed against a free person or a slave (*Ex*. 21.20). In this respect the Hebrew expression of the Masoretic text of the Hebrew Bible that the slave's "vengeance will be avenged" is no less unequivocal than the explicit "death he shall die" of the Samaritan version of the Hebrew Bible. Equally important is the *lex talionis*. This often-misunderstood law of "an eye for an eye" was made as a progressive reaction to the unjust law of the surrounding nations, whereby a slave who wounded or maimed his master was punished by execution. A master who beats and hurts a slave must let him go free (*Ex.* 21.26). There should be no branding or mutilation of a slave except in the case where a freed slave after the Jubilee year knowingly chooses to return to his slave status and voluntarily submits to it.

A slave can have his own business (*1 Sm.* 9.8), be adopted by his master and inherit from him (*Gn.* 15.2ff), and even marry his master's daughter with consent (*1 Chr.* 2.34f). The story of Abraham and his slave girl Hagar (*Gn.* 16.1ff) shows that the practice of masters having slave women to bear children for them and even to be their heirs was regarded as appropriate. In the case of concubinage, the examples of Abraham's maid Hagar and Jacob's maids Zilpah and Bilha in *Genesis* attest that a female slave's status rose after she gave birth to the children of the master.

In spite of the many rights slaves were granted, they remained in a lower social status. For an offense against a slave, compensation went to the owner. For example, "If the ox gores a slave, male or female, he (the owner) shall pay thirty shekels of silver to the master and the ox shall be stoned" (*Ex.* 21.32). Furthermore, the consequences for the offending party would be different depending on whether the victim was free or enslaved: "If a man has carnal relations with a woman who is a slave and has been designated for another man, but has not been redeemed or given her freedom, there shall be an indemnity; they shall not, however, be put to death, since she has not been freed" (*Lv.* 19.20).

Manumission is a very important biblical concept. The Israelites are continually reminded that they had endured slavery in Egypt, but that they were freed by a mighty hand from the land of Egypt, "the house of bondage" (*Dt.* 6.12). The wording varies in different passages, but the emphasis is the same: "The Lord freed you with a mighty hand and rescued you from the house of bondage, from the power of Pharaoh king of Egypt" (*Dt.* 7.8). Thus the Israelites are reminded not only of slavery but also of freedom and redemption.

There are at least five conditions and methods of manumitting a slave in the Hebrew Bible. The comprehensive biblical law has no parallel elsewhere in the ancient world. According to the Code of Hammurabi, a defaulting debtor who has been subjected to slavery must be freed after three years. In the Hebrew Bible, regardless of any unfulfilled debt, after six years of service a slave must be freed (*Ex.* 21. 2–4; *Dt.* 15.12). More importantly, during the year of the Jubilee all slaves must be freed (*Lv.* 25.39–43, 47–55). This law has no parallel elsewhere. A slave who has been injured or maimed by his master must go free (*Ex.* 21.26). A fugitive slave must be freed and granted the right of asylum, not delivered to his master (*Dt.* 23.15, 16). Finally, a slave has the right to acquire freedom through self-purchase (*Lv.* 25.47–54.)

Terms describing manumission, like those describing the treatment of slaves, are specific and detailed. When a slave is to be released, he or she must be given specific provisions. These provisions reflect a fair and compassionate attitude toward slaves. Simply sending forth slaves into freedom or dismissing them from one's household after the designated number of years of service is not enough: "When you set him free, do not let him go empty-handed: Furnish him out of the flock, threshing floor, and vat, with which the Lord your God has blessed you" (*Dt.* 15.13–14). Undoubtedly these gifts not only represented gratitude for the slave's labor and effort but also affirmed the slave's new status as an equally free person. Additionally, the master must not feel regretful or unhappy, since in his six years of service the slave has been worth double the labor of a hired man (*Dt.* 15.18).

A Hebrew slave was manumitted after six years of service. If his wife bore him children during the time of enslavement, she and the children were to remain with the master and the husband left alone. But "if he (the slave) came with a wife, his wife shall leave with him" (*Ex.* 21.3). If, however, the Hebrew had sold himself into slavery because of debt or extreme poverty, "he shall serve with you only until the Jubilee year. Then he and his children with him shall be free of your authority; he shall go back to his family and return to his ancestral holding" (*Lv.* 25.40–41). Moreover, there are specifications that allow manumission to take place earlier than the Jubilee year. For a Hebrew who sold himself to a foreigner, "one of his kinsmen shall redeem him, or his uncle or his uncle's son shall redeem him, or anyone of his family who is of his own flesh shall redeem him; or, if he prospers, he may redeem himself" (*Lv.* 39.48–49). To compensate the master, the purchase price paid for the slave is to be divided by years of expected service; the balance is paid to the owner, and the slave is manumitted (*Lv.* 25.50–52).

When a father sold his daughter as a slave, it was on the condition that after she reached puberty, the master would marry her. When the marriage was consummated, she attained the status of a wife. However, there are three conditions because of which she had to be be freed. "If she proves to be displeasing to her master, who designated her for himself, he must let her be redeemed; he shall not have the right to sell her to outsiders since he broke faith with her" (*Ex.* 21.8). If he had declared that she would become his wife but married another, he was not permitted to withhold from her "her food, her clothing, or her conjugal rights," or she must be freed (*Ex.* 10–11). Finally, if she had been designated for his son, and the latter did not look on her favorably, he "shall deal with her as is the practice with free maidens" (*Ex.* 21.9).

If an owner injured a slave, he was penalized for his actions by having to free the slave. "When a man strikes the eye of his slave, male or female, and destroys it, he shall let him go on account of his eye. If he knocks out the tooth of his slave, male or female, he shall let him go free on account of his tooth" (*Ex.* 25.26–27).

A compassionate commandment concerning manumission pertains to fugitive slaves who are captured: "You shall not turn over to his master a slave who seeks refuge with you from his master. He shall live with you in any place he may choose among the settlements in your midst, wherever

he pleases; you must not mistreat him" (*Dt.* 23.16–17). This is also distinct from many ancient practices regarding the treatment of slaves.

We do not know how extensively the legal provisions, including the emancipation laws and the Jubilee year freedom, and capital punishment for killing a slave, were enforced or practiced. Nonetheless, there is no denying that the Hebrew biblical laws had a theoretically distinctive ethical thrust, different from the ancient Near Eastern laws and other precedents.

The concept of the total abolition of slavery is not propounded in the Hebrew Bible. Some scholars, however, believe that Job might have espoused such an idea when he cried, "Did not He who made me in the womb make him? Did not one fashion us in the womb?" (*Jb.* 31.15). Could this be one "sweeping condemnation of slavery as a cruel and inhuman institution"? Such a view indeed seems to have first been held by a Jewish group, the Essenes. According to Josephus, the Essenes condemned slavery as an unjust system and did not hold slaves.

There are indeed strong anti-slavery sentiments in the Bible. The ancient Israelites were themselves slaves in Egypt, as we know not only from the Hebrew Bible but also from other sources, such as the Nuzi Tablets. This traumatic experience undoubtedly affected deeply the consciousness of the Israelites, and many of their laws revolve around it. It becomes an ever-present theme and motif: "Remember that you were a slave in the land of Egypt and the Lord your God freed you from there with a mighty hand and an outstretched arm"; "Bear in mind that you were slaves in Egypt, and take care to obey these laws"; "Always remember that you were a slave in the land of Egypt and that the Lord your God redeemed you from there; therefore do I enjoin you to observe this commandment" (*Dt.* 5.15, 16.12, 24.22). They built their spring festival of Passover around it (*Ex.* 12; *Dt.* 5.15, 15.15, 24.18; *Jer.* 34.8ff), and the theme of this festival rings down the generations to our own time. The exodus of the slaves from Egypt is regarded as the first slave revolt known from ancient times, and its story influenced American slaves and Christian abolitionists.

The concept of natural slavery, as propounded by Aristotle, is not found in the Hebrew Bible. On the contrary, there is not a single passage in the Hebrew Bible that even remotely implies that a slave is born ethnically, tribally, or racially different from the master. (Throughout this article it is assumed that the term "Hebrew" slave found in the Hebrew Bible refers to Israelites themselves.)

The passage that pro-slavery advocates most frequently quoted as the reason for the enslavement of Africans in the Americas—as people naturally predestined for slavery—is the story of Noah cursing his own grandson Canaan, Ham's son, as a punishment (*Gn.* 9.25–27). Such an interpretation is simply an abuse of the text, far from the original intent of the biblical story and its ethical thrust. What the crime was is not clear from the Hebrew Bible, but various attempts to explain it are found in later Jewish literature (see Isaac in *EB*). The curse, as manifest in later post-biblical Jewish exegesis, was clearly an Israelite political myth directed at their distant relatives, the powerful, seafaring Canaanites, with whom the Israelite peasantry had continual conflict over land-ownership. At any rate, the attribution of the punishment of slavery to the whole family of Ham, the ancestor of Africans according to ancient ethnography, by more recent Jewish, Christian, and Muslim teachers, is not biblical; neither is it supported by the early Jewish rabbinic exegesis in the Midrash or Talmud.

Slaves owned by Israelites, although undoubtedly servile, were never denied the recognition of their humanity. This is marked not only by the laws protecting them but also by the fact that they were required to fulfill the divine commandments given to all Israel. Israelites were commanded to rest on the Sabbath, together with members of their household and possessions: "your son or daughter, your male or female slave, or your cattle, or the stranger who is within your settlements" (*Ex.* 20.8–10, 23.12). That slaves are to keep the Sabbath as a day of rest like their masters is emphasized in the Deuteronomic law, "so that your male and female slave may rest as you do" (*Dt.* 5.13–14).

Slaves are also included in the celebration of the three major festivals and holidays. In regard to Shavuot, the Hebrew Bible directs, "Observe the Feast of Weeks for the Lord your God. . . . You shall rejoice before the Lord your God with your son and daughter, your male and female slave, the Levite in your communities, and the stranger, the fatherless, and the widow in your midst" (*Dt.* 16.10–11); in regard to Sukkot, "You shall hold the Feast of Booths for seven days. You shall rejoice . . . with your son and daughter, your male and female slave, the Levite, the stranger, the fatherless, and the widow in your communities" (*Dt.* 16.14). And for Passover (Pesaḥ), "The Lord said to Moses and Aaron: This is the law of the Passover offering: No foreigner shall eat of it. But any slave a man has bought may eat of it once he has been circumcised" (*Ex.* 12.43–44).

From the story of Abraham we also learn that circumcision applies not only to every one of his free male descendants, but also to his male slaves and each of his children's male slaves as an everlasting sign of divine covenant (*Gn.* 17.11–13). Such a practice would imply that slaves are members of the divine covenant like all Israel, a part of the people of Israel. This view seems to be implied also in the Passover commandment referred to above. Strangers may not share the Passover meal, but a circumcised slave, as a member of the people of Israel, celebrating the freedom from Egyptian bondage, shall participate in it.

The Israelites personalized both slavery and freedom through the ceremony of the Passover: "You shall explain to your son on that day, 'It is because of what the Lord did for me when I went free from Egypt'" (*Ex.* 13.8). Such repetitive reminders of their identity and the bitterness of slavery still did not cause the Israelites to abolish the institution altogether. However, they certainly directed them to be more humane: the people of Israel are told "[You shall] not oppress a stranger, for you know how a stranger feels, having yourselves been strangers in the land of Egypt" (*Ex.* 23.9). Or, "You shall not subvert the rights of the stranger or the fatherless . . . Remember that you were a slave in Egypt and that the Lord . . . redeemed you from there" (*Dt.* 24.17–18). In antiquity there hardly exists a parallel teaching calling for the sense of justice and equity for the slave. Elsewhere, the Israelites are also continually reminded that their own divine master is just and kind: he worked for their manumission from slavery.

The commandment for manumission of a Hebrew slave is based on the metaphor of the divine master who frees the slaves, the people of Israel. Thus, "For they (Hebrew slaves) are My servants, whom I freed from the land of Egypt; they may not give themselves over into servitude. You shall not rule over him ruthlessly; you shall fear your God" (*Lv.* 25.42–43). Furthermore, when a slave offered freedom chooses to remain indentured, the owner is mandated to "take an awl and put it through his ear into the door, and he shall become your slave in perpetuity" (*Ex.* 21.6 and *Dt.* 15.17). According to the ancient *Midrash Haggadol*, this act is performed to indicate the slave's refusing to obey the divine command to serve none but God and choosing a mere human being as his master: "His ear heard God say on Mt. Sinai that Israel is His servant, and must not serve another, and yet this man chooses to remain a bondsman." Moreover, it is done at the door because the door signifies a way out of slavery, and the slave is rejecting an opportunity to go through it (*Ex.* 21.6 *Mishpatim*). This interpretation clearly implies that to remain a slave is a choice, but a wrong and ungodly choice.

What appears to some as the the Hebrew Bible's contradictory attitude toward slaves and slavery is a reflection of the underlying realities the Israelites felt. Slaves are property, yet they celebrate festivals as equals; slavery is a curse, and yet slaves are still divine people; they are taken as war booty, but they are to be treated with compassion; the Israelites were slaves, but they also held slaves. In the last case, contradictions appear even in determining whether the Israelites can own slaves or not: on the one hand, they are allowed to take foreign women and children as captives; on the other hand, they are instructed not to transgress the rights of the stranger.

The problem lies in deciphering a conclusive position on slavery as found in the Hebrew Bible. The best approach might be hermeneutic, drawing aggregate interpretations from different perspectives. On the one hand, slavery is simply a part of the social order of the world of the biblical times, and like many small nations of the time, the Israelites accepted the institution as they found it. On the other hand, as former slaves with bitter experience in Egypt, the Israelites were uncomfortable with the institution. They strongly advocated the humanity and humane treatment of slaves, and they established laws regarding their treatment and manumission. Finally, neither the biblical Israelites nor the later teachers of the Talmud and Midrash considered dogma important, leaving their humane teachings open to misinterpretation and abuse.

It is in this light that we must understand how the Hebrew Bible was used by both abolitionist and pro-slavery movements in the United States. The protagonists and antagonists of American slavery selected the image that best fit their ideology. The abolitionists, members of the Second Great Awakening and adherents of the radical wing of the Protestant Reformation, "inherited the Puritan doctrine of collective accountability and collective judgment," according to James McPherson. Their anti-slavery use of the Hebrew Bible went back to the early 1700s, when it was argued that "casting [slavery] out of doors [would make] the Sons and Daughters of New England . . . more like Jacob and Rachel." (See Samuel Sewall, *The Selling of Joseph.*) Such works as Albert Barnes's *An Inquiry into the Scriptural Views of Slavery* (1846), George B. Cheever's *The Guilt of Slavery and the Crime of Slaveholding* (1860), and numerous sermons used the Bible (both the Hebrew Bible and the New Testament) as their fundamental tool to attack slavery and slaveholding.

It is interesting to note that American rabbis were equally divided in their interpretation of the Hebrew Bible and their attitude toward slavery. Morris Raphall of New York and Southern Reform rabbis like James K. Gutheim were pro-slavery; by contrast, religious traditionalists such as the New York rabbi B. L. Konreuther, and other Northern Reform rabbis like David Einhorn, Bernard Felsenthal, and Gustav Gottheil, were ardent opponents of slavery.

The pro-slavery movement countered that the Bible did not view slaveholding as sin. The Reverend Richard Furman in 1822 held that slavery's "lawfulness is positively stated in the Old Testament . . . (the slaves') respective duties are taught, explicitly, and enforced by eternal Sanctions. By these Rules the former are not directed to claim a Right to Liberation, nor encouraged to use Fraud or Force to effect it; but to be faithful, good, and obedient." The middle, untenable ground was attempted by pre–Civil War Southern ministers who argued that the Hebrew Bible was against "unethical" forms of servitude that treated slaves solely as chattels. They admonished slave-owners not necessarily to free their slaves but to treat them humanely in accordance with the teachings of the Bible.

Each side focused on the biblical images of slavery that best supported their position, while probably aware that their arguments could be refuted by interpretations of yet other passages from the Hebrew Bible. For the slaves themselves, however, the Hebrew Bible was a very potent tool. In spite of the use and abuse of biblical interpretations, what mattered to them were the images of Moses and the victory of the slaves over the Egyptians. Slave songs, stories, and aspirations were ignited by the story of the exodus. In balance, therefore, it is fair to say that the Hebrew Bible had a powerful positive role in the defeat of slavery: the heroes of the Hebrew Bible were role models for African-American slaves and ultimately very important in the struggle to win freedom for them.

BIBLIOGRAPHY

Isaac, Ephraim. "Genesis, Judaism, and the 'Sons of Ham.'" *Slavery and Abolition* 1 (May 1980): 3–17.

Isaac, Ephraim. "Ham." In *Anchor Dictionary of the Bible*, edited by D. N. Freedman, vol. 3, pp. 31–32. New York: Doubleday, 1992.

Josephus, Flavius. *Jewish Antiquities*. Edited by R. Marcus, vol. 18, pp. 18–20. Cambridge, Mass.: Loeb Classical Library, 1961.

Lemche, N. P. "Habiru, Hapiru." In *Anchor Dictionary of the Bible*, edited by D. N. Freedman, vol. 3, pp. 6–10. New York: Doubleday, 1992.

Margalith, M., ed. *Midrash Haggadol*. Vol. 2, *Exodus*. Jerusalem: Mossad Harav Kook, 1953.

Mendelsohn, I. *Slavery in the Ancient Near East: A Comparative Study of Slavery in Babylonia, Assyria, Syria, Palestine, from the Middle of the Third Millennium*. New York: Oxford University Press, 1949.

Mendelsohn, I. "Slavery." In *Interpreters' Dictionary of the Bible*, edited by Keith Crim, vol. 4. Nashville: Abingdon Press, 1976.

Raphall, M. J. *Bible View of Slavery*. 1861.

Westbrook, R. "Biblical and Cuneiform Law Codes." *Revue Biblique* 92 (1985): 247.

—EPHRAIM ISAAC

BLACK CARIBBEANS. Black slavery in the Caribbean was primarily an economic phenomenon, although it had important political and social ramifications. A large, cheap, docile labor force was the ideal the Europeans sought for their sugar, coffee, cocoa, cotton, and other tropical plantations. The sparsity of the indigenous Caribbean populations in most of the islands at the time of the European arrival, and their subsequent decimation by inhuman treatment and epidemic diseases introduced from Europe and Africa, led to a critical shortage of labor for the new European plantations. The geographical location of Africa and the collaboration of the African ruling classes with the European purveyors of the slave trade ensured continuous supply of slaves from that source. Over time the introduction of Africans radically changed the demographic, economic, social, and cultural landscape of the Caribbean. Peoples of African descent today constitute the largest popu-

Engraving depicting Spanish conquistadors attacking and decimating a
native village in the Caribbean, sixteenth century.

lation groups in most of the islands and are significant minorities in the remainder.

The number of slaves introduced into the Caribbean (and the Americas as a whole) during the
four and a half centuries the trade lasted (roughly
the early sixteenth century to the mid-nineteenth)
cannot be determined accurately. Philip Curtin
puts the total New World figure at around nine and
one-half million. He estimates the number of those
introduced into the Caribbean islands at just over
four million, with another half-million introduced
into the Guianas, together amounting to 47.8 percent of the total Atlantic trade. He gives specific
distribution figures for the main territories as follows: Saint Domingue (modern Haiti), 864,300;
Cuba, 702,000; Jamaica, 747,500; Guadeloupe,
290,000; Martinique, 365,800; and Barbados,
387,000. However, these figures are disputed by a
number of scholars, notably Joseph Inikori, who
suggests that the overall estimate needs to be revised upward by 40 to 60 percent.

It is equally difficult to trace precisely the ethnic
origins of the slaves imported into the Caribbean;
however, the main coastal areas from which they
were shipped were the Gold Coast, the bights of
Benin and Biafra, and the region of Congo-Angola.
The best-known ethnic groups in the Caribbean
were the Akan, Fon, Yoruba, and Igbo, along with
the groups from West Central Africa (Loango,
Kakongo, Imbangala, Yaka, and others) commonly
referred to as "Bantu" or "Congolese" in the parlance of the time.

While for most of the slavery period the Africans met the planters' need for a cheap labor force,
they were far from docile. The history of slavery in
the region is punctuated by a large number of

revolts, the Akan gaining the widest reputation for such activities, especially in Jamaica. The most successful revolt was that which occurred in Saint Domingue from 1791 to 1804, culminating in the creation of Haiti, the first independent state in the Caribbean. Other major revolts include those in Antigua (1736), Berbice (1763), Jamaica (1760 and 1831–1832), and Barbados (1816). Equally important in the history of slave resistance in the region were the maroon communities that were established in various territories, including Cuba, Jamaica, Saint Domingue, Santo Domingo (modern Dominican Republic), and Suriname.

The slave system was eventually abolished, first by the slaves themselves in 1804, in the case of Haiti, and later by the British (1834), French and Danish (1848), Dutch (1863), and Spanish (1886). The reasons for abolition are complex and often differ from one European power to another; however, they include changing economic circumstances in Europe and the Caribbean, a new humanitarianism, political pressures from within and outside the region, and slave revolts aimed more frequently than before at the destruction of the entire slave system within a given colony. The post-emancipation period has been an uphill struggle by blacks to rid themselves of the legacies of slavery.

[See also Caribbean Region; Revolts; and Slave Trade, article on Trans-Atlantic Trade.]

BIBLIOGRAPHY

Beckles, Hilary, and Verene Shepherd, eds. *Caribbean Slave Society and Economy: A Student Reader.* Kingston, Jamaica: Ian Randle, 1991.

Curtin, Philip D. *The Atlantic Slave Trade: A Census.* Madison: University of Wisconsin Press, 1969.

Higman, Barry W. *Slave Populations of the British Caribbean, 1807–1834.* Baltimore: Johns Hopkins University Press, 1984.

Inikori, Joseph E., and Stanley L. Engerman, eds. *The Atlantic Slave Trade: Effects on Economies, Societies, and Peoples in Africa, the Americas, and Europe.* Durham: Duke University Press, 1992.

Williams, Eric. *Capitalism and Slavery.* Chapel Hill: University of North Carolina Press, 1944.

—ALVIN O. THOMPSON

BRAZIL. Of all the colonies and nations of the Americas, none was influenced by slavery more profoundly or for a longer period of time than was Brazil. From the mid-sixteenth century until the abolition of the slave trade to Brazil in 1850, about three million (some argue between three and five million) Africans were delivered to its shores, and Brazil had the unenviable distinction of being the last nation in the Western Hemisphere formally to abolish the institution, ending slavery only in 1888. During about three hundred fifty years slavery helped to shape the economy, society, and culture of Brazil.

Portuguese contact with Brazil began in 1500, but no attempt at settlement was initially attempted. Instead, early activities centered on the extraction of dyewood. First contacts with the indigenous inhabitants, especially the Tupi-Guaraní-speaking peoples who predominated on the coast, were organized around barter. Europeans provided trinkets, tools, and weapons in return for Indian labor in the felling and delivery of logs to the coast. By 1533 the Portuguese crown developed a colonization scheme in which private capital and initiative were authorized under royal donations that assigned parts of the coast to certain minor nobles. In some cases, such as in the northeastern captaincy of Pernambuco, sugar plantations or *engenhos* were created. With this new activity, a transformation took place in relations with the Indians. The need for constant agricultural labor conflicted with indigenous concepts of work, and the Portuguese also proved unwilling to meet Indian demands for better compensation, especially since the French were also on the coast bidding for Indian labor. The result was an increasing move toward coercion and the enslavement of Indians as agricultural workers.

By the 1570s sixty mills were producing sugar, and the enslavement of Indians was growing as expeditions swept the interior to bring in new laborers. By this time, however, Jesuit missionaries who had been in the colony since 1549 were opposing the capture of Indians. Royal laws beginning in

1570 prohibited the enslavement of Indians except when captured in a "just war" or under other sanctioned circumstances; although Indian slavery never disappeared fully from the colony and persisted on its northern and southern frontiers, the Portuguese turned increasingly to Africa for labor. Stiff Indian resistance, their high mortality from European diseases, and their apparent low productivity in plantation agriculture all contributed to the Portuguese turn toward African laborers who, while more expensive to obtain, seemed to be more productive, less able to flee, and less susceptible to illness. The first Africans who arrived were often given specialized tasks, and some were already familiar with sugar production through enslavement by the Portuguese on Madeira. The transition of the labor force was not fully achieved until the 1630s, and Indians and Africans often worked together on Brazilian plantations in the late sixteenth and early seventeenth centuries.

The Portuguese had established outposts on the African coast in the fifteenth century and initially drew slaves from the Senegambia region. After 1590 slaves came increasingly from Angola. About seven to eight thousand Africans a year arrived in Portuguese Brazil before 1680, and by that date, the colony had perhaps one hundred fifty thousand slaves concentrated in the sugar-growing areas of the coast. The Dutch, during their occupancy of northeastern Brazil (1630–1654), also supplied roughly twenty-six thousand Africans to the plantations, taking Luanda for a short while and holding El Mina in the Bight of Benin as major ports for the Atlantic slave trade.

The eighteenth century witnessed a great expansion of the Atlantic slave trade to Brazil, especially after the opening of Minas Gerais in the beginning of the century and the development of plantation agriculture in the Amazonian region (Pará and Maranhão) after 1750. Imports of Africans averaged around twenty thousand per year in the eighteenth century and were considerably higher in the second and third decades of the nineteenth century. Demand was so high in the newly opened mining zones that restrictions on supply were imposed by the government in order to ensure a supply of laborers for coastal agricultural zones. In Maranhão a commercial monopoly company controlled the supply of slaves from 1757 to 1777. The Atlantic slave trade reached its height in Brazil in the nineteenth century, when—despite political turmoil and increasing British pressure against the trade—almost a million Africans were landed.

It was a commonplace to say in the seventeenth century, "Without sugar, no Brazil; without slaves, no sugar; without Angola, no slaves." The phrase underlined a basic constant of Brazilian slavery, its dependence on Africa. Although in some places and at some times Brazilian slaves had a positive rate of reproduction (Paraná in the early nineteenth century; perhaps Minas Gerais in the late eighteenth), for the most part they did not, and thus slavery was maintained and expanded only through continual importation from Africa. The imbalanced sex ratios of the trade, favoring males 3:2, exacerbated the low fertility levels of Brazilian slaves. These factors, combined with brutal labor conditions and high mortality (especially among infants) as well as a tendency to favor women in manumission, all contributed to a negative rate of natural growth and continued dependence on Africa. Reliance on the Atlantic slave trade prior to 1850 also meant a continual presence of Africans and the reinforcement of African cultural forms and practices among the slaves in every aspect from language and religion to child-rearing practices. This reinforcement influenced not only slave culture but also Brazilian culture in general, as is evident in its cuisine, language, music, religion, and many other aspects of life.

Although the work of the Brazilian sociologist Gilberto Freyre (*Casa grande e senzala*, 1933) focused on this African contribution to Brazilian culture and brought it to the attention of his compatriots, his presentation implied a certain "mildness" and acceptance in the treatment of slaves and in subsequent race relations. More recent research has concentrated on these issues and raised objections. While it is true that the Catholic Church, Portuguese legal codes, and royal legislation did provide some protection and mitigated the rigors of slavery, there is much evidence of abuse and cruelty associated with slavery in Brazil. Some of this resulted from the whims of sadistic masters, but there is considerable evidence that the basic theory of slave management was to extract the maximum effort and labor from slaves with little concern for maintenance, preservation, or reproduction, and then to purchase replacements for those who became infirm or died. This policy was made possible by the relative effectiveness and low cost of the Atlantic slave trade.

Freyre's work also gave little attention to the slave "community" itself, and much modern research has sought to fill this gap. It is now clear that church-sponsored marriage among Brazilian slaves was rare, and illegitimacy rates often ran at 90 percent of slave births. Nonetheless, slaves formed families and sought to maintain familial ties despite the reality of separation by sale or division of property at the death of the owner. A degree of syncretism developed that allowed the integration of African religious beliefs with Roman Catholicism, and despite active repression, African religions like Yoruba-based Candomblé flourished. Overall, however, slave culture in Brazil seems to demonstrate a fusion of African, European, and occasionally Indian elements rather than the continuation of unchanged African practices. Slave society also imposed hierarchies and divisions that affected the ways in which the slaves saw themselves and their world. Distinctions were made among field hands, house servants, and artisans. The divisions among different African "nations" (ethnicities) were manipulated by slave-owners as a means of control, as were the distinctions between "Africans," *crioulos* (Brazilian-born blacks), and mulattoes. These differences also operated among the slaves themselves in the choice of marriage partners, collaboration in resistance movements, and participation in voluntary associations such as religious brotherhoods. Such distinctions complicated the creation of a slave "community."

How slaves were employed was a key to slavery's nature and its development. The sugar industry absorbed the majority of slaves in the seventeenth century, and by 1710 there were more than five hundred sugar mills operating in the colony. The geography of Brazilian slavery then shifted south and west with the discovery of gold in Minas Gerais in 1695 and subsequent gold strikes in Goiás and Mato Grosso. The gold rush created a great demand for slave labor in all aspects of the economy. By 1800 Minas Gerais alone had a slave population of more than three hundred thousand; even more striking was the fact that the free population of color, freed persons and their descendants, was also growing rapidly, constituting more than one-third of the region's population. Thus by 1800 more than two-thirds of the population of Minas were slaves, ex-slaves, and their descendants. Parallel developments occurred elsewhere in Brazil. Perhaps nowhere else in the Americas, with the possible exception of Puerto Rico, did the free people of color constitute such a large segment of a society's population.

Slaves worked in virtually every occupation in Brazil. On the *engenhos* the majority were field-hands, "slaves of sickle and hoe," but in the technical aspects of sugar-making slaves were used as boilermen, mechanics, and even managers, and they were also employed as household servants. Planters preferred Brazilian-born *crioulos* and mulattoes for the more skilled occupations. Tobacco farms and cattle ranches also made extensive use of slave labor, as did cotton plantations in Maranhão and Pernambuco in the eighteenth and nineteenth centuries. Even subsistence agriculture employed slaves, although in smaller units than found in export crops like sugar. The average size of an *engenho* slave force was eighty to one hundred slaves, and this was also the case on coffee estates prior to the development of very large properties of three to four hundred slaves in Rio de Janeiro and western São Paulo in the late nineteenth century; yet slaves

Drawing showing slaves clearing land on a Brazilian plantation, nineteenth century.

were owned by all segments of the population, and the average holding was probably two or three slaves. Slavery was such a ubiquitous institution that during certain periods of economic expansion even peasants acquired slaves in order to increase production. Owning a slave was a symbol of status as well as an economic investment during most of Brazil's history.

In some segments of the economy, slavery was essential. Gold-mining in Minas Gerais and western central Brazil was distinguished by its heavy use of slave labor, a dependence so marked that the government, faced with contraband and avoidance of taxes, eventually sought in 1735 to control gold production by levying a tax on the number of slaves employed. By the early nineteenth century, when mining was in decline in Minas Gerais, that province still had the largest number of slaves in Brazil, employed in everything from ranching to food production for local and national markets.

Slavery was not limited to the rural areas. By the early nineteenth century slaves were ubiquitous in Brazilian cities, performing a wide range of activities, as cooks and household servants, artisan craftsmen, ambulant street vendors, manual laborers, and stevedores. Rio de Janeiro in 1849 had a population of about two hundred thousand, of whom almost 40 percent were slaves. Similar situations were found in Salvador, Recife, and other large cities. Urban slaves often worked with little supervision as *negros de ganho*, hiring themselves out for service. They sometimes formed themselves into groups or work gangs. These *cantos* were particularly well-organized in Salvador along African ethnic or linguistic lines and controlled the movement of goods within the city. The access of urban slaves to the money economy allowed for some accumulation and fostered manumission by purchase. The presence of slaves on Brazil's city streets caught the attention of many observers, and their participation in a broad range of social activities—such as religious confraternities and public festivals—gave the Brazilian cities a distinctive look and character.

Slaves responded to their situation in a number of ways, accommodating, resisting, or seeking some social space within the constraints of slavery. Slaves in Brazil resisted in a variety of ways. Flight was common, and fugitives often formed small communities or *quilombos* in inaccessible places, raiding nearby plantations and farms and sometimes threatening rural towns. Slave-owning society employed bush captains (*capitães do mato*) to capture fugitives; expeditions usually moved quickly to eliminate the threat of *quilombos* by destroying these communities. Most were relatively short-lived, but there were significant exceptions. While most of these *quilombos* were small, a few reached considerable size. Quilombo Grande, destroyed in Minas Gerais in 1759, had about one thousand inhabitants. Largest of all was Palmares in the mountains of Alagoas. Fighting between the Portuguese and the Dutch in the seventeenth century resulted in many slave runaways and the formation of a series of associated maroon settlements. The so-called "republic" of Palmares lasted for almost a century and was said to have had twenty thousand inhabitants at its height. It was destroyed in 1695 after a heroic defense.

Given the risk and price of repression, large-scale slave rebellions were relatively uncommon. Nevertheless, between 1807 and 1840 slaves in northeastern Brazil, especially in Bahia, mounted a series of rebellions, many of which were organized around African ethnic affiliations. The most serious of these, the Malé revolt of 1835, involved Yoruba Muslims in the city of Salvador.

For many slaves the path from slavery to freedom was entered by manumission. Legal provisions and Catholic tradition made the voluntary freeing of slaves possible, and masters recognized its economic benefits as well. Prior to 1850 perhaps no more than 1 to 2 percent per year were actually manumitted, but the hope of freedom served as both incentive and control. The process favored Brazilian-born slaves and especially mulattoes.

Women were freed at a rate twice that of men. Many manumissions were purchased by the slaves themselves, and about 20 percent of the manumissions were conditional on further service or other obligations. In some periods almost half of the grants were purchased. Manumission provided some hope of freedom, and slaves made great sacrifices to obtain it for themselves and their loved ones, contributing to the growing free population of color in Brazil.

Slavery was still a vigorous institution in Brazil in the mid-nineteenth century, but anti-slavery pressures were building both within the country and outside it. The movement for abolition developed slowly. British pressure had forced Brazilian concessions on abolition of the slave trade in 1831, but despite this pressure, the trade did not effectively end until 1850. This was particularly important in the Brazilian case because of the negative demographic growth rates of Brazilian slave populations. Early attempts to replace slaves with immigrant workers failed because the workers received poor treatment and because European nations imposed restrictions on further immigration. By the 1860s planters in southern Brazil depended on an internal slave trade that moved workers from the declining sugar economy of the northeast to the expanding coffee zones of the south, and by 1880 almost two-thirds of all the slaves in Brazil were concentrated in those zones.

Changes affecting Brazilian slavery were not limited to the situation of the slaves themselves. By the 1860s the national and international contexts were also changing. The service of slaves and freedmen in the war against Paraguay (War of the Triple Alliance, 1864–1870) created new anti-slavery sentiments in Brazil; the U.S. Civil War left Brazil and Cuba as the last slave-owning nations in the hemisphere. The Brazilian monarch, Dom Pedro II, while sympathetic toward abolition, did nothing to upset his traditional political backers, most of whom opposed an end to slavery. New elites, however, were emerging. As fresh plantation zones were opened for coffee, the new planters were less wedded to traditional labor forms and more willing to consider alternatives. Above all, a growing urban middle class and an incipient sector of industrial labor came to view slavery as an atavistic and unproductive system.

The abolitionist movement received considerable impetus from the 1871 Law of Free Birth, which provided that the children born of slave mothers after that date were free. This put the slave-owners on notice about slavery's ultimate end, although the provision that the children so freed had to remain with the master until age twenty-one lessened the immediate impact. A fund set up to purchase the early release of children born after that date was not very effective. Still, the slave population was declining and aging, and the end of the slave system was in sight. In 1872 slaves still made up 70 percent of the plantation labor force, but they were only 20 percent of the total work force and only 16 percent of the Brazilian population.

By the 1880s planters were seeking alternatives to bound labor. In the northeast, sugar-planters began to free their slaves and then to contract them and the large free population of color as tenants, sharecroppers, and wage workers. In the south, Italian immigrants began to appear in large numbers on the coffee plantations. More than one hundred twenty thousand immigrants arrived in São Paulo between 1886 and 1888. These changes were accompanied by a mounting abolitionist crusade carried out in the press and in public meetings, led by people such as the upper-class activist Joaquim Nabuco, the fiery mulatto journalist José do Patrocínio, and the ex-slave lawyer Luiz Gama. After 1885, mass flight by slaves and increasing violence against slave-owners contributed to the final collapse of the system.

It has been argued that abolition eventually came more to relieve Brazil from the problems of slavery than from a wish to emancipate the slaves. Some conservative planters and politicians continued to fight a rearguard action in defense of slavery, but the real debate was over whether former owners would receive compensation. Some prov-

inces (Amazonas, Ceará) moved to abolish slavery in the mid-1880s, stimulating further pressure from the slaves and abolitionists on the national government. Final abolition was decreed without compensation on 13 May 1888. By that time, with slaves constituting only 5 percent of the Brazilian labor force, abolition was in reality simply the formal recognition of a process that was already almost complete. The "Golden Law" was not signed by Dom Pedro II, emperor of Brazil, but by his daughter, Princess Isabel, acting in his name. The monarchy itself fell in the following year.

Slavery's end did not result in a program of land redistribution or other efforts to facilitate the entry of former slaves into the work force of the country. Lacking education, capital, and opportunity, they tended to sink to the bottom of the social ladder. Their dire circumstances were not the product of discriminatory legislation but of discriminatory practices and economic condition.

[See also Abolition and Anti-Slavery, article on Latin America; Confraternities; Emancipation in the Americas; Historiography, article on Latin American and Caribbean Slavery; Maroons; Mining; Slave Trade, article on Trans-Atlantic Trade; and South America.]

BIBLIOGRAPHY

Conrad, Robert. *The Destruction of Brazilian Slavery, 1850–1888*. Berkeley: University of California Press, 1972.

Conrad, Robert. *Children of God's Fire: A Documentary History of Black Slavery in Brazil*. Princeton: Princeton University Press, 1983.

Freyre, Gilberto. *The Masters and the Slaves*. 2d English ed. New York: Knopf, 1956.

Karasch, Mary. *Slave Life in Rio de Janeiro, 1808–1850*. Princeton: Princeton University Press, 1987.

de Queiró Mattoso, Katia M. *To Be a Slave in Brazil*. New Brunswick: Rutgers University Press, 1986.

Schwartz, Stuart B. *Sugar Plantations in the Formation of Brazilian Society: Bahia, 1550–1835*. New York: Cambridge University Press, 1985.

Stein, Stanley. *Vassouras: A Brazilian Coffee County, 1850–1900*. 2d ed. Princeton: Princeton University Press, 1985.

Viotti da Costa, Emilia. *The Brazilian Empire: Myths and Histories*. Chicago: University of Chicago Press, 1985.

—STUART B. SCHWARTZ

CANADA. Canada's historic identification with the Underground Railroad has obscured slavery's earlier existence in the region. Seventeenth-century settlers in New France held native ("Panis") and African bondsmen, even though this slavery lacked legal foundation until 1689, when Louis XIV authorized importing African slaves to stimulate the labor-starved colony's economy. Slavery never became widespread there, however, because the colony failed to develop the kind of large-scale agricultural enterprise that required forced labor in a preindustrial era. Careful scholarship has identified only 3,604 slaves—2,472 Panis and 1,132 Africans—employed mainly as domestics in urban households in Quebec prior to 1759. Along the Atlantic seaboard in the eighteenth century at least 212 Panis and African slaves, mostly domestics, existed on Île Royale (now Cape Breton Island) between 1713 and 1763, and slavery appeared in mainland Nova Scotia soon after Halifax was founded in 1749.

The 1763 peace treaty that ended the French and Indian War, in which England acquired France's eastern North American colonies, left existing slavery intact, but the American Revolution unleashed significant changes. When that conflict ended in 1783, many British loyalists fled from the United States to British North America and the West Indies with their bondsmen. Parliament encouraged the influx with legislation in 1790 permitting free entry for African slaves provided they were retained for one year, and they soon outnumbered Panis in Canada. How many of the several thousand blacks who went to Nova Scotia were slaves is unknown, but most who emigrated to Quebec entered as slaves of fleeing loyalists. The 1784 census counted 304 black slaves in the region that became Lower Canada when Quebec was divided in 1791. In Upper Canada, loyalist families settled along the shores of Lake Ontario with their slaves—three hundred of them in the Niagara region alone by 1791. Arriving loyalists also carried slavery into the St. John River valley, where the province of New Brunswick was created in 1784, and to Isle St. Jean (now Prince Edward Island), where the legislature in 1781, seeking to prevent baptized slaves from claiming freedom, declared that the sacrament did not release them from bondage.

Although slavery expanded momentarily after 1783 in British North America, the American Revolution ultimately undermined the institution in the future Canadian provinces. Coming from areas like New England where slavery was unpopular, some loyalists harbored nascent anti-slavery sentiments. Others found slavery no longer profitable when heavy field-clearance work was done. Moreover, slavery reminded them of the despised republican institutions they had left in the American colonies, and within two decades of arriving the loyalists were restricting slavery in British North America.

Upper Canada led the way after the heartless sale of a young female slave stirred the slavery-hating Lieutenant–Governor John Graves Simcoe to introduce anti-slavery legislation. The 1793 measure ended the importation of slaves, freed the children of slaves at age twenty-five, limited future indentures to nine years, and required those freeing slaves to give bond that they would not become public charges. The law freed no slaves immediately, but it eliminated new recruits from either natural increase or foreign sources, and thereafter slavery declined steadily in Upper Canada.

The courts facilitated slavery's demise in Lower Canada and Nova Scotia. In 1800 Montreal Chief Justice James Monk released an escaped slave, arguing that a 1797 imperial statute that repealed the slave clause of an earlier imperial act in 1732 allowing the sale of slaves to pay estate debts, voided all laws respecting slavery in the province. This decision—a gross distortion of the law because there was no reference to provincial statutes in the 1797 measure—denied Lower Canadian slaveholders legal recourse when slaves sought freedom. Nova Scotian chief justices Andrew Strange and Sampson Salter Blowers, knowing that slavery was legal but unwilling to protect it, delayed decisions on fugitive slaves while encouraging the litigants to sign agreements freeing the slaves after a specified period of service. Failing this, the judges tried cases before juries who often found for the slaves. These resourceful tactics were as effective in hobbling Nova Scotian slavery as Monk's high-handed strategy was in Lower Canada. Even in New Brunswick, where neither legislation nor legal decision impeded slavery, slave-owners were soon paying their slaves and freeing them on limited-term indentures. In 1825 Prince Edward Island repealed the 1781 law preventing slaves from using baptism as a pretext for claiming freedom, although by that time few if any slaves remained in the colony.

These developments virtually ended slavery in British North America by 1820. No more than a handful of bondsmen could have remained when slavery formally ended throughout the empire with the implementation of the British Emancipation Act on 1 August 1834.

BIBLIOGRAPHY

Power, Michael, and Nancy Butler. *Slavery and Freedom in Niagara*. Niagara-on-the-Lake: Niagara Historical Society, 1993.

Riddell, William Renwick. "Slavery in Canada." *Journal of Negro History* 5 (1920): 261–377.

Smith, T. Watson. "The Slave in Canada." *Collections of the Nova Scotia Historical Society* 10 (1899).

Stouffer, Allen P. *The Light of Nature and the Law of God: Antislavery in Ontario, 1833–1877*. Montreal: McGill-Queen's University Press, 1992.

Trudel, Marcel. *L'esclavage Canada français: Histoire et conditions de l'esclavage*. Quebec: Presses Universitaires Laval, 1960.

Winks, Robin W. *The Blacks in Canada: A History*. New Haven: Yale University Press, 1971.

—ALLEN STOUFFER

CAPITALISM AND SLAVERY. Although the title of this essay is the same as that of a famous book by Eric Williams, the two differ greatly in terms of what they identify as their focal problem. Williams defines as his central problem the impact of capitalism on slavery as an economic institu-

tion; by contrast, the central problem addressed in the present article is the contribution of slavery to the development of capitalism. Williams focused on the destructive impact of capitalism on the institution of slavery in the Americas, but he also examined, though to a lesser degree, the contribution of the Atlantic slave trade and African slavery in the Americas to the rise of capitalism as represented by its development in Britain in the eighteenth and nineteenth centuries.

Consistent with the main focus of the work of Williams, scholarly responses since the 1960s have centered largely on the politics of abolition. Studies focused on the contribution of slavery to the development of capitalism are more recent and fewer. There are few detailed studies apart from those on the role of private profits from the slave trade and the employment of slaves in the Americas. This essay examines current evidence and discusses the changing theoretical insights for interpreting the evidence.

Conceptual Issues. Neither Williams nor his critics offer an effective working definition of the central term, capitalism, that would help to focus investigation and analysis of the critical elements of the problem at hand. We may define capitalism as a system of production for market exchange, in which the direct producers separated from the means of production voluntarily sell their labor-power to the owners of capital, whose motivation is profit and the reproduction of capital on an expanded scale. Apart from being consistent with Marx and Weber's identical conceptions, this definition captures the dynamics of the capitalist system precisely and accurately.

Defined in this way, the progress of capitalist development can be measured in terms of the extent of free wage-earners and wage-labor-employing private entrepreneurs in the production process of a national economy. The task for analysis then becomes to explain the circumstances that led to the emergence of free wage labor as the overwhelmingly dominant form of the labor process. The contribution of slavery to the development of capitalism has thus to be assessed in the context of such an analytical schema. The expansion of wage employment implies the creation of jobs, and the creation of jobs means a host of factors, discussed below.

Role of Slavery in the Emergence of the First Capitalist Nation. While writers employing imprecise conceptions of capitalism find it in all sorts of places and time periods, the historical evidence shows clearly that wage-earning workers became the dominant group among the active population of a nation for the first time in history in England in the middle decades of the nineteenth century. Before that time, several parts of western Europe saw the commercialization of socioeconomic life, in which family-based commercial agriculture with self-employed independent producers predominated. Recent demographic analysis from England suggests that as late as 1759, self-employed families still outnumbered wage-earning families there, even in agriculture where capitalist development made most progress before it spread to other sectors. The first capitalist nation in the world was nineteenth-century England, and so this discussion focuses on the contribution of slavery to the rise of capitalism in that place and time. What transformed the economy and society of England by the nineteenth century was the growth of large-scale, mechanized manufacturing, which was totally dependent on wage-earners for its labor.

What was the contribution of the Atlantic slave trade and African slavery in the Americas to the growth of large-scale industrial production in England between 1650 and 1850? In answering this question earlier scholars concentrated on the contribution of private profits from the slave trade and from the employment of slaves in the British Caribbean colonies to the financing of industrial investment. For this reason, historical investigation and analysis were limited to economic relations between England and the Caribbean colonies. More recent writers reject both the emphasis on private profits and the limiting of focus to the

British Caribbean colonies. While conceding that the slave trade and the employment of slaves in the Caribbean were profitable business enterprises, the latter stress that the critical contribution of slavery to the growth of large-scale industrial production in England during the period in question is to be found in the growth of Atlantic commerce, which produced the "Commercial Revolution" of the seventeenth and eighteenth centuries in the Atlantic world. This stimulated the growth of English trade, foreign and domestic, and provided large, rapidly growing markets and vital raw-material sources for English industry; it thereby provided the opportunities and pressures that led to large-scale, mechanized industrial production. The English trading network that expanded between 1650 and 1850 radiated from the Atlantic; the products of African slave labor in the British Caribbean and North American colonies—sugar, tobacco, rice, cotton, and others—were at the center of the trade. Some of England's main trading partners in Europe at the time, Spain and Portugal, were also largely dependent on income generated by the labor of Africans in their American colonies. For this reason, it is not enough to examine slavery in the British Caribbean if we want to have a complete view of the contribution of slavery to the growth of large-scale manufacturing in England. The analysis must be extended to the role of slavery in commodity production for Atlantic commerce in all the Caribbean islands, North America, Spanish America, and Portuguese America (Brazil).

Estimates based on current evidence show that the annual value of Atlantic commerce conducted by western Europe, western Africa, and the Americas was about twenty million pounds (sterling) in the middle decades of the seventeenth century; it rose to forty million in the mid-eighteenth, and one hundred ten million in the last decades of the eighteenth century. These figures do not include the re-export of American products that constituted a large proportion of the trade of England, France, Holland, Spain, and Portugal with other

European countries at the time. In fact, England's exports of manufactures to Portugal depended heavily on Brazilian gold and sugar produced by African slaves; hence those exports fluctuated in exactly the same way that Brazilian exports to Portugal fluctuated. A large part of the English exports to Portugal ended up in Brazil, re-exported from Portugal. To a lesser extent, the same was true of England's exports to Spain. England's re-export of American products to the Baltic helped to pay for imports of vital raw materials, such as high-quality iron and naval materials, from that region.

Demographic evidence makes it possible to estimate the quantitative contribution of African slaves to the production of commodities for Atlantic commerce during the period. The evidence shows that before the nineteenth century, the colonization of the Americas was conducted very largely with forced migrants, the slaves from Africa. They dominated the populations of all the export-producing regions of tropical America. Because land was abundant, the few free migrants from Europe took to self-employment in subsistence agriculture. African slaves, who had no choice, were the forced specialists in large-scale production for Atlantic commerce. Estimates for the export-producing regions of the Americas show that African slaves and their descendants produced about 75 percent of the total value of American products traded in the Atlantic area in the seventeenth and eighteenth centuries.

Other evidence shows that the growth of England's entrepôt trade from 1650 to 1750, based on the re-export of the American products, laid the foundation for the growth of industrial production in the country from 1750 on. It stimulated the growth of urban populations in the trading centers; it led to the development of financial institutions in the port cities, especially London; and it created markets at home and abroad, on the basis of which English industries developed by producing manufactures as substitutes for imports and as re-export-replacing domestic exports. Cotton textiles, the leading industry in the Industrial Revolu-

tion, is a good example, as are several metallurgical industries.

In addition, rapidly growing export of manufactures to the slave-based economies of the Atlantic, especially North America, was the main impetus for the acceleration in the rate of growth of manufacturing output in England in the eighteenth and early nineteenth centuries. As trade statistics show, English manufactures exported to continental Europe were 82.6 percent of the total in the period from 1699 to 1701, and only 12.3 percent went to non-European markets in the Atlantic; by the period from 1772 to 1774, the corresponding proportions were 42.6 percent and 43.4 percent; in 1784–1786 they were 33.8 percent and 45.4 percent; and in 1854–1856 they were 28.9 percent and 41 percent. By contrast, industries producing largely for exports grew considerably faster than those that produced mainly for the domestic market during the period.

Moreover, the growth of employment in commerce and industry, associated with growing exports to the Atlantic world, encouraged peasant families in England to abandon the long-established tradition of tailoring their demographic behavior to access to agricultural land. This gave rise to sustained population growth for the first time in the country's history, based on declining age at marriage and increased incidence of marriage. Thus England's population grew from 5.1 million in 1701 to 16.7 million in 1851. This threefold increase in population contributed immensely to the growth of the domestic market for the products of English industry. It was this enlarged size of the market, and its rapid pace of growth, that made possible the technological innovations of the period, which were critical in the growth of mechanized manufacturing.

Recently discovered evidence and newer analytical frameworks thus make it clear that African slavery in the Americas was a critical factor in the development of capitalism in England between 1650 and 1850. However, there are two main sources of objection to the analysis. One derives from the role of progressive sociopolitical structures that evolved in England from the late medieval period to the sixteenth century. The other is based on a theory of technological development that leads to the argument that technical change in England in the late eighteenth and nineteenth centuries was a matter of chance and was not related to market developments.

The evolution of sociopolitical structures was certainly an important element in the equation, but its role should be seen in relation to the aggressive pursuit of colonies and commerce by the English government. Viewed otherwise, it becomes difficult to explain why countries like Italy and the Netherlands, with similarly progressive social structures at the time, failed to develop industrial capitalism. The social-structure argument becomes even more difficult to sustain in the light of the comparative performance of the English regions during the period. From 1086 to 1650 the most prosperous agricultural and manufacturing English counties were those in the south. Their social structures were also the most progressive. The most backward counties in economic and social development were in the north and the Midlands, especially Lancashire and Yorkshire. Yet the Industrial Revolution occurred in Lancashire, Yorkshire, and the West Midlands rather than in the previously more prosperous southern counties with their progressive socioeconomic structures.

The chance hypothesis of technical change is extremely difficult to demonstrate empirically, and most historians do not support it. It invites a host of awkward questions. For example, why did the technological accident not take place in Italy or France or Holland or China? With special focus on England, why did it not occur in East Anglia or the West Country? Why did it have to occur in Lancashire and Yorkshire, counties that were the most heavily involved in industrial production for export in their respective sectors? It is pertinent to note that, based on the empirical evidence coming from the more recent industrialization processes in Asia and Latin America, economists are now devel-

oping new growth theories that emphasize the role of expanding markets and market size in technological innovation. These new growth theories make it even more difficult to underrate the role of slavery in the rise of English capitalism.

[*See also* Marxism.]

BIBLIOGRAPHY

Inikori, Joseph E. "Africa in World History: The Export Slave Trade from Africa and the Emergence of the Atlantic Economic Order." In *UNESCO General History of Africa*, vol. 5, *Africa from the Sixteenth to the Eighteenth Century*, edited by B. A. Ogot. Berkeley: Heinemann, University of California Press and UNESCO, 1992.

Inikori, Joseph E. "Slavery and Atlantic Commerce, 1650–1800." *American Economic Review* 82 (May 1992): 151–157.

Inikori, Joseph E. *Slavery and the Rise of Capitalism: The 1993 Elsa Goveia Memorial Lecture*. Mona, Jamaica: University of the West Indies, 1993.

Inikori, Joseph E., and Stanley L. Engerman, eds. *The Atlantic Slave Trade: Effects on Economies, Societies, and Peoples in Africa, the Americas, and Europe*. Durham: Duke University Press, 1992.

Solow, Barbara L., ed. *Slavery and the Rise of the Atlantic System*. Cambridge: Cambridge University Press, 1991.

Solow, Barbara L., and Stanley L. Engerman, eds. *British Capitalism and Caribbean Slavery: The Legacy of Eric Williams*. Cambridge: Cambridge University Press, 1987.

Williams, Eric. *Capitalism and Slavery*. Chapel Hill: University of North Carolina Press, 1944.

—JOSEPH INIKORI

CARIBBEAN AGRICULTURE. The use of the labor of enslaved Africans became a part of the strategic economic thinking of European wealth-accumulators in the Americas by the early seventeenth century, as soon as it became clear that indigenous and white servant labor were both numerically inadequate to serve the needs of the expanding agricultural economy. Having conquered the land resources of the indigenous peoples, and with no desire to work this land themselves, Europeans turned to the coerced labor of outsiders to extract returns from the land. The success of the colonization project depended on the export of agricultural commodities to provide raw material and consumer goods for Europe. Sugar, rice, indigo, coffee, cotton, and tobacco were among the crops that provided planters in the Americas with the exportable agricultural commodities they needed. There was no inherent reason why export-led growth had to be associated with slavery. Smallholders in other parts of the world successfully produced cacao, wheat, wool, and rice with the use of free labor. Nevertheless, the Europeans in the Americas believed that plantation crops had production characteristics that gave enslaved labor enormous cost advantages over free labor.

For various military, economic, and political reasons, the enslaved were forced to come to the Americas. When they arrived, they were coerced into doing work that free laborers would not do, in conditions under which free laborers would not work. These factors, as well as the demand for sugar and other plantation crops, caused slaves from Africa to form the bulk of the labor force and slavery to become the dominant mode of production in the Americas. Added to the ample land and the extensive capital investment in the Americas, African labor sparked economic growth.

International Context. Before slavery developed in the Caribbean and the wider Americas, it had long existed around the edges of medieval Europe, in Spain, throughout the Islamic world, in the Byzantine Empire, and in Kievan Russia, as well as anciently in Egypt, Babylonia, Assyria, Greece, Rome, India, China, and Africa. Black slave-labor gangs could be found in some Mediterranean and European economies by the mid-fifteenth century. As long as there was labor to be done that would not be done by members of the family, and as long as surplus production was desired but free labor could not be exploited, coerced outside labor was used.

The labor of enslaved people was utilized in agriculture everywhere that slavery existed, although slaves were not as overwhelmingly concentrated in staple-crop production in the ancient and medieval world and in sections of Africa as

they later were in the Americas. Except for Roman Italy, where the *latifundia* (landed estates) developed as the peasantry was expropriated, plantation slavery was not a feature of the ancient and medieval worlds. In Athens the enslaved worked alongside free laborers to produce a variety of crops on small farms. In Roman Italy, as in Sicily, the *latifundia* were cultivated by slave gangs. Before the development of feudalism in medieval England about 10 percent of the population were slaves, and there was small-scale domestic and artisanal slavery as well as some gang slavery on the large estates. By the tenth century most Europeans countries had ended slavery, although the institution continued to flourish in Spain and Mediterranean areas, where sugar was a significant crop. Slaves also grew sugar cane in the Iberian-controlled Atlantic islands.

In the ancient Islamic world there was no gang slavery, but slaves grew dates and coffee. In Africa slaves cultivated subsistence crops. On the Gold Coast slaves produced kola, palm oil, yams, and cacao; they were involved in peanut production in Senegambia, palm-oil and palm-kernel production in Old Calabar, coffee-growing in Angola, and wine and wheat production in South Africa; in the nineteenth century, in places like Zanzibar and Pemba, slaves cultivated cloves, grain, and coconuts.

The labor of enslaved Africans was deemed essential to agriculture in the Americas, where by the eighteenth century the greatest demand for forced labor came from the agricultural areas. Brazil, between 1580 and 1680 the world's principal producer of sugar, had by 1850 imported about four million enslaved Africans, primarily for work on plantations; these enslaved laborers were also vital to the production of food, cotton, and coffee. In the sugar sector, four-fifths of the laborers were enslaved blacks.

Large-scale slavery in agriculture revived the Spanish-American economies after the end of the mining boom, particularly in eighteenth-century Mexico and Peru. By the 1550s Peru had about three thousand enslaved Africans, mostly in Lima. Africans were used at first in urban Peru, but they later worked on sugar plantations and in vineyards. As the urban population grew, the use of enslaved peoples in agriculture expanded to meet the food needs of the urban population.

Enslaved Africans transformed the economy of the U.S. South, profitably cultivating cotton, rice, indigo, and tobacco. Slavery in the British colonies and the United States they formed existed from 1619 to the end of the Civil War. Enslaved Africans did not immediately form the backbone of the labor force but remained for decades only one of several possible answers to the labor needs of a new colonial society. The early settlements relied on white indentured and free labor, and the staple crop, tobacco, did not require enslaved labor in the way that rice and later cotton would. By the eighteenth century, however, several factors combined to reduce the supply of white servants, resulting in the growth of a largely black agricultural labor force in parts of the United States.

Slave-grown export staples eventually provided 78 percent of British America's commodity exports, bringing prosperity to Virginia, Maryland, South Carolina, Georgia and the lower South. According to the 1850 U.S. census, two million enslaved Africans and their offspring were directly employed in agriculture. Of this number, 350,000 were engaged in the cultivation of tobacco, 150,000 in sugar, 125,000 in rice, 60,000 in hemp, and 1,815,000 in cotton.

Slavery and Agriculture in the Caribbean. Caribbean plantation societies were established in territories formerly occupied and under the control of a heterogeneous indigenous people. Despite their resistance, Europeans subjugated the native groups as a prerequisite for successful colonization, a process that virtually exterminated the indigenous people. By the time staple crops were found on which to base Caribbean economies, indigenous labor had all but disappeared. The decline of indigenous labor and the colonizers' prejudice against manning their own farms and plantations led them to experiment with imported white servants from Europe. By 1750 white servants had been replaced by African slaves. From 1450 to 1888, at least twelve million Africans were captured and shipped to the Americas, with around two million being imported by the British Caribbean.

The period beginning in 1645 and ending in 1886 marked a distinct phase in the development of the Caribbean. It saw the expansion of slavery with the full emergence of the plantation as the basic unit of capitalistic agriculture. A slave-based sugar-plantation regime became the motive force of the region's development.

For most Caribbean colonies, sugar was the most viable export commodity. When the sugar industry started, it was provided with indigenous and European servant labor. Nevertheless, slavery became more closely associated with sugar than with any other agricultural commodity in the Caribbean, although enslaved Africans were also found on nonsugar properties.

Spanish Caribbean. Spain's Caribbean colonies were the earliest to exploit enslaved African labor in agriculture. Slavery had been associated with mining in the early Spanish Caribbean, but the early placer mines were depleted by the end of the sixteenth century. Agriculture then took over as the most important economic activity, with slavery in intimate association with it. The main agricultural crops in the Hispanic Caribbean islands of Cuba, Puerto Rico, and Hispaniola were food crops, cotton, ginger, indigo, cacao, tobacco, and sugar. Sugar was first grown for subsistence purposes, but by the end of the eighteenth century it had become an export crop. By 1860 there were 1,318 sugar mills in Cuba producing about 515,000 metric tons of sugar; by 1895, the number of mills had decreased to 250, while production rose to one million tons.

In Puerto Rico the enslaved population was almost exclusively on the coast where sugar was produced. Slavery played a less important role in the interior, where coffee was the principal crop. Enslaved Africans represented 80 percent of the total work force on the sugar estates of the coastal areas, such as Ponce, by the mid-nineteenth century. The Dominican sugar economy on Hispaniola got a boost during the first Cuban war of independence (1868–1878), which reduced the production of the world's largest sugar producer. Sugar had been profitably produced in Hispaniola in the sixteenth century but had suffered declines thereafter. Cacao and tobacco took over as the important exportable crops in the seventeenth and eighteenth centuries, but by the nineteenth century sugar had re-emerged. The Hispanic Caribbean did not completely abolish slavery until 1886, after all sections of the Americas except Brazil, where slavery ended in 1888.

British Caribbean. By the mid-eighteenth century most of the British Caribbean colonies had become committed to a single economic activity, sugar production for export. In the first half-century or so of settlement, settlers made only modest incomes from food cultivation, tobacco, indigo, cacao, cotton, and livestock farming. From around 1645, beginning in Barbados and spreading to the other territories, Dutch and other external capital and technology, as well as some locally accumulated capital, helped to transform the economies of the region. By 1700 sugar had become the most important and profitable export crop.

Up to the mid-seventeenth century white servants provided a cheaper form of labor for the sugar industry than enslaved laborers. But as the supply of indentured servants eventually failed to keep pace with the labor demands of the sugar industry, the prices of white servants went up; and as more and more slave traders got access to the African coast, Caribbean proprietors gradually shifted to purchasing enslaved Africans. From the mid-seventeenth century to 1834 slavery was inextricably linked with agricultural production in the British Caribbean.

The sugar colonies had a high proportion of the enslaved labor force attached to agricultural units or classified as "praedial" (engaged in agricul-

ture). On the average, about 85 percent of the enslaved worked the land. Of those described as praedial, 74 percent labored in the fields; the rest worked as domestics, tradespeople, supervisors, and wharfworkers.

The occupational distribution of the enslaved labor force is a good indication of the extent to which a colony was dominated by staple-crop production. Of the nineteen British West Indies colonies in the period from 1807 to 1834, only five were not significant sugar producers. British Honduras relied on logwood and mahogany, the Cayman islands on maritime activities such as turtling, the Bahamas on cotton and extractive and maritime industries, Barbuda on livestock, and Anguilla on salt.

By contrast, sugar and its byproducts accounted for 98 percent of exports from Barbados, and sugar occupied 78 percent of the island's enslaved labor force, compared to 11 percent in cotton and 11 percent in the towns. The overall percentage of enslaved Africans in the British Caribbean engaged in sugar ranged from 60 to 90 percent. In St. Kitts, Nevis, Antigua, and Montserrat, few enslaved peoples were occupied other than in sugar cultivation. Other colonies, especially Trinidad, Jamaica, and the British Windward islands, were more diversified, with significant amounts of cotton, ginger, cocoa, coffee, food provisions, arrowroot, indigo, pimento, and cassava being produced; even so, the majority of enslaved Africans were involved in the cultivation of sugar.

In Jamaica, by 1740 sugar had become the dominant export staple. By 1832 the island had 527 sugar estates with 117,670 enslaved Africans. This was in contrast to 176 coffee plantations with 22,562 slaves, fifteen pimento plantations with 1,287 slaves, and 56 livestock farms with 5,529 slaves. Sugar estates employed 49.5 percent of the enslaved population, coffee 14.4 percent, and livestock 12.8 percent, with the remainder distributed among urban centers, jobbing gangs, plantations of minor staples, pimento estates, and the wharves.

French Caribbean. The French colonies of Martinique, Guadeloupe, and Saint Domingue all became sugar producers. By 1789 Saint Domingue had emerged as the most significant sugar-producer in the French Caribbean colonies, and the majority of the enslaved were engaged in agriculture. The switch to sugar, and later the expansion of coffee cultivation, spurred the demand for African slaves as agricultural laborers.

In 1789 Saint Domingue had well over seven thousand plantations: more than three thousand in indigo, two thousand five hundred in coffee, eight hundred in cotton, and more than fifty in cacao. The large plantations had an average of one hundred slaves each. Prior to 1690 Saint Domingue had not one sugar estate; by the mid-eighteenth century it had about eight hundred, and by 1789 it had become the single most important sugar colony in the Americas, surpassing the other French colonies as well as British-held Barbados and Jamaica.

Danish Caribbean. Although significant quantities were produced in the Danish possessions of St. John, St. Thomas, and St. Croix, sugar was not as extensively cultivated as in the British and French Caribbean. Because of its size and geography, St. Croix's economy was more dependent on agriculture than that of the other Danish islands, and the labor of enslaved Africans was used in the production of sugar and other crops. About 26 percent of the population of Charlotte Amalie in St. Thomas, for example, were enslaved.

Dutch and Swedish Caribbean. Dutch colonized the six islands that came to be called the

Cutting the Sugar Cane; painting, William Clark, 1823; West India Committee.

Dutch Antilles, as well as Suriname on the South American coast. Only the latter developed as an agricultural enterprise, the others existing mainly as commercial stations.

In 1784 Sweden came into possession of its only Caribbean colony, St. Barthelemy, an island which used enslaved laborers in domestic service and subsistence agriculture. This colony was later returned to the French.

Distribution of the Slave Population. The numbers of the enslaved work force on an estate varied from territory to territory. For example, in Jamaica around 1832 there were an average of 223 slaves on sugar estates; 128 slaves on coffee plantations, 85.8 slaves on pimento plantations, and 98.7 slaves on livestock farms. In 1832 more than 50 percent of all slave-owners possessed five or fewer slaves, but only 4.3 percent of all slaves lived on the properties of such smallholders. Only 25 percent of slaves lived on properties of fewer than fifty slaves; 25 percent lived on properties with more than 250, and almost 50 percent on those of 150 or more. In the United States in 1860, in contrast, 75 percent of the slaves lived in units of fewer than fifty, and 97 percent of the slave-owners held fewer than fifty slaves (in contrast with 88 percent in Jamaica). Much more than in the United States, then, the typical enslaved person in Jamaica lived on a large estate.

Nature and Organization of Slave Work. The considerable variety in the nature and organization of slave work derived not only from the range of crops under cultivation but also from the sizes of the farms or plantations. On small farms in the United States, the owner worked with the enslaved and supervised them directly. Working relationships were less formalized and regimented; small farms generally lacked an overseer. In the Caribbean, large plantations had white overseers to organize the slaves. Beneath the overseer were the slave-drivers, men who were themselves enslaved but who saw to the everyday running of the plantation. The timing of plantation tasks depended on the vagaries of the weather and the varying hours of daylight, on the health of owners, the enslaved, and their animals, and on agricultural technology.

Among the enslaved plantation labor force in the United States, about half were normally full-time field hands, who were generally young, strong, and healthy. The very young, pregnant and nursing women, the old, and the disabled were classified as less than a full field hand. Both the gang and task systems were used, though on rice plantations the task system was preferred. In some cases this left the enslaved with time to engage in their own agricultural activities. In the Caribbean sugar estates the enslaved worked under the gang system and were assigned tasks on the basis of age, color, gender, skill, birthplace, and health. Females were disproportionately located in the fields, while males were more frequently in skilled and supervisory positions. Women outnumbered men in most field gangs; for instance, on plantation Beaulieu in the French Antilles, there were 141 slaves in 1768, of whom eighty-seven were male and fifty-four female, but only nine males worked in the fields as opposed to twenty women. The men seemed to have been employed primarily in nonfield occupations. There were no differences, however, in the type of field work given to men and women. Women were involved in all the arduous tasks of field and factory. Age and health determined which men and women were placed in which field gangs; skin color determined which men and women worked as domestics and which men worked as artisans; birthplace was a factor in the allocation of domestic work, creoles being preferred to Africans.

Field laborers had the most physically demanding tasks. There were usually three or four field gangs on a sugar estate. In the French Antilles there might be as many as four gangs (called *ateliers*), though three was the norm. The first gang, comprised of the strongest men and women, prepared the soil, dug cane holes, planted and manured the canes, cut canes at harvest time, and performed manual labor in the mills during crop time. The gang laborers used simple agricultural tools such as hand-held bills and hoes; the plow was rare. On coffee and cotton plantations, and on pens (livestock farms) with one hundred or more enslaved workers, the gang system was also used. On the smaller agricultural units producing cocoa and provisions and on small pens, slaves had less clearly defined hierarchies within the field labor force. On coffee estates the first gang planted and picked the coffee; the men in this gang cut and cleared trees and extracted rocks, led by a male slave-driver or *commandeur.*

The second gang, containing males and females who were less robust, included newly arrived slaves and women who were pregnant or nursing. They performed lighter and more varied tasks, including molding, weeding, and gathering cane trash. On some islands this gang planted food crops for the estate's slaves. They carried manure to the cane fields. During crop time they worked in the field, removing trash for use as fuel. At the sugar factory they carried crushed cane stalks to the trash house, dried them, and took them to the furnaces. On some estates weeding was the job of women in the second gang. This second gang was also under the direction of *commandeurs.*

The third gang, consisting chiefly of children aged eight to thirteen and led by an old woman, gathered grass for estate livestock and was thus at times called the grass or hogmeat gang. More individualized field-related tasks included carrying water to the field laborers, cooking their food, and minding their children. Where there was a fourth gang, this was also made up of the very old and the young, who did light tasks.

Sugar cultivation required arduous labor. During crop time the enslaved had to work from eighteen to twenty-four hours on shifts, carrying out the tasks of cutting, hauling, grinding, clarification, filtration, evaporation, and crystallization without interruption. In the French West Indies, for the essential night shift during crop time, the enslaved recruited from the first *atelier* were divided into four sections, the first two working from six a.m. until midnight, and the other two from

midnight until six the next morning. The enslaved on the two shifts alternated. This kind of twenty-four-hour schedule lasted throughout the five or six months of reaping and grinding. In the basic cycle of husbandry, cane was usually planted in the fall, and sometimes also in the spring. It came to maturity after about sixteen months, to be cut down between January and May or June. Then the stumps remaining might either be dug up and the field replanted, or they were ratooned (left to send up new shoots for harvesting the next year). Replanting entailed extra work, so its frequency was dictated in part by the state of the labor supply and in part by soil conditions. Doing night work did not relieve the bondsmen and women from regular labor the next day. The enslaved normally had to turn up for work at five or six in the morning, finishing about 6:30 in the evening.

Until 1807, in the British West Indies the enslaved worked according to set hours per day. After 1807 task work was more usual, with specific tasks measured in terms of distance, area, or volume. Planters believed that task work increased productivity and lowered costs of supervision; it was more suitable where the work could be quantified. Task work was used first in the marginal colonies.

Slavery and Agriculture on Nonsugar Properties. It is clear that slavery was not incompatible with small-scale subsistence agriculture nor with an agricultural regime based on the raising of livestock, logwood, and other commodities. Jamaica provides a clear example of a colony in which subsistence farming assisted by slave labor worked both socially and economically from the seventeenth century. This English colony was not as monocultural as the classic plantation colonies of the eastern Caribbean. Bondsmen and women were used in the cultivation of cotton, tobacco, coffee, and food crops; they raised livestock on pens and exploited logwood and other dyewoods.

The character of slavery was different on nonsugar properties, and striking contrasts were evident between the rural regimes of the two. As in the sugar colonies, the majority of the enslaved in

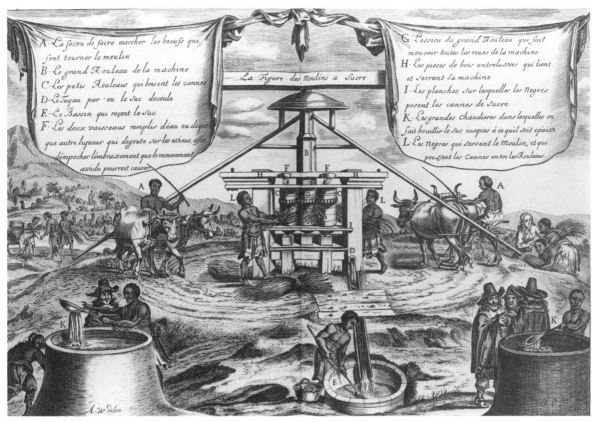

Engraving depicting African slaves laboring at an outdoor sugar mill
in the Caribbean; France, seventeenth century.

nonsugar areas were assigned to field labor. Those not in the field were employed as skilled tradespeople, domestics, slave-watchmen, and in other capacities. Sugar estates had more laborers who were skilled tradespeople than did the other agricultural properties. They also had more bondspeople who served as nurses and watchmen. Males were less often employed in the field on sugar estates than on other units, and females more often in the former.

The slave regime was less regimented on nonsugar properties, though the work was no less hard. Gang labor was less marked on nonsugar properties like pens, where tasks were more individualized. Many of the enslaved on nonsugar properties worked unsupervised. In fact, those on pens often had one white resident, who at times left the property in the care of the black male driver.

On Caribbean nonsugar properties the enslaved tended to live in smaller units. In the Bahamas, not characterized by the sugar plantation, most slaves lived in small units. The factors determining how enslaved labor was used on nonsugar properties seemed similar to those on the sugar estates. Gender was an important determinant in all occupations except field work, where age and color were more important.

Supportive Nonagricultural Activities. Although some of the enslaved were not directly engaged in agriculture, their work supported it. Artisans (called *nègres-à-talent* in the French Caribbean) were needed on the sugar plantations to work as coopers, carpenters, masons, wheelwrights, loggers, and penkeepers. Artisans were male; they made or repaired plantation buildings and equipment, guarded plantation animals, and built plantation houses. There were enslaved people who were full-time or part-time domestics, craftsmen, couriers, and sickhouse attendants. Skilled artisans, often male, were important figures in the enslaved community and on the plantations.

Slaves and Their Own Agriculture. Enslaved Africans and creoles not only worked agricultural estates for their owners; in most slave societies in the Americas bondsmen and women were involved in agriculture on their own account. In most Caribbean colonies, regardless of imperial power, the enslaved were allotted small pieces of land (called grounds or gardens) for customary use. Where the system of rationed allowances was not the dominant mode of providing laborers with food, the provision-ground system assumed great importance. Enslaved workers grew their own food on such plots and developed agricultural skills by tending them. Those who produced surpluses engaged in an internal marketing system. The size of grounds varied, but except in St. Kitts, Nevis, Barbados, Antigua, and Guyana, planters provided the enslaved with land on which they planted a variety of food crops such as plantains, corn, bananas, cassava, eddoes, and potatoes. Kitchen gardens were kept by most of the enslaved, even in islands where there were no individual provision grounds. The aim of allowing the enslaved the customary use of marginal estate lands for cultivating food was not a benevolent gesture on the part of slaveowners, but a way to get bondspeople to provide their own food and save the owners the cost of imported food. In the Caribbean the system of provision grounds diluted white power, because the slave-owners could not use food as a means of control as they did in sections of the U.S. South where slave provisioning was by means of rationed allowance. Enslaved people, conscious of the value of their labor power, engaged in protest action to prevent masters and mistresses from reducing their access to grounds or limiting their marketing activities.

The internal organization of the provision ground was left up to the slaves. Planters sometimes subdivided the grounds and allocated them to individuals; but beyond this, they took no interest apart from making occasional inspection. Grounds were worked by enslaved family groups or individuals. Those too old to work their plots got help from friends and relatives.

Control and Revolt. Freedpersons would not voluntarily undertake the type of work and regimentation required of slaves, no matter what the material incentive offered. Slave-based agriculture was efficient and profitable for many planters, especially when there also existed a favorable climate and demand for the various crops. The profitability of slave-based agriculture caused proprietors to use rewards and incentives as well as threatened or actual punishment to maintain slavery and keep slaves working. Incentives, though present, were secondary to the coercive measures of control. The two basic conditions that set the pattern of slave control were punishment and the generally poor prospects for successful and permanent escape. Bondspeople worked productively, efficiently, and hard; but they resented at the same time the conditions of their enslavement. Consequently, despite the elaborate control mechanisms, enslaved people all over the Americas used a variety of strategies to resist slavery and struggle for its demise. Enslaved people in Saint Domingue successfully revolted against slavery and took their freedom by revolutionary means after 1791. Emancipation came later for the rest of the Americas. Slavery ended in the British Caribbean in 1834, in the other French Caribbean colonies and the Danish colonies in 1848, and in the Dutch Caribbean in 1863. The United States did not abolish slavery completely until after the Civil War. Slaves in the Spanish Caribbean were freed between 1870 and 1886, and in Brazil slavery ended in 1888.

[*See also* Caribbean Region; *and* Caribbean Race Relations.]

BIBLIOGRAPHY

Beckles, Hilary, and Verene Shepherd. *Caribbean Slave Society and Economy: A Student Reader.* Kingston, Jamaica: Ian Randle, 1994.

Fick, Carolyn. *The Making of Haiti: The San Domingue Revolution from Below.* Knoxville: University of Tennessee Press, 1992.

Higman, Barry W. *Slave Population and Economy in Jamaica, 1807–1834.* Cambridge: Cambridge University Press, 1976.

Higman, Barry, W. *Slave Populations of the British Caribbean, 1807–1834.* Baltimore: Johns Hopkins University Press, 1984.

Klein, Herbert. *African Slavery in Latin America and the Caribbean.* New York and Oxford: Oxford University Press, 1986.

Morrissey, Marrietta. *Slave Women in the New World: Gender Stratification in the Caribbean.* Lawrence: University Press of Kansas, 1989.

Parrish, Peter, J. *Slavery, History and Historians.* New York: Harper and Row, 1989.

Shepherd, Verene, et al. *Engendering History: Caribbean Women in Historical Perspective.* Kingston, Jamaica: Ian Randle, 1995.

Solow, Barbara, ed. *Slavery and the Rise of the Atlantic System.* Cambridge: Cambridge University Press, 1991.

—VERENE A. SHEPHERD

CARIBBEAN RACE RELATIONS. Throughout the Caribbean the end of slavery, achieved after a long ordeal lasting from the 1790s (Haiti) to the 1880s (Cuba), left the region's societies deeply divided. Slavery had played a role of widely varying significance in the different islands and mainland colonies, and the effects of its abolition were far from uniform or predictable. Nonetheless, with few exceptions Caribbean societies were largely shaped in the post-abolition era by the legacy of the slave system.

In the classic slave and plantation societies, the large-scale production of export staples had dominated economic life, and the enslavement of Africans had been established as the main system of labor organization since the seventeenth or eighteenth century. Here Africans and their locally born descendants formed the overwhelming majority of the population, and economic resources were concentrated (though never exclusively) in the hands of a few white capitalist landowners. These societies, including all the larger British and French island colonies and the mainland colonies of Suriname and the Guianas, inherited from the slave system a fairly simple three-tiered racial and social structure.

At the top of this structure were the white elites, groups of families that controlled a large proportion of the economic resources, especially land, and dominated the formal and informal political institutions. Except in Haiti, they were predominantly of European descent, and often the descendants of former slave-owners. It should be pointed out, however, that some whites in these territories were far from affluent and not a part of the economic elite. Nevertheless, these "middling whites" (as opposed to the "poor whites" who formed small but distinct communities in a few islands) shared with their more prosperous fellows a social status superior to that of the mixed-race middle stratum. Conversely, there were a few mixed-race landowners (often former slave-owners) in most of these territories; despite their status as planters and employers, they often encountered discrimination and prejudice based on their ethnicity from resident whites. Thus the three-tier model, though broadly descriptive of the former slave societies, must be applied with respect for the unique features of each Caribbean society.

The second or middle tier consisted mainly of mixed-race people descended from unions between white men and African women. Before the end of slavery these "free coloreds" (always including some free blacks who were wholly or predominantly of African descent but were legally free) had faced severe discrimination of different kinds. In spite of this, their legal status as free people, their access to education and literacy, and their ability to carve out certain occupational niches (especially artisanal trades and small-scale commerce) gave them important advantages over the African masses freed by legislative enactments in the 1830s

(Britain), 1840s (France and Denmark) and 1860s (Holland).

The third or lowest tier comprised the ex-slaves and their descendants, the great majority of the population. Entering free society with all the massive disadvantages flowing from two centuries of enslavement, the ex-slaves found their opportunities for economic, social, and cultural improvement harshly limited and always problematic—but nowhere entirely absent.

In the second half of the eighteenth century the largest and most productive Caribbean slave society had been French Saint Domingue, where the three-tier structure was perhaps best exemplified. The upheavals that took place between 1791 and 1804 shattered that structure, and the new state of Haiti entered independent existence with a racial and social configuration very different from the other classic ex-slave societies. In effect, the white elite (the upper tier) was eliminated through war and emigration, and post-slavery Haiti was a two-tier society consisting of a small elite and the rural masses of slave descent. Haiti's elite consisted mainly of mixed-race people, the *anciens libres* (former free coloreds) and their descendants, but it also included some blacks who had emerged from the masses during the wars of liberation, or under the black rulers Dessalines and Christophe (1804–1819), or after 1820 through service in the army. Race relations in nineteenth-century Haiti revolved around struggles between a small, mainly mixed-race, Francophile elite and the African peasant majority.

In Haiti, as in nearly all the British, French, Dutch, and Danish colonies, most of the people at the time slavery ended were of African descent. In the Hispanic Caribbean, however, slavery had never dominated economic and social relations to the same extent. In the Dominican Republic, slavery—permanently abolished in 1822—was never of great importance. In Puerto Rico, though slavery was critical to the sugar industry in the first half of the nineteenth century, slaves were always a relatively small group in the population as a whole, and there was large-scale white immigration all through the century. Puerto Rico had a large mixed-race free population as well as a numerous white peasantry living in the highland interior. The *libertos*, the ex-slaves freed in the 1870s, were a relatively small group who interacted fairly easily with the free white and mixed-race agricultural laborers, estate tenants, and independent peasants. In general, Puerto Rico escaped the rigid racial divisions generated by the slave system; this was also the case in the Dominican Republic, where most people were of mixed race (Spanish-African-Amerindian) but regarded themselves as white, and where persons of predominantly African descent constituted a small minority. In both these Hispanic societies, therefore, blacks were relatively few, while the great majority of the people were either of mixed race, or "white," with considerable fluidity between the two categories.

Cuba presents us with a different pattern. Here massive slave imports from the late eighteenth century and the explosive growth of the sugar industry changed the social and racial configuration profoundly. Cuba became a slave society, with a nonwhite majority by the 1850s, burdened with the racial and caste divisions typical of such a society. At the same time, however, Cuba—like Puerto Rico and the Dominican Republic—had a large white peasantry outside the sugar-growing areas. Moreover, massive immigration from Spain—which, far from ending with the fall of Spanish rule in 1898, actually increased tremendously in the decades between 1898 and 1930—had the effect of "whitening" Cuba's population in this period. Postabolition Cuba was an ex-slave society, but one in which blacks formed a minority of the whole population, and a decreasing minority at that. By 1912 just under 30 percent of Cuba's people were officially classified as black or colored (mixed-race). European immigration to Cuba was encouraged in part precisely to achieve this whitening effect and hence to marginalize Afro-Cubans, whose low social status and political impotence were highlighted in the tragic "war of the races" in 1912.

It would be wrong to study race relations in the post-abolition Caribbean solely with reference to slavery and its legacies, fundamental though these were. Many other variables helped to shape the racial system, notably geographical and environmental factors, the different policies and colonial traditions of the imperial powers, and international economic forces. Moreover, post-abolition developments led to significant differences in the racial composition of the Caribbean territories. Large-scale contract labor immigration to the region, a direct consequence of the end of slavery, established important communities of Asians in several countries. In three territories, Suriname, Guyana, and Trinidad, immigrants from India (and Indonesia in the case of Suriname) and their descendants constituted by 1917 between 30 and 40 percent of the total populations. In Martinique, Guadeloupe, Jamaica, and a few smaller British islands, Indians were present in smaller but still significant proportions. Chinese immigrants, never numerous except in nineteenth-century Cuba, also came to play a highly visible economic role in many territories. By 1920, moreover, immigrants from Syria and Lebanon had established numerically minute but remarkably prosperous communities of traders and retailers in many places. Finally, aboriginal people of the region still existed as a significant minority group in Guyana, Cayenne (French Guiana), Suriname, and Belize, and in Dominica and St. Vincent among the islands. Race relations in the post-abolition Caribbean involved, for the most part, the descendants of Africans and of Europeans (and their mixed-race progeny), but people of other origins were also part of the pattern.

The end of formal slavery presented a challenge to the traditional white elites in colonies where it had been the basis of the social organization. To maintain their hegemony over society, ideological weapons were important. Social distance could be preserved, and hegemony could be reasserted, through a profoundly racist conviction of the superiority of Europeans and their civilization, and the irremediable inferiority of Africans and their culture. Directly related to that conviction was an obsession with skin color and phenotype and with racial "purity" (defined as the absence of any acknowledged African ancestor) as the key index of elite status. This was the legacy of slave society. In the classic former-slave societies, where the elites were overwhelmingly of European descent, the middle strata mainly of mixed race, and the masses of African origin, racism directed against black and mixed-race people, and preoccupation with skin color, were especially salient as elite strategies for social control. This was less marked in the Hispanic Caribbean, but it was by no means absent there, even in the Dominican Republic and Puerto Rico where African slavery had been of far less significance.

Post-emancipation society in the British, French, Dutch, and Danish colonies rested on racism and sensitivity to skin color and phenotype, even though no formal apartheid system existed and in law all were equal. Elite whites felt little compunction about the public expression of their views. In 1900, for instance, a Jamaican member of the island legislature attacked a black candidate, Robert Love, in these terms: "Dr Love must remember that his ancestors were my ancestors' slaves, and as such he could never be my equal. He is aggrieved because my forefathers rescued him from the bonds of thraldom and deprived him of the privilege of being King of Congo, enjoying the conjugal orgies and the sacrificial pleasures of his ancestral home in Africa." A governor of Trinidad in 1869, describing mixed-race Trinidadians as "this strange class," told his superior in London, "impulsive, fickle, and profoundly treacherous in all social relations, it is impossible to trust them."

In general, resident whites maintained a marked social aloofness both from the mixed-race middle stratum and the black masses. Their private life was a closed world; exclusive clubs were established everywhere, and much of white social life was conducted within them and in family gatherings. Interaction with nonwhites was confined to stereotyped relationships in which social distance and superiority and inferiority were clearly demarcated: planter and laborer, mistress and servant, magistrate and offender. The creole whites in particular showed great sensitivity to social relations with black and mixed-race persons; they felt even more acutely than European immigrants the need to maintain distance and to preserve and prove their racial purity, and they had imbibed racist ideas since infancy. Most white immigrants soon adjusted, whatever their liberal intentions, and few ever broke out of the white enclave. As well as racism, there was fear of the masses and their potential for revenge; the Haitian bloodbath was never far from the minds of creole whites in the nineteenth century.

These attitudes lay behind the informal and extralegal yet institutionalized discrimination against nonwhites that existed everywhere well into the mid-twentieth century, despite the absence of official segregation. It was especially strong, among the British territories, in the Bahamas and in Barbados, where a relatively large, long-established and cohesive creole white elite had built up an almost total grip over economic, social, and political life in each colony. W. G. Sewell, an American journalist who visited around 1860, commented, "Distinctions of caste are more strictly observed in Barbados than any other British West India colony. No person, male or female, with the slightest taint of African blood, is admitted to white society. . . . The lineage of every person in the island is known, and remote descent from an African ancestor makes some unhappy creature a pariah from the little world of Barbados." Here and in the Bahamas, exclusion of black and mixed-race persons from clubs, restaurants, hotels, cinemas, and the like was routinely practiced up to the 1950s. Barbados and the Bahamas probably most closely approximated the southern United States' pattern of race relations with rigid (though extralegal) segregation and weakly developed mixed-race middle strata. Dis-

crimination was found everywhere in the British Caribbean, though, in social life but also in the civil service, businesses, banks, schools, and churches. It was especially galling to upwardly mobile, educated nonwhites.

In the French Caribbean islands, too, whites responded to the end of slavery by maintaining social exclusiveness and racial solidarity. One observer noted that Guadeloupe whites in the 1880s refused to go to official functions because they might have to meet "a family of mulattoes or negroes." The women of these often impoverished creole white families might support themselves by making sweets or cakes to be sold by black street vendors, but they would scornfully reject "the honest offers of a colored man in a very enviable situation." Another writer was struck by the refusal of most white creoles in Martinique to send their children to the new government *lycées* established after 1880, despite their evident superiority, because they were racially mixed. These children went to ecclesiastical schools because the Catholic Church "recognizes race-feelings, keeps her schools unmixed, and even in her convents, it is said, obliges the colored nuns to serve the whites."

In the Hispanic Caribbean, where blacks were a minority of the population, racism, preoccupation with skin color, and obsessions about mixing with nonwhites were on the whole less salient. Nevertheless, Cuban whites showed much the same kind of concern about racial purity. The traditional Spanish concept of "purity of blood"—which in Spain had referred to the absence of Jewish or Moorish ancestry—was of great importance in nineteenth-century Cuba in the sense of absence of any African ancestors. To maintain status, white families were anxious to avoid legitimate marriage alliances with those who had known African ancestors. The white Cuban was not so much prejudiced against a particular physical appearance as against "impurity." A *pardo* (mixed-race person) might look white, but as the child of at least one parent whose baptism had been registered in the *pardo* register, he was unacceptable as a marriage partner for a girl from a "pure" family. Conversely, a person of brown complexion who was the child of two parents registered as white (of pure blood) might be perfectly acceptable. Legal color (impurity) signified the taint of slave origins; its absence was symbolized by a family's purity of blood and, consequently, its "honor" in a multiracial hierarchical society where slavery existed up to the 1880s.

Even in the Dominican Republic, where slavery had not been of great importance and where most people were racially mixed, whiteness, or at least a light complexion, remained the social ideal. Contempt for the darker-skinned was far from absent in the national political discourse in the nineteenth century; it was, for example, directed against the dictator Hereaux, who was of part-Haitian descent. Moreover, racism probably increased with large-scale white immigration after about 1870, including that of white Cubans. Blatant racism was evident in the elite reaction to labor immigration from Haiti and the British West Indies after 1880 to serve the expanding sugar plantations. There was anxiety about the threat of "africanization" as a danger not only to the country's white or mulatto ideal but also to its Hispanic-American culture. "This is an immigration which is not needed," wrote a Dominican minister in 1912 of the British West Indians, "because of its inferior race." Dominican race consciousness was also tied up with hostility to Haiti; national identity was defined in opposition to Haitian characteristics as Hispanic, white or fair-skinned, and anti-African. Both racism and concern by the light-complexioned to maintain their distance from the darker-skinned probably increased by the early years of the twentieth century, though neither could be as rigid as elsewhere in the Caribbean given the extensive *mulatizacion* (race-mixing) that had already occurred.

Inevitably, racist attitudes and practices were not confined to members of the white elites in the post-emancipation Caribbean. Upwardly mobile mixed-race persons from the middle stratum typically shared many of these attitudes and often tried to maintain as much social distance as possible from the darker-skinned. In the British, French, Dutch, and Danish colonies, possession of a light complexion and European-type features was a distinct advantage for members of the middle stratum. Other factors were also important for upward mobility—income, occupation, education, and command of European culture—but phenotype smoothed the way. Most of the nonwhites who achieved some financial security, social status, and even political gains in the nineteenth-century colonial Caribbean were of light complexion.

These relatively successful men and women often tried to distance themselves from darker-skinned people and to associate with whites or "their own kind." The Trinidadian scholar C. L. R. James, writing in the early 1930s, put it this way: "There are the nearly whites hanging on tooth and nail to the fringes of white society, and these . . . hate contact with the darker skin far more than some of the broader minded whites. Then there are the browns, intermediates, who cannot by any stretch of the imagination pass as white, but who will not go one inch towards mixing with people darker than themselves." Much earlier, in 1874 another Trinidadian had criticized members of his own mixed-race middle stratum: "Were we less anxious to associate with [whites]; could we feel as much honor in being seen with friends of our own class as with them; were we less ambitious to select our friends from them; . . . we would most assuredly have less of their arrogance. . . . The tendency to believe them a higher order of creation than ourselves is one of the many baneful influences of slavery." The baneful influences of slavery had produced the characteristic self-contempt so widespread among mixed-race and black Caribbean colonials. It was well expressed in a popular calypso sung in Trinidad at the turn of the nineteenth century:

Dan is the Devil, the Devil is Dan
Brown nigger more bad than Bacra (white) man
But black is the baddest
The baddest in the land.
God you is a white man
I want to know the trut'
Who but the Devil
Could mek these nigger brutes.

Divisions between nonwhites based on skin color or phenotype were not absent in the Hispanic Caribbean, and upwardly mobile light-colored persons in these territories might also try to distance themselves from blacks. Prosperous light-complexioned men in mid-nineteenth-century Santo Domingo, for instance, organized their own exclusive social club, La Perla Negra. As Cuba emerged from slavery in the 1870s and 1880s, many of her *pardos*, especially those who had been free long before general emancipation in the 1880s, worked to establish and maintain their social superiority over the *morenos* (blacks). The line between *pardo* and *moreno* was important in Afro-Cuban society, coinciding as it often did with the division between the established free coloreds and the newly emancipated masses. In the political sphere, however, leaders from the *pardo* middle stratum allied with spokesmen for the freed slaves after 1880 to mount a campaign for civil rights for all Afro-Cubans; and many of the mutual-aid societies founded in this period explicitly rejected the color division.

There was a clear tendency for successful mixed-race people in the colonial Caribbean to emphasize their ties (biological, social, and cultural) with the whites and to distance themselves from the blacks. There was an equally clear countervailing development, however: some educated black and mixed-race men began to develop a sense of race pride and to construct an ideology with which to confront white racism. They used the colonial newspapers, as well as the fora provided by the schools, the churches, and political institutions, to articulate their developing sense of racial identity. Men

such as Edward Blyden of the Danish West Indies, Samuel Prescod and J. Albert Thorne of Barbados, J. J. Thomas and Henry Sylvester Williams of Trinidad, Robert Love of the Bahamas and Jamaica, and Hegesippe Legitimus of Guadeloupe, were important precursors of the better-known twentieth-century ideologues of Pan-Africanism and *négritude*. This development was less marked in the Hispanic Caribbean, where blacks were in the minority. The fluidity of Dominican and Puerto Rican race relations as a result of the process of *mulatizacion* made it less likely that an explicit sense of race pride or separateness from the white elite would develop among the black and mixed-race groups. In Cuba, blacks lost ground demographically and socially in the decades after abolition, and after the disastrous "war of the races" in 1912, when thousands of Afro-Cubans were killed, public articulation of a separate racial identity became even more problematic.

Caribbean societies after emancipation were deeply divided along racial lines, and these divisions were to a great extent the legacies of the slave system. Nevertheless, there were also forces and institutions that mitigated or softened these divisions. Rural society was still deeply affected by traditional paternalistic relations between estate-owners and their workers. This paternalism could be found everywhere, from the coffee-growers of the Puerto Rican interior who lived closely with their mixed-race *peones de confianza* in a network of customary obligations and duties, to Trinidadian French Creole cocoa planters who regarded their black workers (the descendants, perhaps, of their parents' or grandparents' slaves) as "their people." Paternalism implied deference and respect, but also obligations and a sense of shared destiny. In Suriname the *kosi* (curtsey) was traditionally extended by black women on meeting a white person; in Martinique a white man was greeted by a black passerby with "Bonjou, missie" (*monsieur*), to which he replied, "Bonjou, mafi/monfi" ("my daughter/my son"), whatever the black person's age. Traditional patriarchal relations between resident estate-owners from old white creole families and their long-established black workers were breaking down in many places around the turn of the century as the forces of modernization, capitalization, and technological change advanced, but they still helped to shape race relations.

In the Catholic countries the institution of ritual kinship also helped to soften divisions between white and black (or brown). Influential men and women in the Dominican Republic or Puerto Rico served as *compadre* or *comadre* (godfather or godmother) to many poor children, building up important ties to their "coparents" (the children's biological parents). The godparent relationship was also important in the French Antilles, where white planters and their wives regularly agreed to sponsor the children of their resident laborers, and probably among Catholics in British islands such as Grenada, St. Lucia, and Trinidad. Language (French-based and English-based creoles and Spanish), various creole cultural blends, and religion also helped to create common ties among black, brown, and white people in the post-emancipation Caribbean.

These societies were hierarchical and authoritarian, based to a large extent on divisions of ancestry and racial origin inherited from slavery; however, they were not static—there was a degree of social and racial mobility in all of them. Cultural and other ties crossed the racial divides. The caste-like divisions of the post-slavery era would slowly but inexorably shift and blur after the end of the eventful nineteenth century.

[*See also* Caribbean Region, *articles on* British Caribbean *and* French Caribbean; *and* Race and Racism.]

BIBLIOGRAPHY

Green, William A. *British Slave Emancipation: The Sugar Colonies and the Great Experiment, 1830–1865.* Oxford: Clarendon Press, 1976.

Hoetink, H. *The Two Variants in Caribbean Race Relations: A Contribution to the Sociology of Segmented Societies.* London: Oxford University Press, 1967.

Knight, Franklin W. *The Caribbean: Genesis of a Fragmented Nationalism.* 2d ed. New York and Oxford: Oxford University Press, 1990.

Knight, Franklin W., and Colin A. Palmer, eds. *The Modern Caribbean.* Chapel Hill: University of North Carolina Press, 1989.

Mintz, Sidney W., and Sally Price, eds. *Caribbean Contours.* Baltimore: Johns Hopkins University Press, 1985.

Moreno Fraginals, Manuel, Frank Moya Pons, and Stanley L. Engerman, eds. *Between Slavery and Free Labor: The Spanish-Speaking Caribbean in the Nineteenth Century.* Baltimore: Johns Hopkins University Press, 1985.

—BRIDGET BRERETON

CARIBBEAN REGION. [*To chart the history of slavery in various European colonies throughout the Caribbean, this entry comprises five articles:*

British Caribbean
French Caribbean
Spanish Caribbean
Dutch Caribbean
Danish and Swedish Caribbean

For further discussion of the scope and documentation of slavery in the region, see Historiography, *article on* Latin American and Caribbean Slavery.]

British Caribbean

Africans were enslaved in all the English colonies of the Caribbean region virtually from the beginning. Black slavery became the predominant system of labor from the time it superseded the use of Amerindians and indentured whites in the mid-seventeenth century, until emancipation was enforced in the period 1834 to 1838. The slave-labor system involved a trade in blacks from West Africa that suddenly surged with the introduction of large-scale sugar cultivation. It increased along with the expansion of plantations to reach an annual peak of around thirty-eight thousand before the abolition of the trade in 1807. Because of mortality that owed as much to the climate and prevalent disease as to the harsh work regime and overt cruelty, a traffic totaling about two million over 180 years left a population of no more than six hundred seventy thousand slaves in 1834 (compared with a slave population of three million in the United States in 1865, from about four hundred thousand imported); however, the slave population in 1834 still outnumbered resident whites by nearly ten to one, and the intermediate class of nonwhite free persons in similar proportion.

The English colonies of the Caribbean region were not only scattered but extremely diverse. Thus their slavery systems (as well as differing from those of the other imperial powers) also varied in important ways—broadly according to the type and intensity of the economic system, but more subtly according to the time and the circumstances of territorial acquisition, the colony's relative stage and pace of development, and the form of its government. The majority were plantation colonies, and sugar (with its byproducts molasses and rum) was by far the most important crop, accounting for as much as 80 percent of exports by value. However, geographical factors such as mountains, low rainfall, or sparse soils determined a degree of diversification into cotton, coffee, spices, stock animals, or provisions, and some of the later-acquired colonies, despite their fertility, had not fully developed plantations before the slave trade or slavery ended. There were also some nonplantation or marginal colonies, dedicated to maritime activity (Bermuda, the Bahamas), logwood cutting (Belize), salt production (Turks and Caicos), or turtling (Caymans).

Politically, all English Caribbean colonies can be termed "plantocracies" in that the white slave-owners ruled, although there were subtle variations among colonies that were English from the beginning and those acquired later from the French or Dutch. The very fact that planters made their own laws in most colonies led to legal variations within a broad general pattern. Toward the end of slavery an important distinction also arose between the original self-legislating colonies and those acquired during the Napoleonic Wars; the latter were directly ruled as crown colonies and thus came more under the influence of an increasingly liberal Colonial Office.

Sociologically, however, just as all English Caribbean colonies were true slave rather than merely slave-owning colonies, all of them were "slave societies" in the sense defined by Elsa Goveia; that is, despite the whites' pretensions to being a socially distinct elite, the entire social fabric was shaped by the slavery system, encompassing whites and free nonwhites as well as the slaves themselves. Slave society, however, was by no means static; it was subject to the overarching process termed *creolization* in both its demographic and its cultural aspects. Confusingly, the adjective *creole* has often been applied narrowly either to local whites or to persons of mixed race; more conveniently, it describes all persons (or even animals) not indigenously native but born and bred in the region, as well as aspects of the creoles' locally shaped and essentially syncretic culture. As a process, the term *creolization* is used both for the gradual increase in the population's proportion of creoles (blacks and whites who were no longer culturally African or European, as well as persons of mixed race), and for the equally gradual evolution of their distinct regional culture. Though limited and covert, racial miscegenation was the most extreme but by no means a necessary feature of creolization. The most general and notable aspect of cultural creolization—which can stand as a paradigm for all other aspects—was the evolution out of the slave-traders' pidgin of genuine creole languages (every colony had its own) in which the lexicon was predominantly European but contained African loans, while much of the grammar, sentence structure, and intonation were generically African.

The slave codes the plantocrats constructed could derive little except general concepts of property, punishment, and the control of labor out of an English legal system from which the ideas of chattel slavery and serfdom had long since faded. The slave laws of the English colonies, unlike those of the other imperial powers, were not codified un-

Vue de Cedarhall dans l'Isle d'Antigoa (View of Cedarhall on the Island of
Antigua); engraving, L. Stobwasser, published by the Société d'Amis
de l'Evangile, nineteenth century.

til the last years of the eighteenth century, when
each self-legislating colony passed its own Consolidated Slave Act. They reflected the planters' pragmatic needs and prejudices as well as borrowing
from Roman law principles also found in the Spanish Siete Partidas and the French Code Noir. The
general purposes of these laws were simple: to define slaves as chattel; to restrict their mobility; to
control their lives and work; and to punish them
for infractions. In many islands slaves were defined
as real estate so that they could be tied to their
owners' other goods, chattels, and land. Everywhere, manumission was made almost impossible;
the "uterine law" that children inherited their
mother's status was generally adopted; and strict
pass laws and savage punishments were enacted

for running away, as well as for acts of sabotage, in-
subordination, and overt resistance.

Until the late eighteenth century, laws remained on the books decreeing or permitting mutilation, and execution by slow burning or starving
to death in gibbets for the worst offenses. However,
these laws were characterized by inequity and impracticality: they punished runaways with lashes
but their harborers with death, or slave insolence
with death but white slave-murderers with fines;
and they never quite determined whether a slave
as a chattel could actually commit a crime like
theft. This meant that usage and custom were always more important, and generally more lenient,
than enacted slave laws. When "ameliorative" laws
were introduced under metropolitan pressure

beginning in the 1780s, they were mostly dead letters, simply codifying what had long been customary, or endorsing changes—such as the wholesale adoption and adaptation of Christianity by the slaves—that were occurring independently.

In the age of the buccaneers, slaves were acquired from foreign plantations or ships, but as English plantations developed, the West African trade was formalized through a series of chartered monopoly companies, of which the Royal African Company (1670–1750) was the most important. In contrast to the continuing protection afforded sugar and other plantation products (thanks to a powerful lobby of merchants and planters) slave-trading was deregulated and thrown open to free trade by 1712. This perhaps explains in part why the slave trade lost its imperial support and was abolished a quarter-century before the institution of slavery itself.

The lethal process of acclimatization called "seasoning" carried off nearly half of all new slaves within three years. Coupled with the steady expansion of plantations throughout the slavery era, this ensured the vigorous continuation of the slave trade until 1807 and, at the same time, continuous cultural links with Africa. However, the wealth of African retentions and the degree of creolization varied greatly among the colonies at any given time. Barbados and the marginal colonies, having become economically fully developed or static and demographically self-sustaining, no longer needed African imports, and as many as 90 percent of their slaves were creoles when the African slave trade ended. By contrast, 37 percent of Jamaican slaves were African-born as late as 1817, and in Trinidad and Guyana (where the labor demand was exacerbated by a natural decrease in the slave population of around fifteen per thousand a year) no more than 45 percent were colony-born.

The slaves' lives were shaped by the dominant economy and their culture reshaped by the creolization process, but within the variations of their Caribbean environment and assigned functions the slaves preserved what they could of their exis-

tential identity. Indeed, they increased their own contribution to the English Caribbean economy and culture as the institution of slavery ran its course.

Domestic and town slaves lived in smaller groups in closer proximity to their white masters and tended to experience a more intimate intercourse with them than did the majority of slaves on large plantations. Mariner and wood-cutting crews also enjoyed to a degree the essential freemasonry of the sea and interior forests—their relative freedom being a transactional equation based on the comparative ease with which they could abscond or arm themselves. Nonetheless, such a large proportion of English Caribbean slaves lived their whole lives within the large community and closely guarded cellular bounds of a single plantation that the plantation may be taken as the quintessential form of their existence.

At the apex of the plantation hierarchy, the owner known by the slaves as "Big Massa" was often an absentee; this was most common in Jamaica, and least common in Barbados. He could therefore exercise aristocratic luxuries, even *noblesse oblige*. When resident he occupied a so-called "great house" proprietarily overlooking his land, slaves, and factory. The harsher realities, however, were handled by subordinate whites—attorney-managers (generally resident in the colonial capital), overseers, and undermanagers called "book-keepers." Those whites set in immediate authority were an isolated and beleaguered minority, non-gentlemen of limited education, dissolute and shiftless for the most part, outnumbered fifty to one by their charges, tied by contract and the requirement to make a profit, with only the parlous rewards of power to offset unpleasant work in a harsh climate, the ever-present threat of lethal or crippling disease, and the perils of insurrection.

In the system of plantation management slaves were graded according to their usefulness, which was roughly equivalent to their monetary valuation. The able-bodied laborers were divided into three or more gangs by age and strength with little regard to gender, with only the roughly 10 percent who were hopelessly diseased, senile, or under six years of age regarded as unproductive. Within the managers' own formulation there was a complex implied hierarchy that separated the domestics and those of mixed race from the laborers, and the factory workers and artisans from the field workers, and gave at least some delegated, if reversible, authority to trusted slave headmen. Africans were regarded as inferior to creoles only to the degree that they were less acculturated, with fewer useful skills and less amenable attitudes. That field headmen were often Africans rather than creoles, however, suggests that there was an underlying hierarchy among the slaves that owed more to traditional canons of reputation than to the simple economic imperatives of the plantation. In the small fraction of their time that the slaves had to themselves, and within their own quarters and grounds, they fashioned a social, economic, and cultural life of which the masters were largely ignorant or dismissive, but which came to have a critical effect on plantation life and culture as a whole before slavery ended.

Much of this influence went unnoticed, not just because it was so gradual but also because it was syncretic and thus more easily accepted by the whites, or even assimilated by them. Besides strongly influencing the development of creole languages, Africans introduced new foods and methods of cooking, and new music and modes of dancing that employed European as well as African instruments and adapted European measures and rhythms. African festivals and festival forms such as Crop-over and Jonkonnu were melded with European celebrations like Harvest Home, Carnival, or Christmas mumming. African games, folklore, proverbs, and beliefs also found their way into the creole culture.

Even more significant was the way the English Caribbean slaves adopted and adapted Christianity. Unlike the slaves of the Catholic imperial powers, the English slaves were not actively proselytized from the beginning, and the established Anglican Church was regarded as mainly for whites, as well as having a secular role in local government and society as it did in England. The Anglican Church had considerable success in attracting slaves in Barbados and Antigua, and there were many nominally Catholic slaves in the colonies acquired from France and Spain after 1763. When Nonconformist missionaries—first invited by planters in the expectation that they would have a socializing or "civilizing" function—became widely active from the 1780s on, the great majority of English Caribbean slaves became baptized Christians. As the more perceptive (mainly Anglican) planters recognized, however, the majority of slaves were attracted to theologies and liturgies that were comparatively consonant with African beliefs and practices, as well as to the more participatory churches. Most popular of all were the Baptists of Jamaica and the Bahamas, whose first congregations were formed by evangelical slave preachers who had come from the United States mainland with their loyalist owners after 1783, a generation before white Baptist missionaries appeared on the scene from England.

Most important of all, however, was the influence the slaves themselves had on English Caribbean socioeconomic patterns both during and after slavery. Despite the intentional jumbling of Africans of various ethnic origins by the traders and slave-owners, Afro-Caribbean slaves quickly reconstituted kinship networks, beginning as early as the "shipmate bond" and soon reinforced by inevitable endogamy and the sense of belonging to a localized plantation community. Contrary to the arguments of some scholars that slave sales inevitably broke up families and that family dysfunction was increased by sexual relations between slave women and whites that were tantamount to prostitution and rape, English Caribbean slaves had a strong commitment to the immediate family, in which the roles of father and mother owed more to African traditions of domestic economy than to any concern on the masters' part.

Of fundamental importance in this respect were the ways in which slave mothers dominated in the domestic economy in and around the family house, and the fact that slave families were able to control and exploit the provision grounds they were allotted by their owners. Slaves cultivated gardens and raised small stock around their hutments, and on some plantations there were "shell blow" grounds near the canefields where slaves were set to grow provision crops during the midday breaks. Slave family heads were assigned more extensive grounds wherever there was sufficient cultivable land on the margins of the areas planted to export crops. It was clearly in the owners' interest to have the slaves be as self-supporting in food as possible, but many slaves went much further. Working as families in the evenings and on the one and one-half weekend days they were released from plantation labor (and surely working with greater enthusiasm than ever for their owners), they raised small stock, fruits, and surplus provisions, collected wild produce, and made simple craft items. These goods were marketed particularly by the slave women, who carried them to the Sunday markets in town and to informal markets at plantation intersections, or even sold them to their owners. The money received was used to purchase small luxuries such as crockery, cutlery, glassware, mirrors, and combs, or fancier items of clothing than were issued by their owners, from itinerant peddlers or market stallholders. So prevalent did the system of informal slave production and marketing become (most notably in Jamaica) that scholars, following the lead of Sidney Mintz, commonly refer to slaves in the late slave period as proto-peasants. One Marxist, Ciro Cardoso, has even referred to "the peasant breach in the slave mode of production."

Other scholars, such as Mary Turner, Nigel Bolland, and Howard Johnson, bearing in mind that the fate (if not the ideal) of ex-slaves was to fill the ranks of a Caribbean hybrid class of "part-peasant, part-proletarian," have stressed the ways in which slaves organized themselves to challenge and mitigate the terms under which they worked and to receive fixed rewards, even cash for work beyond the normal call, to the degree that we may call them proto-proletarians. Considering what slaves did with the money they earned to ease the poverty of their material life—contributing in a small way to the incorporation of the plantation periphery into the industrializing world—one might even term them proto-consumers. In all three ways of anticipating later trends, slaves probably contributed almost as much to the transition out of slavery as did any external actors or forces, quite apart from what they did to discredit and bring down slavery by more aggressive forms of resistance.

The simplest and earliest way to work slaves was to form them into gangs and force them to labor under duress as long as was physically possible. The general substitution for pure gang labor of fixed daily tasks—after which slaves would be free to rest or labor for themselves as they willed—was an early recognition that slaves worked better under some form of incentive. As time went on, slaves showed enterprise in reducing the size of tasks that could reasonably be expected, and in raising the level of incentives by playing on their managers' need to maximize their labor output. At one extreme, slaves in Bermuda and the Bahamas helped to crew privateers during wartime, but they would fight with a will only if they received a seaman's share of the booty. In all colonies, surplus skilled slaves were often hired out and were usually able to command a share of their hire in return for performing satisfactorily. Some were even allowed to hire themselves out and simply pay their owner for the privilege. Even on the strictest plantations, the levels of tasks and rewards (including more time to work the grounds) became so customary that managers risked virtual strikes, or even a sacking from the attorney or owner, if they attempted to extract more than was practicable from their charges.

Beyond the transactional calculus of such primitive industrial relations was the fearsome threat of escalating forms of slave resistance. This ranged from malingering, recalcitrance, and running away to arson, cattle-maiming, and other acts of sabotage, and from individual acts of violence against the whites (including poisoning and the casting of

African spells), to widening plots and the ultimate horror of a general slave uprising. Although there was never a completely successful slave revolt in the English Caribbean like that in Haiti (1791–1804), it is clear that English slaves, like those everywhere, perennially resisted their enslavement however they could; they rose up whenever they could or had to, as when the forces of control were weakened or distracted by war, or when the slaves were driven intolerably; and their resistance ultimately drove home the impracticality of slavery as a labor system compared with its alternatives.

Overt slave resistance in the English Caribbean, as elsewhere in plantation America, went through several distinct phases. The earliest manifestations involved mass running away and the forming of obdurate maroon communities in the forested and mountainous interior, sometimes cooperating with Amerindian survivors. Fighting when they had to, the maroons forced the planters into making treaties, although these were not permanently honored by the whites. The formidable Black Caribs of St. Vincent and the maroons of Dominica were not finally subdued until the 1790s, while the Bush Negroes and maroons of the Guianese and Belizean riverine hinterlands were able to survive permanently beyond the reach of planter imperialism. The fate of the most famous maroons of the English Caribbean, those of Jamaica, was more equivocal. They fought a successful guerrilla war against the colonial regime in the 1730s, but they were divided by the subsequent treaties of accommodation. The more troublesome Leeward Maroons were expelled to Nova Scotia and Sierra Leone after a second war in the 1790s, but the remaining maroons retained a nominal independence as the planters' allies to the end of slavery and beyond, keeping a distinct if fading cultural identity into the late twentieth century.

As long as African-born slaves remained the majority, African-led revolts were the worst threat to plantocratic hegemony, particularly when Akan-speaking "Coromantine" slaves from the warrior culture of Ghana were involved. The most serious such crisis was the island-wide Coromantin-led rebellion of 1760 in Jamaica, which occurred when British forces were heavily engaged in the Seven Years' War. Subsequent plots and localized uprisings were weakened by divisions in aims and leadership between African and creole slaves. The worldwide ferment that included the American, French, and Haitian revolutions did not lead to a general slave uprising throughout the English Caribbean, both because British naval and military forces were heavily mobilized, and because a majority of English slaves were persuaded to stay neutral or actually to fight for the regime by promises, largely unfulfilled, of ameliorated conditions or manumission.

To the consternation of the English planters, however, the progressive creolization of their slaves did not lessen the incidence of overt rebellion, but rather the reverse. As the creole slaves became gradually more aware of abolitionist allies in England and of a changing climate of opinion about slavery in Parliament, the three most serious slave revolts occurred in the three most important sugar plantation colonies of the English Caribbean—Barbados in 1816, Demerara (British Guiana) in 1823, and Jamaica in 1831–1832. These involved tens of thousands of slaves, led by the most creolized and trusted slave headmen, who in the latter two cases included black Christian deacons. What the rebels wanted above all, of course, was freedom from chattel slavery. Nevertheless, there is overwhelming evidence that they did not seek violence, retribution, or the destruction of the plantation system. Rather, they wanted the freedom of choice: to live either as free townsfolk, or more like free peasants, retaining the option of working for wages as and when it suited them.

All three rebellions were suppressed with bloody savagery. Planters and imperial conservatives alike were convinced that slavery must continue and that less rather than more leniency was called for. In the British parliamentary debates rising to a climax even as the Jamaican insurrection occurred, however, the abolitionist minority was joined by two types of allies. Some were realist: economic liberals who believed with Adam Smith that a system of competitive wage labor was superior to the coercion of slavery; others were convinced that if freedom of this kind were not granted from above, it would be seized from below, and the very existence of the colonial empire in the Caribbean jeopardized. In these respects, therefore, the slaves of the English Caribbean can be said to have contributed to their own emancipation.

Emancipation for all slaves in the English Caribbean (as well as in South Africa, Mauritius, and Ceylon) was decreed by the imperial parliament a year in advance, to come into effect at midnight on 31 July 1834. It was endorsed by the colonial legislatures with a promptitude spurred by the fear of losing the monetary compensation voted for the owners (not, of course, for the slaves), and the right to impose a transitional period of compulsory labor called apprenticeship. Apprenticeship was designed to last six years but was terminated after four. This was partly because it proved unworkable and provoked scandal, but mainly because it was deemed unnecessary. The legislators of Bermuda and Antigua, where there was no spare land and ex-slaves had no option but to work for their former owners, even chose to forego apprenticeship altogether. As the disciples of Adam Smith had predicted, labor relations fell into a natural pattern without regulation or physical coercion; however, only in colonies with surplus land and a shortage of workers were these conditions even remotely favorable to the ex-slaves.

With their numbers for the first time increasing everywhere, the ex-slaves of the English Caribbean and their descendants were faced by a rapidly declining economy, an increasingly indifferent imperial government, and a local ruling class able to sustain its hegemony through the control of land and commerce, and usually through the structure of local politics. Though still proudly struggling to construct a life of their own and intermittently continuing the fight against oppression, in an age driven by laissez-faire ideas (as well as the racist dis-

tortions of Social Darwinism), formal slavery's black legatees were condemned to a century or more of a different, and scarcely preferable, form of involuntary servitude. The racism that stemmed from the correlation between functional, class, and ethnic divisions was an even longer-lived legacy.

[*See also* Abolition and Anti-Slavery, *article on* Britain; *and* Caribbean Race Relations.]

BIBLIOGRAPHY

Brathwaite, Edward K. *The Development of Creole Society in Jamaica, 1770–1820.* Oxford: Clarendon Press, 1971.

Craton, Michael. *Sinews of Empire: A Short History of British Slavery.* Garden City, N.Y.: Anchor Press, 1974.

Craton, Michael. *Searching for the Invisible Man: Slaves and Plantation Life in Jamaica.* Cambridge, Mass.: Harvard University Press, 1978.

Craton, Michael. "Reshuffling the Pack: The Transition from Slavery to Other Forms of Labour in the British Caribbean, c. 1790–1890." *Nieuwe Westindische Gids* 68 (1995): 23–75.

Dunn, Richard S. *Sugar and Slaves: The Rise of the Planter Class in the English West Indies, 1624–1713.* Chapel Hill: University of North Carolina Press, 1972.

Goveia, Elsa. *Slave Society in the British Leeward Islands at the End of the Eighteenth Century.* New Haven: Yale University Press, 1965.

Hall, Douglas. *In Miserable Slavery: Thomas Thistlewood in Jamaica, 1750–1786.* London: Macmillan, 1989.

Higman, Barry W. *Slave Populations of the British Caribbean, 1807–1834.* Baltimore: Johns Hopkins University Press, 1984.

Sheridan, Richard B. *Sugar and Slavery: An Economic History of the British West Indies, 1623–1775.* Baltimore: Johns Hopkins University Press, 1974.

Ward, John R. *British West Indian Slavery, 1750–1834: The Process of Amelioration.* Oxford: Clarendon Press, 1988.

Williams, Eric. *Capitalism and Slavery.* Chapel Hill: University of North Carolina Press, 1944.

—MICHAEL CRATON

French Caribbean

France began formal occupation of its West Indian colonies in 1626 when Cardinal Richelieu created the Compagnie de Saint-Christophe. The following year an expedition led by Pierre d'Esnambuc defeated the English and the Spanish and took possession of the island of Saint Christopher for France. The growth and success of the colony stimulated further expansion. In 1635 the Compagnie des Îles d'Amérique was formed to colonize Guadeloupe and Martinique. This company went bankrupt in 1650 and the colonies were sold to their former governors. who administered them as proprietary holdings until 1664.

During this period free colonists and voluntary and involuntary indentured servants of European origin gradually replaced the buccaneers and corsairs who preceded them. By 1640 an economy of small-scale cultivators—growing provisions for local consumption, cotton, and above all tobacco—emerged in the two colonies. In that year the native Caribs were eliminated in Guadeloupe, while they were expelled from Martinique in 1658. Sugar-cane cultivation was also first introduced into the French colonies in 1640, but it was put on a solid foundation only with the arrival of Dutch and Jewish refugees from Brazil in 1654.

The Dutch offered the French colonists sugarcane plants, slaves, refining technology, and access to Dutch markets, shipping, and credit. With the fall of tobacco prices in the 1660s, the sugar plantation and slave labor transformed the colonies. Land was concentrated in the hands of large-scale sugar-planters. Existing estates were converted to sugar. Holdings were consolidated, and the remaining vacant lands were brought under cultivation. Slaves were imported from Cape Verde, Guinea, Senegal, and Angola. The transformation was more rapid and thorough in Martinique than in Guadeloupe. In Martinique the slave population increased from 2,700 in 1664 to 55,700 in 1736, while in Guadeloupe the number of slaves climbed from 4,300 in 1671 to 33,400 in 1739. By the 1720s, the French West Indian colonies were no longer settlements of European smallholders but were dominated by large sugar estates worked by African slaves.

Dutch influence over colonial commerce and the growing prosperity of the sugar industry led the French government to reassert control over the

Black slaves at the table in front of their house in Martinique; painting, Le Masurier, 1775; Ministry of the Oversees Territories, Paris.

colonies. In 1664 Colbert established the Compagnie des Indes Occidentales, which assumed responsibility for the administration of the colonies and enjoyed a monopoly of colonial commerce. By 1674 that company was declared bankrupt, and the colonies reverted to crown control. Despite the company's failure, it eliminated the Dutch commercial presence and opened the West Indian trade to French private merchants.

Colbert's subsequent mercantilist policy (the Exclusif) provided the basic outline for French trade with the West Indies until slave emancipation the nineteenth century. Under its terms the colonies were systematically subordinated to French commercial interests. They were regarded as the sole property of the metropolis and existed only for its benefit. They could not raise or manufacture anything that competed with metropolitan goods, they were forbidden to trade with countries other than France, and they could transport their goods only in French ships. In exchange, the colonists were granted a monopoly of the French market for their produce. This framework encouraged the further growth of sugar plantation and African slavery and contributed to the prosperity of France's Atlantic port cities.

The rapidly growing slave population also led Colbert to formulate the Code Noir. Promulgated in 1685, this was the most comprehensive attempt by a European power to regulate the juridical, moral, and material conditions of slavery in its colonies. Following Roman law, slaves were regarded as movable property. They could be mortgaged and seized for debt. However, family members were not to be sold separately, and slaves on sugar estates could only be seized along with the whole property. The Code did not recognize the slave's juridical personality. Slaves could not own property or sell goods without the authorization of their master. They were forbidden to carry arms. They had no right to assemble, to hold office, or to bear witness in legal proceedings. On the other hand, masters were required to baptize their slaves, to provide for their religious instruction, and to allow them to marry. Marriage between Europeans and African slaves was permitted until 1723. Concubinage was forbidden, and provisions were made to protect the integrity of slave families. Slaves were exempted from work on Sundays and religious holidays. The Code also attempted to regulate the conditions of manumission and the amount and kind of food, housing, and clothing to be provided to slaves by their masters.

Finally, the Code prescribed punishments for slaves and the offenses for which they were to be applied. Running away, theft, and striking the master, his wife, or any free person were regarded as particularly serious offenses. In such cases punishments included whipping, branding, mutilation, or execution to be carried out by public authorities. Masters could chain or flog their slaves when they felt it necessary, but they were forbidden to torture, mutilate, or kill them. Although there were wide discrepancies between the law and practice, and the clauses protecting the slaves' welfare were habitually ignored by planters, the Code Noir remained the fundamental legislation on slavery in the French colonies until emancipation in 1848.

After 1740 the French colonies of the Lesser Antilles were eclipsed in importance by Saint Domingue. This was France's prize colony, yet it was the last of the Caribbean colonies to be established by a major European power. It became French only in 1697, when the western third of the Spanish island of Hispaniola, up to then sparsely inhabited by buccaneers, freebooters, and pirates, was ceded to France by the Treaty of Ryswick. A proprietary colony from 1698 to 1718 under the Compagnie de Saint-Domingue and, from 1718 to 1724 under the Compagnie des Indes, Saint Domingue thereafter was administered directly by the French government.

While early economic activity consisted largely in small-scale production of hides, tobacco, and indigo, capital derived from these sources was soon invested in sugar. Where not a single sugar plantation had existed in 1689, there were eighteen by 1700, 120 by 1704, and 138 by 1713. Saint Domingue thus entered a period of economic takeoff within its first two decades, and one of sustained and unprecedented growth thereafter. By 1730 there were 339 sugar plantations, and roughly 600 in 1754 on the eve of the Seven Years' War, which temporarily interrupted the growth of the sugar sector. From the 1770s to the eve of the revolution in 1789, Saint Domingue again experienced a surge, with another two hundred sugar plantations being established in these two crucial decades, bringing the peak to 793, with more than half of these producing the more lucrative, partially purified clayed, rather than raw or brown, sugar. These plantations were concentrated in the North Province, where the massive slave rebellion of 1791 broke out. By 1789 Saint Domingue was the single most important Caribbean sugar colony, outproducing the entire British West Indies. By all standards it was the world's greatest wealth-producing colony. Of the total French colonial imports, two-thirds were re-exported, allowing for France's commercial supremacy over Great Britain in European markets.

Such expansion of sugar production inevitably brought with it a tremendous influx of African slaves, whose numbers swelled from a mere three thousand in 1687 to almost fifty thousand in 1720 and two hundred six thousand by 1764. The next two and one-half decades witnessed even more spiraling expansion as the slave population reached 465,429 in 1789 by official census figures. During the 1780s close to forty thousand slaves per year were imported into the French West Indies, of whom 80 percent were destined for Saint Domingue. Recent demographic research suggests that by the eve of the revolution, the dominant African groups in Saint Domingue were the Aradas from the Gulf of Guinea and the Congolese from West Central Africa, and that the latter constituted the most numerous of the African groups. By 1789 roughly two-thirds of Saint Domingue's slaves were African-born.

Although the cornerstone of the colony's economy was sugar, it was not the sole source of wealth. About three thousand indigo plantations, two thousand five hundred in coffee, eight hundred in cotton, and fifty in cocoa were in operation in 1789, bringing the number of plantations producing export cash crops to well over seven thousand.

Whereas the sugar estates were owned exclusively by members of Saint Domingue's white and largely absentee planter elite, the *grands blancs*, a significant portion of the colony's free coloreds participated as owners of slave and other property in the expanding secondary sectors of coffee and indigo, concentrated in the South and West provinces in the 1770s and 1780s. The rise of the free coloreds during the second half of the eighteenth century was both economically and demographically significant. At the turn of the eighteenth century they numbered barely six hundred and initially competed with lower-class whites, the *petits blancs*, for employment in the skilled trades

on the plantations. By midcentury their economic advances were perceived by the white plantocracy as a threat to its hegemony and to the rule of white supremacy institutionalized by the Code Noir. By the Seven Years' War their numbers were approximately five thousand, and they rose from seven thousand in 1775 to about twenty-eight thousand in 1789, placing them numerically in near-equal balance with the white population, which stood slightly above thirty thousand. Their numbers in Saint Domingue alone exceeded their totals for the entire British West Indies and the remaining French West Indies combined.

It is often claimed that by 1789 the free coloreds owned one-third of Saint Domingue's plantation property and one-quarter of its slaves. However, research has yet to reveal what proportion of the twenty-eight thousand individuals may be regarded as a free colored "plantocracy." While it may safely be assumed that the prominent political spokesmen for the free coloreds, such as Julien Raimond and Vincent Ogé, came from the property-owning sector, the data are not yet available to analyze the composition of this highly heterogeneous group. Within the same social caste, in addition to the mulattoes, were people of pure African descent; most of them owned some sort of property, and they often had ties to kin and friends still in bondage, so their affinities may have been much closer to the slaves than to their lighter-skinned peers. Terms such as "free coloreds," or "mulattoes and free blacks," frequently used interchangeably in the literature to designate those who had been manumitted as well as those born of free parents, tend to conflate all categories of free persons who had some portion of African blood. Still, phenotype and generational distance from slavery notwithstanding, all persons of color who were not slaves in Saint Domingue were relegated to a subordinate status defined by discriminatory legislation. They were prohibited from holding public office, practicing law, medicine, pharmacy, and certain privileged trades, and taking the surname of a white forebear. Laws restricted their mode of dress, imposed curfews, and made service in the *marechaussée* (an exclusively free colored militia established to capture runaway slaves) compulsory for adult males. Such legislation, passed mainly in the 1770s and 1780s in reaction to the economic and demographic advances of the free coloreds, aimed at erecting an insurmountable barrier between the racial groups and at frustrating the aspirations of the free coloreds to civil equality. As fellow slaveholders, no restrictions were ever placed upon their property rights.

By 1789, with the opening of the Estates General and the Revolution in France, each sector of the colonial population harbored specific and inherently opposing goals: the planters argued for an end to the Exclusif, for local autonomy, and for representation in the metropolis; free coloreds petitioned for full civil rights; and significant segments of the slave population prepared to attack slavery itself. Maintaining an ideology of white supremacy, the planters refused the bid of the free coloreds for equality, leading to armed struggles between the factions. Free coloreds and whites armed their own slaves in the West and South provinces, while slaves in the North, under the indigenous black leadership of Jean-François, Biassou, and Toussaint Louverture (a free black), emerged as an autonomous insurrectionary force.

The French Revolution and the Napoleonic Wars decimated France's colonial empire. In the face of slave insurrection and subsequent invasion by Spain and Great Britain in Saint Domingue, the French civil commissioners, Léger Sonthonax and Etienne Polverel, abolished slavery by decree in 1793. In Guadeloupe, a revolutionary army of freed slaves led by the *montagnard* Victor Hugues defeated royalist planters and their British allies and abolished slavery there. (The majority of slaves remained on plantations, while free mulattoes occupied strategic positions in the new regime.) Abolition was formally ratified by the National Convention on 4 February 1794. In Martinique, the slave plantations remained intact, as the island was occupied by the British. Slavery was restored in Guadeloupe in 1802 by Napoleon Bonaparte; however, an expeditionary army of about twenty thousand troops, led by Bonaparte's brother-in-law, General Victor-Emmanuel Leclerc, was dispatched earlier that year to Saint Domingue to reimpose slavery there. Toussaint Louverture, who had risen to the pinnacle of power as governor-general, was captured and exiled to France, where he died in captivity; however, the blacks and free coloreds continued their defense of freedom, forcing the French to evacuate at the end of 1803. On 1 January 1804 General Jean-Jacques Dessalines proclaimed the colony's independence and adopted the original Taino Arawak name, Hayti, for the New World's second independent nation.

After 1815 France promoted the sugar industry in its remaining colonies in order to compensate for the loss of Haiti and to revive the colonies, port cities, and merchant marine. Protective tariffs allowed colonial sugar to dominate the domestic market. The African slave trade was revived. In the colonies, secondary crops were abandoned as all available land and slaves were devoted to sugar. By 1826 Martinique, Guadeloupe, and Réunion in the Indian Ocean were producing more sugar than Saint Domingue in its heyday. However, high tariffs and the growth of the French market encouraged the revival of the metropolitan beet-sugar industry and created a major competitor in the French market. As the colonies' economic position eroded, the slave regime came under political attack.

After 1830, British diplomatic pressure led to the end of the slave trade, while the new government of the July Monarchy pledged to abolish slavery itself. Although the regime never succeeded in carrying out its intentions, the reforms associated with the Mackau Law (1845) were intended to regularize slave life and to create a transition to free labor. They provided for compulsory manumission, limited corporal punishment, recognized the legal personality of the slave, and made elementary and religious education mandatory. They were supplemented by laws that regulated slave discipline, diet, clothing, and housing, their moral and religious status, and the working day. Although these laws' practical effect was limited, they foreshadowed the end of slavery. At the same time, a small but effective abolitionist movement under the leadership of Victor Schoelcher effectively criticized the slave regime and undermined its legitimacy.

Under these conditions slave resistance assumed new significance. After British emancipation, thousands of slaves fled to neighboring British colonies or died in the attempt. There were plots in Guadeloupe in 1815, 1816, and 1831, and revolts in Martinique in 1821, 1831, and 1848. Sabotage, strikes against night work in the sugar mills, and other forms of daily resistance were persistent. With the revolution of 1848 and proclamation of the Second Republic in France, slavery was finally abolished under the tutelage of Schoelcher, now under-secretary of the navy for colonies, and the freed slaves were declared citizens of France.

[See also Saint Domingue Revolution.]

BIBLIOGRAPHY

Blackburn, Robin. *The Overthrow of Colonial Slavery, 1776–1848*. London: Verso, 1988.

Cohen, William B. *The French Encounter with Africans: White Response to Blacks, 1530–1880*. Bloomington: Indiana University Press, 1980.

Fick, Carolyn E. *The Making of Haiti: The Saint Domingue Revolution from Below*. Knoxville: University of Tennessee Press, 1990.

Stein, Robert L. *The French Slave Trade in the Eighteenth Century: An Old Regime Business*. Madison: University of Wisconsin Press, 1979.

Stein, Robert L. *The French Sugar Business in the Eighteenth Century*. Baton Rouge: Louisiana State University Press, 1988.

Tomich, Dale W. *Slavery in the Circuit of Sugar: Martinique in the World Economy, 1830–1848*. Baltimore: Johns Hopkins University Press, 1990.

—DALE TOMICH AND CAROLYN FICK

Spanish Caribbean

African slaves and their descendants played an important role in the Spanish island colonies of Cuba, Santo Domingo, and Puerto Rico. For a longer time span than anywhere else in the New World except Brazil, they participated in all economic spheres and were centrally involved in the creative and syncretic processes of creole culture-building. Performing the difficult labor of growing and harvesting crops and building military fortresses, leading the festivities that marked the liturgical and secular calendars, and instilling in Spanish settlers the constant terror of maroon attack, slaves punctuated at every turn the social, cultural, and political life of the three Spanish-speaking Caribbean colonies. Paradoxically, however, only for very short periods was slavery the key social institution of these colonies and slaves the most important element in their population.

Three distinct cycles, corresponding to different modes of appropriation of slave labor, may be said to characterize Spanish Caribbean slavery. The first (1493–1575) saw experimentation with Native American slavery, the early introduction of black slaves from the Iberian Peninsula and Africa itself on a commercial scale, and, for a relatively short time, the intensive application of slave labor to key productive tasks in gold-mining and sugar production. The second and longest of the cycles, which spanned almost two centuries (1575–1763), witnessed a diminution in slavery's scope and significance, along with sharp fluctuations in slave importations from Africa. Throughout this protracted period, plantation slavery was less important than the exploitation of slave labor in urban settings. As a result, the brutality of the master-slave relationship was attenuated somewhat, with significant numbers of slaves attaining freedom through various means. The final period (1763–1886) was characterized by the conversion of the Spanish islands (especially Cuba and Puerto Rico) into one of the world's most important sugar-producing areas. At this relatively late date the growth of the plantation system produced more intensive exploitation of slave labor, an unprecedented volume of slave imports from Africa (despite international agreements banning it), a sharp increase in the proportion of blacks in the population, heightened social tensions, and harsh repression of conspiracies and rebellions. This last phase was marked by determined struggles by the slaves themselves, and by others on their behalf, to achieve the final proscription of legal enslavement, which occurred when the last "apprentices" were freed in Cuba in 1886.

The earliest form of slavery practiced by Europeans in the Caribbean involved Taino Indians who had resisted the Spanish on the island of Hispaniola after 1493. As conflicts between the local population and the new settlers escalated into all-out war within a few years of Columbus's initial landfall, thousands of Tainos were subdued and placed in bondage. The Spaniards used their labor in gold-mining, in subsistence agriculture, and in personal services. Later, when the crown proscribed Indian slavery except in cases of captives taken in just wars, the practice of enslaving the natives diminished in scope, and a semifeudal institution known as *repartimiento* became the primary mode of labor procurement.

It is believed that other slaves of either sub-Saharan or North African origin may have arrived with the conquerors of Hispaniola during the first few years of effective colonization. Slaves were ubiquitous in the Iberian Peninsula at the time of Columbus's early voyages to the New World, and they might well have been among the more than twelve hundred persons who arrived at Hispaniola on board the large fleet of the second voyage in 1493.

Commercial shipments of black slaves from the Old World arrived in Hispaniola after 1501. For a time, however, the black slave population remained a small, if steadily growing, portion of the total. The Indians were disappearing at an alarming rate, however, and the Spaniards soon deemed them an insufficient source of labor. The situation became critical after a smallpox epidemic in 1518 and 1519 that spread devastation throughout the four Greater Antilles and decimated the remaining Indians. In 1518, prodded in part by the hu-

manitarian arguments of Bartolomé de las Casas on behalf of the rapidly dwindling Tainos, the crown authorized the first large-scale shipments of African-born slaves. This action coincided with a period of increasing crown and private interest in the promotion of sugarcane cultivation and in the establishment of the mills (called *ingenios* in the Spanish colonies) that processed the sugarcane juice into sugar. Thus, the origins of the large-scale slave trade from Africa to the Caribbean are closely intertwined with the earliest steps taken to develop a viable, export-oriented sugar industry.

For nearly a half century after 1530, sugar production replaced gold as the islands' principal economic activity and the main reason for the survival of Spanish settlements. The slave-based *ingenios* of Hispaniola led the way, with those of Puerto Rico and Cuba following far behind. In all three islands the establishment of a slave-based economy meant that the population of Africans overtook those of Europeans and Indians. At least for a time during the middle decades of the sixteenth century, the island societies became progressively africanized. While African slaves and their descendants predominated in the lowland sugar-producing zones, many escaped slaves (maroons), often in collusion with groups of unassimilated Indians, were among the first nonnatives to occupy the mountainous interior.

The early cycle of slave-based sugar production reached its zenith around 1550 to 1560. At the time there were about thirty or forty *ingenios* in Hispaniola, and about a dozen each in Puerto Rico and Cuba. The larger *ingenios* held one hundred fifty, two hundred, or even five hundred slaves, and were solidly established, well-capitalized operations. Others, much smaller in scale, were less stable affairs whose ownership turned over rapidly. By 1571 slaves accounted for the vast majority of the population in Hispaniola (approximately thirteen thousand out of a total of eighteen thousand), but they constituted a smaller proportion in Puerto Rico and Cuba.

Brazil's entry intro the sugar market around

Engraving of African slaves (depicted with European features) working
inside a sugar mill in Hispaniola, sixteenth century.

1575 marked the beginning of the end for this early cycle of Caribbean slave-plantation history. After that date many *ingenios* were abandoned, especially in Hispaniola and Puerto Rico. Slave imports from Africa into these areas fell markedly. Still, in some portions of the insular Spanish Caribbean slavery remained a vital institution of labor procurement. This was the case in western Cuba around Havana, which became an important rendezvous port for Spanish ships, many of them laden with Peruvian and Mexican silver, as they began their return voyage to Europe. It was also the case in the urban perimeters of San Juan and Santo Domingo, where massive fortresses and their associated wall defenses were put up beginning around 1540 and continuing well into the seventeenth century.

A more diversified exploitation of the slave labor force followed the brief plantation spurt of the mid-1500s. With the insular Spanish Caribbean, except for western Cuba, in demographic and economic recession, the axis of slave exploitation shifted toward the larger urban centers. After 1595 an expanded trans-Atlantic slave trade supplied increasing numbers of slaves to Spain's continental colonies. The strategic port city of Cartagena on the Caribbean coast of New Granada (present Colombia) served as the hub of this expanded trade in slaves. In the more depressed Caribbean, however, the supply of slaves did not rise concomitantly in every area. It may have done so in western Cuba, especially in the city of Havana and its environs, but it subsided in the rural areas of eastern Cuba, Hispaniola, and Puerto Rico, where the sugar industry's prosperity was by the mid-1600s a fading memory.

Slavery's long period of recession in the Spanish islands coincided with the development of a vast plantation complex in the neighboring British and French colonies (Barbados, the British and French Leewards, Jamaica, western Hispaniola, and the continental colonies of the Guianas). As one might expect, slave-master relations followed a distinct course in each of these groups of colonies. In the Spanish Antilles, and to a lesser extent in the French possessions, a predominantly urban slave regimen seems to have provided considerable opportunity for manumission and self-purchase, so that a large group of free people of African descent came into existence. By contrast, in colonies where plantation slavery was intense, interracial unions, while not unheard of, tended to be less frequent than in the Hispanic colonies.

For this reason, by the first decades of the eighteenth century Cuba, Santo Domingo, and Puerto Rico had small minorities of slaves (ranging from 10 to 25 percent of the total population) but large minorities (or even majorities, in Santo Domingo and Puerto Rico) of people who descended from Africans to some degree. Because whiteness was keenly valued as a social commodity, the relative fluidity and vagueness of race relations may have, paradoxically, sharpened racial awareness and made discrimination based on phenotype even more acute, especially among the elite. African ancestry being so common, dominant groups strove to avoid the entry of darker-skinned persons into circles of prestige and power.

All of these conditions changed drastically, especially in Cuba, after 1763. The British capture of Havana during the last months of the Seven Years' War (1756–1763), an event accompanied by heightened opportunities for sugar exports and slave imports, prompted a re-examination of Spanish mercantile policy toward its Caribbean colonies. In the wake of the Havana occupation, Spain's Bourbon monarchs pursued policies of freer trade in export commodities and in slaves. One of the explicit goals of Spanish reformist policy in the last third of the eighteenth century became the need to emulate other European nations' success with slave plantation development in the Caribbean. Partly because of this, slave-based coffee and sugar estates sprang up in increasing numbers in portions of Cuba (especially around Havana), Santo Domingo, and Puerto Rico. An expanded slave trade was a necessary condition of such growth. In Cuba alone approximately seventy thousand slaves were imported between 1763 and 1792, and another three hundred twenty-five thousand were brought in between 1790 and 1820, when slave imports from Africa were banned (without success) by an Anglo-Spanish treaty. For the entire nineteenth century, imports to Cuba amounted to about seven hundred thousand persons, and to Puerto Rico approximately one-tenth that number. When the final slave cargoes were smuggled—into Cuban territory in 1867 and around 1850 into Puerto Rico—both islands had experienced the most significant demographic, social, and economic transformation in their history as a result of their involvement in the trans-Atlantic slave trade.

The heightened pace of slave importations into Cuba reveals the frenzy of plantation development there, a result of the collapse of the world's largest producer of coffee and sugar, the rebellion-racked French colony of Saint Domingue (Haiti). As commodity prices reached unprecedented peak between 1791 and 1815, native landowners, Saint Domingue exiles, and other immigrants seized the opportunity to establish scores of new slave-based estates in Cuba and Puerto Rico. By the second decade of the nineteenth century, both islands were well on their way to social transformation. At about the same time, in 1822, Santo Domingo, having recently gained its independence from Spain, witnessed a Haitian occupation that resulted in the immediate emancipation of its remaining slaves.

By Caribbean standards, the Cuban and Puerto Rican slave regimes of the nineteenth century were peculiar in several ways. First, although the percentage of slaves in the total population increased steadily in both islands until the mid-1840s, it never attained the absolute majority that it earlier had in the British, French, Dutch, and Danish "sugar islands" at comparable stages of development. At the peak of slave importations from Africa during the 1840s, Cuba's slaves accounted for 43 percent of the total population, whites comprised 42 percent, and free people of African descent 15 percent. Comparable figures for Puerto Rico were 12, 48, and 40 percent, respectively. This breakdown contrasts with slave percentages of 80 or more that were typical in the sugar islands.

Second, slaves who lived and worked in cities comprised a larger share of the total in the Spanish colonies (particularly in Cuba) than in their non-Hispanic counterparts. Despite the fact that most slaves lived and worked in rural estates, as many as one-sixth lived in cities, where they were domestic servants, laborers, craftsmen, and the like. Third, opportunities for manumission, whether by the master's will or by self-purchase (through a legal mechanism known as *coartación*) were greater in the Spanish colonies than in surrounding territories, despite the fact that such opportunities had become scarcer at the height of the slave plantation cycle than they had previously been.

Fourth, the majority of slaves introduced in these islands during this cycle were illegally imported, as Spain entered into successive agreements (dated 1817, 1835, and 1845) with Great Britain to suppress its involvement in the trans-Atlantic slave trade. The business's illegality and the danger of repression by a British anti-slave squadron inflated captives' prices, introduced some distortions in the composition of the victimized groups (regarding age, sex, and regional origins in Africa), and shaped the business ventures themselves, reflected by changes in the participants' nationality, their financing sources, the conduct of the business, and ultimately, their profitability. Finally, the long-drawn-out process of emancipation in the Spanish Caribbean allowed slaveholders and colonial officials to institute measures for a deliberate, gradual transition from slavery to free labor. Although ultimately the slave system collapsed faster than most of its supporters had hoped, Cuba and Puerto Rico experienced fewer post-emancipation economic disruptions than their neighbors.

That the system had never been entirely stable was evident in numerous rebellions and conspiracies that kept the master class unsettled and helped ensure their continued allegiance to Spain. As would be expected, these events were more frequent during the period of largest African importations (c. 1790–1850). In Cuba, the Escalera conspiracy of 1843–1844 revealed to the world the unwelcome prospect that slaves could conspire with free people of color and British abolitionists, in an array of converging plots, to bring about a sudden and violent end of the slave system. Only the swift repressive action of Spanish authorities prevented the rebellion. But as thousands of accused conspirators were put to death in 1844, Cuba's fate as a slave society was sealed; it would henceforth measure its sugar wealth against the terror and violence spawned by racial hatred and class feud. Over the next four decades the prospect of emancipation was the central issue occupying the people, free and slave, of both Spanish islands.

Final emancipation arrived in Puerto Rico in 1876, after a three-year apprenticeship period, and in Cuba in 1886, after a six-year transition of a similar sort. Emancipation was the result of a complex interaction of factors, local, imperial, and international. British abolitionist pressure and other forces helped put an end to the Cuban slave trade in 1867, yet despite the loss of a vital source of new slaves, plantation slavery as a system of labor procurement did not immediately deteriorate. The larger Cuban planters of the western and central regions continued to rely heavily on slave labor even as the 1870s approached, as did most of the wealthiest sugar barons of Puerto Rico. Two interconnected events helped to spark the liberation process: Cuba's Ten Years' War (1868–1878), an independence struggle waged primarily by planters and other farmers from the eastern provinces; and the Moret Law (1870), a Spanish statute that called for the freeing of slaves born after September 1868 and those aged sixty and over. Each in its own way helped to undermine Cuban slavery, not least because they armed the slaves themselves with the legal and military weapons to further their long struggle for freedom. When in March 1873 the Spanish *Cortes* decreed the emancipation of Puerto Rio's thirty thousand bondsmen, Cuba's slave population, ten times larger than that, was already on a path of gradual, steady liberation.

Through a process that included the effects of the Moret Law, Puerto Rican emancipation, and freedom decreed by the independence rebels in the east, the slave system of the Spanish Caribbean came tumbling down during the 1870s. By 1877 more than half of the four hundred thousand slaves counted in the 1867 census of Cuba and Puerto Rico had been liberated. The remainder, still active on some of Cuba's most productive estates, would be freed gradually by an 1880 Spanish law that created an apprenticeship system called the *patronato,* intended to last eight years. Under the weight of numerous freedmen's challenges against their *patronos,* however, in 1886 Spain put a premature end to this system, and with it, to the longest-running chapter in the history of New World slavery.

[*See also* Slave Trade, *article on* Trans-Atlantic Trade.]

BIBLIOGRAPHY

Bergad, Laird W. *Cuban Rural Society in the Nineteenth Century: The Social and Economic History of Monoculture in Matanzas.* Princeton: Princeton University Press, 1990.

Bergad, Laird W., Fe Iglesias García, and María del Carmen Barcia. *The Cuban Slave Market, 1790–1880.* New York: Cambridge University Press, 1995.

Corwin, Arthur F. *Spain and the Abolition of Slavery in Cuba, 1817–1886.* Austin: University of Texas Press, 1967.

Klein, Herbert S. *Slavery in the Americas: A Comparative Study of Virginia and Cuba.* Chicago: University of Chicago Press, 1967.

Paquette, Robert. *Sugar Is Made with Blood: The Conspiracy of La Escalera and the Conflict between Empires over Slavery in Cuba.* Middletown, Conn.: Wesleyan University Press, 1988.

Scarano, Francisco A. *Sugar and Slavery in Puerto Rico: The Plantation Economy of Ponce, 1800–1850.* Madison: University of Wisconsin Press, 1984.

Scott, Rebecca J. *Slave Emancipation in Cuba: The Transition to Free Labor, 1860–1899.* Princeton: Princeton University Press, 1985.

—FRANCISCO A. SCARANO

Dutch Caribbean

Dutch participation in the Atlantic slave trade began in 1596, when a Dutch privateer brought a cargo of slaves captured aboard a Portuguese slaver into the town of Middelburg. After some discussion these slaves were "restored to their natural liberty." There are other stories to support the claim that privateers were the first Dutch slave-traders. A Dutch privateer introduced the first African slaves into British North America; twenty slaves are reported to have been landed in Virginia in 1619 and sold "by a Dutch man of warre."

The situation changed drastically when the Dutch West India Company (WIC) was founded in 1621 and between 1629 and 1636 managed to capture part of Portuguese Brazil. In addition, the WIC expanded the Dutch colony of New Netherland along the Hudson River in North America. It also conquered the small islands close to the coast of Venezuela (Curaçao, Aruba, and Bonaire) as well as three even smaller ones in the northern Caribbean (St. Eustatius, Saba, and St. Maarten, the latter shared with France). In order to supply its Brazilian colony with slaves the WIC conquered some of the Portuguese possessions in Africa, such as Elmina on the Gold Coast in 1637, and the islands of São Tomé, São Paulo, and Benguela on the Angolan coast in 1641.

Between 1636 and 1644 the WIC transferred two thousand five hundred slaves a year. The company failed to prosper, however, because the Portuguese slave-owners in Brazil obtained most of these slaves on credit, and the WIC was unable to obtain payment after the Portuguese planters started a revolt against the Dutch in 1644.

As a result the WIC incurred heavy debts and by midcentury gave up its colony in Brazil, as well as São Tomé and its footholds in Angola. The WIC then utilized its considerable shipping and slave-trading capacities to develop a second Brazil in the Caribbean, where both the French and the British had conquered large sections of the Spanish Caribbean. In return for supplying slaves, technology, and European merchandise to the Spanish, British, and French colonists—directly or via Curaçao—the WIC could continue selling unrefined sugar and other tropical products in the Netherlands.

Dutch dominance lasted until the early 1660s, when British merchants aided by the Acts of Navigation were able to oust the Dutch from the trade with the British Caribbean. Somewhat later the French did the same. Finally, the Dutch developed their own plantation colonies. In the Guianas they already were in possession of some small settlements along the Berbice and Essequibo rivers. In addition, Suriname was taken from the British in 1667. The Dutch were able to keep Suriname by an exchange that gave the British New Netherland. The WIC had not derived much profit from its North American settlement colony because it did not produce much in the way of exports. There were slaves in New Netherland, some of whom had come directly from Africa; the majority, however, were brought to the colony via Curaçao. Slaves numbered around four hundred fifty and made up 5 percent of the total population of New Netherland, estimated at nine thousand in 1664.

In addition to transporting slaves to the Dutch Guianas, the WIC remained active in supplying slaves to the Spanish Caribbean, including parts of the mainland, via Curaçao. In 1662 this trade continued on a legal basis when the WIC became the main subcontractor for a succession of merchants who held the official *asiento*. After the Treaty of Utrecht (1713), however, the British obtained the right to provide slaves to Spanish America and no longer needed the WIC as a supplier. During the eighteenth century Curaçao remained an open slave market, mainly catering to the needs of slave buyers from the Hispanic American mainland.

Slavery in the Dutch Colonial World. After the conquest of Suriname the Dutch West India

Company started to deliver slaves to the planters, and in 1770 the number of slaves in the colony reached its peak of about fifty thousand. In each of the three smaller neighboring colonies to the west, Essequibo, Demerara, and Berbice, a maximum of about eight thousand slaves were employed. In all of these colonies slavery was the basis of the economy; the slave-worked plantations in the Dutch Guianas resembled those in the British and French Caribbean, although there were some differences.

The majority of the planters did not come from the Netherlands. The white population was composed of Jews from Brazil and Germany (both Sephardic and Ashkenazic), French Huguenots,

A Surinam Planter with a Female Slave; engraving, William Blake, from John Gabriel Stedman's *Narrative of a Five Years' Expedition against the Revolted Negroes of Surinam* (1796).

Germans, and above all Scots and Englishmen. Another difference pertains to the relatively high percentage of slaves in Suriname who were able to run away, because most plantations were situated close to the jungle. Around 1770 more than 10 percent of the slaves lived as maroons in the undeveloped hinterland of the colony. At the end of the eighteenth century the colonial government was forced to conclude peace treaties with several of the maroon communities. These treaties stipulated that the runaway slaves no longer would be harassed by the colonial army, and that in return the maroons would not accept any new runaways.

The most important deviation of Dutch plantation agriculture from the general pattern of plan-

A Family of Negro Slaves from Loango, Africa; engraving, William Blake, from John Gabriel Stedman's *Narrative of a Five Years' Expedition against the Revolted Negroes of Surinam* (1796).

tation agriculture in the Caribbean was the erratic way in which the plantations in Suriname attracted metropolitan capital. Before 1750 there was nothing abnormal in this respect; most plantation-owners in the Dutch Guianas had brought their own money. However, between 1750 and 1770 a group of Amsterdam investors poured more than forty million guilders into the Suriname plantations in an attempt to increase production. The outcome of this speculative wave of investment was disastrous. The importation of slaves increased, but income derived from the sale of cash crops did not. As a result the colony developed a deficit in its balance of payments, and after 1780 the growth rate of the Suriname plantation economy was considerably lower than in the British and French Caribbean.

Slaves were also important for the economy of the Dutch Antilles, albeit more as a commodity than as a factor of production. The number of slaves on Curaçao came to about seven thousand, roughly half the population of the island. The second-largest group of inhabitants were the free people of color, totaling about four thousand five hundred. The whites numbered twenty-five hundred. The economy of the islands was mainly geared to the transit trade, and there were few plantations producing for export. Slaves also produced salt for export as well as food for the ships and the slaves in transit, but the main destination of the imported slaves was Spanish America. During the first decades of the eighteenth century St. Eustatius gained a similar position as entrepôt. During that period twenty thousand slaves passed through that island, most destined for the French Caribbean.

A third region, one outside the Caribbean, where slavery played a role, though a modest one, in the Dutch empire, was along the Gold Coast in West Africa. Like the British and the French, the Dutch possessed a string of strongholds along the coast that housed about one to two hundred Europeans and about six hundred slaves. These slaves were used for various purposes, but not for the production of export crops.

Slavery was important for the export economy of the Dutch colony at the Cape of Good Hope. Slaves were imported into the Cape Colony from a wide range of areas in the Indian Ocean—the Indonesian archipelago, India, Sri Lanka, Madagascar, and Mauritius—as well as from the East African mainland. On the eve of the British conquest in 1794, there were 14,747 slaves in the colony, compared to 13,830 Europeans; and the slaves provided much of the labor for the large cattle, wine, and grain farms in South Africa.

Finally, the Dutch used slaves in their Asian and South African possessions. A total of seven thousand slaves annually entered the slavery system of Southeast Asia. The role of those slaves was, however, different from that in the New World. Generally, slaves were not used to produce agricultural exports, with the exception of the Spice Islands (Amboina and Banda). Instead, they staffed the houses of the Dutch merchant community in Asia and worked on the docks.

Abolition of the Slave Trade and Emancipation. After the 1770s Suriname's negative trade balance made it impossible for the planters to buy enough slaves to compensate for mortality in the resident slave population. This explains why the Dutch slave trade declined at the end of the eighteenth century. In total, the Dutch slavers had brought about two hundred fifty thousand slaves to the Guianas and about two hundred thousand to the Dutch islands in the Caribbean. After the French occupation of the Netherlands between 1795 and 1813, the resumption of the slave trade was forbidden.

The peace settlements after the Napoleonic Wars made permanent British possessions of several parts of the Dutch empire where slavery dominated the labor supply, including the Cape Colony and Berbice, Demerara, and Essequibo. It is striking to see how this transfer stimulated economic growth in these areas. Obviously the dynamics of nineteenth-century colonial slavery demanded more investment than the stagnating Dutch economy could provide. In spite of the relative decline of the Dutch slaveholding colonies, however, the Dutch were slow in emancipating their slaves. The abolition debate extended over many years, and not until 1863 were the slaves in Suriname and the Dutch Antilles freed. The owners received about three hundred guilders per slave in compensation. The slaves on the Dutch part of the island of St. Maarten already had received their freedom in 1848 by threatening to move to the French part of the island, where slave emancipation already had taken place. In the Dutch East Indies the number of slaves had been in decline and in 1860 slavery was officially abolished. Not slavery but forced labor enabled the Dutch to increase the production of cash crops on Java dramatically. Every village had to devote one-fifth of its acreage to the production of tropical cash crops; in return the villagers were paid a set wage, allowing the colonial government to make windfall profits. Most of the proceeds of this "cultivation system" flowed into the metropolitan treasury. As a result, the expenditure of twelve million guilders to compensate the West Indian slave-owners could easily be paid.

In spite of the revenues, the Dutch parliament abolished the "cultivation system" in 1860, but the plantation and sugar-factory owners on Java remained dependent on the employment of labor gangs offered on contract by their village chiefs because the supply of free labor never became sufficient. After emancipation in Suriname a similar phenomenon occurred: the majority of the ex-slaves preferred to leave the plantations after the period of apprenticeship (1863–1873) had ended. In their place the Suriname colonial government imported about thirty thousand indentured laborers from British India between 1873 and 1916, as well as thirty thousand indentured laborers from Java between 1890 and 1939.

[*See also* Asia, *article on* Southeast Asia; Maroons; *and* Slave Trade, *article on* Trans-Atlantic Trade.]

BIBLIOGRAPHY

Drescher, Seymour. "The Long Goodbye: Dutch Capitalism and Anti-Slavery in Comparative Perspective." *American Historical Review* 99 (Feb. 1994): 44–70.

Emmer, P. C. "The Dutch and the Making of the Second Atlantic System." In *Slavery and the Rise of the Atlantic System,* edited by Barbara L. Solow. Cambridge: Cambridge University Press, 1991.

Goslinga, Cornelis C. *The Dutch in the Caribbean and on the Wild Coast, 1580–1680.* Gainesville: University of Florida Press, 1971.

Oostindie, Gert. "The Economics of Surinam Slavery." *Economic and Social History in the Netherlands* 5 (1993): 1–23.

Oostindie, Gert, ed. *Fifty Years Later: Antislavery, Capitalism, and Modernity in the Dutch Orbit.* Pittsburgh: University of Pittsburgh Press, 1996.

Postma, Johannes. *The Dutch in the Atlantic Slave Trade, 1600–1815.* Cambridge: Cambridge University Press, 1990.

—PIETER EMMER

Danish and Swedish Caribbean

Among the minor slave-trading nations in the Atlantic between 1600 and 1800, the Dutch carried about four hundred fifty thousand slaves and the Danes and Swedes about fifty thousand. The difference between the carrying capacity of the two nations can be partly explained by the fact that of the three Danish West Indies colonies, St. Thomas, St. John and St. Croix, only St. Croix developed large-scale sugar plantations after 1750. The other islands served as transit harbors.

The participation of the Swedes and the Danes in the early slave trade was marginal. Until 1672 neither nation possessed any colonies in the Caribbean. The Swedes began by participating in the Atlantic slave trade in 1647, when several Dutch investors founded the Swedish Africa Company in an attempt to take business away from the Dutch West Indies Company (WIC). The Swedish company employed former WIC personnel and Dutch ships sailing from Hamburg. The activities of the Swedish Africa Company ended when its chief executive, a former WIC employee, changed employers and conquered most of the Swedish possessions on the African coast in the name of the Danish king. In 1663 the Swedes were evicted from their last African stronghold, Carolusburgh. The Danes managed to consolidate their possessions on the African coast; their main fortress, Christiansborg at Accra, was sold to the British in 1850.

The development of sugar cultivation in the Danish West Indies was hampered by a royal decree in 1792 by which the Danish slave trade was to be suspended as of 1803. Slavery was abolished in 1848. The early abolition of the Danish slave trade can be explained as a political move to strengthen Denmark's ties with Britain. In contrast, the relatively long period between the ending of the slave trade and slave emancipation can be explained by the absence of a Danish abolitionist movement. Sweden also abolished slavery for the six hundred slaves on its only island in the Caribbean, St. Barthelémy, in 1847. The island had been obtained from France in 1774 and was returned in 1877. It had no plantations, and most of its French colonists (2,500) were involved in the transit trade.

BIBLIOGRAPHY

Ekman, Ernst. "Sweden, the Slave Trade and Slavery, 1784–1847." In *La traite des Noirs par l'Atlantique, nouvelles approches/The Atlantic Slave Trade, New Approaches,* edited by Walter E. Minchinton and Pieter C. Emmer. Paris: Société Française d'Histoire d'Outre-mer, 1976.

Green-Pedersen, S. E. "The Scope and Structure of the Danish Negro Slave Trade." *Scandinavian Economic History Review* 19 (1971): 149–197.

Johansen, Hans Christian. "The Reality Behind the Demographic Arguments to Abolish the Danish Slave Trade." In *The Abolition of the Atlantic Slave Trade: Origins and Effects in Europe, Africa and the Americas,* edited by David Eltis and James Walvin. Madison: University of Wisconsin Press, 1981.

Oostindie, Gert, ed. *Fifty Years Later: Antislavery, Capitalism and Modernity in the Dutch Orbit.* Pittsburgh: University of Pittsburgh Press, 1996.

Tyson, George F., Jr. "On the Periphery of the Peripheries: The Cotton Plantations of St. Croix, Danish West Indies, 1735–1815." *Journal of Caribbean History* 26 (1992) 1–36.

—PIETER EMMER

CENTRAL AMERICA. Indigenous forms of servitude in Central America preceded the Spanish conquest, but, oppressive and widespread as they were, they should not be equated with the institution of slavery introduced by Europeans between the sixteenth and nineteenth centuries. As opposed to earlier slavery systems, enslavement of indigenous Indians and then of Africans by Spanish and British settlers reflected demands for labor within the culture of capitalist property rights in the developing economies of the Atlantic world. The peripheral nature of the Central American colonies in the Spanish and British empires led first to the massive export of enslaved Indians, and then to the importation of enslaved Africans into the region; the latter was relatively minor in comparison with importations to other parts of the Americas. The net result was a depopulation of Central America that contributed to the region's persistent underdevelopment.

Servitude existed during the Classic period of Maya civilization (c. 250–1000 CE) and perhaps earlier, and slaves were quite numerous at the time of the Spanish conquest in the 1520s. In the Maya area of Central America (present-day Guatemala, Belize, southeastern Mexico, and western Honduras) the capture of prisoners to sell as slaves was an incentive for endemic border warfare. Prisoners of higher rank were generally sacrificed in ritual acts, but commoners were likely to be sold to work in cacao groves in Mexico or Honduras. Some people were enslaved for crimes or the nonpayment of debts; they could be redeemed if relatives paid their debts or if they were mistreated. This indigenous servitude was often temporary, and the servile group did not constitute a castelike stratum in the society. Rather, little distinction was made among war captives, criminals, and "slaves."

After the Spanish conquest, warfare and the capture of slaves became a Spanish monopoly. The Spaniards took over all long-distance trade, including the slave trade, which became one of their chief sources of wealth. The Spanish colonizers conceived of slaves as commodities to be sold and used as expendable resources. At the time of conquest the region between present-day Panama and the Yucatán Peninsula of Mexico (including Belize, Guatemala, El Salvador, Honduras, Nicaragua, and Costa Rica) contained about three million people of diverse cultures. As a result of warfare, social and economic disruption, pandemics of diseases including smallpox, pulmonary plague, typhus, and measles, and a massive slave trade, this population was reduced within fifty years to perhaps less than half a million, and it continued to decline thereafter. This disaster was especially intense in what is now Nicaragua and Honduras, where the population fell from over a million before the conquest to about ten thousand by the end of the sixteenth century.

In this demographic holocaust, warfare, famine, disease, and slavery reinforced one another, but the Spanish search for slave labor may have accounted for as much as one-third of the decline in some areas. As Spain expanded its empire, indigenous people were hunted, enslaved, and transported from areas where the colonists considered them to be a surplus to those where they were most needed. After 1515 Spaniards sought to repopulate the Greater Antilles with slave-raiding expeditions to the Yucatán coast, and within ten years the Bay Islands in the Gulf of Honduras were depopulated. The conquest of Peru in 1533 created further labor needs in the Andes, and also in Panama to staff the transportation of goods across the isthmus. African slaves were too expensive, but the native peoples of Central America were viewed as an expendable and inexhaustible reservoir of labor. Nicaragua became the chief center of this slave trade. By the mid-sixteenth century between two hundred thousand and five hundred thousand enslaved Indians had been exported from Nicaragua, and between one hundred thousand and one hundred fifty thousand from Honduras. Thousands of others died during slaving expeditions. In 1527, for example, the governor of Honduras led an expedition into Nicaragua in which hundreds of people were killed and two thousand captured, but only one hundred people survived to be sold.

From 1542 to 1543 "New Laws for the Good Treatment and Preservation of the Indians" were proclaimed, but much damage was already done. The slave trade was reduced after 1550 less because of humane laws than because there were few people left in Nicaragua and Honduras to be enslaved. Nonetheless, Mayans from Yucatán continued to be transported to central Mexico to meet Spanish manpower needs in farms, mills, mines, public works, and domestic service. Relatively large populations persisted in the less-accessible highlands, so when Spaniards turned to cacao production in the 1560s they coerced thousands of Mayans from the Guatemalan highlands to work on plantations on the Pacific coast. As a result of bad conditions, overwork, diseases, and famine, the population of that coast fell from more than thirty thousand to one thousand six hundred by the 1570s. The Indian population continued to decline in the seventeenth century. In Costa Rica, for example, there were about eighty thousand Indians in 1563, but fewer than one thousand in 1714.

Although Indian slavery was curtailed by law between the 1540s and 1560s, it remained a way of subjugating those who resisted colonization as well as a means of acquiring and controlling labor. Slave-raiding continued in the seventeenth and eighteenth centuries. The Spanish crown sought to regulate labor through royal labor exchanges, requiring Indians to be paid and to be free to return periodically to their villages; in practice, however, many were treated by the colonists as if they were their chattel property.

Despite the labor shortage that resulted from the severe depopulation of the sixteenth century, most owners of workshops, mines, and farms could not afford African slaves, and slave ships called infrequently at the Caribbean ports of Central America. By 1545 about fifteen hundred enslaved Africans worked at gold extraction in the Guayape River valley in Honduras, but most work-

ers were Indians or poor Europeans. The importation of African slaves, never large, declined to almost nothing by the mid-seventeenth century. Of 62,500 enslaved Africans imported into Spanish America between 1551 and 1600, only about three thousand went to Central America. These African slaves mingled with free people of African-European and African-Indian descent and were lumped together as *pardos*. By 1790 Africans and *pardos* were less than 10 percent of the population of Yucatán, compared to 8 percent for Spaniards and 11 percent for *mestizos*, who were of European and Indian descent. In Nicaragua, Honduras, and Costa Rica, the number of enslaved and free Africans and mulattoes increased slowly in the seventeenth century, but it was never large. Indian labor remained cheaper than enslaved Africans in most of Central America, and labor shortages persisted.

The peripheral, underpopulated, and depressed nature of the Spanish Central American colonies provided opportunities for British intervention there. British colonists established several settlements along the Mosquito Coast and at Belize, on the Bay Islands in the Gulf of Honduras, and on Providence Island off the coast of Nicaragua; they were responsible for importing most of the slaves of African origin who came into Central America in the eighteenth century. Jamaica, seized by Britain in 1655, became the center for British trade and piracy in the western Caribbean. Small numbers of British adventurers, some with African slaves, settled on the Central American coasts to cut wood, establish plantations, and trade with Indians.

By the 1680s some Africans had mixed with local people and formed a new group, known as the Miskito Indians, who remained largely independent of Britain and Spain. They inhabited the coast from Honduras to Costa Rica and obtained tribute and slaves from Indians of the interior. British settlers, however, relied chiefly on importing slaves of African origin, obtained in West Indian slave markets, until the end of the slave trade in 1808. These slaves were expensive, but the British had developed a lucrative export trade in logwood and mahogany from the Bay of Honduras. This economy was based on slave labor, and by the mid-eighteenth century slaves of African origin were the majority of the population in these British settlements. In 1779 there were about three thousand slaves in Belize, about 86 percent of the population. After 1787, when 2,214 people, moreo than three-quarters of whom were slaves, were evacuated from the Mosquito Shore to Belize, the latter became the largest British settlement in Central America.

Slave-ownership in Belize, like land-ownership, was highly concentrated by 1816 about 3 percent of the free heads of families owned 37 percent of the slaves, and in 1820 the five biggest owners possessed 669 slaves, or more than one-quarter of the total. There was an unusually marked division of labor by gender among the slaves in Belize. In 1834 more than 80 percent of the men over ten years of age were woodcutters, while most women were domestic workers. Residence patterns, too, were unusual in that men spent long logging seasons in more or less temporary camps in the forest, while the women and children were in Belize Town. The organization of labor thus shaped the slaves' social and cultural life. The period around Christmas, when all the slaves came together in the town at the end of the logging season, provided the chief opportunity for the development of their creole culture.

The slave population of Belize did not reproduce itself. A marked imbalance of the sexes, with two or three men to each woman, and high mortality rates resulting from disease, malnutrition, overwork, and ill-treatment, contributed to the decline of the slave population after the abolition of the slave trade. Further, more than five hundred slaves were manumitted between 1808 and 1830, and many slaves escaped through the bush to Yucatán and Guatemala, and to maroon communities in the interior. There were four slave revolts, in 1765, 1768, 1773, and 1820, but the relative ease with which slaves could escape, especially after slavery was abolished in the newly independent republics after 1821, made flight a more common

choice than revolt. The colonists, who claimed that their slaves were contented and loyal, repeatedly complained that the rate at which they escaped threatened to ruin the settlement. By 1834, when the 1,923 slaves were made "apprentices" by act of the British Parliament, they constituted less than half of the total population.

The British colony at Belize had developed on the basis of African slave labor while the Spanish colonies continued to stagnate, but the abolition of slavery in Mexico and Central America that followed the end of Spanish control in 1821 helped undermine slavery in Belize. The apprenticeship period that followed slavery ended in 1838 in Belize, but other varieties of coerced labor persisted there and in much of Central America well into the twentieth century.

[See also Emancipation in the Americas.]

BIBLIOGRAPHY

Bolland, O. Nigel. *The Formation of a Colonial Society: Belize from Conquest to Crown Colony.* Baltimore: Johns Hopkins University Press, 1977.

Bolland, O. Nigel. "Colonization and Slavery in Central America." In *Unfree Labour in the Development of the Atlantic World,* edited by Paul E. Lovejoy and Nicholas Rogers. London: Frank Cass, 1994.

Newson, Linda. *The Cost of Conquest: Indian Decline in Honduras under Spanish Rule.* Boulder, Colo.: Westview Press, 1986.

Newson, Linda. *Indian Survival in Colonial Nicaragua.* Norman: University of Oklahoma Press, 1987.

Sherman, William L. *Forced Native Labor in Sixteenth-Century Central America.* Lincoln: University of Nebraska Press, 1979.

—O. Nigel Bolland

CHINA. Prior to the communist collectivization campaigns of the 1950s, China had an exceedingly complex system of social stratification marked by regional cultural variation and a rural-urban dichotomy. Localized forms of slavery existed in many provinces, as did systems of hereditary tenancy and debt bondage.

The best-documented cases of chattel slavery were found in southern China, notably in the provinces of Guangdong and Fujian. Two closely related forms of servitude emerged in this region, one male-specific and the other restricted to women. Most of these servile dependents were status symbols, treated much like investments in imperial degrees, stately homes, and ostentatious rituals.

Servile males were referred to as *ximin*, literally "little people" or "minor people"; they were usually purchased as adolescents from poor families who had an excess of male heirs. Wealthy purchasers used intermediaries—older women who also served as matchmakers—to negotiate the exchange, thus keeping the identities of buyer and seller secret. The status of *ximin* was inherited in the male line, which meant that sons became the property of their father's masters. At the death of an owner his *ximin* were divided among his surviving heirs like any other form of movable property.

The social category referred to as *ximin* was male-specific and was not used for slave daughters or wives. *Ximin* unions were arranged by owners, usually with the daughters of other slaves, but were not treated as marriages in the usual sense of the term. Unlike ordinary unions, servile couples were not bound by a formal ceremony and they had no legal control over their offspring.

The primary duties of *ximin* and their female counterparts were to perform domestic service in the homes of their masters. They carried water, gathered cooking fuel, discarded night soil, carried sedan chairs, and pulled the cords of ceiling fans, among other tasks. It is no doubt significant, given what we know of other forms of servile labor, that *ximin* were often expected to cut, peel, and prepare raw foods for the kitchen but were never allowed to cook or serve the final dishes; these tasks were reserved for servile females.

A few *ximin* were lucky enough to be assigned in their childhood to be companions of their master's sons. Occasionally a former companion would be entrusted with managerial authority over other servants, but the majority of *ximin* performed menial tasks throughout their lives.

All *ximin* and their families were assigned to inferior housing clustered near the boundaries of their masters' estates or, on the margins of villages, adjoining pigsties and water-buffalo sheds. *Ximin* had no rights of ownership to any form of property—in people or goods—within the community and passed nothing of consequence to their offspring. Many *ximin* were granted usufruct to small vegetable plots but were not expected to be self-sufficient; most of their food, clothing, and household goods were provided by the master household. Owners were also responsible for the medical and funeral expenses of their *ximin*.

In a purely economic sense, therefore, this form of male servitude constituted a net loss for the ownership class. *Ximin* did not generate a surplus; on the contrary, they consumed more than they produced. *Ximin* did work, of course, and thus freed members of the master household to engage in other activities. Given the lifetime investment required for maintaining hereditary servants, however, it is clear that wage labor would have been a less costly mode of domestic service.

Chinese servitude of the type outlined above did not spread beyond the domestic sphere into the domains of agricultural production and manufacturing. *Ximin* are best understood as expensive status symbols that helped to distinguish the households of wealthy merchants and landlords from their less affluent neighbors. The fact that *ximin* consumed more than they produced does not in itself make this form of servitude unique; Moses Finley and others have demonstrated that slaves in the ancient world were not all "instruments of production" in the strict sense of that term. However, unlike most slave systems, *ximin* servitude does not appear to have been an outgrowth of, or a secondary development from, older forms of labor exploitation in the same society. Premodern forms of slavery that used unfree laborers as "instruments of production" had long since died out in China by the time Guangdong and Fujian provinces were settled by Han Chinese pioneers. *Ximin* servitude was without doubt indigenous to southern China, where it emerged along with corporate patrilineages and clans that had dominated local culture since the twelfth century BCE.

Systems of female servitude and bondage co-existed with the *ximin* phenomenon well into the communist era (mid-1950s). The daughters of *ximin* were treated as chattels of the master households but, as women in a patrilineal system, they had a better chance to break out of the cycle of servitude. Most of these women were purchased on the open market as domestic servants and were called *mui-jai* (also spelled *mui-tsai*), a Cantonese term that has no Mandarin equivalent. *Mui-jai* literally means "little younger sister," but it is perhaps best translated as "maidservant." In some cases maids of this type accompanied wealthy brides when they moved to the households of their husbands; the *mui-jai* were gifts from the bride's parents and constituted an integral part of the dowry. People in many parts of South China made a direct connection between *mui-jai* servants and mistresses with bound feet who, because of their stylish deformities, were not expected to perform domestic labor.

Unlike servile males, *mui-jai* were not expected to spend their entire lives in the households of their purchasers. Most entered into low-status families at puberty, either as wives for adult sons or as concubines for household heads who had not yet succeeded in producing offspring with first wives. There was thus a constant demand in elite households for young maidservants to replace those who had married out. As the historian Maria Jaschok has demonstrated. the relationship between former *mui-jai* and their masters was fraught with tension and ambiguity, but many remained in close touch throughout their lives.

There can be little doubt that the southern Chinese system of male servitude fits most recognized definitions of chattel slavery: *ximin* were owned by specific masters and their labor was extracted by coercion, since unlike servants, they were not paid for services. They were of lower hereditary status than ordinary peasants, and they did not have

legally recognized marriages; nor was it possible for servile males to be adopted into or accepted by the kinship unit of their masters. *Ximin* slavery was, in comparative perspective, more rigid than most forms of chattel slavery found in precolonial Africa and in ancient Eurasia.

It is doubtful, however, that the *mui-jai* system can be categorized as a form of true chattel slavery. Although servile females were often bought and sold as chattels, most were allowed to marry and establish their own families after a period of domestic service. This is true even of daughters born to male (*ximin*) slaves. The relative flexibility of female servitude is due to the patrilineal bias that prevailed in South Chinese kinship systems. Males were the conveyors of property and status; once a male was admitted into the kinship group as legitimate heirs, it was difficult to make changes at a later date. Women, by contrast, did not inherit property and were not deemed to be lifelong members of their fathers' kinship groups: they married out. Thus female servants often played multiple roles in the kinship system: They could be purchased as surrogate daughters in infancy, exploited like slaves in adolescence, and married to their buyer's male relatives in adulthood. The plight of male slaves was fixed for life: once a *ximin*, always a *ximin*—passing from generation to generation, in the male line.

Chattel slavery was formally abolished in China during the final decade of Manchu rule (1644–1911), but the *ximin* system continued in some areas of South China until the communist land reform campaigns of the 1950s. Former *ximin* and their descendants benefited greatly from the inversion of class status that followed in the revolution's wake. Most found themselves categorized as "landless laborers," thereby qualifying for membership in the Communist Party. Although the evidence is sketchy, it appears that many Communist leaders in the southern Chinese countryside traced their origins to *ximin* slaves. It is perhaps no accident, therefore, that households of former slave-owners were singled out for special attention during the anti-rightist campaigns of the 1950s and 1960s.

[*See also* Concubinage; Gender and Slavery; *and* Mui-jai.]

BIBLIOGRAPHY

Jaschok, Maria. *Concubines and Bondservants: The Social History of a Chinese Custom.* London: Zed Books, 1988.

Pulleyblank, E. G. "The Origins and Nature of Chattel Slavery in China." *Journal of the Economic and Social History of the Orient* 1 (1958): 185–220.

Watson, James L. "Chattel Slavery in Chinese Peasant Society: A Comparative Analysis." *Ethnology* 15 (Oct.1976): 361–375.

Watson, James L. "Transactions in People: The Chinese Market in Slaves, Servants, and Heirs." In *Asian and African Systems of Slavery,* edited by James L. Watson. Oxford: Basil Blackwell, 1980.

Watson, Rubie S. "Wives, Concubines, and Maids: Servitude and Kinship in the Hong Kong Region, 1900–1940." In *Marriage and Inequality in Chinese Society,* edited by Rubie S. Watson and Patricia B. Ebrey. Berkeley: University of California Press, 1991.

Wilbur, C. M. *Slavery in China During the Former Han Dynasty.* Chicago: Field Museum of Natural History, 1943.

—JAMES L. WATSON

CHRISTIAN PERSPECTIVES ON SLAVERY. Thanks to the scholarship of David B. Davis, Orlando Patterson, and others, historians acknowledge that European Christian leaders tolerated residual forms of slavery throughout the Middle Ages and sanctioned the establishment of the institution in New World colonies. While the papacy denounced the enslavement of Indians in the sixteenth century, Catholic colonists in Latin America imported millions of African bondsmen. The Roman Catholic church's influence served to ameliorate the treatment of those African slaves, although apparently not as much as historians once believed. In the British West Indies, masters minimized the potential for Anglican church interference by actively discouraging the conversion of slaves to Christianity.

In colonial North America, the Society of Friends stood alone in the religious community in professing that slaveholding was antithetical to piety. The ideological ferment of the Age of Enlightenment followed by the American Revolution, however, led many Christians to equate the slaves' right to freedom with the colonists' demand for independence from arbitrary rule. As a consequence, dissenting sects such as the Methodists and Presbyterians inscribed anti-slavery sentiment into their disciplinary regulations during the last two decades of the eighteenth century. As James D. Essig has shown, Quakers and Congregational clergy strongly supported the gradual emancipation movement in the Northern states of the newly independent union.

In Great Britain shortly before the American Revolution, Quakers and other religious dissenters, especially Methodists such as John Wesley, began raising moral questions concerning the treatment of slaves. Together with Anglicans inclined toward social reform and evangelicalism, such as Granville Sharp, Thomas Clarkson, and William Wilberforce, they led a generation-long campaign that persuaded Parliament first to curtail the slave trade and then gradually to emancipate slaves in the Caribbean colonies.

Although many American denominations made anti-slavery professions in the immediate post-Revolutionary War period, the nation's major religious bodies did not come to terms with slavery until the early nineteenth century. Some Northern churchmen still spoke out against slavery, but they hoped to use the churches' moral influence to encourage Southern Christians to manumit their slaves voluntarily, perhaps under the auspices of the African Colonization Society, begun in 1816. Conservative Northern churchmen even refused to acknowledge that slavery was a proper subject for ecclesiastical legislation. The inclination of most Northern churchmen, as of Northern politicians, was to treat slavery as a problem best trusted to Southern whites' consciences to solve.

In the 1830s, however, the revivals of the Second Great Awakening led many Christians to regard social evils, including slavery, as the product of sin. Inspired by the success of British emancipation, America's new generation of abolitionists sought the churches' endorsement for their moral appraisal of slave-owning as a sin requiring immediate and complete repentance in the form of emancipation. Most abolitionists also called for an end to all official forms of racial discrimination practiced in the churches. In the 1830s the abolitionists' moral suasion campaign concentrated on converting the churches and reaching an evangelically oriented audience. Abolitionist propaganda endeavored to educate religious institutions about the ways in which their practices sanctioned slavery. The immediate abolitionists hoped that the denominations could convince slaveholders to manumit their slaves by threats of church discipline. Early abolitionists believed that once the churches were enlisted in the anti-slavery movement, Southern slave-masters would capitulate to their opponents' superior moral power. Except for the Quakers, Freewill Baptists, and a few other small, traditionally anti-slavery denominations, however, churches resisted any commitment to abolitionism.

Southern church opinion regarding slavery had begun to change even before the rise of immediate abolitionism in the 1830s. Sentiment favoring gradual emancipation declined in the early nineteenth century as the rapid expansion of cotton production restored prosperity to the institution of slavery. The rising status of members of evangelical churches, such as the Methodists, caused them to renounce earlier anti-slavery professions in order to win social acceptance. As Donald Mathews has demonstrated, residual misgivings about slavery were channeled into safer activities, such as support for colonization (the return of ex-slaves to Africa), missionary work with slaves, and advocacy of a slaveholding ethic to guide the masters' treatment of slaves. At the same time, in response to abolitionist chastisement, pro-slavery sentiment grew up in the region, emphasizing biblical as well as racist arguments.

As a result of the indifference and sometimes outright hostility to the immediate emancipation program, the abolitionists' attitude toward the churches underwent extensive change. Still convinced of the righteousness of their cause, anti-slavery militants accused religious institutions of thwarting rather than promoting God's will. Modeling themselves on the biblical prophets, abolitionists began a campaign to save the churches from divine retribution by rousing them from their toleration of the sin of slaveholding.

The frustration produced by the churches' failure to support abolitionism led the abolitionists to reassess their original strategy of moral suasion. While their propaganda continued to expose pro-slavery church practices, the followers of the radical perfectionist abolitionist William Lloyd Garrison abandoned the nation's religious bodies as hopelessly corrupted by slavery. The public's identification of Garrisonianism with Comeouterism, anticlericalism, and a variety of other heterodox views, however, handicapped the group's effectiveness in developing anti-slavery opinion in the Northern churches.

Of greater influence in religious circles were a group of abolitionists who broke with the Garrisonians in the early 1840s and regrouped in a new organization, the American and Foreign Anti-Slavery Society (AFASS). Although many anti-Garrisonian abolitionists concentrated on political anti-slavery activity, the AFASS attempted to continue traditional church-oriented tactics. In their lecturing and writing, AFASS abolitionists concentrated on inducing the churches to take stronger anti-slavery stands.

The AFASS gained valuable allies in the early 1840s in the form of well-organized denominational anti-slavery movements. Methodist, Baptist, and Presbyterian abolitionists lobbied their denominations to expel slaveholders. These movements had important impact in fomenting the sectional schisms of the Methodist and Baptist churches in the mid-1840s and of the New School Presbyterians in 1857. Even after those divisions, however, abolitionists complained that the Northern church branches still tolerated slavery. As evidence, abolitionists noted that none of these denominations condemned slaveholding as sinful and that all retained thousands of Border State slave-owners in their fellowships. The unsatisfactory outcome of these intradenominational efforts, however, did not destroy church-oriented abolitionists' desire to enlist the support of religious bodies; they continued their lobbying of those institutions until the time of the Civil War. Besides approaching the churches directly, these religiously oriented abolitionists attempted to spread their anti-slavery principles through lobbying the nation's network of interdenominational missionary and religious publication societies. When those bodies resisted, the abolitionists created a parallel network of religious benevolent enterprises, such as the American Missionary Association.

Although most religious bodies stopped short of adopting abolitionist principles and practices, there was evidence of growing anti-slavery sentiment in the Northern churches during the 1840s and 1850s. After enduring abolitionist condemnation for decades, the last remaining Southern members seceded from the New School Presbyterian and Methodist Episcopalian churches in the immediate prewar years, effectively ending the fellowship of slaveholders in those denominations. Although the Unitarian, Baptist, and Congregationalist churches still refrained from formally endorsing abolitionism, a large majority of their Northern members publicly condemned slavery and supported anti-slavery political parties. Nonevangelical denominations, such as the Roman Catholics, Lutherans, and Episcopalians, however, remained firm in their longstanding position that slavery was a morally neutral and exclusively secular question. Despite the considerable growth of anti-slavery sentiment in many denominations, undiluted abolitionism remained a minority viewpoint in the Northern churches in 1860. It is significant that the abolitionists had made little progress in winning equal treatment for blacks in most Northern religious bodies.

Southern pro-slaveryism intensified in the face of the abolitionists' unremitting moral condemnation. The biblical pro-slavery argument was used to sanctify slavery and to question the orthodoxy of its abolitionist critics. Toleration for the region's remaining anti-slavery voices, such as the Quakers, practically disappeared in most of the Deep South. Such militancy spurred Southern secessions from the largest Protestant denominations in the mid-1840s when Northerners refused their demands to remove all anti-slavery vestiges from church disciplines and practices. The historian Mitchell Snay has shown that once freed of ties to their Northern counterparts, Southern churches became an important vehicle in promoting the cultural separatism that would contribute to the sectional strife leading to the Civil War.

The Civil War broke down most of the Northern churches' remaining resistance to taking aggressive anti-slavery actions. The secession of the Southern states led most denominations to acknowledge the moral corruption inherent in a slaveholding society. After initial hesitation, most denominations responded to abolitionist entreaties to endorse emancipation. With the exception of the nonevangelical denominations, Northern churches lobbied the President and Congress during the war to put an end to slavery.

Following the Confederacy's defeat, Southern white Christians reconciled themselves to emancipation as God's will. Few Southerners, though, ever acknowledged the validity of the abolitionists' moral critique of slavery. As wartime passions cooled, most denominations began the process of sectional reunification. Northern racism increased in the postwar era, and little pressure was placed on Southern white Christians to make an equal place for African Americans in their churches. Although the churches had contributed to the victory of emancipation in the United States, they would not play the role abolitionists had expected in healing the nation's racial divisions. Following emancipation in the United States, slavery legally existed only in Brazil and the Spanish Caribbean colonies; other Central and South American nations had abolished the institution immediately or soon after gaining independence. The Roman Catholic church offered no challenge to slavery in these countries beyond ameliorative practices such as sanctioning slave marriages. The small abolitionist campaigns in both remaining slave societies were primarily offshoots of anticlerical liberal political movements. Organized churches thus played little role in bringing about emancipation in Brazil and Cuba late in the nineteenth century.

In general, evangelical Christian tenets contributed heavily to the inspiration for the modern abolitionist movement. Members of denominations where the concepts of free will and individual responsibility for social problems were strongest tended to be in the anti-slavery vanguard. Even so, the influence of slaveholding members and other institutional considerations caused most evangelical denominations to refrain from unqualified endorsement of immediate abolitionism. As a consequence, militant abolitionists in most countries generally worked apart from and sometimes in opposition to church leaders. The abolitionist triumph should be attributed more to Christian principles than to Christian institutions.

[*See also* Abolition and Anti-Slavery; Biblical Literature, *overview article*; Emancipation in the Americas; Religion; *and* United States, *article on* The South.]

BIBLIOGRAPHY

Davis, David Brion. *The Problem of Slavery in Western Culture.* Ithaca, N.Y.: Cornell University Press, 1966.

Essig, James D. *The Bonds of Wickedness: American Evangelicals Against Slavery, 1770–1808.* Philadelphia: Temple University Press, 1982.

Mathews, Donald G. *Slavery and Methodism: A Chapter in American Morality, 1780–1845.* Princeton: Princeton University Press, 1965.

Patterson, Orlando. *Slavery and Social Death: A Comparative Study.* Cambridge, Mass.: Harvard University Press, 1982.

Snay, Mitchell. *The Gospel of Disunion: Religion and Separatism in the Antebellum South.* Cambridge: Cambridge University Press, 1993.

—JOHN R. MCKIVIGAN

CLIENTAGE. In the clientage system, also known as *clientelism* and *patron-client relationship*, voluntary, informal alliances are formed between two individuals of unequal status, power, or material resources for the purposes of mutual aid and support. In such relationships the higher ally is termed a *patron*, and the lower one a *client*. Through their interaction each ally can expect favored treatment from his patron or client as compared with outsiders who may appeal for similar aid.

Clientage differs from slavery in that a patron does not own—has no unbreakable hold on—a client, based on force or law. The client is free to seek another patron, can manage without any patron, or may become a patron in his or her own right. Even slaves can hope to become the favorites of their masters, thereby becoming clients while remaining slaves.

Because patron and client are not of equal status, the help given by each to the other is different in kind from that expected in return. Typically the patron gives material benefits and protection to the client, while the latter gives labor and loyal service in return. In a broad sense, the client accepts the patron as a leader, and the latter takes the client as a follower. The most valuable feature of such a relationship to both patron and client, however, lies in their expectation that each will come to the other's aid with all his or her resources in time of extreme need, and without too precise a reckoning of the costs.

Thus the spirit of the relationship is almost—but not quite—familial. Client and patron may even employ terms suggesting kinship in addressing each other. Real children, however, cannot replace their parents, nor real parents their children, whereas patrons and clients have these options. Moreover, their mutual affection is at least partly feigned. At bottom, self-interest underlies altruism in patron-client relationships; therefore, benefits and obligations must be reciprocal.

In practice patron-client ties can be quite fragile, and therefore they must be nurtured through the periodic exchange of small favors. When either patron or client fails to fulfill the other's expectations, especially when help is greatly needed, the relationship ends. Even with the best of intentions, the endurance of a patron-client tie depends on the continuance of the patron's resources. When these are unstable because they are not wholly owned (as in the case of a politician who has lost office and thus access to government patronage), the clients are likely to drift away.

A patron, by definition a person of superior resources, can maintain simultaneous alliances with numerous clients. The greater the patron's stock of resources, the larger the potential number of his or her clients. There can exist multitiered pyramids of clienteles, in which several minor patrons, each with a small band of followers, are themselves the clients of one higher patron. Political parties in many developing countries can be described as such clientelistic pyramids, in which local leaders deliver the votes of their followers upward to higher national leaders in return for the downward flow of patronage.

Patron-client relationships may be found at any level of a social system. The role of client can be filled by a farm tenant or day-laborer who offers special loyalty or provides extra services to his or her landlord or employer in the hope of secure tenure or employment; by a local political leader who becomes the follower of a more powerful national politician; by an ambitious army officer who hopes to speed his or her own career by becoming the aide to a rising general; and among aspirants for membership in the Politburo of a communist state. Similar ties can be formed between collectivities, as in the case of a small country that consistently follows the lead of a superpower in return for the latter's protection.

Because they are very simple and useful arrange-ments, patron-client relationships probably have existed throughout history in all human societies, but they have not always been equally prominent. Clientelism is most likely to flourish in times of general insecurity, when "big men" need followers on whose loyalty they can rely and "little men" need the special protection of persons more powerful than themselves. Such conditions were common before the appearance of the strong modern state.

In premodern societies clientelism was adapted to a wide variety of institutional settings. In medieval Europe and Japan, lords, vassals, and their peasant serfs were bound together in pyramids of reciprocal feudal obligations by ritualized pledges of personal loyalty. In premodern Thailand, clientelism was an integral part of monarchic administration. In Africa, patron-client relationships bound together religious teachers and their followers and placed immigrants under the protection of members of dominant tribes. Similar adaptations may be found in other parts of the world.

In modern industrial societies there is less need for patron-client relationships. Personal security, at least in theory, is assured by the state through its suppression of private armies and the enforcement of contracts. Furthermore, favoritism, the cement of patron-client relationships, clashes with the typical modern beliefs that individuals should be treated equally under the law, that rewards and promotions should be based on unbiased assessments of achievement, and that economic decisions should be guided by the impersonal rules of market.

Nonetheless, patron-client relationships can be observed in modern societies as useful, though extralegal, arrangements within firms and bureaucracies that ostensibly prohibit personal favoritism. They are especially evident in present-day dictatorships and other regimes of dubious legitimacy, where power falls to those who seize it by force or who rise through intrabureaucratic intrigue. There loyal henchmen who are willing to take risks for their patrons are needed by the major power-seekers and can expect to receive substantial rewards.

Patron-client relationships can be found even in modern democracies. The unpaid pre-convention campaign workers of an American presidential hopeful—who may be rewarded with positions on the White House staff—are clients too. The American political system legitimates their presence by classifying them as "political appointees." They are tolerated, but they are placed outside the civil service system, because they have become essential to the American process of choosing a president.

BIBLIOGRAPHY

Gellner, Ernest and John Waterbury, eds. *Patrons and Clients in Mediterranean Societies*. London: Gerald Duckworth, 1977.

Schmidt, Steffen W., et al., eds. *Friends, Followers and Factions: A Reader in Political Clientelism*. Berkeley: University of California Press, 1977.

—CARL H. LANDÉ

COARTACIÓN. The term *coartación* was used in Spain's American colonies to denote the practice of establishing a fixed price at which any slave could purchase his or her freedom on an installment plan. Theoretically this insulated the market mechanism of self-purchase from the individual whim of the master, but theory and practice were not necessarily reconciled in the American world of masters and slaves. Thus the custom varied considerably throughout the Americas (with equivalents existing in the non-Hispanic slave colonies) based on population mix, the nature of the economy, and its demand for slave labor, as well as the locally prevailing mores of masters and slaves.

Exactly when the term established itself in association with Spanish-American slavery is not clear. By the eighteenth century it had entered legal and political discourse. Fernando Ortiz suggests that *coartación* first appeared in Spanish laws in 1712. It formed an important part of the Cuban slave code of 1842.

The practice apparently prevailed in general custom before it found acceptance in common law. In December 1788 the Consejo de Indias, the Spanish crown's advisory council for its American empire, rendered an important opinion on a request from the local governor at Havana, Cuba, who insisted that the offspring of slaves who were *coartado*, or undergoing installment self-purchase, were not automatically included in any previously agreed price.

The system of *coartación*, according to Elsa Goveia in *The West Indian Slave Laws of the Eighteenth Century* (1970), "was widespread in the Spanish islands in the eighteenth century, and it was probably of great importance in increasing the numbers of freed men in these territories at the time." Indeed, a custom sometimes prevailed by which a slave, having publicly established his individual purchase price, could change masters, with or without cause, in order to increase his or her income and thereby more rapidly exercise the right of purchase. Slaves could also change masters to improve the opportunity to purchase their freedom, and they could negotiate the purchase of specific days or periods of time.

The custom of *coartación* introduced significant modifications in the system of slavery, but its overall importance as a conduit of manumission should not be exaggerated. The custom clearly indicated that slaves retained, regardless of their legal status, a legal persona that entitled them to certain stipulated rights and privileges. They could own some property, even property in themselves. They could become and indeed were an increasingly important factor in the expanding world of capital fueled by the trans-Atlantic commerce in Africans and tropical plantation staples. Individual earnings derived from such permitted activities as the sale of produce in Sunday markets or from various jobbing skills could be protected from arbitrary confiscation by the master. Above all, *coartación* established and retained the principle that freedom for some slaves could be obtained through a simple monetary transaction. At the same time, a slave undergoing installment self-purchase enjoyed the dubious protections of all slaves: exemption from royal or clerical taxes; freedom from the responsibilities of any personal debts, and exclusion from automatic service in the militia. While it is difficult to estimate the number who obtained freedom under this procedure, urban slaves, especially females and those with artisanal skills in high demand, were best situated to take advantage of the process of *coartación*.

[*See also* Caribbean Region, *article on* Spanish Caribbean; *and* Manumission.]

BIBLIOGRAPHY

Bergad, Laird W., Fe Iglesias García, and María del Carmen Barcia. *The Cuban Slave Market, 1790–1880*. New York: Cambridge University Press, 1995.

Goveia, Elsa V. *The West Indian Slave Laws of the 18th Century*. London: Caribbean Universities Press, 1970.

Knight, Franklin W. *Slave Society in Cuba During the Nineteenth Century*. Madison: University of Wisconsin Press, 1970.

Nuñez, Benjamin. *Dictionary of Afro-Latin American Civilization*. Westport, Conn.: Greenwood Press, 1980.

—FRANKLIN W. KNIGHT

CONCUBINAGE. The examination of concubinage—the ownership of females by males for sexual and reproductive purposes—calls forth a radical contexualization of slavery, particularly "domestic slavery," with kinship and gender. In much of sub-Saharan Africa the traditional productive systems were marked by extensive hoe cultivation of slash-and-burn fields, while the political landscape was often characterized by a checkerboard pattern of states with economies based on booty and trade rather than on internally generated surplus agricultural products. The remaining sociopolitical blocks were kinship domains where one's opportunities and access to resources were embedded in the corporate kin group; these polities' external relations were grounded in the politics of ratios of persons to land. The accumulation of marital ties and dependents were the "capital" of this kinship domain. Therefore, existing inequalities, such as those of age and gender, were reinforced by the concentration of reproductive power in the control of males who held high rank in kin groups. Concubines as slave wives increased both the kinship unit's labor force and its long-term stability and status, since the group's size grew through the inclusive legitimization of the slave concubines' children.

In Eurasian societies characterized by intensive cultivation of cereals and strong artisanal, commercial, and trading sectors, there was surplus accumulation, stratification, and much greater elaboration of status than in Africa. Concubinage in this global zone was a condition paralleling the practice of dowry and diverging devolution, in which property can be diffused outside the lineage. In China, the presence of heirs for the transmission of property and power was a central concern in legal and ideological constructs of power. Concubinage, even though associated with males' erotic images, was principally a way of obtaining offspring. In the Chinese practice of concubinage, it did not matter who the mother was; it was the father's status that mattered. Rulers and wealthy men surrounded themselves with numerous wives, concubines, and female retainers whose lives were easier and more respectable than those of commoner women. In Asia generally, the children of a concubine might inherit from their father. The inability of a wife to bear children was one reason for taking a concubine. Generally, concubinage as an addition to marriage was associated with high caste or class groups in which polygamy was practiced. Among lower groups, it functioned as an alternative to marriage. Concubines were drawn from the lower groups, including slaves. The accumulation of women as sexual partners and maidservants was not merely a form of conspicuous consumption but also a display of power that provided required work and heirs for the household.

The concubine was ubiquitous in the structured, patriarchal Muslim societies, from the family household to the courts of pashas and the seraglios of the sultans. This made the concubine an integral part of Islamic domestic life. Islamic law tried to provide some safeguards and protection for concubines; for instance, it was stipulated that a concubine could not be sold or alienated after she bore the master's child. After kingship became hereditary in Islamic domains, concubines often had political power that competed with that of royal wives.

The key status of concubines lay in the critical issue of inheritance and security of status, which was intertwined with but still distinct from the masters' predatory sexual access to unwed slave women. It can be said, however, that concubinage, especially the institution of slave concubines, significantly reinforced gender inequality and the general dominance of men. For example, the sharp increase in Africa and Asia in the number of slave concubines and wives in the era of slave exports from Africa and probably also from Southeast Asia served to degrade all affected wives. Some females might be slave, concubine, wife, and prostitute at different times in their lives.

Jack Goody (1990) has distinguished between three types of concubinage relating to the householding property forms with which they are identified: legitimizing, morganatic, and companion concubinage. The first is exemplified in parts of China, where children of concubines were able to inherit equally with those of free wives. Ancient Rome exemplifies the morganatic type; the Romans generally practiced monogamy, and the preference for concubines or slave mistresses derived from the fact that they produced no additional heirs to share in the inheritance, a particular attraction for the rich and powerful.

Although Goody's discussion of kinship, household, and the role of concubines is limited to the Old World, the system of companion concubinage appears to be most characteristic of New World slavery. The acquisition of slave women as sexual partners, primarily by European men, presents some of the more vexing issues in New World slavery. In addition to suffering sexual exploitation, the concubine found herself torn between identities and allegiances in the double vulnerability of

being both slave and woman. Although instances of shared affection existed, in the main women were left struggling to survive and gain some advantage from their victimization. Children of slave women and white masters introduced ambiguity and conflict into the slave society by contradicting the castelike codes of separation, both by status and by race, which functioned together in New World slavery. Unlike women serving as concubines in other slave societies, they received little or no legal protection, and their children inherited their mother's servile status unless manumitted by their fathers.

[*See also* Biblical Literature, *article on* Hebrew Scriptures; China; Gender and Slavery; Law, *article on* Islamic Law; *and* Mui-jai.]

BIBLIOGRAPHY

Goody, Jack. *The Oriental, the Ancient and the Primitive: Systems of Marriage and the Family in the Pre-Industrial Societies of Eurasia*. Cambridge: Cambridge University Press, 1990.

Jaschok, Maria. *Concubines and Maidservants: The Social History of a Chinese Custom*. London: Zed Books, 1988.

Martinez-Alier [Stolcke], Verena. *Marriage, Class and Colour in Nineteenth Century Cuba: A Study of Racial Attitudes and Sexual Values in a Slave Society*. London: Cambridge University Press, 1974.

Meillassoux, Claude. *Maidens, Meal and Money: Capitalism and the Domestic Community*. Cambridge: Cambridge University Press, 1981.

Morrissey, Marietta. *Slave Women in the New World: Gender Stratification in the Caribbean*. Lawrence: University Press of Kansas, 1989.

Reid, Anthony, ed. *Slavery, Bondage, and Dependancy in Southeast Asia*. New York and St. Lucia: University of Queensland Press, 1983.

Robertson, Claire C. and Martin A. Klein, eds. *Women and Slavery in Africa*. Madison: University of Wisconsin Press, 1983.

Watson, Rubie S., and Patricia B. Ebrey, eds. *Marriage and Inequality in Chinese Society*. Berkeley: University of California Press, 1991.

—FRANK MCGLYNN

CONFRATERNITIES. The lay brotherhoods of the Roman Catholic Church are voluntary organizations of the faithful to exercise some work of piety or charity. They have historically been devoted to social benevolence and mutual aid. European brotherhoods of the medieval to early modern period were affiliated with parish churches, monasteries, or convents; they were devoted to a patron saint and performed various charitable activities not performed by the state authorities, such as burying the dead, building churches, and caring for sick and imprisoned members and for their widows and orphans. Confraternities in Latin America, a development from this institution, comprised different social classes, occupations, ethnic groups, and races. These organizations have existed in many societies, but they have been most important in the Iberian Peninsula and in Iberian settlements.

When the first African slaves began arriving in large numbers in the Iberian Peninsula in the fifteenth century, confraternities were created to aid in their conversion. The aristocratic white brotherhoods excluded blacks from their membership. The organization of Iberian society into brotherhoods dependent on social status, color, or occupation was a carryover from the medieval practice of organizing society into different estates or guilds. The earliest slave brotherhoods date from the fifteenth century and were found mainly in urban areas such as Seville, Barcelona, Valencia, and Lisbon. The religious organization of slaves into confraternities in Europe and Latin America was an attempt by the religious orders and church officials to assimilate the slaves into European-dominated societies. By giving the slaves a religious role in the confraternities and a place in religious processions, churchmen hoped that they would be kept from falling back into pagan religious practices.

In the sixteenth and seventeenth centuries there were at least fifteen slave confraternities in Portugal and eleven in Spain. Both the Iberian church and state viewed confraternities as a vital step in the christianization of African slaves only nominally baptized on the slave ships. These early brotherhoods also performed the important function of providing decent Christian burial for slaves. In general, dead slaves were otherwise not buried; their bodies were often tossed into the streets of the cities, or in rural fields, even in dung heaps, with little regard for their humanity. In addition, from the beginnings of the Atlantic slave trade the monarchs of Spain and Portugal encouraged the christianization of African slaves as one justification for the cruel and inhuman traffic in black labor.

Historically, black confraternities owe their existence to missionaries in Africa and Latin America who worked in the evangelization of newly arrived slaves. As mutual-aid societies, they provided spiritual consolation and a measure of defense and protection for the slaves. They were mainly cooperative in nature and owed much to the Jesuits and Dominicans for their founding in the fifteenth and sixteenth centuries. The Dominican order had the special canonical privilege to found lay confraternities for the African population in Portugal and Africa. In the New World this privilege was extended to other religious orders. The Jesuits were especially active in organizing lay confraternities among the African populations in Brazil, Colombia, and Peru.

The lack of adequate burial for slaves was also a public nuisance in the cities of colonial Brazil and an expense for the church. The bodies of dead slaves were often found at church doors, in cemeteries, on beaches, or dumped into rivers or tied to sticks to float out on the evening tides, which presented health hazards for the living population. Customary beliefs in Portugal, Africa, and Brazil held that the souls of unburied corpses would wander accursed as ghosts haunting the living. Africans believed that souls not properly buried would never return to Africa or live in harmony with the spirits of family ancestors.

Black confraternities existed in the major urban centers of colonial Brazil, wherever the black population was large enough to encourage religious devotion to black saints and to support the devel-

Burial of a Slave; painting from João Maurécio's *Rugendas viagem pictoresca através do Brasilian* (1835).

opment of Afro-Brazilian cult houses and the preservation of African customs. The brotherhoods of Brazil were more important than lay confraternities of slaves elsewhere in Latin America because of the larger size of the African population in the northeastern provinces, where nonwhite people outnumbered whites. It is no exaggeration to say that practically every parish in colonial Brazil had a slave sodality attached to its churches and convents. The four provinces of Minas Gerais, Bahia, Pernambuco, and Rio de Janeiro had the largest African populations as well as the greatest number of black confraternities.

The first Jesuit missionaries in Pernambuco started the earliest confraternities for newly arrived African slaves from Guinea as early as 1552. This first slave confraternity in Brazil was dedicated to the patronage of Our Lady of the Rosary, whom the slaves worshipped as Yemanja, an African goddess of the sea. The brotherhood members heard masses together in the Jesuit church on Sundays and feast days; religious processions were organized on Sundays during Lent. Confraternities were attractive to African-born slaves because of the West African traditions of similar Muslim brotherhoods and autochthonous secret societies.

Pope Gregory XIII permitted the organization of brotherhoods in the late sixteenth century to indoctrinate newly converted slaves in the customs and dogma of Catholicism. In 1589 two Jesuit priests who worked in missions on the sugar plantations in Brazil's northeast provinces also created brotherhoods for the African slaves of the *engenho* (sugar mill). The Jesuits believed the slave sodalities had great spiritual utility because in one year the confessions heard in the *engenhos* surpassed eight thousand. The institution of lay brotherhoods was viewed by the crown and church as another important step in the evangelization of slaves. In 1576 the king of Portugal passed a decree ordering that the tithes collected from newly converted Africans should be used for their own churches, lay brotherhoods, and spiritual affairs in Brazil for a span of six years. The church encouraged the organization of slave confraternities (*confraria*) to facilitate their religious conversion and instruction. Membership in the *confraria* obliged the brothers and sisters (there were separate, analogous organizations for women) to meet together in the church to say the Rosary, attend Mass, receive the sacraments, participate in religious festivals and funeral processions, and take religious instruction.

From earliest times in Brazil separate brotherhoods existed for whites, blacks, and Indians. With the growth of race-mixing in Brazil, confraternities were created for the fourth racial category of mulattoes or *pardos*. The earliest brotherhoods dedicated to Our Lady of the Rosary in Bahia were divided into two branches, one for whites and another for blacks. A separate confraternity was later established in Salvador for mulattoes, dedicated to Our Lady of Guadelupe. In the sixteenth and seventeenth centuries the lay brotherhoods of Brazil were divided by racial and ethnic classifications. By the eighteenth century many of the black brotherhoods admitted whites as members, although they usually paid higher entrance fees and annual dues and were barred from positions on the governing boards of the brotherhoods. It was at first customary to reserve the positions of scribe and treasurer for whites, because of the poverty and illiteracy of the African population; however, by the end of the eighteenth century there were enough literate blacks and mulattoes to demand an end to this practice.

Although the earliest brotherhoods were founded by missionaries and secular clergymen, the confraternities of the late colonial period were organized by pious laymen and women, not imposed by church or state, to provide some sense of community and fictive kin for those who had lost families in the slave trade. Afro-Brazilians found in brotherhoods a socially-acceptable outlet for their talents, not available elsewhere in a slaveholding society.

African slaves were bound together in brotherhoods by common kinship ties, common oppression, and ethnic loyalties. Religious associations gave slaves some sense of autonomy, dignity, and transcendence over oppressive earthly conditions. Organization of slaves in brotherhoods helped to preserve African languages, customs, and tribal identities. Owing to tribal rivalries and cultural differences, separate confraternities were organized for people of West African or Sudanese origin; the Portuguese settlers preferred the Bantu people from Angola or the Congo. These mutual-aid and benefit societies were interwoven with extended families, tribes, and churches in the urban areas.

More research needs to be done on brotherhoods in the nineteenth century, when they competed with secular associations such as masonic lodges, manumission societies, and *capoeira* (martial-arts) clubs. Further study could also be done on the connection between brotherhoods and the African cult houses that flourished in the shadow of confraternity churches, meeting secretly at night to avoid censure from church and state. There were political aspects, too: black confraternal brothers and sisters participated in riots and rebellions in 1835 and 1836 in Salvador (Bahia). These societies give a view of the internal lives of slaves and religious rituals of popular religion. Lay brotherhoods functioned as parish and neighborhood associations, providing mutual aid and social benevolence, and as such showed a strong sense of kinship and community spirit.

People of African descent in Brazil and Spanish America organized mutual aid societies based on their tribal origins to maintain their cultural heritage, to acquire social prestige, and to secure death benefits. Slave sodalities acted as a means of community solidarity in times of hardship and economic need. In joyful times they celebrated festivals in honor of their patron saints, syncretizing African gods and goddesses with Catholic saints.

[*See also* Brazil; Race and Racism; *and* South America.]

BIBLIOGRAPHY

Meyers, A., and D. E. Hopkins, eds. *Manipulating the Saints: Religious Brotherhoods and Social Integration in Postconquest Latin America*. Hamburg: Wayasbah, 1988.

Mulvey, Patricia A. "Black Brothers and Sisters: Membership in the Black Lay Brotherhoods of Colonial Brazil." *Luso-Brazilian Review* 19 (1980): 253–279.

Mulvey, Patricia A. "The Black Lay Brotherhoods of Colonial Brazil: A History." Ph.D. diss., City University of New York (Graduate Center), 1976.

Mulvey, Patricia A. "Slave Confraternities in Brazil: Their Role in Colonial Society." *Americas* 39 (1982): 39–67.

Reis, João Jose. "Death to the Cemetery: Funerary Reform and Rebellion in Salvador, Brazil, 1836." In *Riots in the Cities*, edited by S. M. Arrom and S. Ortoll. Wilmington, Del.: Scholarly Resources, 1996.

Russell-Wood, A. J. R. "Black and Mulatto Brotherhoods in Colonial Brazil: A Study in Collective Behavior." *Hispanic American Historical Review* 54 (1974): 567–602.

—PATRICIA A. MULVEY

CONTEMPORARY SLAVERY. In 1975 a working group of the United Nations was established to collect evidence on slavery and a wide variety of practices that have been variously described as analogous to slavery, "slavery-like practices," and, recently, "contemporary forms of slavery." Many are as oppressive, and have at least as long a history, as chattel slavery, but they have been designated forms of slavery in international agreements only in the twentieth century.

By the end of World War I chattel slavery and the slave trade had been largely eradicated. Both were still legal, however, in some areas, most notably in Ethiopia and the Arabian Peninsula. A small-scale illegal traffic continued elsewhere, and slavery itself was tolerated in some of the territories of European colonial powers (Britain, France, Portugal, Spain, Italy, Belgium, and the Netherlands). In most of these, however, it had lost its legal status, and in theory slaves could leave their owners. It was widely believed that those who remained did so voluntarily and that the institution was therefore "benign." In 1919 the victorious allied powers abrogated the Brussels Act of 1890, which had pledged signatories to suppress the African slave trade, on the grounds that it was no longer needed.

It had long been accepted, however, that "native welfare" was a matter of international concern, and it was envisaged that the nascent League of Nations would take up the question under Article 23 of its Covenant. This bound members to secure "fair and humane conditions of labor for men, women and children," not just in their own countries but in all countries to which their commercial and industrial relations extended. Moreover, the International Labor Organization (ILO) had been newly formed to protect labor everywhere.

The colonial powers, however, wanted no interference in their internal affairs and had no wish to negotiate any new treaties against the slave trade, let alone slavery. Probably no action would have been taken had there not been an outcry in the British press in 1922 over revelations of slave-raiding, as well as trading, in Ethiopia, and of an active slave traffic to Arabia. Intensive lobbying at the League of Nations in Geneva by the British and Foreign Anti-Slavery and Aborigines Protection Society—the oldest and foremost anti-slavery organization—resulted in the appointment of a Temporary Slavery Commission to inquire not only into the slave trade, but also into slavery in all its forms all over the world, and to recommend measures to suppress it.

This commission met in 1924 and 1925. The European colonial powers limited its scope and impact by insisting that it was to be a temporary advisory body that met in private and received evidence from approved sources only. They also claimed the right to review its published reports and to reject its recommendations. However, to ensure that it was not simply a tool of these powers, the League appointed the commission's members as "independent experts" rather than government representatives. Most were serving or retired colonial officials who had seen slavery and the colonial exploitation of forced labor at first hand.

The commissioners broke new ground by recommending that the League negotiate a treaty not only against chattel slavery and the slave trade, but also against a range of other practices restrictive of individual liberty, particularly serfdom, African forms of slavery, debt bondage (including peonage and pawning), the acquisition of girls by purchase disguised as dowry, forced marriage, child marriage, and the buying and selling of children for domestic or other labor. Most importantly, they included forced labor, which was widely used by the colonial powers to provide cheap labor for construction projects and export production.

It was this committee, therefore, that first officially designated these practices as forms of slavery against which victims should be protected by international agreement. Trafficking in women and children for prostitution—called the "white slave trade"—was not included simply because it was already the subject of several international conventions and was under the supervision of a League committee.

The main result of the report of the Temporary Slavery Commission was the negotiation by the League of Nations of the first multilateral treaty against slavery, the Convention of 1926. The colonial powers ensured that it was a paper tiger. Signatories were bound to suppress the slave trade immediately but were only required to abolish slavery in all its forms "progressively and as soon as possible." Moreover, although slavery was broadly defined as "the status or condition of a person over whom any or all of the powers attaching to the right of ownership are exercised," the various forms under attack were not spelled out, no time limit was set for their eradication, and there was no

mechanism for enforcing the treaty or even monitoring results.

An important article in the convention, however, strictly limited forced labor for public purposes and condemned its use for private enterprises. This question was now passed to the International Labor Organization, which negotiated the Forced Labor Convention of 1930 and subsequent treaties.

It soon became clear that the 1926 Slavery Convention had limited impact. Although slavery was outlawed in the next few years in Afghanistan, Iraq, Nepal, Kelat, Trans-Jordan, and Iran, it remained legal in Arabia, where victims were still imported from as far away as West Africa and China. Slave-raiding persisted in Ethiopia. Little Chinese girls were still sold as *mui-jai* in British colonies, as well as in China. Workers, under guise of contract labor, were still recruited by force and shipped off to virtual slavery, notably from Liberia to the Spanish island of Fernando Po. Debt bondage remained widespread, including peonage, forced marriages, child labor, and other forms of oppression analogous to slavery. Faced with this, a second and even more circumscribed League committee, which met in 1932 to investigate the results of the 1926 Convention, recommended the creation of a small permanent body to collect information on slavery and offer advice on its suppression.

This led to the appointment of the Advisory Committee of Experts on Slavery, which functioned from 1934 to 1939. The European colonial powers ensured that it was as emasculated as its predecessors. However, its British member conducted his own investigations, building on the work of the Temporary Slavery Commission by calling attention to abuses such as debt bondage in India, child labor in Ceylon, *mui-jai* in China, the virtual enslavement of hunters and gatherers in Bechuanaland, and forms of bride wealth in Africa, as well as continuing chattel slavery. His efforts shamed some governments, particularly British colonial administrations, into amending anti-slavery legislation in their territories and taking some steps to remedy the practices most akin to chattel slavery. Little headway, however, had been made against most of the other practices now designated forms of slavery before the outbreak of World War II ended the work of the committee.

By the end of the war chattel slavery had been outlawed in Ethiopia, but it was still legal in Saudi Arabia, Yemen, Oman, and some of the British satellites on the Arabian coast. It continued in parts of the Sahara, and in areas such as Mauritania, where in theory it had long lost its legal status. A small-scale smuggling traffic still brought slaves to Arabia from Ethiopia, Baluchistan, and elsewhere. The number of victims of this classic form of slavery was small, however, compared to the untold millions suffering from other forms of servitude. Moreover, the need for continuing vigilance was demonstrated by revelations of the use of slave labor in Nazi Germany during the war, growing evidence of conditions bordering on slavery in the penal labor camps of the Soviet Union, and the ongoing use of forced labor in some colonial empires.

Successful lobbying by the Anti-Slavery Society, as the British and Foreign Anti-Slavery and Aborigines Protection Society was now called, brought the question before the newly formed United Nations in 1948. As a result, a small ad hoc committee of experts was established to investigate slavery and related institutions, with the limited aim of identifying the appropriate branch of the United Nations to deal with these breaches of what were now designated universal human rights. However, forced labor—a sensitive issue for both the Soviet Union and the colonial powers—was again passed to the International Labor Organization. Of the ad hoc committee's four experts (from Chile, France, the United States, and Britain), the mainspring was the British delegate, who was the secretary of the Anti-Slavery Society. Attempts to appoint a Soviet member failed. The inclusion of peonage in the committee's agenda led to such strong objections from Peru that its meetings were drastically cut. Nevertheless, its report led the United Nations to negotiate a new treaty signed in 1956, the Supplementary Convention on the Abolition of Slavery, the Slave Trade, and Institutions and Practices Similar to Slavery.

This treaty extended the Convention of 1926, which remained in force, by identifying the various forms of servitude to be eradicated. These were debt bondage, serfdom, forced marriage for payment in money or kind, forced transfers and inheritance of women, and all transfers of persons under eighteen for the purpose of exploiting them, whether paid or not. To reinforce the clauses relating to marriage, signatories undertook to prescribe a minimum marriageable age.

Once more, interested powers saw to it that the convention contained no mechanism for enforcement. In spite of constant pressure from nongovernmental organizations, led by the British society (renamed the Anti-Slavery Society for the Protection of Human Rights in 1957, and in the 1990s called Anti-Slavery International), a permanent working group was agreed to only in 1974. This was after chattel slavery had been outlawed in the last areas where it was still legal, including the strategically vital states of Saudi Arabia in 1962, and Oman in 1970. Significantly, too, by this time the great colonial empires had been or were being dismantled, and the agreement of some African states and the Soviet Union was secured by identifying apartheid and colonialism as collective slavery.

Like its predecessors, the working group can only collect evidence and offer advice. It reports to the Subcommission on the Prevention of Discrimination and Protection of Minorities. This is a subsidiary of the Commission on Human Rights, one of the specialized institutions set up by the Economic and Social Council (ECOSOC) to further the social and economic aims agreed on by the United Nations. A number of treaties besides the 1956 Convention now prohibit practices analogous to slavery. These include the Convention for the Suppression of the Traffic in Persons and the Exploitation of the Prostitution of Others (1949)—which updated earlier treaties against the "white slave trade"—the Abolition of Forced Labor Convention (1957), the Convention on the Elimination of All Forms of Discrimination against Women (1979), and the Convention on the Rights of the Child (1989). The United Nations and the International Labor Organization have also launched a number of programs and investigations on these practices, particularly on the exploitation of women and children.

Theoretically, the working group, like its predecessors, is composed of experts on slavery, but its five members, all drawn from the subcommission, change too frequently to build up expertise. They represent broad geographic regions. During the Cold War they also represented power blocs. In 1984, for instance, the Western democracies, the Soviet bloc, East Asia, Latin America, and Africa each had one delegate. In 1995 members came from Bangladesh, Morocco, Rumania, Brazil, and the United States, but since the American and Brazilian could not attend, a Briton and a Cuban replaced them.

Unlike its predecessors, this committee takes evidence directly from nongovernmental organizations accredited to the United Nations. It thus hears at first hand from people working in the field and even from victims themselves. Its meetings are attended by an array of international organizations, including the International Labor Organization, the United Nations High Commission on Refugees, the United Nations Children's Fund (UNICEF), and Interpol, all of which can be directly faced with problems in their own areas. Most importantly, it meets in public. This is valued by the hard-working, usually understaffed and underfinanced, nongovernmental organizations that send representatives to Geneva to present their reports. Publicity is their most effective means of putting pressure on recalcitrant governments. They hope to attract media attention, although results have been generally disappointing.

During the Cold War and the days of apartheid, much time was spent in political posturing and little attention was given to finding solutions to the many forms of oppression brought before the group. In the 1990s, however, in response to pressure from nongovernmental organizations, the group and other United Nations bodies seemed to be making a genuine effort to promote action. Significantly, more nongovernmental organizations from the developing world are now presenting their own cases and establishing their own priorities, often with the aid of the older Western humanitarian organizations.

The working group has a daunting task. It deals with an ever-widening range of social and economic problems, covering all areas of the world. Some, such as female genital mutilation or the taking of organs for transplants from condemned prisoners in China, bear little relation to chattel slavery. The rationale for their inclusion is that victims are denied control over their own bodies. Other practices clearly approximate chattel slavery. As a byproduct of war in the Sudan, for instance, South Sudanese women and children have been captured and sold or sent north by their captors as domestic labor. In China, thousands of women and girls have been kidnapped by gangs of criminals and sold as brides, often kept under lock and key until they have had babies and are less likely to want to escape.

Child labor is one of the most widespread and cruel forms of contemporary slavery. Children are sold by poverty-stricken, often indebted parents into a wide range of employment. Many suffer from overwork and malnutrition. Some, like the Indian boys riding racing camels in Arabia, face injury and death. Those forced to carry heavy loads as porters in Africa, chained to looms in carpet factories in the Indian subcontinent, or confined in sweatshops in Thailand, may grow up stunted or deformed.

Children of both sexes, as well as women, are victims of forced prostitution. This varies from women and young girls unable to escape from the hands of pimps or brothel-owners in Europe, the United States, or Japan, to children sold into brothels in Thailand, Pakistan, or Brazil. The newest cases involve sex tourism, in which travel agents in the developed world supply tourists in Sri Lanka, the Philippines and other poor areas, with children of either sex for any kind of deviance. Many victims of forced prostitution contract sexually transmitted diseases. The more fortunate are sent home to die; many end up on the streets, while in Myanmar (Burma), it is charged, those who are HIV-positive are killed by the authorities to stop the spread of AIDS.

Unknown numbers of adults and children are trapped in various forms of debt bondage. The terms are often such that the debts can never be repaid and their servitude is not only lifelong, but may even be hereditary in countries where children become responsible for the debts of their parents. The creditor may be a moneylender in East Asia, a landlord in Latin America, a subcontractor clearing the forest in Brazil, the owner of a carpet factory or a stone quarry in the Indian subcontinent, a pimp or brothel-keeper in Europe, Japan, or the United States, a labor recruiter in the Philippines—the list is endless. Contract labor, migrant workers, and refugees are enticed or sold into work from which they cannot escape without repaying the cost of their transport, and sometimes ever-escalating charges for shelter, food, and even the tools with which they work.

Illegal aliens are particularly vulnerable to exploitation. Desperate to earn money for their families at home and afraid of being deported if they complain to the authorities, they may be forced to work long hours for a pittance in appalling conditions, as in the sweatshops of the U.S. garment industry. Similarly, foreigners admitted to work for designated employers only, such as the servants of diplomats and other privileged persons in Britain, the Gulf States, and elsewhere, have been imprisoned and physically abused by their employers.

There are also instances of outright forced labor. Members of the public are simply taken and made to work for little or no pay in bad, even dangerous, conditions by their own governments or by entrepreneurs acting with official support. Some are forcibly conscripted into the armed forces. Very young boys have been sent out to fight, most recently in Myanmar and Sudan.

New forms of contemporary slavery are constantly brought before the working group. Some are the inevitable consequence of rapid economic growth in some areas and stagnation or decline in others, and of disparities in wealth within states and between them. Others are the result of misgovernment, the deliberate oppression of minorities and dissenters, or the hazards of war and rebellion.

Most of these practices, now condemned in international agreements, are illegal, but the laws are thwarted by corrupt officials or simply not enforced. Governments may be too poor or weak to muster the necessary resources. They may need the support of the powerful economic and political interests that benefit from these forms of exploitation, as well as the hard currency generated by the sale of exports produced by cheap labor. They routinely fend off critics by ignoring or flatly denying accusations, by promising action they never take, or—most disarmingly—by asking for financial aid to enforce their own legislation.

Some forms of servitude have proved resistant to attack because they are rooted in long-standing ethnic, class, or caste divisions, such as the continued oppression of former slaves in Mauritania (which outlawed slavery for the third time in 1980). Others are sanctioned by religion and custom. Increasingly coming to the fore in this category are practices that violate the human rights of women and children, including servile marriages, child marriage, forced marriage, and the denial to women of rights to divorce, to have custody of their children, and to own property. Also difficult to eradicate, because of their religious bases, are such practices as the dedication of girls to temples in Ghana (the *trokosi* system) where priests may demand labor and sexual favors; or the use of boys to work and beg for the benefit of Muslim teachers in West Africa. Some practices, such as the transfer of children from poor to rich households for domestic labor, or their apprenticeship in a trade, are simply not perceived as forms of slavery and are defended because they ensure the children a livelihood, even when they are subjected to backbreaking work during the years when they could be at school.

Contemporary forms of slavery thus cover an ever-widening range of social and economic problems as more and more nongovernmental organizations bring their cases to the working group in the endless quest for a more perfect world. Although they differ from what is normally considered slavery, all these forms of exploitation have a strong element of coercion. Children sold by their parents have no choice in their fate. Victims of all ages are recruited by force or trickery, including the escalation of debts. Those who try to escape face intimidation, varying from prosecution for not paying their creditors, to mutilation or even death at the hands of their oppressors.

Although many of these practices remain widespread and deeply rooted, the working group provides an international forum where they can be identified as breaches of human rights and solutions discussed. The resulting publicity has led some countries to amend their laws, and some consumers to boycott goods produced by coerced labor. This is only a start, however, and until action can be agreed upon to enforce even existing treaties these abuses will continue.

[*See also* Capitalism and Slavery; Debt Bondage; Forced Labor, *article on* Soviet Union; Marxism; Penal Slavery; *and* Wage Slavery.]

BIBLIOGRAPHY

Annual Reports (since 1976) of the Working Group on Contemporary Forms of Slavery of the Sub-Commission on the Protection of Minorities of the United Nations Commission on Human Rights.
Annual Reports of the Committee of Experts on the Application of Conventions and Recommendations—Conventions 29 and 105—of the International Labour Office.
Greenidge, C. W. W. *Slavery.* New York: Macmillan, 1958.
Reports and Newsletters of Anti-Slavery International and of other philanthropic organizations, including the International Catholic Child Bureau, the International

Abolitionist Federation, and the various committees of Human Rights Watch.

—SUZANNE MIERS

DEMOGRAPHY. Slave populations were never truly separate from the free populations within which they existed. The number and proportion of persons in a society who lived as slaves depended on a variety of factors, some internal and some external to the enslaved population. Growth in slave populations resulted from the external processes of enslavement, forced migration, and changes in the status of individuals within societies, and from the internal process of fertility (although some of the fathers of slave children were free persons). Population decrease resulted from changes in the status of the enslaved class at large—abolition and partial abolition—or in the status of individual slaves (through manumission, *coartación*, or maroonage), from forced migration, and from mortality. These events and processes linked enslaved and free people in complex ways. In some cases slaves were able to exercise a degree of control over the demographic events, whether by acts of resistance or by simple individual or group choice; very often, however, slaves (and free people who were made slaves) had no effective control over their experience. Any attempt to understand the demography of slavery must take account of this complex interaction of slave and free, and of internal and external variables.

In considering the demography of slavery, four main questions are generally considered to be of central importance. The first concerns the number and proportion of persons enslaved, and their distribution in space and time; the second has to do with the role of slave trades in determining the growth of slave populations; the third considers the reproduction of slave populations by natural increase; and the fourth examines the internal composition and characteristics of slave populations. Answers to these questions depend on the definition of *slavery* employed. Beyond the problem of definition, analysis is also hampered by the fact that the study of slavery remains uneven, with detailed knowledge tending to be confined to particular areas and issues. Firm quantitative answers are not always available, and area specialists are frequently reluctant to offer even rough estimates.

Numbers. Slave populations are generally thought to have been associated with the emergence of relatively advanced agricultural civilizations in which the desire to control labor was associated with the presence of a land-owning and capital-controlling class and a relatively low ratio of people to land resources. The existence of slavery in the hunter-gatherer economy of the Kwakiutl on the Northwest Coast of North America is regarded as an exception based on special environmental conditions with rich food resources. In the post-neolithic economies with which slavery was broadly compatible, the slave populations are often thought to have peaked early. For instance, around 2300 BCE, when slaves accounted for 13 to 35 percent of the populations of Pharoanic Egypt and Old Akkadian Mesopotamia (the estimated percentages vary according to definitions of slave status), the proportion is thought to have been already in decline. The Chinese market in people was vast and complex, and existed from the time of the earliest civilizations with irrigated agriculture, affecting millions of people, but the demographic impact of chattel slavery (Mandarin, *ximin;* Cantonese, *sai man*) was relatively minor. In the ancient world, slave societies with large proportions of enslaved in their populations existed only in classical Greece and Roman Italy. Even here there is dispute. For Athens, the most prosperous Greek polis in the fifth century BCE, recent commentators argue that the number of slaves is a matter of conjecture, to be derived only indirectly from estimates of the economic and social importance of the slaves. Existing estimates range from as low as twenty thousand to as high as one hundred twenty thousand. Taking the more moderate estimates as a guide, the evidence suggests that slaves made up between 20 and 35 percent of the population of

Athens at the height of its wealth and democratic development, with a wider range of possibilities in the rest of Greece. For Rome census data exist, but these censuses were confined to male citizens, excluding women, children, and slaves from their enumerations. Modern estimates suggest that imperial Rome had a total population of about one million, roughly one-third being enslaved. Higher ratios existed in the olive-plantation area of Italy and in some parts of the Roman Empire.

There is no doubt that the slave populations of the Mediterranean shrank dramatically following the fading of classical Greece and the retreat of the Roman Empire. Chattel slavery was increasingly blurred as an institution of unfree labor, gradually merging with serfdom in medieval Europe. Even where slavery was important in the economy, as in medieval Scandinavia, the numbers were small, rarely accounting for more than 10 percent of the population. The creation of an Islamic hegemony stretching from Spain through North Africa to Iran, essentially complete by 800 CE, saw the development of an economy in which slavery was a persistent feature, if not a true slave society. Slaves were used in unusual occupations in this Islamic society, notably as soldiers, but in the absence of firm statistical estimates it seems unlikely that they accounted for more than 5 percent of the total population.

The modern, post-Columbian world witnessed a dramatic increase in the slave population, particularly in the Americas, Africa, and later the Middle East. This growth created slave societies in the Caribbean, Brazil and the United States, in which the number of enslaved people was counted in millions and their proportion exceeded 30 percent. In the antebellum United States the slave population peaked at 4 million and consistently accounted for 33 percent of the population of the Southern states between 1790 and 1860 (though only about 13 percent of the total population of the United States as a nation in 1860). Brazil's slave population peaked in the 1850s at roughly 2.25 million, making up close to 30 percent of the total population, a proportion similar to that in the U.S. South.

Taking the Caribbean as a whole, the slave population reached a maximum of 1.1 million immediately before the revolution in Saint Domingue (Haiti), and slaves accounted for roughly 70 percent of the total population of the region. Saint Domingue alone had a slave population of more than 450,000 in 1791. The British colonies in the Caribbean saw a peak slave population of about 775,000 in 1807 at the abolition of the British Atlantic slave trade, with Jamaica accounting for almost one-half of the total. Smaller slave populations occurred in the colonies of the Dutch (Suriname) and Danish (the Virgin Islands). Cuba had a slave population of only 30,000 in 1760, but this increased rapidly to 370,000 by 1860, growing faster than the free colored sector, so that slaves came to account for almost 50 percent of the total population of the island. Where sugar and slavery were strongly associated over the long term and the growth of the free colored sector was restricted, as in the British West Indies, slaves regularly came to account for more than 85 percent of the total population.

The slave populations of Spanish mainland America generally experienced their maximums much earlier than the major slave societies. At the end of the eighteenth century, the Spanish territories of mainland America had a total slave population of about 270,000, compared to a free colored population of 650,000. The largest slave populations were then in Peru (about 90,000), Venezuela (64,000), and New Granada or northeastern Colombia (54,000). Many of these colonies had seen significantly larger slave populations in the seventeenth and eighteenth centuries, although the proportions had never been really large.

Reliable data on the numbers and proportions of slaves in the populations of Africa and Asia in the modern period are harder to find than for the Americas. At the abolition of slavery by the British in 1834, there were 70,000 slaves in Mauritius and the Seychelles, where they formed a large majority

of the total population; there were 38,000 at the Cape of Good Hope (South Africa), and 10,000 in Ceylon. Chattel slavery was widespread in India, and by the early seventeenth century when abolitionist movements first rose, there were an estimated 8 to 9 million slaves in British Indian territories and as many beyond British influence. China maintained a large chattel slave (*ximin*) population well into the twentieth century, and many women were sold into adoptive servitude (*mui-jai*), but *ximin* never accounted for more than perhaps 2 percent of the total population. Similarly complex patterns existed throughout the agricultural societies of Southeast Asia, but slaves were always a rarity in Australia and the Pacific.

To generalize boldly, it appears that in societies that recognized slavery as a legal institution, there existed a fairly consistent range of proportions of slave to free. In a few examples slavery was truly intense, accounting for 80 to 90 percent of the total populations of the societies, as in the modern plantation colonies established in the Caribbean by the British and the French. These slave societies generally occupied small land areas but affected substantial population numbers. Elsewhere, genuine slave societies covering larger land areas, as in the U.S. South, Brazil, and ancient Greece and Rome, tended to have a very consistent 30 to 35 percent of enslaved people in their populations. The remaining societies with slavery as a legal institution generally had less than 10 percent of their populations held in chattel slavery, and this social relationship was often associated with other forms of unfree labor and a much longer history of slavery over millennia rather than centuries. Looking at the world as a whole, it is arguable that the slave population peaked around the end of the eighteenth century, when it accounted for roughly 5 percent of the world total.

Forced Migration. The long-term tendency was for slave populations to be drawn from increasingly distant sources and from peoples regarded as other by the slave-owning classes. In the ancient world the classical slave societies of Greece and Rome had to some extent taken slaves from communities seen as ethnically distinct, but in Africa and Asia slavery often formed a stage in a process of incorporation into kinship systems, without ethnic difference being a factor; something similar occurred throughout medieval Europe. In modern times, by contrast, long-distance slave trades were the major source of slaves taken to the Americas and the Middle East, and here ethnic difference played a fundamental role in the process of enslavement. Africa became the most important supplier of slaves in this market, and the result was a parallel increase in the size of the slave population within Africa itself and the emergence of plantation slave economies there in the nineteenth century, particularly in northern Nigeria and Zanzibar. Thus slavery became responsible for a major demographic shift in the modern world, through the forced migration that created the African diaspora. Further, by removing people from their ethnic populations, modern slavery made return to the original free population impossible and inhibited insertion into the free, slave-owning society.

Estimates of the size of the slave trades have been and remain a matter of contention among scholars. There is no dispute that the most important of the long-distance slave trades was that across the Atlantic from Africa to the Americas, but the number of people involved has been difficult to establish firmly. The most complete modern estimates of the volume of the Atlantic slave trade are those produced by Philip D. Curtin, but several of the components of his calculations have been called into question, and his critics have mostly argued for larger rather than smaller numbers. Revisions of Curtin's overall estimates by Paul E. Lovejoy show that at least 11.7 million enslaved people were taken from Africa between 1450 and 1900, but 15 to 20 percent died in the Middle Passage, never reaching the shores of the Americas. Many others died in the process of movement from the interior of Africa to the slave ships on the coast. The Atlantic slave trade was distributed over time

as follows: 3.1 percent were taken between 1450 and 1600, 16 percent in the seventeenth century, 52.4 percent in the eighteenth century, and 28.5 percent in the nineteenth century. In the early years of European colonization in the Americas, slaves were less numerous than free people in the trans-Atlantic stream, but enslaved Africans outnumbered free migrants between about 1700 and 1870, and it was not until late in the nineteenth century that the cumulative migration of Europeans exceeded the numbers carried in the slave trade. The Atlantic slave trade was a major event in world demographic history, remarkable for its intensity and impact.

The second major slave trade was that directed to the Muslim areas of North Africa, Arabia, and India, a long-distance trade that took slaves across the Sahara, the Red Sea, and the Indian Ocean, with levels of mortality that probably rivaled those in the Middle Passage. The numbers are less certain, but Lovejoy argues that perhaps as many people were involved in this slave trade as in the trans-Atlantic movement. What is clear is that the slave trade to Islamic countries was never as intense as the trade to the European colonies in the Americas. It was spread over many centuries, with an estimated 4.8 million crossing the Sahara between 650 and 1600, and 2.4 million being taken across the Red Sea and Indian Ocean between 800 and 1600, for an annual average of fewer than 10,000. Until the sixteenth century the Islamic areas remained the most important receivers of slaves, with 550,000 in the trans-Saharan trade, 200,000 crossing the Red Sea, and 100,000 exported from East Africa across the Indian Ocean, compared to just 325,000 crossing the Atlantic. In the seventeenth century, however, the Atlantic slave trade took 1.9 million or 65.1 percent of the total, and in the eighteenth century, 6.1 million or 82.5 percent. The number of slaves taken to Islamic countries in these centuries held fairly steady, with an annual average of roughly 10,000. This average doubled in the nineteenth century, with 1.2 million crossing the Sahara, 450,000 the Red Sea, and

440,000 the Indian Ocean; however, this was still fewer than the 3.3 million crossing the Atlantic in the century that witnessed major attacks on the European slave trades.

Reproduction. Debate has long surrounded the question of whether slave populations could reproduce naturally, by having more births than deaths, or whether they were absolutely dependent on fresh importations through slave trades. This is a question that matters most for the true slave societies, especially those centered on plantation agriculture. Where slaves were taken from local communities and integrated, however painfully, into the societies that took them, the demographic impact was generally thought to be positive, through increasing fertility in the population. Societies that became major sources of slave supply, however, suffered immediate losses; a further question arises concerning the extent of depopulation that followed as a consequence. This last question is most important for Africa, where relatively large proportions of the populations of many regions were removed over a long period of time. Scholars disagree, however, about the demographic consequences. Some contend that the slave trades created long-term absolute depopulation, resulting in the low population density of the West African "Middle Belt," for example. Others argue that losses through the slave trade were quickly made up by increased fertility, and that the overall impact on African population growth was minimal. Resolution of this debate is inhibited by the poor quality of the available data.

For the Americas, the demographic data are much more firmly grounded, but debate continues, mainly because of the difficulty involved in explaining differences among regions. In the Caribbean and Brazil the ratio of slave population to slave imports was relatively low. For example, Jamaica imported an estimated 750,000 slaves between 1600 and 1808 but had a living slave population of just 350,000 in 1808; Saint Domingue took 700,000 slaves from the slave trade to support a slave population of 450,000 in 1791. In the United States, by contrast, the slave population grew as rapidly as the free; the 4 million slaves living in 1860 were descended from a total import of only 400,000. What caused this dramatic difference?

Some scholars have argued that this contrast was largely a product of variations in mortality. It is certain that the heaviest mortality, with deaths regularly exceeding births, occurred in regions of the Americas with a strong concentration on the production of sugar on large plantations. The sugar plantations of Louisiana shared these patterns with those of the Caribbean and Brazil, in strong contrast to the common experience of the cotton-producing areas of the United States. Areas within the Caribbean that produced commodities other than sugar generally experienced low mortality and showed positive growth; indeed, some of them grew even more rapidly than the United States average. As far as it is possible to separate the variables, it seems that environmental and epidemiological factors were less important in determining levels of mortality than the labor regimes associated with different kinds of economic activity. Slaves on sugar plantations worked extremely long hours compared to both other contemporary slaves and to free workers; they experienced a long crop season, lasting up to six months, during which they worked in the field by day and the factory by night; they performed arduous and often dangerous tasks; they were subject to brutal physical treatment while worked in gangs; and many of them were required to produce their own food on provision grounds in time outside the normal extreme demands of sugar production. These factors taken together contributed to high mortality in all age groups, including infants. Some sugar-planters made a conscious accounting calculation that it was more profitable to purchase slaves from the slave ships than to encourage fertility and a positive natural increase, and the slaves were literally worked to death.

Differences in fertility are generally attributed in part to the demands of sugar production, particularly the heavy tasks performed by women and their brutal treatment in gang labor. Other causes of differential fertility included variations in family structure, the length of the period of breast-feeding (which appears to have been significantly longer in the Caribbean than in the United States), and to techniques of contraception and abortion used by women as a form of resistance to slavery. Some of these differences relate to the variations in labor regimes and nutrition that affected mortality. It is also possible to identify links between mortality regimes and fertility. Heavy mortality had an immediate impact on mating patterns and on family and household organization, and these elements of slave life were directly disrupted by the high rates of forced migration through the slave trade that were themselves a consequence of high mortality. All of these patterns reflected the demographic composition of the slave trades.

Composition. Slave-owners almost always and everywhere showed a clear preference for slaves who were young—in late adolescence and early adulthood. These were the people who experienced the lowest rates of morbidity and mortality, were most fertile, and had the best chances of remaining strong and healthy for a number of years. Infants and children were expensive to raise and a risk in survival terms; older adults had a shorter productive span. Where owners captured or purchased through the slave trade, they were able to exercise these preferences. Established slave populations, on the other hand, contained individuals with a much wider range of ages. In cases where the slave population grew through natural increase, as in the United States, infants and children made up a relatively large proportion of the slave population, and because the level of mortality was low, older people also made up a larger contingent. This resulted in a relatively normal age pyramid. By contrast, where heavy natural decrease was the norm, as in most of the sugar-plantation economies of the Caribbean, dependence on the slave trade resulted in an age profile heavily weighted to those in the age range of fifteen to thirty-five years

Sex was also a vital element in the composition of slave populations, but here slave-owners were less consistent in their preferences. Where enslavement was associated with a process of integration into the family and kinship system of the slave-owner, as in India, China, and Africa, females were generally more highly valued than males; but in the most intense plantation-slave economies, the demand was chiefly for field labor, work seen by European slave-owners as best performed by males. The Atlantic slave trade in some periods carried almost twice as many males as females from Africa to the Americas, and the overall long-term total was in the ratio sixty males to forty females. This male weighting of the sex ratio gradually diminished in the established slave populations, however, because of the higher mortality experienced by males. Slave populations with high rates of natural increase and low rates of importation quickly moved toward a situation in which females were more numerous than males.

Age and sex were the most important biological elements in the internal composition of slave populations. Another characteristic that mattered was race or ethnicity, but this was a constructed feature rather than a biological one. In the Atlantic slave trade, and in the slave societies of the Americas generally, race was a vital factor. Black Africans were selected for enslavement and white Europeans were not. Native Americans were also enslaved in the European settlements of the Americas, but the association with Africans was so strong that *slave* and *Negro* came to be synonyms. A similar racial selectivity applied in the slave trade from Africa to the Islamic societies of the Middle East. Elsewhere and in earlier periods, enslaved people often came from the same races as their owners, even though they were universally defined as "outsiders" in one way or another. Racial difference was rarely recognized where slavery was designed to incorporate the enslaved into the kinship system of the free. In cases where race was a vital defining feature of slave status, as in the Americas, children always took the status of their slave mothers, except where the children crossed a legal limit to the number of white ancestors an individual could have and still carry slave status. Where manumission was restricted, slave populations consequently contained relatively large proportions of persons of mixed race, and these individuals were often treated differently by their owners, especially in the allocation of occupations. Thus the proportions of slaves of mixed race in slave populations depended on rates of miscegenation, levels of manumission, the contribution of external slave trades to overall growth, and the very construction of race as perceived difference.

Another element in the composition of slave populations was stature or physical growth. Slaveowners often selected individuals from the slave trades on the basis of perceived strength, and stature was used as a major indicator. Slaves were sometimes allocated to particular occupations on the basis of their height. Slave populations also differed in their average stature as a result of differences in nutrition and epidemiology, the best-fed and least-diseased generally being the tallest. These patterns were clearly revealed in comparisons of the most hostile environments in the Caribbean with the relatively favorable conditions for growth of the United States. Creole slaves in the United States were on average 7 to 10 centimeters taller than their Caribbean counterparts, and within the Caribbean, creoles born in the nonsugar territories were consistently taller than those in the sugar-plantation regions.

These variations in age, sex, race, and stature were not simply a product of the preferences of the slave-owning classes. Supply was often as important as demand in determining the structure of slave populations, the competition between the two sides being worked out in the prices paid for slaves in the market. Unhealthy, short, and aged slaves were sold and purchased, but only at lower prices. On the supply side, young individuals were often enslaved, partly because they were easier to capture than adults. In some cases, however, supply and demand worked together to match the preferences of buyers and sellers; for example, in the Atlantic slave trade the relatively great demand for females within Africa was balanced by the relatively low demand for them in the Americas.

Compared to the free populations of slaveholding societies, slaves were more likely to be concentrated among the young adults and to be from outside the racial or territorial group. It is also probable that slaves generally experienced higher mortality and lower fertility than free people, and were unusual in sometimes suffering natural decrease in periods of human history associated with general growth. The slaves who lived in the most intense examples of the system occupied a demographic disaster area. Other demographic characteristics were not shared in a uniform way across societies, and there was no simple correlation between slave status and demographic performance.

[*See also* Economics; *and* Slave Trade, *articles on* Trans-Saharan Trade, Trans-Atlantic Trade, Volume of Trade, *and* Suppression of Trade.]

BIBLIOGRAPHY

Curtin, Philip D. *The Atlantic Slave Trade: A Census*. Madison: University of Wisconsin Press, 1969.

Hellie, Richard. *Slavery in Russia, 1450–1725*. Chicago: University of Chicago Press, 1982.

Lovejoy, Paul E. *Transformations in Slavery: A History of Slavery in Africa*. Cambridge: Cambridge University Press, 1983.

Phillips, William D., Jr. *Slavery from Roman Times to the Early Transatlantic Trade*. Minneapolis: University of Minnesota Press, 1985.

Watson, James L., ed. *Asian and African Systems of Slavery*. Oxford: Basil Blackwell, 1980.

—BARRY HIGMAN

DOMESTIC SLAVERY. The concept of domestic slavery customarily included household servants rather than skilled craft and industrial workers or agricultural laborers. Existing from ancient times, domestic slavery in North America dated almost from the beginning of African bondage there in the sixteenth and early seventeenth centuries. In the nineteenth century, U.S. slave-owners referred to domestic slavery to characterize their entire institution and to create the argument of slavery as a positive good. With this focus on domestic slavery, they compared the Southern slaveholding household to an extended family.

In many societies domestic slavery was an urban phenomena, but in North America it came to be important on farms and plantations as well as in cities. Domestic service involved a multitude of possible posts: ladies' maids and housemaids, valets, cooks, butlers, housekeepers, dining-room servers, carriage-drivers, coachmen, laundresses and ironers, and nursemaids. While gardeners, dairymaids, seamstresses, and spinners produced goods, they too worked in or near the plantation house and might be considered domestic servants. Even on large plantations, more than one of these functions might be fulfilled by a single person. For example, a housemaid might wait at table in the dining room, while the master's valet might also be the family carriage-driver. For the majority of nineteenth-century Southern slaveholding families who owned fewer than five slaves, their enslaved women would generally be expected to work in both the field and the house. Even on the nineteenth-century plantation, where the division and specialization of functions was greatest in American slavery, the line between domestic servitude and agricultural work was neither clear nor impassable. In times of harvest or when crops were threatened, all hands would be sent to labor in the fields.

In its early guises in seventeenth-century Virginia, North American slavery was primarily agricultural. Domestic slavery was relatively slow to develop in the Chesapeake region, where slaves, outside the wealthiest families, tended to labor in tobacco and other farm occupations. For example, one estimate holds that in Virginia before 1760 only about 10 percent of female slaves worked in occupations around the household rather than in the fields. In contrast, the Northern colonies in the seventeenth and eighteenth centuries had relatively more domestic slavery. Eighteenth-century

slavery, both North and South, had a growing household component.

The expansion of slavery and consumer society by the 1760s began the process of bringing larger numbers of enslaved females to work in the house and its dependencies. The typical domestic servant of late eighteenth-century Virginia was a young woman involved in a multitude of household chores. Indeed, this may be one of the largest changes between early American and nineteenth century Southern slavery. As domestic production of cloth, dairy products, and preserved food products increased in the nineteenth century, perhaps as many as one-third of the female slaves on plantations of the coastal Southeast came to labor in and around the plantation house. The proportion may have been lower on newer Deep South and Southwest plantations, but the combination of prosperity and higher standards of cleanliness and comfort among slave-owners in the nineteenth century meant an expansion of domestic slavery.

Southern white women probably considered the most important domestic post that of the cook. In urban establishments with only a few servants, a cook and maid of all work, sometimes combined in the same person, were deemed essential. When emancipation occurred in 1865, Southern white women were especially daunted by the prospect of having to do their own cooking.

Cooks were such valuable domestic slaves because of their combination of skill and hard work, under often difficult working conditions. An excellent cook reflected well on the status of the family as well as making meals more pleasurable for them. During the nineteenth century much Southern cooking took place in annexes detached or semidetached from the main house, both because of the danger of fire and because of the heat generated by cooking. Southern cooks well into the nineteenth century, even on prosperous plantations, tended to work with open-hearth fireplaces. Just as slavery may have retarded the adoption of labor-saving devices in agriculture, it seems to have done so for the kitchen. The cast-iron range, which allowed more

The Cook; engraving, nineteenth century.

elaborate baking, greater control over temperature, and less bending and stooping, became ubiquitous in other nineteenth-century American kitchens but was slow to arrive in the South.

Although the cook was the most important to contemporaries, the nursemaid or "mammy" has become the best-known symbol of Southern domestic slavery. As this image was perfected in late nineteenth- and early twentieth-century popular culture, this servant came to symbolize the close relationship between slaves and the white family. Southern whites tended to depict the mammy as a somewhat humorous figure, fiercely devoted to the white children and their proper behavior; some descriptions claimed that she was more devoted to the white family than to her own children. Studies of antebellum Southern households, however, have shown that the mammy was a more ambiguous and elusive figure. To be sure, the households of wealthy planters contained nursemaids, some of

whom had extensive power and long-running relationships with the family, but childrearing among even wealthy Southerners was seldom so organized. Many baby nurses were young and inexperienced, often in their teens and hardly more than children themselves. These young women could seldom convey the authority or position of the mammy. Other households saw considerable turnover among nursemaids as plantation wives sought slaves who would suit their notions of proper child care. While some of the nursemaids might be of the requisite age, their tenure in the position was often brief. The mammy of later legend may have always been the ideal child nurse, but her numbers were far more limited and her character far more complicated. Moreover, some of these slave women of authority had positions as housekeepers or cooks rather than as nursemaids.

Some of this Southern mythology presents the mammy as not only the nursemaid but also the wet nurse of the white children, suckling them along with her own offspring. This too appears to have little basis in reality. Antebellum infants appear to have been wet-nursed only when the mother had died or was physically incapable in suckling her children. In such cases, any slave or white woman breastfeeding her own child and able to nurse another child was pressed into service.

In addition to cooks and nursemaids, personal servants—valets and maids—were frequently members of elite households. These valuable servants saw to the toilettes of their mistresses or masters and performed a host of tasks relating to clothing and appearance. In some cases, parents and grandparents gave young slaves to their white children to serve as such personal attendants. Because these were potentially the closest relationships, they could be fraught with tension, resentment, and hatred as well as genuine affection.

Some historians have argued that domestic slaves played a particularly valuable role in the plantation community as sources and conduits of information to the other slaves. Because of their close proximity to the white people, house servants learned not only family and local gossip but also news about political and even military affairs.

Recruitment of domestic servants in the nineteenth century often appears to have come from within their own ranks. Sometimes house servants brought along their own children to help with small tasks such as running errands, playing with the white children, or keeping flies away from food. Such tasks would over time help to teach them the ways of household service, but not all the youngsters who labored in the plantation house would return to it as domestic workers. Domestic production such as spinning, weaving, sewing, and canning foodstuffs may have been a practice ground for possible house servants. By using these women slaves in domestic production, mistresses were able to ascertain some of their skills and discern whether they would be good domestic workers.

The traditional view of domestic slavery, put forward by the slave-owners, was that house servants saw themselves as a group apart from and superior to the agricultural workers on the plantation. The slave-owners believed that proximity to themselves had lifted the house servants in intelligence, manners, morality, and other markers of civilization. Some contemporary observers believed that house servants were more likely than field workers to be mulatto rather than of fully African descent. Recent scholarship has disputed several of these claims for North America. Even on large plantations where specialization was greater, the field hands and house servants were not distinct groups.

Historians recently have tended to focus on the advantages and disadvantages of service in the plantation household and to enumerate the privileges that house servants received. There is little doubt that house servants received better food and clothing. The slaves' owners often gave castoff clothes, furniture, and other personal items to personal servants. Household servants were able to sample the food, and the cook and her helpers tra-

ditionally were able to take leftover food back to their families—a high privilege in a situation in which food distribution was measured and food supplies were normally under lock and key. At times guests gave presents or tips to household servants who had been especially attentive to them.

Some historians have questioned whether the conditions of work were as favorable for domestic servants as for field workers. Under the gang system, agricultural workers worked from daybreak to dusk with specified breaks for meals and rest. Task workers in the rice plantations sometimes finished their specified duties early in the afternoon and then had time for their own chores. In contrast, most domestic slaves worked long hours and were less likely to have weekend days for rest. Some especially pious owners allowed their cooks and maids time off for church attendance, but not necessarily on a regular basis. Personal body-servants often slept in or near their master's or mistress's room, on call during the night.

Women domestic servants, like domestic workers in many societies, lived in close proximity to

Engraving depicting slave women tending to their children and those of their master, c.1854.

men of wealth and power who sometimes made sexual advances. Women household servants seem to have been more vulnerable to rape, sexual assault, or seduction than plantation workers. Enslaved women had no legal protection from forced sexual activity; at best, they could hope that the morality of their owner would forbid this behavior. Harriet Jacobs's *Incidents in the Life of a Slave Girl* is an autobiographical account of the problems encountered by a house servant when her master was determined to force her into a sexual relationship with him.

Punishments may also have differed for domestic than plantation slaves. Plantations with overseers sometimes had formal rules about chastisements that sought to prohibit whippings and floggings when the overseer was still enraged by the slave's action. Instead, punishment was postponed until it could more coolly be applied. No such rules obtained in the plantation house, where masters and mistresses often slapped, choked, beat, whipped, or otherwise assaulted slaves who had displeased them. Moreover, house slaves could become targets when their owners were unhappy or distressed for other reasons.

Nevertheless, there may have been some privileges associated with domestic service. Some scholars have argued that house servants, because of their value and access to their owners, had a greater likelihood of living in unbroken families. House servants with husbands or wives owned by other whites could attempt to influence or cajole their owners into buying the spouse and uniting the family. In other cases, house servants tried to keep a family together by convincing the owner not to sell or relocate their relatives to a faraway plantation. Here the combination of the slave's value and personal relationship with the owner played a role. Skilled cooks and personal attendants were difficult to replace, and some were able to capitalize on their importance. Finally, slave-owners who manumitted a few but not all of their slaves were most likely to free house servants.

In the nineteenth century, slaveholders in the American South held up their domestic servants as examples of the positive effects of slavery. The planters argued that slavery had brought savage people from Africa and had not only tamed them and taught them to work but also introduced them to Christianity. In this view, it was the close relationship of the slave-owners to the enslaved that had lifted the latter to a higher stage of civilization. Yet slavery, in this argument, remained essential for the wellbeing of the slaves, who, according to white Southerners, would otherwise revert to barbarism.

Another area of significance in regard to domestic slavery concerns the personal relationship or bargain that some believe existed between the slaves and slaveholders. In the interpretation made famous by Eugene D. Genovese, a pervasive paternalism and personalism imbued the relationship in which master and slaves held mutual expectations of one another. The lack of absenteeism among the Southern planters, compared to those in the Caribbean, meant that most of them spent a great deal of time on their plantations with their slaves. According to Genovese, it was this personal relationship that made it difficult for the slaves to join together and revolt against the masters' rule.

Although Genovese believed this interaction was true throughout the plantation, other historians have pointed out that the owners' personal relationships with slaves tended to be largely, if not exclusively, with domestic servants. There is no doubt that some of these relationships were very close. Some slave-owners nursed favorite slaves during serious or fatal illnesses; they even erected tombstones over the graves of these servants.

Nevertheless, physical proximity did not necessarily mean mutual understanding, as the Civil War impressed on the understanding of Southern slaveholders. As the war came close to them, they found that their slaves would strike out for freedom, either by leaving the plantation or by refusing to work in the old manner. Perhaps the most unnerving thing for many slave-owners was the fact that their most trusted slaves refused to stay.

Although in the postwar period white Southerners would construct stories about the wartime loyalty of their slaves, at the time they had been dismayed about the behavior of the slaves of whom they had expected most. At the end of the war and with the destruction of slavery, Southern slaveholders were left to ponder the nature of relationships they thought they had understood.

[*See also* Anti-Slavery Literature, *article on* African-American Perspectives; Concubinage; Gender and Slavery; Manumission; Occupations; United States, *article on* The South; *and* Urban Slavery.]

BIBLIOGRAPHY

Fox-Genovese, Elizabeth. *Within the Plantation Household: Black and White Women of the Old South.* Chapel Hill: University of North Carolina Press, 1988.

Genovese, Eugene D. *Roll, Jordan, Roll: The World the Slaves Made.* New York: Pantheon, 1974.

Jones, Norrece T., Jr. *Born a Child of Freedom, Yet a Slave: Mechanisms of Control and Strategies of Resistance in Antebellum South Carolina.* Hanover, N.H.: Wesleyan University Press, 1990.

Shammas, Carole. "Black Women's Work and the Evolution of Plantation Society in Virginia." *Labor History* 26 (1985): 5–28.

Weiner, Marli F. *Mistresses and Slaves: Plantation Women in South Carolina, 1830–1880.* Urbana: University of Illinois Press, 1997.

White, Deborah Gray. *Ar'n't I a Woman? Female Slaves in the Plantation South.* New York: W. W. Norton, 1985.

—JANE TURNER CENSER

ECONOMICS. The agenda for research on many topics in studying slavery in the United States was established during the nineteenth century. The charges and countercharges of the pre–Civil War debate over slavery and abolition left a residue of ideas condemning the "peculiar institution." Hinton Rowan Helper argued that inefficiencies inherent in slavery retarded Southern economic growth, while Frederick Law Olmsted maintained that slave labor was less productive than free labor and that investments in slaves were generally unprofitable. By the twentieth century, themes of growth retardation, inefficiency, nonviability, unprofitability, and the harshness of slave life often appeared in works on antebellum Southern history. Thus when Alfred Conrad and John Meyer in 1958 published their famous paper ushering in the new economic history, they confronted widely held views and ways of thinking about slavery and the Southern economy.

Work conducted in the decade or so following the paper by Conrad and Meyer largely settled the profitability issue and the question of whether economic forces alone would have ended the slave system. Thereafter research turned toward other topics: the productivity of slave labor and economies of scale; slavery and Southern economic performance; interregional trade and plantation self-sufficiency; slavery and the yeoman experience; and the standard of living of slaves.

Research on questions of profitability and viability in the first half of the twentieth century was hampered by flawed conceptual frameworks. U. B. Phillips, for example, argued that closing the African slave trade eventually triggered a speculative rise in slave prices relative to cotton prices, which then significantly lowered profits on slave assets. He and others then considered alternative explanations for slave-ownership, such as conspicuous consumption. The major insight by Conrad and Meyer was to treat the decision to purchase a slave as a standard investment problem in economics. Their work and subsequent refinements showed that the average rate of return to slave-ownership was approximately 10 percent, which compared favorably with returns on alternative investments in railroads and manufacturing. There was no significant long-term trend after 1820 in the return, although it varied somewhat by region and time period.

Additional work showed that current returns on slave-ownership were an unreliable guide to the long-term viability of the institution. If current earnings were low, the institution could be viable if future earnings were going to rise. Similarly, current earnings could be high while low earnings in the future made the institution nonviable in the long run. Given that earnings in the antebellum period were favorable compared with alternative investments, long-run viability also required that the price of slaves exceed their production cost. Quantitative research published in the 1960s showed just this: the market price of slaves substantially exceeded their reproduction cost in the years from 1820 to 1860. The findings on profitability and viability made clear that the institution had no early prospect of demise for economic reasons alone. Therefore, political intervention was necessary to end slavery.

Robert Fogel and Stanley Engerman (1974) crystallized thought and debate on the efficiency of slave labor by expressing efficiency in terms of a geometric index of total factor productivity, which is a ratio of output to a geometric average of inputs. Using data from the manuscript schedules of the U.S. Census of Agriculture collected by William Parker and Robert Gallman, they reported that slave farms were about 40 percent more efficient than Northern farms and 28 percent more efficient than Southern free farms in 1860, and that efficiency of slave farms increased with the number of slaves up to fifty and then declined slightly. Fogel and Engerman suggested that specific features of slavery, such as intensive use of labor and superior management, explained the results. Critics offered alternative explanations, citing temporarily inflated prices for cotton in 1860, a large cotton crop in 1860, poor measurement of the land input, a longer work year for slaves, and regional differences in crop mix. Fogel and Engerman tested the implications of these criticisms and successfully defended their claim of greater efficiency on medium and large plantations, though one may quibble with procedural details and the precise magnitude of the efficiency advantage. Drawing on the work of others, Fogel and Engerman also made a plausible case for the importance of the gang system to efficiency, but they were unable to measure its contribution relative to other factors associated with plantation size, such as managerial skills,

child-care practices, discipline or force, and complementarities in production.

The thesis that slavery substantially retarded Southern economic growth suffered a major setback with the publication of regional income estimates by Richard Easterlin for 1840 to 1860, which showed that Southern per capita income was about two-thirds of that in the North while the rate of growth was slightly higher in the South. The unexpectedly small size of the gap, and especially the growth rate advantage for the South, suggested that slavery may have had little adverse effect on Southern economic performance. Subsequent research addressed the adequacy of the income estimates, special conditions of the late antebellum economy that may have affected measured growth, and the mechanisms through which slavery could have retarded growth. For example, it was argued that underreporting in the 1840 census of agriculture exaggerated Southern performance from 1840 to 1860; however, revised estimates for 1840, 1850, and 1860 indicate that the ratio of Northern to Southern income changed little in each decade. Other critics maintained that the income figures underestimated the Northern advantage and that region's growth rate, but subsequent research showed that this bias was modest. The late antebellum cotton boom might have improved the measured performance of the South, but it has been noted that the period from the depression of the late 1830s and early 1840s to 1860 encompassed a boom that benefited the North. In sum, the available evidence indicates that per capita income was moderately lower in the South compared with the North, but growth rates were roughly equal during the last two decades of the antebellum period.

There is little agreement on the models that should be used to investigate the question of whether Southern economic performance in the nineteenth century would have improved without slavery. Recent additions to this literature suggest, however, that slavery may have retarded long-run industrial development, not because it was inefficient relative to other forms of agriculture, but because it was remarkably efficient relative to industrial pursuits. It has been claimed that the nature of labor markets in the rural North limited farm size and therefore profit levels, which directed entrepreneurs into urban areas and stimulated industrial growth; in the South, however, slavery eliminated the labor constraint on large-scale farming operations, agriculture retained entrepreneurial talent, and industrialization was retarded. Under Eugene Genovese's dictum that slavery required all hands to be occupied at all times, slaves became a form of fixed capital that planters kept busy during lay-by periods through diversification of farm operations. Thus plantations had a high ratio of labor to capital compared with the Northern farms, were largely self-sufficient, and had little need of a transportation system and distribution centers (cities and towns) that would have furthered commercial and industrial development. It has also been suggested that planters may have been reluctant to invest in manufacturing despite high rates of return because they preferred to avoid risks, were uninformed about the benefits of diversification, or felt threatened economically, socially, and politically by industrialization. Because slave property was portable, planters may have had little stake in community life and little to gain from local improvements in roads, marketing facilities, and education. In this view, emancipation was an economic revolution that led to new investment strategies for local development.

The issue of Southern self-sufficiency in food production is a byproduct of hypotheses of growth that stress the contribution of interregional trade in widening the market for manufactured goods, and of claims that Southern agriculture lacked the productivity to feed its population. Estimates of food supplies and demands have shown, however, that with the possible exception of certain coastal areas and strips along the Mississippi River, the South was largely independent of food supplies from the West. One study addressed the widespread belief that planters in southern Louisiana imported much of their food from the West, but analysis of manuscript schedules of agriculture indicates that this rural sector could have been self-sufficient if planters exchanged their excess grain for meat produced by small, local farmers.

Views of antebellum Southern farmers have been dominated by two opposing schools of thought. U. B. Phillips and Lewis Cecil Gray argued that large planters controlled political and economic life in the antebellum South and pushed yeoman farmers into a subordinate position; members of the school of Frank Owsley at Vanderbilt University emphasized the numerical majority and prosperity of small farmers under democratic institutions. Although recent research tends to favor the planter-dominance position, this work also demonstrates oversimplifications and misconceptions inherent in both points of view. Recently historians have identified several biases and shortcomings in the traditional works and placed the new round of research on firm methodological foundations. Gavin Wright's (1986) work on the cotton-growing South showed that the distribution of wealth was more unequal in the South than in the North, and that from 1850 to 1860 there was a shift of slave-ownership away from small farmers toward larger farmers, resulting in greater concentration of wealth. Studies of other regions and cropping patterns within the South reveal a pattern of inequality similar to that in the cotton-growing area. Although several studies show that wealth was highly concentrated among the slave-owner class, yeomen were more prosperous and heterogeneous than depicted by the planter-dominance thesis. Small farmers of the plantation belt devoted much of their resources to cotton production and thereby partook of the cotton boom of the late 1840s and the 1850s, while their counterparts in the Upcountry were substantially self-sufficient until there were railroads and other investments in commercial infrastructure beginning in the 1850s. These late-antebellum changes overcame geographic isolation, broke down a culture that emphasized social and political autonomy, and promoted capital gains that were an important first step away from safety-first agriculture and toward markets.

Because slaves were not paid wages and received no regular income, the debate over living standards has focused on their health and consumption of basic commodities such as food, clothing, shelter, and medical care. For example, studies have examined food and clothing allotments, the size and furnishing of houses, and slave-owners' expenditures on medical care, sometimes with reference to similar quantities consumed by working-class populations elsewhere. Though interesting and useful, these types of studies have not ended debate, in part because they fail to take into account needs or demands on the biological system. Diets can be understood as adequate or inadequate only in relation to work effort and exposure to disease. Similarly, clothing and housing must be judged relative to climate; and medical care in the early nineteenth century was generally of poor quality and in some (perhaps many) instances harmful. Moreover, while plantation records may reveal allocations, little systematic evidence is available on inputs or provisions made by slaves themselves. For these reasons, more recent research has emphasized measures such as mortality rates and stature.

These findings establish the diversity of conditions among slaves. Richard Steckel has shown that slave children's health was comparable to that in the poorest populations ever studied, while working-age slaves were remarkably well off. These conclusions rest on plantation records of births and deaths, measurements of stature recorded on manifests of slaves shipped in the coastal trade, and an approach that combines these data through the concept of net nutrition. The study of human growth and development makes it clear that diet, disease, and work cannot be evaluated in isolation; instead, these factors are components of a package that interact to determine a person's level of net nutrition (or nutritional status). Work, disease, and body maintenance place claims on the diet, and the net result influences growth and stature. Thus instances of growth retardation and illness and mortality tend to occur together.

Plantation records that were adjusted for under-enumeration of deaths occurring soon after birth indicate that slave mortality rates were approximately 350 per thousand among infants and 200 per thousand at ages one to four. These childhood rates were roughly double those of the entire free population in the United States, but the rates of slave and free adults were approximately equal. With regard to stature, the average slave child fell below the first percentile of modern National Center for Health Statistics height standards that characterize Europeans, Americans of European descent, and African Americans who are well-nourished, but the average slave adult exceeded the fifteenth percentile. Comparisons of average heights in studies of growth from childhood to maturity show that slave children were among the smallest ever measured, while growth recovery during and after adolescence was remarkable if not unprecedented.

Recognizing that decisions were made in an environment of poor medical knowledge and that many deaths would have occurred despite the best intentions and the best care that was available, explanations have been sought for the high mortality of slaves. The origins of the unusual age pattern of health can be traced to poor prenatal health and low birth weight. During periods of peak demand for labor mothers returned to work within a few weeks of birth, and to compensate for reductions in breast milk, infants were fed starchy paps and gruels, often supplied in contaminated utensils. Young children who survived the hazardous period of infancy encountered a poor diet and diseases that were often related to poor nutrition. The child's diet emphasized hominy and fat, and owners and medical practitioners often cited nutrition-sensitive diseases such as whooping cough, diarrhea, measles, worms, and pneumonia as causes of death.

By ages eight to twelve work entered the equation of slave health. Other things being equal, work would have placed a claim on the diet that retarded growth, yet it was at the ages when work usually began, initially as a light activity, that some catch-up growth occurred. Other things must not have been equal. As workers, slaves received regular allocations of meat (about one-half pound of pork per day) and other foods. Slaves may have supplemented the allocations by raising garden produce, pigs, and fowl, and by fishing and hunting. The strong growth recovery as teenagers and workers reinforces the view that the diet was at least adequate, if not exceptional, for the disease load and the tasks performed by slaves. Adolescents may have encountered nutritional deficiencies, but they were not widespread or severe enough to impair the substantial recovery of average growth.

Although the health of slave children was poor by the standards of the nineteenth century, one must distinguish effects specific to the region versus the institution of slavery. The disease environment might have been relatively harsh in the South, exposing residents to diseases such as malaria and gastrointestinal infections that caused high death rates. Some information on this question is available from a national sample of nearly sixteen hundred families matched from the 1860 to the 1850 census manuscript schedules of population. Although family members could have left the household for reasons other than death, the presence or absence in 1860 of young children who were recorded in these families in 1850 have been studied as an approximate guide to mortality conditions. Among children aged one to four the expected deaths were 16.3 percent in the South and 13.3 percent in the Northeast. If the South is divided into two subregions, coastal states from North Carolina to Louisiana and the remaining states, expected deaths were higher in the coastal states (18.7 percent) but not in the remaining states of the South, compared with the Northeast. Because the estimated mortality rates of slave children were approximately double those for the

entire free population, the household data suggest that a modest portion of the high mortality of slave children could be attributed to regional factors such as endemic disease.

Economic historians have made great strides in understanding the slave economy. Research in the past two decades has overturned the image of slaves as lazy and inept, established slave-owners as rational capitalists, demonstrated that Southerners were largely independent of Western food supplies, and shown that slave workers were well-nourished while young children had extraordinarily poor health. Progress on these and other topics has raised new issues and suggested additional directions for research. Certain results on regional differences in the efficiency of slave labor await explanation, and the process of quantifying the sources of higher measured efficiency on larger plantations has just begun. The substantial volume of slave manifests lodged in the National Archives has been only partially exploited for insights into the interregional slave trade and into regional and temporal patterns of slave health. The consequences of poor net nutrition for young slaves have been largely unexamined because studies of the subject emphasized the diet alone and perceptions of food intake were reasonably favorable. The investigation of probate records, which depict the occupations, value, and fertility of slaves, has merely scratched the surface of the available data. Designers of models to study the effect of slavery on Southern economic development should look to international comparisons for insights. In addition, the rigor and interest that has characterized study of efficiency, productivity, and self-sufficiency in the cotton-growing South could be extended to areas that produced tobacco, rice, or sugar.

Although discussion of the new economic history of slavery has focused on the United States, many points raised also apply to the Caribbean and Brazil. However, several contrasts are worth noting, including the observation that sugar, rather than cotton or tobacco, was the dominant crop in these areas. It is well established that Caribbean plantations relied heavily on food exported from the United States. Moreover, slave living standards, as measured by stature or mortality rates, were below those in the United States for various reasons, including the presence of large numbers of African-born slaves who were undergoing "seasoning" or adjustment to a new disease environment, and dietary inadequacy in relation to the tropical disease environment and to a heavy workload associated with the production of sugar.

[*See also* Mortality; Slave Trade, *article on* Trans-Atlantic Trade; *and* United States, *article on* The South.]

BIBLIOGRAPHY

Conrad, Alfred H., and John R. Meyer. "The Economics of Slavery in the Ante-Bellum South." *Journal of Political Economy* 66 (1958): 95–130.

Easterlin, Richard A. "Regional Income Trends, 1840–1950." In *American Economic History,* edited by Seymour Harris, pp. 525–547. New York: McGraw-Hill, 1961.

Fogel, Robert William. *Without Consent or Contract: The Rise and Fall of American Slavery.* New York: W. W. Norton, 1989.

Fogel, Robert William, and Stanley L. Engerman. *Time on the Cross: The Economics of American Negro Slavery.* 2 vols. Boston: Little, Brown, 1974.

Genovese, Eugene D. *Roll, Jordan, Roll: The World the Slaves Made.* New York: Pantheon, 1974.

Grey, Lewis Cecil. *History of Agriculture in the Southern United States to 1860.* 2 vols. Wasington: Carnegie Institution of Washington, 1933.

Phillips, Ulrich B. *American Negro Slavery: A Survey of the Supply, Employment, and Control of Negro Labor as Determined by the Plantation Regime.* New York: D. Appleton, 1918.

Stampp, Kenneth M. *The Peculiar Institution: Slavery in the Ante-bellum South.* New York: Alfred A. Knopf, 1956.

Steckel, Richard H. "A Peculiar Population: The Nutrition, Health, and Mortality of American Slaves from Childhood to Maturity." *Journal of Economic History* 46 (1986): 721–741.

Wright, Gavin. *Old South, New South: Revolutions in the Southern Economy Since the Civil War.* New York: Basic Books, 1986.

—RICHARD H. STECKEL

EMANCIPATION IN THE AMERICAS. In Roman society emancipation was the process whereby a son or daughter left the power of the father. In modern parlance the term *emancipation* refers to the ending of any state of oppression or bondage, with particular reference to legislative acts abolishing the slave status and condition. In medieval and early modern Europe slavery became marginal, vestigial, and even, in several kingdoms, extinct. Slaves were manumitted by their masters, or, more exceptionally, they escaped to a free city like Toulouse, where they could claim their freedom after a year. However, the fragmented and layered sovereignty of the medieval polities meant that there was no general slave emancipation, in the sense of legislation freeing all slaves and banning slavery.

With the development of new slave systems in the Americas from the sixteenth and seventeenth century, there were occasions when slaves were freed by purchase or as a reward. In the eighteenth century there were several important cases in which legal action was taken to free an enslaved individual on the grounds that he or she was wrongly held in bondage. Such decisions came close to slave emancipation when they denied the lawfulness of slaveholders' powers in a particular jurisdiction, as with the celebrated Somerset case in England in 1772. This route to the elimination of slavery occurred where the new type of slavery was not clarified by legal precedent and where public opinion was hostile to it. When Vermont seceded in 1777, it became the first state in the world to ban slavery by its constitution. In Portugal and France royal decrees of the 1760s and 1770s sought to ban the entry of slaves to the metropolis. Affecting only a few personal servants, these judgments and decrees dramatized the fact that slavery had already withered away in Europe.

A law adopted by the Assembly of Pennsylvania in 1780 initiated a new type of legislative anti-slavery, although there were only a few thousand slaves in the state and the law freed only children henceforth born to slave mothers once they had reached adulthood. In practice, some slaves acquired freedom because their masters failed to register them as stipulated by the law. Prompted by respect for legitimately acquired property, this was a very moderate law, although one which would, after seventy years or so, end slavery. Although the Pennsylvania act was referred to as an "emancipation law," such "free womb" laws did not in principle free a single living slave. This route to emancipation was later taken by Rhode Island and Connecticut in the 1780s; New York and New Jersey followed in 1799 and 1804 after initial failure and controversy.

Emancipation had its first serious impact on New World slavery when the Jacobin National Convention decreed the immediate ending of slavery, without compensation, throughout the French colonies in February 1794. The decree was enacted following the appearance of an anti-slavery delegation from the large colony of Saint Domingue (later Haiti), where the institution of slavery had been greatly weakened by a large slave uprising in August 1791. This revolt gave birth to a variety of armed groups of black rebels, some of whom were supported by Spain. The coherence of the colonial slave order was also undermined by the claims of a free colored community that was as large of that of the colonial whites. The decree of 1794 aimed to attach the large black majority to the cause of the embattled French Republic and to assist it to repel the treason of royalist planters and the covetous designs of Britain and Spain. The Jacobin decree conferred legal emancipation on about one-half million slaves in the French Caribbean, although in some areas, notably Martinique, British occupation prevented application of the law, while in others, such as Réunion in the Indian Ocean, the law was ignored. Napoleon succeeded in reintroducing slavery to Guadeloupe in 1802, but his attempt to reestablish French power in Saint Domingue, as a prelude to reestablishing slavery there, was defeated by the black revolutionaries who proclaimed the Republic of Haiti in 1804. Since this had been the richest slave colony

in the Americas in 1790, the emancipation of its slaves, won by their own efforts, was a momentous development. According to stern regulations for the slaves, issued by the French Republican commissioners and largely confirmed by the black generals, the lot of the newly emancipated was not enviable. Those on plantations were obliged to work in return for a promise that they would receive one-third of the proceeds of the sale of the crop, but authority on the plantations had broken down and the regulations were widely ignored. While the black military kept some estates going with invigilated labor, in many areas an ex-slave peasantry emerged. The defeat of the French in 1804 showed that despite the flaws of Republican emancipation, those who had freed themselves, or had been freed, had no desire to return to slavery. By the 1820s plantation production had yielded to small farming, the population was growing, and a new elite of military and urban mulattoes vied for control of the fruits of peasant labor.

The new republics of Spanish America generally adopted "free womb" laws in the years from 1814 to 1830, in the course of their struggle for independence against Spain or soon after winning it. The president of the Republic of Haiti helped Simón Bolívar on the condition that he support emancipation. Slaves were offered their freedom if they enrolled in the forces fighting the colonial power, and "free womb" laws were enacted. While many tens of thousands won their freedom in the revolutionary epoch, the "free womb" laws condemned just as many to live out their remaining days in servitude. In several of the successor republics, such as Venezuela, the value of slaveholdings remained for some decades a vital component of the rural credit system. It was not until the period between 1849 and 1856 that remaining slaveholding ended in all the South American republics—except for Paraguay, where emancipation was paradoxically suppressed by invading armies of the slaveholding Brazilian empire in the late 1860s.

The advance of anti-slavery in French and Spanish America exercised a certain influence on

Britain, a country where large-scale abolitionist agitation first appeared in the 1780s. In 1807 Britain forbade its merchants or colonists to participate in the Atlantic slave trade. Under British pressure, the Congress of Vienna (1815) formally condemned the Atlantic traffic. An emancipation law was eventually adopted by Britain's Reformed Parliament in 1833, after a sustained public campaign and in the aftermath of the Reform Crisis. A revolt involving thirty thousand Jamaican slaves at Christmas of 1831 made some West Indian proprietors more willing to accept emancipation with compensation. The law also obliged the former slaves to serve their masters for six years as "apprentices"; however, in 1838, following further agitation in Britain and the West Indies, more than seven hundred thousand former slaves finally achieved their freedom. In Barbados, where the land was effectively controlled by planters, wage-earning freedmen continued to work the plantations. In Jamaica only some of the freedmen, and no freedwomen, were willing to work for wages; others cultivated subsistence crops, often on land allotted to them for this purpose under slavery. While many abolitionists were content that life was better for the former slaves, others were discomfited by the decline of plantation output.

The supposedly abolitionist governments of Louis Phillippe in France were restrained from introducing bolder measures in Martinique and Guadeloupe by respect for slaveholders' property rights and by fears that immediate emancipation would destroy the plantation economy. The 1848 Revolution in France, however, brought more vigorous anti-slavery advocates to the fore. Large numbers of slaves in Martinique abandoned the plantations, and a general emancipation law resulted. The freedmen and freedwomen were to benefit from the institutions of the "social republic," but these were abandoned under Louis Napoleon and compensation was paid to the planters. Instead, the plantation system survived in the French islands, worked by wage and contract labor. The position of the sugar-mills was further bolstered by legislation and by the advanced organization and technology of their central system.

The ending of slavery in the British and French Caribbean, and the increasingly effective ban on the Atlantic slave trade, made abolitionism appear part of the spirit of the age. Nonetheless, in the 1850s the slave plantations of the American South, Cuba, and Brazil were still profitably producing ever-larger quantities of cotton, sugar, tobacco, and coffee. The slave trade to Cuba continued despite an official ban. There were more slaves in the Americas than ever before—nearly six million—and in the United States the slave population was growing without slave imports. The fate of slavery in the hemisphere was only to be sealed by the momentous conflict in North America.

The controversies leading up to the secession of the Confederate states did not directly address the question of emancipation, although Southern slaveholders feared that a Republican administration would not protect their "peculiar institution." Republican support was based in the Northeast and West, where there was no slavery. It was accompanied by proclamation of the virtues of "free labor" and distrust of what were portrayed as the expansionary ambitions of the "Slave Power." However, the Republicans shrank from proposing emancipation as a practical measure. To expropriate the slave-owners would be unjust, it was believed; but where would the money come from to compensate the owners of four million slaves? And what would happen to the freedmen and freedwomen? Abraham Lincoln pondered schemes for introducing a "free womb" law and for "colonizing" the former slaves back to Africa. It was, however, the course of the Civil War that dictated the direct measure of emancipation. The Confederate rebellion, instead of being swiftly crushed, turned into a bitter and hard-fought war. British and French statesmen were tempted to recognize the right of the Confederate states to self-determination. The sentiment of Republicans and Union soldiers toward the rebels became increasingly punitive. Lincoln's Emancipation Proclamation of

January 1863 declared that the slaves held in the rebel states were free; however, only with the victory of the Union and the ratification of the Thirteenth Amendment in 1865 did slaves throughout the United States gain their freedom. Nevertheless, the Emancipation Proclamation had altered the character of the war; it also facilitated the enlistment of two hundred thousand African Americans in the Union armed forces and undermined slaveholders' authority within the Confederacy. The freedmen received not only their freedom but also the vote, as the Republicans enlisted black support in their attempted reconstruction of the South. Despite this, the Southern planters retained their lands. By the 1870s they were able, through the mobilization of a majority of the Southern whites, to impose sharecropping peonage or debt bondage on the former slaves, depriving them in the process of their new political rights.

The destruction of the largest slave system in the New World isolated the last remaining slaveowners in Cuba and Brazil; the slaves of Dutch Suriname had won their freedom (with apprenticeship) in 1863. "Free womb" laws were enacted in Spain in 1870 and in Brazil in 1871. In both countries, however, slavery remained profitable, leading the slaveowners to resort to every device of procrastination and giving them the resources to do so. The slaveholding orders in Cuba and Brazil were eventually brought down, as had been the case elsewhere, in the context of a wider political crisis affecting, respectively, the Spanish monarchy and empire and the Brazilian monarchy and empire. The year 1868 witnessed both a liberal revolution in Spain and a colonial revolt in Cuba. The new authorities in Madrid and the Cuban rebels both made anti-slavery gestures and declarations, but neither were prepared to tackle the slave magnates of western Cuba head-on. In 1873 a decree of the Spanish Republic ended slavery in Puerto Rico, with support from the local possessing classes. In Cuba, the rebels who held out at the eastern end of the island, away from the main plantation zone, attracted the support of blacks and mulattoes, including some runaway slaves, but they failed to make a breakthrough in the west. In 1878 a restored Spanish monarchy brought this first war of Cuban independence to an end. In the following year, however, there was a renewed outbreak of revolt; one of its leaders was the colored General Maceo. In 1880 an emancipation law was introduced; the owners of the one hundred seventy thousand remaining slaves received no financial compensation but were to retain the services of their slaves for another eight years. In 1886 this system, known as the *patronato*, ended. The wealthier planters had built large, modern sugar mills, using not only steampower but also electricity and an extended network of rail lines to bring cane from a wide area. They proved able to survive both emancipation and a drop in sugar prices. They employed wage labor, sometimes on a seasonal basis, and raised overall output to record levels.

Brazilian slavery was brought to an end in 1888 following a wide-ranging mobilization of public opinion within the country. About one-half of the free citizens were themselves people of color, and many resented the stigma of a racial system of slavery. Direct action accompanied public outcry, as when colored boatmen or railway workers refused to transport slaves. In a number of cities abolitionists succeeded in persuading small slaveholders to free their chattels. In 1886 and 1887 abolitionists worked in the main plantation zone around São Paulo, inciting slaves to desert the coffee estates. The empire also faced opposition from a small workers' movement and from republican agitation with backing from the planters of São Paulo. The Empire of Brazil was overthrown by a republican revolution in 1889; the emancipation of the preceding year had not registered the imminent collapse of the slave system and was unaccompanied by any sort of compensation. The coffee barons now sponsored the entry of large numbers of Italian immigrants to furnish their main labor force as the former slaves were relegated to the margins of the plantation economy.

The cycle of emancipations that swept the

Americas between the 1780s and the 1880s did not outlaw racial injustice or exploitation, but it did strike down an extreme form of oppression that sought to control the whole existence of the slave, denying mobility or family life. The freedmen and freedwomen acquired a variety of formal rights, although many were effectively suspended for decades to come. The former slaves sought to acquire small plots of land, as tenants if not proprietors, but except on the smallest Caribbean islands, only a minority realized this ambition.

By the 1770s and 1780s slavery had become an institution that both the enlightened and the pious found offensive. The anti-slavery cause was patronized by leading statesmen in the United States, Britain, and France. This anti-slavery sentiment, however, was generally restrained by respect for property, fear of "uncontrolled Negroes," and considerations of national interest. In times of crisis these restraints were neutralized, especially in cases where slaveholders were traitorous or threatening. When artisans, farmers, or those with little or no property were drawn into political life, they often proved to be unreliable supporters of slavery. Even if they did not pity the slave, they feared and detested the slaveholder. Most of the acts of emancipation coincided with moments of national crisis. At such moments both statesmen and revolutionaries saw the need to redefine the boundaries of citizenship and the scope of the market. In an epoch when capitalist advance was disrupting traditional economies, anti-slavery movements sought to assert at least one important limit on the rights and powers of the propertyholder. The notions of freedom and free labor were attractive and powerful ones, while the ideal of restraining power appealed to those, above all women, excluded from formal political life.

Free people of color might enjoy privileges, or even own slaves, but they were not comfortable with a racial system of slavery. Finally, emancipation invariably rallied support from the slaves themselves; but while slaves and abolitionists were protagonists of emancipation, they did not determine its results. Old or new landed elites, responding to capitalist development based on new forms of dependent rural labor, wrote new racial codes. Almost everywhere, however, the experience of emancipation bequeathed traditions that could be used by former slaves and their descendants in renewed efforts to improve their condition.

In different accounts anti-slavery has been construed as an instrument of industrial capitalists, as conducive to "bourgeois hegemony," as market-inspired middle-class humanitarianism, as an evangelical crusade, as a cloak for the Pax Britannica, as "free labor" patriotism, as a vehicle of black resistance, and as an aspect of an Atlantic class struggle. As research and debate reach out beyond the supposed British prototype and focus on acts of emancipation as much as abolitionist ideology, the scope for combining these different models in new ways will increase.

[*See also* Abolition and Anti-Slavery, *articles on* Latin America *and* United States; Brazil; Historiography, *article on* Latin American and Caribbean Slavery; *and* South America.]

BIBLIOGRAPHY

Berlin, Ira, et al., eds. *Free at Last: A Documentary History of Slavery, Freedom, and the Civil War*. New York: New Press, 1992.

Blackburn, Robin. *The Overthrow of Colonial Slavery, 1776–1848*. London: Verso, 1988.

Drescher, Seymour. *Capitalism and Anti-Slavery: British Mobilization in Comparative Perspective*. London: Macmillan, 1986.

Foner, Eric. *Nothing But Freedom: Emancipation and Its Legacy*. Baton Rouge: Louisiana State University Press, 1983.

Holt, Thomas. *The Problem of Freedom: Race, Labour and Politics in Jamaica, 1838–1940*. Baltimore: Johns Hopkins University Press, 1992.

McGlynn, Frank, and Seymour Drescher, eds. *The Meaning of Freedom: Economics, Politics and Culture After Slavery*. Pittsburgh: University of Pittsburgh Press, 1992.

Scott, Rebecca J. *Slave Emancipation in Cuba: The Transition to Free Labor, 1860–1899*. Princeton: Princeton University Press, 1985.

Scott, Rebecca J., et al. *The Abolition of Slavery and the Aftermath of Emancipation in Brazil*. Durham: Duke University Press, 1988.

—ROBIN BLACKBURN

EUNUCHS. The term *eunuchs* denotes males who were emasculated and thus rendered incapable of sexual relations. Eunuchs were widely used and were valued slaves—primarily because they could be used to guard and supervise women in the harems of sovereigns and rulers—in many diverse regions of the world, ranging from Ming Dynasty China to Ottoman Turkey. Their most frequent function was to ensure that women remained the exclusive sexual property of their masters. Although the word *eunuch* in its original Greek sense meant "bed guard," they were also used as soldiers, personal retainers, administrators, and entertainers. Thus eunuchs were used beyond the harem, and many undertook important political duties well beyond their role as harem-guardians.

Eunuchs were made from young, usually prepubescent, boys. After being captured or sold into slavery, these boys were transformed into eunuchs by undergoing a dangerous operation, often performed by experienced surgeons. Despite the reputed skill of many surgeons, 75 to 90 percent of those operated on died (although the incidence of death decreased if performed on boys before puberty). Although the emasculation procedure varied according to time and place, eunuchs were generally made in one of two ways. The first and most radical procedure involved the simultaneous removal of the testicles and the penis, with a variation where castration preceded the removal of the penis. After the operation, a device (often a lead rod or smooth piece of wood) was placed in the urethra and replaced after each urination until healing was finished. This was done to prevent the tissue from joining around the wound and blocking the passage of urine. The flow of blood from the wound was never staunched, but hot oil (usually sesame oil) was poured over the wound immediately after the penis and testicles were severed. In Egypt the victim was buried in hot sand up to the navel for five days after the procedure. In southern India the operation was similar, except that the subject was given opium and his genitals were clamped between two pieces of bamboo and severed by a razor that slid along the wood. The second procedure consisted of incising and cauterizing the scrotum with a red-hot blade and then removing the testicles. A third and rare form of emasculation was to sever only the penis and leave the testicles intact. Eunuchs fetched high prices as slaves owing to the great demand for them and the high mortality rate after the operation. Generally, the cost of a eunuch was four to ten times that of a regular slave.

The physical ramifications of this surgery were drastic, although it is difficult to pass beyond the stereotypes and stock descriptions of eunuchs recorded by eyewitnesses. Perhaps the most obvious result of the operation was inability to perform coitus; however, eunuchs who underwent the second procedure and were only castrated sometimes retained sexual potency. The sexual act therefore remained possible for some eunuchs, who were reputed to be highly sought after by harem women, who appreciated their guardian's attentions and sexual abilities. Indeed, according to the author Juvenal, Roman women often engaged in sexual relations with their eunuchs.

Eunuchs were often able to transcend the gendered spatial barriers of palace life by virtue of their liminal status as "sexless" beings. Thus they played a role in the private, female sphere and also in the public-political male sphere of palaces in societies as diverse as the early Byzantine empires and Mughal India. While eunuchs were certainly used to guard harem women, their use was also part of a broader system of court slavery wherein elite slaves, not all of them eunuchs, achieved power and authority beyond the reach of the vast majority of slaves and free persons alike. In the Nupe court of West Africa, for example, elite slaves were used as police, tax-collectors, messengers, and bodyguards. Overall, eunuchs were used both as means to control women and as functionaries of state who wielded authority in the name of their sovereign ruler.

Eunuchs were commonly described as obese, resourceful, avaricious, emotionally unstable, and hedonistic. They were reputed to be extravagant dressers and were usually shown in possession of the trappings of great wealth. They were also distinguishable by their smooth, pallid skin and their high-pitched voices. If the operation took place before puberty, secondary sexual characteristics such as beard and body hair never developed. Although psychological and hormonal abnormalities certainly afflicted some eunuchs, their negative image also stemmed from the influence and power they wielded as a group, which often undermined the position of the aristocratic elite in favor of the sovereign and his slave retainers, thus incurring the enmity of many nobles.

The power some highly placed eunuchs wielded was intimately connected with their special relationship to the sovereign they served. They were entrusted with the stewardship of money and possessions because they were unable to produce progeny and thus had no family to which they could bequeath their possessions, titles, or functions.

As a group, eunuchs had no corporate existence among or beyond themselves. Thus while many court slaves were denied progeny by law or tradition, only eunuchs as a group were made physically incapable of producing heirs and descendants. As Claude Meillassoux has noted, the physical state of eunuchs locked them into their legal state as slaves. Although eunuchs were sometimes manumitted, they remained isolated and were physically unable to reproduce themselves; the latter was a fundamental component of slave status. Furthermore, like all slaves, they had no broader family loyalties that could compete with their allegiance to their masters. Nor could they be assimilated into the aristocracy because they were marked by their physical deformity. Eunuchs were valuable because many rulers felt that their loyalty was assured. By using eunuchs, the sovereign could maintain close control over the duties and goods assigned to these people who were highly dependent on the favor of the sovereign for protection

and status. In short, eunuchs were more easily controlled than aristocrats, as well as more easily disposed of should they become troublesome or rebellious.

Many rulers used eunuchs to centralize their own power and control over the bureaucracy by staffing it with officials loyal to them. The use of eunuchs was sometimes linked to a movement from government based on kinship to one based on a more bureaucratic model; in many cases the use of eunuchs was associated with an attempt to subvert the power of the aristocracy in favor of the sovereign or ruler. In Ming Dynasty China, for example, the increased use of eunuchs coincided with an attempt by the emperors to reduce the power of the aristocracy. In the West African kingdom of Damagaram, posts formerly held by aristocrats, such as the chief receiver of revenue or commander of the armies, were passed to elite slaves, including eunuchs. In later Imperial Rome, eunuchs often achieved status and rank higher than the hereditary nobility. The key to political power and influence in later Imperial Rome was the ability to maintain close social and political proximity to the emperor. In this type of situation the eunuchs who served as trusted advisors, confidants, and personal servants could use their freedom of access to the ruler and their powers of informal persuasion to dominate political life at the court and often beyond. Emperor Shenzong (1572–1620) of China transmitted all his imperial decisions to the Grand Secretariat on papers carried by palace eunuchs, a clear example of how the political influence held by eunuchs was often the result of sensitive information they obtained inside the corridors of power.

Although many eunuchs performed routine or simply ceremonial tasks, it was relatively common for individual eunuchs to attain great power and prestige. Their easy access to powerful persons and their role in the management of information gave some of them remarkable political mobility. Those with political acumen, such as Narses, a eunuch-general during the reign of Justinian, could rise to high office, control estates, and manage great wealth and property. In Ottoman Turkey the chief eunuch (*kislar agha*) served as the confidential messenger between the sultan and the grand vizier, held the rank of "pasha with three tails," and was commander of the corps of *baltaji* or halberdiers. The eunuch who occupied this influential position was rewarded commensurably and had other eunuchs and girls as slaves, as well as being allotted three hundred horses for his own personal use. African eunuchs in Medina served as the police of the Mosque of the Prophet, possessed influence in the political affairs of the town, had large stipends sent from Constantinople, and were given presents by the rich. The grand eunuch of the West African state of Oyo controlled the palace and all access to the sovereign; the eunuchs of Oyo eventually gained control of the succession and actually chose which prince would become king.

Eunuchs were not always loyal to the rulers who had enslaved them. As a group, they could act as an independent force against the interest of their sovereign. Rulers sometimes found themselves besieged by powerful factions of palace eunuchs. During the Tang era in China, for example, the power of the eunuchs exceeded that of the emperor; they even managed to gain control of key military units and interfere with the imperial succession. Similarly, on the death of Shāh ʿAbbās II in 1667, the palace eunuchs obtained control of the state, and in 1694 they placed Shāh Sulṭān Ḥusayn on the Persian throne; he in turn left virtually all the affairs of state to his retinue of eunuchs.

Typically, eunuchs were integrated into the social world of the palace at as early an age as possible. In the palace of the Ottoman sultan they were initially placed in a "school for eunuchs" where they learned court etiquette. The graduates of the school began as harem-eunuchs with the rank of *en asagi*, meaning "the lowest." They then could rise through the palace hierarchy, with the most influential achieving unique titled positions that brought with them influence and wealth. Eunuchs began to wield influence in the Ottoman court as early as the sixteenth century and continued to play a key role in political affairs well into the eighteenth century.

With the exception of China, eunuchs were generally supplied from beyond the borders of the state using them. In the Middle Ages eunuchs destined for the Ottoman Empire were sent from Christian Europe and Circassia. Ottoman Turkey was one of the most consistent markets for eunuchs; throughout the nineteenth century it took about ten thousand slaves annually to meet the demand of the sultan. African eunuchs were produced mainly in Egypt, Ethiopia, Darfur, Nupe, and Baghirmi for sale both inside and outside Africa. While it is difficult to determine their precise point of origin, it is clear that Upper Egypt, the Nile Basin, East Africa, and the Sudan were the primary sources of eunuchs for the Arabian Peninsula, the Middle East, and the Mediterranean world by the sixteenth century. After the sixteenth century the number of white eunuchs declined in the Mediterranean and the Middle East, while the number of black eunuchs, mainly imported from Africa, increased. They were part of a larger African diaspora in the region, the result of an extensive slave trade via routes from the Sahara Desert, the Nile Valley, the Ethiopian plateau, the Red Sea, and the Persian Gulf.

As elite slaves, eunuchs represent a fundamental discontinuity in the structure of many slave systems: that slaves, who were by definition property, could hold positions of power and have access to high rank and influence. As surrogates of the sovereign, some eunuchs exercised considerable influence by virtue of their close proximity to the throne, but they gained this access only as a result of their kinlessness and status as slaves. These elite slaves were intimately connected with the maintenance of their respective slave systems, whether in Africa, India, China, or the Arab world. By their participating in the creation of a slave society and bureaucracy, the meaning of slavery had shifted for these slaves. It had moved from a slave system based on outright exploitation and powerlessness to one that provided certain avenues to authority, status, esteem, and upward social mobility. In short, eunuchs altered the social terms on which the institution of slavery was based. From the vantage-point of the sovereign, eunuchs were the most trustworthy of all slaves, dependent on their masters for advancement, influence, and prestige. However, the price of entry into this world was immense; boys and young men had their sexuality, their "maleness," forcibly sacrificed in a profoundly horrific manner. Eunuchs were given opportunities few slaves possessed, but they were only allowed to hold such positions because they performed a number of invaluable duties made possible by virtue of their sexlessness.

BIBLIOGRAPHY

Fisher, Allan G. B., and Humphrey J. Fisher. *Slavery and Muslim Society in Africa*. London: C. Hurst, 1970.

Hopkins, Keith. *Conquerors and Slaves*. Cambridge: Cambridge University Press, 1978.

Lewis, Bernard. *Race and Slavery in the Middle-East*. New York and Oxford: Oxford University Press, 1990.

Meillassoux, Claude. *The Anthropology of Slavery: The Womb of Iron and Gold*. Translated by Alide Dasnois. Chicago: University of Chicago Press, 1991.

—SEAN STILWELL

EUROPE. [*This entry comprises two articles that trace the history of slavery and other forms of servitude in the Greco-Roman world and in medieval Europe.*]

Ancient World

The world of the ancient Greeks and Romans was enormous in time and space. Greek speakers were established on the mainland of Greece by the Late Bronze Age (c.1600–1200 BCE), while the power of Rome lingered until the deposition of the last emperor, Romulus Augustulus, two millennia later (476 CE). In the Hellenistic age (323–31 BCE), Greek ideas and cultural forms that had emerged in the Classical era (c.550–350 BCE) spread widely through much of the Near East and the western Mediterranean. In the second century CE the Roman Empire extended from Portugal and Morocco to Iraq and Jordan on one axis, and from Scotland across Europe to the North African littoral, including Egypt, on the other. There was in antiquity therefore no single "classical" world, but rather a succession of distinct historical epochs in which Greeks and Romans created societies that affected other Mediterranean peoples in varying ways.

Across the vast dimensions of Greco-Roman history, forms of servitude (for example, serfdom or debt bondage) were ubiquitous. They included chattel slavery, the ultimate form of servitude, in which the slave was judged a commodity, akin to livestock, and the slave-owner enjoyed complete mastery over the slave's physical being, the power of life and death included. Slavery in this strict sense was said to have first emerged on a large scale on the Greek island of Chios, but it was not found in all times and places. It was particularly evident in Classical Athens, where it grew in strength as Athens became more democratic, and also in Roman Italy of the late Republic and Principate (c. 200 BCE–200 CE). Often it coexisted with other forms of servitude. Thus in Classical Sparta the elite ruling citizens held in permanent and terror-laden subjection the Helots, descendants of a pre-existing population they had conquered on arrival in the Peloponnese, and against whom they declared war every year. But as a self-reproducing group of indigenous Greeks, not foreigners, the Helots had limited rights (they were allowed to marry and maintain families, for example) and so were not chattel slaves. In contrast, chattel slaves were utterly deracinated and disempowered beings, devoid of any personal or social identity other than that deriving from association with their owners. They had no ties of kin and were forcibly held in shameful subjection at their owners' discretion, without legal rights. In the central eras of Greek and Roman history, slavery stood as the antithesis, and guarantee, of civic freedom; thus from a structural standpoint the societies of Greece and Rome were genuine slave societies, no matter what the actual numbers of slaves in any one era or region.

No reliable statistical information exists on the size of Greco-Roman slave populations. For Classical Athens estimates range from twenty thousand to one hundred twenty thousand, or 15 to 35 percent of the total population, with sixty thousand a plausible compromise. For Roman Italy at the end of the first century BCE, two million from a total population of six million is likewise plausible but still an approximation. The rough ratio of one slave to three free persons known in the slave societies of Brazil and the United States is unlikely ever to have been generally surpassed in antiquity, although the Helots certainly outnumbered the Spartan elite.

To judge from anecdotal literary sources, the scale of individual slave-ownership was smaller in Greece than in Rome. The father of the orator Demosthenes, an unusually wealthy man, kept about ten slaves in his house. The 120 slaves used to manufacture shields confiscated from Lysias, another orator, and his brother at the end of the fifth century BCE were probably an exceptionally large complement. At Rome, however, elite citizens might own hundreds of slaves. The son of Cn. Pompeius recruited eight hundred of his personal slaves and shepherds for war against Julius Caesar, while the senator L. Pedanius Secundus maintained under Nero about four hundred slaves in his urban townhouse alone. In Roman Tripolitania of the second century CE, a wealthy female property-owner could afford to make a gift of four hundred slaves to her sons. Slave-owning, however, was not the preserve of the very rich alone. Athenian peasants in the age of Pericles, it is thought, regularly kept two or three slaves. The same is true of artisans in Hellenistic and Roman Egypt, where inventories surviving on papyrus documents such as tax declarations or wills permit a clearer picture of slave-ownership than in other regions. Owning slaves, therefore, was an expression of status and power, to be sought for its own sake at all social levels. Paradoxically, even

slaves and former slaves might be slave-owners, especially those at Rome who belonged to the household of the emperor and prospered from their favored standing. An ex-slave of the Augustan period is reported to have possessed 4,116 slaves when he died. In the hierarchical social structures of antiquity, the desire to exercise power over others knew little limitation.

Slaves were acquired principally through capture in war, through organized kidnapping (especially piracy), through natural reproduction in the existing slave population, and through trade conducted by merchants. Over time the sources of supply fluctuated, with sustained periods of warfare sometimes producing a glut of slaves on the open market. But there is no evidence, even in late antiquity, of slave-owners ever complaining of serious shortages of slaves.

In the Republican era the growth of Rome's empire through expansionist warfare generated huge numbers of prisoners—men, women, and children—who were transported from all over the Mediterranean to Italy and grain-growing Sicily. The principle of enslavement on capture in warfare was operative at all times. The anguish it entailed was arrestingly portrayed in works of art. Both Greeks and Romans tended to avoid enslavement of conationals and chose to equate slaves with "barbarians," and other peoples they considered their inferiors. Thus the Greeks thought of Thracians and Carians, peoples from the Black Sea and southwestern Asia Minor, as slaves by definition, and to the Romans, Syrians and Jews were born for enslavement. Slavery, however, was not itself racially grounded: anyone, regardless of racial identity, could become a slave.

Piracy is best illustrated by the activities of the Cilician bandits notorious in the Hellenistic period for unloading vast quantities of enslaved victims in the port of Delos, whence traders swiftly redistributed them, particularly to the west. It was said that tens of thousands of slaves could be exchanged there in just one day. A letter of the Christian bishop Augustine reveals that piracy was still rampant in late antiquity, and also that demand for slaves remained high.

Children born to a slave mother were considered born into slavery (the status of the father was irrelevant), so natural reproduction constantly contributed to the slave supply. Such writers as Xenophon, Varro, and Columella, who wrote treatises on estate management that included instructions on how to manage slaves, suggest that some slave-owners encouraged reproduction among their slaves and allowed them to form families, but it is impossible to judge whether there was manipulated slave-breeding. Many slave women must have borne children fathered by their masters, since reports of sexual opportunism by owners are legion. Thus Pliny, in the first century CE, told of a slave woman who after two sexual encounters on the same day gave birth to twins, one resembling her master, the other his steward. Men considered it shameful, however, for free women to have sex with male slaves. The widespread practice of infant exposure, a form of birth control after the fact prevalent at all social levels, also produced new slaves: anyone reclaiming an abandoned infant was at liberty to raise the child in slavery. The Roman grammarian C. Melissus was born free, abandoned as an infant by his parents, and raised as a slave but later manumitted.

Slave-traders such as A. Kapreilius Timotheus—whose funeral monument, of Roman imperial date, shows a dealer (presumably himself) leading along a train of eight chained slaves for sale—were active throughout the Mediterranean in war and peace as distributors of captives and home-born slaves alike. They might combine their interests in slaves with trade in other commodities. Their activities were of little interest to litterateurs, however, so their importance as agents of supply is imperfectly reflected in the historical record. Nonetheless, the sight of slaves on sale was common in the marketplaces of Greek and Roman towns, as documentary evidence of transactions indicates. For example, third-century CE records from the middle Euphrates attest the sale of a thir-

teen-year-old girl, Immedabous, who had previously been sold less than a year before at a site a considerable distance away.

Slaves in antiquity worked in almost every area of human enterprise, and the concept of competition between slave and free labor did not exist. Often, especially in manufacturing, slave and free worked side by side. The one area in which Greeks and Romans tended not to employ slaves, except in crises, was in the military: the dangers inherent in arming slaves were well understood, although Classical Athens had a sort of police force composed of three hundred armed Scythian slaves. Slave occupations were so diverse that a hierarchy of servile statuses resulted, which was continually reinforced by the varying means of recruitment. Consequently, there was never a single slave class recognizably conscious of itself as such.

Agriculture was the mainstay of the ancient economy, and slaves were often involved in farm work; however, the extent to which communities in Classical Greece, especially Athens, depended on slave labor in agriculture is a matter of deep controversy. Xenophon in his book on estate management instructed his reader in the management of agricultural slaves, which implies that wealthy Athenian absentee land-owners commonly had considerable numbers of slaves at their disposal, supervised by slave overseers. But scholarly estimates of the use of slaves in peasant smallholdings, the dominant economic form, range from widespread to almost nonexistent. In contrast, in Italy of the late Republic the extensive development of large slave-run estates that followed the acquisition of empire meant that the rural slave presence was very high—though independent peasant smallholders never completely disappeared—and it continued well into the imperial age.

Slaves were especially associated with domestic work, both the menial tasks of the household and those of administration. Commerce and shopkeeping were also often handled by slaves, many of whom lived and worked independently. Elite Romans kept slaves as secretaries, accountants, doctors, and teachers of their children, while under the Principate some of the emperor's slaves, a privileged corps, were used in the administration of empire. Job titles were often recorded on slaves' epitaphs, and this may mean that their work was particularly important to them in the construction of personal identity. Many slaves were highly educated. The dangerous and heavily exploitative work of mining for precious metals, where physical strength alone was needed, was also a slave preserve. The Athenian silver mines at Laurium had a slave population perhaps as high as thirty thousand by the fourth century BCE, and the gold and silver mines developed by the Romans in Spain consumed slaves at a prodigious rate. Mining slaves worked in conditions so noxious that occasionally sympathy was forthcoming even from the elite. Sometimes cities maintained groups of public slaves who built and repaired roads, cleaned streets, and did other similar jobs.

Greek and Roman slave-owners frequently exercised their prerogative of setting slaves free, and at Rome, though not in Greece, manumitted slaves could become citizens. Nevertheless, most slaves, especially agricultural and mining slaves, were never set free. Many slaves paid their owners in compensation for their freedom from savings accumulated by one means or another, and this allowed owners to replace their losses. The extensive manumission records from Delphi of the last two centuries BCE indicate that as a condition of manumission many slaves had to continue to serve their owners, a pattern well in evidence in Roman legal sources too. Manumission therefore tended to reinforce the slavery system, not to erode it.

At no time was the structural embeddedness of slavery in ancient society seriously questioned. In a weak argument, Aristotle in the fourth century BCE maintained that some human beings were slaves by nature and that they should be enslaved for both their own good and that of society. He was responding to an opposing view, but one that never made a major impact. At Rome the teachings of the Stoics are sometimes said to have mitigated atti-

Roman women with their slave hairdresser, from a fresco in Herculaneum, first–third century; Museo Archeologico Nazionale, Naples.

tudes to slavery and to have inspired humane legislation rendering slavery more tolerable. In reality, moralists like Seneca, writing in the first century CE, were more concerned with the effects of slave-owning on the moral health of elite slave-owners than with the conditions under which slaves actually lived. And although showing an increasing interest in the public regulation of slavery, Roman legislation was driven above all by the object of keeping the slavery system intact. Doubtless some individual slaveowners treated their slaves well—the younger Pliny at the turn of the second century CE is often cited in this regard—but there is nothing to prove permanent betterment in the way slaves were treated over the course of time. Nor did Christianity have any improving effect. Across the generations Christian teachers offered slaves the injunction that they should obey their masters "with fear and trembling," thus vigorously reaffirming the reality that slavery was an institution based above all on violence. Neither Christians nor anyone else in antiquity brought forth a sustained indictment of slavery calling for its abolition as a social evil.

Practically all knowledge of Greek and Roman slavery comes from sources embodying the attitudes and ideology of slave-owners. It is impossible therefore to understand fully what it was like to be a slave in antiquity. Slaves were characterized from century to century as unreliable, lazy, immoral, and criminous (with a special tendency to steal and run away), a reflection of the fact that slave-owners had to contend with an intractable labor force from which they had to elicit service by carefully alternating incentives and rewards with threats and applications of physical punishment. The notion that slaves should pay with their bodies was fundamental. The essential irrationality of the owners' posture is betrayed by the maintenance of slavery as an institution, together with the benefits it brought them, over an immense amount of time. Many slaves must have responded to the oppression and brutality they constantly faced by consciously obeying their masters and accepting such rewards for good behavior as time off from work, extra rations of food or clothing, or even freedom. Many presumably internalized their master's values in the process, but others, as Plutarch realized, knowing that coercion would follow if obedience were not forthcoming, simply assumed a façade of loyalty and concealed their true beliefs. Obedience and passivity did not necessarily go in tandem, and as the record of protest and resistance makes clear, slaves in antiquity made many efforts to assert their human will in the face of adversity.

Resistance to slavery, a relatively little-studied topic in ancient history, is most easily recognizable in the occasional episodes of open revolt on record, the most notorious being that led by the gladiator Spartacus in Italy in the late 70s BCE. The object of such resistance was to remove the disaffected from the rigors of slavery, not to eradicate slavery itself. Nothing suggests that programmatic opposition ever inspired servile revolutionary activity. Revolt, however, was a dangerous form of resistance, jeopardizing slaves' family relationships and guaranteeing severe reprisals if unsuccessful.

As in later slave societies, therefore, Greek and Roman slaves tended to display resistance more commonly by adopting tactics that annoyed and frustrated owners but were less personally threatening—running away, playing truant, working inefficiently, pilfering, and sabotaging property. Running away was particularly endemic, ranging from grand actions like the flight of twenty thousand slaves from Decelea in northern Attica in the late years of the Peloponnesian War, to individual efforts like that of Dionysius, a slave of the Roman statesman Cicero, who escaped across the Adriatic in 46 BCE. In the third century BCE a slave named Drimacus organized and led a community of runaways on Chios in the manner of maroons in later history. Slave-owners advertised rewards for the return of their runaways, engaged professional slave-catchers to find them, or set out in pursuit themselves.

Slaves sometimes preferred death to slavery. The memory was long preserved, for instance, of the captive Spartan boy who chose to kill himself rather than suffer the indignity of bringing the chamberpot to his master, the Macedonian king Antigonus Doson.

At both the material and the psychological levels the lives of most slaves in antiquity were unenviably severe, and relations with owners were by definition tension-fraught and antagonistic. It is important to acknowledge, therefore, not just that the high cultural achievements of the Greeks and Romans, which are still rightly valued today, would not have been possible without the institution of slavery, but also that the creation of this high civilization came at the cost of tremendous human suffering.

[See also Historiography, article on Medieval European and Mediterranean Slavery; Law, article on Roman Law; Mediterranean; and Serfdom.]

BIBLIOGRAPHY

Bradley, K. R. Slaves and Masters in the Roman Empire: A Study in Social Control. New York and Oxford: Oxford University Press, 1987.

Bradley, K. R. *Slavery and Rebellion in the Roman World 140 B.C.–70 B.C.* Bloomington: Indiana University Press, 1989.

Bradley, K. R. *Slavery and Society at Rome.* Cambridge: Cambridge University Press, 1994.

Finley, Moses I. *Ancient Slavery and Modern Ideology.* New York: Viking Press, 1980.

Fisher, N. R. E. *Slavery in Classical Greece.* London: Bristol Classical Press, 1993.

Garlan, Yvon. *Slavery in Ancient Greece.* Ithaca, N.Y.: Cornell University Press, 1988.

Hopkins, Keith. *Conquerors and Slaves.* Cambridge: Cambridge University Press, 1978.

Joshel, Sandra R. *Work, Identity, and Legal Status at Rome: A Study of the Occupational Inscriptions.* Norman: University of Oklahoma Press, 1992.

—KEITH BRADLEY

Middle Ages

Throughout the Middle Ages slavery persisted on both shores of the Mediterranean and in the regions linked with it, even though it occupied a far less important position in society and in the economy than it had in Roman times. From the end of the Roman Empire to the beginning of European expansion in the Atlantic, slavery was a social and physical reality in the Christian world, and it was reinforced by contact with the highly developed slavery of the Muslims. In addition to the actual presence of slaves, the influence of Roman law helped to shape the legal systems of the European West. The persistence of slavery throughout the Middle Ages set the stage for colonial slavery in the Americas and thus influenced the evolution of modern society throughout the Western Hemisphere. Roman slavery and slave laws and the attitudes of early Christianity influenced medieval slavery, despite the major social and economic developments in the European West.

Varieties of slavery are readily apparent in both Islam and Western Christendom. Because of the many ways they were employed, slaves cannot be fitted neatly into a single category, nor did they form a distinct social class or caste. Most were on the bottom strata of society, but a few occupied roles with greater responsibility. Even though all slaves suffered the same or similar legal, emotional, and ideological disabilities, there were gradations in their material circumstances.

Analyzing the differences in slavery through the division between agricultural or rural slavery and domestic or urban slavery is useful only to a certain point, because wide variations can be observed within each category, and because the categories themselves often overlapped. For example, rural slaves worked in manufacturing on the estates of the early Middles Ages in western Europe. There were gradations among domestic slaves as well. Household service performed by slaves continued throughout the medieval period to its end. Much of the employment of domestic slaves must be described as unproductive labor, because slaves were usually assigned to noneconomic tasks; their employment was often totally independent of the normal mode of other laborers in the society. As servants, guards, and sexual partners, their primary function in many cases was to demonstrate the wealth and luxury enjoyed by their owners, yet here too there were exceptions and variations. In the preindustrial world, most manufacturing was artisan production in workshops within the homes of the artisans. In these workshops a few domestic slaves might aid their artisan owners, and collectively their activity made a significant impact on production. There are other variations, such as slaves acting as business agents, state-owned slaves, and military slaves. These varieties were present in the Roman period and appeared at certain times and places in the Islamic world, but less frequently in Europe.

A two-part definition of the most common types of slavery includes small-scale (or domestic) slavery and large-scale (or gang) slavery. Small-scale slavery, in which a few slaves were added to the urban or rural households as domestics and additional workers, was characteristic of both medieval Europe and the Islamic world. Gang slavery, which we associate with the late Roman Republic and early Empire and with plantation slavery in Latin America and the United States, was not present at all in medieval Europe. It was exceptional in the Islamic world, occurring in particular places at particular times (such as in lower Mesopotamia in the early years of Islamic expansion). Both for the medieval West and for the world of Islam, small-scale slavery was the norm.

Islamic slavery drew on pre-Islamic traditions in Arabian society, and also on traditional practices in the areas the Muslims conquered, including some of the Mediterranean lands of the former Roman Empire. Among the Muslims slavery was based on prohibitions on enslaving those considered to be part of the group and, consequently, a need to enslave outsiders. Religion was the great division: free Muslims were not to be enslaved, but conversion to Islam did not necessarily bring freedom to a slave. Muslims therefore sought non-Muslims as their slaves. For most of the Middle Ages acquisition of non-Muslims was relatively easy. In the early years of expansion prisoners of war were abundant and easily enslaved. Thereafter, the trading links of the highly commercialized Islamic world brought in eastern European and sub-Saharan African slaves. The presence of the prosperous Islamic world with its elaborate slave system helped to account for the continuation of slavery within Christian Europe and for the slave trade from parts of Europe to the Islamic world.

In western Europe a progressive ruralization of society and the economy followed the end of the Roman Empire. Cities declined, and the population increasingly moved to rural estates, manors, and agricultural villages. In these circumstances western European slavery lost much of its former importance.

Agricultural slavery persisted only where the government was strong enough to prevent runaways and keep the workers on the land. It was feasible in an economic sense only when a flourishing market system allowed specialized commodities to be sold in the towns for money. In early medieval Europe both conditions were uncommon: governments were weak, and the market economy was restricted. With the cities in decline, there were no great urban markets. From the lord's point of view, it was better to make the manor as self-sufficient as possible. With government and economy weak, the local lords no doubt thought it was better to dispense with the use of slaves and to secure a more dependable, contented, and cheaper labor force by granting improved conditions to the workers, giving them security of tenure and individual houses and plots.

Labor-saving devices invented or adopted in the early Middle Ages, and in general use by the mid-eleventh century, also helped reduce the demand for slave labor. These included better plows to cope with the dense soils of continental Europe, harnesses that permitted horses and oxen to pull heavier loads and to be harnessed in tandem, horseshoes for better traction, and water mills. They reduced requirements for human labor, as did the improved draft animals, products of centuries of selective breeding. As a consequence of these changes, free and semidependent workers provided the labor needed, and slavery ceased to be the normal pattern for rural labor in western Europe.

There remained other slaves who were not involved in farming. Domestic slavery continued. The cities and towns, as well as the larger manors, provided places for skilled slaves. Artisan wares—including glassware, pottery, and metalwork—were produced in the towns in small shops owned by free people and worked at times by slaves. On the estates, too, slave artisans, especially textile workers, labored under the direction of the managerial group of the lords' slaves. Specialized occupations on the manor—managers, record-keepers, smiths, messengers, soldiers, beekeepers, or experts in cattle raising—were filled by the lord's dependents. They had the same servile legal status as the agricultural laborers, but through their skills they attained a better and more highly regarded status than the others. For the skilled occupations, the children of the servile families on the manors formed a pool of potential trainees the lord could tap as needed.

The assimilation of the formerly free and former slaves into a more or less uniform class of serfs was substantially complete by the twelfth century. Language altered as the new social realities were recognized. The word *serf* comes from the Latin *servus* or "slave," but the medieval serf was far different in status from the *servus* of the Romans. Administrators, whose written language was Latin and whose training was in Roman law, simply applied the word the Romans had used to describe their lowest class to indicate the lowest class of medieval society. The word *servus*, and its feminine equivalent *ancilla*, were transformed so completely from their original meanings that they could no longer be used to describe true chattel servitude and ceased to be used in France around the early twelfth century. To describe true slaves, a new word was coined, derived from the most numerous ethnic group in the medieval slave trade, the Slavs. The word has cognates in all western European languages: *slave* in English, *esclave* in French, *esclavo* in Spanish, *escravo* in Portuguese, *schiavo* in Italian, and *Sklave* in German. At the same time, the word *serf* came to be used exclusively to describe dependent peasants.

In the late Middle Ages, from the twelfth century through the fifteenth, Europe's economy continued to develop and strengthen. Slavery was still present, although throughout most of Europe agriculture was the labor of serfs or free peasants. Domestic and artisan slavery continued, particularly in Italy and the Iberian Peninsula, the European areas having greatest contact with the Islamic world.

Several late medieval developments stimulated European slavery and helped to form the background for American slavery. First were the Crusades. In the eleventh century, western European knights conquered and established a series of states in Syria and Palestine that lasted until the late thirteenth century. The presence of the Crusader states allowed greatly expanded commercial activity by Italian merchants, always the most active in the slave trade. More importantly, Europeans gained from the Crusades a taste for cane sugar and learned from the Muslims of Syria and Palestine the techniques for the cultivation and refining it. With the end of the Crusades Europeans introduced sugar-cane planting and refining to several parts of southern Europe and then to the Atlantic islands.

In the late Middle Ages Europeans recovered and assimilated Roman law and its elaborate regulations for slaves into their legal systems. In the eleventh century the Italian legal scholar Irnerius began the academic study of the Roman code, and in the next two centuries knowledge and application of Roman law spread widely in western Europe. In Iberia, the Castilian king Alfonso X in the mid-thirteenth century produced a new law code for his kingdom, known as the Siete Partidas, with heavy influences from Roman law. Although it never fully became law in Castile, the Siete Partidas still had a significant influence on late medieval and early modern legislation in Spain, both for the home countries and later for the American colonies, and thereby ensured that many Roman rules for slavery entered Spanish law.

Another late medieval influence that heightened the use of slaves was the Black Death of the mid-fourteenth century. The plague originated in central Asia and was brought to the Crimea across caravan routes in 1346. Two years later it entered Italy and spread to the rest of western Europe, killing one-quarter to one-third of the European population. Among the consequences was an increase in slavery. Because of the high death rate, the workers who survived could easily find good jobs in the countryside or in the cities and could not be induced to become household servants. Death had not spared the elite, but the rich who remained had a larger supply of money available as fortunes were consolidated through inheritance. Those with money needed servants, and in the absence of free workers willing to accept domestic service, they turned to slaves.

Slavery thus persisted throughout the Middle Ages in Europe, preserved from Roman times and reinforced continually by contacts with the Islamic world. Nonetheless, slavery in the medieval period was less important in terms of numbers and economic significance than it had been in the ancient world or than it would be in colonial America.

[*See also* Historiography, *article on* Medieval European and Mediterranean Slavery; Mediterranean; *and* Serfdom.]

BIBLIOGRAPHY

Bloch, Marc. *Slavery and Serfdom in the Middle Ages: Selected Papers*. Berkeley and Los Angeles: University of California Press, 1975.

Bonnassie, Pierre. *From Slavery to Feudalism in Southwestern Europe*. Translated by Jean Birrell. Cambridge: Cambridge University Press, 1991.

Dockès, Pierre. *Medieval Slavery and Liberation*. Translated by Arthur Goldhammer. Chicago: University of Chicago Press, 1982.

Heers, Jacques. *Esclaves et domestiques au Moyen Age dans le monde méditerranéen*. Paris: Fayard, 1982.

Phillips, William D. Jr. *Slavery from Roman Times to the Early Transatlantic Trade*. Minneapolis: University of Minnesota Press, 1985.

Verlinden, Charles. *L'esclavage dans l'Europe médiévale*. 2 vols. Bruges: De Tempel, 1955, 1977.

—WILLIAM D. PHILLIPS, JR.

FAMILY. For the first six decades of the twentieth century, the historical presentation of the slave family in the United States was dominated by three distinct views of the slave experience, which one might usefully term *conservative, radical,* and *liberal*. The conservative view, exemplified by U. B. Phillips, had a distinct "Southern apologist" tinge. Phillips, a Georgian and son of former slaveholders, presented the slaves in general, and the slave family in particular, as having benefited from the civilizing forces of enslavement. In the radical camp were African Americans W. E. B. Du Bois and E. Franklin Frazier, who, in contradistinction to Phillips, attempted to demonstrate that a dual slave-family structure had existed under slavery: one structure was formed by slaves who worked in the house, and the other by those who worked in the fields. While close proximity to their white masters facilitated the development of family values among house slaves, among the field hands "there was no family life, . . . no marriages, no decency." Dysfunctional characteristics in the African-American family, the radicals argued, were linked not to the slaves' African heritage, as Phillips claimed; rather, they were the product of the slavery experience and of subsequent social and economic developments.

Combining elements of the two camps, Kenneth Stampp's *The Peculiar Institution* (1956) provided a "liberal" approach to the study of slavery that would be ascendant for much of the next two or three decades. In a direct attack on the conservative camp Stampp furthered the environmentalist approach, emphasizing the inherent brutality of slavery and its devastating effects on the slaves. He consulted documents that had been ignored or underused by Phillips and depicted a plantation system in which the slaveholders were not "cavaliers," and the slaves not the loyal and devoted retainers that Phillips had presented. Like the radicals, Stampp distinguished between the slaves' experience and that of their African past: stripped of their African heritage, the slaves had been victimized by owners who had deliberately destroyed the strictly regulated family life and rigid moral code that had prevailed in Africa, and then the owners "more or less encouraged" slaves to live as families and to accept white standards of morality. His summation of the slave family, however, differed little from those of the conservatives or the radicals: the family that emerged was matriarchal and "had about it an air of impermanence."

Under the influence of the radicals, Frazier in particular, there developed a general consensus as to the experience of the black family in slavery. The publication of the Moynihan report (1965) shattered this consensus and signaled what one critic called "the death of white sociology" and the birth of a new radicalism. In countering earlier claims that the slaves had been culturally deprived, scholars in the 1970s looked to identify the African Americans' abilities to retain elements of their

African heritage and to adjust culturally to life in America.

John Blassingame presented a slave family that was continually under attack but demonstrated its resilience: although the family was frequently broken, it was indispensable to the slave, because the family was primarily responsible for survival on the plantation "without becoming totally dependent on and submissive to his master." Eugene Genovese's work revealed the interdependent nature of a paternalistic relationship between masters and slaves out of which "slaves created impressive norms of family life" and entered the postwar world with "a remarkable stable base." It was Herbert Gutman, however, who drew attention to the two-parent slave family, its stability and its smooth transition from slavery to freedom. He argued that the black family, influenced by its African heritage and its experience under slavery, emerged from slavery with an adaptive yet stable family structure.

Among their many achievements, scholars writing in the 1970s shifted the focus away from the slaveholders as the primary cultural force in the lives of the slaves and to the slaves and cultural developments in the slave community. They showed that the system was not so closed, slave-owners not so powerful, and slaves not so powerless that no choices were available to them.

Encouraged by the work of economic historians such as Fogel and Engerman, more and more researchers seemed to be describing the system of slavery and the behavior of slaveholders and slaves as demonstrating a certain rationality (however morally uncomfortable this was for some). In addition, they drew on previously ignored or underused sources, such as the interviews of former slaves collected in the 1920s and 1930s, edited and published early in the 1970s by George Rawick. These sources, and a close scrutiny of plantation journals and runaway slave autobiographies, gave voice to the previously silent slave.

By the early 1980s there was another significant departure. The broad overview that typically ac-

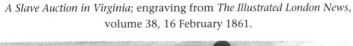

A Slave Auction in Virginia; engraving from *The Illustrated London News*, volume 38, 16 February 1861.

companied the earlier studies of slavery and the family gave way to more local studies that, as Charles Joyner wrote, looked at "large issues in small places." As a result, the 1970s' focus of attention on the slave family in slavery and freedom narrowed in the 1980s as the spotlight settled on questions of family and gender, and in particular on the slave woman, first as mother and increasingly as wife and mother. The work of Deborah Gray White, Suzanne Lebsock, Jacqueline Jones, and Elizabeth Fox-Genovese examined the unique experience of black women in the slave South and considered the choices available to them under the burdens of gender and slavery within a white patriarchal structure.

While the 1980s might be called the "gender years," the 1990s appears to be the "work years." Research in this decade focused on the independent production of slaves—the work slaves did for their own benefit after having completed their owners' work assignments. This departure (although not new or peculiar to the American South) expanded on the theme of "choice" and stimulated a closer look at an area of the slave life in the American South that had been previously underappreciated. The work slaves performed in their spare time, earning cash money from owners or neighbors, or more typically in their garden patches where they produced crops and raised livestock for sale or exchange to their owners (or others), increased the amount of money, goods, and

Engraving depicting slaves with young children at work in the fields; from the *American Anti-Slavery Almanac for 1840*.

services at their disposal. This expansion of goods and services created what Berlin and Morgan term the slaves' internal economy, wherein the slaves established and maintained a regular commercial traffic between themselves and others. Furthermore, the ensuing economic "busyness" of the slaves "offered a foundation for their domestic and community life, shaping the social structure of slave society and providing a material basis for the slaves' distinctive culture." An alternative view on the slaves' cultural autonomy is that of Norrece Jones, who interprets the slaveholders' use of task and garden systems as a deliberate attempt to "hamper the annoyingly cooperative spirit among the enslaved."

Some scholars, morally troubled by arguments that economic benefits could accrue to planters who succeeded in encouraging stable and productive slave families, maintain that slaveholders frequently intruded into the more intimate lives of their slaves. Indeed, a good deal of the literature of the "gender years" dealt with the sexual coercion and rape of black females by white males, which, according to Brenda Stevenson, did not decline over time.

If the masters' only interest in the slave family was the expansion of their slave labor force, the matriarchal structure would have served them well. Desiring more from their slaves than sexual impulse or the whip could muster, however, masters were obliged to interfere more constructively in the intimate affairs of the slaves. This is not to say that they practiced slave-breeding, although former slaves recalled examples of such intrusive behavior. Stevenson supports her claim that the practice existed with the example of a married slave man in Loudoun County, Virginia, whose owner continued to bring "some women to see" him. For John Boles, it was the "shifting labor needs and the desires of slave marriage partners, not calculating slave breeders," that determined slave population increase.

Most planters shunned direct interference in the sexual practices of slaves and tried to influence fertility patterns through a system of incentives. The slaves, with their own ideas and some ability to have them implemented, frequently thwarted these attempts at manipulation. The efforts of James Henry Hammond, who offered a declining bounty to his slaves for first and subsequent marriages, were designed to control the form and function of the slave family. Overwhelmingly, slave-owners reasoned and acted as did the North Carolinians studied by Edward Phifer, who claimed, "Fully realizing that active breeding was an indispensable requisite to successful slave ownership, the investor made certain, insofar as he was financially able, that the female of child-bearing age was an integral part of his slave family and that the male in turn was a part of her environment." With suitable demographics, "no additional planning or plotting was necessary, the natural processes of production went on without urging or prompting" on the part of the slaveowner (1962, p. 146).

The slave family was a major point of intersection in the aspirations of both masters and slaves. Slaveholders may have tended to view the slave family as little more than a means of disciplining and expanding their labor force. The slaves, however, cherished the opportunity to organize their lives around the family group, and they made it the primary institution in the slave quarters. The evolving antebellum slave family was no mere reproductive machine. As Charles Joyner points out, "The strength of the slave family rested upon firmer foundation than the masters' promotion . . . it served the slaves as a mode of structuring sexual and kinship relations and the rearing of children, and as a focus for psychological loyalty and devotion" (1984, p. 137). Slaves consistently took the risk of establishing families and maintaining them; and, as Ann Patton Malone demonstrates, whenever it became necessary, they revealed "a persistent urge within a fragmented slave community to reunite or rebuild despite the pain associated with such efforts and adjustments" (1992, pp. 2–3).

Work and garden systems provided the slaves with a means of accumulating amounts of property sufficient to introduce into the slave quarters significant social differences among the slaves. The study of individual and family work efforts has provided a means of answering a number of questions that in one way or another touch on gender and class. The economic prowess and social status of individual slaves and slave families would have affected the chances of slaves' marrying someone of their choice on the home place. The amount of choice slaves had as to where, when, and whom they married depended to some extent on their economic power: the more the slave enjoyed, the more choices he or she had as to who or when to marry.

Although the arbitrary breakup of slave families by masters continued, evidence suggests that the practice was on the decline as slave-owners, encouraged by the church, and in part as a response to the growing abolitionist attack and the movement to reform the institution of slavery, were making greater efforts to keep families together. Fogel and Engerman estimate that about 13 percent of interregional sales resulted in marriage separations, and Michael Tadman suggests that as many as 20 percent of slaves in the lower South experienced forced family separation. Using data for slave unions collected from Mississippi, Tennessee, and Louisiana, Blassingame estimates that about 32 percent were dissolved by masters, the majority being separated before they reached their sixth anniversary.

Interestingly, despite the fact that neither institution depended for its existence on legal protection, some scholars continue to structure their examination of slavery on the premise that there existed no legal sanctions for slave marriage and family. It was the rules and regulations operating within the slaveholders' immediate domain rather than legal statutes that most affected the familial experience of slaves.

In sum, the recent emphasis on gender and work has placed the slave family at center stage and under a microscope more powerful than ever before. The slave family's existence is no longer a point of contention among scholars, and its more intimate workings are now of primary interest.

[*See also* Gender and Slavery; *and* Slave Culture.]

BIBLIOGRAPHY

Berlin, Ira, and Philip D. Morgan, eds. *The Slaves' Economy: Independent Production by Slaves in the Americas*. London: Frank Cass, 1991.

Blassingame, John W. *The Slave Community: Plantation Life in the Antebellum South*. New York and Oxford: Oxford University Press, 1972.

Fogel, Robert, and Stanley Engerman. *Time on the Cross: The Economics of American Negro Slavery*. 2 vols. Boston: Little, Brown, 1974.

Genovese, Eugene D. *Roll, Jordan, Roll: The World the Slaves Made*. New York: Pantheon, 1974.

Gutman, Herbert G. *The Black Family in Slavery and Freedom, 1750–1925*. New York: Pantheon, 1976.

Hudson, Larry E., Jr. *To Have and to Hold: Slave Work and Family Life in Antebellum South Carolina*. Athens: University of Georgia Press, 1997.

Joyner, Charles. *Down by the Riverside: A South Carolina Slave Community*. Urbana: University of Illinois Press, 1984.

Malone, Ann Patton. *Sweet Chariot: Slave Family and Household Structure in Nineteenth-Century Louisiana*. Chapel Hill: University of North Carolina Press, 1992.

Phifer, Eward W. "Slavery in Microcosm: Burke County, North Carolina." *Journal of Southern History* 28 (1962): 137–165.

Stampp, Kenneth M. *The Peculiar Institution: Slavery in the Ante-bellum South*. New York: Knopf, 1956.

Stevenson, Brenda E. *Life in Black and White: Family and Community in the Slave South*. New York and Oxford: Oxford University Press, 1996.

White, Deborah Gray. *"Ar'n't I a Woman?": Female Slaves in the Plantation South*. New York: W. W. Norton, 1985.

—LARRY E. HUDSON, JR.

FORCED LABOR. [*This entry comprises two articles. The first is a historical and global overview of the various practices that constitute forced labor. The second is an in-depth discussion of the Soviet Union, a society where forced labor was of particular significance.*]

An Overview

To define *forced labor* is not straightforward. In one sense, all labor is forced as we are forced to work in order to survive. In another sense, many people are forced to enter the labor market and work for an employer; if they had sufficient capital, they would prefer to work for themselves as independent proprietors. More commonly, however, we distinguish between forced labor and free labor. Various criteria are used in making this distinction: one is whether labor is offered voluntarily or is obtained without the worker's consent; another is whether the worker is free to leave the employer without threat of physical punishment or criminal sanctions (such as imprisonment).

Slave and convict labor are unambiguously forced-labor systems: their labor is involuntarily obtained, and they are compelled to work under threat of harsh punishment. There are, however, other types of labor that are hybrid arrangements containing elements of free and forced labor—free in the sense of workers voluntarily entering contracts of employment, but forced in the sense that these contracts were subject to penal sanctions. In the seventeenth century, white workers in the British North American colonies were engaged under Masters and Servants acts that included penal sanctions for noncompliance, but in the eighteenth century these penal sanctions were no longer being used. In Great Britain, however, the penal sanction for breach of contract was repealed only in 1875, following trade union pressure. Tracing the genesis of free labor in Great Britain and its North American colonies that later combined to form the United States suggests, therefore, that free labor should be considered the exception rather than the rule in history.

The institution of indentured labor should also come under the rubric of forced labor. Like other workers employed in seventeenth-century British North America under Masters and Servants acts, indentured labor generally involved voluntary contracting, but the contract could be enforced by use of penal sanctions. Many, if not most, British emigrants to the North American colonies financed their passage across the Atlantic by signing indenture contracts. In return for the cost of the passage, they contracted to work for a specific number of years in a specified colony. Remuneration seldom included a cash wage; it usually consisted of food, accommodation, clothing, and medical care during the indenture. In addition, "freedom dues" (in seed, farm implements, or other commodities) were given at the end of the indenture to help the emigrant get settled as an independent farmer. Prospective emigrants negotiated their indenture contracts with a ship's captain or a merchant before departure, and on arrival in the colonies the contracts were auctioned off to employers. German emigrants to North America usually financed their passage under a slightly different arrangement called the redemptioner system. Under this arrangement German emigrants, on arrival in the colonies, were given a few days or weeks to find relatives or friends who would be prepared to pay for their passage; if unsuccessful, they were required to be indentured through the auction process.

The system of indentured labor persisted after the American war of independence on a much-reduced scale, and by the 1820s it appears to have died out in the United States. After the abolition of slavery in British colonies in 1834, however, the system of indentured labor was revived by the British government in order to effect the migration of Asian, African, and Pacific Islander laborers to work on the plantations and in the mines of diverse regions of the world. Between 1834 and 1917 about 1.25 million Indians, primarily from Uttar Pradesh and Bihar in North India and the Madras Presidency in the south, were recruited as indentured laborers for work on the sugar-cane plantations of Fiji, Malaysia, Mauritius, Réunion, Natal (South Africa), Guyana, Suriname, Trinidad, Jamaica, and smaller islands in the Caribbean. Nearly two million Indians, primarily from Uttar Pradesh, Bihar, and Bengal, were recruited as indentured laborers to work on the tea plantations of Assam in North India. Many South Indians also worked on the coffee and tea estates of Sri Lanka, the coffee and rubber estates of Malaya, and in construction and rice mills in Burma, but under more informal arrangements.

Between 1853 and 1884 about eighteen thousand Chinese indentured laborers, mainly from the southern maritime provinces of China, were recruited to work on the sugar-cane plantations of the British Caribbean colonies; during the late nineteenth and early twentieth centuries many more were recruited for the sugar-cane plantations of Cuba, Peru, and Hawaii, the guano mines of Peru, the gold mines of the Transvaal (South Africa), and in the Pacific, where they labored in the phosphate mines of Nauru and the copra plantations of Samoa. Between 1862 and the late 1940s Pacific Islanders were also procured as indentured laborers. Recruits from Vanuatu, the Solomon Islands, and Kiribati worked on the sugar-cane plantations of Queensland (Australia), Fiji, and Hawaii, the copra plantations of Fiji, Samoa, and Tahiti, the nickel mines of New Caledonia, and the phosphate mines of Nauru and Ocean Island. The indentured-labor system similarly facilitated the internal migration of labor within Papua New Guinea for employment on copra plantations and in gold mines, and within Vanuatu and the Solomon Islands for employment on copra plantations. It was used to effect the labor migrations of Javanese to Sumatra, Malaya, New Caledonia, and Suriname, and Japanese to Queensland (Australia) and Hawaii. The internal migration of labor for the gold, diamond, copper, and coal mines of southern Africa was also effected by the indentured labor system.

There were important differences in the organization of these diverse streams of indentured laborers, with considerable variation in the length of the indenture, whether a return passage to their home community was provided, and the degree of supervision by imperial and colonial governments. There was also considerable variation in the age and sex composition of the migrant populations. Indian emigrants, for example, included adult women workers and accompanying children; the streams of Chinese, African, and Pacific Islanders were mostly young adult males. These streams of

Asian, Pacific Islander, and African indentured workers are generally considered forced labor because some (perhaps many) of them were coerced by recruiters or community leaders to sign these contracts, and the contracts were enforced by penal sanctions, notably fines or imprisonment. In addition, although physical punishment was usually not legally permitted, it was difficult to guard against.

As with indentured labor, there has been considerable variation in the organization of convict labor. Before the American war of independence, Britain shipped many of its convicts to its North American colonies. Penal colonies were not established; rather, the convicts were auctioned off as indentured servants and became almost indistinguishable from other indentured servants. When

the newly independent United States refused to accept British convicts, Britain turned to establishing a penal colony in Australia. Between 1788 and 1868 about one hundred sixty-three thousand convicts were shipped to the Australian colonies of New South Wales, Port Phillip (Victoria), Moreton Bay (Queensland), Van Diemen's Land (Tasmania), and Western Australia. Most of the convicts were assigned to private employers, working as shepherds under little direct control; convicts working in chain gangs on public works suffered harsher conditions. Particularly harsh conditions were the lot of convicts who committed further offenses in Australia; they were sent to penal settlements for repeat offenders at Port Macquarie, Port Arthur, Moreton Bay, and Norfolk Island.

After the Civil War various state governments

View from the Summit of Mount York, Looking towards Bathurst Plains, Convicts Breaking Stones, New South Wales; watercolor, Augustus Earle, nineteenth century.

in the U.S. South leased many of their convicts to private employers for a fee. They were usually employed under harsh conditions, and after the many abuses of this "chain gang" leasing system were made public, it was gradually discontinued. More recently, the brutal conditions of prison labor in the Soviet gulags have been well documented.

Another form of forced labor is debt peonage. In many societies poor people, in return for the advancement of a sum of money, undertake to work for creditors until their debt is paid. Even though indebtedness is usually voluntary, people sometimes (perhaps often) find it impossible ever to repay the debt because of coercive practices adopted by the creditor, such as dishonest bookkeeping, overcharging at the creditor's store, and arbitrary imposition of fines for supposedly unsatisfactory work. In these ways an initially voluntary agreement turns into involuntary servitude in which debtors are forced to work to repay ever-augmented debts. Although workers are bound to specific creditors, their debts can be transferred from one creditor to another and even inherited by relatives of a deceased worker. The incidence of debt peonage has been well documented in some societies, such as in nineteenth-century southern Mexico, but scholars differ on its incidence in other societies.

There are many other types of forced labor: serfdom in Europe, child labor disciplined by corporal punishment, apprenticeship arrangements, and the mobilization of labor by the state to build public works (corvée labor) and for military purposes (conscription). Another variant of state mobilization of labor was the "cultivation system" adopted by the Dutch colonial administration in Java in the nineteenth century. Between 1830 and 1870 the Dutch imposed a system of forced cropping on the rural population of Java whereby Javanese villages were compelled to produce cash crops such as sugar-cane and coffee for export.

Recent literature on forced labor has focused on three topics: the variation in punishments and rewards used in different forced labor systems; alternative ways of conceptualizing the extent to which forced laborers were exploited; and the role of epidemiological factors in explaining the mortality suffered by forced laborers. In discussing this literature, examples will be restricted to slave, convict, and indentured labor.

Punishments and Rewards. The lash was the symbol of dominance in slave and convict societies, and the threat of corporal punishment was the main method used to elicit labor. A variety of other punishments supplemented the threat of force, including incarceration (especially solitary confinement), the withdrawal of privileges, and being given unpleasant tasks. Some slaves were also threatened with sale, and convicts who had been assigned to private employers in Australia were threatened with being sent back to government employment, working in chain gangs on public works or in a harsh penal settlement for repeat offenders.

Although the mix of punishments and rewards was heavily biased toward the use of punishments, rewards were also important in the operation of slave and convict-labor systems. These included the granting of privileges (such as the opportunity to earn wages and extra rations, or to obtain passes to go off the estate), the opportunity to acquire preferred jobs, and promises of obtaining freedom. Although few slaves could expect to be manumitted in the United States, an important incentive for convicts in Australia was the early receipt of a "ticket-of-leave" with which convicts could work for themselves in the free labor market.

Employers of indentured laborers were faced with the twin problems of retaining their workers until the end of the contract, and eliciting satisfactory labor during the contract. The first problem—which was of particular importance in remitting labor-recruiting costs—was largely solved by deferring part of the wages (or freedom dues for indentured servants in colonial North America) until the end of the contract, and by making desertion a criminal offense. In addition, free repatriation was made conditional on the completion of the contract.

The problem of eliciting a satisfactory supply of labor during the contract proved to be much more difficult. The mix of positive and negative incentives used to motivate free workers, such as prospects of higher wages, promotion, and preferred jobs, or the threat of dismissal, was of limited efficacy when workers were hired on long-term contracts at predetermined wages, and when substantial recruiting costs had been incurred in procuring these workers. Employers of indentured labor in colonial North America were legally able to use corporal punishment and sale as negative incentives, options not generally available to employers of other indentured laborers. The dominant mode of punishment used by employers of indentured workers was to bring their complaints before magistrates, who regularly visited the plantations, for breach of the so-called "labor laws." Infractions of these laws, such as neglect of work, disobedience, and offensive behavior, were given penal sanction, and convicted workers could incur prison sentences, fines, or having their contracts extended. These penal sanctions placed employers in a position to exercise substantial control over their workforce.

Exploitation. The primary rationale for the existence of slavery was to exploit the slaves in the sense of paying them (in food, accommodation, clothing, and medical care) less than what they contributed to production, and to make them work under harsher conditions than free workers would usually find acceptable. Convict workers were similarly exploited, but there were also other objectives in the use of convict labor: deterrence and reformation. Harsh working conditions in North America and Australia were intended to deter crime in Great Britain, while access to land and greater social mobility in these colonies was to provide opportunities for reformation.

Indentured laborers were also paid less than they contributed to production, but in well-working competitive labor markets this gap between production and consumption does not necessarily indicate that the indentured workers were exploited. Rather, the indentured worker was implicitly repaying the employer for his passage by accepting the lower level of consumption. Exploitation would occur if the laborer's level of consumption was so depressed that the gap between production and consumption was in excess of what was needed for the employer to recoup the capital incurred on passage fares.

In southern Africa and in the Pacific, recruitment of indentured labor followed a circular migratory pattern: recruits were usually young adult males who returned to their home communities after serving their terms of indenture. A number of scholars have argued that these workers were "doubly exploited" because they were paid only a "bachelor's wage" to cover their subsistence during the contract while their home communities supported the worker's wife, children, and the worker himself in his old age. As much of the care and reproduction of the labor force was borne by their home communities, those communities, according to this view, subsidized the capitalist economy, and so imperial and colonial governments attempted to preserve these as recruiting areas. Underlying this argument are three key assumptions: male migrant workers are only paid a bachelor's wage covering their subsistence, so there was no return flow of goods to the worker's home community; employers preferred this circular migrant labor system to a settled labor force at their place of employment because it was the cheaper option; and the choice of labor system was determined solely by employers.

Many scholars, however, have questioned whether this argument fits the facts of African and Pacific history. They have shown that wages usually exceeded subsistence levels and so migrant workers were able to take goods back to their home communities. This return flow of goods places in doubt the conclusion that the home communities subsidized the capitalist sector. They have also shown that although wages appeared to be low, the migrant labor system was not necessarily a provider of cheap labor. As compared to a settled labor force, the migrant labor system was expensive owing to heavy recruiting and repatriation costs, the lack of skill of each new batch of recruits, and heavy losses through mortality. Finally, they suggest that for a full explanation of the emergence and persistence of this migrant-labor system as compared to a more settled labor force at the place of employment, consideration must be given not only to the employer's demand for cheap and tractable labor, but also to the side of supply. The fact that Africans and Pacific Islanders usually had access to land adequate for subsistence meant that the decision to migrate was influenced by the workers themselves. Moreover, their preference was usually not to migrate permanently to their place of employment. In South Africa and Queensland (Australia), opposition to the permanent settlement of workers at their place of employment also came from the political authorities, mindful of the threat posed by a large black proletariat.

Mortality. The term *relocation cost* has been used to refer to the increased mortality associated with the movement of migrants from the disease environment of their childhood to a new disease environment. Exposure to infectious diseases, usually in a mild form in childhood, gives the survivors either lifelong immunity (in the case of diseases such as smallpox and measles) or partial immunity (in the case of diseases such as malaria and cholera). Migration exposed people to new diseases to which they had no immunity, placing them at risk.

The process of migration also brought together people with differing immunities and susceptibilities, and the congregation of migrants in departure depots and on board vessels, often under unsanitary conditions, facilitated the spread of infectious diseases. Furthermore, the congregation of forced laborers on plantations and in mines under unsanitary conditions, and harsh working and living conditions, placed them under additional risk.

The relocation cost of migrant labor can be con-sidered in two steps—while on the voyage, and soon after arrival at their destination. Seaborne populations usually had higher death rates than their equivalent land-based population. The highest death rates occurred on trans-Atlantic slave vessels; the lowest death rates were on convict voyages to Australia. The crude death rate per month was 61.3 per thousand on slave voyages to the Americas between 1817 and 1843, compared to 2.4 per thousand on convict voyages to Australia between 1815 and 1868. The relatively low death rates on the latter were due to the implementation of a series of administrative reforms that included the better screening of passengers on embarkation to prevent the sailing of sick passengers, the establishment of an adequate system of sanitation on board the vessels, reduced crowding, and the provision of adequate and uncontaminated food and water.

Death rates of migrants after arrival at their destination differed markedly, owing to their differing immunities. African slaves had some degree of immunity to malaria and yellow fever but were susceptible to tuberculosis and pneumonia in the Americas; African indentured workers were also susceptible to these diseases when they encountered them in the mining compounds of southern Africa. British convict workers encountered no new diseases in Australia, so they did not suffer high death rates following migration. Indian indentured workers suffered high death rates in some regions but not in others. For Indian indentured workers the highest death rates, usually in excess of 50 per thousand per year, occurred in Assam and Malaya, which had most hostile disease environments: cholera and malaria were endemic in Assam and malaria was endemic in Malaya. Death rates were lowest in Natal and Fiji, which were free of cholera and malaria. Death rates in the Caribbean with its endemic malaria and epidemic yellow fever were higher than in Natal and Fiji but lower than in Assam and Malaya. It appears that Indians were seldom exposed to yellow fever, and when exposed they did not suffer high fatality rates. It also appears that malaria in the Caribbean was less intense and virulent than malaria in Malaya and Assam.

Before contact with Europeans, Pacific Islanders were "virgin soil populations," free of most of the infectious diseases of Europe and Asia such as smallpox, influenza, measles, tuberculosis, and pneumonia. It is thus not surprising that they suffered very high death rates as indentured laborers: migration exposed them to many new diseases. The crude death rates of Pacific Islander workers in Queensland and Fiji were in excess of 80 per thousand between 1879 and 1887. Support for the proposition that their high death rates can largely be explained by exposure to new diseases is given by a variety of types of evidence. When Asian and Pacific Islander workers were employed on the same plantations under similar environmental and working conditions, Pacific Islanders suffered much higher death rates than the Asians. Moreover, death rates were highest in the first year after arrival at their place of work; survivors acquired some degree of immunity to the new disease environment, so death rates in subsequent years steadily declined. Finally, whereas tuberculosis was generally a chronic disease among Europeans and Asians, among Pacific Islanders it usually appeared as an acute, rapidly progressive disease with a high case fatality rate, indicating that the latter had little prior exposure to it.

[See also Asia, article on South Asia and Southeast Asia; Indentured Servitude; Mortality; and Oceania.]

BIBLIOGRAPHY

Ekirch, A. Roger. Bound for America: The Transportation of British Convicts to the Colonies, 1718–1775. New York and Oxford: Oxford University Press, 1987.

Moore, Clive, Jacqueline Leckie, and Doug Munro, eds. Labour in the South Pacific. Townsville: James Cook University of Northern Queensland, 1990.

Northrup, David. Indentured Labor in the Age of Imperialism, 1834–1922. Cambridge: Cambridge University Press, 1995.

Shaw, A. G. L. Convicts and the Colonies: A Study of Penal Transportation from Great Britain and Ireland to Australia and other Parts of the British Empire. London: Faber, 1966.

Steinfeld, Robert J. The Invention of Free Labor: The Employ-

ment Relation in English and American Law and Culture, 1350–1870. Chapel Hill: University of North Carolina Press, 1991.

Tomlins, Christopher L. Law, Labor and Ideology in the Early American Republic. Cambridge: Cambridge University Press, 1993.

—RALPH SHLOMOWITZ

Soviet Union

From its inception Soviet penal policy included the notion of forced labor. From the time of the Civil War (1918–1921) on, two prison systems coexisted in Soviet Russia, and forced labor was a feature of both. Prisons under the jurisdiction of the Main Administration of Places of Detention, a division of the People's Commissariat of Internal Affairs, held common criminals and members of the working classes who had committed their crimes from need or ignorance. Like their American and European counterparts, Soviet penologists emphasized the need to reform rather than punish criminals. Forced labor was supposed to train the inmate for some useful occupation and prevent him from returning to a life of crime. In the 1920s, however, the Soviet economy was still recovering from the devastation of World War I and the Civil War. Prisons were forced to become economically self-supporting. As a result, the corrective nature of forced labor was lost.

The second prison system was under the jurisdiction of the secret police, the OGPU, also a division of the Commissariat of Internal Affairs. During the Civil War the secret police (then called the Cheka) had created labor camps for the regime's political enemies. After the war the population of these camps expanded to include not just Tsarist sympathizers, but also members of other socialist parties and of religious sects. Incorrigible criminals and dangerous recidivists were also kept there. The OGPU labor camps, known as the Northern Camps of Special Designation or SLON, were located in the northernmost part of western Russia, in the region around the White Sea; the most infamous were on the Solovetskii Islands. Forced labor in

SLON camps was meant to be punitive. It acquired economic significance in the mid-1920s, when inmates had to provide for the camps' needs.

An important turning point in the development of Soviet forced labor occurred in 1927 and 1928 with the First Five-Year Plan and the transition to a planned economy. The Soviet government under Joseph Stalin required all sectors of the economy to fulfill economic plans for the rapid industrialization of the USSR. Prisons were also given norms to fulfill. The government expected to help finance industrialization through the export of timber, an abundant natural resource. Given that the forests were located in the far eastern and northern regions of the USSR, free workers were unwilling to relocate there to do hard work in harsh conditions for low pay. A government decree of 7 April 1930 provided the solution to this problem. Lawbreakers sentenced to at least three years' detention, as well as OGPU prisoners, would be sent to the OGPU labor camps in the east and north. To oversee this new camp system, the OGPU created the State Administration of Camps, Gosudarstvennoe Upravlenie Lageriami, or Gulag.

Hand-in-hand with industrialization, the government began to collectivize agriculture, creating collective farms at the expense of peasant and village holdings. As part of this campaign, the prosperous peasants, the kulaks, were to be stripped of their possessions and sent to labor camps. Those who resisted collectivization were also classified as kulaks, and along with their families were subject to deportation to the camps. In addition to kulaks, the camps filled with "wreckers." When the unrealistic production goals of the economic plans were not met, Stalin claimed that "wreckers and saboteurs" were undermining the industrialization campaign in an attempt to restore bourgeois power. "Wreckers" often were technical specialists, particularly engineers, who had received their educations before the 1917 Revolution or outside the USSR.

Prisoners were put to work in the timber industry, farming, factories, and mining (particularly for coal and gold). They were also used on construction projects, such as building highways, railroads, and canals. The construction of the Belomor Canal in 1931, linking the Baltic and White seas, was the most famous of these projects.

At the end of the 1930s Stalin directed a new wave of repression against members of the military, the Communist Party, and ultimately the secret police itself (now called the NKVD). Victims of the Great Terror (1937–1939) were accused of being spies, wreckers, and saboteurs who had collaborated with Leon Trotsky, whose opposition to Stalin in 1927 led to his exile from the USSR. Members of the military high command and some of the Communist Party elite were executed. Lowerranking party members, however, were sent to the labor camps for terms of ten years or more.

The Gulag population decreased with the onset of war in 1941 but began to grow again as the war drew to a close. Victims of this wave of repression included peoples from the occupied Baltic and eastern European states, foreign prisoners of war, Russian prisoners of war who had returned to the USSR, members of religious sects, and national minorities within the USSR (Kazakhs, Volga Germans, Chechen-Ingush, and Kalmyks). The writer Alexander Solzhenitsyn was arrested while fighting at the front for Russia because he had criticized the government in a letter to a colleague. Such arrests continued throughout the 1940s and early 1950s.

After Stalin's death in March 1953 the head of the secret police, Lavrentii Beria, released some high-ranking political prisoners as part of his quest to gain control of the state. To counter Beria, the Central Committee of the Communist Party issued the resolution "On the Violation of the Law by State Security Organs," by which Beria was arrested and convicted for his role in the Stalinist repressions. This resolution also led to the release of a number of camp prisoners and fueled expectations among Russians that more victims would be freed. The Russian dissidents Roy and Zhores Medvedev estimated that four thousand were released in 1953, and another twelve thousand in 1954 and

1955; they also claimed that seven or eight million were released by 1957.

The "thaw" that Nikita Khrushchev and the Communist Party had initiated led to thousands of rehabilitations. Persecutions and the use of forced labor, however, continued under Khrushchev and his successors. Victims included artists who did not present a favorable view of the USSR in their work and who published abroad, and scientists who criticized officially sanctioned scientific theories. Members of religious sects, conscientious objectors, applicants for emigration (especially Jews), and participants in human-rights groups were also arrested and sentenced to hard labor. As late as 1993 two conscientious objectors were sentenced to forced labor.

Available reports on forced labor in the Soviet Union from 1917 through 1980 indicate brutal, often fatal conditions. Most of the camps were in Siberia, where winter temperatures reach –20 degrees centigrade and lower. Even in the summer some ground remains frozen. Memoirs consistently report that prisoners were not issued appropriate clothing for working outdoors. The prisoners' meager diet consisted of bread and some type of soup or porridge, issued based on the type and amount of work they did. Not meeting one's work norm (which was frequently increased) would entail having one's food ration cut. Prisoners lived in wooden barracks or tents that were poorly heated. For breaches of discipline, such as refusal to work or failure to appear at roll call, the prisoner could be subjected to lock-up in an unheated isolation cell for a week, a punishment that often resulted in death.

Given these conditions and the arduous work they had to perform, many camp inmates died. The question of how many people fell victim to repression and how many died is a contentious issue among scholars. Most focus on the repression of the 1930s, particularly the years of the Great Terror. One school of thought (represented by Robert Conquest and the Medvedevs) estimates that by 1939, sixteen million or more had died in the purges and another nine million or more were in the camps. This school has relied on memoirs and, recently, some archival documentation. From those data they have attempted to estimate the number of camps and their capacity in order to determine the total number of victims. Recent research, however, has significantly revised these numbers. Scholars such as Alec Nove and S. G. Wheatcroft estimate that the camp population by 1939 was three million and the number of deaths from repression around ten million; their calculations are based on new information from the archives dealing with the 1937 and 1939 censuses.

No definitive proof exists about the exact number of prisoners or deaths in labor camps, but with the opening of the Soviet archives, the chances for reaching an accurate estimate have greatly improved. Moreover, the availability of previously closed documents allows scholars to examine the roots of forced labor in the 1920s as well as its development in the post-World War II era.

[*See also* Penal Slavery.]

BIBLIOGRAPHY

Dallin, David J. and Boris Nicolaevsky. *Forced Labor in Soviet Russia*. New Haven: Yale University Press, 1947.

Ginzburg, Eugenia. *Within the Whirlwind*. New York: Harcourt Brace Jovanovich, 1981.

Nove, Alec. "How Many Victims in the 1930s?" Parts I and II. *Soviet Studies* 42 (1990): 369–373, 811–814.

Solomon, Peter H., Jr. "Soviet Penal Policy, 1917–1934: A Reinterpretation." *Slavic Review* 39 (1980): 195–217.

Solzhenitsyn, Alexander. *One Day in the Life of Ivan Denisovich*. New York: E. P. Dutton, 1963.

Wheatcroft, S. G. "More Light on the Scale of Repression and Excess Mortality in the Soviet Union in the 1930s." *Soviet Studies* 42 (1990): 355–367.

—ELLEN M. WIMBERG

FREED PERSONS. The term *freed persons* in slave societies denoted men and women who were black or of mixed race (called "brown" in this article) and born free or manumitted. More specific gendered terms to describe this group include *freedmen* and *freedwomen;* in addition, *free colored* is used when discussing men and women of mixed race, and *free black* when referring specifically to blacks. Slaves gained their freedom by self-purchase or were manumitted by their owners. In addition, the state manumitted some slaves who uncovered potential rebellions or fought on its behalf.

In early American colonial slave societies, the number of freed persons was small because freed persons were an unintended byproduct of slave societies. Many of them were the offspring of liaisons between white males and black (and subsequently brown) females, and whites sometimes freed their brown children as well as the slave women who produced them. These sexual relationships reflected the skewed demography of most slave societies, in which a minority of whites controlled a large majority of black slaves. Because the white population often had a surplus of males, relationships developed between white and black, free and slave. The resulting freed population was therefore heavily female and of mixed race.

The proportions of free coloreds and free blacks within slave societies, as well as their growth rates, varied considerably from colony to colony. At one end of the spectrum, more than 50 percent of the total population in several Brazilian provinces just prior to emancipation consisted of freed persons. Elsewhere in the Americas there were also significant proportions of freed persons in the population. At the end of the eighteenth century in Martinique, for example, freed persons constituted about one-third of the free population; in Saint Domingue just before the outbreak of the revolution that established Haiti, they formed nearly 40 percent of this group. Nevertheless, in these societies they were massively outnumbered by the slaves: freed persons were only 5 percent of the total population in the French Caribbean islands. In two of the most significant colonies of the British Caribbean in the last quarter of the eighteenth century, free coloreds and free blacks made up even less of the total population: in Jamaica freed persons were just over 2 percent of this group, while in

Barbados, they formed about 1 percent of the total population.

Despite obstacles, the number of freed persons often increased rapidly. In the United States it rose dramatically after the American Revolution. By 1810 there were more than one hundred thousand freed persons in the South, comprising almost 5 percent of the free population. In Virginia the number of freed persons more than doubled between 1790 and 1810. This was also the case in Jamaica, where the freed population trebled in the first three decades of the nineteenth century. Although some of this increase was due to manumission, freed people were the only group that increased naturally in many slave societies.

Freed persons suffered a variety of legal, social, and economic disabilities. In most slave societies they could not vote, testify against whites, or sit on juries. They were barred from holding political office and from the political life of their societies; moreover, they were often legally proscribed from various trades or jobs. In parts of the American South freed persons were prohibited from working as river pilots or captains; in Jamaica freed people could not work as navigators or drive carriages for hire, probably because these jobs were seen as the domain of whites. In many colonies freed persons were unable to serve in any of the supervisory posts on plantations; they were also forbidden to practice medicine or pharmacy or work in the offices of clerks of court or notaries. It is apparent that white legislators were very careful to limit the rights of freed persons; legal freedom for them was highly circumscribed.

Some of the legislation directed against freed persons went to extreme lengths to identify free blacks and coloreds and had particularly galling effects. In the Danish West Indies a law passed in 1768 made it obligatory for freed people to wear a distinctive cockade or badge at all times. There was also a long list of items freedmen and freedwomen could not wear, including silk stockings, clothing made of silk, chintz, and gold or silver brocade. In Jamaica, an eighteenth-century act required freed people who owned neither land nor a minimum of ten slaves to wear a blue cross on their right shoulders. They also had to register in a parish and to appear before a magistrate for proper certification of their freedom. Freed persons in parts of the American South faced similar requirements; in addition, they had evening curfews much like the slaves.

Freed persons did not constitute an undifferentiated group. For example, the gradations of color among them could be of considerable importance. Free coloreds often had a higher status than free blacks; some had inherited property from their white fathers and themselves owned slaves. In many slave societies free coloreds socialized among themselves and excluded free blacks from these gatherings. Free coloreds were among the refugees from the Haitian Revolution; one of their destinations was Charleston, South Carolina, where they established the Brown Fellowship Society, a benevolent association open only to free coloreds throughout the antebellum period.

Color was one of the differentiating elements among freed persons; another was the nature of their freedom. Freeborn and manumitted freed persons were often treated differently in law as well as in custom. In Jamaica those born free were subject to trial by jury, whereas manumitted freed persons were subject to slave courts. Manumitted freed persons were also unable to give evidence in court against freeborn members of this group.

There were freed persons in Jamaica who appealed against their legal disabilities and were granted privileges that were denied to other members of their group. In some cases, as with a legislative enactment of 1733, the freed people in question and their families were granted all the rights of whites. The acts that followed this one were more demanding: they stipulated that privileged freed people had to marry a white if their children were to inherit their privileges. Other societies had similar categories, but the freed persons who qualified for special privileges were usually light-skinned and had significant wealth and education.

Regardless of their status within the freed population, freed persons worked in a variety of occupations. Many worked on the land, often as farmhands or casual laborers. Freedwomen served as laundresses, housekeepers, and seamstresses, although they also worked in the fields. A significant proportion of freed persons migrated from the countryside to find work in towns. In many cases, they did so not only to escape the difficult conditions in the countryside, but also to distance themselves from the most visible symbol of slavery, the plantation.

Once in the towns, many freed persons occupied a niche between the upper ranks of urban slaves and the lower echelons of whites. Freedmen worked primarily as artisans, and especially as carpenters, masons, tailors, and shoemakers. In Havana, freedmen included cigar-makers, cooks, musicians, stonecutters, harness makers, small truck farmers, blacksmiths, tinsmiths, butchers, and barbers. Freedwomen in Havana had a smaller range of possibilities: they worked as seamstresses, washerwomen, house servants, dressmakers, and midwives. Elsewhere, freedwomen were frequently hucksters or shopkeepers, and some gained considerable notoriety as tavernkeepers. One of them, Rachael Pringle Polgreen, was a well-known figure in Bridgetown, Barbados; her Royal Naval Hotel was frequently visited by Prince William Henry (later King William IV). An astute businesswoman, Pringle Polgreen died a wealthy woman, the owner of at least ten properties in Bridgetown as well as nineteen slaves, six of whom she manumitted in her will.

In the American South certain types of work were seen as the preserve of freed persons. Barbering was one of these: a barber required little capital and depended on white customers. Like other trades dominated by freed persons, barbering required considerable skill, which helped to protect these jobs from competition from the least-skilled white workers. In Richmond, Virginia, most of the skilled freedmen just before the Civil War worked at six trades—barbering, carpentry, plastering, blacksmithing, bricklaying, and shoemaking.

As a result of their occupations and the restrictions imposed on them, freed persons tended to occupy a very different world from the whites. It was apparent that freed people were unable to socialize with whites on an equal basis. Many public institutions were segregated; for instance, whites had special pews in church, as did freed persons. Theaters sometimes held separate performances for whites and freedmen and freedwomen; when they attended the same performance, freed persons entered by a different door from whites and sat apart from them. Each group often had its own burial ground.

There was, however, one area where these rules could not be enforced. Sexual relations between white men and black and brown women fell outside the usual conventions that affected this group as a whole. While some of these relationships were casual and informal, others were longer-term liaisons. Nonetheless, the informal relationships between white males and freedwomen did not improve the standing of freed persons generally. Freedwomen may have prospered personally, but their relationships stemmed from the social inferiority of their group and highlighted the general exclusion of freed people from white society.

Despite this exclusion, wealthy and acculturated freed persons often sought to emphasize their affinity with whites and to distance themselves from blacks. They adopted the culture of the whites, attending church, seeking to marry, and abusing their slaves. Nonetheless, this group formed a small segment of the class as a whole. Most freed persons were unable to acquire the wealth or education to maintain a lifestyle similar to that of the whites.

Freed persons were therefore more likely to interact with the world of the slaves than with that of the whites. This was certainly so in towns, where freed people and urban slaves mixed freely. They not only lived in close proximity to each other but also worked together as artisans, shopkeepers, or hucksters. Free coloreds and free blacks frequently participated in slave social networks, attending slave funerals and religious activities as well as weekend dances. Both groups often had kin in

Portrait of Rachel Pringle, freedwoman, Bridgetown, Barbados; engraving, nineteenth century.

common; many freed persons owned slaves who were their kin and whom they were seeking to manumit. The line between freed persons and slaves was considerably easier to cross than that between freed people and whites. Moreover, in making the transition from slave to freed person, the manumitted slave reinforced the links between the two sectors of the nonwhite population. The freed slave could therefore expect to find significant continuities in the culture of freed people.

Emancipation did not completely eradicate differences among the nonwhite populations. While freed persons no longer enjoyed a different legal status from slaves or had to confront the political and economic disabilities they had faced during slavery, they continued to enjoy advantages over ex-slaves. They often predominated in politics and society. During Reconstruction, for example, freed persons controlled a disproportionate share of

Photograph of a "freedmen's village" in Arlington Heights, Virginia, late 1860s.

black wealth and political power. However circumscribed their freedom during slavery, freed persons continued to be significant after emancipation.

[*See also* Caribbean Race Relations; Emancipation in the Americas; Race and Racism; *and* Segregation.]

BIBLIOGRAPHY

Cohen, David W., and Jack P. Greene, eds. *Neither Slave nor Free: The Freedman of African Descent in the Slave Societies of the New World.* Baltimore: Johns Hopkins University Press, 1972.

Franklin, John Hope. *The Free Negro in North Carolina, 1790–1860.* Chapel Hill: University of North Carolina Press, 1943.

Handler, Jerome S. *The Unappropriated People: Freedmen in the Slave Society of Barbados.* Baltimore: Johns Hopkins University Press, 1974.

Heuman, Gad J. *Between Black and White: Race, Politics, and the Free Coloreds in Jamaica, 1792–1865.* Westport, Conn.: Greenwood Press, 1981.

—GAD J. HEUMAN

GENDER AND SLAVERY. Although there were many commonalities in the experiences of all slaves, there were also important lines of division among slaves. One of these divisions was gender. In any given society men and women, both enslaved and enslaving, experienced slavery differently. The experience of men and women slaves differed both for biological reasons related to their sexual and reproductive use, and for sociocultural reasons related to gender divisions of labor.

In many societies slaves have been predominantly or stereotypically female. In part this is because war was an important source of slaves, and men were often killed rather than captured. Women captives of various social groups were part of the booty of war. Elite women, for example, might become wives or concubines (the distinction was not made in many legal, kinship, and linguistic systems), although they never gained the status of a wife married by agreement with her male relatives. In Africa slaves were predominantly female. While Europeans preferentially purchased males for export in a ratio of 2:1, this may have been an effect rather than a cause of sex ratios among slaves within Africa, which varied locally based on demand for labor. The feminine character of slavery may also, as Gerda Lerner (1986) argues, be partly due to the fact that women were the original subjugated people. It was the subordination of women during the development of the earliest complex hierarchical societies that allowed for the evolution of the institution of slavery itself. Not all slaveholding societies had a surplus of women; where women were considered less useful as laborers, fewer were purchased or imported, and female infanticide was probably common.

One of the uses of female slaves was for sexual relations. In many slaveholding societies it was permissible to purchase or keep a woman solely for the purpose of sexual pleasure, and in all slaveholding societies women slaves, whatever their other functions, were sexually available to their masters. Sexual use of slaves could be violent or coercive but was not considered rape: the slave was the master's property to be used as he wished. Slave-owning society often blamed these sexual relations on the slaves themselves, leading, for example, to a stereotype of African-American women as lascivious and promiscuous.

Slaves for sexual use were considered a luxury item in the slave trade and could command much higher prices than other workers. In the Americas women of mixed race were especially prized. Contemporary stereotypes held that African women were more libidinous than European women, and women of mixed race combined exoticism with an appearance that approached the European ideal of feminine beauty. Such women might be used as household servants or might be placed in their own households by their masters. Some were owned by brothel-keepers and used as prostitutes.

The sexual use of female slaves created tensions between these slaves and the wives of the slaveowners. In some societies women had separate quarters from men, and the slaves and wives lived alongside each other. In the Americas the slaveowner's sexual partner was often given a privileged position as a domestic servant. Such slaves often bore the brunt of white women's anger over their husbands' sexual infidelity.

The sexual use of male slaves has never been as widespread or as accepted as that of female slaves. There are cases of white women in the American South becoming sexually involved with male slaves, but society judged these instances much more harshly. This was true in ancient Rome as well, where a free man who had sex with a slave (of either sex) incurred no punishment, but a free woman who had sex with a slave might be enslaved or put to death. In some slave societies male domestic slaves were castrated in order to avoid this situation, although eunuchs were sometimes created not to protect free men's monopoly on women but in order to create an administrative class without heirs and thus avoid nepotism.

In some societies, particularly ancient Greece and others where there was little opprobrium attached to homosexual relations, it was not uncommon for a man to purchase male slaves for sexual purposes or for brothels to be staffed by male slaves. The Mamluks of medieval Egypt purchased male slaves for incorporation into the military elite but also had sexual relations with them while they were young. In most modern slave societies, however, although we may guess that homosexual behavior between masters and slaves took place, such activity was forbidden and has left little trace in the historical record, in contrast to the substantial evidence for heterosexual master-slave relations.

Sex between masters and slave women had another important dimension besides sexual desire and the assertion of power. It involved reproduction. In the slave societies of the Americas, masters did not generally intend to have children by slave women; such children were regarded as unavoidable accidents. It was not uncommon for the father to free them and help them financially, and in Latin America and the Caribbean, a master might openly acknowledge them as his illegitimate off-spring. In cultures not affected by Roman or common law notions about legitimacy of issue, children (especially sons) were desirable even if not born to the formally wedded wife. Under Islamic law a slave who bore an acknowledged son to her master was freed on her master's death, and the child was free from birth. In some polygamous African societies a man would choose his most capable son as heir, regardless of whether the son was born to a wife or a slave woman. Even in societies that preferred the children of a legal wife, in the absence of such children those of a slave could be accepted as heirs. In matrilineal societies men might want to have children by female slaves because they could control them more directly than they could their wives' children, who were legally part of the wife's kin group. Where women slaves were valued for reproductive purposes, they were more likely than male slaves to be integrated into the kin group. This was especially so in societies with plural marriages, where the distinction between slave and free wives might be small.

The possibility of bearing children was an important aspect of a slave woman's life, whether or not the slave-owner was her sexual partner. In some slave societies slave women were deliberately encouraged to have children in order to increase the slave-owner's work force. This encouragement could take the form of cash bonuses or privileges, or more coercive forms such as being forced to have sex with a male slave who the slave-owner thought would be likely to father healthy children.

In other slave societies the birth of children to slave women might be a disadvantage to the slave-owner. If the cost of purchasing an adult slave was less than the cost of rearing one to adulthood, then slave reproduction would be discouraged. To prevent such births, slave-owners might refuse to lighten working conditions for pregnant women, leading to miscarriages or infanticide. If a slave knew that her child was going to be ill-treated or sold away from her soon after birth, or that it would suffer malnutrition because she was forbidden to

nurse it and instead was used as wet-nurse for the mistress's child, she might do what she could to prevent conception or abort any pregnancy that occurred. There is evidence from the Caribbean that slave women controlled their fertility, as well as that women's work on sugar plantations was so strenuous as to damage their health and fertility.

In most instances masters probably regarded the reproduction of the slave labor force neither as an important goal nor as a disadvantage, but rather as a profitable benefit of owning slaves. The main purpose of female slaves, as of male slaves, in most slave economies was production, but if they reproduced too, so much the better. Slave fertility was often not especially high, and deliberate breeding was rarely practiced.

When slaves did reproduce, the women tended to have much closer contact with the children than did the men. The law usually did not recognize the rights of either parent in regard to the child, who was simply the property of the mother's owner, but custom often recognized the rights of the mother. Roman law and legal systems based on it denied the legality of slave marriage, and therefore there was no presumption of paternity; the child was the mother's alone. Many slave-owners would not think twice about selling a father away from his children, but most would allow at least very young children to remain with their mothers, whether for sentimental reasons, notions of propriety, or economic concerns (it was probably the most efficient way to rear slave children). Childcare was considered to be the responsibility of the slave mother, even if it meant taking a baby out to the field with her while she worked. Slave mothers thus had much more opportunity to bond with their children than did slave fathers, although American history provides numerous examples of slave families who stayed together, or who were separated by the slave-owner and reunited after emancipation. There are also cases in which mothers killed their children rather than have them sold to another owner.

In some societies male and female slaves worked

at the same tasks. This was true especially of plantation slavery in the American South: in the growing of cotton or tobacco women and men were both considered capable of field work. The dominant ideology that women were weaker than men and belonged in the domestic sphere did not apply to African slaves. In more grueling labor such as sugar-cane cultivation and refining, however, men were preferred. When slaves were trained in skilled crafts, or on small plantations where slaves performed multiple household duties, work tended to break down along the same gender lines as in free society—tasks relating to textiles and clothing to women, tasks involving metalworking and woodworking to men. Among domestic servants, women were involved in food preparation, cleaning, and childcare, and men in transportation and heavy lifting. In addition to the stereotype of the lustful black woman, the other important stereotype that emerged of the African-American slave woman was "mammy." Loyal and beloved by the white children she reared, she was sometimes competent but tough and physically unattractive.

The same basic pattern is found in the division of labor in other slave societies: slave women did the same tasks as free women, and slave men the same tasks as free men. The division, however, was always less strict for slaves than for the free. In some societies, for example in West Africa, food preparation, traditionally associated with women, was a very complicated and time-consuming area of the economy, involving everything from hoe agriculture through the grinding of grain to serving meals. A military entourage or a mercantile center required a substantial agricultural labor force, most of which consisted of women and

Engraving of a Southern mistress with her household slaves, nineteenth century.

much of which might consist of slaves. Slavery was more a way of recruiting women for the work force than a way of organizing production.

Within the slaves' own households in the American South, both men and women contributed labor to fulfill the needs of the family, but the labor tended to be divided by gender according to African traditions. When they had the choice, slaves retained separate skills for men and women, a community of women who worked together, and an opportunity for women to care for their families and homes. Because men did not share the same power over their wives as in European-American society (whether because of African tradition or because of the realities of slavery), the slave family was more egalitarian than its white counterpart. Whites found this remarkable, and it served as the basis of the stereotype that slave women dominated their men and gave rise to a pathological theory of the black family.

Where slave women worked to feed and clothe the labor force rather than to produce for the market, their work often accrued to the benefit of slaveholding women as well as men. In the American South slaveholding women sometimes found the burden of managing a household of slaves, combined with the sexual tensions involved, a hardship, calling themselves "slaves of slaves." In parts of Africa, by contrast, wives benefited substantially from their husbands' purchase of female slaves, and women could own slaves themselves and use them to accrue wealth.

Slavery thus in some ways followed existing gender divisions and stereotypes. In other ways,

Costume des Négresses de Saint Thomas (Dress of the Negresses of Saint Thomas); lithograph, C. DeLasteyrie, nineteenth century.

however, slaves were denied special privileges belonging to their gender. Slave women did not receive the protections that free women did; they were never placed on a pedestal, rarely excused from the heaviest labor, and denied special consideration because of childbirth or childbearing responsibilities. They also escaped some of the disadvantages of femininity—they did not have to be weak and submissive within the family, or deny an interest in sexuality—but this escape was not an advantage to them. Rather, it subjected them to forcible dissolution of their families and to rape.

Slave men suffered, too, from not being allowed to live up to contemporary standards of masculinity. In societies where the measure of a man was how well he could support his family, slave men were not allowed to do so; they were often forcibly separated from their families, or never lived with their sexual partner and children in the first place. They were denied the ability to protect their wives and daughters from sexual and other sorts of violent assault, an essential component of masculine honor in many cultures. In some cases sexual aggression by slave-owners or overseers against women slaves was done deliberately to emasculate slave men.

Casting the male slave as feminine could serve not only to dishonor him but also to ennoble him. American abolitionists argued against the enslavement of Africans on the grounds that blacks, like white women, were especially virtuous and moral. The gentle, long-suffering Uncle Tom image embodied Christian characteristics associated with femininity and passivity. Abolitionists took a stereotype that may have had its roots in the necessities of survival, and used it as an argument against the system that took advantage of such natural virtue. Proslavery arguments similarly conflated slaves and women. The subordination of women, considered a natural state of affairs, was used as a metaphor for the subordination of one race to another, and the association of abolitionism with the women's-rights movement was used to discredit both.

In the American South slave women's resistance to slavery tended to be more individual than men's. Women did not play major roles in collective rebellion but rather reacted individually to the violence and domination of masters, mistresses, or overseers. Women also ran away less often than did men, whether out of reluctance to leave children, lack of confidence in their ability to make good their escape, or resignation to their situation.

The denial to slaves of education and of prospects for betterment in life probably made more difference to men than to women, who would not have had those opportunities even if free. Women slaves outside the plantation system did basically the same kind of work they would have done if they were free (although perhaps more of it), because women's work was largely the same across social classes; for men, enslavement made more of a difference because it denied them choice of work.

Both men and women slaves were denied the honor accorded to free people in the respective slave societies. Women were denied it because of their sexual exploitation; men were denied it because of the inherently dishonoring fact of enslavement.

[*See also* Concubinage; Law, *articles on* Roman Law *and* Islamic Law; *and* United States, *article on* The South.]

BIBLIOGRAPHY

Brunschvig, Robert. "'Abd." In *Encyclopedia of Islam*, new ed., vol. 1. Leiden: E. J. Brill, 1960.

Bush, Barbara. *Slave Women in Caribbean Society, 1650–1838.* Kingston, Jamaica: Heinemann Caribbean, 1990.

Fox-Genovese, Elizabeth. *Within the Plantation Household: Black and White Women of the Old South.* Chapel Hill: University of North Carolina Press, 1988.

Lerner, Gerda. *The Creation of Patriarchy.* New York and Oxford: Oxford University Press, 1986.

Morton, Patricia. *Disfigured Images: The Historical Assault on Afro-American Women.* New York: Greenwood Press, 1991.

Robertson, Claire C., and Martin A. Klein, eds. *Women and Slavery in Africa.* Madison: University of Wisconsin Press, 1983.

White, Deborah Gray. *Ar'n't I a Woman?: Female Slaves in the Plantation South.* New York: W. W. Norton, 1985.

—RUTH MAZO KARRAS

HISTORIOGRAPHY. [*To survey the scope of historical research on slavery in major parts of the world, this entry comprises five articles:*
An Overview
African Slavery
Medieval European and Mediterranean Slavery
Latin American and Caribbean Slavery
North American Slavery
The first is a general overview of historiography from the nineteenth century to the present day; this is followed by four articles that focus on key regions. For further discussion of related issues and measures addressed by historians, see Demography *and* Economics.]

An Overview

Because slavery has existed in many places and over long periods of time, much has been written about it, but systematic historical studies have been a feature of only the last century or so. Some of the early writings, not meant as historical treatments, raised issues that have become central in the recent study of slavery—Greek and Roman manuals and literary works dealing with slave personalities, the economic weaknesses of the *latifundia*, and the limited reproduction of slave populations. By the end of the eighteenth century there were attacks on slavery, part of broader philosophic arguments by such writers as Bodin, Montesquieu, Locke, Hume, Franklin, and Smith. Hume argued that slave populations were not able to reproduce themselves owing to the difficulties of "breeding." Smith claimed, in brief remarks that were to become central to the antislavery argument, that slavery did not pay economically because of the slave's lack of incentives relative to the free workers who could benefit from their increased productivity. Many nineteenth-century European and American economists included comments about the economics of slavery; most noted the incentive problem, but several (including Say and Mill) pointed to the implications of the different climates worked in and outputs produced by slave labor and by free labor. None of the economists, philosophers, or religious writers dealing with slavery, however, provided a full-scale analysis of the slave system. Rather, they presented critiques based mainly on a particular set of issues.

The first full works dealing with slavery came in the mid-nineteenth century, generally from an anti-slavery perspective. This literature emerged only after slavery had come to be politically questioned. Henri Wallon's three volumes (1847) dealt with ancient slavery, but he also published an introductory volume on slavery in the European colonies, attacking it as un-Christian. William O. Blake published, in 1857, a large volume on slavery and the slave trade, with particular attention to U.S. slavery. At about this time other works were published in France, Spain, and elsewhere in Europe, dealing with slavery in both ancient and modern times. Perhaps the most influential work to appear in this period was by the Irish economist J. E. Cairnes, writing during the American Civil War to elicit support for Northern efforts against slavery. Using economic theory and data from U.S. sources, Cairnes presented anti-slavery arguments that were to be used by future writers on the economics of American slavery. These related to the limited productive abilities of slave labor, the constant need for slavery to expand geographically, and the extra costs to a society from its being based on the use of slave labor.

Another late nineteenth-century scholar whose brief comments on slavery and slave labor were to have a major impact on subsequent scholarship was Karl Marx. He argued for the initial role of slavery's productivity in the primitive accumulation of capital. Marx also suggested that slavery was a backward form of labor and economic organization that inevitably must decline. Several nineteenth- and early twentieth-century German scholars wrote on slavery, primarily in the ancient world, most significantly Max Weber's essay on the decline of Roman slavery. Also useful for its historical analysis is J. K. Ingram's concise book, expanding on his entry on slavery in the *Encyclopaedia Britannica*.

Much of our information about slavery comes, however, from the anti-slavery and pro-slavery polemics of the nineteenth century, writings that played a large role in the debates over emancipation. These works of advocacy often included detailed empirical information about slave life, and similar information could also be found in government debates and reports. This voluminous literature, with the anti-slavery writings probably exceeding those defending it, generally included comparisons of slavery with other forms of labor organization. The adversarial nature of such writings meant that, useful as they were, they could not be viewed as systematic scholarly studies.

In the twentieth century, particularly after World War II, there emerged a much richer literature on most aspects of slavery. These writings covered a broader range of areas and time periods than did most earlier ones and often rested on detailed empirical study. They considered slavery in comparative perspective and were explicitly concerned with understanding how the "evil" of slavery developed and continued to survive. While maintaining a highly moral tone, they attempted to explain how the slave system was able to function over centuries and what its impact was on slaves, masters, and other members of society.

Rather than attempt to cover the entire range of slavery studies, this article discusses only some of the key problems examined, particularly those issues that have led to further studies by other scholars, mainly concerning the United States and the English colonies, as well as the writings of certain dominant figures who have set the tone and context for new studies and new interpretations. Restricting this analysis to the study of slavery is particularly limiting, given the strong relation between race and slavery in the Americas and the steadily growing interest in the spectrum of forms of coerced labor and free labor.

The first major analytical work on the causes and nature of slavery in broad perspective was by the Dutch ethnographer H. J. Nieboer (1971). He surveyed all slave societies and divided them by stage of agricultural development. He claimed that at early stages of society slavery seldom existed because there was no surplus for potential enslavers. It was only when there was an open frontier and a surplus that could be captured that slavery would pay. This argument was made more formal in an article by the economist Evsey Domar in 1970. Domar pointed to the importance of preventing labor from moving to "free" land in order to maintain a labor force on already-settled land. He noted that the conditions that led to the desirability of slavery could also have led to serfdom or other varieties of unfree labor, the specific form of labor not being predictable on the basis of the model alone. Further, the availability of a surplus above subsistence would influence labor's bargaining power, and, as argued by Adam Smith, Frederick Jackson Turner, and others, this could lead to a more equal distribution of land and income. Thus, while Nieboer and Domar pointed to an important set of conditions necessary for the presence of slavery, these conditions alone could not explain it.

Left unsaid within the Nieboer analysis was exactly who would be enslaved and why. There had long been descriptions of the groups who were enslavable, going back at least to Aristotle; these emphasized distinctions by nationality, religion, and (most important for slavery in the New World) race. It was only with the work of Moses I. Finley (1980) and the detailed analysis of Orlando Patterson (1982) that the concept of the enslavable "outsider" as an essential aspect of slavery became better understood. The definition of those who were considered outsiders has varied over time and place, but the focus on the loss of legal rights and the legal powerlessness of the enslaved remained constant. The relationship of slavery to race in the New World, and the question of whether slavery preceded or was caused by race prejudice, have been examined in detail by Winthrop Jordan, following a major debate in the scholarly journals between Oscar and Mary Handlin and Carl Degler, as well as being important to the arguments of Eric Williams.

The implication of this loss of rights for slave personality and slave culture was long a staple of discussions of slavery, which emphasized the infantilization of the enslaved and the effect of uprooting in their inability to maintain their cultures of origin. This pattern was long believed to have occurred among slaves in the United States and elsewhere; however, it was only after Stanley Elkins presented his analogy between the effects of living on the slave plantation and the impact of the German concentration camps of World War II that there was extensive analysis of the slave's personality and the effects of master-slave interaction on it. These issues have become central to slave studies in the past three or four decades, with differing interpretations of the extent of the master's power and of the slaves' ability to forge their own existence. Writers often seem to emphasize either autonomy or dependence; Eugene D. Genovese's *Roll, Jordan, Roll* (1974) provides the most complete and balanced depiction of master-slave relations. It drew heavily on the WPA interviews with ex-slaves in the 1930s, a source now widely used in the study of slavery. Although Genovese's book concerned slavery in the United States, it was (like earlier and later works on U.S. slavery) influential in the interpretation of slavery in other places and other times. Because of the vast quantity of research on U.S. slavery and the growing international diffusion of ideas about the slaves and the masters, many of the points made below in regard to U.S. slavery have a wider applicability.

Elkins also revived historical interest in another area of slave studies, the comparison of its functioning in different societies. His contrast between North America and Latin America drew on the writings of Frank Tannenbaum, but earlier writers had made similar juxtapositions. At issue in these comparisons were attitudes of masters and others toward slaves, the psychological and material treatment of slaves, the nature of racial attitudes after emancipation, and the role of religion and metropolitan-colony relations in influencing long-term patterns. This comparative work had the immediate effect of challenging an oft-cited earlier classic by Gilberto Freyre on Brazil, which presented a rather romantic view of Brazilian slavery and race relations.

Another set of comparisons, pursuing one of Nieboer's insights, was presented by David Brion Davis in *Slavery and Human Progress* (1984). Davis argued that, in very long-term perspective, slavery was frequently accompanied by economic, political, and cultural benefits to the slave-owning classes and societies. Rather than being economically backward and politically and culturally retrogressive, slave economies were frequently productive and progressive. Moreover, the existence of slavery was consistent with the expansion of freedom among the nonslaves of the society. Indeed, as Patterson argued, the concept of freedom in the classical world was dependent on the prior existence of slavery. Similar arguments have been made that U.S. slavery permitted a *Herrenvolk* democracy of the free at the expense of the slaves.

The debates on the economics of slavery—concerning the economic performance of slave societies and the economic factors in the ending of slavery—became rather heated over the latter half of the twentieth century. The economic debate concerning U.S. slavery begins, as do debates about most aspects of Southern slavery, with the writings of the Southerner Ulrich B. Phillips in the 1910s and 1920s. Phillips accepted that slavery had economic dimensions, but he believed that it was primarily a noneconomic institution. In economic terms, however, he regarded slavery as unprofitable and unproductive because of both the noneconomic goals of slave-owners and the racially limited capabilities of the slave laborers. The expected ending date for slavery could not be predicted, in large part because slave-owners would have been willing to accept losses to maintain the institution.

The probable date of the economically caused ending of slavery had been discussed in the nineteenth century, generally on the basis of simple Malthusian arguments. This line of analysis became of more central historical concern in the 1920s, owing to the continuing debates on the causes of the Civil War. One major question about that conflict was whether it had been unnecessary because of the imminent demise of slavery on economic grounds. Contributions were made by several historians, generally students of Phillips, but the major article was by Charles Ramsdell. He contended that the natural limits of slavery had been reached, reflecting the earlier hypothesis of Cairnes. Ramsdell further argued that by 1860 slavery was approaching unprofitability and would have ended very soon without the need for war. With a few exceptions, these arguments about the unprofitability of slavery and the backwardness of the Southern economy persisted until the 1960s, when they were forcefully reasserted by Genovese.

A major turning point in the study of the slave economy, as on most other aspects of the Southern slave system, came in the mid-1950s. Kenneth Stampp's *The Peculiar Institution,* a study of many aspects of slavery, attacked most of the views presented earlier by Phillips. Stampp emphasized the importance of economic concerns to slave-owners. He argued that the slave-owners were therefore harsh in their treatment of slaves. He also reevaluated most of the points made in the debate on the economics of slavery, concluding that Southern slavery remained profitable up to the Civil War. This general conclusion was reached at about the same time by two economists, Alfred Conrad and John Meyer, who used available data on slave prices and production and the standard economic measure of the profitability of an investment to calculate rates of return from slave-ownership in the late antebellum period. Conrad and Meyer concluded that slavery had been profitable to slave-owners prior to the Civil War, and that there were no economic indications of any imminent demise. Subsequently, economic historians used other economic measures and new data sources to reiterate Conrad and Meyer's conclusions and to extend the analysis to a new range of questions. The most controversial of such studies on the economic and social aspects of slavery was *Time on the Cross* (1974) by Robert Fogel and Stanley Engerman, followed by Fogel (1989) They argued not only that slavery was profitable, but also that the

slave economy was capable of rapid economic growth and was, by standard economic measures, highly productive. The post-Conrad and Meyer conclusions have been applied to the study of slavery elsewhere, verifying the idea that slavery exhibited a dynamic in many places that belied most earlier arguments about the economic defects of the institution in the Americas, in Africa, in Asia, and even in the ancient world. These arguments have also proven useful in examining the consequences of emancipation and of the economic and social adjustments it entailed.

There have been several other recent influential works concerning American slavery, including Edmund Morgan's (1975) analysis of the relation between American slavery and American freedom in colonial Virginia, and Herbert Gutman's (1976) analysis of the slave family throughout the South. Herbert Aptheker's arguments about slave revolts and resistance were first published in the 1930s. While frequently challenged for what some felt to be his overstatements, Aptheker was among the first nonblack historians to provide an extended critique of the notion of slave docility and acceptance of enslavement. Although an earlier generation of black historians, following after Carter Woodson, had made similar arguments, the theme of psychological resistance to slavery, leading at times to outright revolt, is central to many recent reinterpretations. The examination of slave culture and its evolution from Africa to the Americas has also recently become a widely discussed issue in the United States and elsewhere.

The slave trade has been another fruitful focus of historical study. Philip Curtin's *The Atlantic Slave Trade: A Census* (1969), was instrumental in reopening a number of major questions about the magnitude of the trans-Atlantic slave trade, the structure of the trade by African sources of slaves and their New World ports of arrival, and the relative demographic performance of slaves in the United States and elsewhere in the Americas. Works by Curtin and others have led to extensive archival investigations to obtain more data on the various slave trades, including the trans-Atlantic, the trans-Saharan, and other movements within and from Africa; the impact of the slave trade on African populations and economies; mortality in the Middle Passage, and the slave trade more generally. Much of this work is controversial, but it provides a basis for treating slavery as a worldwide institution and for integrating the study of slavery in the Americas and elsewhere.

Much of the recent historical writing about slavery in the British Empire has been concerned with the role of colonial slavery in causing the British Industrial Revolution, and with the motivations for the ending of the British slave trade in 1808 and of colonial slavery in 1834. Both questions were studied by Eric Williams, as were the reasons for the introduction of black slavery in the New World. His *Capitalism and Slavery* (1944) presented strong arguments about these questions, although each topic had a considerably longer history in the debates of contemporaries and in subsequent scholarship. Williams asserted the central role of the British slave trade in financing the Industrial Revolution, using the writings and parliamentary testimony of slave-trade supporters, which proclaimed the importance of the British slave trade and warned of heavy costs if it were ended. The impact of Williams's writing was limited at first; it was about twenty years until his influence was felt. Responses to Williams on the impact of the slave trade, by Roger Anstey and others, argued for a reduced magnitude of the trade's contribution to British growth and pointed to the broad diffusion of economic change in the Industrial Revolution.

The investigation of the causes of British abolition and emancipation continues to be an important historical debate, entailing substantial discussion of the relative roles of economics and of morality. The ending of the British Atlantic slave system was based on arguments concerning the prospective economic fortunes and role of the British West Indies and the relative political power of different economic interests within Britain. Lowell Ragatz argued for the economic weakness and decline of the British slave colonies, drawing analogies to U.S. slavery and pulling together much of the earlier British literature. This view was challenged by Seymour Drescher and, for a later period, by David Eltis. Reginald Coupland's earlier dominating view had given priority to the importance of moral and religious factors, and to the crucial role for the so-called "saints" and evangelical Protestants in Britain's successful attack on slavery. To Williams, however, morality was relatively insignificant in the ending of slavery. The economic decline of the colonies, which facilitated the transition from merchant capitalism to industrial capitalism, was crucial. Williams's focus on economic forces became a dominant view for a period after World War II, but as the writings of Anstey, Davis, Drescher, Eltis, and Fogel demonstrated, the economic arguments are complex, and the ability to convert moral forces into political ones remains a highly questionable thesis.

The cultural history of British West Indian slavery has also flourished. In recent years, following research elsewhere, there have been detailed studies of slave life in the West Indies. Among the leading figures have been Sidney Mintz, Michael Craton, Jerome Handler, and, particularly on demographic issues, Barry Higman.

While this article has focused on slavery and abolition in the Anglo-American world, there have been important recent works on slavery in other times and places. In many ways the developments in the historiography of these areas reflect, or are consistent with, the emerging literature for the Anglo-American world.

[*See also* Abolition and Anti-Slavery, *article on* Britain; Economics; Marxism; Slave Trade, *article on* Trans-Atlantic Trade; *and* United States, *article on* The South.]

BIBLIOGRAPHY

Davis, David Brion. *The Problem of Slavery in Western Culture.* Ithaca, N.Y.: Cornell University Press, 1966.

Davis, David Brion. *Slavery and Human Progress.* New York and Oxford: Oxford University Press, 1984.

Engerman, Stanley L. "Slavery." In *The New Palgrave: A Dic-*

tionary of Economics, edited by John Eatwell et al. London: Macmillan, 1987.

Finley, Moses I. *Ancient Slavery and Modern Ideology.* New York: Viking Press, 1980.

Fogel, Robert W. *Without Consent or Contract: The Rise and Fall of American Slavery.* New York: W. W. Norton, 1989.

Fogel, Robert William, and Stanley L. Engerman. *Time on the Cross: Evidence and Methods—A Supplement.* (Appendix C). Boston: Little, Brown, 1974.

Miller, Joseph C. *Slavery and Slaving in World History: A Bibliography, 1900–1991.* Millwood, N.Y.: Kraus International Publications, 1993.

Nieboer, H. J. *Slavery as an Industrial System: Ethnological Researches.* 2d ed., rpt. New York: B. Franklin, 1971 (2d ed. first published 1910; 1st ed. 1900).

Patterson, Orlando. *Slavery and Social Death: A Comparative Study.* Cambridge, Mass.: Harvard University Press, 1982.

—STANLEY L. ENGERMAN

African Slavery

The early debates on slavery, as rendered into print by whites and blacks in the Americas and Europe, tended to leave aside Africa, neglecting both slavery in Africa and the impact of trans-Atlantic slavery on Africa. Pity for African victims of slavery and the slave trade grew significant only as they were loaded onto ships for the Middle Passage. Archibald Dalzel made his treatment of Africans as "other" explicit in his 1793 pro-slavery interpretation of the history of Dahomey: he quoted the king as arguing that slave trade saved the lives of Africans captured in wars, who would otherwise have been executed.

One early exception to this pattern was the British abolitionist Thomas Fowell Buxton, whose 1836 analysis included a serious (though probably exaggerated) estimate of the population losses in Africa stemming from the export of slaves. He did not, however, account for the enslavement and retention of people within Africa.

Later in the nineteenth century the expansion of European imperial pressures on the continent was linked with the expansion of slavery and the slave trade. David Livingstone's accounts of the expanding East African slave trade, published from 1853 to 1876, gained wide attention and fueled a Western humanitarian campaign to abolish the slave trade in Africa. Writers of this era pictured the continent as ravaged by the slave trade and populated by masses of captives.

With the establishment of European colonial rule in Africa, generally by 1900, the literature again changed tone sharply. The slave trade, assumed to have been abolished by European conquest, was no longer discussed; slavery in Africa was now presented as benign and of little social consequence. The colonial regimes did not emancipate slaves, but they still spoke of having abolished slavery.

Official ethnologists in the first decades of colonial rule collected data on African slavery, often in the form of a balance sheet, setting the disadvantages of slave status against the protections provided for slaves. These reports, written in the era after the abolition of slave trade, emphasized the quiet reproduction of localized slave systems, rather than the rapacious collection of new slaves. The reports became the data base for anthropological studies of slavery. Europeans, willing to believe in the timelessness of African society, projected these images into the past.

From the 1930s into the 1960s neither historians nor anthropologists had much to say about slavery in Africa. Then decolonization in Africa brought into the open the divisions and debates between descendants of slaves and descendants of slaveowners, and there arose a new willingness to discuss slavery in Africa's past. Concurrently in the Americas, rising popular interest in the history of black people brought new attention to the study of slavery and, inevitably, to exploring African connections.

Philip Curtin's 1969 census of the Atlantic slave trade pulled together existing studies of slave-trade volume and presented a comprehensive and controversial overview. The response to this appeared, beginning in 1975, in edited volumes of two types: the first comprised quantitative studies focusing on the Atlantic trade, which were somewhat cut off from the African interior; and the second were anthropological studies treating African slavery as a set of domestic systems, somewhat cut off from the rest of the world. The volumes included several on the Atlantic slave trade and on slavery in Africa, as well as articles and a volume on the slave trade to Africa's east and north, and collections on women and slavery, the ideology of slavery, and the end of slavery. Monographic studies appeared beginning in 1975, providing details on slavery and African society in more than a score of important works.

The various studies—institutional and commercial, African and Atlantic—eventually began to connect. By the 1980s there existed plausible estimates of Africa's export slave trade in all directions, as well as a growing understanding of intracontinental slavery. The specificity of slavery and the slave trade by age and gender linked distinct local patterns of slavery into a broad system. Synthetic treatments were written, providing global and interconnected estimates of the demographic and social effects of slavery in Africa, the Americas, and Asia. Lovejoy (1983) focused on institutional change, Meillassoux (1991) on theorizing social relations, and Manning (1990) on economic and demographic change.

The basic questions under debate in the literature on African slavery remain those of whether slavery was a major or minor factor in African history, and whether African slavery was a major or minor factor in world history. The more specific issues in recent historiography on African slavery and the slave trade are conveniently addressed for three historical periods. First is the period up to 1600 CE, before the Atlantic trade and in its infancy. For that period discussion centers on the size and direction of the trans-Saharan trade, and on the size of slave populations in Africa, especially in the western Sudan and along the Atlantic coast.

The literature remains centered most heavily on the period of the trans-Atlantic trade (1600–1850). There the issues under debate include the migration paths of enslaved Africans; mortality in the Atlantic and in Africa; effects on African population size and structure; effects on African industry,

social organization and states; expansion of African slavery and the slave trade; gender specificity of slavery and slave trade; the impact on Africa of the decline in export slave trade; and the degree of oppressiveness of slavery in Africa. In regional balance, the analysis of slavery in Central Africa has advanced greatly (Miller, 1988).

For the period after the trans-Atlantic trade (after 1850), major issues include the prices and quantities of slave trade within Africa (and to the Sahara, Mediterranean, Red Sea, and Indian Ocean) and the colonial abolition of slave trade. The biggest recent advance is in studies of slavery in colonial Africa (Lovejoy and Hogendorn, 1993).

The African literature on slavery has now become rather strong: local stories are now connected to continental and global trends. Historians of slavery in other regions might do well to treat African slavery more fully as part of a global system of slavery, and to rely more heavily on African cases in comparative and synthetic studies of slavery. For instance, the New World–centered narrative of the end of slavery gives insufficient attention to the persistence of slavery in Africa and Asia, especially the survival of large-scale slave systems in this century.

[*See also* Abolition and Anti-Slavery, *article on* Africa; *and* Africa.]

BIBLIOGRAPHY

Lovejoy, Paul E. *Transformations in Slavery: A History of Slavery in Africa*. Cambridge: Cambridge University Press, 1983.

Lovejoy, Paul E., and Jan S. Hogendorn. *Slow Death for Slavery: The Course of Abolition in Northern Nigeria, 1897–1936*. Cambridge: Cambridge University Press, 1993.

Manning, Patrick. *Slavery and African Life: Occidental, Oriental and African Slave Trades*. Cambridge: Cambridge University Press, 1990.

Meillassoux, Claude. *The Anthropology of Slavery: The Womb of Iron and Gold*. Translated by Alide Desnois. Chicago: University of Chicago Press, 1991.

Miller, Joseph C. *Way of Death: Merchant Capitalism and the Angolan Slave Trade, 1730–1830*. Madison: University of Wisconsin Press, 1988.

—PATRICK MANNING

Medieval European and Mediterranean Slavery

The modern historiography of slavery in medieval Europe addresses two fundamental problems. The first concerns the chronology of and the reasons for the transition from ancient slavery to medieval serfdom by the eleventh century. The second deals with the stubborn persistence of slavery on the frontiers of Latin Europe in the late Middle Ages and its transfer to the New World.

The eventual disappearance of rural slavery in most of Europe after the dissolution of the Roman Empire holds a privileged place in discussions about the early Middle Ages. Following a line of argumentation already traced out during the Enlightenment, historians tend to regard the disappearance of Roman slavery and the emergence that mitigated servitude of European serfdom as a general movement toward freedom throughout the West. Marc Bloch (1995, p.1) claimed that this transformation was "one of the most profound mankind has known." The continued existence of slavery on the margins of Latin Europe during the later Middle Ages, however, contradicts the optimistic view of "medieval liberation." Until interest grew in the medieval background to European colonialism, medieval slavery tended to be dismissed as a peripheral aberration in European society.

"How and Why Ancient Slavery Came to an End," the problem posed succinctly as the title of a famous essay by Bloch, provides a point of departure for all subsequent research. In it he set out the main economic interpretations advanced to account for the shift from slavery to serfdom. Did slavery die out because of the lack of a supply of new slaves? Historians of imperial Rome have pointed out the difficulty of recruitment by the third century and noted the growth of *coloni*, originally free men settled on tenured holdings, at the expense of slave gangs. But as a result of the disturbances produced by the incursions of new people in the Roman world from the late fourth century,

incessant tribal warfare and raiding may well have increased the availability of slaves. Thus, many historians today would agree with Bloch that, far from diminishing gradually from the fourth century, the availability of slaves may have increased in the barbarian kingdoms.

If slavery did not wither from a lack of supply in human chattel, what economic forces led to its decline? Marxist historians helped to set the outlines for the debate; in their view the transition from a slave to a feudal mode of production marked a transition as fundamental as the movement from feudalism to capitalism. Marxist interpretations, however, have varied substantially in explaining this fundamental shift. Charles Parain (see Bonnassie, pp. 10–11) argued that technological advances, including water-mills, heavy plows, and crop rotation, lessened the need for a concentration of slave labor. Stressing class conflict, Pierre Dockès maintained that slave revolts in late antiquity and the declining power of the state lessened the ability of the masters to maintain the slave mode of production.

According to Bloch, however, the expense of maintaining large slave estates became too great a burden as the economy contracted. Rather than house and clothe slaves at central locations, which required high cost and substantial organization, masters gradually settled them on separate tenures and granted them quasi-liberty through "manumission with obedience." Georges Duby and others now argue, however, that even though the early medieval economy exhibited signs of growth, particularly from the seventh century, slavery nevertheless remained an anachronistic presence throughout the early Middle Ages. Only a fundamental change in social structure could bring it to an end.

Cultural and anthropological perspectives have added new dimensions to answer the problem of why ancient slavery came to an end. Although the early medieval Roman Catholic Church, which itself owned substantial numbers of slaves, did not oppose the institution, Pierre Bonnassie (1991) maintains that Christianity indirectly promoted slavery's decline. By insisting on conversion and manumission as pious acts and forbidding the enslavement of other Christians, the church helped to reduce the cultural alienness of slaves by considering them full human beings rather than "tools with voices," to use Aristotle's definition. Conversion, marriage, and flight gradually made slaves indistinguishable from the rest of the peasantry alongside whom they toiled.

Distinguishing between slavery and less absolute forms of servitude has proven a particularly difficult and divisive issue. By the Carolingian period many slaves and descendants of former slaves held tenures and shared the same labor obligations as free tenants. Differences in legal status, therefore, increasingly failed to reflect differences in economic function. Substantial disagreement exists among historians about the continuing relevance of the legal category of slavery in a society that recognized various forms of dependence. Bloch (1995) maintained that the legal distinctions between free and unfree gradually became muddled as slaves improved their lot and the fate of freemen deteriorated to produce medieval serfdom. Léo Verriest (see Bonnassie, pp. 13–14), by contrast, holds that the servile population of the twelfth and thirteenth centuries were direct descendents of the "housed slaves" of the Carolingian period.

The chronology of slavery's decline has proven controversial because it provides an acid test for the transition from the ancient to the medieval world. Against an older historiography that argued for a gradual movement from slavery to serfdom between the fifth and eleventh centuries, French historians influenced by Duby have emphasized a sharp rupture in European society around the year 1000. This sudden transformation, sometimes called the "feudal revolution," finally caused agricultural slavery to disappear. Whereas Duby himself at first emphasized institutional changes, particularly the rapid disintegration of traditional public courts (which helped to distinguish free liti-gants from servile dependents), others following him have argued for an even broader and more abrupt transformation around 1000. Guy Bois recently offered the most far-reaching model of the "feudal revolution." As a result of a profound and dramatic change in the means of production, lords began to extort labor and rents from both free and unfree peasants. The nobility found in serfdom a preferable alternative to the use of slaves. Thus Bois decisively postponed the end of ancient slavery to the threshold of the second millennium. His position, however, quickly provoked criticism. Retreating from a history of sharp ruptures, Dominique Barthélemy, Adriaan Verhulst, and others returned to an older interpretation emphasizing a gradual, even imperceptible evolution from slavery to serfdom from the third to the tenth century. Although the debate about chronology continues today, scholars generally agree that by the eleventh century slavery had given way to radically different means of exploiting agricultural labor.

Nevertheless, slavery did not completely disappear in medieval Europe, although it did move from the heartland of Latin Christendom to its frontiers, and from the countryside to the towns. Historians utilizing the richer archival sources of the late Middle Ages have tried to gauge the nature of the slave market and to determine its economic impact. From notarial contracts recording slave purchases, distinct cycles have emerged in the importation to the Latin Mediterranean of Muslim, Greek, Tartar, and—by the fifteenth century—African captives. Mediterranean towns received the majority of these unwilling immigrants. Because entrepreneurs and artisans found in wage labor a flexible means of meeting their business needs, slaves usually served their masters as domestic help or as occasional, unspecialized laborers. Susan Mosher Stuard (1995), however, maintained that because historians have misunderstood the role of servile female labor, they have failed to stress that women provided a fundamental link in the history of Western slavery. Substantially outnumbering male slaves in the late Middle Ages, unfree women met the needs of masters of large households for display and consumption.

Slavery also took other forms. Verlinden emphasized the importance of servile labor in Genoese and Venetian medieval colonies, such as Chios and Crete. After employing slaves on their island outposts in the eastern Mediterranean, Italians, with Spain's backing, transferred this system to the Canary Islands, which lacked an adequate labor force to cultivate sugar-cane. Spain and Portugal then transferred this incipient colonial slave system to the Americas. Verlinden established substantial structural continuity, despite a difference in scale, between slavery in the medieval Mediterranean and that in the colonial Atlantic.

After exploring questions of recruitment and exploitation, which largely reflect the view of the masters, historians have now begun to turn to other social and cultural dimensions of late medieval slavery. Jacques Heers (1981) placed many slaves in late medieval households on the same footing as domestic servants. Through conversion, sexual intimacy, and manumission, chattels and their descendants were eventually integrated into their host society. Whereas this approach stresses mechanisms for integration rather than the reproduction of a servile class, the fear produced by an alien, resentful population of slaves has drawn scholars to investigate methods of repression, surveillance, and control, and to explore the moral dilemmas these caused for both church and state. Although the medieval church in general did not question the foundations of slavery, individual clerics, especially those concerned with missionary activities, began to raise doubts about the legitimacy of the institution.

Historians at the end of the twentieth century no longer consider the Middle Ages a pleasant intermezzo between the massive movements of ancient and colonial slavery. Transformed but still recognizable, slavery persisted in the West from ancient Rome to the encounter with the Americas.

[*See also* Europe; Mediterranean; Serfdom; *and* Slave Trade, *article on* Medieval Europe.]

BIBLIOGRAPHY

Bonnassie, Pierre. *From Slavery to Feudalism in South-Western Europe.* Translated by Jean Birrell. Cambridge: Cambridge University Press, 1991.

Bloch, Marc. *Slavery and Serfdom in the Middle Ages: Selected Papers.* Berkeley: University of California Press, 1975.

Bois, Guy. *The Transformation of the Year One Thousand: The Village of Lournand from Antiquity to Feudalism.* Translated by Jean Birrell. Manchester: Manchester University Press, 1992.

Dockès, Pierre. *Medieval Slavery and Liberation.* Translated by Arthur Goldhammer. Chicago: University of Chicago Press, 1982.

Duby, George. *The Early Growth of European Economy: Warriors and Peasants from the Seventh to the Twelfth Century.* London: Weidenfeld and Nicolson, 1974.

Heers, Jacques. *Esclaves et domestiques au moyen âge.* Paris: Fayard, 1981.

Stuard, Susan Mosher. "Ancillary Evidence for the Decline of Medieval Slavery," *Past and Present* 149 (1995): 3–28.

Verhulst, Adriaan. "The Decline of Slavery and the Economic Expansion of the Early Middle Ages." *Past and Present* 133 (1991): 195–203.

Verlinden, Charles. *The Beginnings of Modern Colonization.* Translated by Yvonne Freccero. Ithaca, N.Y.: Cornell University Press, 1970.

—STEPHEN P. BENSCH

Latin American and Caribbean Slavery

The historiography of Latin American and Caribbean slavery since 1960 has revealed the enormous diversity of the African slave experience through time, and in the numerous regions and economic sectors where slavery became a major form of labor exploitation. The difficulty of making generalizations about African slavery in Latin America and the Caribbean is perhaps the most important general conclusion that has emerged, and this has encouraged much archival research at the regional and local levels.

In most studies scholars have addressed important themes that reflect the developing historiography of slavery elsewhere. Demographic aspects in different periods and regions are an important focus. Historians comb local archives for data on reproductive rates, fertility, mortality, age structures, sex ratios, and any other data that help them to understand slave life from the vantage point of the slaves themselves. No sweeping conclusions have been drawn, but it is clear that the demographic histories of slave populations varied temporally, by economic sector, and by geographical region. Slaves on rural plantations, in contrast with those on smaller farms and ranches, in mining districts, and in urban centers, demonstrated quite different demographic characteristics. There were also great contrasts in demography between slaves working in export sectors and those in nonexport economies.

There has been a concerted effort in recent historiography to view slaves not as faceless objects but as people struggling to assert their humanity at every turn within the context of the most dreadful of human conditions. Slaves rebelled and ran away to seek freedom, and this theme has been studied in nearly every region and period. They also struggled to preserve African culture and religion, to establish families, to create space for themselves within the slave system to cultivate their crops, and, surprisingly, to market their products or services. There was a relentless and diverse quest for freedom in Latin American and Caribbean slave societies. One manifestation was the constant search for access to cash: Spanish and Portuguese slave codes recognized the rights of slaves to purchase freedom. Entering into *coartación* or self-purchase contracts for themselves, their children, or their spouses conferred on the contractors rights and privileges distinct from those of slaves who had not entered into this process. How widespread this practice was is not yet known, but a number of studies suggest that self-purchase may have been more prevalent than previously believed.

The economic dynamics of slave systems have also been considered through the application of economic theory, an approach made possible by the use of many kinds of data derived from local archives throughout the region. It is now accepted that slavery was a highly profitable system for slave-owners in almost all economic sectors, and

that this continued to be true right up to abolition. The implications of this conclusion have been important for studies on the causes of abolition, which have increasingly been interpreted as involving a complex interplay of ideological factors rather than economic rationality.

The fourteenth- and fifteenth-century antecedents to the development of Latin American and Caribbean slave systems are now well known and provide an important background for understanding how and why the African slave trade initially evolved. The first slaves in the Americas were indigenous peoples of conquered regions, who had no immunity to European diseases and rapidly died off. They were replaced by Africans, who from the beginning of Portuguese exploration of the African coast in the fourteenth century had been traded by African merchants in exchange for European manufactured goods.

Indigenous slavery was outlawed by the middle of the sixteenth century, and this resulted in the legal sanctioning of a race-based slave system stipulating that a person had to be African or of African descent to be legally enslaved. Historians have debated whether racism preceded the evolution of African slavery in the New World or developed parallel to it. They have found that racist ideologies were present prior to the initiation of the large-scale trans-Atlantic slave trade and were refined during the nearly four-century-long tragedy of African slavery in the Americas.

The discovery of silver in northern Mexico and highland Bolivia in the 1540s led to the emergence of a complex colonial economic system that extended through every region of Latin America and across the Atlantic to Spain. It rested on silver-mining but generated a diverse array of ancillary economic activities, all of which demanded substantial labor inputs. In every economic center from Buenos Aires to the Mexican mining districts, African slaves played a critical role in meeting the demand for labor during the sixteenth century. In the two major colonial capitals, Mexico City and Lima, Africans were the second most numerous population group after indigenous peoples during the sixteenth century. African slaves worked in the mines; they were muleteers moving merchandise to and from markets; they raised cattle, grew wheat and corn, and labored in nearly every urban occupation from highly skilled trades to domestic service. African women played critical roles in many urban trades, and these have been carefully documented by local historians.

Slavery declined during the seventeenth century in the Spanish colonies, in part because of the demographic recovery of the indigenous population, the expansion of the mixed or *mestizo* population, and the general development of a free labor market that made slave labor unnecessary. The institution then shifted its center to Brazil, which would become the greatest slave-importing colony in the Americas, accounting for nearly 40 percent of all Africans forced across the Atlantic. Slavery first expanded in the Brazilian northeast, which developed into the world's leading center of sugar production during the seventeenth century. The regions of Pernambuco and Bahía became the first great New World plantation systems, where sugar was produced by African slave labor after the earlier exploitation of indigenous slaves. This Brazilian slave-based plantation system was emulated by the British, French, and Dutch when they established control over various island possessions in the Caribbean and began to produce tropical staple products such as sugar to break the Brazilian monopoly. During the eighteenth century the British colonies of Barbados, Jamaica, and the Leeward Islands, along with the French colonies of Saint Domingue and Martinique, became large-scale importers of African slaves and producers of sugar, coffee, ginger, cacao, and other products consumed in Europe.

Sugar and slavery remained in the Brazilian northeast, but in the eighteenth century the discovery of gold, diamonds, and other minerals in the Brazilian interior region of Minas Gerais shifted slavery and the slave trade to the center of the colony. Slaves worked extensively in mineral production during the boom period to 1750. As during the sixteenth-century silver cycle in the Spanish colonies, African slaves also labored in a diverse array of other economic sectors, urban and rural, skilled and unskilled. The decline of mining and export activities in late eighteenth-century Minas Gerais did not herald the end of slavery in the region. The persistence of slavery in nonexport sectors has been a theme of considerable interest to recent Brazilian historiography.

The growth of coffee production in the valley regions north of Rio de Janeiro in the early nineteenth century, and later in São Paulo, once again spread African slavery to a new region in the country. These slave-based coffee plantations led to a resurgence of the Brazilian slave trade. Slaves also worked in nearly every other urban and rural economic sector in the Brazilian south, and the growth of urban slavery in Rio de Janeiro was particularly important. Slavery within the Brazilian coffee economy and in the country's urban centers has been studied in a large number of monographs.

The last great slave system to develop in Latin America and the Caribbean was in the Spanish Caribbean colonies during the nineteenth century, principally Cuba and to a lesser extent Puerto Rico. African slaves were present in small numbers from the sixteenth throught the eighteenth century, but only in Havana were there great concentrations until the nineteenth century. Havana was the rendezvous point for the Spanish fleet during most of the colonial period, resulting in a high level of economic development and an extensive urban infrastructure, including shipyards and foundries employing large numbers of slaves.

Cuba began to imitate the economic success of its neighbors, British Jamaica and French Saint Domingue, during the eighteenth century by turning to sugar and coffee plantation production based on slave labor. With the great Haitian slave revolt of the 1790s and the ensuing rise in world prices for tropical staples, production expanded, and the large-scale nineteenth-century slave trade to Cuba began in earnest. Cuba, and on a much smaller scale Puerto Rico, became centers of slavery, largely owing to the plantation economy. These two islands were also the final great destination of the trans-Atlantic slave trade. These processes have been extensively examined by recent studies.

Despite a historiography that has matured considerably, there are still many unanswered questions to be addressed by future research. Especially important will be a more detailed portrait of life in slave societies from the perspectives of slaves. Court records, parish archives, notarial protocols, municipal documents, manuscript census records, and many other historical documents which contain valuable data on slavery remain unexamined throughout Latin America and the Caribbean.

[*See also* Abolition and Anti-Slavery, *article on* Latin America; Emancipation in the Americas; Law, *article on* Latin American Law; *and* Slave Trade, *article on* Trans-Atlantic Trade.]

BIBLIOGRAPHY

Bergad, Laird W., Fe Iglesias García, and María del Carmen Barcia. *The Cuban Slave Market, 1790–1880*. New York: Cambridge University Press, 1995.

Eltis, David. *Economic Growth and the Ending of the Transatlantic Slave Trade*. New York and Oxford: Oxford University Press, 1987.

Engerman, Stanley L., and Eugene D. Genovese, eds. *Race and Slavery in the Western Hemisphere: Quantitative Studies*. Princeton: Princeton University Press, 1975.

Klein, Herbert S. *African Slavery in Latin America and the Caribbean*. New York and Oxford: Oxford University Press, 1986.

Miller, Joseph C. *Slavery and Slaving in World History: A Bibliography, 1900–1991*. Millwood, N.Y.: Kraus International Publications, 1993.

Schwartz, Stuart B. *Slaves, Peasants, and Rebels: Reconsidering Brazilian Slavery*. Urbana: University of Illinois Press, 1992.

—Laird W. Bergad

North American Slavery

The United States may never repeat the history of slavery—following George Santayana's dictum that those who do not understand history are doomed to repeat it—but U.S. historians seem doomed to an endless recapitulation of the terms in which slavery was debated before the Civil War. Opponents made the case for slavery's sinfulness and cruelty, its threat to democracy, and its economic irrationality. Pro-slavery ideologues answered that slavery was a benevolent system, superior in most ways to the alternative of wage labor, and a bulwark of democratic equality among free white men. These contrasting positions have reappeared in virtually all the major scholarly studies of slavery written in the twentieth century.

The professional history of American slavery, based on archival research in plantation records, came into its own with Ulrich B. Phillips's *American Negro Slavery* (1918). Phillips was a Southern-born scholar who likened slave plantations to the urban settlement houses set up by progressive reformers in the early twentieth century. His work provided intellectual support for Southern progressives who justified black disenfranchisement and Jim Crow laws by emphasizing the South's continuous history of racial subordination of blacks to whites. The assumption of white racial superiority had been the "cornerstone" of the Confederacy, at least according to its vice president, Alexander Stephens. In Phillips's hands, the same racial hierarchy became the "central theme" of Southern history. He thus depicted slavery as a particular phase in the history of race relations—a phase in which uncivilized blacks were tutored under the benevolent dictatorship of their white superiors. For Phillips, the planters' commitment to the management of race relations prevailed over their economic self-interest, and hence the price of racial "adjustment" in the Old South was a relatively backward economy.

If Phillips reflected the planter's view of slavery, Kenneth Stampp's *The Peculiar Institution* (1956) revived the abolitionist perspective. For Stampp slavery was less a way of life than a system of labor, and, like most systems of labor, slavery was driven by its own internal conflicts. Like Frederick Law Olmsted in the 1850s, Stampp in the 1950s observed on Southern plantations a kind of low-level warfare, centered at the workplace, that pitted masters against slaves in a day-to-day battle of wills. Stampp added a new element, however, when he wrote that the slaves lived in a "cultural void," stripped of their African heritage but excluded from mainstream America. In a subsequent essay Stampp saw evidence of psychological damage in, for example, the large number of slaves who stuttered. After Stampp, much of the historiography of slavery, guided by the so-called "therapeutic" model, focused on the slaves' psychological adjustment to the harsh realities of slavery.

Psychological damage as a barometer of American race relations had already entered public discussion in the Supreme Court's 1954 *Brown vs. Board of Education* decision. Stanley Elkins highlighted the therapeutic theme in his provocative *Slavery* (1959). Elkins argued that the slaves were "infantilized" by the totality of the plantation regime, a totality he compared to Nazi concentration camps. Because slave marriages were illegal and slave parents had no formal authority over their own children, the master became the slave's only "significant other." Thus slavery turned its victims into damaged human beings, the "helpless dependents" captured in the Sambo stereotype, stripped of their capacity for resistance. Rich and complex African cultures were reduced, Elkins argued, to "a point of utter stultification in America." Here was a recapitulation of another powerful theme in the abolitionist critique of slavery: that the slaves themselves were reduced to ciphers by the brutality and oppression of the masters. And just as Frederick Douglass had objected to this line of reasoning among his fellow abolitionists, so too did a number of historians who set out to repudiate Elkins.

The therapeutic model stressed culture over political economy, and so most of those who engaged with Elkins argued for the vitality of slave culture. A series of remarkable studies published between the late 1960s and the mid-1970s took up this theme. Sterling Stuckey (1968) emphasized the persistence of African traditions. John Blassingame (1972) pointed to the strength of "the slave community." Lawrence Levine (1977) uncovered the richness of African-American music and folklore. Herbert Gutman (1976) saw remarkable adaptive capacities in the slave family. Most important, however, was the meticulous reconstruction of "the sacred world" of African-American Christianity by Levine, Albert Raboteau (1978), and Eugene Genovese (1974). Where Stampp had emphasized resistance and Elkins helpless dependency, cultural historians admired the slaves' simple capacity to survive. The study of slave culture thus reflected the increasingly depoliticized nature of the history of ordinary men and women. The slaves, Levine (1977, p. 54) explained, "were prepolitical beings in a prepolitical situation."

Although most studies of slave culture disputed Elkins's argument for slavery's damage, the most influential study of the 1970s, Eugene D. Genovese's *Roll, Jordan, Roll* (1974), took a more ambiguous stance. On the one hand, Genovese argued, slave preachers, drivers, mammies, and others made their peace with the slaveholders' regime and in so doing won slaves a measure of dignity under duress. But the price slaves paid for their accommodation was a high one, Genovese argued, because it encouraged among slaves a stifling pattern of dependency that effectively obliterated an older tradition of revolutionary resistance. Thus Genovese confronted the political question directly. Much of his work was directed to explaining why the slaves failed to rebel, especially during the Civil War. "The record of the slaves and ex-slaves during the war constituted a disaster," Genovese wrote. "Having relied previously on the protection and guidance of the masters, they now threw themselves on the mercies of the Union Army" (1971, p. 139). In *Been in the Storm So Long* (1979), Leon Litwack offered the most detailed, nuanced version of Genovese's interpretation of slavery during the Civil War. Most scholarship since then, however, has stressed the active role slaves played in furthering their own emancipation.

Genovese was one of a long line of distinguished Marxists who contributed to the study of slavery throughout the twentieth century, but Marxism touched different historians in different ways. W. E. B. Du Bois, for example, noted the thousands of runaways during the Civil War and labeled their action "the Great Strike." Herbert Aptheker laid out in impressive detail the number of slave uprisings and, more commonly, insurrection panics, in the antebellum South. Kenneth Stampp's socialist background undoubtedly contributed to the emphasis on labor relations at the heart of *The Peculiar Institution*. But where Du Bois, Aptheker, and Stampp stressed conflict, Genovese emphasized the slaves' relatively quiescent accommodation to the masters' cultural hegemony.

Stampp's book had also opened another line of scholarly inquiry, this one focused on the slave economy. Against Phillips, Stampp argued that slavery was a profitable enterprise, and within a few years econometricians were busily proving that plantations made money year-to-year. The antebellum critics of slavery had been less concerned with the short-term solvency of plantations than with their long-term viability. In the early 1960s Douglass North could still point to the structural weaknesses of the slave economy, but it was Genovese's *The Political Economy of Slavery* (1965) that breathed new life into the antebellum critique. He questioned the system's long-term viability more than its short-term profitability, emphasizing the debilitating consequences of weak consumer demand and an unmotivated workforce.

The counterargument was pressed most forcefully by Robert Fogel and Stanley Engerman in their controversial study of the economics of slavery, *Time on the Cross* (1974). They questioned the distinction between profitability and viability. They argued that slavery had built-in incentives to encourage the slaves' productivity, and that by global standards the antebellum South was a relatively developed economy. *Time on the Cross* was the most methodologically sophisticated neoclassical account of the slave economy, although it

struck some readers as reminiscent of antebellum defenses of the slave regime. Not all economic historians accepted Fogel and Engerman's conclusions. While a number of sharp critiques were published, the most theoretically complete alternative was Gavin Wright's *The Political Economy of the Cotton South* (1978). Although he matched Fogel and Engerman's methodological sophistication, Wright's conclusions were very different. He stressed the South's dependence on the industrial world's demand for cotton; he questioned the productive capacity of the cotton plantation and, by extension, the economic vitality of the slave economy. Nevertheless, it was clear by the end of the 1970s that economic historians were no more in agreement about slavery than were social and cultural historians.

Another major study from the 1970s, Edmund Morgan's *American Slavery, American Freedom* (1975), created an even more glaring contradiction in the historiography. Focusing on the development of slavery in colonial Virginia, Morgan noted that the republicanism of the U.S. founders was actually strengthened by the fact that Virginia's lower class was excluded from the polity by virtue of its enslavement. Racism, Morgan argued, became the ideological rationale for denying black slaves their right to liberty. By contrast, Genovese (1974, p. 5) argued that the irrational features of the slave economy made it a descendent of "the land-oriented world of medieval Europe," and as such increasingly alien to the larger patterns of American political culture. Historians of Southern political culture promptly moved off in two different directions. Kenneth Greenberg, Rachel Klein, and Michael P. Johnson, for example, stressed the distinctive conservatism of Southern political culture, but they often referred to a "republican" ideology that more and more historians located in Northern politics as well. Meanwhile, most students of Southern politics (among them William J. Cooper, J. Mills Thornton, Harry Watson, Lacy Ford, and William Freehling) found evidence that, despite regional variations, the slaveholders largely accommodated themselves to national patterns. As antebellum historians uncovered the outlines of a sustained debate over the merits of wage labor within the North, the decisive struggle between slavery and free labor no longer seemed confined to sectional politics. However, this only reinforced the sense that slave labor and liberal republicanism were fundamentally incompatible. Resolving this contradiction became a major preoccupation of subsequent historians of the slave South.

Comparative history failed to resolve any of these issues. Frank Tannenbaum's pioneering *Slave and Citizen* (1946) argued that the Roman Catholic Church intervened to lessen slavery's harshness in Latin America, but David Brion Davis and others questioned whether slavery really was more cruel in the United States. Carl Degler's study of the United States and Brazil persuaded him that racism was central to the ideological legitimation of Southern slavery, but Genovese's comparisons led him to the opposite conclusion. Peter Kolchin compared Southern slavery with Russian serfdom and found support for Genovese's theory of premodern paternalism. By contrast, Shearer Davis Bowman's equally rigorous comparison of Southern planters and Prussian Junkers suggested that the slaveholders fused a capitalist orientation to a Burkean conservatism that was neither premodern nor paternalistic.

Hoping to bridge the widening chasm between social and political history, James Oakes argued in *The Ruling Race* (1982) that the slaveholders were able to embrace the dominant political culture by using the acquisition of slaves as a vehicle for pursuing the "American dream" of upward mobility. In *Slavery and Freedom* (1990) Oakes invoked the theoretical advances of Moses I. Finley and Orlando Patterson to carry the argument further. Once slavery was understood as a form of social *death*, Oakes argued, it was possible to locate the ways in which liberalism excluded slaves from the dominant forms of social *life*. The political significance of slave resistance could therefore be measured by the degree to which slaves asserted their own social life by forcing the liberal polity to extend to them the basic rights of humanity. At the same time, Oakes argued, the contradictory aspects of the slave economy—its intimate ties to the capitalist world and its intrinsically irrational tendencies—sustained the slaveholders' equally contradictory relationship to American political system. In *The Slaveholder's Dilemma* (1992), Genovese pointed to a similar contradiction: the slaveholder's simultaneous commitment to a retrograde social system and to a modern ideology of progress defined as material prosperity.

The "golden age" of the 1970s left other questions unresolved. Particularly inadequate was the treatment of women and the family in the antebellum South. The effect of slavery on Southern families, black and white, was a persistent theme in antebellum discussions, so it is no surprise that the subject resurfaced in modern debates. Historians of the 1970s were often concerned to demonstrate, in contrast to Elkins, that black men were not emasculated by slavery, but their emphasis on the strength and ubiquity of Southern patriarchy quickly produced a flood of revisionist studies, although once again no consensus. Slave women and their families have been subjected to increasingly detailed treatment, but where some scholars—Deborah Gray White (1981), for example—stressed the relative autonomy of slave women, others, most notably Elizabeth Fox-Genovese (1988), argued for deep interconnections between slave and free within the plantation household. Daniel Blake Smith, Jan Lewis, and Jane Turner Censer all argued that planter families experienced the retreat from patriarchal values familiar to historians of bourgeois domesticity. By contrast, Catherine Clinton and Fox-Genovese both argued, albeit in very different ways, for the persistence of patriarchal assumptions in planter families.

Many of the unresolved questions can be answered only by a fuller appreciation for the colonial background of antebellum slavery, yet the history of slavery in the colonial period has largely remained a subfield of its own. It was dominated for a long time by a stimulating debate over the relationship among class structure, racism, and the origins of slavery in the earliest decades of Virginia's history. In an unusually effective use of the comparative method, Philip Morgan shifted the emphasis from the status of the first slaves to Virginia's transition from a slaveholding to a slave society. In the 1970s social historians such as Peter Wood and Gerald Mullin published important studies of the roots of slave rebelliousness. Both Wood and Mullin tied together social and cultural history, but the emphasis quickly shifted to the latter. Some scholars stressed the degree to which slaves "assimilated" the culture of their masters; some stressed the relative autonomy of slave culture. By contrast, Mechal Sobel argued for a mutual accommodation among masters and slaves.

Despite the continued flow of monographs, however, it is fair to say that since the intellectual ferment of the 1970s the historiography of slavery has settled into a series of analytical ruts. Was slavery capitalist or feudal? Were planter families fundamentally bourgeois, or did the "plantation household" constitute a distinctive social formation? Was slave culture "African" or "American?" Most historians now recognize both the capitalist and the precapitalist elements of the slave economy. By contrast, historians have been needlessly divided over whether slavery was "at bottom" a system of class oppression or racial exploitation.

Thus neither Marxism nor the therapeutic model, and neither cultural nor economic history, could bring consensus to the study of slavery. In each field scholars divided among themselves, and in most cases they recapitulated various elements of the antebellum debate over slavery. This is probably unavoidable, and it is probably a good thing. Slavery forced Americans—just as it forces historians—to be unusually articulate about their deepest political and moral convictions. What does a just society look like? What does it mean to be free? To argue about slavery is to confront the brutal concreteness of these fundamental questions.

[*See also* Caribbean Race Relations; Race and Racism; *and* United States.]

BIBLIOGRAPHY

Blassingame, John. *The Slave Community: Plantation Life in the Antebellum South*. New York and Oxford: Oxford University Press, 1972.

Du Bois, W. E. B. *Black Reconstruction in America: An Essay toward a History of the Part Which Black Folk Played in the Attempt to Reconstruct Democracy in America, 1860–1880*. New York: Harcourt, Brace and Company, 1935.

Elkins, Stanley. *Slavery: A Problem in American Institutional and Intellectual Life*. Chicago: University of Chicago Press, 1959.

Fogel, Robert William, and Stanley L. Engerman. *Time on the Cross: The Economics of American Negro Slavery*. 2 vols. Boston: Little, Brown, 1974.

Fox-Genovese, Elizabeth. *Within the Plantation Household: Black and White Women of the Old South*. Chapel Hill: University of North Carolina Press, 1988.

Genovese, Eugene D. *The Political Economy of Slavery: Studies in the Economy and Society of the Slave South*. New York: Pantheon, 1965.

Genovese, Eugene D. *In Red and Black: Marxian Explorations in Southern and Afro-American History*. New York: Pantheon, 1971.

Genovese, Eugene D. *Roll, Jordan, Roll: The World the Slaves Made*. New York: Pantheon, 1974.

Gutman, Herbert G. *The Black Family in Slavery and Freedom, 1750–1925*. New York: Pantheon, 1976.

Jordan, Winthrop D. *White Over Black: American Attitudes toward the Negro, 1550–1812*. Chapel Hill: University of North Carolina Press, 1968.

Levine, Lawrence. *Black Culture and Black Consciousness: Afro-American Folk Thought from Slavery to Freedom*. New York and Oxford: Oxford University Press, 1977.

Morgan, Edmund. *American Slavery, American Freedom: The Ordeal of Colonial Virginia*. New York: W. W. Norton, 1975.

Oakes, James. *The Ruling Race: A History of American Slaveholders*. New York: Knopf, 1982.

Oakes, James. *Slavery and Freedom: An Interpretation of the Old South*. New York: Knopf, 1990.

Phillips, Ulrich Bonnell. *American Negro Slavery: A Survey of the Supply, Employment and Control of Negro Labor as Determined by the Plantation Regime*. New York: D. Appleton, 1918.

Raboteau, Albert. *Slave Religion: The Invisible Institution in the Antebellum South*. New York and Oxford: Oxford University Press, 1978.

Stampp, Kenneth M. *The Peculiar Institution: Slavery in the Ante-bellum South*. New York: Knopf, 1956.

Stuckey, Sterling. "Through the Prism of Folklore: The Black Ethos in Slavery." *Massachusetts Review* 9 (1968): 417–437.

Tannenbaum, Frank. *Slave and Citizen: The Negro in the Americas.* New York: Vintage Books, 1947.

White, Deborah Gray. *Ar'n't I a Woman?: Female Slaves in the Plantation South.* New York: W. W. Norton, 1981.

Wright, Gavin. *The Political Economy of the Cotton South: Households, Markets and Wealth in the Nineteenth Century.* New York: W. W. Norton, 1978.

—JAMES OAKES

INDENTURED SERVITUDE. The institution of indentured servitude first appeared in use in mainland North America around 1620. The system, developed by the Virginia Company as a solution to the problem of how colonial planters could obtain a labor force, effectively allowed English workers unable to afford the cost of passage to America to borrow the necessary funds. In return for transportation to the colonies, the migrants signed "indentures," or contracts, that bound them to repay their debt by working for colonial planters for specified periods of years. Servitude quickly became a central institution in the economy and society of many parts of colonial British America. It has been estimated that between one-half and two-thirds of all white immigrants to the British colonies between the 1630s and the American Revolution came under indenture. During this period indentured servitude enabled between three and four hundred thousand Europeans to migrate to the New World. Most of these migrants came from England, but during the eighteenth century significant components of the servant population came to be made up of Scottish, Irish, and German immigrants.

This first episode of indentured servitude ended by the early nineteenth century. At the same time that indentured servitude was disappearing from the United States, however, the abolition of slavery in the British West Indies in the 1830s produced a renewed demand for indentured labor. The revival of indentured servitude that followed during the nineteenth century was an episode quite different from the use of servants in British America in the seventeenth and eighteenth centuries. Whereas the indentured system had earlier involved the immigration of Europeans to America, in the nineteenth century it was Asia that provided planters with a source of bound labor. Also unlike the earlier episode, in which bound immigrants moved almost entirely to British America, the receiving areas of the nineteenth-century migration were more diverse, ranging over a very wide area chiefly in the Americas. Table 1 summarizes the major streams among the nineteenth-century indentured migrations. It shows that India was the major country of origin, with more than one and one-half million emigrants, followed by China, with more than half a million, and Japan, with sixty-five thousand.

There were a number of other differences besides race between the two episodes of indentured servitude. As noted above, one basic difference was racial: the first episode involved Europeans, while the second was dominated by Asians. The skill composition of the immigrants also differed. Although some of the European servants of the first episode performed unskilled labor on large plantations, particularly early in the American colonial period, over time the role of indentured labor changed and the European servants increasingly performed skilled work, often on large plantations based on unskilled slave labor. In contrast, the Asians of the second episode almost all performed unskilled work on large plantations, often growing the same crops previously produced by slaves. Another difference involved rates of return migration. In the first episode virtually all of the former servants remained overseas; most of them indentured themselves precisely because they wished to migrate permanently to America but were unable to afford the cost of passage from their own savings. The second episode saw significantly higher rates of repatriation. This was again anticipated at the outset, as in many cases the original indenture agreement guaranteed free return passage for ser-

TABLE 1. *Major Flows of Indentured Labor during the Nineteenth and Twentieth Centuries*

Source	Destination	Dates	Number (thousands)
India	British Guiana	1838–1918	239
	Trinidad	1838–1918	144
	Other British Caribbean	1838–1918	47
	Mauritius	1834–1910	452
	French Caribbean	1853–1885	80
	Réunion	1826–1882	87
	Suriname	1873–1916	34
	Fiji	1878–1917	61
	Natal	1860–1912	152
	Malaya	1844–1910	250
China	British Guiana	1852–1879	14
	Trinidad	1852–1865	3
	Peru	1849–1874	90
	Cuba	1848–1874	125
	Hawaii	1865–1899	34
	California	1852–1884	300
Japan	Hawaii	1868–1899	65
Africa	Caribbean	1834–1867	58
	Réunion	1848–1861	34
United Kingdom	Australia	1788–1868	162

Source: Adapted from Stanley L. Engerman, "Servants to Slaves to Servants: Contract Labor and European Expansion," in *Colonialism and Migration,* edited by P. C. Emmer (Dordrecht: Martinus Nijhoff, 1986), Table 2.

Note: The migration from the United Kingdom to Australia consisted of convicts, sentenced involuntarily to servitude. The other migrations listed all appear to have involved forms of contract labor, in which migrants voluntarily signed labor contracts, either prior to migration or at their destinations.

vants at the end of their terms. Although many Asians chose to remain overseas after servitude, the fact that they had the option of returning to their original homelands often led to the perception of servants in the second episode as sojourners rather than as settlers.

The first episode moved migrants from some of the world's wealthiest nations to areas of recent settlement that were generally undergoing rapid economic growth. These European migrants were drawn from a broad cross-section of the populations of their countries of origin, and many gained considerable prosperity after completing their terms of servitude. In the second episode, mi-

grants moved from some of the world's poorest nations to other poor areas. These Asian migrants were drawn chiefly from among the poorer members of their countries of origin, and the poverty of the receiving areas meant that their chances for economic improvement after servitude were often quite circumscribed.

One basic similarity between the two episodes lay in their demographic composition. Few of the indentured migrants traveled in families, and a substantial majority of indentured servants in both episodes were males in their teens or twenties. These characteristics emphasize the fact that indentured servitude was a form of labor migration that, with few exceptions, a person entered only if there was an immediate demand for that individual's labor.

Recent quantitative research on indentured servitude during the first episode has produced new insights into the economics of the system. It has long been known that the duration of the term of indenture varied considerably across servants, from a normal minimum of four years to as long as ten or more years, yet no systematic explanation for this variation had been given. An economic analysis begins with the observation that all servants incurred debts of similar value in emigrating—principally the cost of passage to America—while in exchange they sold claims on their future labor to repay these debts. Servants whose labor was more valuable could repay their debts more quickly, so the economic analysis predicts that any characteristics that raised their expected productivity in the colonies would shorten their terms. Statistical analysis of surviving collections of servant contracts confirms this prediction. Thus older servants tended to receive shorter terms than younger ones; and those who had skilled occupations recorded on their contracts and who were literate enough to sign their contracts received shorter terms than the unskilled and illiterate. Servants who worked in the West Indies received shorter terms than those bound for the North American mainland. Mortality rates were generally higher in the islands than on the mainland, the work of cultivating sugar was harsh, and the small, densely populated islands offered relatively little opportunity for former servants to obtain land of their own after completing their terms, so servants had to be given an added inducement to travel to these less desirable destinations.

Entry into an indenture involved a substantial sacrifice of freedom for a European migrant. In colonial America, by law a master normally had an unrestricted legal right to determine the work his servant was to do. Servants' living conditions were similarly controlled by their masters, and servants could marry during their terms only with their masters' permission. The treatment of servants varied considerably, depending on factors including the attitudes of their masters, the sizes of the plantations they worked on, the kind of work they did, and their region of destination. Servants on small farms in the early colonial period might live under the same relatively meager conditions as the families of their masters, whereas skilled servants on large plantations in the eighteenth century were often paid wages and treated substantially better than the slaves who made up the bulk of their masters' labor forces.

Unlike slaves, servants in colonial English America had important basic legal rights. Servants could bring suit in colonial courts, their testimony was accepted on the same basis as that of free men, and they were legally entitled to hold property. Colonial laws protected servants from excessive corporal punishment, and masters who killed their servants could be tried for murder, although masters were permitted considerable latitude in beating their servants.

European servants normally appear to have been provided for and treated decently by their masters, in large part because their labor was a valuable asset. Nonetheless, servants had little control over their conditions of work during the years of their terms, and their ability to make decisions about most aspects of their lives in that time was severely limited. At the same time, one of the major consequences of the settlement of North America, and the use of the continent's natural resources, was the promise of genuine economic opportunity for workers. This promise provided an attraction sufficiently powerful to encourage hundreds of thousands of prospective settlers from Europe to enter indentures during the first episode of servitude, voluntarily giving up much of their freedom for a term of years in order to improve their economic and social condition in the New World.

Many controversies still surround the second episode of indentured servitude. Some of its features are clear. Asian servants in the nineteenth century were typically bound for five-year terms, to serve on specific plantations, with severe restrictions on their physical mobility. Breach of these contracts by the workers was punishable by criminal sanctions, including fines and imprisonment. Local colonial governments were often actively involved in the recruitment and distribution of indentured workers; in a number of cases governments actually subsidized the costs of transporting the workers. The economic importance of the system was considerable in a number of places; the sugar plantations of Trinidad and British Guiana, for example, came to depend almost exclusively on indentured immigrant labor during the second half of the nineteenth century.

The persistent controversies that arose almost from the beginning of the second episode of servitude, and that continue today in historical debates, concern the treatment of the workers and the extent to which the indenture system offered them genuine opportunities eventually to improve their condition. There is general agreement that the system was harsher, and prospects for improvement poorer, than for the Europeans in the first episode of servitude. Some contemporaries and later historians have claimed that it was radically different and have condemned the servitude of the Asians as a thinly disguised revival of slavery. These critics have pointed to a variety of abuses to which the Asians were subjected, both legally—with severe laws governing absenteeism, vagrancy, and insufficient work—and illegally, in the form of harassment by vicious masters. Yet other observers have defended the system as a boon to the Asian workers. Voluntary reindenture at the end of their terms was common among the migrants, suggesting that many Asians judged the system to be beneficial to them. Observers in the West Indies also pointed out that the failure of the great majority of Indians to take advantage of their legal right to return to India at the end of their terms implied that they considered their lives in the islands preferable to those they had led in Asia. Many former servants are also known to have prospered economically in their new places of residence.

Systematic quantitative evidence is needed to resolve this debate and to answer such questions as whether the Asians' life expectancies were reduced by their migration, and what the typical economic accomplishments of former servants were in the Americas. This second episode of servitude clearly produced great hardships for some servants and resulted in great gains for others. How many suffered the extreme hardships, and how many enjoyed the successes, remain unresolved questions. This dramatic episode, in which hundreds of thousands of Asian laborers entered societies populated by small numbers of white plantation-owners and large numbers of black freedmen, will certainly attract more study aimed at providing systematic answers to these and other questions about this system of bound labor, which like the first episode lay in a number of respects between slavery and free labor.

[See also Forced Labor, overview article.]

BIBLIOGRAPHY

Engerman, Stanley L. "Servants to Slaves to Servants: Contract Labor and European Expansion." In Colonialism and Migration: Indentured Labour Before and After Slavery, edited by P. C. Emmer. Dordrecht: Martinus Nijhoff, 1986.

Galenson, David W. White Servitude in Colonial America: An Economic Analysis. New York: Cambridge University Press, 1981.

Look Lai, Walton. Indentured Labor, Caribbean Sugar: Chinese and Indian Migrants to the British West Indies, 1838–1918. Baltimore: Johns Hopkins University Press, 1993.

Smith, Abbot Emerson. Colonists in Bondage: White Servitude and Convict Labor in America, 1607–1776. Chapel Hill: University of North Carolina Press, 1947.

Tinker, Hugh. A New System of Slavery: The Export of Indian Labour Overseas, 1830–1920. London and New York: Oxford University Press, 1974.

—DAVID W. GALENSON

INDUSTRIAL SLAVERY. From the colonial era until the end of the Civil War, slave labor was engaged in almost every aspect of industrial activity in the U.S. South. Robert Starobin (1970) estimates that between one hundred sixty thousand and two hundred thousand slaves—approximately 5 percent of the South's slave population—worked in industry during the decade of the 1850s. They filled an amazingly broad range of occupations: construction laborers, ironworkers, miners, woodchoppers, coopers, turpentine hands, tanners, millers, sugar refiners, shipbuilders, and salt and chemical workers, and they labored in tobacco, hemp, and textile factories. Many of the workers who ran the South's transportation system—rafters, canal-boat hands, railroad, steamboat, and turnpike laborers—were slaves, and the blacksmith, carpenter, and harness shops vital to plantation operations were usually staffed by slave artisans.

Industrial work forces were predominately male and were generally composed of a mix of slaves owned by the employer and other slave workers hired for temporary service, usually a year. A well-developed hiring market existed in the nineteenth century, particularly in the upper South. Counties in the Virginia Tidewater and Piedmont, for example, held "hiring days" in late December and early January during which ironmasters, tobacco-factory owners, coal- and gold-mining interests, railroad and canal contractors, and local farmers competed to secure additional slave labor for the coming year.

Historians have debated whether slaves employed at industrial establishments, particularly the hirelings, were subjected to added hardship and abuse. Some scholars have argued that working conditions were often dangerous and that the removal of the hired slave from the immediate control of his owner placed this laborer in a situation where he could be, and frequently was, subjected to a harsh work regimen and deprived of adequate food, clothing, and shelter; employers seeking to minimize cost and maximize production and profit, these investigators maintain, lacked the slave-owner's interest in protecting his valuable human property. Other historians have pointed to the control hired slaves frequently exercised over where and for whom they would work, as well as the necessity of employers' cultivating a good repu-

tation among both owners and slaves in order to secure an adequate labor force year after year. Those who claim that industrial employment was often an attractive option for slaves also emphasize the opportunity it gave most workers to earn compensation for themselves.

Almost all industrial slaves worked on a task basis. Forgemen in the Virginia iron district were required to hammer out a "journey" of 560 pounds of bar iron per day; choppers who provided the wood for the charcoal that ran the South's blast furnaces and forges had to cut nine cords per week; coopers in the Kanawha salt district in western Virginia had to assemble seven barrels a day; turpentine hands worked tasks composed of half-acre squares in the pine forests of North Carolina. Tanners, shinglemakers, tobacco-factory hands, chemical workers, and many others worked on a task basis. Stealey (1993) quotes one Kanawha salt manufacturer who reported in 1854, "We operate a furnace by task work, a coal digger has a prescribed quantity of coal to dig, a hauler, a salt packer a prescribed quantity to pack, and engineer, and kettle tender a certain time to be on watch." Throughout Southern industry tasks were long-established by custom and seem to have been universally recognized by both employer and slave. They were set at a level that an average worker could reach by putting in a day or week of steady labor.

Slaves who exceeded their tasks were paid for their "overwork," as it was usually called, in cash, goods, or a combination of the two. Industrial slaves could also make additional sums by working nights, Sundays, and holidays, and slaves who held supervisory positions were often paid an "allowance" (which amounted to a regular wage) for carrying out their duties. Slaves' earnings could reach impressive levels. Sam Williams, a skilled slave ironworker, made as much as one hundred dollars per year in the 1850s at Buffalo Forge near Lexington, Virginia, and held a savings account in a Lexington bank. This was an exceptional case, but it illustrates an important aspect of the South's industrial slave system: although force and coercion were the cement that held slavery together, employers clearly used overwork payments to try to motivate their slave laborers to work for rather than against their interests. A Tennessee turnpike company even went so far as to refer to the payments it made to its slave workers as "Stimulant & Reward money."

The earnings and expenditures of industrial slaves were recorded in ledgers kept by their employers, and a number of these manuscript volumes have survived. They offer an extraordinary glimpse into the lives of these workers. Their purchases of articles like fine clothing, of "luxury" items like coffee, flour, sugar, and tobacco, their cash withdrawals at Christmas and the purchase of gifts for their parents, wives, and children all tell us a great deal about their priorities and choices. Clearly the "overwork" system afforded these men access to resources they could not normally control as agricultural workers, and this may have been a major reason why many slaves seem to have been willing to work for industrial employers. The hazards of their jobs and, for hired slaves, the separation from their families (and their owners) were balanced against the chance to earn compensation for themselves. It is this same tradeoff that historians seek to measure when they debate the nature of industrial slavery in the old South.

[See also Occupational Mobility; Occupations; United States, article on The South; and Urban Slavery.]

BIBLIOGRAPHY

Dew, Charles B. *Bond of Iron: Master and Slave at Buffalo Forge.* New York: W. W. Norton, 1994.

Lewis, Ronald L. *Coal, Iron, and Slaves: Industrial Slavery in Maryland and Virginia, 1715–1865.* Westport, Conn.: Greenwood Press, 1979.

Outland, Robert B., III. "Slavery, Work, and the Geography of the North Carolina Naval Stores Industry, 1835–1860." *Journal of Southern History* 62 (1996): 27–56.

Starobin, Robert S. *Industrial Slavery in the Old South.* New York and Oxford: Oxford University Press, 1970.

Stealey, John E., III. *The Antebellum Kanawha Salt Business and Western Markets.* Lexington: University Press of Kentucky, 1993.

Whitman, T. Stephen. "Industrial Slavery at the Margin: The Maryland Chemical Works." *Journal of Southern History* 59 (1993): 31–62.

—CHARLES B. DEW

KOREA. In the hierarchical structure of Korean society the "Basic people" (*ch'ŏmin*), the majority of whom were slaves (*nobi*), constituted the bottom layer. Although slavery in Korea is documented from earliest times, its origin is uncertain. Over time, various categories of people were enslaved: prisoners of war captured during the unification wars (sixth and seventh centuries CE) and their descendants, peasants uprooted during dynastic change, and criminals. It was also common for individuals to offer themselves for enslavement to escape dire poverty or to evade taxation. The slaves eventually formed a separate and homogeneous social class, membership in which became hereditary. Uncommon in the context of worldwide slavery is the fact that Korean slaves were ethnically indistinguishable from their enslavers.

Throughout history Korea's ruling class was a hereditary aristocracy (*yangban*) who dominated the two lower classes of commoners (*p'yŏngmin*) and slaves. Status was determined exclusively on the basis of social criteria. Whereas the commoners had to pay taxes, contribute corvée labor, and serve in the military, the slaves were owned by the royal house, government agencies, and private owners and worked under an officially recognized system of coercion and exploitation. Ownership of slaves was not merely of economic significance; it was also an indispensable concomitant of aristocratic status.

Legally, slaves were property. They could be bought, sold, inherited, and given as gifts or bribes. No law, however, prevented slaves from possessing their own property, dwellings, and utensils; rarely, a slave might own land or even other slaves. Slave status was hereditary and derived principally from the mother's status (matrifilial law), regardless of the father's status. A slave's social identity did not arise from membership in a recognized descent group, rather, the slave was perceived as "kinless," lacking antecedents as well as collateral kin. For this reason, the slave did not have a surname (*sŏng*), and was known only by a natal name, often with a pejorative meaning. Despite these strictures, however, most slaves lived for most of their lives with other family members, although a slave family was always threatened by division through sale or inheritance.

Although intermarriage with the commoner population was discouraged, and marriages of male slaves with commoner women were specifically prohibited, mixed marriages were not rare. Mixed offspring, whose status was in principle determined by their mother's status, still posed a problem; their status was manipulated by the government according to whether the commoner population or the slave population needed to be increased. When slave women were made the concubines of elite men, the resulting offspring never gained elite status, but after a long process of "social purification," they eventually were granted commoner status.

Slavery was enormously important economically. Slaves were attached to either private or public owners. Called the "hands and feet" of the elite, private slaves (*sa nobi*) were not subject to state control and were thus exempt from military service, taxes, and corvée labor. They were the actual producers of elite wealth. Individual holdings could range from less than a dozen to many hundreds of slaves. Some of these slaves (*solgŏ nobi*) were attached to their masters' households as servants and cultivators of nearby land. Other, nonresident slaves (*oegŏ nobi*) lived apart and cultivated their masters' far-off landed property or guarded ancestral grave sites. The latter were more independent and, after paying their dues, at times even managed to produce some surplus for themselves.

Public slaves (*kong nobi*) were assigned to the royal palaces and the central and local government agencies. Laboring in the capital's workshops, they produced items needed in government offices and the royal palaces. Within the palaces, male slaves functioned as attendants and performed all kinds of menial functions; their female counterparts engaged in needlework and staffed the kitchens. Outside the capital, public slaves cultivated local government land or palace land. They were also put to work in the many government-supervised potteries; it was slave labor that produced the famous Koryŏ porcelain.

During the Koryŏ period (918–1392) Buddhist monasteries kept large contingents of slaves, often ranging in the thousands, who not only cultivated the vast temple lands but also worked in the monastic workshops, producing such commodities as paper and oil. Large numbers of these slaves were expropriated at the beginning of the Chosŏn (or Yi) dynasty (1392–1910) and distributed among government agencies. Others were given as gifts to meritorious subjects (*kongsin*) who had supported the new dynastic venture.

According to the law, slaves under fifteen and over sixty years of age were not to be put to work and the seriously ill, permanently disabled, and parents of three or more children were exempted from work. They were provided with daily sustenance. Delinquent slaves were punished like commoners for crimes that were not status-related. A slave-owner was held responsible for the upkeep and reasonable wellbeing of his slaves, but he was not held accountable for the death of a slave. A slave had no legal recourse against a master. Private slaves were registered in their masters' household registers (*hojŏk*), which were revised every three years. Public slaves were also registered. A Slave Office was in charge of general slave affairs.

Slaves were distinguishable from commoners by their different (often skimpy) clothing, but they were otherwise fully integrated into society. Although not despised as impure, they were considered morally depraved and unreliable, given to scheming against their masters. In Korea slavery never became a moral issue; occasionally, however, particularly in the second half of the Chosŏn period (eighteenth century), the elite's reliance on slave labor was criticized. The slaves never reacted against their fate in organized opposition. Eight major slave rebellions took place from 1182 to 1232, but none of them was motivated by economic deprivation; rather, the reflected general social unrest and violence prevalent at that time.

Although never large in scale, manumission was a way out of slavery. A private master, grateful for a slave's personal services, might release him or her. With accumulated wealth, slaves might buy their own release (a method that gained currency during the second half of the Chosŏn period). In addition, the government sometimes rewarded a courageous slave for valor in battle by granting him commoner status. In each case, only an individual slave, and not his whole family, was released from base status; manumission was not transferable to the next generation. It was feared that a manumitted slave would turn against his former master.

In the later Chosŏn period (eighteenth and nineteenth centuries), economic change and diversification opened new opportunities, and many slaves simply ran away. No retrieval policies brought the fugitives back, although their names continued to be recorded as their masters' inheritable property. In many areas, where the ratio of labor to land meant slavery was unprofitable, it declined. In particular, government slaves were gradually replaced by hired laborers. In 1801 public slavery was abolished, but private slavery endured, probably because of its high prestige value. Even after it was officially outlawed in 1894, private slavery survived into the twentieth century.

For lack of statistical data, it is impossible to calculate the extent of the enslaved population, but rough estimates suggest that at the beginning of the fifteenth century, slaves constituted about 30 percent of the total population. Whatever the exact figures, compared to China or Japan, slavery in Korea played a much more vital role in the social and economic life of the country; and, although the slave was not marginalized by a caste ideology, his status carried with it an indelible stigma.

BIBLIOGRAPHY

Despite the importance of the topic, no Western-language work deals comprehensively with the subject.

Chŏn, Hyŏng-t'aek. *Chosŏn hugi nobi sinbun yŏn'gu* (Study of the Social Status of Slaves in Late Chosŏn). Seoul: Ilchogak, 1989.

Hong, Sŭng-gi. *Koryŏ kwijok sahoe wa nobi* (Koryŏ's Aristocracy and Slaves). Seoul: Ilchogak, 1983.

Salem, Ellen. "Slavery in Medieval Korea." Ph.D. diss., Columbia University, 1978.

—MARTINA DEUCHLER

LAW. [*This entry comprises four articles that discuss various legal codifications of slavery and servitude in the ancient and modern worlds:*

> Roman Law
>
> Islamic Law
>
> Latin American Law
>
> United States Law

For further discussion of particular reactions engendered by these various statuses, see Revolts.]

Roman Law

Rome of the republic and early empire was one of the few states ever to have an economy based firmly on slavery. The best modern estimates find that slaves constituted around one-third of the population of Italy.

Roman slavery was not racially defined. Anyone could be enslaved who was captured in a just (properly declared) war or who was born to a slave mother. Enormous numbers of prisoners of war were taken, and they became the property of the state or of victorious generals until they were sold to an individual. In typical legal reasoning, a Roman captured in war by an enemy became a slave of the enemy and lost his Roman citizenship. Entering slave status through birth to a slave mother was also frequent, but the rule emerged that if a slave woman was free at any time between conception and birth, her child was born free. The axiom that a Roman could not be a slave to a Roman was not entirely true, and the exceptions are instructive: a citizen who did not enroll on the census (so as to avoid military service) was enslaved; so was a person over age twenty-five who had himself fraudulently sold as a slave in order to gain part of the purchase price. (In this confidence trick, shortly after the sale a friend would come forward and prove that the "slave" was really free.) Although the rules varied from time to time, in the early empire a free woman who cohabited with another's slave and did not desist after notice from his owner became a slave herself.

Despite the social and economic importance of slavery, the Roman authorities took little interest in developing the law in this area and allowed it to grow through the activity of the jurists. Ambiguities were thus established. For some legal purposes slaves were treated as persons, and their position in respect to the master was akin to that of persons subject to paternal power; for other purposes they were treated as property, and their position was akin to that of cattle. For example, as property they were classified like cattle among those important things called *res mancipi,* and ownership could only be transferred by the formal act of *mancipatio* or by the apparent lawsuit called *in iure cessio.* Their produce, whether through work, gifts made them, or offspring they had, belonged to their owner. Slaves could own nothing.

In the last regard, slaves were also treated in the same way as some persons, like sons (of any age) and daughters in the power of the head of the family, the eldest surviving male ancestor. It was common for this head of the family to allow sons and slaves a private fund called the *peculium,* which they administered as if it were their own, though always within limits set by the head of the family. Technically it belonged to the master, but for certain purposes it was treated as a fund apart; for instance, a slave might be freed by will with a legacy of his *peculium,* and then the heir could not subtract from the *peculium.* Within the institution of slavery the *peculium* had a practical function. A master could agree with a slave to let him buy his freedom with his *peculium* when he had acquired a particular amount. The agreement was without legal force, but it could make the slave more obedient and industrious in order to win his freedom, and the owner could then use the *peculium* to buy a replacement.

A slave's humanity, and the similarity of his or her legal position to that of a child, is most clearly seen in the realm of contract and delict (tort). In early law, if a slave entered a contract with a third-party outsider, the third party was bound by the contract to the slave's owner, but the owner was under no liability to the third; nor could the slave be sued at private law, because he had no legal standing. This was obviously unsatisfactory even for the owner, because under such conditions no one would trade with the slave, and so modifications were made to the law. Thus, by the *actio de peculio et de in rem vesso,* the owner was liable under the contract up to the amount in the slave's *peculium,* and to the extent he had benefited from the contract. When the owner had authorized the third party to make the contract with the slave, he was fully liable on the contract by the *actio quod iussu.* Where a slave traded with his *peculium* with the knowledge of his owner, a creditor could demand that the owner divide the *peculium* or the relevant part of it among the creditors.

When a slave committed a delict such as damage to another's property or theft (which was treated as a private wrong rather than a crime), the owner could be sued and was liable to pay damages on the scale that would have applied if the owner had been the wrongdoer. In an exception, the owner could choose to surrender to the plaintiff the slave (or child) instead, provided the owner had not somehow been at fault. This surrender (termed *noxal*) is in effect an early form of limited liability.

Because slaves had no legal personality, they could not marry and so had no legally recognized family ties. However, ties of blood were given legal recognition if the slave were freed. Thus, for example, a freed slave woman could not marry her natural father. During the republic and into the empire there were no legal restrictions on an owner's punishing or ill-treating a slave, but limitations to reasonable punishment came to be imposed by law, and Emperor Antonius Pius declared the deliberate killing of a slave by the owner to be murder. These restrictions probably had little practical impact, because slaves and freed persons could not testify against their owner or former owner. No surviving legal text mentions sexual abuse of a slave, male or female, child or adult, by the owner. Such matters were of no concern to the law.

Christianity brought no improvement to the legal position of slaves. Indeed, it was Christian emperors who ordered that if slaves or freed persons denounced their master for any crime other than treason, they would be burned to death or crucified, and any written evidence would be burned unread.

The state interfered very little with an owner's control over slaves. Thus slaves could be taught to read and allowed to practice any lawful religion or to live far away from the owner. The practical position of a slave could range from being a chained field hand to being a business manager, ship's captain, actor, or medical doctor. Most doctors, in fact, were slaves or freedmen. Although the law was the same for all slaves in practice it affected different groups in quite different ways.

For slaves who were privileged by their training or by being close to their owner, a great incentive to good behavior was the prospect of freedom. Manumission was very common, and in general the state imposed almost no restrictions on owners freeing slaves. This may seem surprising because the freeing of slaves (by the three main ways, and in the later empire by any way) conferred Roman citizenship as well as freedom. More surprising still, the state played almost no role in developing the law of manumission.

The earliest form of freeing a slave, *manumissio vindicta,* was a fictitious lawsuit. An owner who wished to free a slave would have a friend bring an action against his claiming that the slave was free; the owner put up no defense, and the judge declared the slave free. This development occurred simply because individuals created a dodge and the state acquiesced. In *manumissio censu,* the master allowed the slave, when the census was taken, to enroll himself as if he were a free citizen. The censor made no objection, and the slave became free and a citizen.

The third mode was manumission by will. The master declared the slave free and, subject to any condition in the will, the slave automatically became free and a citizen on the testator's death. This was the only way in which a slave could be conditionally freed: manumission could be postponed until a certain date or event, or until the slave fulfilled some condition. In the interim, the heir was not allowed to do anything that would obstruct the slave's freedom.

Emperor Augustus imposed restrictions on manumission. An owner could free by will only a proportion of slaves, which varied according to the number he owned. The restriction applied only to manumission by will. Augustus also enacted that an owner under age twenty could free only slaves in particular categories. These categories were those slaves most likely to be freed in any event: blood relatives, a general business agent, or a woman the owner wanted to marry.

[*See also* Europe, *article on* Ancient World; *and* Manumission.]

BIBLIOGRAPHY

Buckland, W. W. *The Roman Law of Slavery.* Cambridge: Cambridge University Press, 1908.

Watson, Alan. *Roman Slave Law.* Baltimore: Johns Hopkins University Press, 1987.

—ALAN WATSON

Islamic Law

Slavery was practiced in Arabia at the time of the rise of Islam. Although most captives in intertribal wars in Arabia were ransomed, some were probably enslaved. The prophet Muḥammad and his Companions are known to have owned slaves, most of whom were "Ethiopians" (from the lands on the western shore of the Red Sea). The Qur'ān contains numerous references to slaves, calling them "those whom your right hands possess," particularly in regard to concubines, or "necks" (*riqāb*), common slaves freed in expiation or as an act of charity. The principal themes of the Qur'ān in regard to slaves are kind treatment of those possessed and manumission. There is no clear statement about the conditions under which a person may be enslaved, or the process involved. These matters and the many questions concerning the treatment of slaves, their rights and disabilities, the freeing of slaves, and post-manumission clientship, were elaborated by jurists during the third and fourth centuries of Islam (roughly, the ninth and tenth centuries CE, taking their authority from statements of practices attributed to the prophet Muḥammad (*ḥadīth*), the alleged practice of the early Muslim community of Medina, and judgments delivered by early judges and exponents of the law (*fuqahā'*).

It is not possible to deal in this limited space with the various laws concerning slavery in all of the four Sunnī law schools, in Shī'a law, and in Ibāḍī law. Most of what follows, therefore, is based on the rulings of the Mālikī law school, the school with the most elaborated law on slavery, and the one most widely followed in Africa, the continent that produced the majority of slaves over the ages, and a region where slave-ownership was also common. It should be borne in mind that in theory there was no connection between slave status and ethnic origin or skin color. The sole legitimate reason for a Muslim to enslave another human being was that the person enslaved was at the time a non-Muslim (*kāfir*) who had been captured in the course of a *jihād* (battle for the extension of the political domain of Islam), being a member of a group that had rejected peaceful incorporation into the Islamic body politic. Over the centuries Muslims took as slaves not only persons from sub-Saharan Africa, but also from Europe, the Caucasus, Central Asia, India, and elsewhere.

Technically, slavery in Islamic law is a temporary state of legal incapacitation (*ḥajr*). The natural or original state of human beings is freedom, and it is to be presumed that a person is free if it cannot be shown that he or she has been enslaved and has not been freed. The slave's legal incapacitation was not total, although the ability to exercise rights was largely dependent on the owner's good will. Thus, for example, a slave could marry, earn an independent income, or purchase his or her freedom, but only with the owner's permission. The temporary nature of the incapacitation was underscored by legal provisions for emancipation, as well as by the fact that freed slaves immediately assumed all the rights and obligations (religious and otherwise) of a freeborn Muslim. While being a non-Muslim was a condition for enslavement, conversion to Islam did not have freedom as its concomitant. Only a specific act on the part of the owner during his or her lifetime, or upon his or her death by an implicit act, rendered a slave free.

A number of problems arose from the theory that enslavement was lawful only as the product of a *jihād*. The first was the problem of who was authorized to undertake a *jihād*. In theory, this could be undertaken only by a caliph or his lawful deputy. In practice, in Africa at any rate, this rule was observed only in the breach; local African Muslim leaders assumed many of the prerogatives and even the title of caliph ("commander of the Faithful"), following the demise of the 'Abbāsid caliphate. The second problem revolved around the definition of a Muslim. A theoretical literature was developed on what beliefs, utterances, or acts were indicative of "unbelief" (*kufr*), although these were designed to indict individuals rather than groups. In West Africa it was argued that the legal status of a land corresponded to the religious status of its ruler; thus a land ruled by a non-Muslim was *ipso facto* a land of unbelief, against which a *jihād* could be undertaken and prisoners enslaved. The faith or infidelity of the ruler could be judged by competent scholars. This left the door open to abuse and slave-raiding for profit.

The often dubious legality of the origin of slaves raised questions in the minds of purchasers. Aḥmad Bābā of Timbuktu (d. 1627) wrote replies to inquirers in the Saharan oasis of Tuwat and in southern Morocco, advising them how to determine which slaves brought from West Africa might have reasonable claims to being free Muslims. He reviewed the various opinions, including some that gave the benefit of the doubt to the claimant of free status. His own approach was to establish an ethnography of Islam in the region, detailing which peoples were wholly Muslim, which were non-Muslim, and which were only partially or shallowly islamized. On this basis it would be established who might lawfully be owned. The problem endured, however. A nineteenth-century Moroccan writer, the historian al-Nāṣirī, in a passionate attack on the indiscriminate enslavement of black Africans, wrote, "The basic human condition is freedom and absence of any reason for being enslaved. Those who put the case for non-freedom are making a claim in opposition to the basic principle." Such, however, was not the general view.

Legally, a slave was a piece of property to be bought, sold, exchanged, hired, given away, or inherited. Ownership was absolute at the moment of acquisition, unless conditions were laid down; otherwise, the slave's property and any offspring a female slave might give birth to, other than children fathered by her owner, belonged to the owner. A male owner had the unrestricted right of concubinage with his female slaves, but not with those of his wives. Unlike free wives in a polygamous household, who had nights allotted to them on a rotational basis, concubines had no specific time allotted to them. The child of an owner with one of his female slaves was free, on the principle that parenthood and slavery are incompatible. Similarly, one could not own either of one's parents or any other ascending or descending kin. The slave mother of a free child (*umm al-walad*) could not be disposed of in any manner and was automatically free on her owner's death. When a female slave was purchased, it was the buyer's obligation to have her placed in a secure environment until she had menstruated, in order to avoid possible paternity claims. A buyer had the option of returning a slave if a pre-existing fault in the slave were detected within three days, a condition applicable to all goods purchased. Such faults might include undetected illnesses, lack of urinary retention, or in the case of a female destined for concubinage, snoring or vaginal blockage inhibiting intercourse.

The principle of absolute ownership could subsequently be modified in a number of ways. The case of the slave mother of a free child is a clear example: she was thereby granted conditional freedom. She also had security of domicile and maintenance, and, since she was not married to the owner, she could not be divorced. A second case in which absolute ownership was mitigated was that of the *muddabar(a)*, the male or female slave who was promised freedom on the owner's death. This was a unilateral, unconditional promise of freedom, embodied in a document, thereafter the slave could not be disposed of, although the owner might continue to enjoy the slave's services, including the sexual services of a female. When the owner died, the value of the slave was deducted from the one-third of his estate available for bequests before proceeding to the fixed division of the balance among the legal heirs, as enumerated in the Qur'ān.

A slave might also be promised freedom after payment of an agreed sum over a specified period of time. This procedure was called *kitāba*, "by written contract." In such a case he or she was permitted to accumulate money in his or her own right so as to pay the agreed sum in installments. If the slave defaulted on the installments, he or she became a simple slave again, and the owner was allowed to retain whatever installments had been paid. However, if the slave refused to acknowledge insolvency, only the civil authority had the power to do so unilaterally, and had first to allow him or her a respite in which to obtain funds. In the case of a female slave, the owner was not allowed to have sexual relations with her once such a contract had been drawn up, nor might she (or a male slave in the same situation) be sold, though the contract itself could be sold. When the last payment had been made (and it was recommended that the owner forego this), the slave was automatically free. If the owner died before the contract had been completed, the value of the slave was deducted from the value of the total estate before bequests were made and before inheritance shares had been apportioned. If the slave died before paying for his or her freedom, the owner could recoup this from the slave's estate, if it was sufficient, or from the slave's children if they had earning capacity; if they were minors and could not pay, they again became slaves of the former; if payments were completed, they too were free.

Another sort of quasi-freedom was possible, usually but not necessarily predicated on eventual manumission. Under this arrangement, an owner could grant a slave the right to undertake certain specified business dealings on his behalf. The slave was then said to be "authorized" (*ma'dhūn*) and had a large measure of freedom in dealing with third parties. If he incurred debts that he could not pay, they were his responsibility. Mālikīs, followed by Shādi'īs, postponed payment of such debts until the slave obtained funds, even after being freed, while others proposed recovering the debts on the physical person of the slave, by his being sold. This indicates the ambiguous situation of the authorized slave, because although his debt is recognized as his own, it is his owner who in fact pays the debt through selling the slave.

Slaves could be owned by both men and women, since Islamic law granted women property rights. Ownership of a slave could be shared, a situation that arose when the cost of purchasing a whole slave was too great for one person, or when the strict laws of inheritance division made this necessary. Joint ownership of a female slave by males meant that neither owner could take her as a concubine. If two or more persons had a share in a slave and one of them freed his share, the co-

owners might either free their shares simultaneously, or, if not, the one who had first freed his share had to pay the others the value of their shares so that the slave became entirely free. If a man freed only a part of his slave (such as a hand or leg), he was compelled to free the rest. If an owner intentionally mutilated a slave, the slave would be freed by judicial order, unless the owner was feebleminded, a protected person (*dhimmī*, referring mainly to Jews and Christians), or another slave. In Mālikī law only, a slave could own a slave, even though technically all of a slave's property was owned by the slave's owner and could be confiscated at any time. Jews and Christians living under Islamic law could likewise own slaves, though not slaves who had converted to Islam.

Slaves could be freed at any time for pious reasons, for personal reasons, or in expiation of a sin, such as breaking an oath or unintentional homicide. Slaves freed in expiation could not be among those already granted provisional freedom. Freeing a slave was considered to bring reward from God, as a typical formula makes clear: "So-and-so has granted his slave freedom for the sake of God the Generous and in hope of His mighty reward. He has made him one with the free Muslims, partaking of both their privileges and their responsibilities. May God free from the fire of Hell a limb corresponding to the limb set free [of his slave], even his genitals for the genitals [of the slave]."

A slave was permitted to marry with the permission of his or her master. In the Mālikī school, a male slave could have up to four wives concomitantly, but in other schools only two. A female slave who married either another slave or a free man remained the property of her owner, as did her child. She could not marry her owner unless she were freed, because marriage and conjugality are incompatible. The adult Muslim slave was expected to observe the obligatory practices of the faith, such as prayer and fasting; however, he did not have to pay the alms-tax (*zakāt*), since he owned nothing. He could perform the communal Friday prayer or the pilgrimage to Mecca only with his owner's permission. A male slave could lead in prayer, but it was disapproved for him to serve in this capacity as an official salaried imam. He could not hold other religious offices, such as a judgeship, but he might hold civil office, such as a provincial governorship, or any military rank. Prescribed punishments were in general only half of those for free persons, for instance in the cases of fornication and slander, but for theft and apostasy they were the same as those for free persons. If a slave killed another, the owner had the choice of surrendering him for retaliation to the kin of the slain person or paying blood money (*diya*), in the case of a free victim; if the victim was a slave, the blood money went to the victim's owner. If a free man killed a slave, there was no retaliation; the only option was payment of blood money to the victim's owner. A slave's testimony was not acceptable in court, except in the Ḥanbalī school, and then only for less serious offenses.

To ensure the public observance of the law and uphold morality was the province of the *muḥtasib,* an inspector of markets and public places and censor of public morals. It was his task to oversee the slave market and to ensure, among other things, that slave women were not clandestinely prostituted by slave-dealers under the cover of the law governing return of commodities with pre-existing faults; that proper information was made available to buyers to prevent the sale of free persons; and that any conditions attaching to a slave for sale were known. It was also his duty to see that slaves were not worked beyond their capacity, and that they were allowed periods of rest during the heat of the day. A slave could complain to the *muḥtasib* if he or she were inadequately clothed or fed.

When a slave received his or her document of manumission, it was not quite the end of the story in a legal sense (or, for the most part, in a social sense). Freed slaves remained in clientship (*walāʾ*) to the one who freed them for the rest of their lives, and in theory their descendants remained so in perpetuity; such patronage could not be sold or given away. When the manumitter died, patronage passed to the closest of his or her male agnates. Patronage allowed the patron to perform the duties that agnates would otherwise have performed, such as guardianship in marriage for women; conversely, the owner could inherit from an emancipated slave who had no natural heirs.

Although insisting that a slave is an item of property, Islamic law clearly recognized the slave's humanity, and there was a strong moral tone to the law. As Joseph Schacht remarked, "The Islamic law of slavery is patriarchal and belongs more to the law of family than to the law of property." The moral attitude is well summed up in a *ḥadīth:* "Fear God in regard to your slaves. Feed them with what you eat and clothe them with what you wear. Do not work them beyond their capacity [and] . . . to not cause pain to God's creation. He caused you to own them, and had He wished, He would have caused them to own you."

[See *also* Abolition and Anti-Slavery, *article on* African Slavery.]

BIBLIOGRAPHY

Brunschvig, Robert. "ʿAbd." *Encyclopedia of Islam,* new ed., vol. 1, pp. 24–40. Leiden: E. J. Brill, 1960.

Crone, Patricia. *Roman, Provincial and Islamic Law: The Origins of the Islamic Patronate.* Cambridge: Cambridge University Press, 1987.

Hunwick, John O. "Wills, Slave Emancipation, and Clientship." Translation of section from the *Risāla* of Ibn Abī Zayd al-Qayrawānī with the commentary of Abūʾl-Ḥasan al-Mālikī and the supercommentary of ʿAlī al-Saʿīdī. In *The Global Experience,* edited by Philip Riley et al., 2d ed., vol. 1, pp. 189–192. Englewood Cliffs, N.J.: Prentice-Hall, 1992.

Khalîl ben Ishʾâq. *Abrégé de la lois musulmane selon le rite de l'imâm Mâlek.* Translated by G. H. Bousquet. Algiers, 1956–1962.

Lewis, Bernard. *Race and Slavery in the Middle East: An Historical Inquiry.* New York and Oxford: Oxford University Press, 1990.

Schacht, Joseph. *An Introduction to Islamic Law.* Oxford and New York: Oxford University Press, 1964.

—JOHN O. HUNWICK

Latin American Law

In 1946 Frank Tannenbaum published the influential book *Slave and Citizen: The Negro in the Americas.* Tannenbaum's central concern was to explain the etiology of the "divergent position" of people of African descent in Ibero-America and the United States, differences that he claimed could not be "a mere accident." According to Tannenbaum, the contrast between the positions of blacks in North and South America was to be explained by the two regions' dissimilar systems of slavery. In Latin America slavery had developed against a moral and legal backdrop that was several centuries old, and slaves were considered human beings who enjoyed the protection of the state and the church, whereas in North America slavery was not constrained by such traditions, and slaves were denied legal personality. The separation between the two systems of systems of slavery and race relations, Tannenbaum argued, was "a moral one."

Slave and Citizen became the subject of heated controversy. At stake was not only the assumption that blacks' position in contemporary societies could be explained by dissimilar slave systems, but also the possibility of characterizing slavery through legal analysis. As some critics argued, a great deal of difference existed between legal ideals and the harsh realities of everyday life. Moreover, Tannenbaum's study, and those of some of his early followers, rested on an undifferentiated body of legal evidence drawn from different places and periods, and this approach soon came under attack. As a result, by the late 1960s new comparative studies were focusing on more concrete territorial units. Examples are Carl Degler's critically important *Neither Black nor White* (1971), comparing slavery and race relations in Brazil and the United States, and Herbert S. Klein's *Slavery in the Americas: A Comparative Study of Virginia and Cuba* (1967).

Although these studies brought law legal structures to the attention of students of slavery in Latin America, one of their insufficiencies was the way in which legal systems were defined. The study of slave laws was usually restricted to their medieval Castilian precedents, which were transposed to the New World, and to the royal *cédulas* and *pragmáticas* generated by the Consejo de Indias and endorsed with the king's signature. As Klein wrote, referring to Cuba, "The source of its slave code was fundamentally royal enactments and prior metropolitan law." Even in Alan Watson's (1989) comprehensive survey of comparative slave law in the Western Hemisphere, this problem persists.

This is not to say that Castilian precedents or royal regulations are unimportant. The transplantation of slavery to Ibero-America took place within a legal, ethical, and religious framework that had developed in the peninsula for centuries; at the time of the American conquest slavery was very much alive in southern Spain and Portugal. More to the point, in both places the regulation of slavery rested on a long common tradition of Roman law, readily accessible in Justinian's *Corpus Juris Civilis.*

This legal tradition played a fundamental role in the New World. Justinian's compilation was employed as a supplement to the *Ordenaçoes Filipinas,* the Portuguese laws applicable to her colonies, and it was the main source of the Siete Partidas, the monumental Castilian legal codification conducted under Alfonso X ("the Wise") during the thirteenth century. The incorporation of most colonies into the kingdom of Castile implied that its slave laws were to be translated to America, so the Siete Partidas became the most important normative reference to regulate slavery in the colonial world.

The Partidas, as they became known, recognized that humans were naturally free, "the most noble and free creature, among all creatures, that God made," and that freedom was "the dearest" thing they had, and they defined slavery as "the most evil and despicable thing which can be found among men." Based on these principles, the law recognized limited legal personality for slaves. They had, for example, the right to appeal to the courts if their masters exercised undue cruelty toward them or their family; they could marry even against the will of the master, and might even marry free persons; and they could initiate, in certain limited cases, legal suit before a court or testify against another person. Additionally, although slaves did not have the right to own property, following Roman tradition they were frequently allowed a *peculium* or funds set aside by the master for the slave's use. The Castilian laws transplanted to the colonial world also regulated slaves' access to manumission, which could be granted by either the master or the state.

Although these European legal precedents were observed in Latin America for several centuries, the new social and administrative realities of the colonies soon generated additional normative efforts. New issues like the Atlantic slave trade, the legal condition of Indians, and the relationship between African slaves and the indigenous population became the subjects of extensive legislation. The crown acted on these issues in a casuistic way, producing a vast amount of legislation that was selectively complied later in the *Recopilación de leyes de los Reynos de las Indias,* promulgated in 1680. Although the *Recopilación* became the universal law to be applied in all the Indies, what it actually did was to convert into general rules a number of regulations that were originally designed to be applied to particular territories and cases. Therefore, the relevance of this legal body to the understanding of slavery in Latin America is rather limited.

The restricted value of these regulations is better understood when careful attention is paid to the way they were generated. Many of these rules were born in the colonies. In a typical case, a colonial authority of any rank would send a report to the Council of Indies or the king, asking them to regulate a specific situation, to correct a wrong, or to legitimize a local ordinance or practice. The council might study the issue, gather additional information, and hear the prosecutor's opinion before making a recommendation to the king, who then regulated the issue in a *real cédula*. What the *Recopilación* contains is usually a summary, or an abridged version, of this legislative material. Given the social, economic, and demographic diversity of the colonial world, the real applicability of many of these rules was almost nil. Hence students of slave law in colonial Latin America should use the *Recopilación* just as a general reference; they will do better to study some of the previous compilations, where the original *cédulas* are fully reproduced. Among the latter, Diego de Encina's *Cedulario Indiano* (1596) is very valuable.

The study of slave law should not be restricted to royal regulations. Although, in the strictest technical sense, "law" was only a rule promulgated by the king, other colonial officials and institutions in the administrative hierarchy, from viceroys and *audiencias* to town councils, also had limited legislative functions. Royal regulations are useful for understanding larger administrative concerns and imperial policy, but pressing social issues were better covered by the legal production. The best and most comprehensive legislative efforts to regulate slavery in the colonies are found in these local ordinances and regulations, not in the royal *cédulas*. To cite only a few early examples, slavery is extensively regulated in local ordinances approved in Santo Domingo in 1528, 1535, and 1544; in Panama City in 1574; and in Havana in 1570, 1600, and 1690. Regarding slavery, the only royal law comparable in scope to these lower regulations is the late "Royal Cédula of His Majesty, on the education, treatment and occupations of the slaves in all his dominions of the Indies," promulgated in 1789.

Because they responded to concrete social realities in an immediate way, local regulations were usually harsher than general laws and their medieval precedents. Central to these rules was the need to regulate and systematize the subordination of slaves and free blacks in colonial societies. As a result they developed a set of racist juridical principles and ideas that was absent from the Iberian legal precedents. They emphasized the unacceptability of slaves' practices and activities, which contradicted local elites' vision of what the colonial order should be, and above all, they repressed marronage and other forms of resistance. Some of the punishments established by these regulations, such as castration and other forms of physical mutilation, openly clashed with the Iberian legal heritage.

The gap between local and royal regulations was occasionally bridged through the juridical figure of the *real confirmación* (royal confirmation), by which a local rule got royal approval and became law in the fullest sense of the term. But even without such confirmation, these rules were enforced. The Havana ordinances, for instance, were promulgated by the local council in the 1570s but were not confirmed until 1640. During the intervening seventy years, however, the ordinances constituted the fundamental normative reference in the city's life and were constantly enforced by the local authorities. These ordinances are also a good example of the emergence of a distinct body of colonial juridical rules that went beyond the narrow limits of individual jurisdictional units. The author of these ordinances was an *oidor* (judge) from the *audiencia* of Santo Domingo who, as part of his official duties, performed a *visita* (tour of inspection) to the governorship of Cuba in 1570. The result was that Havana's ordinances were heavily influenced by legal precedents from Santo Domingo. Quite often these local rules referred to similar problems and solutions in other colonial territories; however, these intercolonial legal and cultural links have not been systematically studied.

Finally, slavery was also affected by a third body of legislation, canonic law. Church regulations exerted considerable influence over spiritual matters, preventing both masters and slaves from sinful practices. Because of their sacramental character, some fundamental slaves' rights, such as Christian baptism and marriage, were regulated and protected by the church. On the repressive side, the church also restrained cultural practices opposed to Catholic dogma through its inquisitional courts, organized throughout the colonies during the sixteenth and seventeenth centuries. Again, it is in the local canonic production, such as the very valuable *Sínodos Diocesanos* (Diodesan Synods), that these normative efforts are fully developed.

The concrete application of these often conflicting norms created a number of practical problems. On the one hand, local regulations considerably limited slaves' autonomy. On the other, a clear set of juridical principles and legal customs provided slaves with opportunities to protect themselves from abuses, and instances of slaves making use of legal recourse to advance their claims are not uncommon. In the uneasy coexistence of these distinct and often contradictory bodies of legislation and in their concrete interaction lie vast possibilities for innovative future research.

[*See also* Abolition and Anti-Slavery, *article on* Latin America; Emancipation in the Americas; *and* Historiography, *article on* Latin American and Caribbean Slavery.]

BIBLIOGRAPHY

Delger, Carl. *Neither Black Nor White: Slavery and Race Relations in Brazil and the United States.* New York: Macmillan, 1971.

Klein, Herbert. *Slavery in the Americas: A Comparative Study of Virginia and Cuba.* Chicago: University of Chicago Press, 1967.

Tannenbaum, Frank. *Slave and Citizen: The Negro in the Americas.* New York: Vintage Books, 1946.

Watson, Alan. *Slave Law in the Americas.* Athens: University of Georgia Press, 1989.

—ALEJANDRO DE LA FUENTE

United States Law

The relationship between the enslavement of people of color and Anglo-American law began early in the seventeenth century, and it did not end until the constitutional crisis of the 1850s led to one of the bloodiest wars of the nineteenth century. The precise origin of the relationship remains controversial. Some scholars, for example, find the relevant laws outside the common law of England, and some ground the system within the common law. Some see the presence of slavery as dating from the introduction of Africans into Virginia, while others place it later. The "origins debate" is unlikely to be settled to everyone's satisfaction because of the sparsity of records for the first few years after the first Africans appeared in British America in 1619.

One thing, however, is clear: both Africans and Native Americans were reduced to slavery at one time or another before the end of the seventeenth century in England's continental colonies. Moreover, although slavery was confined to the South by the nineteenth century, it existed throughout the English settlements before the American Revolution. In some respects, however, the institution was more notable for its diversity than its universality in the English colonies of North America. While it replaced white indentured servitude in the Southern colonies, which became true slave societies where the basic social and economic order rested on the coerced labor of slaves, it did not expand in the Northern colonies. Southern slaves worked in the rice swamps of South Carolina and the tobacco fields of Maryland and Virginia, but generally slave labor was of less significance north of those colonies. By the end of the eighteenth century slavery had disappeared from the North—either gradually, as in Pennsylvania, or almost immediately, as in Massachusetts. With the collapse of Northern slavery after the Revolution came a separation of geographical sections based on different social and moral orders and the legal systems that were interwoven with them. In the South the notion remained that the ownership of human beings was normally defensible, while in the North contrary conceptions of property claims had taken hold. After the 1780s two separate legal, moral, economic, and social systems confronted each other within the same federal union. In the end the mix proved volatile.

Slavery is the most extreme form of social dependence and subordination. It was undergirded by English and colonial, and later Southern law, common law, equity, and statutes all bore some of the weight imposed by human bondage. Some of the legal and equitable rules were specific to slaves and some concerned property generally, or even persons generally (absent words of exclusion, for instance, some judges applied general criminal statutes to slaves). There never was a simple body of law one can call "the law of slavery," as in a section of a code. Statutes, in fact, were of far less importance in the colonial English world than was the common law, which was made by judges and involved such things as successions to property. Statutory lawmaking did not become important until the nineteenth century. English legal traditions of both law and equity helped to define the policy options used to uphold the slavery of people of color, but legal traditions are malleable, and rules and norms were changing throughout the history of American slavery.

Legal norms and rules changed in response to a variety of pressures, some internal and some external. Evangelical Christianity was one source of pressure that increasingly constrained the power of owners after the American Revolution. At the same time, American slave systems were embedded in a capitalist world that itself changed the master-slave relationship, as well as the rules of law that were involved in the relationship. Rules of succession held primacy throughout the eighteenth century, but by the nineteenth century, with the spread of capitalism, rules on the exchange and alienation of property became ever more important. Market transactions (sales, mortgages, and bailments or hires of slaves) assumed greater significance during the nineteenth century. Even though they were commercially oriented, the Northern colonies bore few marks of the later legal development that governed market transactions in slaves in ways rarely used before. That development was confined to the post-Revolutionary South.

Throughout the history of American slavery there were inconsistencies, contradictions, and simple differences among (and within) the slave jurisdictions. One level of inconsistency and contradiction that we need to know more about is that between doctrine defined by judges and lawmakers and the day-to-day practice in Southern counties. At a fundamental level, however, a key question was what rule of law, or what legal or equitable notion, or analogy would be used when slaves were the objects of legal or equitable claims. Such a basic notion as the slaves' legal category was unsettled. Moses I. Finley (1980, p. 95) noted that powerlessness was an essential element of slavery, and one of the most effective means to that end was to reduce the person to the position of a thing, an object of property claims, to chattelhood. This view is correct in a nontechnical way, to note the status of the slave as property. But to divine the precise rules of law applied to the slave it is important to understand that some American slave jurisdictions defined slaves as real estate, and Louisiana (in a civil law and not a common law jurisdiction) defined slaves as "immovables." The rules of inheritance, too, were significantly different for realty and for chattels, or personal property. Virginia defined slaves as realty for many purposes, but not for all, from 1705 to 1792. Although most Southern states in the nineteenth century defined slaves as chattels personal, not all did so (Kentucky defined them as realty for most of the period, and Arkansas did the same for a brief time). Moreover, some Southern judges, such as John Belton O'Neall of South Carolina, applied rules of real property law to slaves even though slaves were defined as chattels within their state.

Slaves at any rate were property. Although some scholars argue that there are many property claims in people who are not slaves, such as indentured servants, defining slaves as property was significant. One vital element in the law of property was the notion of heritability: people of color inherited the status of slavery, and this made the system perpetual. After some initial experiments all the American colonies and later states held that a person derived status from his or her mother. But that only began the problem for judges and lawmakers. What kind of property? For what purposes?

Slaves were property with souls. Although they were degraded persons, they were held to have du-

ties according Southern law. (This distinguished Southern slave law from Roman law, to take a prominent comparative example: under Roman law slaves were held to be dutiless as well as rightless.) American slaves had a legally significant duty of obedience to masters first of all, and often to all whites. Southerners increasingly articulated a defense of their "peculiar institution" as it came under attack beginning in the late eighteenth century, and as they did so, they emphasized the reciprocal duties of slaves and masters and enforced them at law. Masters were obligated to feed, clothe, and provide medical care for slaves, and in many slave jurisdictions they had to provide counsel for slaves on trial for crimes.

Southern law in regard to slaves was built on English common law, equity, and statutes. Legal treatises became of increasing importance in the common law world after the work of Sir William Blackstone, the *Commentaries on the Laws of England,* in the mid-eighteenth century. These treatises, in turn, were of real importance in the decisions of Southern judges confronted with questions involving slaves. Among the most important of the treatises used in slave society, but not specific to slaves, were Sir William Jones on bailment, John Joseph Powell on contracts and mortgages, and Joseph Story on equity and agency. Perhaps it is surprising that treatises limited to slavery and the law were rare. Abolitionists, for their part, resorted to treatises to attack slavery; examples are George Stroud's *Sketch of the Laws Relating to Slavery* (1827) and William Goodell's *The American Slave Code* (1853). Jacob Wheeler collected a few leading cases in *Practical Treatise on the Law of Slavery* (1837), but his work contained little synthesis. The leading pro-slavery work was Thomas R. R. Cobb's *An Inquiry into the Law of Negro Slavery in the United States of America,* but it did not appear until 1858, and even then it was incomplete; Cobb promised to write about the slave as property in the future but died before he could do so.

A large study of slavery and law by a Northerner was John Codman Hurd's *Law of Freedom and*

Contrabands in the Swamps; engraving from *Harper's Weekly*,
volume 32, April 1866.

Bondage (1858–1862). Hurd's work was an effort by a legal positivist and a proponent of liberal capitalism to uncover the basic principles of the public and private law of slavery. One of his most important observations was, "Every recognition of rights in the slave, independent of the will of the owner or master, which is made by the state to which he is subject, diminishes in some degree the essence of that slavery by changing it into a relation between legal persons." Nonetheless, slaves were increasingly recognized as possessing some limited rights as the Civil War approached. One of the highest barriers to any truly significant grant of rights, however, was race. A significant expression of this was the exclusion of the testimony of slaves against whites in all court cases. Southern slavery rested firmly on race, as evident in the way Southern judges and lawmakers dealt with cases in

which a person designated a slave claimed that he or she was free. A widely used legal presumption was that color raised a presumption of slavery. This problem became important during the nineteenth century as manumission became more frequent.

There were numerous inconsistencies in the ways Southern judges and lawmakers dealt with slaves as persons with moral personality, and as persons in whom others had property claims. The contradictions increased during the nineteenth century, but none of them created a national crisis, because the slave South coexisted with the free North in a federal union. Public or constitutional law in the republic was used in some cases to accommodate slave-owners in order to secure the union. In others, it gave Northern states permission to challenge the notion that human beings could be dealt with as things. The conflicts centered around three issues: fugitive slaves, who remained in the possession of their owners, according to the Constitution; the extension of slavery into the common territories of the United States, an explosive issue that emerged in its starkest form after the war with Mexico in the 1840s; and the issue of the right of slave-owners to travel through free states with their slaves.

One of the sharpest conflicts over fugitives erupted in 1842 in the U.S. Supreme Court in *Prigg v. Pennsylvania.* Justice Joseph Story held that the fugitive slave clause of the Constitution was self-executing and therefore slaveowners could recover their property anywhere in the country without going to the courts. Congress could reinforce this guarantee as it had done in 1793 with the first fugitive slave law, and states could not intrude into the process, as the state of Pennsylvania attempted to do by protecting free blacks at the same time as it carried out its perceived duty to aid slave-owners in recovering their property. Justice John McLean of Ohio argued that the law of Pennsylvania did not intrude into the process in any illegitimate manner because all persons in that state were presumed to be free. It was, in his view, a case of the presumption of the state against the claim of the master. But no other justice agreed with McLean, and eight years later Congress adopted a new fugitive slave law that left Northern law subordinate to the demands of slave-owners. Blacks seized as fugitives in the North were brought before federal fugitive slave commissioners who heard the slave-owner's claim that they were fugitives, while the commissioners were not entitled to hear the testimony of the slave. This issue was so explosive that some in the North urged the adoption of state laws repudiating the constitutional obligation to return fugitive slaves.

The issue of sojourning slave-owners accompanied by their slaves was also hotly contested, especially from the 1840s on. By the 1850s the notion of comity, a crucial one in the federal union, had all but collapsed. Comity is the notion that one jurisdiction will respect the laws, and the claims aris-

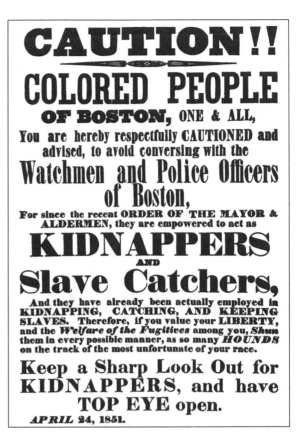

Broadside warning colored citizens of Boston about slave catchers and kidnappers, 24 April 1851.

ing under the laws, of another jurisdiction. Northern states, however, increasingly turned away from any recognition of slavery by refusing even to allow a slave-owner to cross the state with a slave. If the owner brought a slave onto the free soil of some Northern states, he or she risked the immediate loss of the slave property. Southern states retaliated when they refused, as the Mississippi Supreme Court did in 1859 in *Mitchell v. Wells,* to recognize the free status of blacks who acquired freedom on the soil of a free state. In that case, blacks whose Mississippi owner had provided they would be set free in Ohio tried to claim their estate in Mississippi. The end of any binding relationship between the free and slave states was near when the court of Mississippi could declare that "suppose that Ohio [conferred] citizenship on the chimpanzee or the ourang-outang? . . . Are we to be told that 'comity' will require [Mississippi to] forget their own policy . . . and lower their own citizens?" Ohio, the Mississippian judge wrote, "can neither confer freedom on a Mississippi slave, nor the right to acquire, hold, sue for, nor enjoy property in Mississippi."

The issue of the expansion of slavery into the common territories of the country proved to be the most explosive of the public law issues involving slavery. Southerners rallied around the doctrine of state sovereignty as developed by John C. Calhoun of South Carolina. This approach to the problem of the status of slavery in the territories was grasped by the United States Supreme Court in *Dred Scott v. Sandford* (1857). The doctrine held that the federal government was the agent of the sovereign states that created it, and it could do nothing to jeopardize the institutions of those states nor exercise any power not clearly granted to it. Chief Justice Roger Brooke Taney concluded that Congress had only the "power coupled with the duty of protecting the owner in his rights" in the common territories. This was translated by the more aggressive Southerners into a claim that Congress should adopt a territorial slave code patterned after the laws of the Southern states. Northerners, however, tended to adopt either the view of Stephen A. Douglas of Illinois—who outlined a doctrine of squatter or popular sovereignty whereby the residents of the territories would decide for themselves whether they would admit slavery—or the view of Abraham Lincoln, who advocated a doctrine of containment in which Congress had the duty to prohibit the expansion of slavery into the territories. With Lincoln's election, Southern leaders chose to leave a union they believed held them and their institutions in contempt and granted their laws and the claims under those laws no respect. In the end, the contradictions involved in treating people of color as property were resolved in civil war.

[*See also* Property; Race and Racism; Segregation; *and* United States, *overview article and article on* The South.]

BIBLIOGRAPHY

Finkelman, Paul. "Slavery." In *The Oxford Companion to the Supreme Court of the United States,* edited by Kermit L. Hall et al., pp. 791–798. New York and Oxford: Oxford University Press, 1992.

Finley, Moses I. *Ancient Slavery and Modern Ideology.* New York: Viking Press, 1980.

Higginbotham, A. Leon, Jr. *In the Matter of Color.* New York and Oxford: Oxford University Press, 1978.

Morris, Thomas D. *Southern Slavery and the Law, 1619–1860.* Chapel Hill: University of North Carolina Press, 1996.

Tushnet, Mark. *The American Law of Slavery, 1810–1860.* Princeton: Princeton University Press, 1981.

Schwarz, Philip J. *Slave Laws in Virginia.* Athens: University of Georgia Press, 1996.

Watson, Alan. *Slave Law in the Americas.* Athens: University of Georgia Press, 1989.

—THOMAS D. MORRIS

MANUMISSION. Manumission is the granting of freedom by an owner to a specific slave. It is an individualized, personalized concession of freedom. An act of manumission results in a legal, publicly acknowledged change in an individual's civil status from enslaved to free. Manumission is not general emancipation, which ends slavery as an institution, thereby freeing slaves en masse. Notwithstanding this very useful distinction, manumission has often been described and indexed in slave studies as "emancipation" or "liberation." Serfs during the Middle Ages were also on occasion said to be manumitted when they were formally released from labor and other traditional obligations by a bishop or lord.

Manumission occurred because of an agreement, an intention, or a contract between an owner and a slave. The term *manumission* in Western languages derives from the Latin *manumittere,* which means "to let out of the hand." The word evokes the image of the owner's grip on a slave being loosened, as well as the image of a hand extending the gift of freedom. That sense of gift should be noted, as manumission implied in all slave societies that it was the owner's choice to bestow freedom; it was not an agreement reached by social equals. Moreover, the bestower of freedom and the one who received it were bound together in a unique interdependence resulting from the granting and accepting of so unusual and valuable a gift.

Scholarly comment on manumission has almost invariably appeared as subsections of larger works focusing on free people of color, demography, miscegenation, assimilation, and race relations in New World societies. Information on manumission has also appeared within broader discussions of law and legal traditions, religious movements and traditions, and miscegenation. Historians of New World slavery often have referred to manumission in the course of studying other aspects of slavery, generally agreeing that manumission was not and was never intended to be an attack on slavery as an institution.

The seminal interpretation of manumission as practiced in the Western Hemisphere was offered by Frank Tannenbaum in *Slave and Citizen* (1946); Tannenbaum searched for the root causes behind the contrast between the hostile, negative race relations he saw in the United States and the milder, more relaxed interracial behaviors he observed during his long experience in and study of Latin America. He posited that manumission policy was the key indicator of how various European nationalities perceived the humanity of their slaves, how they treated them, and therefore ultimately how they would deal with the descendants of those slaves in the post-emancipation era. In his view, the Catholic Iberian Latins had a body of law and an interracial tradition that favored manumitting slaves and recognized the innate humanity of the slave to a far greater degree than did French Catholics, and even more so than the English and Dutch Protestants, who appeared to have produced little legislation and theology to favor either manumission or the intent to grant full citizenship to ex-slaves as part of the recognition of their humanity.

Tannenbaum's book provoked a long line of works dealing with the English, Spanish, Portuguese, and (much less so) Dutch in the New World, written by scholars who tested Tannenbaum's thesis. This new scholarship questioned the value of legal statutes on manumission in predicting or conditioning race relations in post-emancipation societies. Other works disputed Tannenbaum's perceived dichotomy of the "mildness" of Catholic Iberian slavery in the New World on the one hand, and the "cruelty" of the Protestant English and Dutch on the other; these writers found that how slaves were actually treated differed little from one national or religious group to another, and that treatment was contingent on other, generally economic, factors that varied over time even within a single area. Moreover, economic opportunities were more important than owners' piety or compassion in determining the frequency of manumission.

What has withstood the tests of scholarship was Tannenbaum's observation that slaves were generally more able to purchase their freedom in Latin America than in British North America. The U.S. South emerged as the most severely opposed to manumission of all New World slaveholding societies, as well as the most hostile to former slaves after they obtained their freedom. Recent studies of New Orleans and the Gulf Coast substantiate that slaves under Spanish regimes in this region were more able to attain their freedom than under subsequent British rule.

Manumission has been studied for various reasons: as a point of law; as an indicator of how well or badly slaves were treated; to show that manumission is an inadequate indicator of slave treatment; to explain the nature of race relations after general emancipation; to show that manumission is an inadequate predictor of race relations after emancipation; as an interesting but minor aspect of slavery; and, most often, as one component in a broader study of the free colored and black communities that evolved in all New World societies that held Africans and their descendants as chattel.

Whatever reason motivated the study of manumissions, the essential objects of scrutiny were white owners. How frequently did they free their slaves? What were their motives? How did European civil and religious laws envisage freedom for slaves? In what ways did whites regulate access to freedom?

Because of the questions asked and the sources used, the writers on manumission (including Tannenbaum) often implied that white owners were the active players in manumissions, whereas slaves were the passive recipients of their largesse. Manumission was treated as a legal *event* that changed the legal status of a person from slave to free. Often neglected until recently was the importance of manumission as a *process* and indicator of social relationships among whites, free people of color, and enslaved people of color, of all ages and occupation, urban and rural. The development of social history within the historical profession, and the important contributions of women's history, refocused studies of New World slave societies toward African slaves and their descendants. The study of manumission as a social process allows unique insights into the meaning of freedom within slave societies, the active participation of slaves in acquiring their own freedom, the family life of people of African descent, patronage networks, ethnic and occupational coalitions, and even multiracial alliances and familiar affection. Because women were the majority of the manumitted in almost all New World slave societies, manumission studies open windows on the activities of women, families, children, and slaves in ways not readily approachable through censuses, journals and travel logs of whites, plantation letters, and legal tracts.

Throughout the New World, manumitted people constituted a very small minority of the total population of enslaved people. Most who were manumitted were women and children, with those of mixed race disproportionately represented, especially among children, suggesting the importance of miscegenation and sexual relations between enslaved and free people. All the free black and "colored" (mixed-race) communities before general emancipation in the nineteenth century were descended from one or more ancestors who had themselves been manumitted, and all such communities continued to expand because of manumissions. Consequently, manumission constituted a shared origin and experience, regardless of the differences of age, gender, color, and economic standing that divided these free men and women one from another. Moreover, the manumitted everywhere suffered the stigma of having once been slaves, and often their connection to the enslaved majority of the population was suspect. The manumitted also constituted a model for slaves of what freedom in their societies might allow a person of color. The study of manumission also throws light on creolization and urban life; manumission was largely an urban phenomenon, with some unusual exceptions, such as gold-mining areas, which provided economic opportunities for self-purchase. It is also useful to remember that some of the manumitted were famous and influential in their own times, such as Denmark Vesey, the leader of an aborted large-scale rebellion in South Carolina, and the authors and abolitionists Frederick Douglass and Equiano.

The massive increase in studies of slavery has expanded knowledge tremendously, especially about slavery in the Americas, but cross-cultural comparisons of slavery worldwide have also questioned our very definitions of slavery and freedom and, by extension, manumission. Orlando Patterson's *Slavery and Social Death* (1982) is particularly valuable in this regard. A historical and comparative sociologist who had already published on Jamaican slavery, Patterson analyzed slavery throughout the world, ancient as well as modern. He assembled data on a variety of societies: those in which slavery "attained marked structural significance, ranging from those in which it was important for cultural, economic, or political reasons, or a combination of all three, through those in which it was critical though not definitive, to those in which it was the determinative institution" (p. iv). The last, the "large-scale slave systems," provided much of the data, especially quantitative; they included the classical Mediterranean and Europe; the Atlantic Islands, to which the Mediterranean experience of plantation sugar production and slavery spread; scores of African societies; Asia and Oceania; and all New World colonial societies. Patterson distinguished further between "primitive" and "advanced" societies, premodern and modern, precapitalist and capitalist. His conclusions about manumission are particularly valuable for a number of reasons. The comparisons his data made possible raise questions about how manumission should be defined—indeed, how slavery and freedom should be defined, because New World models and definitions are inadequate for other places and times. Patterson's comparative perspective identified both the commonalities and the range of variability in manumission practices over time and space. His categorizations and conclusions make it easier to compare and to test hypotheses, with the potential of making manumission studies more comparative and important in the broader field of slave studies.

Defining slaves as people who were socially and culturally "dead" as a result of their alienation from kin to whom they would otherwise belong and by whom they would have been protected, Patterson noted that a very few premodern societies understood slavery to be as permanent as physical death, and no manumission was possible in those societies. All modern societies, and most premodern ones, practiced manumission that "restored" life by creating a new person—a freed person. The rituals of manumission, often negligible in modern societies, expose the meaning of manumission, which was almost universally understood and stated to be a gift from the owner. All these "rituals of redemption" were communal and emphasized the owner's giving of freedom as a gift (even if the slave paid for freedom). The manumitted gained a new status and the power to act as a free person, as well as "the capacity to compete for honor" and to act autonomously—although with perpetual gratitude to the owner and his family.

Almost all manumissions occurred by one of seven procedures. The first, postmortem manumission, served as an incentive for slaves to behave and work effectively in the hope of being freed when the owner died, even when few slaves in a household might actually be freed. Patterson identified this form as probably a substitute for sacrificing slaves at the death of the owners. The most widespread and perhaps the earliest form of manumission in human history, it remained very important in modern slave societies, where it appeared as testamentary manumission in its literate form. In fact, most modern studies of manumission rely heavily on testamentary and probate records. Islam was quicker than Christianity to embrace manumission. Muḥammad encouraged such manumission to soften the harshness of slavery and to redefine manumission as an act of piety, and not just as an act that would bring honor on the giver and his heirs. Christianity widely encouraged manumission as an act of piety only in the ninth and tenth centuries. In both religious traditions, the emphasis on piety was new to the meaning of manumission; it appears to have been added as a way of redefining older, pagan traditions by infusing them with new religious meanings appropriate to Islam and Christianity. In both religious traditions, manumission at the death of the owner became important.

Manumission based on marriage or concubinage was common in many premodern societies. This form favored women and their children; adult males were rarely beneficiaries. Islam more than Christianity emphasized the importance of freeing concubines and even institutionalized the practice. This mode of manumission implied the sexual exploitation of female slaves, which is recorded for almost every slaveholding society, including Europe in the Middle Ages and the Americas after the arrival of Europeans. Patterson attacked as a myth the thesis that Latins had a greater proclivity toward concubinage in the Americas than did northern Europeans (although Latins had higher manumission rates). Nonetheless, no New World slave society granted freedom authomatically to concubines, and the findings of many scholars demonstrate that most female slaves who had sexual relations with free men were never freed.

Manumission via adoption was absent in Islamic societies, but common among preliterate peoples, among whom slaves were often incorporated as junior members into the owners' kin groups. Unusual in the Greco-Roman world and rare in Romanized Europe, it was almost unknown in the modern slave societies of the Americas.

Political manumission was usually accomplished by the ruler or an agency of the state. This type would include cases in which slaves were freed for bravery in defense of the state, for exposing treason, or in celebration of royal births or victories. It was always rather unusual. The highly visible and influential role of the Mamluks of the Ottoman Empire, manumitted as a condition of their service to the sultans, was a form of political manumission.

Manumission through collusive litigation was an institutionalized legal fiction in which freedom was granted a slave after a trial in which the slave claimed he was really a free man, and the owner did not contradict the testimony. The subsequent acquittal in effect declared the slave a free man and citizen. Except for the manumissions by the oracle of Delphi, this was the most common form of manumission in classical Greece, and the second most common in Rome (after testamentary manumission).

Sacral manumission was the most common form in Delphi, though not throughout classical Greece, where collusive and testamentary manumission seem to have been more common. Slaves bought their freedom for very large sums in installments, while in theory the god would be the divine patron of the manumitted, sanctifying what would have normally been a secular act.

Manumission by formal contract developed out of earlier informal verbal or written statements by private owners attesting to a desire to free a particular slave. The practice evolved in the Roman Republic even though it was not legally binding. Emperor Justinian codified these customs, making them legally valid, provided legal form was followed and the acts were witnessed. This form of manumission steadily grew more popular until it became the most important form in the modern world, particularly in the Americas.

One of the most important contributions of Patterson's comparative work was to clarify the way in which the act of manumission created not only a new (freed) person but also a new status within society, the freedman or freedwoman. Patterson noted that almost universally, the most important factor determining the position of the freed person in the free community was the nature of the relationship he or she had with the former master. Everywhere the former owner established a strong patron-client bond with the manumitted slave. The kind and degree of the continued dependence of the manumitted slave was most affected by economics (such as the price and the terms the slave paid for freedom), the sex of the slave (women being more dependent on owners as a rule than males), and the former slave's occupation and control of work and income.

Whether more customary or more legalistic in practice, all slave societies demanded that the manumitted honor the former master. This constructed a permanent tie between freed people and former owners that endured during their lifetimes, and sometimes through their descendants over generations. This special relationship was to a large degree involuntary and therefore not a typical patron-client relationship that could be broken. Slaveholding societies varied in the range of conditions allowed the manumitted, from full incorporation into existing kin groups to perpetual dependence and scorn.

In the modern world, the Dutch transferred Roman legal traditions to their American colonies, which incorporated into the legal manumission procedure the requirement binding the manumitted to honor former owners, with the threat of re-enslavement for those who violated this oath. In

Latin America, this relationship of dependence was not formalized by statute but conditioned in social and economic ways such that dependence (and a threat of re-enslavement) was the reality for the many of the manumitted. In the more capitalistic slave systems of South Africa, the English colonies of the Caribbean, and the U.S. South, the other extreme was reached: there were very few manumissions, but the large majority of those were without conditions, and the majority of the manumitted lived in poverty and without the full civil rights accorded whites and other freeborn people. Whether formalized or not, the manumitted generally found it difficult if not impossible to escape their dependence and condition of partial citizenship. As a result, masters anywhere rarely lost any economic or political advantage in freeing slaves, because the dependencies that had bound owners and slaves together tended to continue after manumission.

What, then, did freed people gain? How free was their freedom, and how full their citizenship in the community they joined? Where freed people were legally and politically accepted, social acceptance generally did not follow; social acceptance, where possible, did not gain them legal or political acceptance. This is particularly the case for women, who were manumitted in greater number because of their gender but suffered a double disenfranchisement in freedom because of their gender and their status as manumitted women (and in American societies, a triple indemnity as women of color). Patterson found that in more than 80 percent of major slaveholding societies, freed persons never attained full citizenship.

All former slaves were tainted by their previous status, a condition inherent to the manumitted, no matter the form of manumission. However, manumission is also usefully understood as a stage in a journey that could take many generations. The slave became the manumitted; the manumitted's progeny achieved greater enfranchisement and acceptance as they were freeborn, putting generational space between them and their enslaved ancestors. In this regard, manumission, like slavery, was fluid and changing, in meanings and conditions.

The rate and degree of acceptance of the manumitted and their freeborn descendants by the broader society varied, depending on variables such as the degree of institutionalized and formalized dependence between the former master and slave, the demography and social formation of the society (especially sex ratios and proportion of the population enslaved), occupations, and residence (urban areas generally providing more occupational opportunities for slaves to acquire skills and money for manumission than rural areas). The literature is much less clear about the importance of ethnicity, age, and even gender, especially in large capitalist slaveholding societies, despite the majority of manumittees being female.

Race, which is often thought of as an independent variable that determined the low manumission rates of the Americas and the continued disabilities of those descended from enslaved ancestors, appears to be less important than the global status of once-enslaved. The same discrimination found in many New World societies to the detriment of Africans and their descendants can also be found in societies where phenotype does not distinguish former owners from former slaves, suggesting that former slave status is key and race more a marker of such ancestry.

Who was most likely to be manumitted? In most slave societies, women were freed more often than men, in part because of women's domestic roles, which put them in closer contact, including sexually, with masters, and because of their roles as mothers. Women, given their gender roles in society, were often more dependent on males and less able to break those ties of dependency, especially when some of their kin were still enslaved and greater independence would have meant moving away. Being a child of a master only infrequently resulted in manumission, even in Latin America, where children were freed at a relatively high rate. The skills possessed by a slave were important, but the freedom a slave had to use those skills and the control he or she had over the money earned were just as important. Most of the manumitted historically were urban residents; this is particularly clear among modern slave societies of the Americas. Patterson found that neither race nor religion directly affected manumissions; rather, they were usually justifications for manumissions. In this regard, the argument that owners in the Americas freed slaves who looked most like them has less to do with race than with the nature of the previous relationship with the owner.

The actual rate of manumission is a separate though related issue. Here race was an important factor, and the rates of manumission in individual societies appear to have depended on a number of variables. Modern studies suggest reasons for changes in rates. Patterson, based on information about many societies, ultimately concluded that the only positive indicator of rates of changes in manumission was its correlation with "structural shocks" to either the economic or the political-military system. The shocks in effect stimulated manumissions that would not have occurred in the normal course of affairs. For example, warfare, such as the American Revolution, opened the possibilities for more manumissions to occur; the Napoleonic Wars and the campaigns against maroons in the Caribbean forced imperial powers to manumit male slaves in return for military service. Another instance is the rapid economic decline of plantation sectors, as in Suriname after the 1770s, which contributed to raising the rate of manumissions.

[*See also* Emancipation in the Americas; Gender and Slavery; Historiography, *article on* Latin American and Caribbean Slavery; Law, *article on* Roman Law; *and* United States, *article on* The South.]

BIBLIOGRAPHY

Bergad, Laird, Fe Iglesias García, and María del Carmen Barcia. *The Cuban Slave Market, 1790–1880.* New York: Cambridge University Press, 1995. See especially chap. 6.

Brana-Shute, Rosemary. "Approaching Freedom: The Manumission of Slaves in Suriname, 1760–1828." *Slavery and Abolition* 10 (1989): 40–63.

Hunefeldt, Christine. *Paying the Price of Freedom: Family and Labor among Lima's Slaves, 1800–1854.* Berkeley: University of California Press, 1994.

Johnson, Lyman. "Manumission in Colonial Buenos Aires, 1776–1810." *Hispanic American Historical Review* 59 (1979): 258–279.

McGlynn, Frank, ed. *Perspectives on Manumission*, special issue of *Slavery and Abolition* (Dec. 1989).

Nishida, Mieko. "Manumission and Ethnicity in Urban Slavery: Salvador, Brazil, 1808–1888." *Hispanic American Historical Review* 73.3 (1993): 361–391.

Patterson, Orlando. *Slavery and Social Death: A Comparative Study.* Cambridge, Mass.: Harvard University Press, 1982.

Queiros Mattoso, Kata M. de. *To Be a Slave in Brazil.* New Brunswick, N.J.: Rutgers University Press, 1986.

—ROSEMARY BRANA-SHUTE

MAROONS. The man who was to become the first African-American maroon arrived on the first slave ship to reach the Americas, within a decade of Columbus's landfall; one of the last maroons to escape from slavery was still alive in Cuba in the 1970s. For more than four centuries the communities formed by escaped slaves dotted the fringes of plantation America, from Brazil to the southeastern United States and from Peru to the American Southwest. Known variously as *palenques*, *quilombos*, *mocambos*, *cumbes*, *mambises*, or *ladeiras*, these new societies ranged from tiny bands that survived less than a year to powerful states with thousands of members that survived for generations or even centuries. Today their descendants still form semi-independent enclaves in several parts of the hemisphere—for example, in Suriname, French Guiana, Jamaica, Colombia, and Belize—remaining fiercely proud of their maroon origins and, in some cases at least, faithful to unique cultural traditions that were forged during the earliest days of African-American history.

The English word *maroon* derives from Spanish *cimarrón*, itself based on an Arawakan (Taino) Indian root. *Cimarrón* originally referred to domestic cattle that had taken to the hills in Hispaniola, and soon after that to American Indian slaves who had escaped from the Spaniards as well. By the end of the 1530s the word had taken on strong connotations of fierceness, of being wild and unbroken, and it was being used primarily to refer to African-American runaways.

During the past several decades scholarship on maroons has flourished, and new historical research has done much to dispel the myth of the docile slave. The extent of violent resistance to enslavement has been documented rather fully, from the revolts in the slave factories of West Africa and mutinies during the Middle Passage to the organized rebellions that began to sweep most colonies within a decade after the arrival of the first slave ships. There is also a growing literature on the pervasiveness of various forms of day-to-day resistance, from simple malingering to subtle but systematic acts of sabotage.

Maroons and their communities hold a special significance for the study of slave societies. While they were, from one perspective, the antithesis of all that slavery stood for, they were at the same time a widespread and embarrassingly visible part of that system. Just as the very nature of plantation slavery implied violence and resistance, the wilderness setting of early New World plantations made marronage and the existence of organized maroon communities a ubiquitous reality. The large number of detailed newspaper advertisements placed by masters seeking runaway slaves attests to the level of planters' concern, while at the same time affording the critical historian one important set of sources for establishing the profiles of maroons, which varied significantly by historical period and country. Individual maroons not only fled to the hinterlands; many, especially skilled slaves, escaped to urban centers and successfully melted into the freed black population, while others became "maritime maroons," fleeing by fishing boat or other vessel across international borders.

Planters generally tolerated *petit marronage*, repetitive or periodic truancy with temporary goals such as visiting a friend or lover on a neighboring plantation. Within the first decade of the existence of most slaveholding colonies, however, the most brutal punishments—amputation of a leg, castration, suspension from a meathook through the ribs, or slow roasting to death—had been reserved for long-term, recidivist maroons, and in many cases these were quickly written into law. Marronage on the grand scale, with individual fugitives banding together to create communities of their own, struck directly at the foundations of the plantation system, presenting military and economic threats that often taxed the colonists to their limits. Maroon communities, whether hidden near the fringes of the plantations or deep in the forest, periodically raided plantations for firearms, tools, and women, often permitting families that had formed during slavery to be reunited in freedom. In a remarkable number of cases, the beleaguered colonists were eventually forced to sue their former

Pacification with the Maroon Negroes; engraving, nineteenth century. The scene shows British military officers conferring with Haitian Maroons.

slaves for peace. For example, in Brazil, Colombia, Cuba, Ecuador, Hispaniola, Jamaica, Mexico, and Suriname, the whites reluctantly offered treaties granting maroon communities their freedom, recognizing their territorial integrity, and making some provision for meeting their economic needs in return for an end to hostilities toward the plantations and an agreement to return future runaways. Of course, many maroon societies never reached this stage; they were crushed by massive force of arms, and even when treaties were proposed, they were sometimes refused or quickly violated. Nevertheless, new maroon communities seemed to appear almost as quickly as the old ones were exterminated, and they remained, from a colonial perspective, the "chronic plague" and "gangrene" of many plantation societies right up to final emancipation.

To be viable, maroon communities had to be inaccessible, and villages were typically located in remote, inhospitable areas. In the southern United States, isolated swamps were a favorite setting, and maroons often became part of Native American communities; in Jamaica, some of the most famous maroon groups lived in the intricate terrain called "cockpit country," where deep canyons and limestone sinkholes abound but water and good soil are scarce; and in the Guianas, seemingly impenetrable jungles provided maroons with a safe haven. Throughout the hemisphere maroons developed extraordinary skills in guerrilla warfare. To the bewilderment of their colonial enemies, whose rigid and conventional tactics were learned on the open battlefields of Europe, these highly adaptable and mobile warriors took maximum advantage of local environments, striking and withdrawing with great rapidity, making extensive use of ambushes to catch their adversaries in crossfire, fighting only when and where they chose, depending on reliable intelligence networks among nonmaroons (both slaves and white settlers), and often communicating by drums and horns.

The initial maroons in any New World colony came from a wide range of societies in West and Central Africa; at the outset, they shared neither language nor other major aspects of culture. Their collective task, once off in the forests or mountains or swamplands, was nothing less than to create new communities and institutions, largely via a process of inter-African cultural syncretism. Those scholars, mainly anthropologists, who have examined contemporary maroon life most closely seem to agree that such societies are often uncannily "African" in feeling, but at the same time largely devoid of directly transplanted systems. However "African" in character, no maroon social, political, religious, or aesthetic *system* can be reliably traced to a specific African ethnic provenience; rather, they reveal their syncretistic composition, forged in the early meeting of peoples bearing diverse African, European, and Amerindian cultures in the dynamic setting of the New World.

The political system of the great seventeenth-century Brazilian maroon kingdom of Palmares, for example, which R. K. Kent (1965) has characterized as an "African" state, "did not derive from a *particular* central African model, but from several." In the development of the kinship system of the Ndyuka Maroons of Suriname, writes André Köbben, "undoubtedly their West-African heritage played a part . . . [and] the influence of the matrilineal Akan tribes is unmistakable, but so is that of patrilineal tribes . . . [and there are] significant differences between the Akan and Ndyuka matrilineal systems" (Köbben in Price, 1979). Historical and anthropological research has revealed that the magnificent wood-carving of the Suriname Maroons, long considered "an African art in the Americas" on the basis of many formal resemblances, is (in the words of Jean Hurault) in fact a fundamentally new, African-American art "for which it would be pointless to seek the origin through direct transmission of any particular African style" (Hurault in Price 1979). Moreover, detailed investigations both in museums and in the field of a range of cultural phenomena among the Saramaka Maroons of Suriname have confirmed the dynamic, creative processes that continue to animate these societies.

Maroon cultures, however, possess a remarkable number of direct and sometimes spectacular continuities from particular African peoples, ranging from military techniques for defense to recipes for warding off sorcery. These are of the same type as those that can be found, if with lesser frequency, in African-American communities throughout the hemisphere. In stressing these isolated African retentions, there is a danger of neglecting cultural continuities of a far more significant kind. Roger Bastide (1978) divided African-American religions into those he considered "preserved" or "canned"—like Brazilian Candomblé—and those he considered "alive" or "living," like Haitian Vodun. The former, he argued, represent a kind of "defense mechanism" or "cultural fossilization," a fear that any small change may bring on the end, while the latter are more secure of their future and freer to adapt to the changing needs of their adherents. More generally, it can be shown that tenacious fidelity to "African" *forms* is in many cases an indication of a culture finally having lost meaningful touch with the vital African past. Certainly one of the most striking features of West and Central African cultural systems is their internal dynamism, the ability to grow and change. The cultural uniqueness of the more developed maroon societies (for example, those in Suriname) rests firmly on their fidelity to "African" cultural principles at these deeper levels—whether aesthetic, political, religious, or domestic—rather than on the frequency of their isolated "retentions." With a rare freedom to extrapolate African ideas from a variety of societies and to adapt them to changing circumstances, maroon groups included (and continue to include today) what are in many respects both the most meaningfully African and the most truly alive and culturally dynamic of all African-American cultures.

Maroons and maroon societies hold a special place within the study of slavery. Marronage represented a major form of slave resistance, whether accomplished by lone individuals, by small groups, or in great collective rebellions. Throughout the Americas, maroon communities stood out as a heroic challenge to white authority, as the living proof of the existence of a slave consciousness that refused to be limited by the whites' conception or manipulation of it. It is no accident that throughout the Caribbean today, the historical maroon—often mythologized into a larger-than-life figure—has become a touchstone of identity for the region's writers, artists, and intellectuals, the ultimate symbol of resistance to oppression and the fight for freedom.

[*See also* Brazil; Revolts; Saint Domingue Revolution; *and* South America.]

BIBLIOGRAPHY

Agorsah, E. Kofi, ed. *Maroon Heritage: Archaeological, Ethnographic and Historical Perspectives*. Kingston, Jamaica: Canoe Press, 1994.

Bastide, Roger. *The African Religions of Brazil*. Baltimore: Johns Hopkins University Press, 1978.

Heuman, Gad, ed. *Out of the House of Bondage: Runaways, Resistance and Maroonage in Africa and the New World*. London: Frank Cass, 1986.

Kent, R. K. "Palmares: An African State in Brazil." *Journal of African History* 6 (1965): 161–175.

Price, Richard. *Alabi's World*. Baltimore: Johns Hopkins University Press, 1990.

Price, Richard, ed. *Maroon Societies: Rebel Slave Communities in the Americas*. Baltimore: Johns Hopkins University Press, 1979.

Price, Richard, and Sally Price, eds. *Stedman's Surinam: Life in an 18th-Century Slave Society*. Baltimore: Johns Hopkins University Press, 1992.

—RICHARD PRICE

MARXISM. Karl Marx (1818–1883) was a German-born philosopher, political economist, and revolutionary whose writings explicated European capitalism as an economic, political, and ideological system. Although Marx frequently used slavery as a metaphor for the ultimate degradation of labor, he wrote relatively little about slavery directly. Scholars who have followed in his wake have utilized the concepts and analytical tools developed by Marx to illuminate problems in the history of slavery.

Marx wrote about slavery in antiquity as a mode of production (the primary means by which a ruling class extracts surplus value from its workers). He differentiated slave societies, in which a ruling class relied on the labor of slaves, from societies with slaves who were not essential to the dominant process of production. Marxists insist on the importance of slavery in ancient societies, especially classical Greece and Rome. They assert that few if any aspects of ancient life can be understood without reference to slavery, which constituted the economic base of those societies. Even the definition of citizenship developed in relation to its opposite, enslavement: a citizen was a free man who worked for himself or for whom others worked. Marxists also reject arguments that the rise of Christianity ended ancient slavery. They focus instead on material changes that undermined slavery, such as declining markets and problems of slave supply; or they refer to class relations, noting that over time the distinction between slave and citizen faded as people lost their land and were forced to work for rural magnates, who increasingly ignored the former meanings of citizenship.

Marx's few writings about New World slavery have given rise to two distinct interpretations. One is that modern slavery was an anomaly within a capitalist order based on wage labor. The second and perhaps more useful conception, which Marx developed at the end of volume 1 of *Capital* (1867), is that slavery was part of the primary (or primitive) accumulation of capital. Primary accumulation occurs before or in relation to a capitalist economy and serves to limit workers' ability to labor for themselves as well as to produce wealth that would become capital. Although slavery did not create capitalism, or vice versa, Marxists stress the importance of slavery in the growth of capitalism because slave labor produced commodities, profits, and markets that were vital to North Atlantic economies. It was no coincidence that Britain and France, the most dynamic capitalist powers of the eighteenth century, also possessed the most dynamic slave empires.

If one defines capitalism by commodity production (the production of goods not for the needs they satisfy but for what they will bring on the market), rather than by the emergence of wage labor, then most New World slavery was decidedly capitalist. Of course, slaves were also commodities to their masters, and this commodification had enormous effects both on New World plantations and in Africa, where slavery became more harsh and widespread as the slaves were seen not only as human beings who could produce wealth or provide services by their labor, but also as things that had a market value.

Nevertheless, many Marxists argue that slavery was a precapitalist mode of production within capitalism. For Eugene D. Genovese (1974), precapitalist relations of production enabled a peculiar form of paternalism to emerge between the U.S. South's slaveholding class and their slaves. This paternalism, unlike capitalist wage relations, produced a type of hegemony that limited the autonomy and political initiative of slaves. Other scholars influenced by Marx, such as Herbert G. Gutman (1976) and George Rawick (1972), focus on the possibilities of slave culture in allowing for resistance and autonomy. Genovese, Gutman, and other Marxists played a large role in refuting the stereotypic notion of docile and psychologically destroyed slaves in the U.S. South.

Notions of class relations and resistance are crucial for Marxist arguments concerning abolition. Some Marxists focus on the presumed declining profits of slave plantations or the inherent limitations of slavery, such as its supposed incompatibility with advanced technology (because of sabotage), or the expense of investing capital in slaves instead of industrial machinery for sugar mills. These interpretations challenge the idea that British benevolence and religious attitudes alone were responsible for abolition. Other Marxist interpretations focus on class relations and class struggle within the slave societies. The most powerful example is the Saint Domingue (Haitian) revolution; C. L. R. James (1963) portrays a slave class taking advantage of metropolitan crisis and elite division to make the modern world's first successful slave revolt. Marxists such as Robin Blackburn also have begun to examine class relations in European countries, where governments acted against slavery to try to retain legitimacy in the eyes of their own laboring populations.

As these interpretations of abolition suggest, Marxism is not one single intellectual tradition, but rather an ideological current whose adherents share many concerns and analytical methods yet often develop very different interpretations of historical problems. New investigations emphasizing the role of slavery in capitalism, the role of the slave as a worker, and class relations promise continued contributions from Marxist scholars.

[*See also* Capitalism and Slavery; Historiography, *article on* North American Slavery; *and* Wage Slavery.]

BIBLIOGRAPHY

Finley, Moses I. *Ancient Slavery and Modern Ideology.* New York: Viking Press, 1980.

Genovese, Eugene D. *Roll, Jordan, Roll: The World the Slaves Made.* New York: Pantheon, 1974.

Gutman, Herbert G. *The Black Family in Slavery and Freedom, 1750–1925.* New York: Pantheon, 1976.

James, C. L. R. *The Black Jacobins: Toussaint L'Ouverture and the San Domingo Revolution.* 2d rev. ed. New York: Vintage Books, 1963.

Marx, Karl. *Pre-Capitalist Economic Formations.* With an introduction by Eric. J. Hobsbawm. Trans. by Jack Cohen. New York: International Publishers, 1964.

Miller, Joseph C. *Way of Death: Merchant Capitalism and the Angolan Slave Trade, 1730–1830.* Madison: University of Wisconsin Press, 1988.

Moreno Fraginals, Manuel. *The Sugarmill: The Socioeconomic Complex of Sugar in Cuba, 1760–1860.* Trans. by Cedric Belfrage. New York: Monthly Review Press, 1976.

Rawick, George P. *The American Slave: A Composite Autobiography.* Westport, Conn.: Greenwood Press, 1972.

—JAMES SANDERS

MEDITERRANEAN. Throughout the Middle Ages, slavery persisted on all shores of the Mediter-

ranean and in the regions linked with it, even though it occupied a far less important position in society and in the economy than it had in Roman times. From the end of the Roman Empire to the beginning of European expansion in the Atlantic, slavery in the Christian world was reinforced by contact with the highly developed slavery of the Muslims. In addition to the actual presence of slaves, the influence of Roman law helped to shape the legal systems of the European West. The persistence of slavery throughout the Middle Ages set the stage for colonial slavery in the Americas and thus influenced the evolution of modern society throughout the Western Hemisphere. Despite major social and economic changes in the medieval west, Roman slave laws and the writings of early Christian theologians continued to influence the practice of slavery.

During the early centuries of its existence, the Islamic world experienced a golden age. Thanks to its great wealth and the advantages it possessed over its neighbors, it could afford to import what it needed from outside. The necessities included timber for fuel and construction, metals (iron and gold above all), and slaves. Slaves formed an important component of the Islamic commercial system; even though they were seldom used in agriculture, they still were imported in large numbers for artisan labor and for domestic and military service. One reason for the great demand for slaves was the equally great accumulation of riches the Islamic elite acquired during the period of the conquest, a wealth preserved through many generations by their descendants. To meet that demand, the Muslims looked beyond their frontiers to four regions of slave supply in this period: Europe, the area of the Russian rivers, the east (particularly Turkestan but also India), and sub-Saharan Africa.

Slaves were most commonly used as domestic servants, an occupation free people shunned. Domestics, especially females, were often well treated. At times they became members of the family through adoption, and domestic slaves were generally sold only if they offended the family. Male slaves often served as business agents of their masters. They could engage in business on their own account, and they also could be put to a variety of other uses, including menial tasks at times. The slaves had their own hierarchy, equivalent to and dependent on the status of their masters.

One economic feature of the Islamic world, the expansion of sugar-cane cultivation, was to be of lasting importance for the later history of slavery, although the Muslims ordinarily did not use slaves in sugar production. When they conquered Mesopotamia in the seventh and eighth centuries, they established an imported labor force of blacks from East Africa to work in the cane fields, although in both the Islamic world and in the Christian Mediterranean, free labor predominated in sugar production. Cane could be planted on lands too poor for grain, and it helped to improve the soil in the process. There were special requirements for sugar-cane production, including large tracts of land, irrigation projects, mills, and machinery, and only the rich were able to pursue it.

The fourteenth- and fifteenth-century decline in Egyptian sugar production was attributable in part to internal changes in the Islamic economy. Another factor was the increasing sugar production by Europeans, who from the time of the Crusades had begun to develop sugar plantations and refining centers.

From ancient times to the seventeenth century, Italy knew slavery. While slavery declined in Europe north of the Alps and serfdom rose, the trade in and the use of slaves persisted in Italy. One reason was the durability of urban life in the Italian peninsula; urban life in preindustrial societies often included domestic slavery. More important was Italy's geographic location and the propensity of many Italians for long-distance trade.

The Italian use of slaves was widespread, and most were recruited by the slave trade. In the late eleventh century, when the Normans conquered southern Italy, they often enslaved members of the defeated population, but this was an atypical situation. Wars in the Italian peninsula only rarely ended with the enslavement of the defeated. Italians mainly imported their slaves from outside. Already by the twelfth century, Venice had a slave population that was recruited from a wide area, though it was a small percentage of the total Venetian population. By the mid-twelfth century Genoa possessed Muslim slaves.

In the fourteenth and fifteenth centuries, slaves in Italy came from a number of areas and ethnic groups. In the Italian states, probably the greatest number of slaves were used as domestic servants, and a percentage of these acted as concubines for their masters. Small numbers of others were used in artisan and craft workshops. There is little evidence of slave use in agriculture. Small market farmers may have employed a few slaves as laborers, but plantation agriculture was not important in the peninsula. Italians did make use of a limited number of slaves in agricultural pursuits on the islands they controlled in the Mediterranean, but the practice was not often translated to the mainland. Finally, there were in Italy additional victims of the slave trade, acquired elsewhere and present in Italy only until they could be transshipped for sale elsewhere.

The slave trade to Italy was almost exclusively in the hands of long-distance traders who purchased people in distant markets. In later centuries, prisoners captured in the wars among the Italian states were at times held for ransom and threatened with slavery, but these were exceptional cases. Italian merchants were among Europe's most energetic and successful traders in distant regions. An important part of their trade was devoted to slaves, and while the bulk of their slave trade was concerned with supplying third parties (especially Egyptian Muslims) with slaves purchased in other regions (especially the Balkans and the northern ports of the Black Sea), they also brought slaves home to Italy to be sold.

The existence of slavery in Renaissance Italy was pervasive. Account books and notarial records have preserved evidence of the presence of numerous slaves of various ethnic origins in the peninsula, and their existence also intrigued the portrait painters of the Renaissance. Nonetheless, the Venetian census of 1563 listed only 7 to 8 percent of the population as servants, and this included free persons as well as slaves. Within Europe in the late Middle Ages and the Renaissance, slavery was never crucial for social or economic development, and it was not practiced on any great scale in Europe proper.

Christian Spain and Portugal were part of the European world where slavery gradually declined as serfdom and free labor grew. For most of the early Middle Ages, the economies of the Christian states of Iberia were weak, and as a result the possibilities of slave use in large-scale ventures producing goods and commodities for urban markets was restricted. Unlike other parts of western Europe, however, the Iberian kingdoms were frontier states, sharing borders with non-Christian states whose inhabitants could be raided and enslaved with complete legality. This meant that slavery persisted there longer and more vigorously than elsewhere in Christian Europe. When the Iberians began their overseas expansion in the fifteenth century, slavery was a living institution that could be transplanted with ease to the Atlantic and Caribbean islands and the American mainland.

In the early phases of the Christian reconquest of Iberia, from the eighth century to the twelfth, two distinct slave systems coexisted in the Christian states. One was a continuation of traditional Roman and Visigothic slavery; its victims were primarily Christians, whose conditions were virtually identical to those of the Visigothic slaves. By the twelfth century the use of Christian slaves had almost ended, but slavery as a system persisted. Even during the early period, numbers of Muslim slaves had been present in the Christian states, but after the twelfth century most of the slaves were Muslim prisoners of war, captured in the fall of conquered cities and in the course of Christian raids into Muslim territory.

Portugal also played a vital role in the spread of sugar production. In the later Middle Ages sugar was being produced with some profitability in the Algarve (southern Portugal), and the desire to tap the wealth of Morocco's sugar plantations may have entered into the motivations of Portuguese expansion in Africa. Beyond this, the major importance of Portugal and Spain in the expansion of sugar production came as a result of their discovery and exploitation of the islands of the eastern Atlantic. To a lesser extent the Azores and the Cape Verdes, and to a much greater extent Madeira and the Spanish-held Canaries, were to be staging areas on the eve of the discovery of America. For both Spain and Portugal, slavery would only experience an upsurge when Africa and the Atlantic became important theaters of action in the fifteenth century.

Several late medieval developments had stimulated European slavery and helped to form the background for American slavery. First were the Crusades. In the eleventh century, western European knights conquered and established a series of states in Syria and Palestine that lasted until the late thirteenth century. The presence of the Crusader states allowed greatly expanded commercial activity by Italian merchants, always the most active in the slave trade. More important, Europeans gained from the Crusades a taste for cane sugar. From the Muslims of Syria and Palestine, Europeans learned the techniques of cultivating and refining cane sugar. With the end of the Crusades, Europeans introduced sugar-cane planting and refining to several parts of southern Europe and then to the Atlantic islands.

In the late Middle Ages, Europeans recovered and assimilated into their legal systems Roman law and its elaborate regulations for slaves. In the eleventh century, the Italian legal scholar Irnerius began the academic study of the Roman code, and in the next two centuries knowledge and application of Roman law spread widely in western Europe. In Iberia, the Castilian king Alfonso X in the mid-thirteenth century produced a new law code for his kingdom, known as the Siete Partidas, with heavy influences derived from Roman law. Although it never fully became law in Castile, the

Siete Partidas still had a significant influence in the late medieval and early modern legislation in Spain, both for the home countries and later for the American colonies, and thereby ensured that many Roman rules for slavery entered Spanish law.

By the end of the Middle Ages, Iberia had ample historical experience with slavery, a legal code for operating a slave system, and sugar-cane agriculture. All were necessary for a great expansion of slavery in the overseas colonies.

[*See also* Europe; Historiography, *article on* Medieval European and Mediterranean Slavery; Law, *article on* Roman Law; *and* Slave Trade, *article on* Medieval Europe.]

BIBLIOGRAPHY

Bloch, Marc. *Slavery and Serfdom in the Middle Ages: Selected Papers.* Berkeley: University of California Press, 1975.

Bonnassie, Pierre. *From Slavery to Feudalism in Southwestern Europe.* Translated by Jean Birrell. Cambridge: Cambridge University Press, 1991.

Dockés, Pierre. *Medieval Slavery and Liberation.* Translated by Arthur Goldhammer. Chicago: University of Chicago Press, 1982.

Heers, Jacques. *Esclaves et domestiques au Moyen Age dans le monde méditerranéen.* Paris: Fayard, 1982.

Phillips, William D., Jr. *Slavery from Roman Times to the Early Transatlantic Trade.* Minneapolis: University of Minnesota Press, 1985.

Verlinden, Charles. *L'esclavage dans l'Europe médiévale.* 2 vols. Bruges: De Tempel, 1955, 1977.

—WILLIAM D. PHILLIPS, JR.

MIDDLE PASSAGE. The Atlantic slave trade remained one of the least studied areas in modern Western historiography until the 1960s. This late start was not due to any lack of sources: the materials available for its study were abundant from the very beginning. Rather, it was ignored because it presented a morally difficult problem and because historians lacked methodological tools with which to analyze the complex quantitative data.

In the last three decades of the twentieth century, however, the demography, economics, and politics of the Atlantic trade have been systemati-cally explored. It is now known that from 1444 to 1860 an estimated 11.7 million Africans were carried from Africa across the Atlantic. Of these about 380,000 were taken before 1600, 1.9 million in the seventeenth century, 6 million in the eighteenth century (the peak of the trade was in the last quarter of that century) and about 3.3 million after 1811. About 9.8 million of these Africans arrived in the Americas, with the largest contingent going to Brazil (3.9 million); another 3.8 million went to the non-Hispanic West Indies, 1.6 million to the Spanish American islands and mainland, and fewer than one-half million to the United States. Portuguese, English, and French slave-traders carried the overwhelming majority, although slave-traders from the Hanseatic League and Scandinavia to Newport, Rhode Island, and Rio de Janeiro also outfitted ships for the trade. No national or religious group active in the Atlantic commerce failed to participate in the trade.

Although the volume and direction are now known, major debates remain concerning the basic economics of the trade, its demographic impact, and the causes and consequences of its abolition. Still controversial is the question of who benefited from the slave trade. Initially it was assumed that the trade was a European monopoly from which Africans received little compensation. Profits were astronomic, the argument ran, because slaves could be bought with castoff, second-hand, or shoddy European products, often at a fraction of their real value. It has now been proven, however, that slaves purchased in Africa were not a low-cost item. The goods exported to Africa to pay for the slaves were costly manufactured products and were the single most expensive factor in the outfitting of the voyage. Moreover, African demands dictated European exports to the sub-Saharan region, and the most preferred goods were fine East Indian textiles. It is in fact their role as Asian trade ports that explains why Liverpool and Nantes emerged as the premier slave-trading ports of England and France in the eighteenth century.

Next in economic importance after textiles

were bar iron, agricultural tools, household implements, weapons, gunpowder, brandy, rum, and other liquors, tobacco, and a host of other relatively costly products. Furthermore, the terms of trade between Africa and Europe moved in favor of the Africans over the course of the eighteenth and early nineteenth centuries. Not only were slaves not cheap, but the mix of goods that went into the trade tended to vary over time and reflected changing conditions of demand and supply. Thus African merchants adjusted their demands for goods in response to market conditions. Africans also successfully prevented the Europeans from creating monopoly conditions. The European forts in West Africa and even the Portuguese coastal and interior towns in Southwest Africa were ineffective in excluding competing buyers from entering the local market.

The actual purchase of Africans was a complex affair, involving everything from fixed coastal fort or port locations to open-boat traders who sailed the rivers and coastal waters for several months, purchasing slaves in small lots. Some African states were strong enough to tax the trade heavily, but in other areas a free market existed. Nevertheless, it was the Africans who controlled the volume of slaves on the coast and determined the characteristics of the slaves who would be offered.

It had been assumed that the low cost of the slaves made it profitable to pack in as many as the ship could hold and to accept high rates of mortality during the Atlantic crossing. If the slaves were not inexpensive, however, then the argument about "tight-packing" loses its force. Even more convincing than these theoretical arguments is the fact that no recent study has yet shown a systematic correlation of any significance between the numbers of slaves carried and mortality at sea. Nevertheless, slaves had less room than did contemporary troops or convicts transported. It appears that after much experience in the exigencies of the trade, slavers took on only as many slaves as they could expect safely to cross the Atlantic. From scattered references in the period be-

fore 1700, it seems that provisioning and carrying arrangements were initially deficient; but studies indicate that after 1700 slavers carried water and provisions for about double their expected voyage times, and that they usually carried slightly fewer slaves then their legally established limits.

This increasing sophistication in the carrying of slaves was reflected in declining rates of mortality. In the pre-1700 trade the average mortality rates over many voyages tended to hover around 20 percent. This mean rate reflected quite wide variations, with many ships coming in with very low rates, and many others experiencing rates in excess of the mean figure. After 1700 the mean rates dropped, and the variation around the mean declined. By the mid-eighteenth century the mean stood at around 10 percent, and by the last quarter of the century all trades were averaging a rate of 5 to 8 percent. Moreover, the dispersion around these mean rates had declined, and about two-thirds of the ships were experiencing a mortality rate quite close to the mean figure. It should be stressed that even a 5 percent mortality rate for young healthy adults during a voyage that lasted thirty to fifty days is still an extraordinarily high rate. In addition, while troop, immigrant, and convict mortality rates in the eighteenth century approached the slave death numbers, in the nineteenth century they consistently fell to below 1 percent for trans-Atlantic voyages. For slaves, however, these rates never fell below 5 percent for any large group of vessels surveyed. There thus seems to have been, paradoxically, a minimum rate due to the special conditions of slave transport, which the Europeans could never reduce.

Over time the degree of standardization in slave-trading vessels increased. Specialized vessels were constructed for the slave trades of all nations. From the second half of the eighteenth century, slave ships were averaging two hundred tons among all European traders, a tonnage that seemed best to fit the successful carrying potential of the trade. These ships averaged more than 2.5 slaves per ton. Slave-traders were also the first of the com-

Engraving depicting the interior of a slave ship, nineteenth century.

mercial traders to adopt copper sheathing for their ships, a costly new method to prolong the life of the vessels and guarantee greater speed. These slave-trade vessels were much smaller ships than Europeans used in either the West Indian or East Indian trades. This specialization and tonnage difference explains why the famous model of a triangular trade (European goods to Africa, slaves for America, and sugar for Europe all on the same voyage) is largely a myth. The majority of American crops reached European markets in much larger and specially constructed West Indian vessels designed primarily for this shuttle trade; the majority

of slavers returned with small cargoes or none at all; and in the largest slave trade of all, that of Brazil, no slavers either departed from or returned to Europe.

All traders carried similar numbers of slaves per ton, and while there was some variation in crew size, most slave trade ships had double the number of seamen needed to sail a vessel of that tonnage. This was necessitated by the need to control the slave prisoners. All the European slave traders also used similar provisioning, health, and transportation procedures, building temporary decks for housing the Africans and dividing them by age and sex. Europeans traders adopted smallpox vaccination at about the same time; all carried large quantities of African food provisions to feed the slaves, and all used the same methods for daily hygiene, exercise and the care of the sick. This standardization explains the common experience of mortality decline.

Death on the crossing was due to a variety of causes. The biggest killers were gastrointestinal disorders, which were often related to the quality of food and water available on the trip, and fevers. Bouts of dysentery were common, and the "bloody flux" could break out in epidemic proportions. The increasing exposure of the slaves to dysentery increased both the rates of contamination of supplies and the incidence of death. Dysentery accounted for the majority of deaths and was the most common disease experienced on voyages. The astronomic rates of mortality reached on occasional voyages, however, were due to outbreaks of smallpox, measles, or other highly communicable diseases that were not related to time at sea or the conditions of food and water supply, hygiene, and sanitation practices. The randomness of epidemic diseases prevented even experienced and efficient captains from eliminating high mortality rates.

Although time at sea was not usually correlated with mortality, there were some routes in which

At the Water Tub; engraving from *Harper's New Monthly Magazine*, volume 15, August 1857.

time was a factor. Simply because they were one-third longer than any other route, the East African slave trades that developed in the late eighteenth and early nineteenth centuries were noted for overall higher mortality than the West African routes, even though mortality per day at sea was the same or lower than on the shorter routes. In addition, the carrying together of slaves from different epidemiological zones in Africa meant the transmission of local endemic diseases to all those who were carried aboard. In turn, this guaranteed the spread of all major African diseases to America.

Women represented on average one-third to one-quarter of the Africans forced to migrate, and children represented on average about 10 percent. These age and sex ratios were determined primarily by African supply conditions. Women were in higher demand than men in the internal and East African trades.

The ethnic composition of the slaves was also African-determined. Except for the Portuguese in Angola and Mozambique, Europeans had little idea of the nature of the societies with which they were dealing. In most cases Africans were simply designated by the ports from which they were shipped rather than by any accurate language, group, or national identity. Most European traders had no conception of what went on a few miles inland from the coast, and even those who established forts and fixed settlements dealt with local African governments. On a few occasions, such as the collapse of a large state or after a major military defeat, whole nations of well-defined and clearly delineated groups entered the slave trade and were known by their proper names in America, but these cases were the exception rather than the rule.

These biases in the age and sex of the migrating Africans had a direct impact on the growth and decline of American slave populations. The low ratio of women in each arriving ship, the fact that most of these slave women were mature adults who had already spent several of their fecund years in Africa, and the fact that few children were carried to America meant that the African slaves who arrived in America could not reproduce their numbers.

As for the larger impact of the trade on Africa and Europe, there is much debate. The discussion can be divided into three general questions. Was the slave trade profitable at the firm level and were these profits excessive? What impact did the slave trade have on the economic growth of Europe? And finally, what impact did the slave trade and slave labor have on African growth?

Profits in the slave trade were not extraordinary by European standards. The average 10 percent rate obtained was considered a good profit rate at the time, but not out of the range of other contemporary investments. Although key industries may have relied heavily on the African trade, it is now the consensus that British industrial growth was not financed with profits from the slave trade. But did the trade exacerbate African warfare? Did it promote the spread of epidemics across the continent, and did it depopulate large zones of potential agricultural growth?

Finally, discussion about the trade involves questions of African-American cultural origins. Given the European confusion on African ethnographic information, it has been difficult to reconstruct the cultural elements brought from Africa to America. There is little question that popular religious beliefs and basic cultural components crossed the Atlantic, but the policies of dividing groups and forcing all to work in the lingua franca of the local Europeans tended to dilute the coherence of whole belief systems, especially those tied to state power. Thus local deities and those associated with health and the family had a better chance of surviving the crossing. Moreover, even the most isolated African runaway communities tended to mix their beliefs with popular European ideas, as well as with local Amerindian cultural features.

[*See also* Mortality in Transport; *and* Slave Trade, *article on* Trans-Atlantic Trade.]

BIBLIOGRAPHY

Curtin, Philip D. *The Atlantic Slave Trade: A Census.* Madison: University of Wisconsin Press, 1969.

Eltis, David. *Economic Growth and the Ending of the Transatlantic Slave Trade.* New York and Oxford: Oxford University Press, 1987.

Gemery, Henry A., and Jan S. Hogendorn, eds. *The Uncommon Market: Essays in the Economic History of the Atlantic Slave Trade.* New York: Academic Press, 1979.

Inikori, Joseph E., and Stanley L. Engerman, eds. *The Atlantic Slave Trade: Effects on Economies, Societies and People in Africa.* Durham, N.C.: Duke University Press, 1992.

Klein, Herbert S. *The Middle Passage: Comparative Studies in the Atlantic Slave Trade.* Princeton, N.J.: Princeton University Press, 1978.

Postma, Johannes. *The Dutch in the Atlantic Slave Trade, 1600–1815.* Cambridge: Cambridge University Press, 1990.

—HERBERT S. KLEIN

MINING. Whatever the object of extraction, mining has always been demanding on workers. In the past the hours were long, the work arduous, and conditions insalubrious and often dangerous. Whenever and wherever the institution of slavery coexisted with the potential for exploring mineral deposits, bondsmen were utilized from the onset of development.

The earliest recorded evidence of slaves employed in mining comes from Greece in the fifth century BCE, when several thousand bondsmen were put to work in the silver and lead mines of southeastern Attica. Slaves were also vital to the exploration of mines and quarries throughout the Roman Empire. Whether government monopolies, concessions, or purely private enterprises, these mining operations were highly dependent on slave labor, often constituting notable concentrations of captive populations. In Asia Minor, southeastern and central Europe, Egypt, the Greek islands, Sicily, Spain, and Lusitania, bondsmen extracted and refined gold, silver, copper, emeralds, and feldspar, and quarried marble and granite. Unskilled slaves, sometimes along with common free workers, made up the bulk of the work force, but bondsmen also frequently performed specialized tasks; they might act as foremen, overseers, and administrators and could even rise to the position of lessees of mining concessions. Although the fate of most of these slaves was an early death caused by overwork and harsh living conditions, it is nevertheless true that skilled workers and supervisors were afforded a reasonable chance of obtaining manumission, usually through self-purchase financed by savings (*peculium*) accumulated by way of payments for overtime labor or productivity incentives. Manumission rates approximated those experienced by the artisan and domestic chattel slaves of urban centers and distinguished both groups from the vast majority of slaves, who were engaged in agriculture on the Italian and Iberian peninsulas and in Gaul. Similar features of large concentrations of population, the emergence of a skilled slave elite, and a certain flexibility in the slave condition were later to characterize slave-based mining in the Western Hemisphere.

As early as the 1520s, slaves, both African and Native American, were employed at the silver and gold strikes made by the Spanish in central Mexico, Honduras, and northern Nicaragua. Simple placer mining methods prevailed in this early period, as they would in the strikes of the 1540s in northern Mexico, western Colombia, and Venezuela. Official Spanish prohibition of Indian enslavement eliminated this form of chattel, although free native workers, when available, were always welcomed by mine owners. Silver and mercury mining increasingly depended on various forms of Native American labor. In Bolivia and Peru slaves were virtually absent from mining operations, whereas in Mexico up to the mid-eighteenth century, African and creole bondsmen were an important supplement to the Native American labor force. There, owing to the high turnover of Indian labor, slaves often occupied skilled positions.

Black slaves continued as the mainstay of gold and copper mining in Hispanic America during the entire colonial period. Major gold deposits in the western Colombian region of Chocó were explored with slave labor throughout the eighteenth century. In the last quarter of the century the value of the platinum associated with auriferous deposits was finally recognized. Slave miners and their families comprised the largest group in the regional population, followed by Indians, who were largely dedicated to commercial foodstuff production. As the eighteenth century wore on, manumissions and miscegenation resulted in the emergence of a substantial free colored population. Owing to widespread absenteeism among mineowners, few whites resided on the Chocó. The region sheltered numerous maroon communities (*cimarrones*) and on several occasions was rocked by slave revolts in which free blacks also participated.

The mountainous hinterland of southeastern Brazil was the site in the eighteenth century of the emergence of an enormous slave-based mining society. Following the initial discoveries of gold in the 1690s, the region, aptly denominated Minas Gerais ("General Mines"), became a magnet for successive waves of immigrants, free and slave, African, Portuguese, and Brazilian. The discovery of diamonds in 1728 lent further impetus to this migration and led to the establishment of a separate, harshly administered Diamond District. In the far interior of Goiás and Mato Grosso, additional gold deposits were found, but in terms of population and wealth, these regions would never compare to Minas Gerais.

The extent of the colonies' dependence on slave labor is reflected in the fact that the size of legal claims granted by the crown varied according to the number of slaves possessed by the grantee. Rudimentary placer mining predominated throughout most of the century, although sluicing operations became increasingly complex as extraction followed veins up the hillsides ringing the region's

Drawing depicting the process of washing diamonds in Diamantina, Minas Gerais, Brazil, eighteenth century, from *Pequeno mapa de demarcação diamantine . . . Minas Gerais, século XVIII.*

countless rivers and streams. Underground exploration seems to have begun around the mid-eighteenth century and was subject to frequent cave-ins and flooding. Whether chilled from panning in cold waters, baked in the tropical sun of the hillsides, or forced to toil in precarious shafts, the slaves endured dreadful working conditions. As a result, there is little wonder that dozens of maroon communities (*quilombos*) flourished and rebellion was rampant.

At the same time, however, bondsmen were allowed to mine for personal gain in their free time, and substantial numbers were able to accumulate savings that were used for self-purchase or buying the freedom of family members. In order to stimulate production, slaves lucky enough to encounter diamonds weighing 17.5 carats or more were granted immediate freedom by the crown. The stealing of gold and diamonds by captive workers was a major headache for mine-owners and administrators. The towns and small cities that characterized the settlement of Minas soon overflowed with free coloreds, white proprietors, and adventurers, and the omnipresent slaves who performed every sort of economic activity. Slaves and free coloreds of diverse racial origins formed a veritable army of artisans and were largely responsible for the magnificent baroque art and architecture of colonial Minas. Although manumission and miscegenation were longstanding Brazilian traditions, in the mining region they took on unprecedented dimensions, despite a relative shortage of women in the early decades of the eighteenth century. By the nineteenth century free coloreds, among them numerous slaveholders, comprised the largest segment of the population, lending credence to the notion that mining societies were more permissive and freewheeling than those based on export agriculture.

Around the mid-eighteenth century gold yields declined precipitously, and the Minas economy began a transition toward agriculture and ranching geared to subsistence and the domestic market. Nevertheless, both gold- and diamond-mining

Engraving showing slave miners processing gold near Ouro Preto, Minas Gerais, Brazil, from João Maurécio's *Rugendas viagem pictoresca através do Brasilian* (1835).

persisted as important sectors of the economy well into the nineteenth century. Following independence in 1822, about sixteen firms, mostly financed by British capital, were established in order to explore subterranean gold mines. Organizational and technological improvements were introduced, and the predominantly slave labor force proved fully capable of accompanying them, even in highly skilled positions. Owing to the ultimate inadequacy of nineteenth-century mining techniques, most of these ventures were dismal failures, but the most successful of them, the Morro Velho Gold Mine, was extremely profitable and in the 1860s relied on a work force including more than seventeen hundred bondsmen. Independence also eliminated the severe colonial restrictions on diamond extraction. A second diamond boom took place from the 1820s to the 1860s, when Brazilian gems were dislodged from the international market by lower-priced stones from South Africa. Slaves were undoubtedly an important element in the nineteenth-century boom in Minas Gerais, but the entire phenomenon remains virtually unstudied.

In the United States during the eighteenth century increasing numbers of slaves were employed in mining coal and iron ore destined for the foundries of Maryland and Virginia. In the nineteenth century, Virginia exported coal to northeastern cities, and the Richmond region's iron works would prove vital to Confederate war efforts. European immigrants substituted for bondsmen in Maryland, but Virginia's industrial labor needs were largely supplied through temporary slave-rental contracts. This was also the case for the coal-mining operations associated with the saltworks of western Virginia. Southerners were wary of the large concentrations of bondsmen in these industries, particularly of the freedom of movement afforded the slaves in their free time. Gold strikes were made in North Carolina and Georgia during the first half of the nineteenth century. Although slaves were clearly present in the prospecting that ensued in both states, it appears that white adventurers greatly outnumbered them. Finally, it should be noted that the possibility of utilizing slaves in diverse mining operations in the unoccupied West fired the imagination of Southern politicians during the congressional debates over the slave or free status of newly incorporated territories and states that marked the antebellum period.

[*See also* Brazil; *and* South America.]

BIBLIOGRAPHY

Boxer, C. R. *The Golden Age of Brazil, 1695–1750.* Berkeley: University of California Press, 1962.

Lewis, Ronald L. *Coal, Iron and Slaves: Industrial Slavery in Maryland and Virginia, 1715–1865.* Westport, Conn.: Greenwood Press, 1979.

Russell-Wood, A. J. R. "The Gold Cycle, c.1690–1750." In *Colonial Brazil,* edited by Leslie Bethell. Cambridge: Cambridge University Press, 1987.

Sharp, William Frederick. *Slavery on the Spanish Frontier: The Colombian Chocó, 1680–1810.* Norman: University of Oklahoma Press, 1976.

—Douglas Libby

MORAL ISSUES. In 1869 W. E. H. Lecky offered his famous verdict on the relationship between morality and slavery: "The unwearied, unostentatious, and inglorious crusade of England against slavery may probably be regarded as among the three or four perfectly virtuous pages in the history of nations" (vol. 1, p. 161). A century later Lecky's now famous dictum was as frequently used to illustrate anti-slavery's screening function for capitalist-imperialist exploitation as it was offered as evidence of moral progress. Only a century before Lecky's *History* was published, however, the moral crusade he referred to was unimaginable, and for thousands of years before that slavery's relation to morality was discussed within an entirely different context.

The distinguishing features of the status of slavery are the permanent, natal alienation of the slave from the community, and the availability of the slave's body, labor, and offspring to the master. Long before the status was systematized in law, various forms of servitude existed in the Americas, Asia, Africa, and Europe. Law codes and customs were primarily concerned with making the condition of servitude conform to a desired optimum model of the slave's powerlessness and dishonor. Enslavement meant a convergence of the status of dependent humans with property or domestic animals, as in Aristotle's casual reference to oxen as the slaves of the poor. In societies with highly developed interregional markets, captives spared from death were routinely shipped, priced, and marketed like livestock without regard to prior familial and communal connections.

Sparing the lives of captives became a fundamental rationale in the legitimization of enslavement. The process of physical enslavement was usually accompanied by psychological debasement. The ideology of separation and degradation led to endless analogies of slaves with animate property or otherwise "incomplete" human beings. A characteristic of all systems of slavery in male-dominated societies was the total elimination of any hint of manhood from the enslaved. They were culturally designated as "Sambo" types, docile but irresponsible, loyal but lazy, humble but chronically given to lying, stealing, and immature silliness. The slave's putative relationship with his master was one of utter dependence. However, whatever the imputed analogues to inanimate property, domestic animals, children, or women, slaves were used as administrators, business agents, household guardians, and soldiers. These were all functions that maximized an individual slave's autonomy and power. Precisely because of this broad range of roles, stark behavioral extremes of pure coercion or positive incentives never existed where the institution was of any size and duration.

Most scholars agree that in complex premodern societies, permeated by relations of dependency, there was no moral interest in universalizing liberation. Principled rejections of slavery were confined to ascetic fringe groups like the Jewish Essenes. A social condition of slavelessness might be envisioned as having prevailed at the beginning of time, as in the Roman juristic reference to slavery as being contrary to nature. This reference to a Golden Age was quickly defused by the observation that slavery was an institution of the *ius gentium* (the common law of all peoples) and "what natural reason prescribed for all men" (Finley, 1980, pp. 99–100). This rationale reverberated through centuries of ancient and medieval philosophy and civil law commentaries, producing no extended literature on the morality or immorality of continuing slavery as an institution.

Classical philosophy viewed slavery as an aspect of an assumed hierarchy of the natural moral order, rather than as a problem demanding moral scrutiny. For Plato both the social order and the human personality were arranged in a hierarchy of virtue from ruling rational elements to unruly affective elements. The worst societies and individuals were those in which the lower, or slave element ruled, inverting the natural moral order. Slaves were best off when governed for their own good.

Aristotle offered the most extensive surviving attempt at an ancient justification of slavery. Slaves fulfilled the function of animate instruments in sustaining life and the institutions (household and village) necessary for the existence of a higher institutional form, the polis. The properties of ruling and subordination belonged to the system of nature itself: some people were naturally slaves, and for them, the institution was both beneficial and just. Aristotle acknowledged that there was a contrary contemporary opinion, asserting that slavery was not natural but conventional, being based on force and not on justice. Aristotle retorted that even though some people were exceptionally and unjustly enslaved, the institution itself was natural and just. He referred to the general Greek consensus that "barbarians" were "everywhere and inherently slaves" (*Politics*, I, 6, 19, 1255a).

Aristotle significantly produced the last, as well as the first, surviving Classical analysis of the morality of institutional slavery. Post-Aristotelian philosophy made a clean break between morality and the social order, psychologizing slavery and locating virtue and vice within the individual soul.

Slavery was sometimes envisioned as a morally desirable model. Ancient Mesopotamian rulers regarded slavery as the universal model of human society itself, with all of their subjects as slaves. Hebrew Scripture conceived of Israel as collectively bound to a single, all-powerful deity who had liberated them from collective servitude and would always redeem them. This tradition passed into Christianity as a powerful metaphor. Rulers and disciples of Jesus alike were positively described as "slaves of God." Institutional slavery stimulated Christian conceptions of slavery as morally bivalent. One might be fettered to the devil, or a redeemed slave of God. In both cases, slavery was envisioned as inherent in humanity's relationship to God.

This legitimation still allowed for a great deal of discussion about the proper behavior of both slaves and masters within the context of the institution. Discussions about the proper treatment of slaves included homages to the "faithful slave" who exceeded the demands of normal obedience. The tradition of both Seneca and St. Paul exhorted slaves to obedience. Chaos and sin were themselves kinds of slavery, and accommodation to enslavement was a form of moral virtue. Regarding the imputation of degradation, however, it has been argued that there is no evidence to suggest that slaves ever internalized the conception of degradation attributed to them by their masters.

In conventional accounts, the late eighteenth-century emergence of anti-slavery marks a dramatic revolutionary shift in moral perceptions of slavery. In this account, the great rationalizing tradition of Plato, Aristotle, and Aquinas continued, in the form of natural law theory, through Grotius, Hobbes, Pufendorf, and, implicitly, Locke (Davis, 1966, pp. 120–121). This perspective overlooks a long-term historical development outside the mainstream of the classic philosophical tradition. What made Europe the probable locus of a moral revolution against slavery was the gradual disappearance of slavery and servile labor during the six centuries after the year 1000. The movement against bound labor, which Adam Smith, writing toward the end of the eighteenth century, called a "revolution of the greatest importance to the public happiness of mankind," was not instituted by any sustained moral, political, or religious movement. This movement certainly did not flow from the dominant philosophical or theological tradition of the time, which remained almost impervious to the whole process.

By the mid-sixteenth century, however, the new social reality was being registered in a self-conscious manner. In France, John Bodin not only expressed hostility to slavery *per se* but also described the institution as historically superseded in northwestern Europe. Bodin delighted in challenging the entire Aristotelian tradition on slavery. Moreover, he explicitly disavowed any originality whatever in his assessment of slavery as unnatural, unproductive, and anachronistic. Bodin argued within a long French juridical tradition, asserting the freedom of French soil. Across the Channel, Chief Justice Sir John Fortescue had articulated the same juridical principle for England a century before: the laws of England favor liberty in every situation. English "custom" liberated all servile foreigners as soon as they reached the island.

By 1600 this "free soil" tradition had been "naturalized" throughout most of northwestern Europe; however, a new dimension of slavery was simultaneously being nurtured into existence under European sponsorship. Mediterranean Europe had maintained an unbroken continuity of slavery, acquiring enslaved Muslims, Slavs and sub-Saharan Africans. With the fifteenth-century expansion of European markets to Africa, Asia, and the Americas, Europe's investment in overseas slaveholding expanded rapidly.

Although the Aristotelian moralizing principle of natural slavery still prevailed in philosophy and theology at the time of Iberian overseas expansion after 1450, Christendom had narrowed the scope of "natural slaves" to include only infidels who had rejected the true faith. The great mid-sixteenth-century debate held at Valladolid in Spain, on the legitimacy of enslaving Indians, was the last prominently to invoke Aristotle's authority on natural slavery. Insofar as traditional arguments were thereafter offered in favor of New World slavery, they were drawn from Scripture and the redemption of idolaters.

Although western European juridical theory favored metropolitan liberty, Classical civil law provided a great reservoir of precedents for the revival of overseas slavery. While rejecting Roman slave law as invalid in their own homelands, northwestern European governments accepted slave codes as applicable to their extra-European territories. Slavery was geographically and racially marginalized during the first one and one-half centuries of northwestern European colonial expansion (c. 1600–1750). The situation was epitomized in John Locke's *Two Treatises on Government.* The philosopher explicitly denounced slavery as too vile an estate for an Englishman to plead for, yet his work implicitly justified, either outside the social contract or by the claims of proprietorship, even the vigorous expansion of slave colonies by Englishmen like himself.

The difference between antiquity and modernity was crucial. Slavery was now morally precarious. The world had been made safe for modern overseas slavery by a geographical bifurcation rather than by ubiquitous practice. Within northwestern Europe the assumption of slavery as morally polluting and historically anachronistic strengthened even while slavery expanded abroad. Slavery was no longer sustained by a consensual accepted sense of universality and centrality, but by geographical and climatic difference and distance (Drescher, 1986, chap. 1).

Although the moral valuation of slavery as vile and polluting was not an invention of the mid-eighteenth century, three developments during that century caused the emergence of a moral crusade to reconstruct the entire world in the image of "free" western Europe. The first development was the breakdown of the geographic bifurcation between Europe and the overseas world. Although slavery was legal in all of the European colonial world, some English settlements on the coast of continental North America resembled their metropolis in the preponderance of European inhabitants, European political culture, and free laborers. Meanwhile, thousands of Africans were transported to northwestern Europe, especially to England, stimulating judicial crises over the possible erosion of free-soil principles in Europe. Finally, major political revolutions in North America, France, and the Caribbean created opportunities for dramatic action against trans-Atlantic slavery. The American Declaration of Independence (1776) and the French Declaration of the Rights of Man and Citizen (1789) provided a new framework for collective challenges to slavery by slaves and free citizens alike.

The second major development was the eighteenth-century de-moralization of slavery. The rise of secular and materialist social philosophy undercut the traditional value systems that had supported slave systems. More than any other thinker, Montesquieu put the issue of modern slavery on the agenda of the European Enlightenment. Invoking the criterion of general human happiness, he encouraged the imaginative experiment of role reversal between masters and slaves. The fundamental premise of such a reversal was Bodin's emphasis on universally shared human characteristics, rather than the classical notion of sharp interpersonal hierarchy of virtue. Dismissing appeals to a natural order favoring slavery, Montesquieu left intact only the "modern" argument—that tropical climates made men unwilling to do heavy labor without coercion.

Montesquieu's reframing of slavery was part of a more extended argument about human nature being developed in the seventeenth and eighteenth centuries. It involved the universalizing of individual autonomy as the point of departure for evaluating the human condition. The satisfaction of individual material needs, collective wellbeing, and the ordinary happiness of ordinary people displaced the Classical concern with virtue and the Christian concern with sin. The beginning of this perspective dates from Locke's generation, but it reached full fruition in the second half of the eighteenth century.

Procuring life's basic requirements, the needs of the household, which antiquity had deemed as the inferior concern of animals, foreigners, women, and slaves, became the natural business of humanity. One had to be concerned, as never before, with the motivation of all in order to achieve efficient production and the happiness of the greatest number. When Adam Smith taught his students that "opulence and freedom" were the two greatest blessings men can possess, he meant that liberty was linked to individual desires and accumulation, to the everyday goals of private, self-interested economic activity.

Slavery was less efficient than free labor; it undermined the growth of population, failed to stimulate productivity, and diminished the collective demand for greater comforts. Slavery also corrupted the wealthy by valorizing idleness and cruelty. Slaves, wrote Benjamin Franklin, "pejorate the families that use them; the white children become proud, disgusted with labor, and being educated in idleness, are rendered unfit to get a living by industry" (Franklin, 1751, quoted in Finley, 1961, p. 231). Alexis de Tocqueville made the same conflation of economics and morality a century later in his comparison of lethargic slave Kentucky and energetic free-labor Ohio. Their "modern" presumption was that getting a living by industry was an honorable and crucial virtue. In antiquity, the only comparable concern among philosophers and moralists was about the harmful effects of any excess in behavior. In Finley's words, "No ancient moralist would have thought it harmful to be unfit for getting a living by industry; on the contrary, that was precisely the ideal for the truly free man" (1980, p. 100). Antiquity's morality was now deemed as "peculiar" as its slavery. Romans held "peculiar" notions of honor, according to whether a citizen, stranger, or slave were involved. Morality was premised on universalizing choice, and on substituting the anonymous constraints of interdependence for the relationships of personal domination. The ancient ideal of slaveholding had been devalued in favor of free producers and consumers.

Nevertheless, this line of argument by no means made a virtue of *anti-slavery*. Having argued in naturalistic terms for the superiority of free labor, the same eighteenth-century writers offered naturalistic accounts for slavery's persistence and expansion into their own time. At best, the ending of slavery would be the slow effect of imperceptible change, as in European history. Moreover, one of the moral ambiguities propounded by the Enlight-

enment economists was the fact that in their schema, improvements in human freedom were coincidental with improvements in both wealth and the security of property rights. The continuous expansion of overseas slavery produced a clear ideological conflict between any attack on slavery and masters' rights to their property in persons.

Another development was required not just to de-moralize slavery, but to moralize anti-slavery. It came from within the very religious tradition that had repeatedly renewed its compromise with slavery for seventeen centuries. Theologians had occasionally pressed for mitigation of one aspect or another of slavery, but abolition of the status of slavery had never been a formal objective of institutionalized Christianity. The first collectivities to denounce the principle of slavery were the heirs of earlier perfectionist sects. Most such sects disintegrated or withdrew from radical economic commitments; the Anglo-American Society of Friends, or Quakers, were the only radical seventeenth-century sect to become institutionally stabilized, politically powerful (in America), and deeply entrenched in the Atlantic slave system. A mid-eighteenth-century crisis over the coercive requirements of slaveholding resulted in a collective Quaker decision to withdraw from the system. Similar developments in late-eighteenth-century Protestant revivalism created a broad ecumenical front against the slave system in areas of the Anglo-American Atlantic where it was least entrenched economically.

The greatest moral innovation of the religious turn against slavery was its invention of the guilt of nonslaveholders. Some popular religious groups succeeded in convincing large numbers of individuals who did no more than consume the sugar grown by slaves that they were guilty of mortal sin and capital crimes. Ordinary people were asked to internalize emotionally what Montesquieu had asked his elite readership to imagine intellectually—the reversal of roles between slave and master, of coerced producer and free consumer. The new mass consumption of sugar in late-eighteenth-century England was repackaged as an act of cannibalistic communion in which one stirred the blood of slaves in one's coffee or tea.

For the first time in history the discussion of slavery also became feminized as well as consumerized. As guardians of the table and as embodiments of compassion, women called on themselves to become active moral and political agents. Late eighteenth-century Britain produced the first public debates and polemic writings by women on the question of slavery. Other contentious reform movements quickly invoked slavery for their own domestic purposes. When people were asked to identify with the sufferings of slaves, slavery became a central metaphor in moral discourse about other sufferings: workers ("wage slaves"), women, children, and animals (Drescher, 1986, pp. 158–161).

Within a generation of the first successful attack on the British Atlantic slave trade (1807), British abolitionists envisioned a total eradication of slavery from the entire world. The succession of events marking the demise of slavery and of the Atlantic slave trade between the 1780s and 1880s struck contemporaries as one of the most extraordinary processes in human history. By 1890 slavery had been legally abolished throughout the New World, and anti-slavery was globally linked to the official policy of European imperialism. The explicitly altruistic character of the anti-slavery crusade, pitting morality against profit, seemed to prove that popular enlightenment could keep pace with humanity's moral advance. For Tocqueville, it was decisive that British economic and political interests had resisted emancipation until "popular mobilization swept it along." For John Stuart Mill, it was

L'Abolition de l'Esclavage à la Guadeloupe (Abolition of Slavery in Guadeloupe); engraving from Jean Jaurès's *Histoire socialiste: La deuxième republique français*, vol. 9, *La republique de 1848*.

"not by any change in the distribution of material interests but by the spread of moral convictions, that slavery has been put to an end in the British Empire and elsewhere" (Mill, 1861, p. 382). The abolition of slavery was hailed as irrefutable evidence of the power of moral imperative.

During the age of slave emancipation after 1780, the most unequivocal defense of slavery on moral grounds emerged in the U.S. South between 1820 and 1860. Southerners developed a twin defense of slavery in terms of paternalism and racism. Their argument was framed in far more moral terms than was Aristotle's. The Southern planter's household was more than the prerequisite of public action; it was the site of intense slave moralization. The master was expected to elicit complete dependence and loyalty from his slaves. Ideally, only those who deviated or resisted this moralizing order were punished. In their own moral defense, slaveholders embraced the "natural" group foundations of the institution far more rigorously than did Aristotle. They grounded their argument for slavery on the existence of a single inferior race, providentially designed for enslavement, domination, and moral improvement.

Southern pro-slavery thought also developed a distinctively "modern" dimension. Slaveholders subscribed to the contemporary notion that the spread of Western power, religion, and economic innovation was positively transforming the world. Nevertheless, they fundamentally rejected the notion that free labor afforded the best foundation for a free republic. Pointing to the ravages of Northern and trans-Atlantic industrialization, they presented the Southern social system as a model of a morally superior world order. Slavery offered the only organization of labor in which the interests of capital and labor were harmoniously combined, avoiding economic immiseration and moral disorientation. Because every society required a "mud-sill" of degraded labor on which to stand, the South had fortunately "found a race adapted to that purpose" (Genovese, 1992, p. 93). Southern defeat in the Civil War was also widely interpreted outside the South as decisive evidence for the linkage of moral progress and the ending of slavery.

By 1890, when slavery had legally ended in the Americas and European colonialization was linked to abolitionism by international treaties, the moral hegemony of anti-slavery seemed assured. Nonetheless, at the very moment that civil liberty seemed to be both ideologically hegemonic in Europe and expanding in tandem with Western imperialism, a serious devaluation of the moral foundations of anti-slavery emerged. Germany, remote from the anti-slavery mobilizations of the early nineteenth century, was the locus of an intense academic revival of classically oriented humanism. In this milieu, slavery was rationalized as the historical prerequisite of "that liberal [Greek] spirit which has not reappeared to a similar extent among any other people, that is to say the spiritual role of noble and great attitudes truly worthy of a free man" (Finley, 1980, p. 57). Building on that humanistic assessment, Friedrich Nietzsche devalued the entire humanitarian frame of reference, whose emblematic achievement was the abolition of chattel slavery. The Southern pro-slavery argument was rooted in scripturalism and Christianity; in the Nietzschean perspective, Christian toleration of slavery for seventeen centuries was insignificant when compared with the Judeo-Christian subversion of the "master-morality" of the ancient world. Pagan antiquity's admiration of natural differences of rank, power, and virtue had been subverted by an opposing morality that valued weakness, meekness, and submissiveness. In this perspective, all sufferers, all lower classes—slaves, prisoners, or women—were slavishly alike. Their "slave morality" was born of a religion that supremely valued its slave origins, and it triumphed politically with the French Revolution. Democracy, feminism, humanitarianism, and socialism, with their languages of rights, compassion, and universal suffrage, were only contemporary versions of slave morality. If the modern world had developed a "guilty conscience" about slavery, that was merely a reflection of the decadent nature of modernity and its values.

However controversial the connection between the Nietzschean revaluation of slavery and Europe's twentieth-century upheavals, the most significant resurgence of slavery in the twentieth century occurred in continental Europe. Nazi German ideology designated some groups for servitude to a master race, and World War II briefly stimulated one of the most rapid and massive expansions of slavery in human history. By 1945, after four years of Nazi domination, there were more than seven and one-half million captive laborers in Europe, compared with fewer than six million slaves of African descent in the Americas in 1860. Jews were designated for annihilation, but Slavs and other captive minorities were racially ranked as servile. Their bodies, when not selected for mass annihilation, remained at the disposal of the state for experiments as well as for labor brigades and brothels.

The defeat of the Nazis strengthened the prewar public consensus against slavery. The United Nations' Universal Declaration of Human Rights (1948) placed slavery high on its list of fundamental violations. All sovereign states have now legally abolished chattel slavery. Anti-slavery remains a model of the most successful moral crusade in human history. Those wishing to mobilize against everything from abortion to war invoke anti-slavery's victory as a measure of the mutability of moral attitudes. The moral consensus against slavery has abetted popular claims for compensation by descendants of the enslaved; retrospective accusations of guilt or concealment of guilt are also launched against descendants or putative descendants of the masters.

In scholarly circles, a major movement linked to anti-colonialism emerged after World War II. It aimed to *de*-moralize traditional anti-slavery. The pity, compassion, and empathy that Nietzsche considered emblematic of feminized, democratized, socialist, Judeo-Christian, slave morality, became for some anti-imperialists only the mask of economic interest, imperialism, or racism. Much empirical historical scholarship on slavery over the past half century has undermined this perspective. Economic historians have transformed the nineteenth-century view of slavery as a pathological economic system, sustained by extraordinary noneconomic motivations, into one sustained by economic motives quite similar to those of capitalists everywhere during the past five centuries. The striking economic success of New World slavery until destroyed by political abolitionism, therefore, still poses a central historiographic paradox. Economic historians have ironically reaffirmed the moral indictment of slavery and emphasize noneconomic causes in its ending (Fogel, 1989, pp. 393–406). Contemporary historians of slavery, like contemporary governments, tend to refer less to recent refinements in moral philosophy than to the reiterated concepts of human rights that gained popular assent over the past two centuries. The new moral indictment remains embedded in the old modern consensus of universal accessibility to happiness propounded by the Enlightenment.

Among moral philosophers, slavery itself seems to have lost considerable interest as a theme for systematic discussion. There are so many more recent examples of human behavior at their disposal—genocide, racism, poverty, nationalism, and so on. Where philosophers like Aristotle and Nietzsche remain attractive as catalysts of moral discourse, their specific views on slavery do not figure prominently. However, as formal philosophy becomes ever more sensitized to the robustness of relativist critiques of morality, slavery retains its scholarly status as one of humanity's most morally depleted institutions, and anti-slavery retains its popular status as one of the most successful movements in history.

[*See also* Abolition and Anti-Slavery; Anti-Slavery Literature, *overview article;* Christian Perspectives on Slavery; *and* Slave Trade, *article on* Suppression of Trade.]

BIBLIOGRAPHY

Aristotle. *The Politics of Aristotle.* Oxford: Clarendon Press, 1950.

Davis, David Brion. *The Problem of Slavery in Western Culture.* Ithaca, N.Y.: Cornell University Press, 1966.

Drescher, Seymour. *Capitalism and Antislavery: British Mobilization in Comparative Perspective.* London: Macmillan, 1986.

Finley, Moses I. *Ancient Slavery and Modern Ideology.* New York: Viking Press, 1980.

Fogel, Robert W. *Without Consent or Contract: The Rise and Fall of American Slavery.* New York: W. W. Norton, 1989.

Franklin, Benjamin. *The Papers of Benjamin Franklin.* Edited by L. W. Labaree. New Haven: Yale University Press, 1961.

Genovese, Eugene D. *The Slaveholder's Dilemma: Freedom and Progress in Southern Conservative Thought 1820–1860.* Columbia, S.C.: University of South Carolina Press, 1992.

Lecky, W. E. H. *A History of European Morals from Augustus to Charlemagne.* 2 vols. London: Longmans, Green, 1869.

Locke, John. *Two Treatises of Government.* Edited by Peter Laslett. Cambridge: Cambridge University Press, 1970.

Mill, John Stuart. *On Representative Government.* [1861] Repr. in *Collected Works of John Stuart Mill,* vol. 9. Toronto: University of Toronto Press, 1977.

Patterson, Orlando. *Slavery and Social Death: A Comparative Study.* Cambridge, Mass.: Harvard University Press, 1982.

—SEYMOUR DRESCHER

MORTALITY IN TRANSPORT. Slaves destined for the New World were captured or purchased in the interior of Africa, transported to the coast, and carried by sailing ship. Estimates of the number of deaths, based on a limited amount of data, have been calculated for each stage of this process. It is thought that 20 to 40 percent of the slaves died while being transported to the coast, another 3 to 10 percent died while waiting on the coast, and about 12 to 16 percent of those boarded on ships died during the voyage. Although the exact figures varied by season, route, and the length of time the entire process took, the estimates suggest that at least one-third and perhaps more than one-half of the slaves acquired in the interior of Africa died before arriving in the New World. More deaths occurred in the period immediately following arrival as slaves were exposed to the disease environment of the New World.

The mortality estimates for the sailing voyage (the infamous Middle Passage) are the most accurate. The first significant scholarly attempt to estimate shipboard mortality was by Philip Curtin in *The Atlantic Slave Trade* (1969). Since then a number of researchers have examined archival records in Europe, Africa, and the New World. Records have been found for ships carrying a substantial number of all slaves shipped to the New World; many of these are discussed by Herbert S. Klein in *The Middle Passage* (1978). Ignoring deaths that occurred on ships that never arrived in the New World, the average mortality estimates fall in the range of 12 to 16 percent, although they vary from 5 percent to 24 percent. Mortality has also been calculated as a rate per thirty-day period. These figures show that slaves died on the ships at a rate of sixty per thousand boarded per thirty-day period, with no consistent variation evident over time or by country. The rate of mortality suffered by slaves was substantially higher than that for other groups of travelers, such as immigrants, and for nontravelers. For example, Cohn (1989) shows that the thirty-day rate of mortality on a slave ship was about six times higher than that on an immigrant ship sailing from Europe to the United States.

Slaves died primarily from disease rather than from direct abuse, starvation, suicide, or shipwreck. A limited number of logs kept by slavers mention various types of diseases, but lack of medical knowledge at the time makes interpretation somewhat difficult. One of the major causes of death was dysentery. Smallpox and scurvy are the next most frequently mentioned, followed by a wide variety of other diseases including yellow fever, measles, yaws, pneumonia, and influenza. The reasons that disease was so prevalent on slave ships are somewhat unclear and controversial. Epidemiological factors, movement into a new disease environment, were contributors, as some contagious diseases spread quickly through a group that had never developed an immunity. Other diseases were caused or intensified by the treatment slaves received. While the epidemiological and treatment factors are not mutually exclusive, scholars disagree on their relative importance.

Differing disease environments were also important in causing mortality in situations other than the Middle Passage. Although almost any new disease environment increased mortality for Europeans, their death rates were especially high in Africa and the Caribbean. In addition, slaves went through a "seasoning" (acclimation) process after arrival in the New World. Within Africa at the time of the slave trade, distinct epidemiological regions existed owing to differences in climate and the limited interaction of individuals

from different parts of the continent. Slaves captured in the interior of Africa and moved to the coast were exposed to diseases they had never before encountered. Lacking immunity, many slaves caught these diseases; given the incubation period, the actual outbreak of the disease and the resulting deaths often did not occur until on board the ship. Eltis (1989) suggests that the specific disease environment through which slaves were moved was affected by location and weather, factors that caused shipboard mortality to vary by port and month of embarkation. Movement at the worst times significantly increased the number of slave deaths.

The treatment received after capture or purchase also contributed to the deaths of slaves. Travel to the coast was usually a forced march in

Gang of Captives Met at Mbame's on Their Way to Teffe; engraving from *Harper's Weekly*, volume 32, May 1866.

groups. The inability to keep up at times resulted in death or meant that the survivors arrived in a weakened condition. Health conditions did not improve once the slaves were on board the ship. Unfamiliar food and small amounts of (sometimes tainted) water weakened and dehydrated them. Further, the hot, crowded, unsanitary conditions below deck led to the spread of disease, especially dysentery. While Klein (1978) failed to find any direct relationship between higher crowding and higher mortality on slave ships, slave ships were four to five times more crowded than other passenger ships, a factor that probably contributed to the higher slave mortality. In addition, mortality was particularly low on British slave ships in the 1790s, when Dolben's Act limiting crowding was in effect. For these ships, Steckel and Jensen (1986) found that death rates were highest during the middle portion of the voyage, not at the start as epidemiological factors would suggest. It is uncertain how representative their findings are, however, because of the unusually low slave mortality during the voyages they studied. In summary, though the relative importance of the various factors is unclear, slaves died both from coming into contact with diseases for which they possessed no immunity and from the treatment they received during their ordeal.

[See also Demography; Middle Passage; and Slave Trade, articles on Trans-Atlantic Trade and Volume of Trade.]

BIBLIOGRAPHY

Cohn, Raymond L. "Maritime Mortality in the Eighteenth and Nineteenth Centuries: A Survey." *International Journal of Maritime History* 1 (1989): 159–191.

Curtin, Philip D. *The Atlantic Slave Trade: A Census.* Madison: University of Wisconsin Press, 1969.

Eltis, David. "Fluctuations in Mortality in the Last Half Century of the Transatlantic Slave Trade." *Social Science History* 13 (1989): 315–340.

Klein, Herbert S. *The Middle Passage: Comparative Studies in the Atlantic Slave Trade.* Princeton: Princeton University Press, 1978.

Steckel, Richard H., and Richard A. Jensen. "New Evidence on the Causes of Slave and Crew Mortality in the At-

lantic Slave Trade." *Journal of Economic History* 46 (1986): 57–77.

—RAYMOND L. COHN

MUI-JAI. The Cantonese term *mui-jai* (also spelled *mui-tsai;* possible Mandarin equivalent, *meizi*) literally means "little maid, little younger sister." A *mui-jai* was a young girl from a poor family who was sold to a well-to-do family to become a household servant. Considering the unconditional ownership held by the master, such persons should be more appropriately called "young female domestic slaves." This was a widespread custom, practiced throughout China at least from the time of the Han dynasty until the late 1940s, when it was ended with the establishment of the People's Republic of China. *Mui-jai* was more generally known in other parts of China and in Chinese literature as *yatou*. The term *mui-jai* was used within the province of Guangdong and in the Cantonese-speaking communities in Hong Kong and parts of British Malaya.

This system rose out of the interaction between overpopulation and the subordination of females in China. Overpopulation created extreme poverty in rural China, while the subordination of females led poor families to dispose of surplus female children. These unfortunate girls were sold directly or indirectly through agents by their parents to rich families as domestic slaves at between four and ten years of age. Young maids did tasks such as cleaning, laundry, making tea, and caring for young children of the master's household. They received neither wages nor education and were kept illiterate. The abuse of *mui-jai* was common. They were subjected to all forms of ill-treatment, ate leftovers, wore shabby clothing, and were beaten for making mistakes or failing to obey orders. The punishment was even more severe if one attempted to escape from her servitude. Usually it was the mistress rather than master who inflicted more cruelty.

The owner had absolute power over the *mui-jai*. He could take her as a concubine, give her away as a gift, sell her to brothel for profit, or employ her himself as a prostitute. A *mui-jai*'s bondage was supposed to end when she grew up and was married to a man chosen by her owner, but the owner might decide to sell her or continue to keep her instead of giving her freedom.

The *mui-jai* system was more widespread in urban centers than in rural villages. This was particularly evident in cities such as Guangzhou, Hong Kong, and Singapore. In 1918 the governor of Hong Kong informed the British government that practically every Chinese household in the colony that could afford the expense had a *mui-jai*. In 1922 ten thousand *mui-jai* were estimated to be present in Hong Kong alone. Owing to increased reports of the abuse of *mui-jai*, agitation for suppression of the system began in 1917. The crusaders included some British parliamentarians, missionaries, former British residents in Hong Kong, and Chinese Christians. The result was the adoption of an ordinance banning the practice by the Hong Kong government in February 1923. Although the British authorities suppressed the system after that time, it continued to exist under the cover of the "adopted daughter" (Cantonese, *yeung nui;* or Mandarin, *yang nü*) system in Hong Kong and British Malaya.

[*See also* China; Concubinage; *and* Gender and Slavery.]

BIBLIOGRAPHY

Chang Liang-tsai. *Chung-kuo feng-shu shih (A History of Chinese Custom)*. Hong Kong: T'ai Hsing Book Store, 1963.

Jaschok, Maria. *Concubines and Bondservants: The Social History of a Chinese Custom*. London: Zed Books, 1988.

Jaschok, Maria, and Suzanne Miers. *Women and Chinese Patriarchy: Submission, Servitude and Escape*. Hong Kong: Hong Kong University Press, 1994.

Miners, Norman. "The Attempts to Abolish the Mui Tsai System in Hong Kong, 1917–1941." In *Between East and West: Aspects of Social and Political Development in Hong Kong*, edited by Elizabeth Sinn. Hong Kong: Centre of Asian Studies, Hong Kong University, 1990.

Watson, James L. "Transactions in People: The Chinese Market in Slaves, Servants, and Heirs." In *Asian and African Systems of Slavery*, edited by James L. Watson. Oxford: Basil Blackwell, 1980.

Watson, Rubie S. "Wives, Concubines, and Maids: Servitude and Kinship in the Hong Kong Region, 1900–1940." In *Marriage and Inequality in Chinese Society*, edited by Rubie S. Watson and Patricia Buckley Ebrey. Berkeley: University of California Press, 1991.

—CHING-HWANG YEN

NATIVE AMERICANS. Slavery of various kinds was common on both sides of the Atlantic long before the European invasions of the Americas. Among the many diverse native American cultures slavery was often temporary or specific, with people assigned to the service of others, sometimes for identified tasks or for predetermined periods of time. Some people sold themselves into slavery as a means of paying off debts or other obligations, or of recouping personal, family, or community fortunes. Slavery could be extremely harsh. In Mesoamerica, for example, war captives and others were enslaved in great numbers for the purpose of sacrificing them, sooner or later, in large public ceremonies. The practice of enslaving enemies and then eating them, even allowing for exaggeration in Portuguese accounts, was common in interior parts of the Amazon Basin. Many seminomadic groups practiced raiding for women, some of whom were then enslaved. These examples provide only a small illustration of the great variety within pre-invasion American slavery.

Europeans, especially Iberians, had also become accustomed to slavery over the centuries. The Portuguese had raided for slaves in North Africa. The Spanish conquest of the Canaries was a foretaste of what would happen in the Americas. At first many Guanches (Canarians) were enslaved and shipped to Spain for sale. Others were kept as slaves on the islands. Slavery in the Canaries (one of the pioneer conquests against non-Christians outside Europe) and then later in the Americas, provoked debate as to how to deal with conquered heathens. Some observers felt they should have few rights; others believed they should be treated as "new" Christian vassals. These arguments were often irrelevant, however, to what happened during and after European invasions in the Americas. When confronting powerful, densely inhabited native states, apart from the conquest years and war prisoners, Spaniards (and other Europeans) generally treated sedentary peasant natives as a labor force to be manipulated by means other than enslavement. When they encountered natives in reduced numbers, or when they met types of social organization such as bands and nomads, to whom they felt greatly superior, Europeans drove them away, killed them off, or enslaved them. Enslavement was especially common when there was a local shortage of labor and an attractive local source of wealth that required labor.

Almost everywhere on the Atlantic coasts of the Americas, first contacts soon led to sporadic kidnapping, transportation back to Europe, or enslavement. Prisoners were often lured on board European ships with promises; some were purchased from local leaders; and others were simply seized. A few, if they survived shipboard conditions and the onslaught of European diseases, found their way home again or were returned as they had been promised. Most were kidnapped to be shown off in Europe as curiosities or as proofs of discovery. Some adventurers, including Columbus, obviously thought of these captives as a potential labor force, but labor for Europe was not a great concern in the sixteenth century.

The first massive use of slaves by Europeans in the Americas occurred in the Greater Antilles. The early Spanish occupiers found relatively large Native American populations, especially in Hispaniola, although the size of the population at contact is fiercely debated, and a very productive *conuco* or tuber agriculture, which they did not exploit. More importantly, they also found that many of the streams carried gold silt. As a result, extensive enslavement of the local inhabitants was accompanied by massive dislocations of people, harsh working conditions in gold-panning, and a severe decline in both human and agricultural fertility.

All the large islands experienced precipitous population declines because of mistreatment and the apparent inability of native peoples to withstand immunologically the invasion of Eurasian disease. As the islands emptied, gold production dropped too, largely because the streams were panned out. Spanish entrepreneurs failed to recognize this, however, and sought to replace their vanished slaves by raiding other parts of the Caribbean. The Bahamas, Florida, Pánuco, the Gulf of Honduras, Margarita, Cubagua, and the Venezuelan coasts suffered heavily, and the new slaves brought to the islands died off like their predecessors. These islands, now occupied by large herds of feral cattle, pigs, and horses, lost their importance except as way stations for the fleets until the rise of the sugar industry roughly two centuries later.

Dismayed by the tragedy of the islands, the Spanish monarchs, knowing little about immunology, tried to restrict and then to abolish Native American enslavement. In this they were aided by church reformers and propagandists led by the famous Dominican, later bishop of Chiapas, Bartolomé de las Casas. However, the anarchy of the conquest years on the mainland made crown supervision impossible. Using the pretexts of previous enslavement, or of the legitimacy of enslaving captives taken in a "just war," conquistador bands seized, enslaved, and branded great numbers of natives all over Mesoamerica. Many were used for gold-panning and for the building of new Spanish cities. Nuño de Guzmán and Pedrarias Dávila were notorious as two of the most ruthless slave raiders. In areas such as Pánuco, Honduras, and Nicaragua, natives were shipped abroad, some to restock Panama, badly in need of labor for its trans-isthmian trade after its own severe population losses.

After the first chaotic years, royal legislation was able to make a somewhat greater impact. The new settlers realized that slave exports were wasteful, and as they shifted to trade, agriculture, and silver-mining, they came to appreciate that coerced labor from a permanent village source was preferable to slave labor. By the time of the "New Laws" (1542), which forbade further enslavement and ordered the release of many illegally held slaves, other forms of assigned labor and tribute (*encomienda*), and, later, of rotational draft labor (*tandas, repartimientos,* or *mitas*) had come to replace Native American slavery in the areas of dense population and preconquest empires. Nevertheless, dire warnings and even riots by settlers and royal officials led the crown to suspend implementation of the New Laws. New decrees from Charles V (1553) banned illegal slaving again, and by around 1558 Native American slavery had all but ended, except in some frontier areas of the Spanish empire. (Sentencing to slavery as a punishment for criminal offenses and revolt continued, however, especially in times of labor shortage.)

On open frontiers, enslavement of Native American peoples survived, sometimes almost to the end of the colonial period. The Amazon slopes of the Ecuadorian Andes, the southern Chilean frontier, and especially northern New Spain used the pretext of justified war. Because of labor shortages in New Spain's desert north, slave-hunting sometimes yielded substantial profits. Seminomadic peoples could not be persuaded or induced to work for Europeans by other means, and slave-raiding, although it created the endemic violence of attacks and counterattacks, predominated.

There were also brief recrudescences of slaving, some of them in peripheral areas in dispute between European nations. Thus the English on Jamaica attempted to obtain cheap labor not only by buying Native American slaves from the North American English colonies but also by using captives from Talamanca in Costa Rica, who had been seized by their allies, the so-called Sambos-Mosquitos. In other areas the murder of a missionary, or even an invented border incident, could send a troop of Spaniards into unconquered territory to punish the alleged wrongdoers and "bring them out" for christianization and temporary slavery.

In Portuguese Brazil, slavery of native peoples began more hesitantly than in the Spanish Carib-bean but survived longer as the dominant form of labor. In Bahia, the heart of the first sugar boom, Brazilian coastal peoples were the main workforce for almost a century. In the northern and southern peripheries of colonial Brazil, where sugar did not flourish and where capital accumulation was difficult, the enslavement of native peoples lasted much longer.

There were a few incidents of early kidnapping of trophies for Portugal, but at first, when Portuguese and French settlement was thin and sometimes only seasonal, barter with the Tupi-Guaraní of the coast dominated. As permanent towns and sugar plantations developed, Portuguese settlers began to capture and coerce local natives to work for them. The Brazilian Jesuits, of whom Antonio Vieira was the Brazilian counterpart of Bartolomé de las Casas, sought to legislate and create a relatively free but subordinate peasantry to be settled in new villages under their tutelage. The colonists told the crown repeatedly that prosperity, and thus royal taxes, depended on a sufficient labor force for the sugar industry, which, they added, was not yet productive enough, in the years up to the 1570s, to pay for large numbers of African slaves. The crown ignored the question or wavered, repeatedly banning the enslavement of natives but then allowing exceptions that were fully exploited by slave-raiders and those who bought from them. To supply these demands, the coastal areas of Brazil and their immediate hinterlands were plundered of their original inhabitants.

To the Portuguese colonists of the main sugar zones, however, Native Americans were an unsatisfactory labor force. They suffered from enormous mortality rates, and those who survived often escaped to nearby "wild" areas. Moreover, many of them were seminomadic forest peoples who could not or would not adapt to heavy plantation labor. Thus Native American slaves in South America, as elsewhere in the Americas, were almost always valued at a lower price than Africans and paid less when "free." From the 1580s to the 1630s, with native populations disappearing and local planters beginning to accumulate enough profit, Africans gradually replaced the coastal peoples.

In Maranhão to the north and São Paulo to the south there was no sugar prosperity, and so African slaves never fully replaced local slave labor. As a result, Native American slavery lasted much longer, and, given the Indians' reluctance to work and their mortality, slave-raiding ranged much farther afield. Slavers continued to use the old pretexts of captives taken in "just wars," but they were able to add to this in the Amazon region by claiming that they were ransoming or saving captives from cannibals by purchasing them. The Amazon River was the scene of frequent upstream canoe expeditions in which the riverine interior was demographically devastated, and large numbers of forest natives were "brought down" to work on the northern coasts and elsewhere. Slave-raiding based in São Paulo was even more widespread and destructive. These *bandeirantes* from the São Paulo region sacked the Jesuit Guaraní missions in neighboring Spanish America, and in their lengthy expeditions seeking slaves and precious metals they were the European explorers and pioneers of much of the interior of South America.

Enslavement of native peoples by Europeans never reached the dimensions in English and French America that it did in the Caribbean, in Central America, and in Brazil. In Quebec the institution lasted throughout the colonial period, but numbers were not large and gradually waned as black slavery increased. Most native slaves were war captives, and from time to time some were sent to Cap François (now in Haiti) in exchange for more valuable African slaves, a common exchange rate being three for two. Native American population decline, flight, and absorption by other groups gradually reduced the slave population.

In the English colonies, Indian slaves were most numerous in New England and especially the South. The Carolinas held the largest numbers of all. Warfare, kidnapping, purchase from other Native Americans, and sentencing to slavery for criminal offenses were all methods of acquisition.

More than in French Canada, Native American slaves in the Carolinas were exported, some north to New England and New York, but most to the English West Indies. Population decline, the preference for African slaves or white indentured servants (when there was money to pay for them), flight beyond the frontier, and Native American refusal to adapt to field labor, all led to the decline of enslavement of North American natives.

The enslavement of native peoples accompanied warfare, labor shortages, and comparative poverty on many frontiers throughout the period of European colonialism. In areas where larger, settled European communities developed, the dominant groups found native labor to be unsatisfactory when African slaves were available and affordable. Native resistance, through flight or nonconformity, and high native mortality reduced their availability and work. In areas where large numbers of Native American agriculturists survived, Europeans found that tribute-paying peasants who could provide seasonal labor were a more satisfactory workforce than slaves. Thus, except on the frontiers, the enslavement of large numbers of Native Americans was a phenomenon of the first fifty to one hundred years of European occupation.

[*See also* Brazil; Caribbean Region, *article on* Spanish Caribbean; *and* United States, *overview article*.]

BIBLIOGRAPHY

Alden, Dauril. "Indian Versus Black Slavery in the State of Maranhão during the Seventeenth and Eighteenth Centuries." In *Iberian Colonies, New World Societies: Essays in Memory of Charles Gibson*, edited by Richard L. Garner and William B. Taylor. Privately printed, 1985.

Arenal, Celestino del. "La teoría de la servidumbre natural en el pensamiento español de los siglos XVI y XVII." *Historiografía y Bibliografía Americanistas* 19–20 (1975–1976): 67–124.

Cuello, José. "The Persistence of Indian Slavery and Encomienda in the Northeast of Colonial Mexico, 1577–1723." *Journal of Social History* 21 (1988): 683–700.

Hemming, John. *Red Gold: The Conquest of the Brazilian Indi-*

ans, 1500–1760. Cambridge, Mass.: Harvard University Press, 1978.

Lauber, Almon Wheeler. *Indian Slavery in Colonial Times within the Present Limits of the United States.* 2d ed. New York: AMS Press, 1969.

Saco, José Antonio. *Historia de la esclavitud de los indios en el nuevo mundo: Seguida de la historia de los repartimientos y encomiendas.* 2 vols. Havana: Cultural, S.A., 1932.

Schwartz, Stuart. *Sugar Plantations in the Formation of Brazilian Society: Bahia, 1550–1835.* Cambridge: Cambridge University Press, 1985.

—MURDO J. MACLEOD

NAZI SLAVERY. Between 1939 and 1945 slavery was a fundamental component of the domination of Europe by Adolf Hitler and the National Socialist German Workers' (Nazi) Party. At the height of its power the German Third Reich controlled almost all of the European continent. Ruling over such vast territory, with its tens of thousands of industrial and agricultural operations, required that more than thirteen million Germans be drafted out of industry and agriculture and into the armed forces. To fill this labor gap the Nazi state became one of the largest slaveholders in history. The Nazi regime exploited the unfree labor of millions of civilians and prisoners of war from Nazi-occupied territories by subjecting them to compulsory labor laws and deporting them to work in German fields and armament factories. Jews, Gypsies, prisoners of war, and other inmates in the Nazi concentration camps also constituted an important source of slave labor. Under the leadership of Heinrich Himmler, the military wing known as the SS rented hundreds of thousands of concentration-camp inmates to German industrial concerns like I. G. Farben, Krupp, and the Herman Göring Works.

The ideological foundation for these forms of slavery is found in Adolf Hitler's *Mein Kampf.* Hitler wrote that the history of humankind could only be understood as a series of interactions between the culture-founding, culture-bearing, and culture-destroying races of the world. In the distant human past these races had been separate and homogeneous, but interactions throughout history had generated racial hybridization, which, for the culture-founding Aryan race, had caused physical, intellectual, and cultural regression. As the descendants of the Aryan race, Hitler and the National Socialists strove to reverse racial and cultural regression by purifying the German *Volksgemeinschaft* (racial and cultural community) and by guaranteeing the possibility of pure racial reproduction.

To ensure the purity and vitality of their race, the National Socialists fought to increase the *Lebensraum* (living space) of the German *Volksgemeinschaft.* Conceptually, *Lebensraum* translated into agriculturally usable land, settled and cultivated by Germans, and it was intimately linked to Hitler's military strategy of *Blitzkrieg.* Wanting to avoid a long war of attrition, Hitler tried to expand the German borders through a series of *Blitzkriegs* or "lightning wars." Theoretically, the German army would launch these quick military actions after having diplomatically isolated the target nation, but shortly before the harvest season. With the successful completion of the campaign, the army would collect as its spoils the harvested crops and any industrial output. Racially pure Germans would follow the army, settling the new *Lebensraum* for future generations of the German *Volksgemeinschaft.*

Labor was also an important component of the process of racial purification. According to Hitler, the creative capacity of the Aryan race lay primarily in its ability to subjugate *Untermenschen* or "inferior races" and to turn them into "mechanical tools." In newly conquered territories, Hitler planned to isolate all able-bodied members of inferior races and to use them temporarily in the process of reconstruction. During this period of forced labor, the inferior races would receive a minimum of nutrition and would be prohibited from reproducing. Once the German population in a given region constituted a sufficiently large labor force, they would expel or annihilate the non-Aryan population and with them all possibilities for racial hybridization in the new *Lebensraum.*

The Jewish population was the immediate tar-

Photograph of German troops looking on as a group of Jews digs ditches in a fenced-in lot in Kraków, c.1939–1940.

get of Nazi racial hatred. To the National Socialists the Jews constituted a culture-destroying race and thus the gravest threat to the Aryan race and culture. In 1935, two years after the Nazi seizure of power in Germany, the regime promulgated the Nuremberg Laws to protect German racial purity. These laws forced the segregation of Jews from German social, cultural, and political life, prohibited the employment of Jews, and required Jews to wear the yellow star of David as an outward sign of their racial identity. Hatred for Jews reached the level of widespread violence in November 1938, when thousands of Nazis across Germany burned synagogues and beat Jews. For Jews who did not have the means necessary for emigration, such discrimination and violence meant exclusion from the German economy and society.

The increased *Lebensraum* acquired from the defeat of Poland enabled the Nazis to move forward with their policy of destroying the Jewish population. In December 1939 the German General-Government of Poland issued a compulsory labor decree for Jews. According to this decree all Jews between the ages of fourteen and sixty were subject to compulsory labor in labor camps and ghettos. Jews from Poland, Germany, and other occupied territories were shipped in packed cattle cars to these camps and ghettos, which became the center of a Nazi bureaucratic maelstrom during the first years of the war. Some Nazi bureaucrats wanted to use these camps and ghettos to revolutionize the procedures for racial annihilation, while others envisioned them as centers in which annihilation was achieved through exploitation. The latter group insisted that exploitation might reduce the ultimate war debt shouldered by the future generations of the German *Volksgemeinschaft,* while at the same time furthering the German war effort.

Between 1939 and 1941 the SS organized ghetto-dwellers into working gangs and rented them to German industries and the German army, typically at a daily rate of four Reichsmarks per slave. By early 1941 more than four hundred thousand Jews in Polish ghettos labored for the German army and the German war effort. In 1942 the entire Warsaw ghetto was held collectively responsible for producing the uniforms for the German Luftwaffe (air force). The Jews themselves, working twelve to eighteen hours a day, received little or no remuneration, and Nazi officials restricted the food supply as well as access to water and bathing facilities. These inhuman conditions led to high death rates from starvation and disease.

Hitler's *Blitzkrieg*s rapidly increased the territorial holdings of the Third Reich, while also increasing its supply of labor through the capture of prisoners of war. Although the Geneva Conventions expressly prohibited the use of prisoners of war as forced laborers, the German army avoided violation by forcing prisoners to sign contracts that essentially converted the former soldiers into civilians subject to the compulsory labor laws of Nazi occupation. Throughout the war, prisoners labored in every region and every segment of the German war effort. Hundreds of thousands of

Photograph of prisoners from Buchenwald concentration camp building the
Weimar-Buchenwald railroad line, 1943.

French prisoners of war worked as agricultural laborers in western Europe, while thousands of Soviet, French, and Polish prisoners of war slaved to dig the huge underground Mittelwerk facility at Peenemünde, where slave labor was also used in the construction of Germany's secret A-4 rockets. Huge German industrial concerns like Krupp and I. G. Farben also exploited the forced labor of tens of thousands prisoners of war.

During the winter of 1941–1942 Hitler's army stalled deep within Soviet territory, bringing the debate over racial annihilation and exploitation to a crisis point. The failure of the *Blitzkrieg* against the Soviet Union entangled Germany in a two-front war of attrition, pitting the productive ca-

pacity of the German Reich against that of the Allies. Many argued that a change in military strategies required a corresponding change in labor policy, in particular the abandonment of the policy of racial annihilation in favor of greater exploitation of the labor potential of racially inferior groups. The Nazi regime was slow to alter its course of racial purification, even though the surrender of more than three million Soviet soldiers presented the Nazi regime with a very large pool of labor. In February 1942, after more than two million Red Army soldiers had died in German prisoner-of-war camps, Hitler himself attempted to redirect the war effort by appointing Albert Speer as Reich minister of munitions and Fritz Sauckel as plenipotentiary general for the utilization of labor. These appointments signaled the adoption of a more aggressive policy concerning slave-labor productivity. Over the next three years more than five million non-Jews, most of whom were prisoners of war from eastern Europe, were deported to Germany from occupied territories and forced to labor in German industries and agriculture.

In 1942, despite the apparent bureaucratic move away from the policy of annihilation, Hitler and the Nazi regime hastened the pace of their "final solution to the Jewish question." In that year the German economy employed the unfree labor of more than 2.6 million foreign laborers and 1.4 million prisoners of war; by the end of the war, five million foreign laborers and nearly two million prisoners of war labored in the German war effort. The success of Sauckel and Speer in recruiting unfree foreign labor translated directly into the acceleration and rationalization of the Nazi killing process against the Jews. In 1942 the SS opened death camps at Chelmno, Belzec, Sobibor, Majdanek, and Treblinka and approved the use of the vermin-killing gas Zyklon B. They also expanded the camp at Auschwitz and built a crematorium capable of destroying ten thousand human bodies a day. With respect to the Jewish population, the policy of annihilation was so dominant that 750,000 prisoners were murdered at Auschwitz between 1941 and 1944, while during that same period only a little more than 57,000 labored for firms outside the camp, a figure that includes some who ultimately died at Auschwitz.

In camps like Auschwitz, where the policies of annihilation and of exploitation operated concomitantly, the concept of enslavement took on an entirely new meaning for prisoners. In his book *Night* (1960) Elie Wiesel documented the process of dehumanization that took place when trainloads of men, women, and children walked in lines toward the SS officer who decided on the life or death of each prisoner arriving at Auschwitz. With the wave of the baton, Wiesel was chosen to be a slave, and for this fate he experienced joy. As the SS guard told Wiesel, "Remember, here you have got to work. If not, you will go straight to the furnace. To the crematorium. Work or the crematorium—the choice is in your hands." In this world *"Arbeit macht frei"* took on a macabre reality.

[*See also* Contemporary Slavery; Forced Labor, *article on* Soviet Union; *and* Penal Slavery.]

BIBLIOGRAPHY

Herbert, Ulrich. "Labour and Extermination: Economic Interest and the Primacy of *Weltanschauung* in National Socialism." *Past and Present* 138 (1993): 144–195.

Homze, Edward L. *Foreign Labor in Nazi Germany*. Princeton: Princeton University Press, 1967.

Levi, Primo. *Survival in Auschwitz: The Nazi Assault on Humanity*. Translated by Stuart Woolf. New York: Summit Books, 1986.

Speer, Albert. *Infiltration (Der Sklavenstaat)*. Translated by Joachim Neugroschel. New York: Macmillan, 1981.

Wiesel, Eli. *Night*. Translated by Stella Rodway. New York: Hill and Wang, 1960.

—PATRICK S. DOWD

OCCUPATIONAL MOBILITY. Few issues put in sharper relief the contradictions of slavery than does mobility of the slaves themselves within the institution. However alienated or dehumanized the slaves were supposed to be, they were still expected to act responsibly, often with intelligence and initiative. Slaves in various systems were expected to learn intricate cultural codes of station and performance, to gain new skills of labor, and even under the most brutal of labor regimes to show attributes of obedience that could mark them as suitable to supervise their fellows. Understanding these things gives new meaning to the varied forms that linked slaves to one another and that were developed to regulate both slave task performance and the encounter between slave and free. To claim that certain individuals were incapable of performing certain tasks both misreads the evidence and misunderstands the nature of social relations.

The ways in which slaves could attain upward mobility or promotion depended on the manner of servitude and its structural forms. Sometimes, from the moment of enslavement, the slave was intended for a specialized role that conferred high status in the formal hierarchy of a social or religious order, as when slaves were used as soldiers, officers, administrators, court functionaries, or monks. There were also instances of bondage in which slaves who were the status personnel of a high-ranking member of a kin group might gain the prerequisites of the corporate kin group by pleasing the master.

This discussion refers principally to slave systems in which the great majority of slaves constituted a labor force in market agriculture, mining, manufacture, or hard service labor. No occupation in Roman society was closed to slaves. In practice, domestic servants were overwhelmingly slaves, but every kind of job, especially in agriculture, was done by both slave and free workers. This great diversity of slave work roles was not limited to Roman slave society. Because the slave systems of the New World were particularly concerned with market crops, it is easy to assume that, save for a few domestics, slaves were fieldhands and nothing more, but this assumption is false. In American cities slaves worked in many service industries and in trades of every level of skill, portering, street-cleaning, milling, skilled manufacturing, commerce, slave management, and personal service.

However elaborate the occupational hierarchy may have been, the majority of slaves worked in some variant of the gang system. The nature of the crop and regional variations influenced the size of the plantation enterprise and therefore the opportunities for being recognized as a skilled or privileged slave. The dynamics of slaves' occupational mobility can be reckoned from the following variables. What skilled tasks were available to the slaves? In which occupations did they compete with free labor, and which were reserved for free persons? What was the relationship between the scale of agricultural enterprises and the slaves' opportunities for upward mobility and enhanced quality of life? What was the discriminatory base

of promotion decisions, such as gender, skin color, ethnic stereotyping, or propinquity, that operated to channel selection for advancement? What were the differences in quantity of opportunities and quality of life between rural and urban slaves? Could elite or skilled positions be inherited within a slave family or kin group? These questions need to be posed in a manner that recognizes the dynamics of both upward and downward mobility. Although the answers will invariably involve the use of statistical data, scholars should also make full use of slave narratives, journals, owners' diaries, or logbooks, which may display the social processes with varying interpretations of procedures and motivations among both slave and free.

Because slaves worked from childhood to adulthood, it was possible to progress from one job to another and to gain greater responsibility. Conversely, slaves thought to be in need of punishment could be demoted. Slaves on the bottom of the scale of wealthy households ranked higher than top slaves of less prosperous households, and mulattoes often ranked higher than blacks. Field workers had little opportunity to gain wealth, power, or status. Competition between slaves for the favor and support of the master could be fraught with mutual antipathy, suspicion, and fear, which was not an inducement to unity of purpose.

The diversity of slave jobs and slave status served to disperse rather than unite the slave population, which never constituted a solid, undifferentiated mass. Slaves with no options but field work felt cheated of the chances of internal promotion, especially when aware of instances in which slaves who did not work as hard in other positions were given higher status.

The practice of placing slaves in positions of skilled labor and management may have degraded manual labor in society as a whole. The acquisition of special skills was an important economic and social resource for the slave. As a consequence of the skilled nature of their work, artisans tended to form a more stable and closed group than the domestics or the field slaves. Apprenticeships were often long and represented a great expenditure that would be lost if the slave were sent back to the field. The permanence and stability of the group of artisans depended, among other things, on the size of the estate, the planting and manufacturing routine, and the patterns of recruitment and formation of the labor force.

Women slaves not only labored in the fields and the great houses; they were also involved in production for themselves. There are important unanswered questions concerning women's control over the provision grounds (slaves' produce gardens) and the operation of the internal market. Women's sexual availability under slavery sometimes offered them the potential of mobility, but at great cost: today's favorite could be tomorrow's reject. Perhaps no other elite occupation so penetrated the boundaries between slave and free than that of the woman who had charge of her master's children, who were perhaps her future masters.

[See also Occupations and Urban Slavery.]

BIBLIOGRAPHY

Bradley, K. R. Slaves and Masters in the Roman Empire: A Study in Social Control. Oxford and New York: Oxford University Press, 1987.

Fogel, Robert W. Without Consent or Contract: The Rise and Fall of American Slavery. New York: W. W. Norton, 1989.

Higman, Barry W. Slave Populations in the British Caribbean, 1807–1934. Baltimore: Johns Hopkins University Press, 1984.

Meillassoux, Claude. The Anthropology of Slavery: The Womb of Iron and Gold. Translated by Alide Dasnois. Chicago: University of Chicago Press, 1991.

Mintz, Sidney, and Richard Price, eds. An Anthropological Approach to the Afro-American Past. Philadelphia: Institute for the Study of Human Issues, 1976.

Morrissey, Marietta. Slave Women in the New World: Gender Stratification in the Caribbean. Lawrence: University Press of Kansas, 1989.

—FRANK MCGLYNN

OCCUPATIONS. Stuart Schwartz (1985, chap. 6) has summed it up very well: "Work was the core of slavery." Overall, a much higher proportion of slaves than of free people worked in the labor force.

An estimated two-thirds of all slaves worked, because any slave capable of working was compelled to do so.

Because slaves in the Americas were chattel, the property of others, they were not free to engage in any occupation they chose. Instead, they were forced to labor for masters who determined what they would work at and who could ruthlessly exploit the labor of slaves for their own benefit. Nor could slaves change occupations on their own volition. Because of these severe restrictions on the occupational mobility of slaves in the Americas, they were heavily overrepresented in some occupations, notably agricultural labor and domestic service, and almost invisible in others, such as the professions. In plantation economies, the overwhelming majority of slaves were forced to be agricultural laborers, although the work varied with the crops grown.

In the three most important slaveholding countries of the nineteenth century, the United States, Brazil, and Cuba, slave labor was used mainly to grow plantation crops for export: cotton, tobacco, sugar, and rice in the United States, coffee and sugar in Brazil, and sugar, tobacco, and coffee in Cuba. Slaves were the primary producers of these crops, just as they had been the primary producers of plantation crops in the Caribbean colonies of Britain, France, Spain, and other European powers since the seventeenth century.

Richard Dunn's Sugar and Slaves: The Rise of the Planter Class in the English West Indies, 1624–1713 (1972) includes an occupational census of 450 slaves in the Caribbean island of St. Kitts for the year 1706. It reveals characteristics that would be equally true in many other slave societies right up to abolition. The majority were field slaves, comprising 81 percent of the women and 57 percent of the men. Male slaves had greater access to crafts or skills than female slaves, for whom the range of occupations was much narrower. Nearly all the women who were not field slaves were domestics. The youngest slave worker was a nine-year-old footboy, illustrating that for slaves the regime of work began early in childhood.

The concentration in agricultural labor changed little in the British West Indies prior to emancipation in 1834. More than three-quarters of Jamaican slaves were employed in plantation agriculture in 1832. Slaves living in urban centers had a greater variety of occupations open to them, although the majority, usually female, worked in domestic service. On large plantations, slave gangs performed the field work. They were compelled to work by force and forced to work at a high level of productivity. Robert Fogel (1989, p. 26) has calculated that in 1860, on the eve of the Civil War in the United States, rural gang laborers constituted 50 percent of the adult slave population. In Jamaica and Trinidad earlier in the nineteenth century, it is estimated that one-half of the slaves worked in field gangs. These rural laborers worked longer hours and were more productive than free farmers.

Even where plantation agriculture was not dominant, slave labor was in great demand. Slaves in Peru during the later seventeenth century provided much of the agricultural labor. They farmed the *chacaras*, or market gardens, that provided food for the Spanish towns. Slaves cultivated Peruvian vineyards, orchards, and sugar estates; they were the laborers on many *estancias* raising livestock, and they were essential to colonial Peru's transportation system as muleteers, seamen, and stevedores. Slave fishermen were employed on Peru's coasts, and slaves worked in slaughterhouses and meat markets, some as butchers. Slaves in Peru's capital, Lima, were primarily domestic servants, but domestic service for female slaves included the occupations of cook, laundress, maid, and wet-nurse, while male slaves worked as valets and coachmen. Institutions like convents and hospitals owned slaves. The hospital of Santa Ana in Lima, early in the seventeenth century, owned slaves who were nurses, cooks, laundresses, and bookkeepers. Slaves with particular artisanal skills were employed in Peru's cities, especially Lima. They could be found as carpenters, shipwrights, joiners, and caulkers, and also as tanners, leather-workers, tailors, and hatmakers. Talented slave craftsmen in high demand commanded the highest prices and often were hired out by their masters. Viceroy Chinchon, writing to the Spanish government in 1636, summarized the value of this slave labor for colonial Peru: "All this black labor is necessary for the maintenance of human life." The slaves performed work that no one else would do.

In seventeenth-century Mexico, slaves were primarily employed as laborers on sugar estates, in textile workshops (*obrajes*), and in silver-mining. The Spanish relied increasingly on African slave labor not only for field labor, but also for more specialized tasks such as boilers and refiners, woodcutters, cartwrights, and blacksmiths. Slaves were certainly in demand for the more strenuous labor and found themselves working alongside Indians both in the textile workshops and in the silver mines.

Urban skilled slaves commanded higher prices in nineteenth-century Cuba than rural field slaves. The most expensive slaves sold in Cuba prior to 1850 were masons. Other trades in high demand there were shoemakers, cigar-rollers and muleteers. Slaves predominated in some of Havana's trades: three-quarters of the city's bakers in 1836 were slaves, and 185 slaves worked as shoemakers. The bakers, shoemakers, and cigar workers made up 70 percent of Havana's skilled slave artisans, but the great majority of Havana's slaves were employed in domestic service. By 1846 these numbered nearly nineteen thousand, with 65 percent of them female.

Urban slaves in the United States also pursued a variety of skilled trades. Approximately four thousand slaves lived in the northern seaport colonial capitals of New York, Boston, and Philadelphia on the eve of the American Revolution. Gary Nash (1986) has estimated that 25 percent of the slaves living in pre-Revolutionary Philadelphia had artisan skills. They worked as carpenters, millers, distillers, bakers, blacksmiths, and sailmakers; one even managed a bloomery. Nash also concludes that the colonial American merchant marine may have had a large component of black slave labor.

The greater variety of occupations available to urban slaves continued in the United States after the Revolution, although opportunities for slaves to become skilled craftsmen may have declined in the South during the nineteenth century. Hiring-out practices gave urban slaves more opportunities to learn crafts; although Southern cities tried to stop hiring out, they were unable to eliminate it. Frederick Douglass was one slave who benefited, learning how to caulk, which meant that he could seek employment himself. The Charleston census of 1848 categorized 17 percent of the city's nearly four thousand slaves as skilled and identified a wide range of occupations in which slaves worked. Male slaves represented significant percentages of Charleston's coopers, blacksmiths, painters, carpenters, and butchers. Female slaves in Charleston, as in other urban centers, had a narrower range of occupations open to them, nearly all connected to domestic service. Richmond, Virginia, had the largest industrial slave labor force in the pre-Civil

Photograph of slave women doing laundry on a Southern plantation, nineteenth century.

War South, employing slaves in the ironworks and in tobacco manufacturing.

Across the American South and in other slave societies, urban slaves could be found working at many different tasks. Slave labor built railways in the American South and in Cuba; in New Orleans slaves ran the city's gasworks. The Levee Steam Cotton Press in New Orleans owned more than one hundred slaves in 1850. Charleston had slave jockeys and grooms. Slaves in Louisville worked in the Marine Hospital. Travelers to New Orleans commented about finding slave butchers, fishmongers, and market vendors. Richard Wade (1964) cites a New Orleans bookseller whose slave was his clerk and "knew all the current literature." Nearly all Southern cities employed slaves on public works, and slaves commonly were employed as stevedores in ports. Wade concludes that in Southern cities, "slave labor could be found nearly everywhere there was a task to perform."

Slavery reinforced gender stereotyping of occupations. Slave women predominated in domestic service, and male slaves dominated the skilled crafts. However, field labor is the exception to gender stereotypes. In the British Caribbean plantation colonies, slave women often constituted half or more of the field gangs. These female field slaves were confined to the lower ranks of the plantation hierarchy with very little opportunity for occupational mobility. Slave women cleaned and did the laundry; slave men were the valets and the coach drivers. Female slaves looked after the children. The head overseer was always a male. On the plantations the men dominated the elite positions. They were the craftsmen, the drivers, the sugar-mill workers, or those who possessed some craft skill. They amounted to no more than 5 percent of the plantation slave population, but all of them were males. Occupational opportunities for female slaves were limited to cooks, midwives, housekeepers, or gardeners, although female slaves played important roles in planting provision grounds, which were common throughout the Caribbean, and in selling produce at the weekly markets.

In the United States as well, gender stereotyping of slave occupations did not include field labor, in which most slaves were employed. Jacqueline Jones's (1985) study of female slaves' work patterns found that slave women "spent a good deal of their lives plowing, hoeing and picking cotton." There were exceptions. Thomas Couper, a Sea Island cotton-planter, employed his male slaves exclusively in digging ditches and his female slaves in moting and sorting cotton. On most plantations, however, the field gangs were composed of both sexes, who did whatever work was prescribed for them. Equal proportions of male and female slaves hoed the land and harvested the cotton on the Kollock plantations of Georgia in 1850 and 1851. For the slaves who worked at the Big House, labor was divided clearly by gender. Female slaves worked in domestic service, while males were footmen or skilled craftsmen. The pattern was similar in other slave areas. Slave women were included equally with men on the slave gangs, or *ateliers*, in the French West Indies. This was true also on the *grands ateliers* that were responsible for the heavy work on the plantations. Female slaves were often in the forefront in the dangerous grinding process on the sugar plantations of Saint Domingue.

Slave children began work as servants as early as three or four years old. They could be employed in the children's field gang at less arduous tasks, such as weeding. Their owners believed in training them at very young ages for the field work that awaited them. More than 40 percent of male slaves and 50 percent of female slaves in the U.S. South prior to the Civil War were working by age seven, and by the age of twelve slaves generally were performing adult tasks in field labor.

Economic development played a crucial role in determining slave occupations in Brazil, as it did in other areas of the Americas. Slave labor was concentrated on the sugar plantations of Bahía and Pernambuco during the sixteenth and seventeenth centuries. With the discovery of gold and diamonds in Minas Gerais, thousands of slaves were brought to work these mines in Brazil's interior during the eighteenth century. The resurgence of a plantation economy, especially in São Paulo in the nineteenth century, created an enormous demand for slave labor. The number of slaves on the São Paulo plantations rapidly increased, and the region became the last redoubt of Brazilian slavery. While the field work on Brazilian plantations was similar in its numbing character to field work elsewhere in the hemisphere, nearly all slaves in the mining districts worked as miners, under the control of overseers. Some, however, labored as itinerant prospectors, forced to turn over their profits or to share them with their masters; others acquired skills as goldsmiths.

Male urban slaves in Brazilian cities such as Rio de Janeiro, like their counterparts in the Caribbean or the United States, plied skilled trades as barbers, carpenters, joiners, and blacksmiths. *Negros de ganho,* slaves who worked for hire for others than their masters, also functioned as porters and messengers. Slave barbers dominated the profession in Rio. Female urban slaves could be found in Brazilian cities peddling wares as hawkers, although the largest number were employed in domestic service. Because black wet-nurses were especially prized by prosperous Brazilian families, slave women could be hired out or sold as wet-nurses, often leading to other forms of domestic service. In Brazilian cities and mining districts, female slave prostitutes were common.

The Brazilian census of 1872 classifies more than five hundred thousand of the estimated eight hundred thousand slaves in the country as agricultural laborers. It also reveals that the Brazilian textile and clothing industry employed nearly fifty thousand slaves, most of them females, which accounted for the more than forty thousand seamstresses listed in the female slave occupations. For female slaves in the last days of Brazilian slavery, the textile and clothing industry ranked behind domestic service and agriculture as the main form of employment. Male slaves in Brazil, like their counterparts in other areas of the Americas, engaged in wider variety of occupations than females. The Brazilian census of 1872 lists more than fifteen hundred male slave artists and nearly eighteen hundred male slave fishermen.

Slaves served as soldiers in the Americas from the Spanish conquest to the U.S. Civil War. In times of emergency, slaves might be forcibly enlisted for military service. One of the most famous experiments with slave soldiers was the formation of the British West India regiments in Britain's Caribbean colonies during the wars of the French Revolution and Napoleonic eras. The slaves who were purchased for military service by the British government effectively became military slaves. Between 1795 and 1808 the British government purchased about 13,400 slaves to man these regiments. Far from undermining the slave system in the islands where the soldiers served, they reinforced it. They enjoyed a high military reputation, no doubt in part because their status as soldiers imbued in them a pride of accomplishment and helped them to transcend the limits of their condition as slaves.

Slaves were regularly utilized as auxiliaries, as military construction workers, and as laborers, called "pioneers." Peter Voelz (1993) has found more than eighty occasions on which slaves were employed as auxiliaries during the colonial period. Slave labor built many of the great fortifications of the Caribbean under the supervision of European military officers. The Portuguese and the French military fleets used slave sailors. The military service of slaves and their work as auxiliaries and as construction workers made them indispensable for the European armies and navies who carried out almost endemic warfare in the Caribbean during the seventeenth and eighteenth centuries.

Emancipation did not bring immediate occupational liberty to the former slaves. The decades after freedom in the United States brought a restriction of occupations. The occupational rigidity and gender stereotyping that slavery had imposed, along with centuries of racial prejudice, were formidable barriers to change. Even the move from slave to wage labor was prolonged and complex.

The transition has been painful and lengthy in each of the former slave societies, with a legacy that has endured until the present.

BIBLIOGRAPHY

Dunn, Richard S. *Sugar and Slaves: The Rise of the Planter Class in the English West Indies.* Chapel Hill: University of North Carolina Press, 1972.

Fogel, Robert W. *Without Consent of Contract: The Rise and Fall of American Slavery.* New York: W. W. Norton, 1989.

Jones, Jacqueline. *Labor of Love, Labor of Sorrow: Black Women and the Family from Slavery to the Present.* New York: Basic Books, 1985.

Nash, Gary B. *The Urban Crucible: The Northern Seaports an the Origins of the American Revolution.* Cambridge, Mass.: Harvard University Press, 1986.

Schwartz, Stuart. *Sugar Plantations in the Formation of Brazilian Society: Bahia, 1550–1835.* Cambridge: Cambridge University Press, 1985.

Voelz, Peter Michael. *Slave and Soldier: The Military Impact of Blacks in the Colonial Americas.* New York: Garland, 1993.

Wade, Richard C. *Slavery in the Cities: The South 1820–1860.* New York and Oxford: Oxford University Press, 1964.

—DAVID MURRAY

OCEANIA. Within the southern Pacific region of Oceania, slavery occurred in both indigenous and colonial contexts. Although it was associated with warfare, indigenous slavery was relatively rare; it was more common to kill, sacrifice, or eat prisoners. Many local terms for "slave" properly refer to captives. Captives were commonly regarded as dead by their own communities, so escape was rarely attempted. Slave or captive status was not hereditary; however, the social positions of slaves' descendants differed according to local forms of social distinction. Especially in the more hierarchical Polynesian societies, it was probably difficult for descendants of slaves to acquire high status, except by hypergamy (marrying up in the hierarchy). In Melanesia, they were absorbed into their captors' or spouses' lineages, and here it is often difficult to distinguish between enslavement and captive kinship.

Probably the greatest elaboration of Polynesian slavery occurred in the Maori societies of New

Zealand, where captives not cannibalized or sacrificed performed menial labor for their captors, who retained powers of life and death over them. Otherwise, they generally were well treated and had many normal social rights, such as forthright speech. The children of captives who married locally were members of their free parent's group. Slaves (*tuarekareka*) also acted as carriers on raids and sometimes even fought against their former kin. Maori slavery apparently escalated between the late eighteenth century and the mid-nineteenth, when local demands for European firearms developed. During this period slaves worked in producing flax and provisions for ships, and female slaves were exploited as prostitutes aboard ships. Many were also killed to satisfy European demands for tattooed Maori heads.

Elsewhere in Polynesia, captives, refugees, or the dispossessed were forced into dependent relationships with the victors, but local distinctions among slaves, vassals, and dependents were often ambiguous. Brief examples include Easter Island, where captive labor built the gigantic *ahu* statues; the Society Islands, where menial labor was performed by the lowest orders (*manuhune*), including war captives; and Hawaii, where an order of outcastes (*kauwa*) were regarded as worthless slave descendants. Common to these diverse forms of subjugation were the notions that they were debased statuses, lacking honor, worth, or spiritual power. This was reflected in Hawaiian references to *kauwa* as "corpses," Mangaian descriptions of dependent captives as "fatherless people" (*ivi panga*), and Maori references to slaves as "pets" (*mokai*).

In Melanesia captives were usually taken for sacrifice or adoption. It is notable that the two places best known for slavery, the western Solomon Islands and south-coast New Guinea, were both maritime head-hunting areas. The Marind-anim of New Guinea ranged long distances in search of enemy heads and young women and children for resocialization as Marind-anim. At times captives constituted around 8 percent of the Marind population. The situation was similar in the New Geor-gian Islands in the Solomons, where the word *pinausu* referred to anyone who was adopted or fostered, including captives. In the late nineteenth century some *pinausu* were purchased from distant islands, usually in exchange for firearms. Those who were ultimately sacrificed to ancestral spirits were treated well until their deaths. A second category of captives, who acted as ritual specialists or lieutenants to powerful leaders, often acquired considerable wealth. Others, especially children, were adopted into local kinship groups and were entitled to inherit, like their adoptive siblings.

In the nineteenth century a form of commercial slavery occurred in the Vogelkop Peninsula of western New Guinea, where Papuan slaves were sold into Southeast Asian trading systems. This appears to be the only Oceanic instance of indigenous commercial slaving. However, Europeans were involved in three forms of labor relations that have been likened to slavery: the Peruvian slave trade of 1862–1864, the Southwest Pacific labor trade, and indentured Asian labor.

The Peruvian slave trade in Polynesia followed the abolition of slavery (1854), the curtailment of Chinese immigration, and the expansion of Peruvian cotton and rice production in response to the American Civil War. Peruvian law obliged recruiters to hire Pacific Islanders as voluntary laborers, but most were kidnapped. Maude (1981) estimates that about six thousand people died for reasons directly or indirectly attributable to the trade. This entailed phenomenal depopulation, ranging from 24 percent on Pukapuka to 79 percent on Nukulaelae.

The "labor trade," centered on the Solomons and Vanuatu, developed in the 1870s in response to demands for cheap labor in the Queensland and Fijian cane and cotton fields. The trade was initially known as "blackbirding" because of its early kidnapping, violence, and disregard for the humanity of its victims, but by the 1890s Islanders voluntarily contracted to work for a fixed period. By the turn of the century, Islanders were also working on plantations in British, Dutch, French, and German colonies. Although this was contracted employment, the laboring conditions, endemic violence, and death rates have often led writers to refer to this trade as a form of slavery. By 1911 the Australian "white Australia policy" and the effects of abolitionist agitation saw the end of the long-distance labor trade to Queensland and Fiji. However, various forms of indentured Islander labor continued elsewhere, with Papua and New Caledonia notable for the brutal treatment of laborers.

Other forms of indentured labor involved the movement of Asian workers into the Pacific, the best-known being the Indian *girmitiyas*' emigrations to Fiji, where many took up residence after their indentures had ended. Here too the typical working conditions, persistent violence, and high death rates often evoke coerced slave labor as much as free contract labor.

The word *slavery* should be used cautiously in regard to indigenous Oceanic societies. The term often reflects moralistic glosses for indigenous practices by colonial administrators, missionaries, and others with vested interests in denouncing local cultures. Likewise, there is much rhetoric in the literature on the indentured labor trades. These relationships all entailed degrees of bondage, violence, abuse, coercion, or abduction. It is perhaps most fruitful to look at indigenous and European "slavery" as continua, ranging from the unambiguous enslavement of the Vogelkop and Peruvian slave trades to the more nuanced labor and social relationships of war captives and indentured laborers.

There has been little analysis of indigenous slavery, and much remains to be done on indentured labor. Future research into these subjects requires cultural and linguistic study of indigenous concepts of freedom, captivity, and relationship, and empirical and analytical studies of labor relations in European colonial settings.

[*See also* Forced Labor *and* Indentured Servitude.]

BIBLIOGRAPHY

Goldman, Irving. *Ancient Polynesian Society*. Chicago: University of Chicago Press, 1970.

Knauft, Bruce. "Melanesian Warfare: A Theoretical Perspective." *Oceania* (1990): 251–311.

Lal, Brij V. *Girmitiyas: The Origins of the Fiji Indians*. Canberra: Journal of Pacific History, 1983.

Maude, H. E. *Slavers in Paradise: The Peruvian Slave Trade in Polynesia, 1862–1864*. Stanford: Stanford University Press, 1981.

Vayda, Andrew Peter. *Maori Warfare*. Wellington: Polynesian Society, 1960.

—Christine Dureau

PAWNSHIP. The legal category of social and economic dependency known as *pawnship* was, in various forms, common in many preindustrial societies, including Africa, South and Southeast Asia, and parts of Latin America as well; in the last it is usually referred to as *debt bondage*. The pawn was a person held as collateral for a debt or loan, and as in the case of trees and farms that were pledged under a similar system of credit, the pawning of individuals constituted the transfer of productive assets for the duration of the debt as security, unlike a mortgage, in which assets are transferred only in case of default.

The labor of the pawn constituted interest on the debt and covered the costs of subsistence, but it did not contribute to the principal. The principal usually had a fixed value at the time of the contract and had to be paid off in full before the pawn was free from service. There could be disputes over the amount of the principal; if the loan had been originally calculated in terms of a commodity whose value subsequently increased during the period of servitude, the creditor might insist that repayment be made on the basis of the inflated value, thereby adding an often substantial increment to the debt. It was also possible for the original debt to include a monetary component for interest, in which case the pawn did not usually live with the creditor. However the principal and interest were calculated, the pawn continued in bondage until the full debt had been repaid or otherwise canceled. Although the period for repayment was usually indefinite before the twentieth century, colonial laws in some parts of Africa attempted to fix a terminal date for repayment, thereby establishing the principle that the labor performed by the pawn included both interest and capital.

The contract that controlled the labor of the pawn represented an investment that was realized through the labor-power of the pawn. That contract was property and hence was owned and could be transferred, although the permission of the debtor was required before a pawn could be transferred. Pawns themselves were not property and were not owned. In most instances, it would be more accurate to refer to "creditors" who "controlled" pawns rather than to "masters" who "owned" pawns, as if pawns were slaves. A debt that resulted in pawning involved the implicit recognition by the debtor and the creditor that a specific amount of capital was owed, and that the loan arose from property rights enjoyed by the creditor. Food, money, shelter, trade items, or some combination of these goods and services were extended to the debtor in lieu of full repayment. In short, the transaction was based on the commoditization of these goods and services.

Because interest continued in the form of labor until the debt was repaid in full, pawnship had some similarities to slavery. In each case the creditor or master had relatively full control over the output of the pawn or slave; the labor-power of the pawn or slave belonged to the creditor or master. Nonetheless, there is an important distinction between pawnship and slavery. From a theoretical perspective, the pawning contract, not the pawn, was the property of the creditor, while under slavery the slave was the direct property of the master. Pawns, or more often their kin who had placed them in pawn, had legal recourse in the case of abuse or dispute on the basis of the contract, and the contract could be terminated on repayment of the original debt. Slaves had no such legal re-

course, although they could achieve emancipation in a variety of ways if a master was so disposed. This proprietary difference between the pawning contract and the slave as property had important ramifications in different historical contexts, although it should be recognized that the fine theoretical distinction that is drawn here often broke down in practice. Pawns could end up as slaves, and slaves were sometimes pawned.

Pawns were generally drawn from within the society in which they were in bondage; either pawns were freeborn members of society, or they were slaves of long standing whom their masters pawned in the expectation of redeeming them and reincorporating them into their households. In order for an individual to have use as collateral, it was essential that the debtor want to redeem the person. This commitment to paying off the debt was clearly established in the case of self-pawning, whereby a person agreed to pledge himself or herself as collateral. Whether or not a person was always able to pay off the debt is another matter. The commitment to redemption was also operative in the case of close kin, where the debtors usually intended to pay off the debt. But chronic financial difficulties might prevent redemption, and thus there was considerable risk that the transaction might involve the total alienation of the pawn. A domestic slave had value to his or her owner because slaves were an investment; moreover, the relationship might well evolve so that the personal attachment might become almost as strong as that based on kinship. Nonetheless, potential alienation was certainly more extreme for slaves than in instances of self-pawning or the pawning of close relatives.

Pawns were usually individuals who were recognized as constituent members of society, even if they were subordinates or people of low status. Unless they were full members, they had little chance of being protected from sale into slavery or otherwise abused. Individuals had to have value deriving from their social relationship to the debtor in order for them to have value to the creditor as collateral. Self-pawning intrinsically emphasized this value, even though those who pawned themselves were often in the worst position to honor a debt. They were preoccupied with service to the creditor and hence were usually able only to cover the costs of subsistence and to pay the interest on the debt. Time had to be allowed for additional work if there was any hope of recovering the principal, or relatives had to be willing to repay the original debt. The individuals who were the most effective pawns were close relatives of the debtor, because the debtor was still free to concentrate on acquiring the resources to repay the debt. Social pressures and affection between debtor and pawn were effective instruments that promoted redemption.

This identification with the society in which individuals experienced their subordination further distinguished pawnship from slavery as an institution. Newly acquired slaves were foreigners or otherwise defined as outsiders, unlike individuals who were reduced to the status of pawn. As already noted, slaves could be pawned, but when masters arranged to use slaves as collateral, they were acting on the basis of their investment in slaves as property. Usually, slaves could serve this function only if they were acculturated and therefore members of society, albeit of servile status. In a sense, pawned slaves were being treated like quasi-kin; otherwise, a master would be more likely to sell the slave in order to pay a debt or to raise capital. Because pawns were of domestic origin, social obligations and public pressure served to limit their exploitation in a manner that was similar to the protection provided for kin.

Despite the social position of pawns as familiar members of a community, pawnship was still a system of exploitation and servility. Kinship, marital bond, or some other clearly recognized social status was supposed to safeguard individuals from excessive abuse, prevent the transfer of pawns to third parties, and obstruct other acts that the debtors might consider inappropriate or illegal. The ideological and legal constraints on pawnship did not always operate effectively, however. Social

and legal restrictions might restrain creditors, but market forces could well counteract these safeguards. In short, pawns were vulnerable to greater alienation than their legal position implied.

According to the historical record, the major victims of pawnship were destitute individuals who pawned themselves, children of the poor, social or religious outcasts, and domestic slaves. Self-pawning seems to have been most prevalent among males, and many cases of pawning to secure commercial debts involved males. Nonetheless, it is likely that most pawns were female; moreover, whether male or female, pawns were usually children or teenagers.

The selection of individual pawns suggests a link between labor mobilization, social stratification, and gender. Pawns were a source of labor; they were required to work for the creditor, performing specific tasks depending on the nature of the contract that had been reached at the time of the loan, or at some subsequent date when repayment of the loan was in arrears. Usually pawns were of lower social status, often because they were younger, and hence their acquired status of pawn did not necessarily alter their living and social conditions significantly. Children, for example, were subject to the supervision of adults, whether parents, other relatives, or creditors. Pawned slaves had to obey the creditor of their master just as they had to obey their master. Gender mattered because the creditor was concerned with the recovery of the loan, and marriage, either to the creditor or a relative, was a means of capitalizing on an investment.

Because creditors were usually the wealthiest members of society, relationships of pawnship tended to correspond to class and other social divisions. This stratification was clearest in the case of slave pawns, but since most pawn dependents were of lower social status than their masters, the flow of capital from the wealthy to the less fortunate inevitably reinforced class and social differences. Because social factors, usually involving kinship ties, enabled individuals to be held as collateral, pawning was often associated with gender relationships, particularly marriage. Females were prime candidates for pawning because they could be married, besides being made to work.

The use of slaves as pawns represents a special case of debt bondage. Under these circumstances, slaves were used as collateral in the same way that other property, including land and economically valued trees, could be used as surety for a debt. The slave, as the property of the debtor, had a monetary value that could be realized in case of default, and as was the case with the pawning of other property, the creditor had use of the slave until the loan was repaid. As with the use of relatives as pawns or with self-pawning, however, the labor of the pawned slave serviced the interest on the debt and covered costs associated with subsistence. On repayment, the slave continued in slavery, having temporarily worked on his or her master's behalf for someone else.

It is difficult to calculate the returns to the creditor in cases of pawnship, although in most cases it was probably considerable. The labor of the pawn was composed of two factors—the subsistence costs of the pawn and interest. In addition, the creditor sometimes had to recover administrative and witness fees, and occasionally the expenses associated with religious rituals and other ceremonies. The interest that was realized, moreover, depended on the age and gender of the pawn. Children were less likely to contribute substantially to the income of the creditor, and there was always the risk of ill health or injury, which could temporarily or permanently reduce the ability of the pawn to cover the cost of subsistence or to provide interest on the debt. Because of these risks, creditors did not always benefit from the pawns under their control. Moreover, creditors sometimes took in pawns for social reasons involving costs that could not be fully recovered. Children of destitute relatives, for example, were not necessarily "exploited" in an economic sense, and a creditor might well spend considerable money on educating and clothing them without expecting to recover these costs.

The prevalence of pawnship during any period appears to have had some correlation with poverty and the inability of families and individuals to secure the necessities of life. Famine, disease, political insecurity, and economic miscalculation were frequent causes of poverty and the need to borrow. It should be noted, however, that poverty was not always the cause of indebtedness. Sometimes merchants borrowed to promote their trade. Their expectation was to repay the loan sooner or later out of profits. People also borrowed to meet funeral expenses, ritual obligations, and court fines. In these cases, however, failure to repay debts quickly was often a sign of deteriorating economic circumstances and hence was ultimately related to poverty. Second, pawnship involved control over the labor of the individual held in pawn. As a mechanism for obtaining access to labor, pawnship has to be considered in the context of other mechanisms of labor supply, including slavery, communal activities, corvée, and wages. Pawnship was only one form of labor mobilization. Third, gender issues are paramount in understanding the context for pawnship because much of the labor mobilized through this institution was performed by women. Furthermore, women and their children were often the ones to suffer most from famine and political instability, and gender and indebtedness were often associated. Because of this vulnerability, women were exposed to sexual exploitation and other abuse that sometimes resulted in their reduction to slavery. Fourth, pawning was only one mechanism for obtaining credit, and hence an examination of its economic role must take into consideration other institutions and practices and how these changed in different historical contexts.

Pawns were an important supplement to slaves in Africa and elsewhere before the twentieth century; thereafter, they often became substitutes for slaves with the decline of slavery in Africa and Asia. Pawnship existed alongside slavery, experiencing levels of resurgence and intensity that initially depended on changing economic conditions. When slavery was dominant, pawnship fed individuals into servitude. After slavery subsided, pawnship briefly surfaced as an alternative to slavery, its appearance fluctuating with the vicissitudes of the market economy.

[*See also* Africa; Asia; *and* Clientage.]

BIBLIOGRAPHY

Falola, Toyin, and Paul E. Lovejoy, eds. *Pawnship in Africa: Debt Bondage in Historical Perspective.* Boulder, Colo.: Westview Press, 1994.

Kamble, N. D. *Bonded Labour in India.* New Delhi: Uppal, 1982.

Klein, Martin, ed. *Breaking the Chains: Slavery, Bondage and Emancipation in Africa and Asia.* Madison: University of Wisconsin Press, 1993.

Marla, Sarma. *Bonded Labour in India.* New Delhi: Biblia Impex, 1981.

Miers, Suzanne and Igor Kopytoff, eds. *Slavery in Africa: Anthropological and Historical Perspectives.* Madison: University of Wisconsin Press, 1977.

Patnaik, Utsa, and Manjari Dingwaney, eds. *Chains of Servitude: Bondage and Slavery in India.* Hyderabad: Sangam Books, 1985.

Reid, Anthony, ed. *Slavery, Bondage and Dependency in Southeast Asia.* St. Lucia: University of Queensland Press, 1983.

—PAUL E. LOVEJOY

PENAL SLAVERY. Societies have often faced a dilemma regarding the punishment of criminals, particularly those possessing little property with which to pay fines. Physical chastisement, such as whipping, beating, branding, dunking, using stocks and thumbscrews, bodily mutilation, and execution, while inexpensive, are frequently considered too harsh and uncivilized. Moreover, except for execution, such punishments do not prevent criminals from being a continuing threat to the public. Incarceration, while more civilized and more successful in removing criminals from social intercourse, is costly. Prisons are expensive to build, staff, and maintain, and prisoners must be fed and clothed. In addition, while criminals are in prison society loses the productive value of their labor, and the idleness of prison life may not reform criminals or deter recidivism. Thus incarceration is often coupled with the demand that criminals be compelled to work; however, the level of punishment required to make prisoners work may be worse than the physical chastisement that incarceration replaced. These controversies surrounding penal slavery have continued to the present day, as can be seen by recent debates over the reintroduction of convict chain gangs in the United States, the importation of goods made by Chinese prisoners, and the continuing plight of Korean and Russian prisoners in labor camps.

Incarcerated convicts forfeit most of their rights and control over their persons. The quantity and quality of their food, clothing, and shelter, the location of their persons, how their time can be spent, and the level of compulsion that can be used to extract obedience and effort are determined largely by their overseers. Their condition resembles that of slaves more than of free persons, with the exception that convicts have legally fixed termination dates to their slavery.

Because the sight of fellow members of society forced to labor like slaves can disturb society's self-image and domestic tranquility, convict labor has typically been removed from public view to prison compounds, isolated locations within the realm, or distant colonies. During the eighteenth and nineteenth centuries Russia moved roughly one million prisoners to the Siberian territories, while England, France, and Spain sentenced more than one-quarter million convicts to be forcibly transported to overseas colonies. Overseas transportation was attractive because it defrayed the expense of building prisons at home, and because it provided needed labor for new colonies, both for public works and for private commercial agriculture. Spain sent convicts to North Africa, Cuba, and Puerto Rico. France maintained approximately 3,000 to 6,000 convicts in French Guiana between 1854 and 1920, and it sent 20,000 to New Caledonia in the South Pacific between 1864 and 1897. Britain, however, was the largest participant in this overseas transportation. From the 1718 Transportation Act to the American Revolution, Britain shipped roughly 50,000 convicts to Virginia and Maryland. Thereafter, Australia became Britain's principal convict colony, receiving approximately 160,000 convicts between

1787 and 1868. Another 18,000 were shipped to Bermuda and Gibraltar between 1824 and 1875. From 1787 to 1920, Britain also transported between 30,000 and 50,000 native convicts from India to colonial outposts ringing the Indian Ocean.

Penal slavery via overseas transportation came close to resembling the trans-Atlantic trade in African slaves. Like slavery, the convict trade involved the trans-oceanic movement of involuntary, forced labor. Both trades peaked at roughly the same time. Like slaves, convicts were sold, rented, or assigned to private shippers and colonial employers, thus transferring the convicts' transportation, maintenance, and supervision costs from the public purse to the private sector. Because private employers had an incentive to extract work from convicts in excess of their maintenance and supervision costs, convict laborers, like slaves, could be sold for a positive price. Once convicts left their home shore, private profit rather than penal policy largely determined the institution's character. While the total volume of the trans-oceanic and transcontinental convict trade pales against the volume of the African slave trade and the movement of free immigrants in this period, convicts nevertheless represent an important component of European colony-building, particularly in regions that initially attracted few voluntary immigrants.

Most British transportees had been convicted of minor theft, for which the penalty of death was

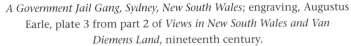

A Government Jail Gang, Sydney, New South Wales; engraving, Augustus Earle, plate 3 from part 2 of *Views in New South Wales and Van Diemens Land*, nineteenth century.

commuted to seven years' servitude in the colonies. A few transportees had been convicted of capital crimes; their death sentences were commuted to colonial servitude for fourteen years to life. The majority of convicts were males between the ages of sixteen and thirty-five, and roughly one-third were Irish. Their range of skills was similar to, and their literacy rate greater than, those of free workers in Britain. They were at least as tall as free workers in England, and taller than indentured servants who emigrated voluntarily. Because height is a positive measure of net nutrition in childhood, and because literacy and skill are measures of social status, convicts may not have experienced a uniquely destitute upbringing. Although exposed to harsher physical coercion than free workers in Britain, convicts, once settled, experienced similar if not better food, health, and work conditions. Finally, the voyage mortality rate for convicts was similar to that for free immigrants.

Agitation to end the transoceanic trade in convict labor came from several sources. Social reformers sought to replace transportation with model penitentiaries. Maturing colonies became reluctant to accept convicts for fear they would pose a threat to public safety and retard the flow of free immigrants. Finally, transportation's deterrent effect on crime may have waned, because the chronic shortage of labor in the colonies sometimes made the convict's lot appear better than that of a law-abiding subject at home. More research into the success convicts experienced after their sentences expired is still needed.

[See also Forced Labor, article on Soviet Union; Nazi Slavery; and United States, overview article.]

BIBLIOGRAPHY

Coldham, Peter Wilson. Emigrants in Chains, 1607–1776. Baltimore: Genealogical Publishing Co., 1992.

Ekirch, A. Roger. Bound for America: The Transportation of British Convicts to the Colonies, 1718–1775. New York and Oxford: Oxford University Press, 1987.

Hughes, Robert. The Fatal Shore: The Epic of Australia's Founding. New York: Random House, 1986.

Nichols, Stephen, ed. Convict Workers: Reinterpreting Australia's Past. New York: Cambridge University Press, 1988.

Smith, Abbot Emerson. Colonists in Bondage: White Servitude and Convict Labor in America, 1607–1776. Chapel Hill: University of North Carolina Press, 1947.

—FARLEY GRUBB

PROPERTY. Slavery is an institution and a practice that was defined by the League of Nations Covenant of 1926 as "the status or condition of a person over whom any or all the powers attaching to the rights of ownership are attached." Although this definition concurs with the usual analytical and common-sense understanding of slavery in the Classical world and the plantation regimes of the modern world, is the property nexus the necessary definition of all slavery at all times? How do we distinguish slavery from all other forms of dependency and involuntary labor?

Nieboer (1971), in his pioneering comparative examination of slavery, stated the property issue of slavery most succinctly: "We may define a slave in the ordinary sense of the word as a man who is the property of another, politically and socially at a lower level than the mass of the people and performing compulsory labor" (p. 5). Significantly, he was compelled to rephrase this definition as "slavery is the fact, that one man is the property or possession of another beyond the limits of the family proper" (p. 30).

Westermarck (1906), also writing at the beginning of the twentieth century, chose to de-emphasize the property-based definition of slavery, preferring the understanding that the slave is a human being and that there are restrictions on the owner's rights regarding the slave. These two positions, with their resonance in anthropology and history, have bracketed the discussion of slavery ever since.

The anti-property, anti-economic position of Westermarck misses the essential fact that although the slave is a human being, he or she is property, albeit a peculiar kind of property. All slave systems regarded the slave as an alienated and alienable commodity yet recognized the master-slave relation as unique among property relations. As to the legal restrictions regarding the slave, all property is a matrix of rights, rarely unlimited and indeed necessarily limited as a manner of codifying, regulating, and protecting the common interests of ownership at large.

Orlando Patterson (1982) shifted the definition of slavery from the minimalist consideration of property to a perspective describing slavery as "the permanent, violent domination of natally alienated and generally dishonored persons." Nieboer's and Patterson's definitions are not mutually incompatible, but they differ significantly in the approach they bring to the peculiar institution. While Nieboer emphasized the political economy of slavery, Patterson stressed its social relational basis, examining the exercise and codification of authority that result in the slave being inferior to the master and to the slavery-holding society in general.

Patterson did well to draw attention to the need to gloss, shade, and ritualize the concept of slavery in a manner that registers the paradox of defining humans as property. What is distinctive about slavery as a social construction is the comprehensive property rights the slave-owner exercises in regard to his property, the slave. The processes of slavery, requiring concomitant ideological constructs by which a human is defined as a social isolate, the ultimate outsider, subject to the authority (even the whims) of the master, are culturally and systemically necessary in order to render a person a piece of property.

Even in instances in which the duties of slaves may include military service or imperial administration, wielding power unknown to the overwhelming number of slaves, they were still the master's property. Those so raised could be reduced and therefore were always humbled before their owner.

Miers and Kopytoff (1977) culturally relativized the concepts of ownership, property, and the purchasing of people when considering African slavery, because there these categories can also be applied to free persons within lineage groups. Distinguishing "slavery" (in quotation marks) from (true) slavery, they differentiated the institution in Africa from slavery elsewhere; they gave preference to local terms for slaves, thereby stressing the slave condition as merely another form of subordination. In all cases, however, the alienation of the individual comes about through unredeemed pawnage, purchase, or capture. Again, the question of property rights in an individual is paramount. The slave "belonged" to a person or group as a piece of property, not as a member with an identity and ancestry of his or her own. If this is true of slavery in kinship societies, the elaboration of concepts of absolute property found in the slave societies of the Classical world and the plantation zones of modern times reflect the innovations of market relations and the consequent wide deployment of slave labor. The slave can then be defined in the terms of Finley, who distinguished between slaves and other kinds of unfree persons by calling the former "a privately owned commodity, denied in perpetuity the ownership of the means of production, denied control over his labor or the products of his labor and over his own reproduction" (1980, p. 74).

[See also Abolition and Anti-Slavery, *article on* Southeast Asia; *and* Law, *article on* United States Law.]

BIBLIOGRAPHY

Finley, Moses I. *Ancient Slavery and Modern Ideology.* New York: Viking Press, 1980.

Meillassoux, Claude. *The Anthropology of Slavery: The Womb of Iron and Gold.* Translated by Alide Dasnois. Chicago: University of Chicago Press, 1991.

Miers, Suzanne, and Igor Kopytoff, eds. *Slavery in Africa: Historical and Anthropological Perspectives.* Madison: University of Wisconsin Press, 1977.

Nieboer, H. J. *Slavery as an Industrial System: Ethnological Research.* 2d ed. Rpt., New York: B. Franklin, 1971.

Patterson, Orlando. *Slavery and Social Death.* Cambridge, Mass.: Harvard University Press, 1982.

Ste. Croix, G. E. M. de. *The Class Struggle in the Ancient Greek World: From the Archaic Age to the Arab Conquests.* Ithaca, N.Y.: Cornell University Press, 1980.

Watson, James L., ed. *Asian and African Systems of Slavery.* Oxford: Basil Blackwell, 1980.

Westermarck, Edward. *The Origin and Development of the Moral Ideas*. London: Macmillan, 1906.

—FRANK MCGLYNN

PSYCHOLOGY. Humankind throughout history has been fascinated by what drives its species to perceive, feel, and act as it does. Until the nineteenth century speculation on these questions of personality and motivation were largely the domain of philosophers, both folk and formally trained. By the mid-1800s a group of scholars claimed these concerns as their own, and the discipline of psychology was established. Its practitioners argued that through careful observation and interaction with their subjects they could uncover scientifically the answers to each ancient query.

From the beginning, the least powerful in society were not infrequently subjected to the probing of privileged men of science. Clear precedents had been set for this attention. In the eighteenth century newly enslaved Africans were examined to discover why their mortality was so high in the British and French Caribbean. The English diagnosed hypochondriasis; their European counterparts suggested *mal d'estomac*. Both believed that this usually fatal disease stemmed from slow-working poisons that black captives administered to one another.

Challenging this view, Benjamin Rush, a prominent Philadelphia physician whose groundbreaking studies of the mentally ill have earned him the title "father of American psychiatry," wrote that the real culprit causing slave deaths in the Caribbean was an extreme and deadly melancholy triggered by Africans' sudden separation from their loved ones and the traumatic trans-Atlantic voyage. Depression was understandable: often transported in a state of complete nakedness, human cargoes of women, men, and children were gener-

Drawing depicting Africans being forced to "dance" on board ship, from Grehan Amedée's *France maritime* (1855).

ally shaved, branded, and made to lie chained in suffocating holds where festering sores, excrement, and harrowing shrieks contributed to a symphony of horrors.

During the thousands of years during which slavery existed, and it appears that every culture experienced it, relatively few victims of this form of coerced labor left records of how they perceived themselves and others, or of what determined the particular courses they chose to take. It is perhaps for this reason that the classicist Moses Finley stated, "Nothing is more elusive than the psychology of the slave" (1980, p. 117). Nonetheless, in the case of the ten to twelve million Africans who survived their forced migration, there is a vast array of testimony, especially from the descendants of the small minority taken to North America. Because no other slave population provides such singularly rich documentation, we will probably never know more about slave psychology than what we learn from those who made Spanish, Portuguese, French, English, Dutch, and Danish colonization a success. The focus of this entry is on the slaves for whom the most definitive evidence exists.

Between 1502 and 1867 slaves from Africa populated an African diaspora that eventually comprised both Old and New World Africans. Whether native-born or creole, the enslaved, like other human beings, struggled to understand their world. In the process they found happiness in friends, cherished the admiration of peers, worried about loved ones, and engaged in all the trivialities between birth and death. For slaves, however, there was another battle: unfree workers had to withstand the coercion and power on which all systems of slavery ultimately rest. The key to unlocking the psychology of New World slaves is contained in their devastatingly simple desires to be free and to survive. The tension from these potentially explosive ambitions goes further to explain the range of behaviors and personalities among bondspeople than all the theories that generations of pro-slavery thinkers, nonslave observers, and post-emancipation scholars have proffered to explain the actions of slaves.

In reaction to their slaves' quest for freedom, white captors devised an endless range of physical and psychological mechanisms of control to keep them enslaved. They also waged incessant campaigns to make sure that their human property knew that any unsanctioned moves toward liberty would always be a matter of life and death. While there is nothing new about the enmity and resistance bred by slavery, those steering the trans-Atlantic slave trade introduced a novel dynamic. They made the very color of slaves a weapon against them: blackness became not only a mark of enslavement but an immutable biological determinant of why they were slaves.

North American enslavers added a special twist to this racial slavery. Drawing on a long history of disparate oppressors who used familial imagery to justify their rule, a wealthy segment of slaveholding males declared themselves "patriarchs" who lovingly protected both their white *and* black families. The consequences were lethal: racist characterizations of nonwhites became more believable, and the most sinfully inconsistent acts of the fathers more acceptable. In his 1838 book, *Morals of Slavery*, the Southern intellectual William Gilmore Simms extolled the benevolence and benefits of black enslavement. He argued that it ensured the sanctity of white women by providing sons their pick of black women in whom they "harmlessly" could sow their oats. How high a price bondswomen paid on behalf of free white women is revealed by the hundreds of thousands of mulattoes throughout the American South in 1860.

More than a century of psychological research has established that there is no abstract individual or group psychology. Behaviors can be connected to specific circumstances and conditions. This is particularly apparent when one compares the challenges that different New World slaves faced in trying to balance their ambition for freedom and their determination to live. These usually conflicting ideas may not have been so unsettling to enslaved blacks on the Pacific coast of sixteenth-century Mexico (then known as New Spain), where there was an abundance of self-emancipated "fugitive" slaves, a paucity of whites, and many Amerindians (the Spanish had largely been unsuccessful in fomenting hostility among the native peoples toward blacks). North American slaves never had the opportunities to escape that were afforded to their Caribbean and South American counterparts by the inaccessible mountains and jungles that provided safe havens for thousands of runaways. They were, however, better able to establish families and to reproduce themselves than any other New World slave population; and for transplanted Africans as well as their descendants, nothing provided greater relief than the psychic comfort of the family.

Whether Ibo, Bambara, Kongo, or any other African ethnic group, the family was the cornerstone of their Old World identity, and they turned first to it in trying to make sense of their sojourn in bondage. During the infamous Middle Passage those on the same slaving vessels frequently went from particular kin identities to "shipmates" to "brothers" and "sisters" in one journey. Without any biological or often even ethnic connection, this new relationship took such strong root that thereafter, even when on the same farm or plantation, people in such a relationship deemed sexual relations with each other incestuous. Thus began their transformation from divergent African ethnicities into a single people. Just how this feat was accomplished is still being explored. That they succeeded, there is no question.

The building blocks for this evolution were the diverse cultures that accompanied each slave to the New World. What helped considerably to forge their faith in eventual freedom was a common intellectual thread that linked diverse African religions and philosophies. Life was not a composite of sharp contrasts and dichotomies but an array of ever-changing forces: families comprised the living and the dead in the same way that good and evil as well as fortune and misfortune were simply part of

an eternal continuum. These beliefs and newer ideas saved not a few from spiritual drowning. In fusing their identity, these blacks made resistance to slavery an essential feature.

Slave elders socialized girls and boys to do all they could to evade the wrath of whites, but later they taught them to engage in stratagems, individually and together, that affirmed their opposition to slavery and support of one another. Naturally, not all could or chose to adhere to this complex message. For the vast majority, self-interest alone dictated that they do so.

Navigating slavery's dangerous waters was no easy task, and staying afloat without the aid of fellow slaves was a hazard most decided early on they did not want to risk. They had witnessed too often how unfree blacks, and sometimes free blacks, provided relief for the distraught victims of rape, brutal lashings, mutilations, and other sufferings. In addition to the high death rates sparked by harsh labor and disease-filled environments, countless slave families were ruthlessly torn apart through sale. While much has been written of the elaborate funeral services in which Africans and their descendants reaffirmed themselves as a people, less has been noted about the equally important ceremonies of mourning that consoled those who suffered the loss of loved ones in domestic trades. In Brazil alone an estimated two hundred thousand slaves were sold from the country's northeast and removed to southern coffee plantations between 1850 and 1888. In North America, approximately 875,000 women, men, and children were marketed within the South between 1820 and 1860. Without the systems of support that the black world offered the steady streams of unrelated but strikingly familiar members of the African diaspora, the emotional, mental, and physical consequences would have been difficult to survive.

The most ubiquitous weapon in the slaveholding arsenal was the lash. To maximize its physical and psychological effect, both women and men were generally stripped at least to the waist, adding sexual titillation for at least some of the floggers.

Slaveholders made sure that all slaves, victims or otherwise, were familiar with flogging. The aim was not simply to punish poor work or bad behavior, but to strike fear into every slave. Encounters with the terrified or grieving were inevitable. After resisting the sexual advances of her South Carolina master, a slave woman named Charlotte was made to sit naked on a pile of manure until she complied. She bore her tormentor a child, and then he decided to pass the mother on to his cousin; she became pregnant again and added another slave to the two men's holdings.

While the struggle to survive and gain freedom was never easily resolved, many slaves concluded that their best course was to stay as far away from whites as possible. Nevertheless, the greatest autonomy was in liberation, and the least dangerous way to obtain it was through cooperating with the masters. Some chose to earn manumission or at least to secure the privilege of buying themselves. Both ambitions apparently motivated the slave whom Harriet Beecher Stowe cited as proof that *Uncle Tom's Cabin* was no fiction. Like Stowe's protagonist, the bondsman Josiah Henson appears to have imbibed an interpretation of Christianity alien to most blacks. Whereas the majority of black Christians did not view appropriations from enslavers as immoral, Josiah believed that stealing from masters was a sin. No doubt because of this refreshing attitude, Henson's Maryland owner delegated him to transport several slave families to Kentucky. Despite a perfect opportunity to escape, Henson kept his trust and delivered them safely. Only after exhausting all legal channels to secure his freedom did Henson break state law and risk federal apprehension by fleeing.

Nowhere in the African diaspora could slaves assume that all blacks were allies or that whites were friends. Even the early abolitionist Benjamin Rush could not help but see his own color as normative: in his research on the causes of blackness, he concluded that blacks suffered from a leprosy-like disease, for which he urged fellow scientists to find a cure. Some idea of the prevailing racism can be

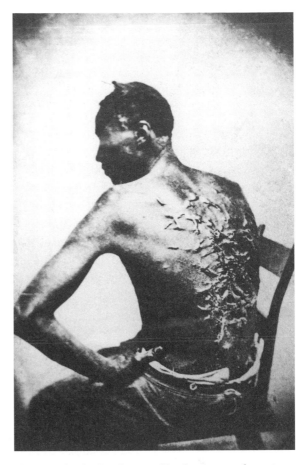

Photograph of a slave's scarred back, nineteenth century.

gathered in the 1840 United States census. It contained the first study of mental illness among blacks and presented data (later proven false) that a disproportionate number of Northern black men had been committed to insane asylums. This evidence was then used to prove the inability of African Americans to live sanely *and* free. Although a prominent physician, Edward Jarvis, refuted the data, first in an 1844 article in the *Journal of the Medical Sciences* and, and eight years later in the *Journal of Insanity*, his findings were largely ignored. The sentiments driving such widespread acceptance of negative depictions of blacks could be found throughout the New World.

To protect themselves from the dangers inherent in such hateful group portraits, countless slaves and free blacks hid their true sentiments behind smiles of contentment and words of servility that confirmed white images of them as infantile, harmless, and contented "boys" and "girls." What lay beneath the surface of some disguises was revealed in the recollections of a Nashville, Tennessee, woman who many years earlier had been a slave in the area. She recalled the men on one plantation whose owner, "old Sam Watkins," would visit their cabins, "ship" them out, and rape their wives. Although he "knew it was death," but reasoned, "it was death anyhow," one husband finally strangled Watkins to death. This made his wife a widow, for killing a white was a capital offense. Because there were always bondswomen and bondsmen who opted to die, like this slave, New World enslavers could never rest easily.

The slaveholders found support in the scientific establishment of their time. Commissioned by the Medical Association of Louisiana to report on "The Diseases and Physical Peculiarities of the Negro Race," the physician Samuel A. Cartwright led a four-man team that produced a detailed twenty-four page study. Aided by "the knife of the anatomist at the dissecting table," these scientists made some striking discoveries. Publishing their findings in the May 1851 issue of the *New Orleans Medical and Surgical Journal*, they disclosed certain "unalterable" physiological and psychological laws about blacks and introduced to the world two new diseases. One was a mental illness that they named *dysaesthesia aethiopis*. The symptoms included "careless movements," destruction of property, poor work, and a "stupidity of mind." The remedy for this free black and slave illness was "the compulsatory authority of the white man," that is, bondage.

Slaveowners sought to shackle their slaves both physically and psychologically. By diagnosing the rebellious as "mad" and the noncompliant as aberrant, they exerted monumental pressures on the slave mind. Nonetheless, these efforts at mass psychological enslavement failed. According to the so-

ciologist Orlando Patterson (1982) in his global history of slave systems, "There is absolutely no evidence from the long and dismal annals of slavery to suggest that any group of slaves ever internalized the conception of degradation held by their masters."

Since the emancipation of African-American slaves in 1865, the majority of what has been written about them reveals more about the culture of racism, sexism, and elitism that continues to inform American life than about slaves' psychology. Even at the end of the twentieth century, a distinguished line of European American scholars have kept alive the paternalistic paradigm of slavery. In a remarkably persistent tradition of scholarship, the patriarchal slaveholding world is almost always focused on men, white and black, slave and free, with little attention to the role of slave females in shaping the psychology of girls, boys, men, or themselves. Those who ran away were not fleeing slavery but "shirking duty." Those who destroyed planter property were not protesting but indulging in "nihilistic" behavior. Rape, a word that for decades never even appeared in the literature, is now being replaced increasingly by substitutes like "interracial sexual intercourse." One recent historian refers to such unions as a never-defined "racial solvent." No antebellum or Civil War battle was as effective in preserving the fantasies of Southern patriarchs as the intellectual rally to do so after the Confederacy lost its war.

There is still much to learn from the testimony of slaves. By discarding paternalistic blinders and utilizing the insights of literary scholars who have been mining the words and silences in slave texts to great effect, historians may begin to answer key questions. How did African concepts of gender change in the New World, and what impact did these ideas have on the psychology of slaves? In what way were feelings of guilt resolved by those who fled bondage but left behind friends and loved ones? Can we discern the effects on women who used sex with masters to secure better treatment, freedom, or promises against sale? What role, if any, did slavery play in intraracial color dynamics among blacks?

Slaves in the New World were victims of a system designed as much to steal their labor as to break their spirits. Some idea of how they survived and propagated a worldview that positioned them to combat the multiplicity of horrors entailed in their captivity is suggested by an anonymous African philosopher. Describing the aphorisms that countless generations of black forebears learned and passed on, this Old World teacher spoke volumes in six short words: "Proverbs are the daughters of experience."

[*See also* Caribbean Race Relations; Moral Issues; *and* Race and Racism.]

BIBLIOGRAPHY

Andrews, William L. *To Tell a Free Story: The First Century of Afro-American Autobiography, 1760–1865.* Urbana: University of Illinois Press, 1986.

Finley, Moses I. *Ancient Slavery and Modern Ideology.* New York: Viking Press, 1980.

Hall, Gwendolyn M. *Africans in Colonial Louisiana: The Development of Afro-Creole Culture in the Eighteenth Century.* Baton Rouge: Louisiana State University Press, 1992.

Jones, Norrece T., Jr. *Born a Child of Freedom, Yet a Slave: Mechanisms of Control and Strategies of Resistance in Antebellum South Carolina.* Hanover, N.H.: Wesleyan University Press, 1990.

Patterson, Orlando. *Slavery and Social Death: A Comparative Study.* Cambridge, Mass.: Harvard University Press, 1982.

Stuckey, Sterling. *Slave Culture: Nationalist Theory and the Foundations of Black America.* New York and Oxford: Oxford University Press, 1987.

—NORRECE T. JONES, JR.

RACE AND RACISM. The idea of race as applied to humans has undergone a number of changes since the early sixteenth century, when the term first appeared in the English language as a way of referring to human groups. Until the mid-eighteenth century *race* was a classificatory word, like *type* or *kind.* From this period on, popular consensus has held that races are groups of people who differ from one another in such inherited physical characteristics as skin color, hair texture, eye shape, and other physiognomic features. Thus certain biophysical traits are seen as the symbols or markers of racial identity.

Throughout the nineteenth century and much of the twentieth, the biological and anthropological sciences confirmed the popular view, holding that the bases for race classifications are physical variations among populations originating in different geographic areas; however, scientists have never been able to agree on the specific criteria for determining race differences, or the number of races of humankind. With the rise of the science of genetics in the mid-twentieth century, races were redefined as populations that differed from one another in the relative frequencies of genes that all members of the species share.

These benign and neutral definitions do not, however, deal with the total social reality of race and the associated phenomenon of racism. Ideas and attitudes about race and racial differences clearly go beyond mere biophysical, or phenotypic, traits. One of the beliefs about race experienced in modern society is that each race has its own culture or forms of behavior, including moral, temperamental, and intellectual characteristics. Moreover, in modern "multiracial" societies, there is a certain lack of clarity about race identity at the individual level; physical features are not always congruent with the typology of existing race groups. In the United States, it is taken for granted as part of folk belief that everyone belongs to a race, and only one race, but a large number of individuals do not fit easily into conventional racial categories. To complicate matters, the term *race* has been applied loosely to national and ethnic groups, religious groups, and even linguistic groups. The result is that at the end of the twentieth century *race* has become an increasingly ambiguous and elusive term.

In the last decades of the twentieth century, scholars have developed new approaches and understandings about the origin and meaning of the idea of race. Using historical data and ethnographic methods, they concluded that race is a culturally invented construct that bears no intrinsic relationship to biophysical differences. Race is one way of looking at the cultural and physical diversity of humankind, dividing it into exclusive and discrete groups, ranking them, and arbitrarily associating them with distinctive behavioral, moral, temperamental, intellectual, and spiritual qualities. Thus *race* is being redefined as part of a society's belief system or world view. One major component of this prevalent belief system is the notion that both the physical features and the behavioral ones are innate and inheritable.

Such fabricated beliefs constitute an ideology about human group differences that is a pervasive part of our cultural heritage and affects our attitudes and behavior. The component of race beliefs that holds that behavior is inherited renders all differences, putative or real, profound and unbridgeable. This makes race a major dimension of social differentiation that, in its permanence and immutability, outranks other forms of social division.

History of Race and Slavery. New scholarship has revealed that race is a modern idea having its roots in the era of European expansion over the past five hundred years. It has been linked with slavery in the New World colonies, both in the popular mind and in much of American scholarship. This occurred because after the initial settlements in the North American colonies, only Africans and their descendants were by law and popular choice kept in a state of permanent servitude. Nonetheless, slavery existed long before the concept of race, reaching back into antiquity more than four thousand years. Moreover, although people of all physical variations have been enslaved, there is no evidence before the last four centuries that any society invented race ideology as a reason for enslaving others.

In the seventeenth-century New World colonies, as the English were institutionalizing a form of slavery for which they had no precedents, they were also constructing the ideological components of race. This historical linkage gave rise to a new form of servitude known as *racial slavery*. However,

both slavery and race were incompatible with the Christian principles and social values of the English colonists. The result was that slavery and the idea of race functioned to reinforce each other in complex ways.

The term *race* first appeared in the English language with reference to human beings in the sixteenth century, although its use then was rare. It was a rudimentary form of classification relating to what were thought to be common characteristics of a class of people; but it was arbitrary and had no clear referents or definition. In some sixteenth- and seventeenth-century literature, for example, one finds such phrases as "a race of saints," "a race of womankind," or "a race of priests."

During the eighteenth century a classificatory mode of approach to the study of living things characterized most of the early sciences, and the human species was not exempt. Early taxonomists, such as Carolus Linnaeus and Johann Friedrich Blumenbach, attempted to classify the diverse human populations encountered by Europeans in their overseas expansion. Because of the strength of the biblical theory of human origins, virtually all early scholars believed that different human populations were but variations within a single species, and so their categories reflected the geographic regions these populations inhabited. Some classifications (such as Blumenbach's "Caucasian," "Mongolian," "Ethiopian," "American," and "Malay") merged into both scientific and popular discourse and tended to rigidify thinking about subgroups of the human species, creating essential categories.

In the same century European settlers in North America increasingly employed the word *race* for the different peoples thrown together in the colonies. At the heart of European attitudes were inequalities of power and status between themselves, the conquered indigenous peoples (Indians), and a collectivity of peoples imported from Africa as slaves. Colonists had early begun to construe Indians as "savages," subject to annihilation, too weak to provide slave labor, and incapable of assimilating into European colonial communities. Africans were in great demand as slave labor because of their knowledge of tropical farming and other skills, their immunity to Old World diseases, and the large numbers made available in the slave trade.

The practices and policies of the early British colonists were driven by an insatiable desire for land and a desperate need for labor, both of which were the primary sources of wealth. To reach these objectives the English followed a policy of structuring separation and inequality between these populations. Precedents for such practices, and the attitudes that governed them, had been formed in their long centuries of conflict with the Irish; as early as the fourteenth century they had established apartheid-style laws to segregate Irish countrymen from English colonists. In the sixteenth and seventeenth centuries many Englishmen involved in wars with the Irish had come to view them as inferior "wild men," similar to the "savages" of ancient writers. They brought these attitudes and beliefs with them to the Virginia colonies. Because both Indians and Africans were also "heathens," colonists felt justified in their degrading treatment of them. This provided a fertile context for the crystallization of the English sense of human differences that came to be expressed in the term *race*.

Native Americans were conquered or removed from their lands by treaties. Although many were also enslaved, they often escaped to familiar territory or died of overwork or diseases to which they had no immunity. The decision to restrict chattel slavery to those of African ancestry was a pragmatic one. Africans were visibly different; they were on alien soil with no familiar places to go even if they escaped; and they had no powerful political supporters or allies in the international Christian community to object to their enslavement. Indeed, other Europeans were deriving great wealth from the use of slaves from Africa. Finally, the trade in slaves seemed unlimited.

Laws forbidding intermarriage between "racial" groups, laws increasingly restricting the freedom of slaves, and practices prohibiting the education and training of slaves exacerbated the cultural differences between slaves and free whites. Despite the fact that there were always a few African people who were free, blackness became linked with slave status. The conditions of chattel slavery so degraded people of African ancestry that a vast status gulf was created between blacks and free white men. Moreover, the English emphasis on the superior rights of property rendered legally invisible the human rights of slaves, who came to be viewed only as property.

By the end of the eighteenth century, despite the egalitarian rhetoric of the Revolutionary era, some supporters of slavery began searching for naturalistic evidence to confirm and validate this ranking of human groups, in part because most slaves had converted to Christianity and heathenism was no longer a tenable argument for slavery. Some educated men revived an older model of a natural hierarchy, the "Great Chain of Being," and applied it to their situation. Because such ranking was accepted as a natural and unassailable model of all living things, virtually everyone was conditioned to this new paradigm of human differences. All living things occupied different positions on the Chain of Being and thus were of unequal status. By allocating some groups to positions of natural inferiority, based on their physical features and place of ancestral origin, policymakers sought to justify the devastation and removal of Native Americans and the preservation of Africans and their descendants in slavery.

The catalyst for this development was the rise in the late eighteenth century of a powerful antislavery movement on both sides of the Atlantic. The opponents of the slave trade, and later the radical abolitionists, argued that slavery was immoral and contradictory to the emerging ideologies of freedom, equality, justice, and democracy growing in Europe. It was in reaction to the strength of abolitionism that some learned men began to promote the belief that "the Negro" was a different and lower order of being.

Although U.S. slavery ended after the Civil War, race as a dominant feature of human identity remained and was intensified. The success of European imperialism in the nineteenth century strengthened the belief in racial determinism so that all human achievements, or lack thereof, came to be explained by race. Confronted on all sides by brown and black peoples whom they now dominated politically, many Europeans became obsessed with race, especially with the idea of maintaining white racial purity. Racial exclusiveness was considered essential for preserving white "civilization."

In a world where scientific knowledge was gaining in stature and prestige, the creation of an ideology of naturally inferior and superior beings had to be buttressed, if not vindicated, by science. Furthermore, those who had misgivings about slavery had to be assuaged by evidence of innate African

Title page of *What Miscegenation Is!*, New York, c.1865.

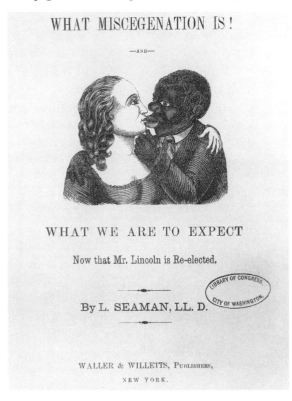

inferiority and the supposed wellbeing that slavery brought to blacks. Thus, in the nineteenth century a whole new field of scientific studies arose in the form of anthropometry, the objective of which was documenting the physical differences between the races. Scientists measured heads and other body parts to find support for claims that low-status races had degenerated from the "normal" human condition. The outcome was a series of averaged quantitative measurements that gave rise to definitions of "racial types." Differences were exaggerated and interpreted in ways designed to confirm the fundamental elements of racial ideology. By the mid-nineteenth century popular opinion and the scientific establishment had demoted all blacks to a separate species, closer to apes than to "normal" (European) humans.

At the beginning of the twentieth century, anthropometric techniques gave way to measuring the inner workings of the mind in the form of "intelligence" (IQ) tests. Morphological and other physical traits lost most of their validity in the first decades of this century when it was demonstrated, by the anthropologist Franz Boas and his students, that they were malleable from one generation to the next and subject to external forces such as nutrition and climate. It was then in mental abilities that the most critical race differences would come to reside. The language of IQ, thought to be an objective measure of fixed, innate intellectual ability, became the new arbiter of race differences and continues as such in certain circles today.

In colonial Latin America, the European, Indian, and African populations did not experience the same degree of separation, although slavery was widespread. The peoples of Spain and Portugal had a long, unbroken tradition of Old World slavery, the customs and practices of which differed in many important ways from the racial slavery of the English. The genetic mixing of people took place on a much larger scale, and individuals were described by their perceived degrees of intermixture. Most people were *mestizos* (mixed), but some societies used phenotypic traits (various combinations of skin color, facial features, and hair texture) to establish numerous descriptive categories that came to have social meaning. Because these categories were not seen as exclusive, the nature of "racial" classifications differed from those in North America. However, in the late nineteenth and early twentieth centuries, new immigrants from Europe helped to rigidify and to reify the superiority of "whiteness" as a category, and to degrade those with more Negroid characteristics. Many scholars see this development of color preferences as a form of racism.

The European colonization of South Africa also led to the establishment of slavery and of racial categories, but these emerged later and largely under the influence of the racial worldview that had spread throughout the United States and Europe. In addition to black and white, South Africans invented a category called "coloured" that reflected the historical intermixture of Dutch sailors and native women, as well as the importation of laborers from India and Southeast Asia. The power relationship of whites over all people of color was as critical to South Africa as it was to North America, with or without slavery. Because of linguistic and cultural differences, and major demographic differences, racial segregation and ideas of separate development advanced further in South Africa than in the United States.

Racism and the Extension of the Racial Worldview. Racism may be seen as any behavioral manifestation of the ideology of race, where those in power seek to portray inequality and all differences as profound and unbridgeable. It is manifest in a wide range of behaviors, from the put-downs and contempt shown by some whites to all blacks and Native Americans, through subtle or overt acts of prejudice and discrimination, to large-scale intergroup hostilities. Expressions of racism have varied from region to region and over time. Experts have perceived generational differences in attitudes toward race and race differences.

Race was predicated initially on a belief in white superiority and dominance over all nonwhites, es-

pecially those who had been conquered or colonized. But because race is an invented concept that is ambiguous, imprecise, and fluid, it can be and has been extended to apply to almost any situation of potential or real conflict of interests, competition, or confrontation between peoples.

In the mid-nineteenth century some Europeans began to interpret their populations and internal power struggles as "racial," even though differences in physical appearance were slight or nonexistent. In France the upper classes were seen as racially different and superior to the lower classes. In Germany race became a matter of nationality, with people of German background asserting a sense of racial superiority over non-Germans. Some scholars saw all of Europe as divided into Nordic, Alpine, and Mediterranean "races," each having distinctive innate characters and behavior, with Nordics (or Teutons) exercising dominance over all others. Many modern ethnic or religious conflicts, whether occurring in Asia, Africa, Europe, or South America, have been portrayed or interpreted as "racial" in nature. As a way of perceiving human differences, race is powerful, simple, and easily assimilated.

Contemporary Scientific Positions on "Race." Scientists have been divided over the use of the term *race* and whether or not biological races really exist. Some scientists maintain an essentialist position. They continue to believe that biogenetically distinct "races" are real phenomena and that we must persist in a search for those fine or subtle differences between such groups that will precisely identify and define them. These scientists (called "splitters") focus on the gross physical characteristics of widely separated populations, genetic features such as hereditary diseases, certain morphological traits, and immunities found in limited areas, and argue that this is sufficient to retain the use of the term. Many of these scholars believe that there are indeed intellectual and other inherited behavioral differences between the major races, and that we should continue searching for their genetic bases. Splitters tend to focus on differences rather than similarities, and to see racial "types" rather than continuous variations in specific traits.

At the end of the twentieth century, splitters may well represent a minority of scientists. Sol Katz, one of the authors of the new UNESCO statement on race, has pointed out that a wide consensus on race now exists among biological anthropologists, human biologists, and geneticists. These scientists (called "lumpers" as opposed to "splitters") agree that the biological concept of race as applied to humans has no validity in science. In the twentieth century science has greatly advanced our understanding of human biophysical variations and their causes. The field of genetics has revealed that the differences among human populations are in fact very small. There are greater genetic differences between individuals within a given population than there are between populations. Skin color and hair texture are indeed only skin deep and account for only a minuscule portion of genetic differences. All humans share a complex ancestry, and the mechanisms of evolution, especially gene flow, have kept us one species. Our contemporary physical diversity reflects the adaptive patterns of the past, and the infinite intermixtures of peoples, especially over the past five hundred years.

Because of the acknowledged complexity of human heredity, most experts argue that it is impossible to place scientific boundaries around human populations. There are no discrete human races, and there never have been "pure" races. Race thus has no meaning in the biological sense. Scientists today study physical and genetic variability as continuous gradations (or clines) that overlap population boundaries. Their interests are no longer in classifying people but in understanding the ecological conditions that gave rise to the diverse physical features of the human species. For these reasons, and because of our greater understanding of race as a social phenomenon, a growing number of scholars have argued since the 1940s that the word *race* should be eliminated from the vocabulary of science. This seems to be taking place in an-thropology textbooks. But whether the scientific findings will lead to the demise of the sociocultural meaning of *race*, a belief system or world view about human differences that is very powerful, remains to be seen.

[*See also* Caribbean Race Relations; *and* Segregation.]

BIBLIOGRAPHY

Alland, Alexander, Jr. *Human Diversity*. Garden City, N.Y.: Anchor Books, 1973.

Banton, Michael. *Racial Consciousness*. London and New York: Longman, 1988.

Fredrickson, George M. *The Black Image in the White Mind*. Middletown, Conn.: Wesleyan University Press, 1987.

Haller, John S., Jr. *Outcasts from Evolution*. Urbana: University of Illinois Press, 1970.

Littlefield, Alice, Leonard Lieberman, and Larry Reynolds. "Redefining Race: The Potential Demise of a Concept in Physical Anthropology." *Current Anthropology* 23 (1982): 641–656.

Mörner, Magnus. *Race Mixture in the History of Latin America*. Boston: Little, Brown, 1967.

Noel, Donald L., ed. *The Origins of American Slavery and Racism*. Columbus, Ohio: Charles E. Merrill, 1972.

Smedley, Audrey. *Race in North America: Origin and Evolution of a World View*. Boulder, Colo.: Westview Press, 1993.

UNESCO. *Racism, Science and Pseudoscience*. Paris: UNESCO, 1983.

—AUDREY SMEDLEY

RELIGION. [*This entry takes as its focus the encounter between African slaves and Christianity in the New World. For treatments of slavery in other religious traditions, see* Biblical Literature, *article on* Hebrew Scriptures; *and* Law, *article on* Islamic Law.]

As oppressive as the conditions and the institution of slavery were in the Western Hemisphere, enslaved Africans dictated, in large measure, the shape and nature of their own religious beliefs and practices. This was possible because of the will and capacity of the slaves to incorporate into their established religious beliefs and practices features from a range of other religions, including Christianity.

To begin with, the traditional religions practiced in Africa were inclusive and open to incorporating insights and practices from other systems. This receptive nature was perhaps unwittingly exploited by Catholic missionaries, who, seeking to convert enslaved Africans, emphasized similarities between Catholicism and traditional African religious systems. For Africans from Yorubaland (present-day Nigeria), *orisha*, or deities who controlled aspects of daily life, appeared much like the saints of Roman Catholicism. In parts of Haiti, for example, Catholic iconography that depicted Saint Jerome wielding a metal sword in battle promoted his connection with Ogun, the Yoruba warrior god of iron. To enslaved Africans from the Kongo region (present-day Congo, formerly Zaïre, and the People's Republic of Congo-Brazzaville), similarities between Catholicism and their own religious practices were also evident. Their traditional use of *minkisi* (charms used to effect healing and other phenomena) seemed similar to the ritual use of holy water, oil, candles, crucifixes, and the Eucharistic elements by Catholic priests.

Demographic, economic, and societal differences led to differences in the types of religion practiced by the enslaved populations. Major differences developed among areas settled by European Catholics (Spanish, Portuguese, and French), and those settled by Protestants (primarily the British). The influence of Catholicism encouraged the development of new religions that were recognizably African in places like Haiti (where the mixed religion came to be known as Vodun), Cuba (Santería), and Brazil (Candomblé).

In South America and the Caribbean, the confluence of traditional African religions with Catholicism, along with important demographic factors (a high ratio of Africans to Europeans, work patterns that minimized interracial contact, and a constant infusion of native-born Africans), made it possible for slaves to maintain, albeit in altered forms, African religious practices and beliefs. Although Catholic missionaries continued to press for adherence to orthodox Catholicism, the inclusive nature of African religions allowed slaves to participate simultaneously in Catholic rituals and African religious practices with no sense of dissonance. Feasts and festivals for Catholic saints would be celebrated with rites and rituals for their African counterparts. The extent to which slaves truly mixed elements of African and Catholic practices (true syncretism), or merely used Catholic names and forms as a safe cover for their African beliefs, remains a point of contention among scholars.

In the British colonies to the north, a lower black-to-white ratio, a smaller proportion of African-born slaves (due to a higher rate of natural increase), and a Protestant milieu discouraged but did not completely eliminate the retention of African religious practices. These practices can be discerned in the African-American traditions known as *hoodoo* and *conjure*, and particularly in the ring shout, which combines African rhythms and dancelike movements with Christian expressions.

Organized attempts to convert the slaves in North America began as early as 1701, with the formation of the Society for the Propagation of the Gospel in Foreign Parts (SPG), the missionary arm of the Church of England. The SPG, in its efforts to convert slaves, encountered resistance from slaveholders, who held deep economic and social concerns about such conversion. Would baptized slaves have to be freed? Would slaveholders have to share church membership with slaves and allow them reading skills? And would that not make the slaves unruly and ungovernable? Early missionaries to slaves tried to convince slave-masters of the contrary, arguing that religion would produce a more productive and docile work force. Although adopted legislation ensured that conversion and church membership of slaves would not cure their slave status, most of the slaves were deterred from conversion to Christianity by a literacy requirement and by the staid form of prevailing Christian worship.

Still, the inclusive nature of African religions availed Protestant Christianity to the slave popula-

Vue de l'Etablissement des Missions à Saint Johns dans l'Isle d'Antigoa (View of the Mission at Saint Johns in the Island of Antigua); engraving, L. Stobwasser, published by the Société d'Amis de l'Evangile, nineteenth century.

tion (increasingly so during the Great Awakening, a series of revivals that occurred throughout the colonies in the latter half of the eighteenth century). Through these revivals, along with conversion efforts by Methodists and Baptists, the number of slave conversions began to rise. The new evangelists stressed a *personal* conversion experience rather than the memorization of catechisms, and their more active worship style allowed for the emotionalism of the African-American slaves. Evangelistic preaching, which was conducted in the language of ordinary people rather than the prose of theologically trained scholars, was more accessible to both black and white congregants, who were encouraged to participate in worship by praying, exhorting or giving testimony, leading

singing, and even preaching. A number of the early Baptist and Methodist preachers were no doubt attractive to slaves because of their condemnation of slavery, but intense opposition by slaveholders soon caused these early religious reformers to abandon abolition as an immediate goal. Their focus then went to the conversion of both slave and master, in the hope that Christian masters would treat their slaves with benevolence.

Some African Americans, both slave and free, received licenses to preach and became popular with both black and white audiences. The illiterate Harry Hosier, an African American who often accompanied Bishop Francis Asbury on his tours of Methodist societies, was praised by the Oxford-trained Thomas Coke as "one of the best preachers in the world." The oratorical feats of John Jasper, who like Hosier was born a slave, were widely known in his day. Slave preachers, including some women, were indispensable in disseminating a distinctively African-American Christianity and in establishing independent African-American churches.

The earliest independent African-American church was started between 1773 and 1775 by David George in Silver Bluff, Georgia. He left Georgia with retreating British forces during the Revolutionary War and moved on to Nova Scotia and later to Sierra Leone. In each location he established a black Baptist church. After the war the church in Silver Bluff relocated to Augusta under the leadership of Jesse Galphin, where it became the First African Baptist Church. While these events were taking place in the South, events in the North were leading to the creation of the first African-American denomination.

In the North slaves and ex-slaves became members of established churches. In Philadelphia, the increasing membership of St. George's Methodist Episcopal Church required an expansion of church facilities, a project to which its African-American membership contributed. In 1792, on the Sunday following the completion of the work, one of the African-American members, an ex-slave named Absolam Jones, was dragged from his knees during prayer for violating the church's segregated seating policy. In protest, African-American members walked out of the service. Jones separated from the Methodists, received ordination in the Episcopal Church, and established St. Thomas African Episcopal Church, the first African-American church in that denomination. Richard Allen, an ex-slave who along with Jones had been a leader among Philadelphia's African population, also left St. George's. Allen, the first African American to receive deacon's orders in the Methodist Episcopal Church, was reluctant to forsake the Methodist system. He soon established the Bethel African Methodist Episcopal Church. In 1816, at a meeting of delegates from several cities in which African

Methodists had suffered indignities similar to the incident at St. George's, a new denomination, the African Methodist Episcopal Church, was formed with Richard Allen as its first bishop. In 1821 several black Methodist groups uncomfortable with Allen's leadership formed the nation's second black denomination, the African Methodist Episcopal Zion Church. From their inception these denominations condemned slavery and became advocates for the rights of African Americans.

Scholars have debated the degree to which religion helped or hindered enslaved Africans in their resistance to slavery. In South America and the Caribbean the coincidence of prevailing African-based religious systems with numerous slave rebellions suggests that religion was not a hindrance to the slaves' resistance. It is likely that a shared religious system that included deities who empowered believers, and charms that offered protection from injury, encouraged a range of anti-slavery activities, including outright rebellion.

In North America, where outright rebellions were relatively scarce, the role of religion in fostering or hindering slave resistance has been hotly debated. Slave-masters had come to promote Christianity among the slaves in an effort to induce obedience and docility, but throughout the antebellum South, law proscribed African Americans' preaching to slaves without white supervision (or even gathering for worship). It is likely that whites were responding to a real threat, for slave preachers were implicated in well-known plots of slave rebellion and insurrection. The Gabriel Prosser plot in Richmond, Virginia, in 1800, included Gabriel's brother Martin, a preacher. Denmark Vesey, a freedman and African Methodist Episcopal class leader in the Charleston, South Carolina, church, was the leader of an aborted plot that resulted in the arrest of 131 Africans and African Americans in 1822; as in the Prosser incident, religious meetings were used to help organize the rebellion, and appeals to Scripture were made to justify the attack against slavery. (The Vesey conspiracy also included in its leadership a slave from Angola, "Gullah" Jack Pur-

Engraving depicting a Southern plantation owner and his family attending
church services with their slaves, nineteenth century.

cell, who reportedly equipped conspirators with
charms and rituals that would make them immune
to injury.) In retaliation, the local African Methodist Episcopal church, which had more than three
thousand members, was burned to the ground, and
its pastor, Morris Brown, was forced to flee the state.

The most famous slave rebellion took place in
1831 in Southampton County, Virginia. Its leader
was a literate slave preacher named Nat Turner,
who had observed miraculous signs and heard the
voice of the Holy Spirit directing him to fight. After
laying plans with five others, the rebels struck on
August 21. They were joined by about seventy
other slaves, and fifty-seven whites were killed before the revolt was crushed. These well-known in-

cidents indicate that religion was not just a tran-
quilizer of the freedom passions aroused in slaves,
but a purveyor of those passions when channeled
through slave preachers able to mobilize followers
against their enslavers.

Slaves, in exerting and maintaining considerable influence over their religious lives, often
risked punishment by stealing away to secluded locations for prayer and worship. The content of
such clandestine services is evident in the body of
religious music created by the slaves. This music,
known as "spirituals," was first recorded and compiled during the Civil War. Thomas Wentworth
Higginson, the commanding officer of one of the
Union Army's black regiments, wrote down the

songs sung by his men, many of whom were recently freed. He noted how images in *Exodus* and the *Book of Revelations* held special meaning and relevance for an enslaved people, from the story of Moses and the liberation of the children of Israel from Egyptian bondage, to the violent images of the Apocalypse and the triumphant image of Jesus as a valiant warrior who would conquer the enemies of God—a God to whom that enslaved race of people turned faithfully for deliverance from the evil they suffered.

This appropriation of biblical images and events by slaves was demeaned as "religious rubbish" by William Kephart, a white Union army chaplain. He observed the religious life of the ex-slaves and wrote Northern sponsors about the "excessive effervescence of emotional feeling" and the lack of theological sophistication among them. In particular, Kephart complained that African Americans saw Jesus as a physical liberator and not a spiritual one. He reported, too, that Moses was viewed by the ex-slaves as a recent historical figure, whose person they confused with Abraham Lincoln.

The clandestine worship services of the slaves necessarily demonstrated a lack of Western sophistication on their part, as these slaves made Christianity their own by resisting the interpretations emphasized by their owners and used the Bible selectively to that end. Far from being passive receptors of religious traditions passed down from whites, African slaves in North America, as well as throughout the Western Hemisphere, actively shaped their religious lives from a mélange of religious influences, fashioning an independent religious voice that spoke directly to their abject circumstances.

[*See also* Christian Perspectives on Slavery; Revolts; *and* Slave Culture.]

BIBLIOGRAPHY

Raboteau, Albert J. *Slave Religion: The Invisible Institution in the Antebellum South.* New York and Oxford: Oxford University Press, 1978.

Sernett, Milton C. *Afro-American Religious History: A Documentary Witness.* Durham, N.C.: Duke University Press, 1985.

Thompson, Robert Farris. *Flash of the Spirit: African and Afro-American Art and Philosophy.* New York: Random House, 1983.

Thornton, John. *Africa and Africans in the Making of the Atlantic World, 1400–1680.* New York: Cambridge University Press, 1992.

—IAN B. STRAKER

REPRODUCTION. Slavery was probably the first systematic form of labor and social subordination to be matched with a mode of reproduction inherent in that form. Slavery was grounded in the continuous supply of mature individuals carried off from their societies of origin and becoming, in their societies of reception, a servile class assigned to different tasks by a native-born class of masters. This mode of reproduction distinguishes slavery from serfdom, which reproduces by the demographic growth of a native-born class of serfs.

The slave mode of reproduction, which seems to have been recognized for the first time by Chayanov (1986, pp. 13–20), derives from an economic logic that engenders its social logic. In domestic agricultural society, economic and social reproduction is assured from within through the raising of children by older generations. Adolescents physically embody this investment, whose value is realized during their active years by means of their labor within the community. In slave society the replacement of the work force was accomplished not by demographic processes nor by the nurturing of preproductive individuals, but by the importation of young adults seized from their own communities and already bearing this investment in nurturing.

The perpetual demand for captives induced by this mode of slave reproduction created and fed on an active cosmopolitan trade based on the captives themselves, on the commodities necessary for their purchase, the instruments of enslavement, the products of slave labor, and the goods for which they were sold. In return, slave reproduction sustained continuous pillage and war, bringing about the demographic degradation of domestic societies located within the captors' sphere of action. The disappearance of these slave-supplying communities also entailed the end of slavery. The political economy of slavery was based on this violent relationship.

Reproduction by Capture versus the Laws of Political Economy. Slave reproduction depended on two complementary institutions—war and the market. It functioned in pillaging societies by means of the capture of individual outsiders, and in merchant societies by means of the purchase of captives. The activity of seizure was decisive because it appropriated, in essence, the price of replacing a slave.

Slave reproduction based on the theft of the living is not amenable to classical economic analysis. Economic exchange assumes that the producer of a commodity receives in return for the product a value that permits its further reproduction. Human life can be reproduced only by life-regenerating agents or goods, that is, women and the means of subsistence. Whatever inert material goods are received in exchange for a living being, none has the capacity to produce other human beings. Societies despoiled of their children receive no corresponding compensation. The uprooting of an individual from the domestic society that has engendered, nourished, and raised him, and his subsequent acquisition by the slaving society that exploits him, simultaneously creates both an organic link between these two societies and the disjuncture between their respective economies.

No market exists between pillaging and pillaged societies. The market begins only where the pillagers sell their captives to traders, who resell them to commodity-producing societies. By virtue of this rupture, slavery engenders several types of returns. In all slaving societies, whether pillaging or purchasing, a portion of the slaves' labor was devoted to subsistence agriculture in order to ensure both their own survival and that of their masters. Slave rent was captured in the monopolization of the total agricultural net surplus (the amont beyond the subsistence requirement) produced by the slave during his or her active life; no provision needed to be made to ensure the maturation of new servile generations. To this rent was added (in pillaging societies) the value of additional pillaging in which slave soldiers shared. In mercantile societies, in addition to the rent, profits were added; these profits included both gains from the exploitation of slave labor through the mechanisms of the ordinary market, and gains from the purchasable reproduction of the slaves, which was more selective, more flexible, and, above all, more rapid than demographic reproduction.

The trade in captives, although it resembled a market in goods, excluded from the market the societies from which captives had been seized. Once extracted by violence from their communities of origin and thrust into the slave market, the captives had only an exchange value within the bounds of that market, and this exchange value was not in essence their demographic replacement and social value; rather, their cost of reproduction was merely the cost of their capture. Their price was that of goods exchanged in a marketplace detached from the place that engendered them. In order to obtain captives in the market, it sufficed for the buyer to offer, in exchange, material goods that could be made by producers; and unlike slaves, these goods could be produced by either men or women. Thus the "effective" population that produced the material goods was of different demographic composition than that which produced the equivalent value in adult slaves, and goods and slaves were created at different social costs. Moreover, slaves used to produce goods for sale reproduced themselves at a "mercantile rate" (the relation of their purchase price to the price of the goods they procure) and not according to the "demographic" growth rate of a population able to replicate an equal number of human beings of comparable ages and sexes. An adult slave could produce the equivalent of his market price (in other words, the price of another adult slave) within a much shorter time than would be required for an infant's maturation. Historical examples show that in certain contexts, slaves could produce the equivalent of their own purchase price within three to five years. The demand for slaves on the market could therefore greatly exceed the growth potential of any demographically stable population. The sexual imbalance in slave populations is evidence of the indifference of enslavers to natural reproduction, and of their preference for "market" reproduction. Captors of slaves responded to this demand by raiding societies at an accelerating rate, which sooner or later exceeded the demographic potential of the raided society.

Reproduction by Acquisition and the Demographic Shaping of the Slave Class. Because slave reproduction operated independently of demographic imperatives, the captor and, even more, the buyers were free to select the sex and age of the captives. Hence there were more women than men in Asian and African slave systems. Aside from the fact that feminine domestic tasks were normally more numerous and restricted in those areas, the slaves were not subject to conventional sexual divisions of labor. Slave women, reputedly more docile, could be assigned to masculine activities, even hauling and fishing. This preference for female slaves did not always imply their use as reproducers of slaves. Children born of concubines or of courtesans might be either freed or placed in the vernacular class (see below). Relatively few slave laborers were in a position to procreate and to raise children (Robertson and Klein, 1983); instead, plantation slavery was characterized by a majority of adult men who were subjected to close discipline.

The age profiles of male and female captives also reflected criteria that were unlike those of demographic reproduction. In Asian slavery, infants of women captives were generally killed. Males between infancy and adolescence were generally enslaved, but not adult males, who were regarded as dangerous. The Atlantic trade favored young adults. The unproductive old age of slaves was not willingly prolonged.

Slave Reproduction and the Neutralizing of the Slave. Slaves, being separated from reproduction and therefore lacking familial links, were deprived of the elementary prerogatives of social membership. Neither ancestor nor spouse nor child belonged to them. They had no claim on inheritance. Everything they used belonged to the master. They were permanent strangers, nonpersons, and nonparents. They were incapable of entering the family network by birth, by marriage, or by succession. They were not, as relatives can be, in a position of potential rivalry with holders of authority.

This lack of connection sometimes led slaveholders to place slaves in positions of trust rather than rely on brothers or sons who were well positioned to succeed them in authority. Slave ministers and slave generals owed their positions to their social nonexistence. From this perspective, the eunuch, rendered physically incapable of procreation, best embodies the state of slavery, even when not legally a slave.

The Vernacular, Another Mode of Reproduction. In almost all slave societies, the children of slaves (here termed the *vernacular*) often enjoyed certain informal privileges (though not usually legal rights), such as the opportunity to live in the household and care for children. This class, neither free nor emancipated but sometimes manumitted, was rarely distinguished from that of slaves, although it was generally designated by a distinctive term. The notion of "domestic slave," sometimes applied to vernacular, is not precise. It may variously denote slaves assigned to household tasks, subsistence agriculturalists, household servants, or those who lived in intimacy with their masters. The emergence of a vernacular prefigured a form of serfdom (sometimes with a paternalistic element) within a slave society, the extension of which required a demographic mode of reproduction and the growing productivity of labor (Meillassoux, 1991, pp. 43–54, 239–248). It is the vernacular who survived the disappearance of the slave trade. They seem to have formed the majority of the servile population of the United States as early as the eighteenth century (Fogel and Engerman, 1974, p. 25). Because they were the only bondspeople who left descendants to bear witness to their existence, the vernacular condition is often conflated with that of slaves, permitting historians to posit the existence of "natural slave reproduction." The absence of descendants of slaves only adds a silent and incorporeal contradiction to this belief.

Conclusion. Slavery affirmed its uniqueness by its mode of reproduction. It is at this level that slave profit was realized, independent of the productivity of labor. It was the means of reproduction, pillage, and commerce, that created the geographic, economic, and political context of slavery. Slave reproduction reveals the opposition between two essentially distinct economic fields, that of the reproduction of life (and of the power of labor) and that of material production. The articulation of these two fields, the source of supplementary gains, eludes classical economic analysis. The requirement of reproduction by seizure, tearing slaves from familial relations, deprived slaves of their condition as men and women, transforming them into social eunuchs. The exclusion of slaves from social reproduction affected their relation with free society and with each other, following a paradoxical logic whose import goes beyond the boundaries of slavery. It is through the transformation of the mode of reproduction that slavery disappeared in favor of generic forms of servility still poorly explored.

[See also Demography and Economics.]

BIBLIOGRAPHY

Chayanov, A. V. *The Theory of Peasant Economy.* Madison: University of Wisconsin Press, 1986.

Fogel, Robert W., and Stanley L. Engerman. *Time on the Cross: The Economics of American Negro Slavery.* Boston: Little, Brown, 1974.

Meillassoux, Claude. *The Anthropology of Slavery: The Womb of Iron and Gold.* Translated by Alide Dasnois. Chicago: University of Chicago Press, 1991.

Robertson, Claire C., and Martin A. Klein, eds. *Women and Slavery in Africa.* Madison: University of Wisconsin Press, 1983.

—CLAUDE MEILLASSOUX

REVOLTS. Prospective slave rebels always confronted an imposing array of hostile forces that militated against revolt. By definition, slaves lived vulnerable and deracinated, as outsiders or degraded beings in a highly personalized relation of domination by an allegedly all-powerful other; yet wherever slavery existed, slaves struggled to reclaim themselves from social death by forging bonds of solidarity with fellow slaves and other disaffected people. These bonds, under favorable conditions, could yield revolt and other forms of rebellion on a continuum of collective slave resistance. Work slowdown and stoppage, conspiracy, demonstration and riot, banditry, mass flight, and marronage, as well as bloody revolt, occurred in virtually every slave society. Slaves revolted in ancient and modern civilizations, in Europe, Africa, Asia, and the Americas, on plantations, in mines and urban centers, aboard ships, and in the ranks of the military. Some revolts burst forth more or less spontaneously from local conditions; others matured within a much wider network of influences, revealing impressive size, organization, and planning. Although hardly commonplace and usually short-lived, slave revolts happened with sufficient frequency to place slave-owners in recurring fear for their own security and dread of social upheaval.

Before the European discovery of the Americas mass enslavement did not typically lead to concentrations of slaves in plantation agriculture, but rather to their dispersal through households for use in a wide variety of domestic occupations. Internally divided in this and other ways, slaves rarely developed the necessary cohesion to raise thousands in large-scale revolt. In the ancient Near East, early modern Russia, and pre-European West

Africa, where household slavery predominated, no evidence of an essentially slave insurrection has yet surfaced. Thucydides wrote of the mass flight of thousands of Athenian slaves during the Peloponnesian Wars, but ancient Greece appears to have had few violent revolts among its largely urban slave population. The great uprisings originated with the rural helotry (bound autochthones). Ancient Rome's grandeur, however, rested on a massive foundation of slave labor fed by chronic expansionist warfare. A succession of slave revolts shook Republican Rome: the First Sicilian Slave War (137–132 BCE), the Second Sicilian Slave War (104–100 BCE), and the legendary Spartacus revolt (73–71 BCE). Ranking among the largest in history, each involved tens of thousands of slaves, and Spartacus's movement threatened the city of Rome itself. Imperial Rome, by contrast, left a meager record of slave revolt. Whether the so-called Bagaudae rebellions, which began in the late third century CE and lasted well into the fifth century, joined bands of slaves with other low-status groups in Gaul and Spain remains a matter of scholarly contention, as does the Bagaudae's contribution and that of slave resistance generally to the decline of the Roman Empire and the transition in some regions from slavery to other forms of dependency. Little evidence of slave revolt exists for medieval Europe, despite the continued strength of slavery in Anglo-Saxon England, among the Germanic peoples, and in lands of the Mediterranean basin. The myths and legends of medieval Scandinavia speak of slave revolt, and a few minor cases have been documented for Denmark and Iceland.

Slavery lasted in non-Muslim Asia for three millennia, although not typically as the central form of labor. A slave society emerged in medieval Korea, and during the Koryŭ Dynasty (918–1392), the number of enslaved Koreans may have approached one-third of the total population. Hundreds of slaves rose in the most serious revolts, which clustered within a fifty-year interval from 1182 to 1232, a period of military coups and Mongol invasions. In China, the strength of slavery varied considerably by time and region. Under the Manchus around the mid-seventeenth century, household slaves may have predominated in uprisings in several provinces.

The lengthy history of Islamic slave-trading and slavery contains explosive moments of collective slave resistance. Probably the largest slave revolt in world history between the time of Spartacus and the 1791 slave revolution in Saint Domingue erupted in 869 in what is now southern Iraq. Near Basra thousands of rebel Zanj (slaves of East African origin), who had been pressed into brutal gang labor for agricultural reclamation projects, created a state, coined money, and held out against reconquest by the ʿAbbāsid Caliphate for fourteen years. Military slaves, a common feature of Islamic societies, became so powerful in mid-thirteenth century Egypt that they overthrew the Ayyūbid rulers and created the Mamluk slave dynasty. Collective slave resistance in precolonial and colonial Africa remains an understudied subject, but revolt, mass desertions, and formidable maroon resistance unsettled various states in the nineteenth century. Muslim Hausa slaves rebelled against the Oyo Empire during its first decades, and after its collapse, Fon officials foiled a major rebellion of Yoruban plantation slaves in 1855. During the nineteenth century, expanding commodity production within Africa was based on the use of slaves, whose prices had been cheapened by the suppression of the Atlantic slave trade. The Sokoto Caliphate in West Central Africa experienced several rebellions, including hundreds of plantation slaves, between 1850 and 1870. In Zanzibar and neighboring islands and on the Swahili coast, East African plantation slaves rebelled against Omani Arab masters during the mid- and late nineteenth century and established a number of maroon strongholds near Mombasa. Muslim Maraka masters of the middle Niger Valley confronted revolt and mass desertions by thousands of plantation slaves during the first decade of the twentieth century. British penetration of Africa under an anti-slavery banner also contributed to significant slave resistance in the western Sudan around 1850, in Zanzibar in the 1870s and 1880s, and in the Sokoto Caliphate after the British conquest (1897–1902). The largest slave revolt in the Cape Colony in southern Africa happened two years after Britain seized the colony in 1806; several hundred rebels marched on Cape Town to demand an end to slavery.

By far the richest record of slave revolt derives from the Western European expansion of the plantation system into the Americas and the attendant growth of the Atlantic slave trade. About twelve million African slaves suffered the infamous Middle Passage. No one knows how frequently they broke out of coastal holding depots or mutinied in transit. To date, more than three hundred risings have been documented in all branches of the trade during its four-hundred-year history; many of these happened on anchored ships before their African departure. Sugar, more than any other crop, determined the location of the survivors of the Atlantic crossing. A majority of the great slave revolts in the Americas occurred where the sugar-planters had built ganged slave labor into an over-whelming majority of a region's total population. Portugal's pioneering explorations of West Africa and the Atlantic during the fifteenth century had prepared the way by transforming the islands of Madeira and São Tomé into colonial slave societies that ultimately served as steppingstones for the trans-Atlantic migration of sugar culture. Also portending the future, stubborn maroon resistance and revolts of imported African slaves dotted São Tomé's landscape during its sixteenth-century sugar boom. One revolt, led by Amador, destroyed scores of sugar plantations in 1595 and placed the city of São Tomé itself under siege by hundreds of rebels.

By this time, in the Americas Portugal had followed Spain in narrowing the legal ground for enslaving Indians, but their predominance on large estates in some regions of Brazil continued into the eighteenth century. In 1567 a major insurrection of Indian slaves in Bahia destroyed sugar plantations and killed whites. A millenarian movement known as Santidade caused mass desertions of Indian slaves from the same region beginning in 1584. While African slaves gradually replaced Indian slaves on Bahian sugar plantations during the seventeenth century, farther south a rash of Indian slave rebellions around mid-century affected the grain-producing captaincy of São Vicente. For Brazil and other plantation zones in the Americas, collective resistance by runaway African slaves overshadowed all-out slave insurrection for much of the colonial period; by serving as an outlet for slave discontent, such resistance often reduced the potential for large-scale insurgency.

No American slave society surpassed Brazil in producing maroon societies. With dozens and even hundreds of members, they dotted the hinterland from northern to southern Brazil. Palmares, the largest maroon community in the history of the Americas, emerged in northeastern Brazil during the seventeenth century. Before its destruction in 1694 it had become a confederation with thousands of residents, challenging Portuguese hegemony in the region. In central Jamaica and the interior of Suriname in the eighteenth century and in eastern Cuba in the early nineteenth century, maroon communities became so powerful that colonial authorities were forced to negotiate treaties with them. For most of their history, however, maroons possessed neither the overall unity nor the inclination to mobilize plantation slaves in revolutionary projects or to end slavery *per se*, however much they struggled against their own enslavement. In the Americas maroon enclaves largely aspired to restore a traditional and hierarchical African or qualified-African society in a new world. Some maroons incited plantation slaves to insurgency; others had poor relations with plantation slaves and acted with whites as agents of slave repression.

Slave revolts with a distinctive African ethnic flavor stand out during the rise of plantation slavery in the Americas and remained prominent during its fall in the nineteenth century. However, many of the larger acts of collective slave resistance in the eighteenth and nineteenth centuries allied African and creole slaves and merged with more general liberal-democratic movements and wars of national liberation. A revolt by enslaved Wolofs from the Senegambian region of West Africa has pride of place as the first major revolt of African slaves in the Americas. It began in December 1521 on a sugar plantation in southeastern Hispaniola owned by the son of Christopher Columbus and at its height involved about forty slaves. Maroon activity afflicted Santo Domingo's sugar region for decades thereafter, but not until the end of the eighteenth century did Dominican masters face a more dangerous insurrection, which started in 1796 on a big sugar estate called Boca Nigua.

The heyday of slave revolt in Puerto Rico coincided with the expansion of sugar cultivation during the first half of the nineteenth century in coastal districts to the south and north. The actual revolts proved to be few and minor, however, and were outnumbered by conspiracies that never got off the ground.

Colonial Cuba has an impressive record of slave revolt. As early as 1533 a handful of African slaves revolted in a gold-mining area in eastern Cuba, and more than three centuries later, during the Ten Years' War (1868–1878), rebel slaves allied with rebel whites to deliver blows that contributed to the end of slavery and Cuba's gaining national independence. The transformation of western Cuba into a black belt of coffee and sugar plantations during the first half of the nineteenth century precipitated one of the most intense periods of collective slave resistance in the history of Latin America; this included ethnic revolts by Yoruban slaves, the revolutionary conspiracies of Aponte (1812) and La Escalera (1843–1844), and an 1825 insurrection in which hundreds of African and creole slaves killed fifteen whites and laid waste to more than twenty estates.

Spanish Louisiana boasted prosperous tobacco and indigo plantations upriver from New Orleans in the Pointe Coupée district. These generated an ethnic revolt of Mina slaves in 1791 and a far more extensive and revolutionary conspiracy in 1795.

Mexico City acquired a large and growing population of African slaves before the death of Hernando Cortés. Slave conspiracies—though no open revolts—were allegedly uncovered there in 1537, 1608, and 1612. African slaves populated a sugar-planting zone around the port of Veracruz soon after the conquest, and by the end of the sixteenth century maroon forays had turned the area into a battleground. Five violent insurrections, the largest of which (1735) may have involved more than a thousand slaves, shook the sugar heartland of Veracruz province from 1725 to 1768.

In Venezuela the seaboard provinces seem to have had more serious slave revolts and conspiracies than any other region in Spanish South America. Government forces in 1555 crushed an attempt by a runaway slave from a mining district near the Yaracuy River to ally maroons and Indians in an anti-Spanish rebellion. By the early 1730s the river's bottomland had given rise to cacao estates and a revolt led by Andresote, an enslaved Zambo. His movement, which lasted several years, received Dutch support, conjoined with a larger popular uprising against Spanish commercial restrictions, and was finally put down by a campaign of fifteen hundred men. Slaves and free people of color combined to plot conspiracies in Caracas (1749) and Maracaibo (1799), and in 1795 a free Zambo led a major slave revolt in the western province of Coro.

Conspicuous resistance in colonial Colombia may have started with the burning of the port of Santa Marta by African slaves in 1529. By 1600 gold-mining had pulled thousands of African slaves into the region drained by the Cauca River. A number of small slave revolts flared up near the interior mining town of Popayán around the mid-sixteenth century. These paled next to a rising in 1598, reportedly involving thousands of slaves, in a gold-mining zone near Zaragoza. A revolt of about forty slaves in a gold mine in 1728 quickly expanded before suppression by government forces from Popayán. Cartagena, the central port that supplied African slaves for the mines, was the site of conspiracies in 1619, 1693, and 1799, but apparently of no serious revolts.

In Peru, the viceregal city of Lima seems to have been spared significant slave resistance, but during the second half of the eighteenth century several coastal estates had minor uprisings. Two slave revolts in 1851 on sugar plantations in Peru's Chicama and Cañete valleys count among the last in Spanish America.

Students of slave revolt in Brazil have tended to focus either on maroon resistance, particularly the fate of Palmares, or on a close succession of about twenty revolts in and near the sugar heartland of early nineteenth-century Bahia. The culmination came in 1835 in the city of Salvador with the revolt of perhaps five hundred slaves, mainly Yoruban and Hausa Muslims. Previously, in the same city, creole slaves had entered into a complex revolutionary conspiracy named the Tailors' Revolt (1798) with skilled free people of color and a few disaffected whites. Inspired by liberal-democratic currents emanating from the French Revolution, the betrayed movement revealed conflicts within its mixed leadership over methods and goals. Ample opportunity to escape into a vast interior frontier may have kept the number of Brazilian slave revolts down during the colonial period, but before the end of the sixteenth century several small uprisings of African slaves had disturbed the nascent sugar industry in Bahia and Pernambuco. African slaves flooded into Minas Gerais after the discovery of gold there in 1695. They subsequently constructed perhaps the densest stretch of maroon settlements in the history of Brazil. Nervous officials avoided a major slave insurrection in Minas Gerais but uncovered conspiracies in 1711, 1719, 1729, and 1756. Numerous conspiracies and revolts in the 1830s and 1840s unsettled plantations in Minas Gerais, Rio de Janeiro, and São Paulo. One of the more remarkable examples ended in pitched battle when Manuel Congo and two hundred estate slaves were vanquished by regular troops dispatched from Rio de Janeiro. During the last decades of slavery in Brazil, mass protests and desertions, some involving thousands of slaves, and small local uprisings hastened slavery's *de facto* end before official emancipation in 1888.

By extending slavery in the Caribbean and on the mainland, French, Dutch, and English colonists, beginning in the seventeenth century, extended the sphere of slave rebellion. The first slave revolt in French America appears to have been a minor uprising in 1639 by African slaves in a transitory French zone of settlement in northern St. Kitts. Martinique and Guadeloupe served as more permanent footholds and before the end of the century had developed into slave-based sugar colonies. In Guadeloupe, Angolan slaves reached out to Senegambian slaves in an islandwide plot of 1656 that seems to have contemplated the division of the island into two African-style kingdoms. At the moment of violence, however, the Angolans found themselves abandoned and were quickly crushed by local forces. Bad treatment and food shortages contributed to several scattered rebellions from 1726 to 1748. Slave conspiracies were uncovered in Martinique in 1699, 1710, and 1748. A privileged slave named Samba organized Bambara slaves in an unsuccessful bid to take French Louisiana in 1731. Before the slave revolution of 1791, Saint Domingue, like Martinique and Guadeloupe, had witnessed considerable slave marronage but, paradoxically, few serious insurrections. In the most famous case, MacKandal, a maroon leader and religious figure, was burned to death in 1757 for attempting to join maroons and estate slaves in a plot that involved mass poisoning of whites.

During the age of democratic revolution, Europe and the Americas experienced unprecedented political upheaval and social transformation. The French Revolution had expanded the realm of the possible for disaffected groups on both sides of the Atlantic. War, insurgency, and anti-slavery politics in Europe converged with emancipationist struggles in the Americas, most notably in France's richest colony, Saint Domingue. By 1791 it had become the world's leading producer of coffee and sugar. On the fertile northern plain, where the largest slaveholdings and sugar plantations existed, the slave revolution began and from there spread to other provinces. Weeks of planning, largely by slave-drivers and other elite slaves, had preceded the onset. Many different kinds of slaves with different goals would eventually rally and coalesce into slave armies. Although much particularist resistance to enslavement mobilized Saint Domingue's oppressed masses, the revolutionary process, like that in France itself, manifested a universalistic crusade against the system of slavery itself and thereby bore witness to the revolutionary politics and ideology of the wider world. Saint Domingue's rebel leaders asserted the rights of their people by looking well beyond their own insular community. The triumph of the slaves and their creation in 1804 of a black nation raised a standard by which subsequent collective slave resistance in the Americas would be reckoned. Slaves now had evidence that they could win a confrontation with their supposedly invulnerable masters; masters now had evidence that collective slave resistance, no matter how small in its beginning, could turn their world upside down.

In this context, slaves in the French Windward Islands also asserted themselves. Indeed, the French Caribbean's first slave revolt with connections to the tumultuous political changes in France occurred in Martinique in August 1789 when hundreds of slaves responded to false rumors of metropolitan emancipation. Whites in both Martinique and Guadeloupe had to quell assorted slave plots and revolts again in the 1790s. After the first French emancipation in 1794, thousands of Guadeloupe's people of color died in an 1802 war trying to prevent Napoleon from reestablishing slavery. Several outbreaks of slave rebellion marked the early 1820s in Martinique. After the July Revolution in France in 1830, the slaves in both islands the following year committed acts of collective violence, the more serious of which involved hundreds of slaves in Martinique. When France issued a final emancipation in 1848, a mass demonstration of thousands of slaves forced an official announcement out of the island's hesitant provisional governor.

Unlike the French, the Dutch concentrated on the carrying trade in the Americas at the expense of their plantation sector. Few slave revolts of consequence broke out in the Dutch Caribbean before the eighteenth century. St. Eustatius, an island trading post with marginal plantation activity, experienced minor disturbances in 1688 and 1770. Demonstrations on the island in response to rumored emancipation turned violent one year before the formal Dutch abolition of slavery in 1863. St. Maarten's slaves took advantage of the divided island with group escapes to the French section after the second French emancipation of 1848. A flare-up by plantation slaves of the Dutch West India Company in Curaçao in 1750 resulted in the execution of more than thirty slaves, among them thirteen women. Curaçao had the largest slave revolt on the Dutch islands. About two thousand slaves swept over the upper half of Curaçao in 1795 under the command of Tula, a plantation slave who had been inspired by the revolutions in France and Saint Domingue. Five years later, when pro-French forces including black soldiers from Saint Domingue and Guadeloupe landed in upper Curaçao, slaves rose again to support them but could not stave off a brief interregnum of English rule. In the Dutch mainland colonies, revolutionary contagion in 1795 helped spark a slave rebellion in Demerara. Its greatest slave revolt, however, came in 1823 under English rule and during a sugar boom. From 1690 to 1863, several dozen conspiracies, mass flights, and revolts took place in Suriname, although these usually involved only one or two plantations; an exception was the slave rebellion in the logging camps along the Tempati River in 1757. By the end of the century Suriname boasted maroon societies that could compete with Brazil's in size and number. Isolated plantation revolts hit Berbice in 1733, 1749, 1751, and 1762 before a great insurrection embracing thousands of slaves in 1763 nearly created an independent black state. Ethnic tensions between African and creole slaves and between Akan-speaking and Angolan slaves undermined the revolt, which lasted for more than a year.

The Danes almost became the first European power to lose a sugar colony to slave revolt. In 1733 Mina slaves erupted on the island of St. Johns. The revolt lasted well into the spring of the next year, cost scores of white and black lives, and was snuffed out only with French support from Martinique. With this scare still in mind, St. Croix's sugar-planters ruthlessly suppressed slave conspiracies in 1746 and 1759. The last major outbreak of collective slave resistance in the Danish Virgin Islands occurred in St. Croix in July 1848 on the eve of legislated emancipation. Thousands of slaves directed by a former estate driver forced an official announcement of freedom from the lips of the reluctant governor.

An ill-fated Puritan experiment in tobacco planting on tiny Providence Island off the coast of Central America provided the first slave revolt in English America in 1638. Before the final abolition of slavery in the British Empire two hundred years, later the British Caribbean alone had given rise to more than fifty slave conspiracies and revolts. Rebellions in Barbados (1816), Demerara (1823), and Jamaica (1831), among the largest in the history of the Americas, intensified metropolitan debate about legislating slavery to an end. Barbados became a slave society and one of the world's leading sugar-producers within three decades of English settlement in 1627. Before the end of the century colonial officials had stamped out an assortment of slave conspiracies: the first, during a provision crisis, in 1649; an ethnic plot of primarily Akan-speaking slaves from the Gold Coast in 1675; one that allied slaves and Irish servants in 1686; and the largest, masterminded by skilled creole slaves, in 1692. On a small, flat deforested island that came to support one of the more reliable militias in

the Caribbean, relative calm prevailed for more than a century until 1816, when an elite African-born slave named Bussa led thousands of primarily creole slaves in a war of liberation. Between the decline of Barbados and the rise of Jamaica as sugar economies, the Leeward Islands vaulted to the fore of world sugar production. After the number of slaves in each island had soared to more than 80 percent of the total population, noteworthy collective resistance struck Antigua in 1701, 1729, 1736, and 1831; Montserrat in 1768; Nevis in 1725 and 1761; and St. Kitts in 1738, 1778, and 1835.

Plantation slavery had transformed the Windward Islands of Dominica, Grenada, and St. Vincent before their acquisition by the British in 1763, even though their rugged interiors proved hospitable to maroon resistance but less so to sugar cultivation. Large slave majorities inhabited each island before the end of the century, when fallout from the French and Saint Domingue revolutions affected their stability. Then, as was frequently the case, slaves took advantage of war and imperial rivalries to advance their own agenda, by themselves or in alliance with other malcontents. Grenada offered a memorable example in 1795 when Julien Fedón, a French-speaking free person of color, initiated a rebellion against British rule that turned into a larger anti-slavery revolt.

In Tobago, another British acquisition in 1763, localized rebellion by recently imported African slaves broke out repeatedly in the early 1770s after the island's breathtaking transformation into a sugar colony. Elite creole slaves brought rural and urban slaves together in a failed movement to take the island in 1801. A similar plot in neighboring Trinidad, its most notable act of collective slave resistance, occurred four years later. In the British Virgin Islands, tiny Tortola stands out with three major slave revolts and a conspiracy from 1790 to 1823, during its rapid rise and decline as a sugar colony. After Britain took possession of the former Dutch colony of Demerara in 1803, a sugar boom concentrated slave-based production on the windward side of the Demerara River. There more than ten thousand African and creole slaves rebelled in 1823. Whites blamed an agent from the London Missionary Society for stirring up trouble; some of the elite slaves who organized the revolt had congregated in his chapel.

Jamaica's experience with slave rebellion includes two maroon wars (1730–1740 and 1795–1796) and at least a dozen conspiracies and revolts involving one hundred or more rebels. Akan-speaking slaves called Coromantees rebelled with unparalleled frequency in the eighteenth century. About two hundred Coromantees in 1673 precipitated Jamaica's first major slave revolt. In size, destructiveness, and bloodshed Tacky's revolt (1760) ranks as Jamaica's greatest ethnic rebellion. It lasted for months, came to embrace thousands of Coromantees throughout the island, resulted in the deaths of scores of whites and hundreds of slaves, and took the combined effort of militia, regular troops, and maroon mercenaries to put it down. After Britain abolished its trans-Atlantic slave trade in 1807, ethnic slave revolt continued in Jamaica, including a plot by Ebo slaves in 1815, but the composition of other movements proved more diverse. By the time of the great slave revolt of 1831, perhaps only one-quarter of Jamaica's slave population was African-born. This revolt, also called the Baptist War because of the prominence of recent slave converts to the faith in the front ranks of the movement, had few rivals in the Americas in its toll of death and destruction. It had a rural center; more than five hundred slaves either died during the conflict or were subsequently executed; probably as many as fifty thousand slaves were ultimately involved; and hundreds of estates were destroyed before it was extinguished. Elite slaves initiated the first blows in the sugar parish of St. James, whence the violence spread to other western parishes.

Britain's sugar colonies proved to be the prime sites of slave rebellion, but more marginal possessions with smaller slave populations produced significant episodes as well. In the seventeenth and eighteenth centuries, Bermuda's maritime-related

Soulevement des Negres à la Jamaïque (Uprising of the Negroes in Jamaica); engraving by David after a painting by Jacques-Louis David; eighteenth century. The work depicts a revolt against the British in 1758.

economy survived scattered slave conspiracies, the most ambitious of which, uncovered in 1761, followed intermittent poisoning scares. Open revolt disrupted slave logging camps in colonial Belize in 1765, 1768, 1773, and 1820. About fifty slaves escaped the salt-pans of the Turks and Caicos Islands in 1822. Groups of Bahamian slaves resisted attempts in the early 1830s to relocate them away from their peasant-like communities.

In Britain's North American colonies, where slave majorities were a rare exception, slave revolt centered in the tobacco-producing Chesapeake region and the rice-producing Carolina Low Country. Official records speak of small slave plots and disturbances in Virginia before 1700. The largest slave revolt involved about one hundred African slaves who in 1739 fought their way south from South Carolina's Stono River plantations. England

and Spain were at war, and the Catholic Congo rebels, led by Jemmy, may have been looking to Spanish Florida for freedom and refuge. Earlier that year, perhaps two hundred mostly African slaves in Maryland entered into a plot formulated by a creole slave named Jack Ransom. Farther north, New York City, where slaves accounted for 15 percent of the population during the first half of the eighteenth century, experienced a revolt by dozens of African slaves in 1712 and an exaggerated conspiracy in 1741.

Two conspiracies and a revolt have dominated the literature on slave rebellion in the United States. In the late summer of 1800, during one of the most divisive presidential campaigns in U.S. history, whites in Richmond, Virginia, uncovered a sizeable plot masterminded by a slave blacksmith name Gabriel. Hundreds of mostly skilled creole slaves rallied around his secular republican vision of freedom; more than twenty paid with their lives by hanging. Denmark Vesey's conspiracy in 1822 proved larger and more successful in uniting rural and urban slaves. It had a pronounced religious dimension. Several members, including Vesey himself, had served as class leaders in Charleston's persecuted African Methodist Episcopal Church. Vesey, a literate freedman and skilled carpenter who had used winnings from a lottery to purchase his own freedom, had, like Gabriel, gathered around him a core of skilled slaves. They had tapped into the debate about slavery sparked by Missouri's admission into the Union and may have intended an escape to Haiti after striking at Charleston and its white inhabitants.

Nat Turner and his band of about sixty followers from Southampton County, Virginia, sent shock waves throughout the antebellum South in 1831 by killing more than fifty whites, many of them women and children. A slave prophet who had an apocalyptic vision of white and black conflict, Turner confessed to his captors that he was doing the Lord's work, "for the time was fast approaching when the first should be last and the last should be first." Scores of innocent slaves died as whites con-

ducted frenzied investigations in several states; Nat Turner and twenty other rebels were hanged.

Though the bloodiest slave revolt in U.S. history, Turner's revolt was not the largest. In January 1811 perhaps as many as five hundred slaves revolted in the sugar parishes of St. Charles and St. John the Baptist in lower Louisiana. Led by a mulatto slave-driver named Charles Deslondes, the rebels marched with drums beating and banners flying down the east bank of the Mississippi River to New Orleans, destroying property along the way. More than sixty slaves were killed in battle or executed after summary trials.

Although no major slave revolt broke out in the United States after Nat Turner, a larger number of small-scale rebellions and plots occurred than has been commonly appreciated, including mass desertions to Union lines and other acts of collective resistance during the Civil War. Still, with a largely resident master class, which by 1860 held on average only ten slaves per unit, and with white minorities in only two states, the antebellum South produced slave revolts with lesser frequency and magnitude than did the Caribbean, where the balance of forces proved far more favorable for slave insurgents.

Wherever slavery existed, certain general conditions favored slave revolt: master absenteeism, abrupt reversals in living standards, high concentrations of slaves, real or perceived weakening in the forces of control, divisions within the ruling class or between elite social groups, favorable terrain for establishing lines of communication and conducting subversive activity, the existence in certain regions or slave communities of strong warrior or militant traditions, and sufficient space within slavery for the creation of a viable leadership. Few cases of slave revolt lacked privileged slaves in leadership roles. Hence, what some considered slave accommodation did not necessarily preclude slave revolt but could serve as a prerequisite to it. Enslaved agricultural foremen, for example, headed many of the large slave revolts in the history of the Americas. The more complex revolts developed multiple lines of authority as rural and urban slaves, mulattoes and blacks, Africans and creoles, privileged and unprivileged, men and women were recruited to the cause.

Prophetic or millennarian religious visions informed some slave revolts such as the First Sicilian Slave War and Nat Turner's revolt. Religious authorities performed crucial rituals, extracted blood oaths, and supplied magical objects to bind slave recruits and steel them for the battle ahead. Gullah Jack, a slave conjurer, used his powers to aid Denmark Vesey in 1822. Muslim leaders of slave revolt in Bahia in 1835 furnished their people with amulets that contained sayings from the Qur'ān.

Sometimes slave rebels attached themselves to a charismatic leader from outside their ranks. The Zanj followed 'Alī ibn-Muḥammad, a freeborn Muslim and religious dissident. Before the Saint Domingue revolution, Toussaint Louverture had obtained his freedom and become a land-owner with at least one slave. Free people of color, in an inherently ambivalent position, led some slave revolts in the Americas, but, like maroons and Indians, also helped whites to suppress them. Free coloreds, for example, drew public praise for their performance in the suppression of the Louisiana slave revolt of 1811, and Indian trackers were employed to hunt down escapees. Slave women can be found at every stage of revolt, from planning to combat, but gender conventions shaped the content; slave men predominated and slave women usually filled supporting roles. In some cases male rebels consciously kept females out of the plotting, whether for fear of betrayal or as a way to protect loved ones and the larger slave community from the horrific retaliation that came with failure.

The specific reasons for slave revolt differed markedly from one slave to another, and from the leadership to the soldiery. Within or between movements, slave rebels could seek different goals, including personal liberation, material gain, access to land, extermination of oppressors, a return to the homeland, or the creation of a new society. Tension and conflict within movements helps to account for the large number of many betrayed or aborted slave revolts. As far back as ancient Rome, ethnic rivalry between slaves of Germanic origin and Spartacus, a Thracian, weakened his great revolt. While masters exploited differences among their slaves to divide and rule, paternalism acted to legitimate authority by binding individual slaves to the master rather than to one another. If such authority failed, masters could fall back on some combination of whips, torture devices, patrols, bloodhounds, mercenaries, informers, militia, and regular troops to keep slaves in line.

Against overwhelming odds, every rebel leader had to deal with acute problems of communication, mobilization, and coordination. Elite and urban slaves used their enhanced mobility and contacts to acquire strategic information and convey it to more isolated comrades. In planning revolt, slaves showed sensitivity to troop redeployments, weakened fortifications, and vulnerable caches of arms. Clock time did not govern slave rebellions, but leaders organized them to take advantage of the cover of darkness and heightened moments of ruling-class distraction. Many revolts in the Americas broke out on Christmas or Easter. Slaves in the British Caribbean also liked to rebel at Whitsuntide, while their brethren in Latin America preferred to rebel on saints' days. Nat Turner and his band targeted the Fourth of July as the day of reckoning. Subversion spread at night, on Sundays or holidays, at funerals and religious gatherings, at taverns, dances, and social clubs, in the fields and on the docks, along roads and waterways, and between ports. Many times hard information taken from the master's own loose talk mixed with volatile rumor to incite revolt. Indeed, in the aftermath of the French and Saint Domingue revolutions a rumored metropolitan emancipation triggered more than a dozen slave revolts throughout the Americas. The birth of a radical new anti-slavery ideology in England radiated outward to groups in continental Europe and the Americas and decisively conditioned the discrete struggles that brought about emancipation in both hemispheres. Nonetheless, slave revolt figured among the range of initiatives undertaken by the slaves themselves that contributed to slavery's ultimate demise.

[*See also* Brazil; Caribbean Region, *article on* French Caribbean; Europe, *article on* Ancient World; Maroons; Saint Domingue Revolution; *and* United States, *article on* The South.]

BIBLIOGRAPHY

Bradley, Keith R. *Slavery and Rebellion in the Roman World, 140 b.c.–70 b.c.* Bloomington: Indiana University Press, 1989.

Craton, Michael. *Testing the Chains: Resistance to Slavery in the British West Indies.* Ithaca, N.Y.: Cornell University Press, 1982.

Genovese, Eugene D. *From Rebellion to Revolution: The Afro-American Slave Revolts in the Making of the Modern World.* Baton Rouge: Louisiana State University Press, 1979.

Paquette, Robert L. *Sugar is Made with Blood: The Conspiracy of La Escalera and the Conflict Between Empires over Slavery in Cuba.* Middletown, Conn.: Wesleyan University Press, 1988.

—ROBERT L. PAQUETTE

RUSSIA. Slavery, primarily of the household type, was an important institution in Russia from earliest recorded times until the 1720s, when it was merged into the institution of serfdom and effectively abolished. The basic Russian word for "slave" is *rab,* which is common to other Slavic languages such as Serbo-Croatian, Polish, and Czech. The modern Russian verb "to work," *rabotat',* initially meant "to perform slave labor." Another Russian word for "slave" is *kholop,* which is also found in other Slavic languages. In the sixteenth through early eighteenth centuries, the words were used more or less interchangeably.

Russia in historic times has been sandwiched between various Turkic peoples on the south and east and other Slavic peoples on the west. Although peaceful relations existed from time to time, warfare (with its goal of booty, often primarily slaves) and outright slave-raiding fill much of the historical record of the many centuries be-

tween the ninth and early eighteenth. Russia, along with Africa, was one of the great reservoirs of slaves for the Islamic and Mediterranean worlds. The Kievan Russian state was founded in 882 by Swedish Vikings, for whom the slave trade was a primary livelihood. After 1136 the Kievan state collapsed into more than a dozen warring principalities, with slave-taking a major object of that warfare. From this time through the fifteenth century there was a great flow of Slavic slaves through Novgorod into the Baltic and from there to Spain and North Africa.

From earliest times to the end of the fifteenth century most slaves were probably military booty. The Russian plain was always sparsely settled, and labor was a very scarce commodity. For many centuries this meant that landholding was not prized, and serfdom did not begin to develop at all until the middle of the fifteenth century. Without labor, land had little value, with the result that private ownership of land did not develop until some time in the late tenth century at the earliest. The breakup of the Kievan Russian state in 1136 provided a considerable stimulus to the private ownership of land, because the great supply of East Slavic slaves that eventuated from the resulting civil wars were sometimes herded into barracks and forced to farm for their captors and buyers. Most slaves, however, still worked in the household.

In addition to captivity, people could be enslaved by marrying slaves, by self-sale into slavery as a result of the inability to pay debts or fines, or through birth from slave parents. The concept that a slave or his offspring should be manumitted by right after serving for a certain number of years or generations did not develop until the end of the sixteenth century. Manumission existed but was limited to instances in which the slave-owner had no heirs or the slave was no longer able to work owing to infirmity.

Until the middle of the sixteenth century, the basic form of slavery was "full slavery," meaning for the life of the slave and heritable by offspring. This gradually came to be replaced by the most interesting form of early modern Russian slavery, limited-service contract slavery (*kabal'noe kholopstvo*). Initially this was a form of antichresis or debt bondage: a free person borrowed a sum for a year and served for the interest. At the end of the year, the slave either repaid the loan (which apparently happened very infrequently), sold himself to someone else, or defaulted on the loan and became a full slave (apparently the typical scenario). Welfare and other forms of charity were almost nonexistent in sixteenth-century Muscovy, with the result that slavery was the major alternative to starvation. Labor remained scarce, owning slaves became a major status symbol, and the demand for slaves remained high. About half of the slaves in the sixteenth century were these limited-service contract slaves, of whom approximately two-thirds were male. This sex ratio held for both adults and children, forcing one to conclude that female infanticide (which was not illegal or condemned until 1649) was practiced on a fairly large scale.

The enserfment of the productive peasantry accelerated in the second half of the sixteenth century, resulting by the 1590s in a peasantry bound to the land and diminishing the differences between serfs and slaves. One difference was that serfs were supposed to pay taxes whereas household slaves were not. This provided an incentive for lords to convert their peasants into slaves and was probably the major impetus for a change in the essence of limited contract slavery in the 1590s. Instead of the contract being for a year and servitude becoming perpetual and hereditary on default, the government changed the nature of the institution. The limitation ceased to be for a year and became the lifetime of owner. The slave could not pay back the "loan" but was automatically freed on the death of the owner. Essentially, the owners (really, their heirs) were expropriated. Owners tried all types of subterfuge in the first half of the seventeenth century to overcome this expropriation, such as multiple ownership by brothers or by a father and all his sons, but the government remained adamant. The slave had to be freed on the death of

one owner. It so happened, of course, that slavery created such dependency that most freed persons (freed without any property or other assets) soon sold themselves either to the heirs of their former owners or to someone else. Nonetheless, the freed person (while that status lasted) was nearly the sole person not bound to any caste in the years between 1649 and 1720.

In the seventeenth century the government, for unknown reasons, began to set the price of limited-service contract slaves, first at two rubles apiece and later at three. This greatly raised the price of families who wanted to sell themselves and reduced the market demand for them. Whether the government anticipated this consequence of price-fixing or approved of it afterward is not known. Throughout the century the median daily wage was four kopeks, which meant that a slave cost the equivalent of fifty to seventy-five days' wages.

How the Russians were able to violate the basic social-scientific "law" forbidding the enslavement of one's own people remains to be satisfactorily explained. It probably had something to do with the great permeability of what it meant to be a Russian, and thus the social indicators of "insider" (who normally could not be enslaved) and "outsider" (who often could be enslaved) failed to function.

Besides "full slaves" and their successor "limited-service contract slaves," there were other forms of slavery in early modern Russia. By law, estate stewards had to be slaves, a rule probably initiated in the sixteenth century to satisfy the norm that in many societies free people can not give orders to other free people (in this case, the peasants before their enserfment). There were also formal debt slaves, who worked off their obligations at the legally stipulated rate of five rubles per year for adult males, two and one-half rubles for adult females, and two rubles for children over age ten. In addition, there were indentured slaves, who sold themselves for a term with the provision that they were to be manumitted at the end of a term, often with a wife and a cash payment. There were so-called "hereditary slaves," people whose parents (and perhaps other predecessors for generations before) had been slaves. All of these categories were numerically subsidiary to the *kabal'nye kholopy*.

The institution of slavery was so prominent that Russia was the only country to have a special central government office whose sole task was the management of slavery, the Slavery Chancellery. Perhaps 10 percent of the total population consisted of slaves. Slaves filled many roles in Russia: they fought as cavalrymen in the sixteenth century and then were converted into baggage-train guards in the seventeenth. They essentially expanded the lineages of merchants by acting as their agents. They gave advice in courts and aided their owners in state administration. They carried messages and ran errands. They served as ornaments in the houses of the rich, who had dozens, even hundreds, of chattel for this purpose. For lesser owners, they acted as body servants on military campaigns and presumably cooked and cleaned for their owners.

The peasants were completely enserfed by the Law Code (*Ulozhenie*) of 1649, and serfdom increasingly borrowed many of the features of slavery. A census was taken in 1678, and the government discovered that there had been a massive conversion of peasant serfs into slaves. Therefore, in 1679 slaves engaged in agriculture were by fiat converted into serfs.

This left the household slaves. In his search for recruits to fight the Swedes in the Northern War (1700–1721), Tsar Peter the Great proclaimed that household slaves would be freed if they joined the army, which reduced their numbers. But a census taken in 1719–1721 revealed that massive numbers of serfs had been converted into house slaves. In response, Peter decreed that all slaves had to pay the poll tax levied on serfs. This converted them into house serfs and effectively abolished the institution of slavery in Russia.

[*See also* Serfdom.]

BIBLIOGRAPHY

Hellie, Richard. *Slavery in Russia 1450–1725*. Chicago: University of Chicago Press, 1982.

Hellie, Richard, trans. and ed. *The Muscovite Law Code (Ulozhenie) of 1649*. Irvine, Calif.: Charles Schlacks Jr., 1988. Slavery permeates the 1649 Law Code, and chap. 20 is devoted to the institution.

Iakovlev, A. I. *Kholopstvo I kholopy v Moskovskom gosudarstve XVII v.* Moscow and Leningrad: AN SSSR, 1943.

Kolycheva, E. I. *Kholopstvo i krepostnichestvo (konets XV–XVI v.).* Moscow: Nauka, 1971.

Paneiakh, V. M. *Kabal'noe kholopstvo na Rusi v XVI veke.* Leningrad: Nauka, 1967.

Paneiakh, V. M. *Kholopstvo v XVI–nachale XVII veka.* Leningrad: Nauka, 1976.

Paneiakh, V. M. *Kholopstvo v pervoi polovine XVII v.* Leningrad: Nauka, 1984.

Zimin, A. A. *Kholopy na Rusi (s drevneishikh vremen do kontsa XV v.).* Moscow: Nauka, 1973.

—RICHARD HELLIE

SAINT DOMINGUE REVOLUTION. The slave revolt that between 1791 and 1803 transformed France's immensely wealthy colony of Saint Domingue was among the largest in world history, and the sole fully successful one. It brought about the first wholesale act of emancipation in a major slave society (August 1793) and the creation in January 1804 of Haiti, the first modern black state. Of all the American struggles for colonial independence it involved the greatest degree of mass mobilization, and it caused the greatest degree of social and economic change. In twelve years of devastating warfare, the world's major producer of sugar and coffee was economically ruined and its ruling class entirely eliminated. For slaves and slave-owners throughout the Americas, the Saint Domingue or Haitian Revolution was an inspiration and a warning.

Historians have disagreed about the extent to which the revolution resulted from internal factors and how far it was a byproduct of the French Revolution of 1789. Saint Domingue was for much of the eighteenth century the most populous and productive colony in the Caribbean. By 1791 it had a population of approximately one-half million slaves, forty thousand whites, and thirty thousand free coloreds. Although it had imported unprecedented numbers of Africans during the previous five years, its social structure and the character of its slavery remained typical of the sugar colonies. Haitian nationalist historians have argued since the 1920s that maroon slaves played a critical role in stimulating and leading the uprising, but this is unproven. Fugitives kept alive a tradition of resistance, but revolution did not so much emerge out of marronage as become an alternative option, as the mountain forests were felled for coffee production and marronage became more difficult. The role of Vodun ("voodoo") is also disputed. Religion divided as well as united slaves, and it is unclear when the fusion of different ethnic cults into modern Vodun came about. The use of amulets (which the wearers believed would protect them from injury) and religious ritual facilitated mobilization, but defeat of European armies resulted more from cautious guerrilla campaigns than suicidal fervor. Some Vodun priests became minor rebel leaders, but the most important leaders were hostile to Vodun.

French scholars stress the French Revolution's impact on Saint Domingue. It weakened the colonial government and split white society into warring factions. Its influence then caused a civil war between white colonists and the strong free colored community, who demanded political equality with whites. These divisions were successfully exploited by the slaves. The influence of French libertarian ideology on the slaves is less obvious. While some invoked the Rights of Man, the rebel leaders generally adopted a counterrevolutionary rhetoric, posing as defenders of king and church against colonial radicals (perhaps to gain assistance from their conservative Spanish neighbors in Santo Domingo). Some rebels also claimed that the king had abolished slavery or granted them an extra free day per week, but that the colonists were blocking these reforms. Similar rumors were associated with more than twenty other slave conspiracies and revolts in the period from 1789 from 1832; this reflected the growth of the European anti-slavery movement as much as the French Revolution.

Beginning in August 1791, the slave uprising on Saint Domingue rapidly mobilized tens of thousands of slaves, and in one month more than a thousand plantations were burned. Military sorties proved ineffective against the rebels' guerrilla tactics, but the rebels in turn were generally unable to capture towns or fortified posts, and the insurrection was confined to the central region of Saint Domingue's northern province. Soldiers sent from France arrived slowly and died rapidly in fever epidemics that decimated European troops throughout the revolution. Elsewhere in the colony, whites and free coloreds armed slaves to fight for them in the separate struggle over racial equality (1791–1793), which led to the burning of the capital, Port-au-Prince. Smaller slave rebellions broke out, but they were usually pacified with limited concessions. Outside the north, the plantation regime was shaken but remained intact. Although Africans predominated in the adult slave population, the main rebel leaders were locally born creoles from the slave "elite," often drivers or coachmen. Several black freedmen also led rebel bands, and in some regions free colored insurgents made temporary alliances with slaves. However, because free coloreds were often slave-owners, they usually opposed slave emancipation, especially once the French government conceded racial equality in April 1792.

The situation was transformed when the French Republic went to war with England and Spain (February–March 1793). British and Spanish forces invaded Saint Domingue, and in an attempt to conquer the valuable colony cheaply, they sought to recruit the slave rebels. The Spanish offered them and their families guns, land, and freedom, but proposed to preserve the slave regime. To outbid the invaders and rally the entire slave population, radical French officials then abolished slavery outright; but France seemed close to defeat, and most insurgents still joined the Spanish. The rebels' willingness to act as mercenaries and to sell other blacks as slaves, their royalist rhetoric, and their leaders' previous attempts to negotiate a compromise peace, have led some scholars to consider these early years of the slave uprising a rebellion rather than a true revolution aimed at completely ending slavery. Early in 1794, however, the French government ratified the local abolition of slavery; thereupon a minority of the rebels, led by the black freedman Toussaint Louverture, rallied to the French, and the balance of power decisively shifted. Thereafter the forces of black self-liberation were unambiguously identified with the libertarian ideology of the Age of Revolution.

The period from 1793 to 1798 was one of continuous warfare fought to expel the Spanish and British and to end slavery in the districts the slaves controlled. More plantations were destroyed, and thousands more blacks became soldiers. Toussaint Louverture emerged as a brilliant military and political tactician and was made deputy governor in 1796. Although the mass of ex-slaves preferred to become independent peasants, plantation production continued, using a system of compulsory but remunerated labor enforced with corporal punishment. The new black officer corps took over abandoned estates and became a nascent landholding class, rivaling the former free coloreds, who were mainly of mixed racial descent and French in culture. In the War of the South (1799–1800), Toussaint Louverture defeated the free coloreds, his erstwhile allies, and was perforce recognized as colonial governor by the French. Outwardly loyal to France, he promulgated his own constitution, made himself governor for life, and traded freely with France's enemies. He did not declare outright independence, probably because he feared the United States and Britain, major slave-owning powers, would cut off his supply of munitions in retaliation. Export agriculture alienated the rural masses but provided the funds that financed Toussaint's army.

Admirers see Toussaint's rule (1800–1802) as a period of racial harmony, innovation in imperial relations, and humane economic progress. Critics see him either as too wedded to the old colonial model, or as a duplicitous power-seeker who bought his soldiers' loyalty by letting the army exploit the masses. The experiment ended when Napoleon Bonaparte came to power and overthrew Toussaint in a brief but costly campaign. Many black generals and former free coloreds collaborated with the French, until it became clear that they wanted to restore slavery and white supremacy. Thereafter, most nonwhites united under the ex-slave general Dessalines in an apocalyptic War of Independence (1802–1803). The French were expelled, and Saint Domingue was given the Amerindian name Haiti to emphasize the rupture with European colonialism.

Perhaps the main impact overseas of the Saint Domingue Revolution was in forcing racial equality and slave emancipation onto the agenda of the French Revolution. This extended its benefits to all French Caribbean possessions and led the French Republic to encourage rebellions in Britain's slave colonies, adding a new dimension to colonial warfare. The Haitians' example inspired nonwhites and alarmed slave-owners across the Americas; it was instrumental in several conspiracies and revolts. Haitian assistance to Simón Bolívar in 1816 furthered decolonization and slave emancipation in South America. In the anti-slavery debate, both sides used the Haitian case for propaganda. Scholars disagree as to its long-term influence, but the removal of France as a commercial rival probably facilitated the progress of abolitionism in Britain. Conversely, the migration of refugees from Saint Domingue and the massive destruction there helped to stimulate slave-based production in Cuba, Jamaica, Louisiana, and elsewhere. More than eighty thousand Europeans perished in the revolution; the number of black dead is unknown.

La Révolte des Nègres à Saint Domingue (Revolt of the Negroes on Saint Domingue); engraving by Jean-François Pourvoyeur after a painting by Martinet, from *Histoire universelle du XIX siècle*.

[*See also* Caribbean Race Relations; Caribbean, *article on* French Caribbean; Maroons; *and* Revolts.]

BIBLIOGRAPHY

Fick, Carolyn. *The Making of Haiti: The Saint Domingue Revolution from Below*. Knoxville: University of Tennessee Press, 1990.

Gaspar, D. Barry, and David Geggus. *A Turbulent Time: The Greater Caribbean in the Age of the French and Haitian Revolutions*. Bloomington: Indiana University Press, 1997.

James, C. L. R. *The Black Jacobins: Toussaint L'Ouverture and the San Domingo Revolution*. 2d rev. ed. New York: Vintage Books, 1963.

Ott, Thomas. *The Haitian Revolution*. Knoxville: University of Tennessee Press, 1976.

Pluchon, Pierre. *Toussaint L'ouverture: Un revolutionnaire noir d'Ancien Regime*. Paris: Fayard, 1989.

—DAVID GEGGUS

SEGREGATION. *De jure* or codified racial segregation bedeviled American society from the colonial era until the mid-twentieth century. Backed by custom, local and state ordinances treated African Americans and whites unequally. Under these laws, African Americans suffered harsher penalties than whites who committed the same crimes, and public and private institutions served African Americans and whites separately or excluded African Americans altogether. In many ways, segregation laws merely enshrined customary, or *de facto*, social relations and practices. Segregation's persistence despite deep economic change and national wars, however, ought not to imply that it was static. Movements to codify racial segregation aimed at much more than shrouding tradition with law. Patterns of racial segregation varied across time and from place to place, and their legalization always encountered opposition. *De jure* segregation originated in the concrete ideological, political, and social realities of particular localities and promoted certain interests. As such, the adoption of segregation statutes reflected the balance of political and social power at specific historical moments.

Colonial segregation laws coincided with the maturation of racial slavery and colonial economic structures. During the early stages of colonization, common work experiences and cultural values produced flexible relations between African Americans and whites. Planters feared, with good cause, that frequent and unguarded interaction among white, African, and African American laborers might foment social unrest. A rebellion in 1676 confirmed these misgivings. Led by Nathaniel Bacon, white indentured servants and African-American slaves attacked the sources and symbols of concentrated wealth in Virginia. Planter elites crushed the uprising, and in its wake they took steps to prevent recurrence. Planters increasingly relied on African-American slaves rather than white indentured servants to produce tobacco, and they passed laws designed to foster antipathy toward African Americans. By 1700 Virginia outlawed interracial marriages and barred African Americans from holding "white, Christian servants." After the Stono slave rebellion in 1739, South Carolina's legislators blurred distinctions between free and enslaved African Americans. They adopted a draconian slave code that treated all African Americans equally, regardless of whether they were slave or free. These early attempts at segregation represented a response to labor insurgency and the fluid race relations that encouraged it.

Following the American Revolution, shifts in social thought and urban growth spurred new forms of segregation. By the mid-nineteenth century an increasing number of whites believed that racial differences were innate and impervious to environmental modification. Frequent interracial contact, endemic to the North's growing cities, raised the haunting specter of white racial degradation. Moreover, the growth of Northern, urban African-American communities led to demands for equal treatment and respectability and greater competition with whites for working-class jobs. To many white Northerners, racial amalgamation no longer seemed a remote possibility.

To meet this perceived danger, Northern state legislators took steps to exclude or segregate African Americans. Before 1790 New Jersey closed its borders to free African Americans, while Massachusetts allowed the entrance of only those African Americans who possessed state citizenship. Ohio in 1804 and Illinois in 1814 required all free African Americans to post good-behavior bonds of five hundred and a thousand dollars, respectively. Under pressure from white convicts, Philadelphia officials segregated the city's prison facilities. As African Americans' potential political strength grew, Northern states curtailed their suffrage rights. By 1830 approximately 80 percent of Northern African Americans lived under governments that barred their formal political participation. In some Northern cities, custom acquired the force of law. In Boston, New York City, and Philadelphia, local and state courts sanctioned the exclusion of free African Americans from restaurants, hotels, and theaters, as well as the segregation of public conveyances.

Southern state legislators wrote similar codes to control the permeable boundaries between slavery and freedom and to buttress racial inequality. A wave of manumissions occurred throughout the South from 1780 to 1810, and the number of free African Americans residing in the Upper South increased from four thousand to ninety-four thousand during those years. After the Haitian

Revolution and Gabriel's Rebellion, Southerners viewed emancipation as a social evil and slavery as the final bulwark against racial warfare. African-American freedom seemed inimical to slavery and racial subordination. Actions taken by free African Americans further substantiated these fears. Within Southern cities and towns, free African Americans exercised some citizenship rights and harbored fugitive slaves.

New state laws, adopted after 1810, restricted the mobility and residence of free African Americans and made suffrage rights contingent on whiteness rather than free status. Free African Americans in North Carolina wore shoulder patches inscribed with the word "Free." In a scheme pioneered by Virginia, Southern states required African Americans to carry passes certifying their freedom; local courts fined, jailed, and hired out persons found without them. Criminal codes across the South prescribed different punishments based solely on the offender's race. Among the free, only African Americans risked sale into servitude or public whipping for robbery, insolence, and other crimes. Legal segregation was most apparent in Southern cities. New Orleans, for example, segregated street railway cars, prisons, and cemeteries, and barred the employment of free African-American workers on city-sponsored projects. Complete segregation proved impossible, however, and laws and practices varied from state to state. Nonetheless, the segregation laws that developed after the American Revolution apprised African Americans of their social and racial status and alerted whites to the tangible and psychological benefits guaranteed to them by law and race.

During the 1840s and 1850s Northern African Americans and some white abolitionists launched sporadic attacks on legal segregation. Bowing to this pressure, Massachusetts legislators repealed restrictions on interracial marriage. However, efforts to desegregate railroad cars, theaters, and public lecture halls failed to overcome legislators' reluctance to tread on private property rights. Only when economic expediency and public pressure

mounted by 1860 did voluntary desegregation of these facilities occur. Outside Massachusetts, such direct pressure proved less successful. In New York City and Philadelphia public conveyances remained segregated, despite legal pressure applied by African Americans. Desegregation movements in Boston, New York City, and Philadelphia occasionally breached the very racial barriers the laws sought to sustain. They demonstrate as well that segregation statutes did not result from an unthinking acceptance of tradition. Rather, they reflected the balance of political and social power at specific historical moments.

Arguments over the propriety of segregation continued during the Civil War. Republican and Northern military leaders faced a chronic manpower shortage, and they enlisted African-American men to fill Union ranks. African Americans believed military service would hasten the end of slavery and legitimate their claims for legal equality and citizenship rights. Regiments quickly formed in Massachusetts, Rhode Island, and Connecticut. In all, approximately 179,000 African-American men joined the Union army, 33,000 of them from the Northern states.

Military recruitment and service reflected prewar racialist ideals and practices. If African-American men shared the horrors of battle equally with whites, they did so in segregated units commanded by white officers. Racial hatred and violence from within the ranks led to the expulsion or transfer of any African-American troops from otherwise all-white regiments. Union policies also denied commissions to African-American men and granted African-American soldiers a lower rate of pay than whites of equal rank. As before the war, African Americans and white abolitionists protested. The Massachusetts 54th and 55th regiments refused their pay vouchers until they matched those of white regiments, and some African-American troops threatened mutiny. Although segregated units remained inviolable, the agitation bore some fruit. In June 1864, Congress agreed to pay African-American and white soldiers

equally, and in 1865 the War Department promoted Stephen A. Swails, a light-skinned freedman, to lieutenant. The overall conduct of the war
showed the willingness of Republican leaders to
segregate free African Americans and whites as an
expedient practice.

This same inclination guided federal oversight
of the defeated South. Southern whites fashioned a
series of "black codes" to govern race relations in
the postbellum South. These laws segregated public accommodations and greatly restricted African
Americans' physical mobility and civic rights. City
ordinances further excluded African Americans
from schools, theaters, the militia, and welfare institutions. Victorious Republicans, however, ne-
gated the "black codes" and required cities to open
facilities for African Americans. If Republicans dis-
allowed the exclusion of African Americans from
public services and conveyances, they tolerated
their *de facto* segregation and separate-but-equal facilities. Redeemers and Democrats maintained
these patterns after the federal government officially abandoned its Reconstruction policy in
1877.

African Americans responded to their new but
segregated freedom in a variety of ways. Through
annual Emancipation Day parades and Republican
rallies, they asserted their political autonomy and
occasionally denounced racial inequality. While
some protested, most initially accepted segregation as an improvement over exclusion from hospitals, theaters, and the like. Savvy and shrewd,
African Americans used local courts to press not for
integrated accommodations but for funding and
resources equal to that provided white institutions.

If the general contours of race relations had
solidified before 1877, technological and industrial developments created new situations in which
custom served as an inadequate guide. Railway
travel, for example, exposed the limitations of the
separate-but-equal doctrine. By the mid-1880s a
new, primarily urban African-American middle
class demanded railroad accommodations com-
mensurate with their status and social respect-

ability. When white women traveled by first class,
railroad companies regularly expelled African-
American riders, relegating them to second-class
smoking cars. Dissatisfied and angered, middle-
class African Americans used federal courts to force
railroad companies to provide them with equal facilities. This only partially solved the dilemma created by African-American activism and the expansion of rail travel. Some railroad companies refused
to run segregated cars, placing profits above racial
propriety, but infuriated white Southerners pressured state legislators to force companies to com-
ply with their racism. Laws mandating racially segregated cars spread across the South, and by 1891
nine Southern states required separate-but-equal
rail cars.

Economic and social change also created political interests and coalitions that breached customary color lines. In New Orleans and Richmond,
confrontations over the reorganization of work,
wages, hours, and conditions spawned uneasy alliances between white and African-American workers. Although single unions were often racially exclusive and Southern rallies and strikes sponsored
by the Knights of Labor fractured repeatedly along
racial lines, white and African-American workers
sustained some partially successful cooperative
strikes. This trend peaked in Richmond, where a
political reform party based on white and African-
American workers defeated Democrats in the 1886
city elections. Interracial unionism and political
activism, no matter how tenuous, directly challenged the power of local urban employers.

Urban working-class activism was part of a
much broader political challenge to Democratic
party supremacy during the 1880s and 1890s. Attempts at cooperation and fusion among Republicans and independent African-American and
white voters persisted throughout the South. In
the early 1880s between 30 and 46 percent of
voters in the deep South supported independent candidates. Building on dissatisfaction with
the Southern economy, corporations, banks, and
Democratic rule, agrarian radicals formed the

Populist Party in the 1890s. Populism electrified independent voters and frightened Southern Democrats. In the ensuing political contests Populists like Tom Watson appealed to African-American voters for support. Riding this wave of political excitement, the moribund Republican Party revived itself in North Carolina and Mississippi. Democratic elites hurled racial invective at Populists and Republicans but remained unable to destroy their base of support.

Faced with political turmoil and opposition, Democrats sought to eliminate the voters who fueled it. Democrats sponsored a series of constitutional conventions to disfranchise "unworthy" voters, starting in 1890 in Mississippi. Well-educated, wealthy, and frequently from Black Belt counties, advocates of disfranchisement used poll taxes, tests of comprehension, grandfather clauses, and registration requirements to impede African-American voters. Written in colorblind language, these restrictions also reduced the poor-white vote, the primary foundation of Populism. Strong opposition from counties with large white majorities emerged, but disfranchisers employed a variety of measures to ensure passage of their handiwork.

Once in place, disfranchisement more than fulfilled the hopes of its creators. It virtually barred African Americans from formal political participation and reduced white voter turnout in Louisiana, Florida, and Texas by more than 30 percent. Coupled with the precedent set by railway laws, this movement released an avalanche of segregation legislation covering hospitals, schools, courtrooms, and almost every other area of Southern life. Beginning as a response to systemic changes within the Southern economy and the tentative organization of urban workers and rural Populists across racial lines, these new laws segregated African Americans and whites from cradle to grave.

Unlike previous segregation laws, those adopted after 1890 were applied almost uniformly throughout the South and received the support of the federal government. In 1892 Homer Adolph Plessy, seven-eighths white, refused to surrender his seat in the white car provided by the East Louisiana Railroad. Arrested by police, Plessy took his case to the Supreme Court, arguing that the Fourteenth Amendment's equal protection clause made segregated cars unconstitutional. The Supreme Court disagreed. In 1896, in *Plessy v. Ferguson*, it ruled that the Civil Rights Act of 1875 required only separate but equal facilities. This conclusion sanctified a system of American apartheid that had both deep and immediate roots in Southern and national politics and culture. A virulent system of racial oppression, the segregation laws of the late nineteenth and early twentieth centuries redrew the political map of the South. This system remained in force until the post–World War II civil rights movement successfully challenged its intellectual, moral, and political foundations.

[*See also* Anti-Slavery Literature, *article on* African-American Perspectives; Caribbean Race Relations; Historiography, *article on* North American Slavery; Law, *article on* United States Law; *and* Race and Racism.]

BIBLIOGRAPHY

Ayers, Edward. *The Promise of the New South.* Oxford and New York: Oxford University Press, 1992.

Kousser, J. Morgan. *The Shaping of Southern Politics.* New Haven: Yale University Press, 1974.

Litwack, Leon. *North of Slavery.* Chicago: University of Chicago Press, 1961.

Rabinowitz, Howard. *Race Relation in the Urban South, 1865–1890.* Urbana: University of Illinois Press, 1980.

Woodward, C. Vann. *The Strange Career of Jim Crow.* New York and Oxford: Oxford University Press, 1955.

—MICHAEL NARAGON

SERFDOM. The term *serfdom* refers to the ties of dependence of servile, or unfree, peasant family farmers to their landlords. In numerous local, regional, and temporal variants, serfdom existed in one part of Europe or another for more than a thousand years, from at least the ninth century to the nineteenth.

In all of preindustrial Europe (prior to the nineteenth century), agriculture was the primary pursuit of the overwhelming majority of the population. Although often described as a traditional society in which custom dictated many practices and the environment severely constrained choice, Europe was not static and unchanging. For landlords in particular, profit from agriculture depended to a great extent on their obtaining a labor supply and on their adapting labor practices to changing economic, demographic, social, and political circumstances. Moreover, because the level of technology was low, labor was a much more significant factor affecting agricultural output than is the case today.

Many different terms were used for serfs in various European lands, including Latin *servi* ("slaves," the source of the word *serf*). This reflects the fact that among the servile peasants of European society there were many gradations and varieties of servitude. In fact, medieval jurists expended much effort in attempting to define servile status; in later times legislators often tried to codify long-standing realities. Unfreedom was not a simple concept, and even modern historians remain sharply divided over its meaning.

Europe experienced two great periods of serfdom. By the eleventh century serfdom was clearly in place in much of western Europe and was distinct from earlier Roman and Carolingian forms of slavery. By the end of the thirteenth century, however, many western European serfs had become free tenants. By the fifteenth century, although vestiges of serfdom still remained, with few exceptions it was no longer very important. Precisely at the time when serfdom was waning in western Europe, much of the population in eastern Europe, the region east of the Elbe River, was sinking into dependent status. Often called the "second serfdom," this state of agrarian servitude spread rapidly in the seventeenth century and lasted in many places well into the nineteenth century.

Serfdom in Western Europe. One of the great transformations in western European history was the gradual shift from slavery to serfdom between the sixth and eleventh centuries. Slavery had existed in the Roman Empire, in the barbarian states that followed, and in the Byzantine Empire. A slave was not simply unfree, but in the words of Marc Bloch, "an ox in the stable, always under his master's orders." Slaves were considered movable, personal property, along with livestock, crops, and money. Gangs of slaves worked the large plantations or manors of their owners and received all their food, clothing, and housing from their masters.

With growing demand from the Muslim world for slaves and a general economic depression throughout much of Europe from the eighth century onward, it became more profitable for landowners to settle their slaves on plots of land in exchange for a rent in cash, in kind, or in labor services on the lord's manor (a system called *seigneurie*). Slave-owners were thereby freed of the costs of maintaining their slaves. Slaves now became tenant serf farmers, responsible for their own livelihood and possessing their own means of subsistence. The use of dependent labor by landlords to farm their own land, known as the *demesne*, still continued, but on a reduced scale; it would continue to decrease throughout the medieval period.

The political instability and fragmentation of early medieval society, marked by the growing weakness of central or state authorities and their institutions of public law, also caused numerous *coloni* (peasants not owned by a master but bound to specific lands) and many free peasants to seek protection from powerful local landlords. Once established, this personal bond was hereditary and indissoluble. This act of submission often entailed free peasants or *coloni* transferring their lands to a protector and becoming dependent tenants.

It is important to realize that all medieval European peasants, both free and unfree, had lords and paid rents. But the free peasant could choose his lord, while serfs were restricted in their movement by ties of personal dependency that were socially degrading, legally incapacitating, and economically burdensome. Some historians hold that the key attribute of serfdom, or, in Marxist parlance, the feudal mode of production, was the particular means by which landlords extracted wealth from their serfs. Because serfs provided for their own subsistence, to obtain an income lords had to resort to noneconomic or extra-economic forms of compulsion. In contrast, slaves, like domestic livestock, depended completely on their owners for survival. Slaves could be deprived of their means of subsistence if they failed to perform as desired. Free peasants, on the other hand, sold their labor power in the marketplace in order to live. Their relationship to their landlords was primarily economic and contractual, even if unequal.

This extra-economic coercion, reflecting the power of the lords as a social class, took on a variety of forms in medieval western Europe, so that no general common law or practice of serfdom can readily be deduced. Restricting freedom of movement, imposing an elaborate system of fines, confiscating serfs' property, levying poll and inheritance taxes, and limiting marriage only to serfs tied to the same lord: all were methods by which medieval landlords laid claim to a substantial portion of serf labor and income. Moreover, serfs were increasingly made subject to their lord's jurisdictional or legal authority. Landlords set up manorial courts to control the lives of their serfs and claimed monopolies on the rights to mill grain, press grapes into wine, or sell certain products. In fact, in the eleventh and twelfth centuries lordship or seigneurial authority became an important dimension of serfdom as income from the direct use of serf labor on the demesne declined, increasingly replaced by wage labor or cash rents.

Numerous scholars have found the interpretation of extra-economic coercion wanting. To some historians, the supply and demand for labor—that is, demographic factors, especially population expansion and decline—governed the state of peasant dependency. When the population grew, as it did in Europe from at least the eleventh century on, wages fell, food prices rose, landholdings fragmented, more marginal lands were cultivated, and the soil was increasingly exhausted. In this environment lords were not so concerned with limiting the mobility of their tenants as in getting the most out of them. For the peasants, as a result, the terms of dependency deteriorated. But with the agricultural crises of the early fourteenth century and then the Black Death at mid-century, a major shift in the demographic balance occurred. Labor became scarce and valuable, existing forms of servitude no longer proved viable, and peasants certainly became freer and more mobile. This marked the end of the medieval world and its practices; "to custom succeeded competition, to status contract."

Some historians have even called into question the usefulness of serfdom as a concept in comprehending medieval society. In this view, medieval peasants were first and foremost subsistence-oriented farmers living on land specifically allotted for their family's use. This, it is argued, gave them a degree of autonomy that neither dependency nor lordship could significantly penetrate. Subsistence farming left them free at times from a master's supervision and allowed them to control the intensity of their labor. In fact, many of the peasants' obligations to their lords were fixed by custom and not readily changed. Peasants could sell and exchange their produce, inherit property, and marry within their own group. Moreover, they formed small rural communities that advanced and protected their interests and exercised rights over common and arable lands. Thus these peasants were not part of a distinctly feudal or medieval society, but peasant farmers in a stable, preindustrial economy in which family-oriented, subsistence values regulated behavior and attitudes. The dynamic elements in society were both demographic and social, especially the mechanisms for family control and survival within a small rural community. The key distinction among peasants was not between freedom or servitude, but between those who had access to enough land to provide for their family's subsistence needs and those who did not.

Serfdom in Eastern Europe. In the thirteenth and early fourteenth centuries, growing population pressures in western Europe encouraged many German peasants to move eastward into the Baltic plain, Bohemia, and Hungary. Landlords there offered favorable terms for settlement, often issuing exemptions for many payments and dues. Labor services, if they existed at all, were light; most land was rented out to peasants for cash. The peasants had few restrictions on their right to move or change lords, and they certainly enjoyed greater freedoms than most of their western European counterparts.

The demographic collapse of the fourteenth century, followed by two centuries of devastating wars, produced quite dramatic changes in eastern Europe. Here the scarcity of labor prompted landlords and the state to resort to desperate and often harsh methods to secure a labor supply. By 1500 these efforts proved successful. Throughout eastern Europe, the terms of servitude were far more burdensome than ever seen in medieval England, France, Spain, or western Germany. In Poland, Hungary, and Russia, many peasants experienced a dependency often compared with New World slavery.

When Europe finally began to recover from crisis in the end of the fifteenth century, the economy changed, and with it the lives of the peasants. Subsistence agriculture still predominated, and the peasant family remained the dominant social organization. In parts of western Europe, however, trade and commerce, money, and banking had taken on new importance. Attendant to these structural changes in the western European economy, the demand for grains and foodstuffs increased, a trend some historians view as necessarily associated with the rise of market-oriented, moneyed entrepreneurs and the increased use of wage laborers.

Landlords in much of eastern Europe, who had seen their cash incomes from renting land decline substantially from the fourteenth century on, also sought to take advantage of this new opportunity by exporting agricultural products to the West. Lacking capital to invest in their lands, lords in the fifteen and especially the sixteenth century ex-

panded demesne production largely by resorting to compulsory labor, which meant imposing new and heavier obligations on the peasantry. Land abandoned during the population decline was incorporated into the manors. To compel peasants to work, the right to change landlords was gradually restricted. Lords often agreed not to entice peasants away by offering better terms. Some peasants became financially indebted to their lords, thereby losing the ability to move elsewhere. Serfdom increasingly came to mean both personal dependency on a lord, subject to his legal authority, and the obligation to perform compulsory labor.

Feudal lords were transformed into a new, modern nobility. They became closely involved in the management of their lands and their labor supply. Most serfs in eastern Europe were obligated to work three days per week on the demesne, leaving them only three days a week to toil for their family. In Mecklenburg, Upper Silesia, and Pomerania, however, serfs were forced in summer to work five or six days for the lord. Recent scholarship has suggested that land in many places was abundant and that many free peasants had substantial amounts of free time on their hands. When they became serfs, this argument contends, they were forced to work much harder, but their material circumstances were not necessarily diminished.

In Poland, the nobility accomplished its goal of enserfing the peasantry by usurping the authority of the crown. In Brandenburg-Prussia and Russia, serfdom was associated with the process of state-building and the rise of absolutism. In the former, the Junker lords ceded political power to the state in exchange for substantially increased authority over their serfs. In Russia, the state lacked the money needed to maintain an armed force capable of defending the realm and a civil bureaucracy able to assert political control. The early Russian state established its authority by compelling the land-owning nobility to serve it. These nobles were rewarded with land, and the peasant population became their serfs to labor on the new estates.

Throughout eastern Europe lords became state

agents, collecting taxes, levying recruits, and administering justice. Often peasants had no right to appeal manorial decisions to state authorities. Until the end of the eighteenth century, most states did little or nothing to interfere in relations between lords and their serfs. In Russia, serfs could be beaten, flogged, or exiled to Siberia; on occasion they were sold apart from their families. Although serf resistance, both active and passive, placed limits on manorial authority, the social conditions of serf life at times resembled New World slavery.

Nevertheless, even at its harshest, serfdom entailed security. Above all, serfdom for most meant freedom from being landless, a vital aspect of life in an economy in which land remained the key productive asset. Obligations, even if heavy, rarely changed abruptly, providing an economic stability many free peasants in western Europe would have envied. Equally, serfs had a powerful patron with a direct interest in their ability to labor and survive and often willing to aid in times of crisis.

It was growing state power that marked the end of serfdom in eastern Europe, and emancipation came primarily from above. Emancipating serfs allowed states and their professional bureaucracies to extend their power by becoming less dependent on the nobility. It was also widely thought that freedom would decrease the economic inefficiencies often associated with servile labor. It allowed for greater peasant mobility in a society becoming more urban and industrial. The state, and often the emancipated peasantry, became wealthier. Ruler and ruled were bound by a greater sense of loyalty to each other. With the emancipation of Russian serfs in 1861, serfdom essentially came to an end in Europe.

[See also Europe; Historiography, article on Medieval European and Mediterranean Slavery; Mediterranean; Russia; and Slave Trade, article on Medieval Europe.]

BIBLIOGRAPHY

Blum, Jerome. *The End of the Old Order in Rural Europe.* Princeton: Princeton University Press, 1978.

Bonnassie, Pierre. *From Slavery to Feudalism in South-Western Europe.* Translated by Jean Birrell. Cambridge: Cambridge University Press, 1991.

Duby, Georges. *Rural Economy and Country Life in the Medieval West.* Translated by Cynthia Postan. Columbia: University of South Carolina Press, 1968.

Hilton, Rodney. *Class Conflict and the Crisis of Feudalism: Essays in Medieval Social History.* London: Hambledon Press, 1985.

Postan, M. M., and H. J. Habakkuk, eds. *The Cambridge Economic History of Europe,* vol. 1, *The Agrarian Life of the Middle Ages.* 2d ed. Cambridge: Cambridge University Press, 1971.

—STEVEN L. HOCH

SLAVE CULTURE. Slaves came to the Americas from a great variety of African backgrounds. Certain regions predominated, however, and particular ethnic, linguistic, and cultural forces were thus more apparent than others among the slaves. However, the development of slave culture in the Americas derived from much more than this heterogeneous African background. Slaves fashioned a complex cultural life based on myriad elements, including local topography, the nature of work, the languages and cultures of their white owners, and, in places, the still poorly understood relationship with local Indian peoples.

Africans were shipped into the slave colonies as individuals and not in family groups. Most landed sick and near-naked, having endured abduction from their homes and the unspeakable torment of the Atlantic crossing. While we can describe the African captives' material and physical wretchedness, we can only guess at their state of mind. Over the long history of the Atlantic slave trade, the great majority of imported Africans were destined (initially, at least) for the sugar fields. A very high proportion of new arrivals died within a few years of landing. Nevertheless, the survivors and their descendants made possible the agricultural and economic transformation of large tracts of the Americas. Indeed, until the late eighteenth century the African, not the European, was the typical immigrant into British colonial America. From such miserable and unpromising beginnings there emerged a varied and vibrant slave culture, shaped from the memories and experiences of Africa, mediated by the experience of the Atlantic crossing, and blended with life in the slave quarters of the differing slave colonies.

Work formed the crude ingredient from which all slaves had to fashion their lives. It dominated their existence, though rarely so completely that they had no time to fashion an independent cultural life. Much depended on the nature of work: the crop, the size and location of the slave-based economic unit, and the ratio of black to white were added to the crucible from which slave culture emerged. Not surprisingly, there were enormous variations, not least because slave work itself varied greatly by region and economic activity. What was true of Caribbean sugar slaves, working in large gangs, was not always the case for the smaller-scale Chesapeake tobacco plantations, nor for domestic or urban slaves. The pace, rhythm, and tone of work, and general social life as well, differed greatly for each of those groups, yet it is possible to make some useful generalizations.

Family became the bedrock on which slave cultural life was built. Although this notion was long denied by influential commentators, recent scholarship has focused on the importance of slave families. Family structure differed across time and among different societies. Throughout the Americas in the early days of settlement, the predominance of male slaves, working alongside whites and Indians in harsh frontier conditions, militated against settled family life. That changed with the stabilization of local economic life, notably the establishment of slave-based monoculture in sugar, tobacco, rice, and later cotton. These staples became major economic enterprises and required a network of slave skills and energies simply to function. All required transport slaves on land and water, craftsmen, laborers to handle production, and skilled men and women to provide services for resident white people and visitors.

This mosaic of slave-based economic activities was the context from which slave communities emerged. While Africans imported their own ideas about community and family from their specific home regions, they also had to adapt to the peculiarities of local life. Europeans tended to belittle slave families, not least because those family structures often did not resemble families as Europeans recognized them. It seems clear enough now, however, that the slave family became central to slave life. From that foundation there emerged a broadly based slave culture of beliefs, social organization, and private and communal values, which enabled slaves to cope with the rigors of their life. It is no accident that in the later years of slavery, the breakup of slave families by sale or relocation was perhaps the most bitterly contested aspect of slavery, disliked by sympathetic outsiders and hated by the slaves themselves. Those who doubt the importance of slave family life need only listen to the anguished voices of slaves forcibly separated from family and loved ones.

Religion too lay at the heart of slave culture. Many whites were initially uneasy about sharing their Christian faith with slaves. After all, one justification for bondage was African heathenism. Such objections became more overtly political, notably where sugar predominated. Christianity, it was feared, might offer slaves a creed and an organization that could be used against slavery itself. West Indian planters were especially resistant to the idea of Christian slaves, even though the stiffest and most obdurate resistance, until the very last years of slavery, came from unacculturated Africans. Sugar-planters did not like slave churches, black preachers, or slaves voicing biblical ideals and images. Elsewhere, notably in North America, black Christianity emerged and thrived within local slave systems without ever posing the fundamentally disruptive threat feared by planters in the West Indies, where the ratio of blacks to whites was much higher.

Slave religion, however, was not solely Christian. Africans brought their own beliefs into the Americas. In the practice of private or communal

African customs, whites saw evidence of all they feared about African-based slave life. Customs like *obeah* (a type of sorcery of African origin) were most strikingly evident in regions where the Atlantic slave trade continued to pour new Africans into the slave quarters; yet even long after direct links with Africa had been severed, the residual echoes of African beliefs continued to surface and worry the slave owners. More common than this stark polarity of African versus Christian cultures was the blending of the different traditions, the transfusion of European Christianity into a belief system that was often African in essence. Where Africans predominated, local slave religions seemed more African than European even when nominally Christian. In the English-speaking Americas Christianity came to dominate most slave quarters, and it eventually it provided the ethical framework for the changing culture of slave life in general.

The Bible became a centerpiece in many slave homes. Similarly, the Sabbath was a special day of rest, important for people designated solely for labor. The christianization of slave life, however, often incorporated older African beliefs and practices. Slave Christianity lived comfortably (in the slave mind, if not always in the white) with a host of practices and attitudes carried over from older African systems. Medical customs, the casting of spells, the designation of local healers, and the acceptance of distinctive spiritual forces all seemed to sit comfortably with the emergence of black Christianity. The whites who actively promoted black Christianity hoped that it would lull the restless slaves and soothe them into an accepting mood. The evidence for this is mixed. In the British West Indies the most savage slave rebellions (in the early nineteenth century) erupted among slaves suffused with Christianity. For them, Christian vernacular, imagery, promise, and reality all spoke to more urgent demands. More than that, black preachers had it within their power to galvanize their flocks, persuading them to take matters into their own hands. Christian slaves were not always

prepared to wait in the hope of salvation in the hereafter.

African religious beliefs ("superstitions" in the minds of many whites) were only one element of a broadly based African cultural infusion into the Americas. Africans arrived with few material possessions but quickly shaped a meaningful material and social world from memories of their earlier lives and from the resources of life in the Americas. It is much easier to describe the material artifacts of slave culture—the objects that were basic to their domestic and social lives—than it is to tease out the less visible, less concrete aspects of cultural existence. Nonetheless, there is a wealth of material that permits the historian to explore the subtleties of slave culture. Slave narratives and the writings of contemporary whites (even when hostile) provide insight into the world the slaves made for themselves.

The attachment to family and other loved ones was a recurring theme of slave experience. The naming process, marriages, escape, grieving, affection for different branches of the family, and other aspects of slave life form a skein of slave family sensibility. It was from within the family that successive generations of slaves were reared to face the hostile and dangerous world of slavery. Slave parents, elders, siblings, and others inculcated the lessons vital if the young slave were to thrive, or indeed survive, in a world filled with practical and ethical ambiguities. It was important from the earliest days to learn what could and could not be done, in front of whites or behind their backs. Slave-owners taught their own lessons, and the young quickly learned to appreciate the dangers, potential brutalities, and violations that lay at the heart of slavery. A slave culture emerged that was based on clear moral and practical precepts, but these precepts generally bemused slave-owners because they seemed so contradictory. Lying and theft, duplicity, untrustworthiness, and laziness were all characterizations leveled at slaves by outsiders. Masters puzzled over their slaves' apparent addiction to social values that seemed to fly in the teeth of white cultural norms. Slave life evolved in step with cultural norms that, though confusing to the slaveowners, were practical and sensible for the slaves themselves.

It was important, for example, to learn how to accommodate to the peculiarities of slave life. Africans and local-born slaves were made aware of the practical dangers they confronted. Capricious blows, persistent violence, and sexual violations formed a background to slave life that young slaves had to learn to deal with. The strategems and codes of slave life evolved in large measure to cope with these practical problems. They were at once a shield against life's ubiquitous threats and a code of behavior that, however unattractive to outsiders, was perfectly attuned to slave needs. In time, precautionary tales became the warp and weft of slave culture, transmitted at a mother's knee and through a rich folk culture of narratives, songs, and memory that characterized slave communities throughout the Americas. Much of that oral culture is familiar today in the tales, rhymes, songs, and folk characters that have become part of a world far removed from the slave system. They remain important historical features, offering a guide to a cultural environment determined by physical violence and the threat of social dislocation. For children especially, it was a confusing world. Loyalties to family were often challenged by more immediate loyalties to local whites. It was important for adults to rear their young in the art of allocating those loyalties, teaching them how (or how far) to accept the unpalatable and how to make the appropriate responses. It was a precarious balancing act that could go wrong, and often did.

Slave culture, then, was anchored in the family and the local slave communitiy. Those communities varied enormously, from large slave villages often described as "African" to small gatherings of homes near the master's home. The closer the physical proximity to local whites, the more directly slave culture was affected by prevailing white values in spheres from religion to child-rearing; yet however close the physical relationship (even when much of the working day was spent under the same roof as the white family), slave culture was determined by a need to keep slavery at arm's length. Despite the frequent view that there were only two alternatives, resistance or accommodation, slave culture embraced a complexity of strategies designed to make slavery more tolerable (though never acceptable). Slaves resisted in whatever form seemed appropriate, though sometimes an outraged slave, provoked beyond endurance, burst into spontaneous defiance. It was again part of slave culture to teach the limits, to persuade slaves of what was possible and what was unacceptable. This was a form of socialization to an institution that was so distorted as to defy simple explanation. On the whole, slaves knew how far they could go and what were the best tactics. These ranged from overt acts of resistance such as violence, rebellion, or escape, to covert foot-dragging, which might merely perplex the owner but please the slave.

Violent slave resistance was feared by slave owners everywhere. When it erupted, it could be volcanic in its destructiveness, as in Haiti, Jamaica, or Brazil. Such outbursts, however, were unusual. Slave society was preserved by a range of laws that prescribed terrible punishments for resistant slaves. Slaves everywhere understood what awaited them if they ventured down the road to violence. Gruesome reminders in the form of dead and mutilated slaves merely added detail to lessons all slaves learned at their mothers' knees: slave violence, even if only hinted, begat white violence on a terrifying scale. Slaves were not so much taught to be docile as to be prudent. Slave culture told them from their earliest years what was in their own best interests, and in the interests of other slaves. Here was the essential communalism of slave life: they needed one another and needed to respect one another to survive and to make the best of a hostile world. Their loyalties were not to those who demanded the most obvious, overt displays, their white owners, but to those whose communal support secured their wellbeing: their family and the local slave community.

The many slaves who ran away could often rely on fellow slaves for material comfort and assistance in their trek to distant loved ones or to freedom. Slaves provided shelter, assistance, and food, at great risk to themselves, for transient fugitive slaves. There was a network of slaves in many slave societies that provided essential help for runaways.

From the huddle of buildings housing the slaves there emerged a local community. It was the basis of social virtues and foibles, as found in most communities; but slave communities were different in that they formed a world within a world. They offered a society that kept the outside world of slavery at bay as much as possible. They provided reprieve from slave life when work was done. In the evenings, on weekends (especially on the Sabbath), and on holidays, the community came into its own. It has been tempting for historians to describe slave communities in terms of their more spectacular outbursts of collective pleasures, the communal religious celebrations and the raucous drinking and dancing parties that were common throughout slave communities in the Americas. However, the slave family and community also need to be recalled for inculcating more mundane features of slave life, teaching cooking and childcare, nursing the young, sick, and old, and providing a forum for the rituals of courtship, marriage, and other events of the family life cycle.

In a way, the family, at the heart of the slave community, was the crucible for the evolution of all the personal and social characteristics of slave life. Whatever planters and slave-owners might try to do, however they might seek to steer their human possessions, the key to the understanding of slave life was slave community. Within it lay another crucial ingredient in slave culture: the range of independent social and economic actvities that enriched material life and enhanced slave cultural activity.

In and around the home, in the yards and the communal spaces, from the plots and gardens, there emerged a material culture of slavery that surprised visitors by its diversity and apparent bounty. Most slaves were granted some time free from work, providing the opportunity to improve their material standard of living and to enhance cultural life in many ways. Plots and gardens, animals and fowl, all yielded food and goods for barter or sale. Skills in clothes-making, metalworking, woodworking, cooking, drawing, instrument-making, and music were put to profitable use. Slaves bought and sold goods at the nearest town markets or via traveling hawkers and peddlers, in return acquiring products they needed or desired. They also accumulated money. There was an independent slave economy thriving on slave effort and enterprise. The energy devoted to this economy contradicts the allegations of laziness common to white comments on slave life everywhere. The enhancement of material well-being that gradually took place in slave communities throughout the Americas was due in large part to their own enterprise.

Slaves' material culture was not only important in the acquisition of consumer goods. Such items made domestic life more tolerable and acceptable, the results of the slaves' spare-time activities also enriched their social lives. The clothing reserved for special days or for Sundays, the food set aside for feast days, the accouterments for ritual communal displays, the money saved for essentials, luxuries, or even self-purchase, the special gifts for loved ones, and the musical instruments bought or crafted, created a web of cultural activities and aspirations that characterized slave life across the hemisphere.

[See also Anti-Slavery Literature, article on African-American Perspectives; Caribbean Slavery; Maroons; Psychology; Religion; Revolts; Slave Trade, article on Trans-Atlantic Trade; and United States, article on The South.]

BIBLIOGRAPHY

Genovese, Eugene D. Roll, Jordan, Roll: The World the Slaves Made. New York: Pantheon, 1974.

Palmié, Stephan, ed. *Slave Cultures and the Cultures of Slavery.* Knoxville: University of Tennessee Press, 1995.

Sobel, Mechal. *The World They Made Together: Black and White Values in Eighteenth-Century Virginia.* Princeton: Princeton University Press, 1987.

Stuckey, Sterling. *Slave Culture: Nationalist Theory and the Foundation of Black America.* New York and Oxford: Oxford University Press, 1987.

Thornton, John. *Africa and Africans in the Making of the Atlantic World, 1400–1680.* New York: Cambridge University Press, 1992.

—JAMES WALVIN

SLAVE TRADE. [*This entry comprises seven articles that trace the principles and practices associated with slaving in major world regions and historical periods and that consider the flow and abolition of the trade in Europe and the Americas:*

> Asia and Oceania
> Medieval Europe
> Trans-Saharan Trade
> Trans-Atlantic Trade
> Brazil and the United States
> Volume of Trade
> Suppression of Trade

For discussion of the manner in which artists and illustrators have depicted the slave trade, see Art and Illustration.]

Asia and Oceania

The slave trade in Asia involved the enslavement of many different peoples and their shipment to diverse places. Slave-trading routes criss-crossed the Indian Ocean: Africans were shipped to the Persian Gulf, India, the Mascarene Islands (Mauritius and Réunion) just east of Madagascar, and the Dutch East Indies (modern-day Indonesia); Indians were shipped to the Mascarene Islands, the Dutch East Indies, and the Cape of Good Hope (the southwestern region of modern-day South Africa); and Indonesians were shipped to India, the Mascarene Islands, and the Cape of Good Hope. Routes also crossed the South China Sea and other waters of Southeast Asia as slaves were shipped from less powerful societies in the region to stronger ones. East Asian countries such as China and Korea, however, did not participate in this slave trade; their recruitment of slaves was local and they did not export them.

Asian slaves were used in a wide variety of urban and agricultural jobs. Few worked on European-owned farms and plantations, which were confined to the sugar-cane plantations of the Mascarene Islands, the vineyards and wheat farms of the Cape of Good Hope, and the nutmeg plantations of the Banda Islands in eastern Indonesia. The slave trade in Asia preceded European penetration of the region, and although Europeans actively participated in this trade in the seventeenth and eighteenth centuries, it was largely through European intervention in the nineteenth century that it was eventually abolished.

Islamic Slave Trade. For many centuries slaves had been shipped out of East Africa by Muslims to Asian and other destinations. With the nineteenth-century expansion of date-planting and pearl-fishing in the Persian Gulf and the Arabian coast of the Red Sea, this Islamic slave trade out of East Africa peaked: about half a million slaves were shipped across the Red Sea and Gulf of Aden, while about three hundred thousand were shipped from the Swahili Coast (a region extending from northern Mozambique and Madagascar in the south to southeastern Somalia in the north, including offshore islands, notably Zanzibar) to Asian destinations during the nineteenth century. The main destinations were the Persian Gulf, Yemen, and Hejaz (in modern-day Saudi Arabia), though transshipments were made to other destinations, including India. The end of the Islamic slave trade from East Africa was a protracted affair, with European colonization of East Africa in the late nineteenth century providing the major curb.

Mascarene Islands and Cape of Good Hope. Although the slave trade to the Mascarene Islands accompanied the initial Dutch settlement in the seventeenth century, its main impetus came during the 1730s, when the French established sugar-cane plantations. Between 1610 and 1810, about 160,000 slaves were sent to the islands. Of these 45 percent were from Madagascar, 40 percent from mainland East Africa, 2 percent from West Africa, and 13 percent from India. Despite the British prohibition of the slave trade in 1808 and British attempts to suppress it, it persisted until slavery was abolished in Mauritius in 1835 and Réunion in 1848. More than 130,000 slaves were shipped to the Mascarene Islands after 1808; the main source of illegal shipments was mainland East Africa, but shipments were also made from Madagascar and from Indonesia. In contrast to the Mascarene Islands, the British prohibition of the slave trade was generally effective elsewhere, as in the case of the Cape of Good Hope. Before prohibition, from 1652 to 1808, about 63,000 slaves were shipped to the Cape, roughly evenly divided between Madagascar, mainland Africa, India, and Indonesia.

India. Whereas estimates have been made of the export of Indian slaves to the Mascarene Islands and the Cape of Good Hope, they have not been made of the export of Indian slaves to Burma, Sri Lanka, and Indonesia, nor of India's imports of slaves from Africa, Nepal, and Indonesia. Great Britain's first attempt to end this slave trade was its prohibition of the export of slaves from Bengal in 1789, extended to Bombay and Madras in the 1790s. The import of slaves was prohibited in Bengal in 1811, and in Bombay and Madras in 1813. The prohibition of slave imports was extended to Nepalese slaves in 1833. Legal prohibitions combined with naval patrols curbed the import and export of slaves, but the effective ending of the slave trade came only with the abolition of slavery as a legal institution in 1843 and the prohibition of slave-ownership in 1860.

Southeast Asia. In the sixteenth and seventeenth centuries, the urban populations of indigenous maritime trading cities of Southeast Asia—Melaka and Patani in Malaysia, Aceh in Sumatra, Banten in Java, and Makasar in Sulawesi—were largely comprised of imported slaves. Similarly, the population of the Dutch city of Batavia (modern-day Jakarta) in Java had a slave majority in the seventeeth century and the first half of the eighteenth. In the seventeenth century the Dutch imported slaves from India, Sri Lanka, Arkan (a kingdom on the eastern shore of the Bay of Bengal, bordering Bengal and Burma), and Madagascar (for gold-mining in Sumatra). In the eighteenth century they turned to the islands of the Indonesian archipelago (other than Java) for their supply. Between 1620 and 1830, about one hundred thousand slaves were shipped from Bali, primarily to Batavia, while between 1660 and 1810, more than one hundred thousand slaves were shipped from southern Sulawesi. A slave register compiled by Dutch authorities for tax purposes in 1816 shows the place of origin of Batavia's slave population. Of the 12,480 slaves listed, 16 percent were born in Batavia, 43 percent were from Sulawesi, 20 percent from Bali, 13 percent from the Lesser Sunda Islands of eastern Indonesia (including Timor), and 8 percent from other places (including New Guinea). The virtual absence in the register of slaves born in Java outside Batavia accords with a ruling of the Dutch in the seventeenth century that Javanese were not to be enslaved.

The Dutch tapped into established slave-trading networks of Southeast Asia in which slaves were taken from stateless hill peoples—the Orang Asli of Malaya, the Batak of Sumatra, the Toraja of Sulawesi, and various Dayak groups of Borneo—and other relatively defenseless groups. A number of states rose and prospered primarily on the traffic in slaves. These included Aru in Sumatra, Onin in New Guinea, Buton in Sulawesi, Tidor in the Melakas, and Sulu located between Borneo and the Philippines. Slave-raiders from the Sulu Sultanate ranged over the waters of Southeast Asia, the South China Sea, and even the Bay of Bengal, procuring between two and three hundred thousand slaves in the period from 1770 to 1870. Many of their captives later manned the raiding vessels that enslaved others.

The slave trade in Southeast Asia was gradually brought to an end by pressure from the European colonial powers and by European colonization. Beginning in the 1860s, Spanish, English, and Dutch steam gunboats limited the freedom of Sulu raiders. In 1875 the Spanish occupied Jolo, the Sulu capital. Slave-raiding persisted, however, until its annexation by the United States in 1898. Earlier, in 1813, during the temporary British occupation of Java, the import of slaves had been abolished, and in 1818 the Dutch prohibited the slave trade in the rest of Dutch-occupied Indonesia. As the Dutch extended their control to the rest of Indonesia in following decades, so was the prohibition of the slave trade extended. In Malaysia, Burma, and Cambodia, abolition of the slave trade also came with effective European colonization.

Oceania. Before European penetration of Oceania (the islands of the Pacific Ocean, including Australia and New Zealand), warfare and raiding led to the capture of slaves in both Melanesia and Polynesia, and such slaving persisted into the nineteenth century. Whereas New Guinea participated in the slave trade in Southeast Asia, slaving elsewhere in the Pacific region was on a more local scale. In the Solomon Islands, for example, slaves could be acquired through warfare or purchase from neighboring peoples; war captives and offenders against the norms of a society provided the supply of slaves for sale. A well-documented instance of how slavery was furthered by warfare is the Musket Wars of the 1820s in New Zealand. In these intertribal conflicts, Maoris who had acquired muskets from Europeans took slaves as a spoil of war. European colonial expansion in Oceania curbed and eventually ended the slave trade in this region.

Following European penetration of Oceania in the nineteenth century came the establishment of sugar cane, cotton, and copra plantations in Queensland (Australia), Fiji, New Guinea, Samoa, Vanuatu, the Solomon Islands, Hawaii, and Tahiti; gold mines in New Guinea; nickel mines in New Caledonia; and, in the twentieth century, phosphate mines in Nauru and Ocean Island. These enterprises used migrant labor recruited through indenture contracts from Asia and various Pacific Islands in what contemporaries and historians have called the Pacific labor trade. Humanitarian groups in Great Britain and Australia accused recruiters of using coercive practices, including kidnapping, to procure these migrant workers, resulting in a thinly disguised slave trade in the Pacific region. The most notorious episode of kidnapping was the forced removal of more than three thousand five hundred Pacific Islanders, mainly from Easter Island and the Cook Islands, for work in Peru in 1862 and 1863. In the following two decades, there were also episodes of kidnapping in the recruitment of Pacific Islanders from Vanuatu and the Solomon Islands for work in Queensland and Fiji, but labor recruitment eventually settled down to a normal, albeit often dangerous for recruiters, business relationship based on the voluntary decisions of recruits and their communities.

Humanitarian groups also accused European employers of Aboriginal workers on pastoral stations in Australia of using coercive practices, equating such practices with slavery. There was, however, no organized slave trade in Aboriginal workers in Australia. They did not become property that could be bought and sold, and they were not bonded for life. The short-term nature of indentured labor contracts in the Pacific labor trade, as well as the freedom of Aboriginal workers to leave their place of employment in Australia, makes it difficult to equate these labor arrangements with slavery.

Further Research. In comparison with the literature on the trans-Atlantic slave trade, a number of topics in the slave trade in Asia and Oceania remain under-researched. Studies are needed on the organization of the various segments of the slave trade as a business, with information needed on how it was financed, on buying and selling prices of slaves, and profits being earned. Studies are also needed on the demography of the slave trade: on sex ratios, the age distributions of the slaves, and the mortality suffered by slaves in transit. Furthermore, studies are needed on the epidemiological consequences of slave migration: slaves may have encountered new diseases to which they had little or no immunity as they moved from their childhood disease environments to new ones; they may have also carried diseases with them that were new and dangerous to the inhabitants of slave-receiving regions.

[*See also* Abolition and Anti-Slavery, *article on* India; Asia, *article on* South Asia; Indentured Servitude; *and* Oceania.]

BIBLIOGRAPHY

Clarence-Smith, William Gervase, ed. *The Economics of the Indian Ocean Slave Trade in the Nineteenth Century.* London: Frank Cass, 1989.

Klein, Martin A., ed. *Breaking the Chains: Slavery, Bondage, and Emancipation in Modern Africa and Asia.* Madison: University of Wisconsin Press, 1993.

Reid, Anthony, ed. *Slavery, Bondage and Dependency in Southeast Asia.* St. Lucia: University of Queensland Press, 1983.

Warren, J.F. *The Sulu Zone, 1768–1898: The Dynamics of External Trade, Slavery and Ethnicity in the Transformation of a Southeast Asian Maritime State.* Singapore: Singapore University Press, 1981.

Watson, James L., ed. *Asian and African Systems of Slavery.* Oxford: Basil Blackwell, 1980.

—RALPH SHLOMOWITZ

Medieval Europe

The medieval slave trade in Europe may be divided into two periods. The sale and purchase of slaves for domestic and agricultural work was common in the early period, from the end of the Roman Empire to around the year 1000. From 1000 to the early modern period, trade was restricted primarily to the Mediterranean and was on a smaller scale, with slaves primarily bought for domestic service.

Distinguishing early medieval slaves from serfs is not always easy, but the sale of humans is an acid test of slavery. Early medieval charters and wills might distinguish between "slaves" (*servi, mancipia,* or *ancillae*) who were movable wealth and might be sold independently, and those who were "housed" (*casati*) and stayed with the estate.

Evidence for slave-trading is surprisingly varied. Early medieval saints' lives abound in stories of saints purchasing slaves to set them free, thus demonstrating their humanity and piety. Letters written by such famous men as Alcuin and Pope Gregory the Great mention the purchase of slaves. An English penitential grappled with marital complications caused by partners captured or sold off as slaves. A bawdy eleventh-century satire was written about a poet and his wife who were captured and repeatedly sold. Church councils, such as one held at Clichy in 626 or 627, threatened excommunication to Christians who sold their slaves to Jews or pagans. Early medieval law codes mention the sale of slaves, often as part of a list of other commodities, even under the title "beasts." Charlemagne prohibited the sale of swords, warhorses, and slaves abroad to potential enemies of the state. Most directly, there are documents called formularies, which were example texts for drawing up legal documents. A seventh-century formulary from the French city of Angers has a model for the sale of a domestic slave (*vernaculus*), "to possess, gift, sell, or exchange." Another, called the Marculf Formulary, provides an example of a sales document in which the seller guarantees that the slave is "no thief, no fugitive, no epileptic, but is healthy of body and mind." Finally, there are import-tax documents, such as the Tonlieu of Raffelstätten (906), requiring a toll on slaves "as was always custom." A Lombard king of Pavia levied a tax of one-tenth the value on horses, slaves (male and female), textiles, tin, and swords entering his Italian kingdom around the year 900.

It is often assumed that the sale of humans as chattels was carried out predominantly by merchants engaged in large-scale and long-distance trade, traditionally by Jews and Syrians or Frisians and Vikings. Only occasionally, however, do we know an individual's nationality or name, such as the Jewish merchant Basilus mentioned by Gregory the Great, or the Christian merchant Christopher mentioned by Gregory of Tours. The Christian Frank Samo, who became king of the Wends, a Slavic tribe, in the seventh century, is thought to have been leading a private army in search of captives to sell as slaves. That many slaves derived from conquered political peripheries of Europe is seen in the very word *slave*, from *Slav*, or in the Anglo-Saxon equivalent *wealh* from "foreign" or "Welsh." References to the sale of Christian slaves abroad or to "pagans" are assumed to mean the Mediterranean traffic, especially to the Arab world, Spain, and North Africa. In the first half of the tenth century, the Spanish city of Córdoba is calculated to have had fourteen thousand slaves. Liutprand of Cremona called the French city of Verdun a veritable "manufacturing center" of eunuchs, who were almost certainly destined for the Islamic market.

Although Archbishop Wulfstan thought the lines of young men and women in chains bound for sale at Bristol would make one weep, perhaps most of the buying and selling of humans was done on a small scale. At the most personal level, the formulary from Angers has a model text for a convicted thief who sells himself into slavery to raise money to pay his fine. Pope Hadrian I wrote to Charlemagne that some Lombard families had "sold" themselves to Byzantine merchants to avoid dying in a famine. Incidental tales, like the sale of Leo told by Gregory of Tours in his *Histories of the Franks*, often mention private individuals' selling single slaves.

There were certainly great centers for the early medieval European slave trade, such as Marseille and Bristol, but selling was more widely spread than is generally recognized. For instance, positive evidence exists for slave-trading in probably every episcopal city in France. At a church council held in Lyon in 583, bishops throughout Gaul were told to keep all bills of sale, with price and date recorded, of the captive slaves they bought. The eleventh-century *Domesday Book* unusually records tolls from the sale of slaves in the small English town of Lewes.

Quantifying the early medieval slave trade is al-

most impossible. In general terms, the trade greatly diminished between the years 500 and 1000. Textual references become fewer and fewer. Unlike seventh-century formularies, there is no model document for the sale of slaves in the ninth-century formulary from the French city Sens. Similarly, the holy act of buying and freeing captive slaves disappears as a topos from saints' lives as the millennium approached. The decline in medieval slave-trading is sometimes explained as due to a drying-up of sources of new slaves, but there was hardly any measurable decline in the frequency or duration of wars in the Middle Ages, and much of the slave population was self-perpetuating or locally derived.

The church was active in condemning the sale of Christians to Jews and pagans. Wulfstan opposed the sale of slaves abroad, but not until 1102 did a church council at Westminster take the radical step of forbidding the sale of slaves altogether. However, by the twelfth century the traffic of slaves had all but ended in temperate western Europe. Never abolitionist, the church probably had a much larger effect in curbing the slave trade by insisting on the sanctity of marriage, thus inadvertently undermining slavery: slave families were kept together, making sales more cumbersome and denying masters one of their greatest coercive powers—the threat of separation. The decline in the slave trade throughout much of Europe in the central Middle Ages was more likely the result of a decline in slavery generally, rather than its cause, as is sometimes supposed.

The demand for slaves in the Muslim world continued and was met through the central Middle Ages largely by the trans-Saharan trade, although for many centuries the Iberian Peninsula saw Muslim raids on Christian territories, aimed at capturing new slaves. The slave trade in the later medieval Christian Mediterranean world was largely directed at supplying an urban demand for domestic servants, especially females. In 1363 Florence allowed unlimited importation of slaves provided they were not Christian, and later medieval European trade in slaves had a marked "racial" aspect. Barcelona, Genoa, and Venice played a major role in the sale above all of "Muslims," but also "blacks," "Bulgars," and "Tartars," with a shift in the sources of slaves from the western Mediterranean to the east through time.

[*See also* Europe; Historiography, *article on* Medieval European and Mediterranean Slavery; Mediterranean; *and* Serfdom.]

BIBLIOGRAPHY

Holm, P. "The Slave Trade of Dublin, Ninth to Twelfth Centuries." *Peritia: Journal of the Medieval Academy of Ireland* 5 (1986): 317–345.

Pelteret, David A. E. "Slave Raiding and Slave Trading in Early England." *Anglo-Saxon England* 9 (1980): 99–114.

Samson, Ross. "The End of Medieval Slavery." In *The Work of Work: Servitude, Slavery, and Labor in Medieval England*, edited by Allen J. Frantzen and Douglas Moffat, pp. 95–124. Glasgow: Cruithne Press, 1994.

Verlinden, Charles. *Wo, wann und warum gab es einen Grosshandel mit Sklaven während des Mittelalters?* Cologne, 1970.

Verlinden, Charles. *L'esclave dans l'Europe médiévale*. 2 vols., Bruges: De Tempel, 1955, 1977.

—ROSS SAMSON

Trans-Saharan Trade

Slaves were brought across and settled in the desert regions of northern Africa for almost twelve centuries, beginning with the Islamic conquests of the eighth century and ending only in the early twentieth century. This system of slavery has attracted more than its share of debate because it touches on questions of European attitudes toward Islam, the unity of the African continent, and the ability of modern scholars to measure and evaluate developments for which we have limited and often far from "objective" records.

What we know for sure about the Saharan slave trade is that its victims were black-skinned inhabitants of the regions south of the great African desert, and that most of them were settled in the Arab-speaking countries of Mediterranean Africa (Morocco, Algeria, Tunisia, Libya, and Egypt).

Many of these slaves did, however, remain within the desert. Others, especially those entering Libya, were sold on to ships that took them to the Islamic lands in the eastern Mediterranean, and even, around the fourteenth and fifteenth centuries, north into Italy and other European territories.

Slaves were brought across the desert in camel caravans organized by the Berber and Arabic-speaking peoples of North Africa and the Sahara. For the most part, the slaves themselves had to transport themselves on foot, and the evidence suggests that many of them perished along the way. Descriptions of the trade as well as the price data from various markets indicate that the majority of this human cargo consisted of women, sought for domestic labor and concubinage. However, males were also recruited for rural agricultural and mine labor (including oases and salt mines within the Sahara), construction, street-cleaning, and porterage in North African cities, and especially for military service under various North African and Egyptian regimes that relied on servile black troops.

We have records of slaves and the slave trade in the Sahara from quite early Islamic times. The precise routes varied over time and were often quite complex, depending on shifting physical conditions of the desert, political alliances with local Berber communities, and integration of long-distance trade with local movements of camels for commercial and pasturage purposes. The demand for slaves varied with the fortunes and specific needs of North African and Saharan societies, but there appears to have been a major increase during the eighteenth and nineteenth centuries, when the entire region from the Mediterranean to the West African Sudan was experiencing economic growth. During this same period, the Islamic world was cut off from alternative sources for slaves in the Caucasus by the expansion of the Russian Empire. On the supply side, the emergence in the western and central Sudan of militant Islamic regimes that waged *jihād*s against their pagan neighbors appears to have made more slaves available for the Saharan markets.

A consistent factor in creating demand for all categories of slaves in North Africa and the Middle East was the need to replace existing servile populations. Forced immigrants from tropical Africa seemed particularly susceptible to the diseases of the Mediterranean zone, had remarkably few children while in captivity there, and were much more frequently manumitted in Muslim societies than in the European plantation colonies of the New World.

The Atlantic trade, when first undertaken by the Portuguese in the fifteenth century, drew on slaves who would otherwise have been transported across the Sahara. In the long run, however, the two trades seem to have complemented each other, in part because European buyers had a strong preference for male over female slaves. More important, European overseas expansion stimulated the growth of non-European economies, thus increasing both the capacity to sell slaves and the demand for them in the receiving areas.

One of the most controversial issues surrounding the trans-Saharan slave trade is its actual size. This question has arisen in response to attempts by Philip Curtin, his followers, and his critics to calculate the scale of the Atlantic slave trade. The Saharan counts have been restricted to slaves crossing the desert or at least reaching its northern edges, because, in standard terminology, these were also being removed from sub-Saharan Africa. In any case, it is harder to count slaves within the Sahara or even to distinguish its southern edge (where most such slaves were settled) from the adjacent Sahel and Sudan.

Even if we restrict ourselves to the trans-Saharan slave trade, we can never produce statistics as precise as those for the Atlantic, because researchers of the Sahara have little access to commercial accounts, customs records, or census counts. Our best estimates are based mainly on observations by European travelers and diplomats, which are concentrated in the period after 1700. For earlier centuries we can only make projections, based on scattered numerical statements in Arabic sources and a

consideration of supply-and-demand conditions. The resulting uneven calculations suggest that something in the region of three and one-half to four million slaves crossed the Sahara throughout the twelve-century history of trade. By comparison, the Atlantic slave trade took at least ten and one-half million people out of Africa, three times as many in less than four centuries; another comparison might add the Nile Valley, Red Sea and Indian Ocean trades to the "Islamic" or "Oriental" total, which then comes to around eight million. Even if we add about 10 percent to this sum, to take into account deaths in the Sahara crossing (which appears to have been more dangerous than the notorious Atlantic Middle Passage), the final figure is still well below that of the Atlantic and spread out over a much longer time period. Nonetheless, when compared to systems other than that of the Atlantic, the Saharan slave trade remains one of the major examples of enslavement in world history.

The words *sub-Saharan*, *Islamic*, and *Oriental* indicate some of the other issues involved in studying Saharan slavery. In addition to the moral questions that frame modern views on all histories of slavery, this topic calls into question the very identity of the participants on both sides. The immediate recipients of Saharan slaves and the overwhelming majority of those who ultimately held them were non-Europeans and at least nominally Muslim; but to speak of an "Islamic" trade suggests that Islam as a religion and cultural system is somehow to blame for the abuses of slavery. Such a view was held by many of those who documented the trade while it was in progress, and it fits well into contemporary Western polemics about the problems of the Third World. In fact, it should be noted that a number of prominent Islamic scholars and political leaders of both North and West Africa publicly criticized the abuses of the Saharan trade (especially where it victimized free Muslims), even if they never argued for its abolition.

The geographical terms for this system likewise raise questions. Patrick Manning (1990) and others call all the trades out of Africa not controlled by Europeans "Oriental," but this term, besides being literally inaccurate about the spatial direction of Saharan commerce, raises the entire specter of "Orientalism" as a demeaning Western form of knowledge about the exotic and amoral "other."

One critic of Manning's terminology, the African economic historian Tiyambe Zeleza (1993), is even more concerned about the use of the Saharan slave system to draw what he sees as a "racist" line between those portions of Africa on either side of the desert. For Zeleza, slaves are just one of many items of a commercial traffic that linked North Africa and West Africa more closely than any other links between regions within the African continent. Another group of historians, members of the Saharan Studies Association, have attempted to draw attention to the great desert as a region in itself rather than merely a "sea of sand" connecting places of denser human habitation.

If we accept the notion of a more or less integrated North African–Saharan–West African precolonial world, we may then ask what was the role of slavery in shaping its cultural, political, and economic development. Slavery certainly influenced racial perceptions in this region, as indicated by disputes over the meaning of the term Ḥarāṭīn (sing. Ḥarṭānī), which may refer either to native black populations of the desert or to former slaves. The latter designation is linguistically based on a folk etymology linking its Berber root to the Arabic ḥurr ("free"), thus yielding ḥarāṭīn or "freedmen." The real source of this understanding is the social history of enslavement, which has produced an association of blackness with at least a former condition of servitude. When the seventeenth-century Moroccan Sultan Mawlāy Ismāʿīl recruited a large number of Ḥarāṭīn (along with an unknown quantity of Sudanic slaves) for his army, the resulting formation was known as ʿabd or "slaves" (officially they were ʿabd al-bukhārī, devotees of the book containing the main extra-Qurʾānic sources for Islamic law).

The source of most of the slaves entering the Sa-

hara was violent capture. However, the captors were usually not Arab or Berber warriors but rather Sudanic state elites, who sold their booty to caravan merchants. The commodity most commonly named as an item of exchange for slaves (although much of the actual trade used other media of exchange, especially Saharan salt) was a horse. One horse was always worth some multiple of slaves, because raising riding horses in the Sudan was difficult, and it was the horse (along with accompanying imports of armor and steel sword-blades) that provided Sudanic rulers with the military capacity to capture slaves. Thus, while other items of export—such as gold in medieval times and later gum, hides, ivory, ostrich feathers, or even manufactured cloth and leatherwork—may have exceeded the monetary value of slaves, Sudanic political life was strongly marked by the slave trade.

Islam may also have played some role here because slave supplies rose in the times and places associated with religious war or jihāds. However, it was the most famous of the jihād leaders, the Fulani cleric Usuman Dan Fodio of present-day northern Nigeria, who argued against contemporary practices of enslavement by his Hausa predecessors. Moreover, in the western Sudan center of present-day Mali, one of the states most involved in slaving was the Segu Empire, a regime whose rulers did not profess any serious commitment to Islam and were themselves the victims of jihād in the mid-nineteenth century. It might more plausibly be argued that the violence encouraged by slave-raiding created a climate that encouraged jihād in West Africa (long before they were common in other parts of the Islamic world), rather than that Islam had any significant role in bringing about the Saharan slave system.

At its core, Saharan slavery seems best explained in economic terms. Precisely because the Sahara provided an effective but costly link between the Mediterranean and Sudanic portions of Africa, it encouraged trade in export commodities that could bear the expenses of caravan transport. Gold served this purpose particularly well and, because it was in greater demand in the Mediterranean than slaves, it probably had greater influence on the development of trans-Saharan commerce. However, slaves could be supplied by a wider range of Sudanic trading partners and, even if not in as much demand in the Mediterranean as in the Atlantic, they could fetch a price that covered the relatively low cost of feeding them while they walked into or across the desert.

As a byproduct of this trade, slaves were also accumulated by communities within the desert or in the Sahel and Sudan to the south, where they could be used for both military and economic purposes. Thus some slaves supported the trade by serving in the armies of Sudanic raiders or provisioning desert merchants and transporters. Others, however, contributed to the intensification of local agricultural, salt, and handicraft production, thus providing alternative commodities for markets within the region and the Mediterranean.

Whether such industry would eventually have discouraged slave exports by raising the value of local labor, as argued for all of Africa by Stefano Fenoaltea, is difficult to determine. As it turned out, the Saharan trade was terminated by a combination of exogenous political and economic forces. During the second half of the nineteenth century European abolitionists gradually imposed restrictions on the Mediterranean dealers in African slaves, cutting off much if by no means all of the demand. By the early twentieth century, colonial railroads provided transport from the Sudan to the Atlantic that was less costly than caravan carriage across the desert, thus reducing the entire Saharan commercial system to very local dimensions. Colonial governments then interfered directly with slavery in the desert regions, although they never eliminated entirely the traffic in human beings, to say nothing of its social residue.

Slavery and attendant race relations are still a major issue in postcolonial Mauritania, but even by the standards of an impoverished Africa, Mauritania (lying entirely in the Sahara) is a very marginal country. Saharan slavery is thus one of the longest-lasting of the world's major servile systems, but by the end of the twentieth century, it too had largely passed into history.

[*See also* Abolition and Anti-Slavery, *article on* Africa; Africa, *articles on* West Africa, Central Africa, *and* East Africa; Demography; *and* Law, *article on* Islamic Law.]

BIBLIOGRAPHY

Austen, Ralph A. "Marginalization, Stagnation and Growth: The Trans-Saharan Caravan Trade in the Era of European Maritime Expansion, 1500–1900." In *The Rise of Merchant Empires*, edited by James D. Tracy, vol. 1. Cambridge: Cambridge University Press, 1990.

Austen, Ralph A. "The Mediterranean Slave Trade Out of Africa: A Tentative Census." *Slavery and Abolition* 13 (1992): 214–248.

Colin, G. S. "Ḥarṭānī." In *Encyclopaedia of Islam*, new ed., vol. 3, pp. 230–231. Leiden: Brill, 1966.

Fisher, Humphrey. "A Muslim William Wilberforce? The Sokoto Jihad as Anti-Slavery Crusade: An Enquiry into Historical Causes." In *De la traité à l'esclavage*, vol. 2, *XVIIIe—XIXe siècles*, edited by Serge Daget. Nantes: Centre de Recherche sur l'Histoire du Monde Atlantique, 1988.

Manning, Patrick. *Slavery and African Life: Occidental, Oriental and African Slave Trades*. Cambridge: Cambridge University Press, 1990.

McDougall, E. Ann. "Salt, Saharans and the Trans-Saharan Slave Trade." *Slavery and Abolition* 13 (1992): 61–88.

Taine-Cheikh, Catherine. "La Mauritanie en noir et blanc; petite promenade linguistique en *hassaniyya*." *Revue du Monde Musulmane et Méditerranée* 54 (1990): 95–96.

Webb, James L. A. *Desert Frontier: Ecological and Economic Change Along the Western Sahel, 1600–1850*. Madison: University of Wisconsin, 1995.

Zeleza, Paul Tiyambe. *A Modern Economic History of Africa*: vol. 1, *The Nineteenth Century*. Dakar: CODESERIA, 1993.

—RALPH A. AUSTEN

Trans-Atlantic Trade

Slavery is only one form of coerced labor, but the extreme powers of the slave-owner and the rightlessness of the slave have made it the most abhorred social status of all. Its odium is such that although in some societies slave status could be earned by or assigned to individuals born into the society, slavery was usually reserved for members of other societies, or "outsiders." This implies that forced movement of peoples is a usual accompaniment of slavery. Large-scale transportation of the unwilling certainly predates the agricultural revolution and was practiced in most regions of the world long before European expansion. Such relocation at first took the form of captives carried into servitude after raids or wars, as in early Greece and Rome. In the Americas, the Aztec Empire received slaves as tribute from subservient societies, usually those on the fringe of Aztec influence. Similarly, a traffic in slaves is likely to have existed in Africa before 1400. Organized and continuous markets drawing on distant provenance zones, however, came later.

Slave-trade routes in the Old World linked markets in the Mediterranean with provenance zones to the north and south for millennia before 1500. As European societies became more powerful, and as the Ottoman Turks interfered with the flow of slaves to Mediterranean markets from the north, the African share of all captives sold in Mediterranean markets, particularly in Islamic societies, increased. By the mid-fourteenth century the traffic in slaves flowed overwhelmingly from south to north, as states in the Middle East, North Africa, and the Iberian Peninsula drew on sub-Saharan African regions.

The trans-Atlantic slave trade constituted both an extension and a reorientation of a well-established commercial pattern. Initially, Europeans carried slaves to the Iberian Peninsula, to the Atlantic offshore islands of Madeira, the Canaries, and São Tomé, and from one part of the African coast to another. Later, they carried them to the Americas. Slaves of African origin, but almost certainly brought through Spain, were present on the Columbian voyages, but large-scale transfer of Africans awaited the leap of the sugar-plantation system from the African offshore islands to northeastern Brazil in the mid-sixteenth century.

Thereafter, the economic and geographic determinants of the traffic are clear: the slave traffic ex-panded westward from the shortest of the trans-Atlantic crossings between Brazil and West Africa beginning in the sixteenth century, to the eastern-most Caribbean islands in the seventeenth century, then to the more westerly (and distant) Greater Antilles, the North American mainland, and the Rio de la Plata in the eighteenth century. This pattern is disturbed only by large-scale arrivals in Spanish Central America in the period from 1595 to 1610, when bullion exports peaked. In the last years of the trans-Atlantic traffic, steamships built in the industrial centers of Europe carried slaves to Brazil and Cuba as cost-effectively as did their passenger-carrying counterparts in the North Atlantic. Until attempts to suppress the slave trade increased shipping costs, the transportation cost "wedge" between the prices of slaves on either side of the Atlantic tended to fall over time, implying improved efficiency in the carrying phase of the business. Nevertheless, slave prices did increase over the four and a half centuries of the trade, with those in Africa rising faster than in the Americas, at least until 1807.

The basic explanatory framework for the trans-Atlantic trade is similar to that of other trans-Atlantic migrations, and indeed of European expansion as a whole. Both the populations and the population densities of the Americas were much smaller than those of the Old World. Moreover, the aboriginal population of the Americas declined severely in the two centuries after European contact. From first contact to the twentieth century, labor—whether free or coerced—was more productive and more valuable in the New World than in the Old. As aboriginal populations declined, transportation innovations gradually lowered barriers between the Old World and the New. Europeans expanded toward eastern Europe, another area of low population densities, as well as westward in the sixteenth century. In both areas, migration was associated with forced labor.

Nevertheless, while such factors explain expansion in general terms and the trans-Atlantic population shift in particular, they cannot explain why part of the shift was voluntary and part involuntary, and much less why almost all those who chose to go the Americas were European, and why most of those who made the trans-Atlantic voyage against their will were African. At the eastern margin of European expansion, coerced labor emerged in the form of serfdom (with the serfs invariably of European origin) rather than slavery. Clearly, there were tasks that free individuals would choose to avoid unless the rewards were very high. Extended field labor on plantations, particularly those producing sugar, and in gold and silver mines, attracted few people from Europe, and those who were prepared to cross the Atlantic to perform such work usually agreed to do so for a limited time period under a regime of indentured servitude. Neither servants nor transported convicts ever faced a lifetime of servitude in the Americas, and in no case did the progeny of these migrants inherit the status of their parents.

European organizers of the trans-Atlantic traffic in people made no effort to impose slave status on the destitute, victims of war, or prisoners convicted of capital crimes in their own continent. They chose instead the relatively expensive and hazardous alternative of sending merchant ships to buy people on various parts of the African coast. Epidemiology is often cited as a factor in this decision; Africans had better protection against tropical fevers than Europeans and could expect to live longer and thus provide more labor in the subtropical Americas. Even so, while Africans and Europeans died for different reasons in the Americas, it seems unlikely that migrants from Africa outlived their European counterparts in the plantation regions of the early modern Americas. From a broad three- or four-continent perspective, the African slave trade appears rooted as much in cultural perceptions and social norms as in economic and demographic imperatives.

African as well as European social and cultural patterns were important in shaping the trade. Slaves, but not many plantations, were present in most African societies, and African conceptions of insiders and outsiders were as well developed as in any European society. The critical difference was that in the slave trade era, the conception of an insider within Africa was more likely to be limited to kin in a limited geographic area. In Europe, insider status, at least on the slavery issue, was accorded to all Europeans. In no case did an African group define the concept in terms of all peoples living in sub-Saharan Africa. "Africa" as a social construction was a European rather than an African concept. Europeans sailed to Africa to find "outsiders" and subsumed them all under the name *African*. African slave-traders also traded in outsiders. Indeed, African kinship structures evolved in part to absorb individuals and enlarge the kin group, so that some exchange in people had long existed in Africa.

Perhaps twelve million people were forcibly removed from Africa for Atlantic destinations between the mid-fourteenth century and 1867, when the last slave ship made the crossing to Cuba. By the early nineteenth century at least two Africans had crossed the Atlantic for every European who did so. About half of the Africans sailed in the eighteenth century and another quarter in the nineteenth. The major carriers were British, Portuguese, and French, with Dutch, Americans, and Danes playing supporting roles. Most slave ships set out from a wide range of European ports—from Whitehaven in the northwest of England to Odessa in the Black Sea—though the English trade was heavily concentrated in the ports of Liverpool, Bristol, and London. Two out of every five slave ships set out from the Americas rather than Europe. New England slavers carried slaves to all parts of the Americas, and Barbados merchants regularly sent ships to Africa from the 1680s on. Brazil, however, contained the most important centers of the slave trade in the Americas. The massive Portuguese traffic was in reality largely Brazilian, or at least based in Brazil, especially Bahia. The goods exchanged for people came from all over the world, including Brazilian tobacco and rum, Indian textiles, cowries from the Indian Ocean, and a wide range of manufactured goods from Europe. Marked regional preferences were apparent in Africa from the outset, and trading occurred among European slave ships before or during the assembling of a slave cargo to ensure that each ship would have a mix of goods that African traders deemed acceptable.

On the African side, people embarked from ports between the mouth of the Senegal River to Mombasa in present-day Kenya, but the trade was nevertheless geographically concentrated. Embarkation points around Luanda, the Zaïre (Congo) River, the Niger Delta, and the lagoons along much of the Bight of Benin coastline probably accounted for at least three-quarters of the total traffic. Ports such as Ouidah (Whydah) on the slave coast and

Luanda in Angola saw far more slave ships than any ports in Europe or the Americas. Provenance zones within Africa that supplied these regions were at their greatest extent in the late eighteenth century. Over time, the demographic center of gravity of the trade shifted south, with Senegambia entering and leaving the trade first, and West Central Africa dominating the last years of the trade. This suggests that, as with Europe, the ethnic or national composition of the trans-Atlantic population shift changed markedly over the centuries. For example, the Yoruban peoples, one of the largest of West African groups, did not occupy a major share of the trade until the early nineteenth century.

There is no scholarly consensus on the nature of the trade's impact on Africa. Despite the trade's far-

Study for the Slave Trade; drawing, Theodore Géricault, nineteenth century; Ecole Nationale Supérieure des Beaux-Arts, Paris.

ranging effects, any assessment of its total value, relative to plausible estimates of the precolonial sub-Saharan African population, suggests that quantitatively the trade was never of overall economic importance to the subcontinent, except in relatively small coastal trading enclaves. African societies had diverse and resilient economies, with strong social structures and cultures before, during, and after the slave-trade era. Nevertheless, Africa's role in the Atlantic trading system relative to Europe and the Americas was probably greater in that era than in any subsequent period.

On the American side, Brazil and the Caribbean took 90 percent of the coerced migrants, with the United States and the colonies preceding it accounting for no more than 8 percent. Brazil took more slaves than any other nation or colony in the Americas, although there was a marked southern shift over time from the sugar regions around Bahia (Salvador) to the coffee-growing areas south of Rio de Janeiro in the nineteenth century. Within the Caribbean and Central America, the Spanish dominated the early trade; British colonies were dominant between the mid-seventeenth and mid-eighteenth centuries, and again briefly in the late 1790s and early 1800s, with the French islands, especially Saint Domingue, filling the interval. After 1807, nine-tenths of all slaves were carried to Cuba and Brazil. Sugar cultivation on plantations was by far the most important demand factor behind the slave trade. Activities associated with tobacco, rice, and coffee-growing, together with the mining of precious metals, probably absorbed less than 20 percent of Africans carried across the Atlantic. Cotton cultivation was least important in generating trans-Atlantic slave traffic, with almost all of the expansion of this crop occurring in the United States after the ending of the slave trade.

The links between the Americas and Africa formed by the slave trade may have changed over time, but they were not random. Particular parts of the Americas drew heavily on particular parts of Africa: Jamaica on the Bight of Biafra and Angola; Barbados on the Gold Coast and the Bight of Benin; Saint Domingue and the Reconcavo of Bahia (the lands surrounding the Bay of All Saints) on the Bight of Benin; and southern central Brazil overwhelmingly on West Central Africa. Areas drawing on a very wide range of African provenance zones, such as Spanish America and the United States, emerge as exceptions to the overall pattern. Normally, one or two African regions predominated in the supply of slaves to a given part of the Americas, and when there was more than one such provenance zone, these regions were often adjacent to each other. Taken together with the relatively evenly balanced demographic structure of the traffic, these patterns suggest that involuntary migrants were able to carry more African cultural and social practices to the Americas than earlier scholarship has recognized.

Nevertheless, in its size and durability, but also in the sheer awfulness of the conditions to which slaves were subjected, the Atlantic slave trade stands alone in history of human migration. Although remarkably balanced demographically compared to most long-distance migrations (females and children being far more common than in the pre-nineteenth-century trans-Atlantic migrant flow of Europeans), most African-American populations did not become self-sustaining until late in the slave era, if at all. Moreover, mortality before and during the voyage was high if compared with any other measurements arising from known movements of peoples. Transporting people within Africa into epidemiologically unfamiliar territory, holding them in large numbers for shipment across the Atlantic, and then packing them into slave ships ensured very heavy mortality. The one phase of this process for which reliable data exist, the Middle Passage, indicates annual average losses of 10 to 20 percent of those embarked during the six- to fourteen-week voyage. In the worst Irish famine year, by contrast, losses on ships arriving at New York and at Quebec from European ports averaged 5 percent of those embarked. Neither convicts, nor troops, nor indentured servants, and certainly not free migrants sailing from European ports, ever experienced crowding as severe as that typical in the African trans-Atlantic slave trade. Dehydration from gastrointestinal diseases, a direct consequence of the appallingly unhygenic conditions, appears to have accounted for most of the deaths, although epidemics of smallpox were always possible. Mortality among the European crew was almost as high as for slaves, with most of it occurring off the African coast, but the cause of European death was typically tropical fevers. Voyage time fell from a little under three months in the seventeenth century to about a month in the mid-nineteenth century, with much of the decline occurring after 1800, yet many severe cases of human suffering occurred in the last years of the trade, when attempts to suppress the traffic disrupted trading patterns and practices.

Like slavery, the slave trade did not die a "natural" economic death. Rather, it was suppressed through legal and politically ascribed sanctions. From the first Danish initiatives in the 1790s down to the effective closing of Cuban ports in the aftermath of the American Civil War, the pattern of the slave traffic followed the vagaries of abolition as much as shifts in trans-Atlantic labor markets. Although a widespread international effort to suppress the trade, spearheaded by the British, began in 1807, direct action in the form of naval policing proved less effective than domestic sanctions enforced by the nations providing the chief markets for slaves. One by one, markets in the Americas closed, together with some African provenance zones, particularly Senegambia.

Neither Africa nor the Americas appeared to derive economic gain (narrowly defined) from the ending of the slave trade. Despite the growth of African produce exports in the nineteenth century, almost all African regions experienced a fall in export earnings when the slave trade came to an end. Most American regions that managed to sustain plantation output in the aftermath of suppression did so only by turning first to an intra-American trade in slaves, as in Brazil and the United States, or to contract Asian and European labor. These were clearly second-best alternatives. Seventeenth- and nineteenth-century indentured labor thus "sandwiched" the slave trade. In most cases, domestic sanctions evolved from a new international climate shaped in turn by the same powerful ideological forces that put an end to slavery in the Americas and eventually elsewhere. Such a climate eventually overtook the traffic in contract laborers as well. In the absence of such pressures, the peopling of the Americas might have continued to be primarily African and primarily slave in content.

[*See also* Asiento; Brazil; Demography; Middle Passage; Mortality in Transport; *and* United States, *article on* The South.]

BIBLIOGRAPHY

Curtin, Philip D. *The Atlantic Slave Trade: A Census*. Madison: University of Wisconsin Press, 1970.

Eltis, David. *Economic Growth and the Ending of the Trans-Atlantic Slave Trade*. New York and Oxford: Oxford University Press, 1987.

Miers, Suzanne, and Igor Kopytoff, eds. *Slavery in Africa: Historical and Anthropological Perspectives*. Madison: University of Wisconsin Press, 1977. See especially pp. 3–77.

Phillips, William D. *Slavery from Roman Times to the Early Trans-Atlantic Slave Trade*. Minneapolis: University of Minnesota Press, 1985.

Solow, Barbara, ed. *Slavery and the Rise of the Atlantic Economy*. Cambridge: Cambridge University Press, 1991.

—DAVID ELTIS

Brazil and the United States

Although the slave systems of Brazil and the United States differed in many ways, both countries in the nineteenth century engaged in extensive internal slave-trading that transported hundreds of thousands of human beings from region to region, locally, and from urban to rural areas. This practice of buying and selling slaves and transferring them to new locations occurred wherever slavery existed in the Americas, but it was most prevalent in these two countries, particularly after the ending of the international slave trade to the United States in 1808 and the suppression of that trade to Brazil in 1850 and 1851. In the case of the United States, the era of large-scale domestic slave-trading continued for half a century (roughly from 1810 until the Civil War); the bulk of the Brazilian internal migration lasted nearly forty years, from 1850 until just prior to abolition in 1888.

The ending of the African slave trade to the two countries stimulated a large increase in domestic trafficking; however, the primary cause of this internal trade was the emergence early in the nineteenth century of two extraordinarily valuable cash crops, coffee in south-central Brazil and cotton in the American South, both of which created large and continuing demands for agricultural labor. In the years following the Napoleonic Wars, coffee rapidly replaced sugar as the most important source of wealth in the broad hinterland of Rio de Janeiro, soon spreading into the nearby provinces of São Paulo and Minas Gerais. In the same period, cotton cultivation, facilitated by the cotton gin, expanded into the Carolinas and Georgia and then relentlessly into the Deep South states or territories of Alabama, Mississippi, Louisiana, Arkansas, and Texas.

Until the early 1850s a massive slave trade from Africa to Brazil supplied most of the black workers who toiled on plantations. However, once that three-hundred-year-old commerce was suppressed, Brazilian coffee-planters, like cotton-growers in the American South, quickly turned for labor to the parts of their own country where slaves were abundant and agriculture far less profitable, and thus slave prices were much lower. "Everyone knows," the Brazilian Naval Minister told the national Chamber of Deputies in 1852, "that coffee planting occupies many workers, and with the increasing need and high value of the slaves employed in this service, the large number of them that come from Bahia is very well explained." Similarly, a decade earlier a British traveler in the United States, J. S. Buckingham, wrote that the slaves of Virginia were being sent away from places "where their labor is not in demand, to the rising states and territories, in which labor is in request."

Thus, he added, in the Washington newspapers "every day are to be seen advertisements, offering 'Cash for likely negroes.'"

Although coffee and cotton were the major stimuli of internal slave trading, other factors invigorated the traffic. In the first half of the century, as coffee took center stage in Brazil, the advent of beet-sugar cultivation in Europe and the expansion of cane production in Louisiana and Cuba created an oversupply of sugar in world markets. This seriously reduced the profits of Brazilian sugar-planters and their ability to compete for slaves in local markets, a situation exacerbated by the ending of the African slave trade in mid-century. In those same decades, the circumstances of Brazilian cotton-farmers were also dismal, because markets for Brazilian cotton were greatly reduced by American-grown cotton. Agricultural practices in both countries also led to soil exhaustion and diminished agricultural production in long-settled regions, such as Brazil's Northeast and the border states of Virginia and Maryland. This induced farmers to sell selected workers or to migrate along with their households and slaves to more promising parts of their own countries, a solution more common in the United States than in Brazil. Obviously, too, transfers of slaves within states and provinces were frequent, and, as economic or demographic conditions changed, sections of states and provinces became net exporters of slaves, while other parts were net buyers.

Similarly, disasters, natural and otherwise, could alter the direction and character of the traffic. For example, a devastating drought in the Brazilian Northeast in the late 1870s impoverished slaveholders and set off a wholesale disposal of slaves at rock-bottom prices, reducing the regional commitment to slavery and helping to end that institution sooner than even ardent abolitionists might have anticipated. No less decisive was the American Civil War, which by drastically diminishing cotton production gave Brazilian cotton-farmers an interlude of comparative prosperity in the 1860s, prompting many to keep their slaves at work in their own fields instead of selling them to their more affluent countrymen. At the same time, the conflict in North America reduced both slave prices and the volume of slave sales in the beleaguered Confederacy, though remarkably, some slavery enthusiasts continued to buy slaves until the last days of the war. The origins of slaves transferred to the more prosperous regions thus varied over the years in response to changing conditions, but patterns of movement began early and persisted until the end. In the United States, most slaves began their journeys in the Carolinas and the border states from Delaware to Kentucky, and most were destined for farms and plantations of the Deep South. Similarly, the Brazilian capital, Rio de Janeiro, and presumably every major town and province outside the coffee zones, sent slaves to coffee-producing areas.

The day-to-day operations of the internal trade in the United States and Brazil consisted of a variety of procedures that began, as a rule, in the towns and rural districts of slave-exporting areas and culminated at places far removed from the victims' former homes. The first step in this process was the procurement of slaves in exporting states or provinces for delivery to markets in nearby towns and cities, there to be sold or auctioned to interregional traders. In both countries this initial acquisition of slaves was the work of local traders who used tactics designed to arouse the greed of potential sellers. In the United States, according to the historian Michael Tadman (1989), "roving speculators . . . toured villages and the countryside" in search of opportunities to acquire slaves directly from owners or at local

Slave Sale, Charleston, South Carolina; engraving from a sketch by Eyre Crowe, *The Illustrated London News*, 29 November 1856.

auctions and judicial sales, in many cases offering cash to hasten the process. In his classic study of the domestic traffic, Frederic Bancroft (1959) drew a powerful portrait of the highly motivated slave buyer, always on the lookout for profitable deals, "chatting at the country stores and taverns, loitering, treating and asking questions at the barrooms, looking in at the county jails to see the latest arrivals, cordially greeting the slaveholding farmer," but always aware of his basic purpose: to acquire slaves for much less than interstate traders would willingly pay for them. As one witness recalled, "It has become a settled trade for men whose occupation is to buy slaves, to travel through the 'Old Dominion', from estate to estate. Here he gets one, there another, and in a few weeks he enters Lynchburg, Alexandria or Richmond with a hundred or more."

"Every city" in the South, according to Richard Wade (1964), had large numbers of slave depots where traders carried on their business. Among the most important in the buying areas of the eastern border states were Baltimore, Richmond, Norfolk, Washington, and Alexandria, with numerous secondary suppliers at work in and about such towns as Fredericksburg, Lynchburg, Warrenton, Petersburg, and the county seats of Maryland's Eastern Shore. In the early 1830s, for example, fifteen or more "large buyers" were active in the small town of Cambridge, the seat of Dorchester County, along with several times as many petty traders, agents, or helpers. Slave-dealers were particularly common on the Eastern Shore, wrote Bancroft, because nowhere else could they find as many slaves so cheap, and because "choice" young men and women bought in that part of Maryland could be sold in Mississippi or Louisiana for twice their original purchase price.

In Brazil, procedures were much the same. Soon after the start of the new traffic, the British consul in the province of Pernambuco advised the Foreign Office, "The coasting traders have their establishments at the ports, and purchase their slaves from men of the lowest order, generally horse-dealers,

who bring them down from the interior; this is the real source whence the coasting traffic is derived." About the same time, a Bahian planter-politician, João Mauricio Wanderley, informed the national Chamber of Deputies that organized companies in the capital and in the provinces were sending agents into every town and provincial center to buy slaves for transport to the slave markets of Rio de Janeiro. Slave sales, he claimed, were the result "of repeated provocations and enticements" on the part of buyers, who traveled from door to door to tempt small farmers and city-dwellers to part with some of their workers. Among the unfortunate results of these transactions, he claimed, was a rapid decline in the number of slaves owned by small farmers and urban dwellers, which in time, he predicted, would deprive the "great planters" of local reserves of slaves, whom they would eventually have to buy if they hoped to replenish their own diminishing work forces.

In both countries, slave-buyers and sellers advertised in newspapers, giving posterity insights into their aims and methods. Frequently employing tiny engravings of slaves, both male and female, to attract the public eye, these notices typically contained such information as the number of slaves the trader wished to buy, the genders and ages he desired, promises of high or "the highest" prices, and such information as the preferred method of payment (normally cash), the buyer's name or firm, the hotel, tavern, or other location where he carried on his business, and often the city, state, or province where the slaves would likely be sent. These announcements reveal that the slaves in greatest demand were the young and the very young, with a general preference for males, but, particularly in the United States, also women of reproductive age who might contribute both labor and children. Typical was an advertisement of one Ansley Davis, based in Louisville, Kentucky, who in 1848 offered to buy a hundred slaves of both sexes from ten to thirty years of age, to pay exceptionally high prices, and even to visit adjacent counties "to see any property." Similarly, in

1879 the firm of Olympio and Irmão, located in the interior town of Baturité in the province of Ceará, offered to buy a dozen slaves ranging in age from twelve to twenty-six for a consignment to São Paulo, and to pay a better price than any other trader.

After the roving slave-buyer had disposed of his collection of slaves at some nearby town or port, a new phase of the trade began, this time conducted by auctioneers and interregional traders. Among the most important trading centers were the two national capitals, whose roles in the trade differed in important ways but were alike in others. Before the onset of Brazil's large-scale internal trade about 1850, Rio de Janeiro and nearby ports had long been among the principal entry points for slaves arriving from Africa. Thus when the internal trade replaced the African, Brazil's capital, with its nearly seventy-nine thousand slaves, shifted to the new traffic with a readiness derived from long experience, maintaining its position for more than thirty years as the country's principal slave mart and a major source of workers for nearby coffee estates. The city of Washington, on the other hand, was at an incipient stage of development early in the nineteenth century when the large-scale interstate trade began, and unlike Rio, it never had an abundance of slaves to sell to buying areas. In fact, Washington's importance as a slave-trading center was primarily the result of its favorable location in the heart of the most active slave-exporting region, as well as its nearness to the Potomac River port of Alexandria, then a major commercial center accessible to oceangoing vessels and the best place, according to Bancroft, to begin both coastwise and overland slave shipments.

Unlike slave-trading in Rio, however, Washington's involvement in domestic trafficking aroused constant disapproval until this highly conspicuous business was at last prohibited in the District of Columbia as part of the Compromise of 1850. Most distasteful to its critics, including members of Congress, were the many ugly scenes of slave-trading in and about the town: gangs of chained or bound

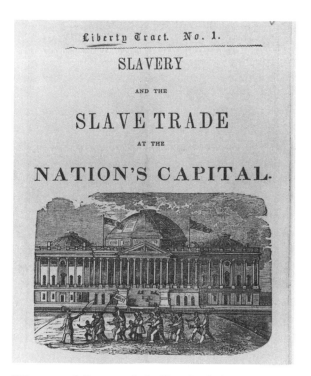

Title page of *Slavery and the Slave Trade in Washington, D.C.*, a pamphlet distributed by the American and Foreign Anti-Slavery Society, c.1850s.

human beings driven through city streets, utilization of private slave pens and public prisons for housing slaves (a common practice throughout the South), the kidnapping and selling of free people, the spectacle of public auctions, incessant slave-advertising, and, perhaps most offensive, the federal government's open sanctioning of slave-trading in the city. "By authority of Congress," said the well-known educator and congressman, Horace Mann, in a speech to the House of Representatives in 1849, "the city of Washington is the Congo of America."

Slaves in the two countries were sent to market both overland and by sea. In the case of Brazil, coastal steamers and sailing ships providing scheduled passenger service to ports up and down the coast were the most common means of transporting slaves in the interprovincial traffic, since the coastal voyage offered major advantages over the mule and cattle trails of inland Brazil. Although conditions aboard ship were at times reminiscent of the African traffic, for a variety of reasons the coastal voyage differed significantly from the grim Atlantic crossing. Most importantly, perhaps, the coastal journey required much less time than voyages from Africa (as little as four days from Bahia to Rio), and so slaves on coastal ships, who often traveled with their owners or were consigned in groups for delivery to designated agents at their destination, could be better fed and cared for than their African predecessors. Moreover, slaves transported in the internal trade were far more expensive than those brought from Africa, and so they were not normally subjected to the levels of abuse and brutality common to the African trade.

None of this means that the victims of this traffic did not suffer great hardship and deprivation. Stanley Stein (1985), in his pioneering study of slavery in a Brazilian coffee county, has suggested that in some respects the internal trade "differed only in minor details" from the African. In fact, despite the many opportunities to ameliorate conditions on coastal voyages, critics sometimes deplored the conditions suffered by slaves at sea and in the marketplaces on both ends of the journey. "The new internal slave trade in the province of Maranhão," wrote the contemporary historian, João Francisco Lisboa, soon after the new traffic began, "retains the greater part of the horrors of the former without any of its problematic advantages." An article in a Pernambuco newspaper published in 1857 described the conditions of slaves newly arrived at Recife on a ship from Maranhão: "The deck of the steamer appeared like one of those vessels coming from the coast of Africa loaded with human flesh; we saw one unhappy child combatting with death, and others miserably naked!" As late as 1880 a São Paulo newspaper complained that the embarkation of slaves in northern provinces was a repetition of the painful scenes once witnessed on the African coast, and that in Rio the slave depositories invoked memories of those formerly used by Africans—"less sub-stantial now because the importation is not carried out on the same scale, but with the same tearful scenes, the same barbaric acts on the part of those who direct them, the same customs and the same instruments of violence."

Although most slaves who experienced Brazil's domestic trade traveled by sea, overland marches were also common. After their sale to slave-buyers, many slaves experienced a forced march to a port of embarkation, and once the voyage by sea had ended, they underwent another journey on foot inland from Rio de Janeiro, Santos, or some other coastal town before being sold to a new master. Others were made to trek long distances through the hinterland in slave gangs or coffles (*cáfilas* in Portuguese, from Arabic *qafilah,* a caravan). Some were marched overland, for example, from the provinces of Goiás and Mato Grosso in the far interior, and others through the backlands of Bahia to the São Francisco River, where they were shipped on riverboats to Minas Gerais. Many more from the southern province of Rio Grande do Sul were driven north on an ancient trail to Sorocaba in São Paulo, traditionally a marketplace for mules. Finally, slave traders often conveyed slaves clandestinely through the interior to avoid the heavy taxes levied on slaves shipped from provincial ports or taken across provincial borders.

In the United States, slaves were also transported by coastal vessel, by flatboat or river steamer down the Ohio and Mississippi rivers, in railway cars (in the final years of the trade), and, probably most often, in overland coffles, some of which lasted for many weeks and obliged slaves to trek hundreds of miles cross-country from Maryland, Virginia, and other border states to such major slave-trading towns as Natchez and New Orleans. This was the most grueling and infamous method of transporting slaves; the constant prospect of flight or rebellion demanded a lavish use of chains and manacles and other injurious forms of restraint, and the forced marches of pitiful men, women, and children along the roads and trails of the American South were highly visible and often the subject of critical comment. Finally, as in Brazil, a large percentage of the American slaves carried in the domestic trade traveled by sea from Atlantic ports to Southern markets. Some slave-trading firms possessed their own specially constructed ships for this purpose and carried not only their own slaves, but, for a fee, those belonging to other dealers and to farmers acquiring slaves for their own use. These ships normally carried perhaps one hundred to one hundred fifty slaves, but sometimes as many as two hundred or more. Such overloading and the lengthy voyages, lasting perhaps two to three weeks, could cause hardship, illness, and even death, even though most slaves shipped on American vessels arrived at their destinations in far better health than slaves brought from Africa. Still, observers in the United States also encountered conditions on American ships that resembled those of the African trade. For example, a British traveler, Basil Hall, who in the 1820s had witnessed conditions on a slaver at Rio de Janeiro, later described a brig docked in New Orleans after arriving from Baltimore with more than two hundred slaves. "Her decks," he wrote, "presented a scene which forcibly reminded me of Rio de Janeiro. In the one case, however, the slaves were brought from the savage regions of Africa; in the other, from the very heart of a free country. To the poor negro the distinction is probably no great matter."

How many people were victims of this traffic? Michael Tadman (1989) has calculated that in the United States close to a million slaves were transferred across state borders between 1810 and 1860. Similarly, the Brazilian scholar Jacob Gorender (1978) estimated that from 1850 to 1885 three hundred thousand slaves were supplied to coffee-producing counties by the interprovincial and intraprovincial trade. These statistics do not include the many slaves in the United States who were sold but never crossed a state line, or the many in Brazil who passed to new owners but never entered a coffee county. Therefore such estimates, large as they are, do not tell the full story.

The internal slave trade had other effects. In both countries it broke up thousands of families, separating husbands from wives and children from parents. The constant danger of sale caused great fear and anxiety and encouraged kidnapping and the sale of free people. In the United States (more than in Brazil) it was alleged that the high values put on slaves encouraged sexual manipulation by owners, including forced mating, the granting of rewards and other benefits to prolific women, the joining of couples based on desirable physical attributes, and even the temporary hiring of strong, well-built men to improve the "quality" of offspring and enhance their potential value. Finally, in both countries the traffic may have contributed to the ending of slavery: in the United States because it aroused intense anti-slavery sentiment in the North, deepening regional divisions that led to the Civil War; and in Brazil because the trade concentrated slave-ownership and commitment to slavery in limited areas of the country, creating by the 1880s a situation that permitted a rapid and generally nonviolent solution to the slavery problem.

[*See also* Reproduction; United States, *overview article and article on* The South.]

BIBLIOGRAPHY

Bancroft, Frederic. *Slave Trading in the Old South*. New York: Ungar, 1959.

Conrad, Robert. *The Destruction of Brazilian Slavery, 1850–1888*. Berkeley: University of California Press, 1972.

Conrad, Robert. *World of Sorrow: The African Slave Trade to Brazil*. Baton Rouge: Louisiana State University Press, 1986.

Gorender, Jacob. *O Escravismo Colonial*. São Paulo: Editora Ática, 1978.

Gutman, Herbert G. *The Black Family in Slavery and Freedom, 1750–1925*. New York: Pantheon, 1976.

Karasch, Mary C. *Slave Life in Rio de Janeiro, 1808–1850*. Princeton: Princeton University Press, 1987.

Slenes, Robert Wayne. "The Demography and Economics of Brazilian Slavery, 1850–1888." Diss., Stanford University, 1976.

Stein, Stanley J. *Vassouras: A Brazilian Coffee County, 1850–1900*. Second edition. Princeton: Princeton University Press, 1985.

Tadman, Michael. *Speculators and Slaves: Masters, Traders, and Slaves in the Old South.* Madison: University of Wisconsin Press, 1989.

—ROBERT EDGAR CONRAD

Suppression of Trade

The Napoleonic Wars in the early nineteenth century provided the background and context for what became a protracted international struggle to abolish the Atlantic slave trade. Denmark was the first country formally to end its involvement in the slave trade (1803). Britain passed legislation to prohibit slave-trading within its empire from the beginning of 1808, and the United States also prohibited the slave trade in 1808. The Dutch outlawed the slave trade by decree in 1814, and the French followed in 1815. At the Congress of Vienna (1815), the British succeeded in persuading the other European powers to sign a declaration condemning the slave trade as "repugnant to the principles of humanity and universal morality." This condemnation did not yet represent widespread public opinion across Europe, although it articulated what an aroused British public had impressed on its government. Not until the Brussels Conference (1889–1890), however, did all the countries involved work out a set of international principles to enforce the prohibition on slave-trading, and by then the trans-Atlantic slave trade had been dead for twenty years. From 1815 until the Brussels Conference, British diplomacy concentrated on bilateral agreements with individual slave-trading countries to achieve the international abolition of the slave trade.

By the end of the Napoleonic wars the major Atlantic countries, except for Spain and Portugal, had prohibited the slave trade. Making it illegal, however, did not end it. The nineteenth-century Atlantic slave trade was transformed into an illegal, contraband trade that transported an estimated 2.9 million African slaves across the Atlantic, primarily to Brazil and Cuba. Slaves were also shipped to various Caribbean islands, particularly before slavery was abolished in the Caribbean colonies of Britain and France in 1833 and 1848, respectively.

As a contraband trade, the slave trade was highly lucrative to the slave-traders and ship-owners who were involved in it. Nor was it confined to one or two nations. Capital, ships, and sailors from a variety of countries, including the United States, Cuba, Brazil, Spain, and Portugal, flowed into the Atlantic slave trade until its termination. Large amounts of money and goods used to facilitate the illegal slave trade actually came from Britain, the leading country in the struggle to abolish it, an irony that did not escape Britain's opponents. David Eltis (1987, p. 59) has calculated that at least 90 percent of the manufactured goods used in the nineteenth century trans-Atlantic slave trade to Brazil and Cuba came from Britain, and he estimates that British credit financed half of the Cuban and Brazilian slave trade.

After prohibiting the slave trade within the British Empire, the British pursued what they regarded as the miscreant nations, such as Spain and Portugal, along with their American possessions, especially Cuba and Brazil, and attempted to force the abolition of the slave trade on them. Britain succeeded in getting these countries to sign treaties pledging to abolish the slave trade, Spain in 1817, Portugal in two treaties of 1815 and 1817, and Brazil, following its independence, in 1826. Portugal committed only to prohibit the slave trade north of the Equator in the treaty of 1815. Spain insisted on a three-year period of grace. The prohibition on the trade to Cuba did not take effect until 30 May 1820. Even the treaty Britain signed with Brazil in 1826 did not come into force until 1830.

The initial treaties soon proved ineffective. British diplomacy then worked to strengthen them, in the absence of any other means to end the Atlantic slave trade. Britain signed a second treaty with Spain in 1835, authorizing the seizure and condemnation of any ships equipped for the slave trade, even if no slaves were found on board. This gave new powers to the British West African

Squadron and resulted in a marked increase of captures of slave ships flying the Spanish flag. Slave-traders, however, quickly resorted to the Portuguese or the U.S. flag to evade the British navy; Britain did not have treaties with Portugal or the United States permitting a mutual maritime right of search. To counter what it regarded as an abuse of the Portuguese flag, the British government passed legislation in 1839 giving British naval vessels the power to capture any Portuguese slaving vessels or slavers without nationality and take them to British vice-admiralty courts for adjudication. But even this did not succeed, as slavers increasingly resorted to the U.S. flag.

The United States refused until the Civil War to sign a treaty with Britain permitting a mutual right of maritime search, but in 1842 it agreed to station a naval squadron off the western coast of Africa. This arrangement had little effect in deterring American slavers, and in 1862 the United States and Britain agreed to a mutual right of search and the creation of joint mixed commission courts. The two dominant maritime nations of the Atlantic now signaled their determination to eliminate the slave trade.

Issues arising from the illegal slave trade regularly spilled over into the growing tensions created by slavery in the United States. The U.S. Supreme Court stated in 1825 that the law of nations sanctioned the slave trade, which justified the return of a captured Cuban slave ship, the *Antelope*, to its owners along with its cargo of slaves. In 1839 a slave mutiny aboard a Cuban slaver, the *Amistad*, had a different outcome. After a U.S. surveying ship captured the *Amistad*, it was taken to Connecticut. Eventually the case went to the Supreme Court, where the Africans won both their acquittal and their freedom.

The United States was the only Atlantic nation to pass a law (in 1820) declaring participation in the Atlantic slave trade piracy and punishable by death. Not until 1862, however, was a slaver executed under this law. Nathaniel Gordon, who captained the Cuban slaver *Erie*, became the only person in the history of the Atlantic slave trade to face capital punishment for his crime.

British pressure ultimately forced first Spain and then Brazil to pass legislation outlawing the slave trade. The Spanish penal law was passed in 1845, and Brazil's came into effect in 1850. The Brazilian law quickly shut off the Atlantic slave trade to Brazil, although a domestic slave trade within Brazil continued until the abolition of slavery in 1888. The Spanish law continued to be ignored or evaded in Cuba until the American Civil War brought emancipation in the United States. Spanish officials then began to enforce the anti-slave-trade law in earnest, hoping to preserve slavery and their Cuban colony. Spain passed a stronger law against the slave trade in 1867; by then, the Atlantic slave trade had been choked off on both sides of the Atlantic.

The treaties Britain signed with the maritime powers engaged in the Atlantic slave trade made the British navy a maritime police force, charged with catching suspected slavers on both sides of the Atlantic. Any ships seized by a naval vessel were to be taken before courts of mixed commission. These were located at various centers in Africa and in the Americas, including Sierra Leone, Havana, Rio de Janeiro, Loanda, Boa Vista, St. Helena, and later New York. The courts pronounced on the legality of the seizure and, in theory, freed any slaves taken. After 1845, most slavers captured by British naval vessels were tried in British vice-admiralty courts, because the "mixed commission courts" functioned in name only. Historians disagree on how effective British pressure was in reducing the Atlantic slave trade in the nineteenth century, but they agree that without British actions it would have been much larger.

The fate of the slaves ostensibly freed by these courts (about ten thousand in Brazil and more than twenty-five thousand in Cuba) is another tragic chapter in the history of the Atlantic slave trade. Legally free, the *emancipados*, as they were known, became in practice a new class of slaves, continuously deprived of the freedom promised to them by the courts of mixed commission. A much larger number, exceeding one hundred thousand, were liberated in Sierra Leone. The British embarked on a variety of emigration plans, transporting these liberated Africans either across the Atlantic to meet the post-emancipation labor needs of their Caribbean colonies or to the Cape of Good Hope.

Backed by militant and articulate public opinion, Britain occupied the moral high ground in its unremitting campaign to force the abolition of the slave trade on the rest of the Atlantic world. Britain continually pressured other states to impose tougher anti-slave-trading measures. The actions of the British navy in enforcing the slave-trade prohibition were often perceived in European countries such as France, Spain, and Portugal, and in the United States, Cuba, and Brazil, as high-handed and arbitrary, even as violating accepted international law. Lacking a similar abolitionist public opinion and convinced of the value of slaves for the plantation economies of Cuba and Brazil, defenders of slavery and the slave trade, especially in Spain and Portugal, as well as Cuba and Brazil, argued that patriotic nationalism required their countries to defend what they viewed as a nominally illegal trade against British seizures of vessels on the high seas. The criminality of the Atlantic slave trade was largely accepted in Britain by 1808; but in the Iberian world, no broad-based abolitionist movement existed for much of the nineteenth century. Patriotism cloaked the pursuit of profit in a contraband trade in human slaves.

When the institution of apprenticeship in the British Caribbean colonies ended in 1838, British abolitionists formed the British and Foreign Anti-Slavery Society in 1839, dedicated to the worldwide elimination of the slave trade and slavery. Among other ideas that surfaced at the time for attacking the foreign slave trade was an ingenious plan put forward in 1840 by David Turnbull, who was subsequently appointed British consul in Havana. Turnbull focused on the inherent right to freedom of any slave who had been brought across the Atlantic after the prohibition of the slave trade. He believed that the mixed commission courts should be given the power to hear legal suits brought by or on behalf of individual Africans seeking their freedom on the grounds of illegal importation. His proposal was aimed specifically at Cuba and at cutting off the demand for slaves.

Turnbull's appointment as consul in 1840 and knowledge of his plan had an extraordinary impact in Cuba. It underlined the tenuous legal foundation of slavery in the island (by 1840 most of Cuba's slaves had been illegally imported), and it created a climate of fear among Spanish officials and the planting class. The Spanish government rejected the plan and blamed Turnbull for instigating a slave conspiracy in 1844. Turnbull's abolitionist commitment may have incited slaves and free blacks in Cuba to plan the Escalera conspiracy (1844) in the belief that British emancipation would be extended to Cuba. Whatever their hopes, they were cruelly dashed. Instead of helping Cuban slaves to freedom, Turnbull's abolitionist machinations contributed to a bloody repression of slaves and free blacks in Cuba and the continuation of the Cuban slave trade until after the American Civil War. Spanish legislators included a clause in the 1845 penal law forbidding any searches for illegal slaves inside plantations. This protection for slave-owners made it very difficult even for well-intentioned Cuban officials to prosecute the illegal slave trade successfully.

In the third quarter of the nineteenth century a constellation of international forces finally suffocated the Atlantic slave trade. The end of the trade foretold the end of slavery in the Americas, although another twenty years would pass before emancipation in Brazil in 1888 completed this process. David Eltis has concluded that the Atlantic slave trade "was killed when its [economic] significance to the Americas and to a lesser extent to Europe was greater than at any point in its history" (1987, p. 15). According to this argument, it did not die a natural death; its termination occurred only because the most powerful nations of the Atlantic world came together to combat it. The end of the Atlantic slave trade occurred in the same time period that theories of scientific racism surfaced in Europe, presaging the partition of Africa and the pervasive influence of racist ideas in the late nineteenth and twentieth century.

[*See also* Abolition and Anti-Slavery, *articles on* Britain *and* United States; *and* Asiento.]

BIBLIOGRAPHY

Bethell, Leslie M. *The Abolition of the Braziliam Slave Trade: Britain, Brazil and the Slave Trade Question, 1807–1869.* Cambridge: Cambridge University Press, 1970.

Drescher, Seymour. *Econocide: British Slavery in the Era of Abolition.* Pittsburgh: University of Pittsburgh Press, 1977.

Eltis, David. *Economic Growth and the Ending of the Trans-Atlantic Slave Trade.* New York and Oxford: Oxford University Press, 1987.

Murray, David R. *Odious Commerce: Britain, Spain and the Abolition of the Cuban Slave Trade.* Cambridge: Cambridge University Press, 1980.

—DAVID MURRAY

Volume of Trade

During the course of the British Parliament's enquiries in 1788 and 1789 into the state of the Atlantic slave trade, a Liverpool merchant, Robert Norris, provided an estimate of annual slave shipments from Africa to America. Norris suggested that at that time, about 74,200 slaves were loaded each year at ports along the Atlantic seaboard of Africa. Of these, he estimated, the British shipped 38,000, the French 20,000, and the Portuguese 10,000, with the remainder being shipped by the Dutch and Danes. According to Norris, more than two-thirds of the slaves came from ports east and south of the Gold Coast, with ports in the Bight of Biafra and along the coast south of Cape Lopez supplying nearly 45,000 slaves each year to European carriers.

Norris's estimate of the slave trade was incomplete; for instance, he omitted North American slave-carriers from his calculations. Moreover, the basis on which he estimated slave shipments of other carriers is unclear. Despite this, modern re-search suggests that his figures provide a reasonably accurate indication of annual shipments of slaves from the western coast of Africa to the Americas in the 1780s, as well as their distribution among slave-carriers and along the continent's Atlantic seaboard. The real significance of Norris's data, however, lies not so much in their accuracy than in their demonstration that interest in quantifying the slave trade began at least two hundred years ago and is not simply a feature of modern scholarship on the trade.

In estimating the Atlantic slave trade, scholars have focused primarily on the numbers of slaves loaded at the African coast or disembarked in the Americas; those killed or maimed during enslavement processes in Africa or sold within Africa are usually excluded from calculations of the trade. Until the 1960s the general consensus of scholars was that about fifteen to twenty million enslaved Africans may have been landed in the Americas during the three hundred fifty years of the trans-Atlantic slave trade. A survey by Philip Curtin (1969) of the existing literature revealed, however, that this figure was based on weak foundations, originating in fact from a calculation made by Robert Norris's contemporary Bryan Edwards, on the basis of Jamaican imports from 1700 to 1786, and from an unsubstantiated estimate made in 1861 by an American publicist, Edward Dunbar. The Edwards-Dunbar figures had been largely repeated, with occasional modifications, by later historians, thereby investing them with, in Curtin's words, "a weight of authority and tradition." Curtin noted that the consensus surrounding the figure of fifteen to twenty million had been broken at times, perhaps most notably by the historian of sugar, Noel Deerr (1949–1950, vol. 2, p. 284), who calculated in 1949 that perhaps twelve million Africans arrived as slaves in the Americas between 1500 and 1861. Deerr's calculations had, however, been neglected by other historians. Believing that other estimates of the trade were insecurely based, Curtin went on to produce his own estimate or "census" of the Atlantic slave trade. In doing so, he relied solely on published data, using figures on slave shipments where these were available, and where they were not, projecting estimates of slave arrivals in the Americas from colonial census data and trends in colonial commodity output and exports.

Published in 1969, Curtin's census suggested that between 1451 and 1870, about 9.4 million enslaved Africans were landed by European and American ships at ports in the Americas. Given the imperfect data underlying his calculations, Curtin believed that any estimate of the trade "falling within 20 percent of actuality" was "right," although he went on to suggest that "it is extremely unlikely that the ultimate total will turn out to be less than 8 million or more than 10.5 million" (1969, p. 86). However, on the assumption of a margin of error of ±20 percent (Curtin, 1986, p. 111), his calculations imply that slave imports into the Americas probably fell within a range from 7.5 million to 11.3 million between 1451 and 1870. It should be noted that the higher range of these figures is broadly consistent with the estimate of slave imports into the Americas offered by Deerr, but it is still nearly 45 percent lower than the figure proposed by Bryan Edwards and subsequently adopted by several other historians. Based on estimates of slave arrivals in the Americas, Curtin's census thus proposed a radical revision of the prevailing view of the volume of the Atlantic slave trade. The census did not provide an estimate of how many slaves were loaded in Africa; but if one assumes that 10 to 20 percent of those shipped from Africa died in the Atlantic crossing, then his figures of slave imports suggest that 8.3 million to 14.8 million slaves may have been shipped at the African coast, with the headline 9.4 million import figure suggesting that 10.4 million to 11.8 million were shipped.

In addition to revising previous estimates of the total volume of the trade, Curtin also offered detailed breakdowns of the trend of slave shipments through time. These are important because they indicate how any revision of Curtin's figures is likely to affect his global estimate of the trade. According to Curtin, slave deliveries in the Americas rose on average from less than 1,000 a year before 1600 to 13,000 a year between 1601 and 1700, and 55,000 a year between 1701 and 1810, before declining to less than 32,000 a year during the final six decades of the Atlantic traffic. These figures of course disguise major fluctuations in slave arrivals from year to year. Overall, however, Curtin's data suggested that from small beginnings before 1600, the trans-Atlantic traffic in African slaves rose to a peak during the eighteenth and nineteenth centuries, with 60 percent of all the slaves arriving in the Americas being shipped between 1721 and 1820, and 80 percent in the century and a half after 1700.

The publication of Curtin's census has inspired similar assessments of other export slave trades from Africa. At the same time, the radical revision of earlier estimates of the Atlantic traffic proposed by Curtin has provoked further investigation of slave shipments to the Americas. Research in both these areas continues and may affect current estimates of the volume of the slave trade from Africa.

Prominent among studies of other export trades have been Ralph Austen's assessments of the trans-Saharan, Red Sea, and Indian Ocean slave trades. Calculating the numbers of African slaves involved in all of these trades, as Austen acknowledges, presents major problems because the surviving evidence relating to them is often anecdotal and even flimsier than that for the Atlantic trade. Censuses of the non-Atlantic slave trades have to be treated, therefore, with considerable caution. Nevertheless, from the available evidence, slave exports via the Sahara, Red Sea, and Swahili coast were far from insignificant and probably reached unprecedented levels in the eighteenth and nineteenth centuries. Thus Austen's censuses suggest that perhaps 2.2 million African slaves entered the trans-Saharan trade from 1700 to 1900, while 492,000 and 313,000 may have entered the nineteenth-century Red Sea and Swahili coast trades, respectively. Comparing these figures with Curtin's, slave shipments to America clearly dominated slave exports from Africa from 1700 to 1867, but exports of slaves to other destinations, notably the eastern Mediterranean and the Middle East, clearly added significantly to the extraordinary exodus of enslaved labor from sub-Saharan Africa that occurred between 1700 and 1900.

While Austen's work has helped to clarify the scale of slave exports through North and East Africa, most recent research on the volume of the slave trade has followed Curtin in focusing on the trans-Atlantic traffic. Seeking to evaluate Curtin's findings, historians have uncovered in European and American archives major new sources of quantitative data on the Atlantic slave trade. Particularly important has been the discovery of new shipping records, which are usually seen as the most reliable means of measuring the trade's volume. Unlike Curtin's census, which sought to quantify the whole Atlantic slave trade, most recent studies have focused on the trade of particular national carriers or on the magnitude of the trade in particular periods. Even within this narrower framework, heated debates have arisen over new estimates of the trade as historians have attempted to assess the impact of even partial revisions of Curtin's figures on the overall total he projected. Some of these debates have still to be resolved, but on the basis of the studies completed so far, some readjustment of Curtin's estimates of the numbers of slaves attributable to specific groups of carriers would seem to be appropriate. On balance, however, the broad thrust of recent estimates of the trade seems to confirm rather than challenge Curtin's assessment of the overall magnitude of the Atlantic slave trade.

Most recent research on the trans-Atlantic traffic in slaves has centered on the last two centuries of the trade. This reflects the increased availability of shipping and other records relating to the slave trade in this period. It is also appropriate, however, because it is commonly accepted that the vast majority of slaves shipped to America left Africa between 1660 and 1850. As a result of this research, it

is now possible to provide an essentially new estimate of the Atlantic slave trade for the two centuries after 1660. This new assessment allows, in turn, a reappraisal of the general reliability of Curtin's census.

What, then, are the new findings regarding the volume of the trade during its last two centuries? Some of the most recent estimates of the trade from 1660 to 1867 are presented in Table 1. These estimates are based on fuller and more detailed sources of evidence than were available to Curtin and may therefore be seen as having superseded his findings. Some commentary on the figures is necessary, however, before their implications for Curtin's census are explored. Two points may be noted.

First, whereas Curtin was largely concerned with slave arrivals in the Americas, most recent studies have produced estimates of slave exports from Africa as well as landings in the Americas. Table 1 presents estimates of slaves shipped from Africa. To compare these figures with Curtin's, it is

TABLE 1. *Estimated Exports from Africa to America, 1660–1867*

Period	Carrier	Total
1660–1699	British	329,600
	Dutch	123,200
	French	40,000
	Portuguese	263,700
Total:		756,500
1700–1810	British	2,954,700
	British colonial	47,200
	Danish	51,000
	Dutch	380,100
	French	1,052,000
	North American	208,000
	Portuguese	1,903,000
Total:		6,596,000
1811–1867	All carriers	2,737,900
Total (all periods):		10,090,400

necessary to adjust his estimates to allow for slave mortality in the Atlantic crossing. Losses of slaves seem to have averaged around 10 to 20 percent of slaves shipped and seem to have declined from the seventeenth century on.

Second, some of the estimates of slave shipments contained in the table remain controversial. This is particularly so with regard to Portuguese shipments before 1700 and French and British shipments from 1700 to 1810. In each of these cases, the figures here are lower than those estimated by some historians. Charles Becker (1986) has suggested that the French may have shipped about 1.5 million slaves from 1700 to 1809, while Joseph Inikori (1992) has recently argued that the British shipped at least 3.4 million slaves from 1698 to 1807. If correct, the estimates of Becker and Inikori would add nearly one million slaves to the total projected for the eighteenth century in the table. For some historians, therefore, the figures on slave exports presented here represent a significant underestimate of the Atlantic slave trade in the two centuries after 1660.

The table suggests that from 1660 to 1867, almost 10.1 million slaves were exported from Africa to America. Of these, some 750,000 were shipped in the last forty years of the seventeenth century, nearly 6.6 million from 1700 to 1809, and more than 2.7 million from 1811 to 1867. Among national carriers, the British, Portuguese, and French dominated the trade in the century and a half before Britain abolished its slave trade in 1807. The precise nationality of carriers from 1811 on is less easy to distinguish, but Portuguese, Spanish, French, and U.S. ships almost certainly dominated the traffic during its final six decades. Overall, the British, Portuguese, and French, in that order, were the principal trans-Atlantic carriers of slaves from Africa from 1660 to 1867.

How do the totals presented in the table compare to Curtin's figures? Precise comparisons are difficult because Curtin gives figures from 1650, not 1660, and concentrates on arrivals in the Americas rather than shipments from Africa. His data suggest, however, that from 1650 to 1870 about 8.9 million slaves arrived in the Americas. Of these, 970,000 landed between 1650 and 1700, just over 6 million from 1701 to 1810, and just under 1.9 million from 1811 to 1870. Assuming 20 percent slave mortality before 1700 and 15 percent thereafter, these figures give an estimate of slaves exported from Africa to America in the period 1650–1870 of 10.5 million slaves, with 1.2 million being shipped from 1650 to 1700, 7.1 million from 1701 to 1810, and 2.2 million from 1811 to 1870.

Comparing these projections from Curtin's figures with those presented in the table, it appears that Curtin underestimated the nineteenth-century slave trade and exaggerated slave shipments before 1700. Overall, however, his global estimate of the Atlantic slave trade between 1650 and 1870 is remarkably close to that suggested by more recent research in this field. Moreover, even if one were to substitute the higher estimates of the eighteenth-century French and British slave trades proposed by Becker and Inikori for those assumed here, Curtin's estimate of the trade from 1650 to 1870 would still appear remarkably accurate, given the evidence available to him in 1969.

The publication of Curtin's census in 1969 prompted a wave of research into the magnitude of slave exports from Africa to America as well as to other parts of the world. Information about the volume of the trade before 1650 still remains patchy, and further research is needed to clarify the level and pattern of slave shipments across the Atlantic during the first century and a half of European colonization of the Americas. Recent research has, however, reduced significantly the margins of error that Curtin was forced to assume in his calculation of the volume of the Atlantic slave trade. This research suggests that about 10 to 11 million slaves were shipped from Africa in the two centuries after 1660 and, on the assumption that 10 to 20 percent died in the Atlantic crossing, eight to ten million landed in the Americas. To these totals, one should also add an estimate of slaves shipped before 1660. According to Curtin's calculations, about 471,000 African slaves arrived in the Americas in the century and a half before 1650. Allowing 25 percent mortality in the Atlantic crossing, this suggests that about 630,000 slaves left Africa for America in this period. The reliability of this figure is difficult to gauge, because the early slave trade has attracted much less attention than that after 1660; however, erring probably on the side of generosity, one might suggest that perhaps one million slaves—or 50 percent more than Curtin's calculations implied—left Africa for America prior to 1660. Adding this figure to the ten to eleven million shipped after 1660, it appears that perhaps as many as 12 million Africans entered the Atlantic slave trade between 1500 and 1867.

[*See also* Demography *and* Middle Passage.]

BIBLIOGRAPHY

Becker, Charles. "Note sue les chiffres de la traite atlantique française au dix-huitième siècle." *Cahiers d'études africaines* 26 (1986): 633–679.

Clarence-Smith, William Gervase, ed. *The Economics of the Indian Ocean Slave Trade in the Nineteenth Century.* London: Frank Cass, 1989.

Curtin, Philip D. *The Atlantic Slave Trade: A Census.* Madison: University of Wisconsin Press, 1969.

Deerr, Noel. *The History of Sugar.* 2 vols. London: Chapman and Hall, 1949–1950.

Eltis, David. *Economic Growth and the Ending of the Trans-Atlantic Slave Trade.* Oxford and New York: Oxford University Press, 1987.

Inikori, Joseph. "The Volume of the British Slave Trade, 1655–1807." *Cahiers d'études africaines* 32 (1992): 543–688.

Lovejoy, Paul E. *Transformations in Slavery: A History of Slavery in Africa.* Cambridge: Cambridge University Press, 1983.

Postma, Johannes. *The Dutch in the Atlantic Slave Trade, 1600–1815.* Cambridge: Cambridge University Press, 1990.

Richardson, David. "Slave Exports from West and West-Central Africa, 1700–1810: New Estimates of Volume and Distribution." *Journal of African History* 30 (1989): 1–22.

Savage, Elizabeth, ed. *The Human Commodity: Perspectives on the Trans-Saharan Slave Trade.* London: Frank Cass, 1992.

—DAVID RICHARDSON

SOUTH AMERICA. Slavery did not exist on a large scale in South America until after the European conquest of the continent. Prior to the arrival of the Spanish and Portuguese, Native American chiefdoms and tribal societies held small numbers of war captives as slaves, and the Inca Empire included a hereditary class of unfree laborers, the *yana* or *yanakuna*, who worked as servants or agricultural workers for the nobility; however, the role of the *yana* in economic production was marginal compared to that of the peasant kinship units (*ayllu*) who held and worked land collectively. The position of the latter in Inca society was closer to that of serfs than slaves: they could not be bought or sold as individuals (there was thus no slave trade before the arrival of the Europeans) and remained tied to the estate on which they lived.

Spaniards arriving in the Andean region in the 1530s and after retained the institution of *yanaconaje* and supplemented it with other forms of forced Indian labor, such as the *encomienda* and *repartimiento*, which required Indians to work for employers or the state while granting them the legal status of free subjects of the Spanish monarch. Efforts to enslave Indians proved so disastrous, in terms of loss of Indian life, that Spain terminally outlawed Indian slavery in 1542; following an equally catastrophic experience in Brazil, Portugal followed suit in 1570. Both prohibitions, however, included a substantial loophole: Indians taken as captives in "just wars" (that is, those who resisted Spanish or Portuguese claims of sovereignty) remained subject to enslavement and could legally be bought and sold. This opened the way for a small (in comparison to the African trade) but active trade in Indians captured in frontier wars, or falsely alleged to have been captured, that lasted in much of the continent until the early 1800s.

As the colonial economies developed, their demand for labor far exceeded the supply of Indian war captives. Moreover, those captives, many of whom were taken from nomadic societies based on hunting and gathering, were not well adapted to the demands of intensive, disciplined labor in

Engraving depicting workers in a Peruvian silver mine, sixteenth century.

mines, plantations, and urban workshops. Particularly along the Atlantic, Caribbean, and Pacific coasts, Native American populations had been virtually annihilated by epidemic disease and forced labor. Slaves imported from Africa proved to be the answer to local labor needs.

The initial demand for such slaves was greatest, not surprisingly, in areas where economic development was most intense: Peru during the silver boom of 1570–1630, and northeastern Brazil (Bahia and Pernambuco), which between 1580 and 1680 was the world's principal producer of sugar. Of the two colonies, Brazil received by far the greater number of Africans, an estimated four hundred fifty thousand during those hundred years, as compared to seventy to eighty thousand to Peru.

Until the termination of slavery in the late 1800s, Brazil overwhelmingly dominated the experience of South American slavery, importing far larger numbers of Africans (by 1850, an estimated four million) than all of Spanish South America combined (slightly over half a million). In part, this reflected the absence in Brazil of the large Indian populations found in the Andean regions, and thus the demand for an alternative source of labor. It was also the result of Portugal's colonial presence in sub-Saharan Africa and its early involvement in the African slave trade. This greatly facilitated the subsequent linkage of its American colony to that trade, a linkage further reinforced by Brazil's proximity to Africa. In addition, during the 1400s Portuguese merchants, planters, and administrators on the offshore islands of Madeira, the Azores, and São Tomé had acquired extensive experience with African slave labor in the plantation cultivation of sugar. That expertise proved readily transportable to Brazil, where a rapidly growing plantation complex fueled the demand for ever more slaves.

A final factor stimulating slave imports into Brazil was the gold and diamond rush of the 1700s in the interior region of Minas Gerais. As during the Peruvian silver boom a century before, precious metals and gemstones helped to pay for slaves, and 1.7 million Africans were imported into Brazil between 1700 and 1800. But unlike Peru, where African slaves were not used as a labor force in the silver mines, in Brazil slaves were sent directly into the gold fields. This reflected both the lack of alternative sources of labor, and the less hazardous conditions of gold-mining, which was carried out in rivers and streams or in shallow pits rather than in deep underground shafts. Indian silver-miners in Peru risked their lives every time they entered the mines; gold-mining was not nearly as dangerous and was viewed by many slaves as preferable to field labor on the plantations.

As a result first of the sugar boom in the northeast, then of the gold boom in Minas Gerais, by the end of the colonial period Brazil's slave population was much larger, and formed a higher proportion of the total population, than that of the rest of the continent combined. Its 1.1 million slaves (1819) represented 31 percent of the colony's total population; Spanish South America's quarter of a million slaves (89,000 in Peru, 64,000 in Venezuela, 54,000 in Colombia, and about 40,000 in the rest of the continent), by contrast, formed a mere 4 percent of the total: 7 or 8 percent in Peru and Venezuela, 5 percent in Colombia, and 1 or 2 percent in Chile, Ecuador, and the Río de la Plata region.

In both Brazil and Spanish America, the number of slaves present in the early 1800s was less than half (43 percent in Brazil, and 48 percent in Spanish America) the number of Africans imported over the course of the colonial period. This reflects a fundamental aspect of slavery in South America, as in most of the New World: the inability of the slave population to grow by natural increase, or even to maintain itself at fixed levels. This was a function in part of the harsh conditions of slave life, and in part of the gender imbalance in the slave population. On average, only about one-third of the Africans whom the slave trade brought to the New World were female. This was an insufficient number of childbearing women to compensate for the high levels of mortality suffered by the slave population as a whole; in most of the continent, the number of slave deaths consistently exceeded the number of slave births. Simply maintaining slave populations at a fixed level required constant infusions of new arrivals from Africa; and increasing those populations required ever larger numbers of imports, which in turn reinforced the gender imbalance and the slave population's inability to reproduce itself.

This vicious demographic cycle was most strongly felt in Brazil, which received almost 90 percent of the Africans brought to South America. More than in any of the Spanish colonies, slaves and slavery were absolutely central to Brazil's society and economy; and that centrality was reflected in the immense variety of uses for slave labor. Most slaves worked in the plantation sector, growing sugar, coffee, cotton, tobacco, and other tropical commodities for export, but even on the planta-

tions, the responsibilities filled by slaves were quite varied. Although most plantation slaves worked as field laborers, a significant minority—on the sugar plantations, 30 to 40 percent—worked in transport and refining, as skilled and semiskilled craftsmen and technicians, and as domestic servants.

Outside of the plantations, slaves worked in truck-farming (production for local consumption), as well as in cattle-ranching and the processing of meat in the *charqueadas* (drying and salting factories) of Rio Grande do Sul. Slaves were a large proportion, perhaps the majority, of the work force in the gold mines. They were also ubiquitous in towns and cities, working at every variety of manual occupation, from the most unskilled (day laborers and porters) to the most highly skilled (master artisans, artists and musicians, and barber-surgeons). Many worked as domestic servants; others participated in retail commerce as street vendors, often selling articles of their own manufacture, such as foodstuffs and candies, brooms, candles, combs, lace, and other items.

Much the same variety of slave occupations was found in Spanish America. Slaves worked on sugar plantations in coastal Peru, in the Cauca Valley of Colombia, and in the interior province of Tucumán in Argentina, and they grew cacao on coastal plantations in Venezuela. They mined for gold in Colombia and for copper at the Cocorote mines in Venezuela. They worked as cowboys in Argentina and Venezuela. In every major city of the empire they could be seen working as skilled craftsmen, street vendors, domestic servants, and day laborers.

The diversity of slave occupations translated into a corresponding diversity of living conditions and "life chances" for slaves. Conditions were most severe for plantation field laborers. On Brazilian sugar plantations, workdays of sixteen hours, and even longer during the harvest season, were common. The effects of overwork and exhaustion were compounded by hunger and malnutrition. Stuart Schwartz's research on plantations in Bahia concludes that "evidence is consistent from the beginning of the sugar economy to the end of the colonial era that slaves did not receive an adequate ration" (1985, p. 137). Overwork, inadequate nutrition, and poor or nonexistent medical care combined to produce high levels of mortality, especially infant mortality, and average life expectancy in the high teens to low twenties.

These central tendencies, however, conceal considerable variation of conditions, both from plantation to plantation and within individual plantations. Many planters allowed, and indeed encouraged, slaves to supplement their rations with vegetables grown on garden plots; some slaves were able to raise pigs and chickens for their own consumption or for sale. While field workers lived a hard and often miserable life, slaves who worked as domestic servants, acquired artisanal or technical skills, or rose into management positions as foremen and overseers, improved their status and position accordingly.

Possibilities for upward mobility and advancement were even greater in towns and cities, where most slaves participated either directly or indirectly in the cash economy. Many were "rented out," either by their owners or by themselves, and were allowed by law to keep whatever sums they earned over the daily quota they had to provide to their master. Slaves were also permitted to keep money they earned on Sundays and religious holidays, or in whatever spare time remained after fulfilling their obligations to their owners. Traveling about the city to carry out their work afforded slaves greater freedom of movement than on the plantations; and many urban slaves received permission to live apart from their masters and make their own arrangements for housing. Although such slaves remained legally tied and obligated to their owners, to whom they turned over most of their earnings, in many ways their conditions of daily life did not differ greatly from those of free blacks and mulattoes.

As a result of their greater ability to generate cash income and savings, urban slaves were granted their freedom by owners at higher rates than slaves in the countryside. Most such freeings, or manumissions, were made in response to cash payments or promises of future service by the slave to the master. Urban slaves were thus relatively advantaged in their pursuit of freedom, as were slaves in the mining zones of Brazil and Colombia, where cash circulated freely and there were numerous opportunities to earn money. Several groups in particular were favored for manumission: women, who were freed at rates higher than men; skilled workers, both in the city and the countryside; creole (American-born) slaves, in comparison to Africans; and slaves of mixed race, mulattoes or *pardos* ("browns")—over slaves of unmixed African ancestry.

Research by historians suggests annual manumission rates ranging from 0.6 percent in Brazil as a whole in the 1870s to 1.0 percent in late colonial Bahia, 1.2 percent in early nineteenth-century Lima, and 1.3 percent in early nineteenth-century Buenos Aires. In comparison to the United States or the non-Hispanic Caribbean, these were relatively high rates, which by the end of the colonial period had produced large free black and mulatto populations. Such populations were particularly noticeable in the gold-mining zones (by 1810, 75 percent of blacks and mulattoes in the Colombian Chocó and 45 percent of blacks and mulattoes in Minas Gerais were free) and in the region's major cities, where free blacks and mulattoes formed 10 to 20 percent of the total population (Lima, Rio de Janeiro) or more (Bahia, Caracas, Cartagena, Recife).

Still, most South American slaves exited slavery not through manumission but through death. Only a minority of slaves succeeded in winning their freedom; the rest remained enslaved and had to deal with that fact as best they could. As elsewhere in the Americas, this produced a variety of responses by slaves to their situation, some individual, some collective. One set of responses centered on the workplace and sought to capitalize on slaves' ability either to expedite or to impede production. Many slaves sought individual upward mobility and possible manumission by acquiring skills and abilities that would increase their earning power and improve their position in the slave labor force. Others negotiated with owners, either subtly or overtly, for better working or living conditions in exchange for higher levels of service or labor. If such improvements were not forthcoming, slaves could slow down their rhythm of work or engage in actual sabotage of production. Such tactics were not without risk and were often met with punishment.

A second set of responses centered on home and family, which slaves actively sought to create even in the face of enormous obstacles. The greatest such obstacle was the gender imbalance of the slave population. The gender balance was normal (a slight excess of females) among American-born slaves, but these were a minority among the slave populations of most of the region. Wherever Africans predominated, men outnumbered women, leaving many men without mates. Contemporary observers, and until recently many historians, concluded from this, and from the very low rates of formal marriages among slaves, that slaves were unable to forge any kind of stable family structure. During the past twenty years, however, research in plantation, notarial, and court records has yielded clear evidence of family formation among slaves, though at rates lower than in the free population. Slaves strove to form nuclear families wherever possible, and to maintain extended kinship networks spanning multiple generations.

A third set of responses centered on the community and on collective social and cultural activities. Prominent among these was religion. Many slaves took active part in the rites and rituals of Catholicism. Especially in towns and cities, slaves and free blacks formed lay brotherhoods or sodalities, often devoted to black saints or to the black Virgin of the Rosary, that built and administered churches and performed other community functions. Many slaves continued to worship African deities as well, often in conjunction with Catholic saints, the Virgin, and Jesus. In the process they created new syncretic religions, such as Brazilian Candomblé and Cuban Santería, that form a major part of Latin American religious life down to the present.

Closely tied to religion were music and dance. Catholic holidays were celebrated with African-style public dances, often presided over by elected monarchs-for-a-day. Slaves preferred to attend dances organized by members of their own African ethnic group and to dance to the music and rhythms of their nation. Some of the Catholic brotherhoods adopted specific African ethnic identities; by the late 1700s formally incorporated African national associations, independent of the Catholic Church, were appearing in Buenos Aires, Montevideo, Rio de Janeiro, and elsewhere. The dances and festivities sponsored by these organizations formed the basis for styles of music and dance that today are central components of national popular culture, including samba in Brazil, cumbia in Colombia, and tango in Argentina. Brazilian Carnaval, with its raucous celebrations carried out by massed corps of drummers and dancers, is the lineal descendant of those early African street dances.

Yet another response by slaves to slavery was flight and attempted escape. Colonial and nineteenth-century newspapers carried frequent advertisements asking for information on runaways and offering rewards for their return. Most of these escapes were short-lived and soon resulted in the return of the runaway to his or her owner. Others were more successful, particularly when slaves were able to make their way to encampments or settlements of runaways and find shelter there. These maroon settlements, called *quilombos* in Brazil and *palenques* in Spanish America, were found throughout the coastal regions. Most were small and had brief lifespans; some proved more durable, lasting for decades or more and providing shelter for hundreds or even thousands of runaways. In Ecuador such communities were concentrated in the Esmeraldas region on the Pacific coast, and in Colombia in the Cauca Valley and on the Caribbean coast near Cartagena. Runaway communities, or *cumbes*, were abundant in the coastal forests and interior plains of Venezuela: Spanish officials and foreign visitors reported about twenty thousand runaways at large in the colony both in the early 1700s and a century later in the early 1800s, representing at both points one-third of the slave population in the colony. The largest and best known *quilombo* was in northeastern Brazil at Palmares, a federation of West African-style villages housing twenty to thirty thousand ex-slaves, Indians, and even white fugitives from colonial rule. Palmares survived for more than seventy years until its conquest by the Portuguese in 1694 and 1695, at which point its inhabitants were forced back into slavery.

A final form of response, and the least common, was violence. Most slave violence was directed against other slaves, for reasons both of physical proximity and of the lower risk of punishment. Occasionally, however, individuals or small groups of slaves lashed out against overseers and masters; and on even rarer occasions, slaves rose up in armed rebellion. In all the Americas, only one such rebellion was ultimately successful—the Haitian Revolution (1791–1804). All others were put down, sometimes even before they had begun. Nevertheless, events in Haiti served as a striking example to both masters and slaves of what might be achieved through armed violence, and it seems to have contributed to a wave of slave rebellion that swept through northern and eastern South America in the 1790s and early 1800s. Slave conspiracies were uncovered in Bahia, Buenos Aires, and Coro (Venezuela) in the 1790s. Between 1809 and 1840 a number of slave rebellions, and more generalized rebellions in which slaves and free blacks played a conspicuous part, erupted up and down the Brazilian coast from Amazonian Pará in the north to Rio de Janeiro and São Paulo in the south. In a near-repeat of the Haitian rebellion, slaves in Venezuela rose en masse during the independence war, in 1812, and virtually destroyed the plantation sector of the economy.

Nonetheless, such rebellions were the exception rather than the rule. Peter Voelz (1993) has argued that slaves were far more likely to fight alongside their masters than against them; and evidence in support of this assertion can be found in the South American independence wars from 1810 to 1825. Offered their freedom in exchange for military service, thousands of slaves volunteered for the rebel armies in Argentina, Colombia, and Venezuela; many served in the Spanish forces as well. The rebels' need for slave and free black recruits, and for black political support for the cause of independence, resulted in abolition decrees and the termination of the slave trade throughout Spanish South America in the 1810s and early 1820s. Only in Chile, however, was abolition immediate and total. All other countries enacted "free womb" laws that granted freedom to the children of slave mothers while requiring the *libertos* to serve their mothers' masters until the age of majority. Slaves born before the decrees were enacted remained slaves; and Argentina and Peru even briefly reopened their slave trades in the 1830s and 1840s. Still, by the middle of the century the "free womb" laws had their effect. Slave populations had dwindled to a fraction of their former size (by the early 1850s, there were 24,000 in Peru, 16,000 in Colombia, and 12,000 in Venezuela) and were composed of middle-aged and elderly individuals. During the 1850s and 1860s, as part of larger programs of liberal reforms enacted at that time, all the Spanish South American nations followed Chile's earlier example in decreeing the final abolition of slavery.

The Spanish American experience, in which governments decreed gradual abolition and the termination of the slave trade in return for slave and free black support in the independence wars, was at sharp variance from that of Brazil. Owing to the relatively peaceful and uncontested nature of Brazil's gaining independence from Portugal in 1822, slavery, the slave trade, and plantation agriculture were able to continue undisturbed, and indeed strengthened, into the post-independence period. The destruction of Haiti's sugar plantations during the Haitian Revolution, and the ending first of slavery and then of apprenticeship in the British Caribbean in the 1830s, both reduced Caribbean sugar production, opening the way for increased production in Brazil. Even more important in maintaining slavery was the explosive growth of coffee cultivation in Rio de Janeiro, Minas Gerais, and São Paulo. By 1850 Brazil accounted for approximately half of the world's coffee supply; its plantations were sustained by the most intensive importation of slaves in the country's history, 1.1 million Africans between 1820 and 1850.

These imports took place in the face of intense pressure from Great Britain to bring the slave trade to an end. In 1850, following incursions by British cruisers into Brazilian territorial waters, the Brazilian Parliament finally agreed to end the Atlantic trade. Cut off from their African sources of supply, during the 1860s and 1870s coffee planters bought slaves from the cities and from the Brazilian northeast. As this internal trade increasingly concentrated the slave population in the coffee zones, political support for slavery weakened in the rest of the country. Parliament enacted a "free womb" law in 1871, and during the 1880s two northern states and a number of towns and cities abolished slavery within their borders. Urged on by abolitionists, slaves began to flee en masse from the plantations in 1887, taking refuge in the free cities; and in 1888 Parliament acknowledged the impending collapse of slavery by passing the "Golden Law" (*Lei Aurea*) of final abolition, thus bringing to an end the largest and longest-lasting slave system in the Americas.

[*See also* Abolition and Anti-Slavery, *article on* Latin America; Brazil; Confraternities; Emancipation in the Americas; Historiography, *article on* Latin American and Caribbean Slavery; Law, *article on* Latin America Law; Manumission; Mining; *and* Slave Trade, *articles on* Trans-Atlantic Trade *and* Brazil and the United States.]

BIBLIOGRAPHY

Andrews, George Reid. *The Afro-Argentines of Buenos Aires, 1800–1900*. Madison: University of Wisconsin Press, 1980.

Bethell, Leslie, ed. *Cambridge History of Latin America,* vol. 2, *Colonial Latin America*. Cambridge and New York: Cambridge University Press, 1985.

Klein, Herbert S. *African Slavery in Latin America and the Caribbean*. New York and Oxford: Oxford University Press, 1986.

Rout, Leslie B. *The African Experience in Spanish America: 1502 to the Present Day*. Cambridge and New York: Cambridge University Press, 1976.

Schwartz, Stuart B. *Slaves, Peasants, and Rebels: Brazilian Slavery Reconsidered*. Urbana: University of Illinois Press, 1992.

Schwartz, Stuart B. *Sugar Plantations in the Formation of Brazilian Society: Bahia, 1550–1835*. Cambridge and New York: Cambridge University Press, 1985.

Voelz, Peter M. *Slave and Soldier: The Military Impact of Blacks in the Colonial Americas*. New York: Garland Publishing, 1993.

—GEORGE REID ANDREWS

UNITED STATES. [*This entry comprises three articles. The first is an overview of the history of slavery and slaving in the United States. This is followed by two articles that focus respectively on the impact of these practices in the North and the South.*]

An Overview

Slavery varied enormously in the United States. The variations were most significant across space and over time. It is thus necessary to identify the many slave systems within the present boundaries of the United States and to sketch the salient features of their respective histories.

Slavery existed on a small scale in aboriginal North America. Many Indian societies consigned to servile status a few war captives who failed to get incorporated into clans; although these captives might escape torture and death, they lived on the margins of society. Northwest Coast Indians, who developed the most extensive form of hereditary slavery in North America, treated slaves harshly. Elsewhere, slaves, if they existed at all, generally formed a minor component of the workforce. Once Europeans arrived, aboriginal slavery changed dramatically. Indians began to sell war captives to the whites instead of torturing, adopting, or keeping them. Europeans also began enslaving Indian prisoners, either for domestic use or for foreign export. Tens of thousands of Indians were enslaved to meet European labor demands. By the late eighteenth century, some members of Indian nations such as the Cherokee emulated Anglo-American culture and began purchasing black slaves to perform manual labor. Among other Indians, slavery was mild: slaves among the Seminoles, for example, enjoyed considerable liberties. Indian slavery was a multifaceted phenomenon.

A second slave system arose when the first slaves of African descent arrived in North America. They landed in 1526, not 1619, and the site was not Jamestown but San Miguel de Gualdape, near present-day Sapelo Sound in Georgia. These slaves were probably not *bozales* or recently arrived Africans, but rather *ladinos* (artisans and domestics)— from Spain. The settlement was not a success; the slaves rebelled, and some may have taken up residence among the Guale Indians. Slaves were part of subsequent Spanish expeditions to the Southeast and were integral to the first permanent settlement, St. Augustine, established in 1565. In the late seventeenth century the Spanish government organized a black and mulatto militia in Florida, and in 1738 Spain established a town for freed slaves named Gracia Real de Santa Teresa de Mose, which served as an early-warning station against English attack.

Slaves thus played an important pioneering and military role in Spanish Florida. For a twenty-year period from 1763 to 1783, Florida became an extension of the rice and indigo plantation system then flourishing in the Lower South, but after the American Revolution it reverted to Spanish rule for almost four more decades. After the United States acquired Florida in 1821, it became a frontier area for slaveholding cotton-planters. Although possessing only sixty-two thousand slaves in 1860, Florida was 44 percent black and ranked fifth in

median holdings of slaves, with twenty-eight the median number per owner.

A third slave system emerged in 1619, when the first known African slaves arrived in the Chesapeake region. Slavery was slow to take root in the Chesapeake, and not until the late seventeenth century were Africans brought there in any numbers. Overall, fewer than one hundred thousand Africans reached Virginia and Maryland. By the early eighteenth century, however, the slave population was self-sustaining—the first large slave population in the Americas to grow quickly through natural increase. As a result, by 1780 more than three hundred thousand African Americans resided in the region; Virginia alone contained almost half the black population of the United States. Even on the eve of the Civil War, the Old Dominion still held more slaves than any other state. Most slaves in the Chesapeake worked first in tobacco and increasingly in mixed farming; they generally lived on small units, in close proximity to whites. Most tobacco plantations had fewer than twenty slaves. Over the course of the nineteenth century, the region began to fragment, with blacks acquiring more independence and opportunity, even freedom, in the upper than in the lower Chesapeake. The Chesapeake also became the primary seedbed for the Southeast, exporting its surplus of slaves.

Slavery came early to the mid-Atlantic region, a fourth slave system. The year 1626 marks the first record of African slaves in New Netherlands. Some of the 420 skeletons from the recently discovered African Burial Ground in New York seem to be seventeenth-century in origin. Slave numbers increased steadily for 175 years, so that by the end of the eighteenth century New York state contained the largest slave population of the postrevolutionary North. Slavery also took root in New Jersey, Pennsylvania, and Delaware. By 1780 more than forty thousand blacks lived in those four states. Most worked as farm laborers or domestic servants, although a sizable minority labored in the cities and towns. With the exception of Pennsylvania, slavery died a slow death in the mid-Atlantic region; not until the early nineteenth century were most slaves freed, and even then almost two thousand slaves lived in Delaware on the eve of the Civil War.

In adjoining New England, a fifth system, slavery was weakly rooted in the society yet important to the overall economy. Blacks arrived in New England in the early 1630s, but throughout the seventeenth and eighteenth centuries they were never more than a small fraction of the total population; only in Rhode Island were blacks more numerous, owing to the slave-trading significance of Newport, the rum-distilling industry, and large-scale dairying and ranching around Narragansett Bay. Slaves arrived in New England in large part because of an active trade with the West Indies, and that trade was central to the New England economy; indeed, even after the Revolution, trade with slave-based economies promoted significant growth in the region's wealth. However, slavery's marginality in New England society helps explains the institution's rapid demise after the American Revolution. Only fifteen thousand blacks lived in New England in 1780, and most of them were freed in the next two or three decades.

A sixth slave system developed in the late seventeenth century in the Low Country region of the Carolinas, and later in Georgia and eastern Florida. The Low Country, like Spanish Florida and French Louisiana, depended on slavery from the earliest colonial days. More than half of the slaves brought to North America in the eighteenth and early nineteenth centuries landed in the region. Most Africans arrived in Charleston, aptly termed the Ellis Island of African Americans (if due recognition is given the involuntary character of their migration). The weighty African presence, together with the large rice plantations, helps explain why Low Country slaves developed a widely spoken creole language and African-influenced customs. In Charleston, too, unlike any other city in the United States, slaves generally comprised a majority of the population. In 1780 the Lower South's

black population stood at almost 210,000. By 1860 Georgia and South Carolina ranked as the second and fifth leading slave states in the nation, and no state was as heavily black as South Carolina.

A seventh slave system crystallized early in the eighteenth century, when in little more than one decade French Louisiana received nearly all its African slaves. They entered a rough-and-tumble, violent world of military outposts, maroon camps, and interracial alliances that made the lower Mississippi Valley one of the most racially flexible societies in the Americas. The slave population grew sharply under Spanish rule from about five thousand in the mid-1760s to twenty-four thousand in 1800. From the early nineteenth century on, sugar was king in Louisiana; the state boasted the largest and richest plantations and the most active slave market in the South. Subject to the harshest work regime in the United States, Louisiana slaves at least could point to their rich community life, their creole language, and their heavily African-influenced folkways, typified in the Congo Square dances of New Orleans.

The American Revolution freed whites to evict Indians from lands west of the Allegheny Mountains, and thousands of slaves accompanied their masters into Kentucky and Tennessee, making this region the eighth slave system. Before 1820 perhaps as many as one hundred fifty thousand slaves arrived in this Upper South interior, some from Africa and some from North Carolina, but the vast majority from the Chesapeake. During the 1810s perhaps as many as one in five Chesapeake slaves moved to Kentucky or farther south. In 1776 the population of this Upper South interior region was about 10 percent black; by 1800 that proportion had doubled. It remained at 20 percent down to the Civil War. Most slaves in this region grew tobacco and hemp and engaged in mixed farming. In 1860 the median plantation size in Tennessee and Kentucky was about thirteen slaves.

The last slave system to arise in the United States was by far the largest; it sprawled across the huge Southern interior, especially on that fertile crescent of rich land stretching from upcountry Carolina through Georgia and Alabama to the Mississippi Delta. Waves of development, in response to a rising demand for cotton, drew settlers and slaves to the region: the invention of an improved cotton gin in 1793 was one catalyst as back-country Georgia and South Carolina opened up; in Alabama and Mississippi, major growth did not occur until after the War of 1812; and on slavery's last frontier, rapid expansion occurred only after the Texas Revolution. At the beginning of the nineteenth century about one in ten U.S. slaves lived on cotton plantations; by 1860, two in three did. In every decade between 1810 and 1860, more than one hundred thousand slave migrants moved into this huge Southern interior. Cotton plantations averaged just over thirty slaves in 1860. On the eve of the Civil War, the cotton South had become the largest regional slave system in the United States.

At least nine major slave systems, then, existed at one time or another within the present-day boundaries of the United States. It is possible to subdivide further: the Chesapeake had become at least two systems by 1860; the cotton South was not a uniform entity, with its ever-expanding frontier; and the Cape Fear region of North Carolina had much in common with the Low Country, but the middle and northern parts of the state can be regarded as a separate system. Additional slave systems might also be identified, such as urban, maritime, industrial, and highland systems. Conversely, it is possible to lump rather than split: New England and the mid-Atlantic can be seen as part of a Northern farming and urban system; and by the early nineteenth century, Florida had lost much of its distinctiveness and had become part of the cotton South. Finally, all these systems originated at different times and developed at varying rates. Slavery in the United States was not cut out of whole cloth but rather was a constantly changing patchwork.

BIBLIOGRAPHY

Berlin, Ira. "Time, Space, and the Evolution of Afro-American Society on British Mainland North Amer-

ica." *American Historical Review* 85 (1980): 44–78.

Berlin, Ira, and Ronald Hoffman, eds. *Slavery and Freedom in the Age of the American Revolution.* Charlottesville: University Press of Virginia, 1983.

Fogel, Robert W. *Without Consent or Contract: The Rise and Fall of American Slavery.* New York: W. W. Norton, 1989.

Kolchin, Peter. *American Slavery, 1619–1877.* New York: Hill and Wang, 1993.

—PHILIP MORGAN

The North

The Northern colonies of British North America adopted slavery almost as early as Virginia. Although involuntary bondage never became the dominant labor system of the North, from first settlement to the late eighteenth century it provided an important source of workers in Northern cities and their commercial hinterlands. Like its counterpart in the South, Northern slavery was racially based. The Dutch and English who settled along the Atlantic seaboard from Massachusetts to Pennsylvania kept Africans and Native Americans, but never whites, as slaves. Most Northern bondspeople were Africans imported in the West Indies trade.

New York and eastern New Jersey, founded as New Netherland by the Dutch, employed enslaved Africans earlier than other Northern colonies and retained the institution longer. The Dutch imported Africans into New Netherland by 1626; at the time of the English conquest in 1664, slavery was firmly rooted in the colony. Fifteen percent of the New York population was black in 1723, compared with 19 percent in Virginia and Maryland. After that date, the New York African-American population declined slightly—to 14 percent in 1760—while slavery expanded in the Chesapeake region. In New Jersey, enslavement of African Americans was more dominant in the eastern section close to New York City than in the western counties near Philadelphia. New York passed a gradual abolition act in 1799; five years later, New Jersey became the last northern state to abolish slavery.

In the New York region, and indeed throughout the North, black bondage was concentrated in the cities and commercial farming areas where merchants, craftsmen, and farmers possessed sufficient capital to afford the high purchase price of slaves and had sufficient work to keep them occupied year round. Enslaved African Americans performed many different jobs in urban areas, including domestic service, a wide variety of crafts, and such occupations as mariner, longshoreman, carter, and laborer. On commercial farms they raised grain and livestock, the North's most significant products. Many rural slaves were artisans and domestic workers, producing household manufactures such as textiles, cheese, butter, and beer.

New England slavery developed as early as 1641, remaining a marginal institution throughout the colonial period. In 1660 blacks numbered six hundred of a total New England population of thirty-three thousand; by 1770 they were still less than 3 percent of the region's inhabitants. Sons and daughters of farm owners supplied most of the region's labor; farmers who required additional help employed day workers for planting and harvest or, with enough capital, purchased a few indentured servants or slaves. Only in Rhode Island's Narragansett country and the lower Connecticut River valley did planters own considerable numbers of Africans.

New Englanders, like other English people, were prepared by their ethnocentric attitudes to regard Africans as "strangers" (or "outsiders") who could justifiably be enslaved. The Massachusetts Bay Colony, in its Body of Liberties of 1641, permitted enslavement of "lawful Captives taken in just wars, and such strangers as willingly sell themselves or are sold to us" (quoted in Greene, 1942, p. 63). Connecticut and Plymouth adopted the same policy, which permitted the sale of Native Americans whom they took as prisoners of war as well as the purchase of Africans who were captured by someone else. Even in Rhode Island, where the government tolerated Europeans of various religions and attempted to deal fairly with Indians, slavery and the slave trade flourished.

Although slavery was milder in New England than in the West Indies or Southern mainland colonies, legal codes defined enslaved and free blacks as a separate and subordinate caste. For example, the penalty suffered by New England slaves for striking whites was less severe than in the plantation colonies, but still the law favored Europeans of every status. On the other hand, masters were subject to a charge of murder if they killed a slave, including their own. And while Massachusetts banned sexual relationships and marriages between whites and blacks, none of the other New England colonies followed suit. The marriages of slaves had legal standing and could not be disrupted legally; blacks were allowed (in fact required) to marry under the same rules as whites. The New England states abolished slavery during the Revolutionary era, by court action in Vermont, Massachusetts, and New Hampshire, and by gradual abolition acts passed by Connecticut and Rhode Island in 1784.

Involuntary bondage flourished in Quaker Pennsylvania, despite warnings against the institution by some members of the Society of Friends. During the half-century after the colony's founding in 1681, many of the Quaker elite owned slaves. In 1720 blacks comprised approximately 12 percent of Philadelphia's population and were a sizable proportion of the rural work force. A number of wealthy immigrants to the new colony came from the West Indies, bringing their slaves and their trading connections with the islands. Like New England and New York, Pennsylvania found a market for its livestock, lumber, and foodstuffs in the sugar islands, a trade that included importation of blacks. After 1720 the proportion of African Americans in Philadelphia dropped as the number of manumissions slowly grew and slave-ownership came under increasing attack by Quakers as a sinful and unjust practice. The influx of Germans and Scots-Irish from the 1720s to the 1750s provided employers with the option of purchasing white indentured servants rather than slaves. By 1770 bondspeople were approximately 5 percent of the population of Philadelphia and 2.3 percent of Pennsylvania's inhabitants.

Most Pennsylvanians simply accepted the practice of slaveholding as worked out in other English colonies. The colony's constitution and first legal code neither legalized nor banned slavery. Slave-owners relied on custom to protect their property rights. At first, blacks were subject to the same laws as whites, but gradually the colony established the racial line, including a comprehensive slave code in 1726. Although this was more lenient toward slaves than were Southern codes, it seriously restricted the activities of free blacks, who could be returned to bondage for vagrancy or marrying a white. Pennsylvania did not force freed people to leave its borders, however, nor did it restrict immigration from other regions. With private manu-missions and passage of the gradual abolition act of 1780, slavery declined. Although the law limited emancipation to children subsequently born of slave women—and then only after they served their mother's master for twenty-eight years— most Pennsylvania slave-masters conformed to its provisions by manumitting all of their slaves after a term of years. Enslaved African Americans also freed themselves by running away. Pennsylvania became a haven for freed blacks and escaped slaves from other jurisdictions. Nevertheless, by law and by custom, Pennsylvania, like the rest of the North, established a caste system based on skin color that was as rigorous as that of the South.

[*See also* Historiography, *article on* North American Slavery; *and* Law, *article on* United States Law.]

BIBLIOGRAPHY

Greene, Lorenzo Johnston. *The Negro in Colonial New England*. New York: Columbia University Press, 1942.

Jordan, Winthrop D. *White Over Black: American Attitudes Toward the Negro, 1550–1812*. Chapel Hill: University of North Carolina Press, 1968.

McCusker, John J., and Russell R. Menard. *The Economy of British America, 1607–1789*. Chapel Hill: University of North Carolina Press, 1985.

Nash, Gary B., and Jean R. Soderlund. *Freedom By Degrees: Emancipation in Pennsylvania and Its Aftermath*. New York and Oxford: Oxford University Press, 1991.

Soderlund, Jean R. *Quakers and Slavery: A Divided Spirit*. Princeton: Princeton University Press, 1985.

White, Shane. *Somewhat More Independent: The End of Slavery in New York City, 1770–1810*. Athens: University of Georgia Press, 1991.

—JEAN R. SODERLUND

The South

In many important respects, the character of North American mainland slavery was distinctive from its beginnings in the seventeenth and eighteenth centuries. It is well known that mortality conditions on the mainland were favorable in comparison with those of the Caribbean islands. Long before the African slave trade was terminated by the U.S. Congress in 1807, natural population increase was the primary source of growth of the slave population, which grew at rates roughly similar to those of the free population. Of the total number of slaves transported from Africa (at least ten million), no more than about 6 percent went to the area that became the United States, yet by 1860 this same territory had the largest slave population in the New World. These slaves were overwhelmingly American-born rather than foreign-born—more so, in fact, than any other ethnic group in the country. As the literature on comparative slave systems has established, material conditions of slavery in the U.S. South were uniquely favorable; at the same time, legal rights and potential access to free status were uniquely limited. This contrast has been seen as paradoxical, yet both sets of conditions flowed from the same underlying context: scarce and valuable slave labor in a setting of strong demand, relatively favorable health conditions, and (after 1807) restrictions on new imports from Africa or other slave countries. Whereas in the Caribbean, Brazil, Cuba and elsewhere, closing the African slave trade was a decisive blow against slavery itself, in the United States the identical step helped to create the strongest slave system in the hemisphere.

In another sense, however, North American slavery was less essential to the economy than was true for most other major slave systems. North American slavery grew up around the labor demands of two staple crops, tobacco and cotton, but neither of these was intrinsically linked to slavery on either a technological or geographic basis. Tobacco was a high-value, care-intensive crop without major capital requirements or scale economies in production. It has continued as the epitome of a family-farm cash crop in modern times. Nonetheless, North American slavery in the eighteenth century was primarily tobacco slavery, production on plantations coexisting with production on small farms with few slaves or none. When cotton emerged as an alternative cash crop in the 1790s, it filled a nearly identical economic and social niche. It is a standard interpretation among American historians that Eli Whitney's cotton gin, which allowed successful commercial cultivation of upland cotton in the Piedmont region, broke down the economic barrier between the coastal plantations and the small-farm interior, giving both groups a common interest in cotton markets and giving slavery a new lease on life. Slavery thus fits very differently into North American economic history than it does elsewhere. In the sugar colonies of the Caribbean and Brazil, slavery made possible the development of commercial production in locations and under conditions that could not have attracted free labor; but in the U.S. South, the expansion of slavery displaced what would otherwise have been an expansion of small cotton-growing family farmers on the pattern of the North. One can analyze the effects of slavery relative to this alternative in terms that are meaningful in historical context (which is not to imply that this alternative history nearly happened).

The relative nonessentiality of slavery was also reflected in the fact that the institution in the U.S. South was embedded in a society with a large free white farming population, displaying a full range of stratification from wealthy planters to landless tenant farmers, and a developed political culture.

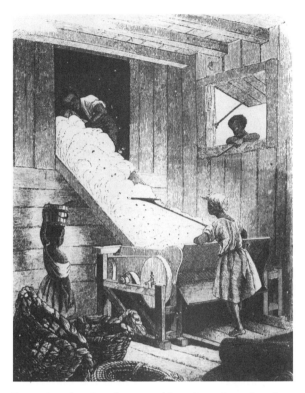

Engraving showing slaves working at a cotton gin, nineteenth century.

Unlike the British and French sugar islands, the antebellum South was not a society in which a small planter elite exercised power over a vast slave-majority population. To be sure, wealth in the South was more concentrated than in the agricultural North, but in 1860 there were 380,000 slave-owners in the Southern states, averaging ten slaves each. The great majority (88 percent) were small-to-moderate farmers owning between one and twenty slaves. In the cotton areas, more than half of the farm-operators owned slaves, a level of dispersion substantially broader than (for example) stock ownership in the United States today. Although the slave societies of Cuba and Brazil also had large coexisting free populations, in both cases there was a much more exclusive link between plantation slavery and export crops than in the South.

At the same time, in 1860 there were on the periphery of the cotton belt large numbers of non-slaveholding farmers, most of them owning land but participating only marginally in the market economy. In the east these areas had been left behind as backwaters when slave-owners leapfrogged onto the best cotton-growing soils farther south and west. In the Southwest, the vast potential of Texas and Arkansas as cotton states had barely been tapped at the time of secession. Although the region as a whole thus had great potential for agricultural expansion, commercial cultivation in much of it was limited by poor transportation and an absence of local credit and marketing facilities. The slave population, however, was heavily concentrated in the plantation region of the Deep South, a reasonably well-defined belt running from South Carolina to Louisiana, with smaller concentrations in Virginia and Tennessee. Here the crop transportation provided by natural waterways was generally sufficient.

Economic aspects of slavery in the South have long been objects of study by American historians and economists. Broadly speaking, the major issues may be grouped under three headings: the profitability of slavery; the efficiency of slavery as a method of production; and the impact of slavery on economic development. In all three cases, achieving clarity in the answers depends at least as much on defining the questions and concepts appropriately as it does on the outcomes of historical research.

"Profitability" refers to the private economic return to owners of slaves. For many years American historians entertained the idea that antebellum slavery was "unprofitable." Loosely based on the observation that slave prices tripled between 1807 and 1860 while cotton prices drifted downward, the notion of unprofitability was also associated with the view that the slave system was in a state of economic decline at the time of secession. (These doctrines are linked with the name of Ulrich B. Phillips, although in fact his position was more subtle than that of many of his followers.) In 1958

two applied economists, Alfred H. Conrad and John R. Meyer, published calculations intended to refute this claim, showing that at prevailing prices, yields, and life expectancies, investments in slaves would have paid rates of return about equal to those available from alternative investments, such as railroad bonds.

Subsequent research revealed, however, that Conrad and Meyer had merely obscured the underlying issue. If rates of return based on market prices were too high or too low, this imbalance could be readily corrected in the market for slaves. The more fundamental question was how these prices were determined. The analysis first presented in 1961 by Yasukichi Yasuba has since become generally accepted: After the closing of the African slave trade, the size of the aggregate slave population was fixed in the short run, independent of price. The slave population did, of course, grow over time, but only through the slow process of natural population growth; there was no short-run mechanism of elastic supply in response to changes in demand. The implication is that the observed rise in slave prices must have been the result of increases in the *demand* for slaves, and hence it could not very well be the basis for an "unprofitability" that would cause the decline of slavery. Indeed, the high profitability of slavery is itself reflected in the rising slave prices, the bulk of which are "capitalized rent" captured by owners at the time of birth or at the time of the price increase in the form of capital gains. In prosperous decades like the 1830s and the 1850s, capital gains were a major component of the profitability of slavery, and because of the operation of regional slave markets, these gains were enjoyed by virtually every owner, whether efficient in production or not.

The now-accepted finding of vigorous profitability during the antebellum era does not necessarily imply that this profitability was firmly rooted in sustainable sources of growth, such as productivity. There is reason to believe that the two-generation history of rising slave prices was not sustainable, because with the aid of hindsight it appears that the antebellum era was unique in its growth rate of demand for cotton, a crop for which the U.S. South had a strong geographic advantage. Cotton demand grew at 5 percent per year from 1820 to 1860, but the rate fell to between 1.5 and 2 percent per year from 1866 to 1895. This development seems to have been largely independent of the American Civil War; it reflects the inevitable slowing down of the first great wave of the Industrial Revolution in cotton textiles. The census year 1860 was at the very crest of this wave; a season in which cotton yields were far above normal combined with record demand to produce the most prosperous year in Southern history, and the highest slave prices. But these extremes of performance and price would surely not have continued, even if there had been no secession and Civil War.

"Efficiency" is a ratio of output to input; however, the *measurement* of efficiency generally entails the aggregation of several outputs and several inputs, and therein lies the conceptual problem. Slavery in the South might have been profitable to the owners despite inefficiency, if a higher ratio of expropriation from the slaves' labor made up for a lower level of output per slave. Indeed, a long-standing tradition in Western thought holds that slave labor is inherently inefficient because it is reluctantly supplied. Antebellum Northerners, including those who visited the South, were convinced that the inefficiency of slave labor was virtually self-evident. However, productivity measurements by Robert W. Fogel and Stanley L. Engerman, published in *Time on the Cross* (1974), indicated that slave plantations were as much as 30 percent more efficient than free family farms in the North or South. The subsequent debate has clustered around two interpretive positions: that of Fogel and Engerman, who attribute the productivity advantage to scale economies, gang labor methods, and the intensity of labor time; and that of Gavin Wright (1978) and others, who attribute the differential to the allocation of labor time between production for the market on the one hand, and food production, household activities, and leisure

time on the other. *Efficiency* may seem an inappropriate term to apply to either of these conceptions, since the desires of the slaves are clearly excluded from the values (or weights) used to aggregate outputs and inputs. Nonetheless, within the logic of a slave society (the logic of the master class) both views agree on the conclusion of efficiency. The first sees it as "productive" efficiency, and the second as primarily "allocative" efficiency, that is, a closer match between resources and market demands.

As Fogel and Engerman approached the issue, scale economies and labor intensity are inferences drawn directly from the statistical data. The productivity differential is largest on large plantations, while Southern slaves do not seem to have worked significantly more days or hours per year than Northern family farmers. The alternative view rests on certain regularities in the economic structure. The main points are that slave-using operations planted a substantially larger share of their acreage in cash crops as opposed to food crops (mainly cotton versus corn), and that a larger share of the labor time of slave households was allocated to market production than was true for free families (mainly the result of women doing fieldwork instead of housework). Direct tests indicate that cotton was a more profitable choice than corn for farms at all levels, but for a variety of reasons, smaller farms chose to grow less cotton than they might have. Some were too far from markets or transportation facilities. Others were simply cautious. Production of cotton for the market at the expense of self-sufficiency was a risky choice for a small farmer with little in reserve. The rule of thumb they followed is known as "safety first": plant enough corn to meet the farm's requirements (with a reasonable margin for error), then plant the remainder in cotton, treating it as a "surplus" crop.

Concerning the intrafamily division of labor and the length of the work year, comparisons with Northern farmers are not necessarily germane, because the seasonality of agriculture was so different in the two regions. Nonetheless, slavery did increase the number of fieldwork hours per family, or so adjustments after emancipation would suggest. Black women withdrew from field work in large numbers after emancipation, while hours worked per day and per week declined. Roger Ransom and Richard Sutch (1977) estimate the decline in black labor supply at 28 to 37 percent per slave.

If these two effects, crop mix and family labor, are both valid, the crucial productivity effect comes from the interaction between them. A number of studies have shown that both large and small Southern farms were self-sufficient in foods, at about the same levels of consumption per person, per hog, or per mule. Because of its ability to collectivize such duties as food preparation and child care, however, the plantation was able to put additional labor into the fields. In effect, all of this additional labor went into the high-payoff cash crop. Thus the two effects jointly had an impact substantially greater than the sum of their separate effects would have been.

The plausibility of this view is enhanced by two additional observations. First, the sizes of cotton-farming operations did not cluster around a large "optimal" scale, as they did in crops like sugar and rice, where technological scale economies were important. Second, in economic activities with homogeneous outputs and inputs, such as mining, manufacturing, and grain-farming, there is no evidence of a productivity differential between free and slave labor.

If slave labor was productive, mobile, and efficiently allocated according to market principles, and if production and wealth were growing rapidly under the slave regime (albeit with the aid of strong cotton demand), the question arises as to why so many Northern observers (and some Southerners) felt so strongly that both slavery and the South were economically backward. It is possible that such views reflected only bias, ignorance, racism, or lack of economic sophistication. More plausibly, these perceptions arose from the objective fact that patterns of Southern economic development under slavery were indeed quite different from those in the North. The South invested far less in transportation facilities relative to its area than did the North. The canal boom of the 1830s almost completely bypassed the South, and the density of its railroad mileage even in 1860 was only about one-third that of the North. Urbanization rates were markedly lower, and this difference was steadily widening over time. Even more notable was the contrast in numbers of small towns: crossroads communities with stores, post offices, libraries, and schools dotted the countryside across the Northern states, but they were few and far between in the South. To be sure, economic progress and backwardness are relative concepts, and by many of these conventional measures, the American South was well ahead of Brazil and other slave economies in the mid-nineteenth century. Nevertheless, the regional contrast was so great in such visible manifestations of progress as towns, railroads and factories, that it is not difficult to see why Northerners thought the slave South was backward.

Equally important was the difference in population growth, almost entirely the result of the fact that foreign immigration went overwhelmingly to the North. Immigrants were actively recruited by Northern land-owners, as well as by owners of fixed manufacturing capital looking for cheap labor. These motivations were virtually reversed under the high-price slave regime of the U.S. South. Slave-owners in all parts of the South actively opposed the campaign to reopen the African slave trade. They may have had many reasons for doing so, but an aspect that was not lost on them was that such a proposal would instantly wipe out a large fraction of their accumulated wealth by reducing slave prices. Thus the incentives of slave-ownership led the South to remain isolated from outside labor flows, and for this reason the South was "falling behind" in the specific sense that the Southern share of total national population or economy was steadily declining.

Slower population growth was directly related to Southern backwardness in manufacturing.

Slaves could and did work effectively in factories, including skilled jobs, but their value was still greater in the cotton-fields, especially in the rich new lands of the Old Southwest. The ability to tap into an elastic supply of foreign labor was crucial to the survival and growth of manufacturing in the North, even while opportunities in farming were expanding. The slave South, however, rejected this option, and hence manufacturing languished during times of agricultural prosperity. A specific example is the textile industry, which grew at a 6 percent annual rate during the 1840s, only to have its progress stifled in the 1850s. Recent studies link the regional lag in manufacturing more comprehensively to differences in the extent of markets, associated in turn with limited development of networks of cities and towns.

Another way in which the economic effects of slavery may be ascertained is by noting the changes in economic structure that began immediately after emancipation. A reorientation toward land-intensity occurred on many fronts. Railroad investment accelerated, and interior towns began to spring up. A new interest in mineral exploration led to a wave of discoveries and development schemes, from the phosphorus deposits of South Carolina to the coal and iron ores of Alabama and Tennessee. Phosphorus mining was associated with another striking new development, the fertilizer revolution that revived or initiated commercial cotton-growing in many parts of the Southeast that had been previously abandoned or passed over. In both the Southeast and Old Southwest, town-building efforts were closely linked to new progress in manufacturing, especially in the textile and iron industries. These departures make it clear that the institution of slavery had a major influence on the pattern and structure of the Southern economy.

Emancipation did not, of course, immediately bring the South into the mainstream of national economic development. The Reconstruction period accentuated the geographic divide between the plantation belt of the Deep South and the newly energized cities and towns of the Upper South. Although the former had originally been the richest and most prosperous section of the slave South, by the end of the nineteenth century it was the most impoverished region in the country. These developments clearly reflected the effects of the slavery era, not just in physical infrastructure but also in the political and cultural legacies of both races. These are chapters in the economic history of the postslavery era. Exactly what shape the slave economy might have taken had it survived into the twentieth century will always be a matter for speculation. What we can say is that slavery in the American South did not create an economy well-suited for rapid integration into the capitalist world.

[*See also* Economics; *and* Historiography, *article on* North American Slavery.]

BIBLIOGRAPHY

Fogel, Robert W. *Without Consent or Contract: The Rise and Fall of American Slavery*. New York: Norton, 1989.

Kolchin, Peter. *American Slavery, 1619–1877*. New York: Hill and Wang, 1993.

Oakes, James. *Slavery and Freedom: An Interpretation of the Old South*. New York: Alfred A. Knopf, 1990.

Ransom, Roger L., and Richard Sutch. *One Kind of Freedom: The Economic Consequences of Emancipation*. Cambridge and New York: Cambridge University Press, 1977.

Tadman, Michael. *Speculators and Slaves: Masters, Traders, and Slaves in the Old South*. Madison: University of Wisconsin Press, 1989.

Weiman, David. "Staple Crops and Slave Plantations." In *Agriculture and National Development*, edited by Lou Ferleger. Ames: Iowa State University Press, 1990.

Wright, Gavin. *The Political Economy of the Cotton South*. New York: W.W. Norton, 1978.

—GAVIN WRIGHT

URBAN SLAVERY. The subject of urban slavery has attracted much less attention than rural slavery. This is unfortunate, because slavery in cities has been as widespread and ancient as its rural counterpart. The greater number of slaves lived and worked in the countryside largely because until recently, most people, whether slave or free, lived in rural areas and engaged in agricultural pursuits. Urban slavery demonstrates how adaptable the institution has been over the millennia. In adapting to the city, however, urban slavery became converted into something quite different from what it had been in the countryside.

Prevalence of Urban Slavery. Some scholars, notably Richard Wade, have argued that city life was incompatible with slavery. In *Slavery in the Cities* (1964), Wade argued that in the United States, urban labor markets required skilled workers and flexible work conditions, both of which tended to undermine slavery. The publication of Wade's book stimulated a group of scholars who have devoted themselves to showing that Wade's thesis was not necessarily true. Claudia Goldin (1976), for example, attributes the relative decline of slavery in Southern U.S. cities to a greater demand for their labor in the countryside rather than to any incompatibility between slavery and urban life. The census bears out Goldin's argument: in 1860 U.S. slaves were as likely as the rest of the population to live in cities. This was true for a cotton state like Georgia, where 8 percent of slaves and 11 percent of freeborn persons lived in cities, and it was almost as true for a tobacco state like Virginia, where the corresponding figures were 7 and 14 percent. It was probably true as well in the Caribbean. In the British West Indies, the percentage of urban slaves was as high as in the United States, and in the Spanish colony of Cuba the percentage was perhaps twice as high.

In addition to being widespread, urban slavery was quite ancient. Slaves were present in the courts and urban centers of ancient Mesopotamia, Egypt,

Engraving of a view of the waterfront of Christiansted, Saint Croix, Danish West Indies, nineteenth century.

Israel, India, and China. In ancient Greece and Rome, they formed as large a proportion of the population as in the U.S. South. In Athens, slaves were an important, perhaps indispensable, part of the economy, and provide early evidence that slavery for some and freedom for others—even in an urban setting—were quite compatible. In the Middle Ages, urban slavery was less common in Europe than it had been in Athens and Rome. This was especially true for northern Europe; Germans had a saying, *"Stadtluft macht frei"* ("city air makes one free"). In Mediterranean cities such as Venice, Genoa, Florence, Marseille, and Córdoba, however, slavery and the slave trade continued into the modern era. In Islamic lands (including southern Spain), urban slavery flourished more than in medieval Europe, partly because Islam was a more urban society than medieval Europe.

Occupations of Urban Slaves. One reason for the persistence of urban slavery was its flexibility, including its effective use of women. Most urban slaves worked as household servants, a majority of whom were women. Male slaves typically served as laborers, artisans, servants, and personal retainers of their masters, sometimes rising to positions of prominence in the master's household.

Another reason for the persistence of urban slavery was the ability of slaves to perform many of the most skilled and demanding tasks of urban society. Some have argued that slave labor almost always was inferior, either because of slaves' personal inadequacies or because of the system's lack of incentives. The historical record belies both assumptions. Slaves proved themselves quite capable of carrying out complex tasks. In ancient Greece, they were widely used both as domestic servants and as skilled workers. We get some idea of the scope of this practice from Thucydides's report that during the siege of Athens about twenty thousand Athenian slaves, most of them craftsmen, ran away.

Similarly, urban slavery flourished in ancient Rome. The great majority of Roman urban slaves were household servants, owned not just by the elite and the aristocracy, but by a wide swathe of Roman society, including the middle class and artisans. They performed a remarkably broad range of duties, working as maids, guards, and repairmen but also as teachers and physicians. Some, both male and female, became concubines or lovers of their master; quite a few of the women became prostitutes. The especially talented and lucky became imperial household slaves, who handled much of the administration of the empire—staffing the bureaucracy, handling record-keeping and correspondence, collecting taxes, disbursing money, and running the libraries and postal system.

In Han China (c. 100 BCE), slavery was not particularly important to the economy or society, but it clearly existed. It is not possible to get a sense of the urban nature of Chinese slavery, but slaves worked in a wide range of occupations that could well have had an urban connotation. Wilbur (1943) reports that, in addition to work in agriculture and public construction projects, slaves worked in commerce, in handicrafts, and especially as personal domestic servants. Some were the possession of the imperial court and the government, where they worked as clerks, accountants, and petty bureaucrats.

In the Islamic world, slaves performed a wide variety of functions. Most worked as domestic servants and artisans; a few had special highly prized functions, notably as musicians and dancers. One function was distinctive: female slaves in harems were overseen by slave eunuch guards. In the Sudanic kingdoms of medieval Africa, cities like Timbuktu, Jenne, and Gao served as major transshipment centers for sub-Saharan slaves being shipped to cities of the Arab Mediterranean.

In the modern era, slaves in cities like Lima, Peru, were found in virtually any job involving artisanry or labor, whether skilled or unskilled. While most of the women worked as domestic servants, the men performed a wide range of occupations. They made shoes, adobe bricks, and chocolate, in addition to working in bakeries and pastry shops and as general laborers, porters, water-carriers, painters, bricklayers, shoemakers, night-watchmen, and soldiers. Both men and women sold food and produce in the city markets.

In the U.S. South, urban slaves worked at what Wade (1964, chap. 2) has termed "an enormously varied number of positions." In 1848 a special census for the city of Savannah listed slaves in such occupations as boatman, coachman, domestic servant, fisherman, gardener, huckster, market seller, porter, sailor, stevedore, washerwoman, apprentice, baker, barber, blacksmith, bookbinder, bootmaker, brass founder, bricklayer, butcher, cabinetmaker, carpenter, cigar maker, coachmaker, confectioner, cook, cooper, mechanic, nurse, painter, plasterer, printer, saddler, seamstress, ship carpenter, shoe maker, tailor, tinner, upholsterer, wharf-builder, engineer, and pilot. Goldin (1976) calculated that in Charleston 17 percent of the male slave labor force "had substantial skills" and made up 43 percent of the city's carpenters, 73 percent of its coopers, 87 percent of its blacksmiths, 32 percent of its painters, and 49 percent of its ship carpenters. The tobacco factories and iron foundries of Richmond, Virginia, were manned almost exclusively by slave labor. Slaves' prominence in urban trades and industrial occupations prompted long complaints from white artisans, to no avail.

Treatment of Urban and Rural Slaves. In adapting to urban conditions, as Wade claimed, urban slavery became different from rural slavery. Not the least of these differences involved treatment. Urban slaves, especially those who were house servants, generally received better food, clothing, and housing as a result of living in closer proximity to their masters. An owner who held slaves for reasons of prestige and status had an incentive to ensure that slaves appeared happy and well cared for, because their appearance reflected on their owners' wealth and position.

Another difference involved flexibility and work incentives. Urban slavery required a flexible labor force and developed the institution of hiring out; sometimes owners allowed their slaves to hire themselves (self-hire) in return for a payment to the master. Such institutions and flexibility provided incentives for slaves to perform skilled tasks under moderate supervision. Thus urban slavery increased the contacts and independence of the urban slave beyond those of his rural counterpart. Urban slaves performed a wider range of occupations and had a larger percentage of skilled workers than did rural slaves, largely because of the more elaborate nature of urban labor requirements. Skilled work and the related possibility of hiring out provided urban slaves a greater degree of control over their work and leisure. In addition, public opinion operated more strongly in urban areas to curtail the worst excesses of slave-owners, simply because there were persons around to hear the abused slaves' screams. Frederick Douglass lived and worked in both the city of Baltimore and in the countryside of nineteenth-century Maryland. Having experienced slavery in both settings, Douglass concluded that "compared to the rural slave, the city slave is half-free," partly because of this force of public opinion. He also felt that the city offered the slave more opportunities for learning and provided more varied experiences to which the slave could contrast his condition. In the New World, free blacks were more frequently city-dwellers than rural; because of this, interaction of slaves and free blacks occurred more frequently in urban than in rural areas.

Nonetheless, one should not romanticize the condition of urban slaves. In Rome, in the Islamic world, in ancient China, and elsewhere, female slaves were often turned into prostitutes. Others who became concubines and mistresses might suffer not only sexual abuse by their masters but also cruel punishment at the hands of jealous wives. The hours required of domestic slaves, typically round-the-clock service, exceeded those of rural agricultural slaves. White artisans in the American South complained bitterly of slave artisans because they could not compete with them, being unwilling to tolerate the low wages and poor working conditions forced on slaves. Of course, these conditions prevailed also for rural household servants and artisans, but to the extent that urban slaves were more likely to engage in these occupations than their rural counterparts, they constituted an important factor in the quality of urban slave life.

Urban Slavery and Emancipation. Urban slaves were more frequently manumitted than their rural counterparts. Partly this was a result of closer contact with their masters, permitting ties of friendship and even kinship to develop. In the New World, urban slaves who hired themselves out for wages were more able to acquire funds with which to purchase the freedom of themselves and their families. In Cuba this practice became institutionalized as *coartación*. The combination of greater occupational skills, greater access to institutionalized means for self-purchase, and greater contact with masters resulted in urban slaves being freed at a substantially higher rate than their rural counterparts.

Frederick P. Bowser maintains that in Latin America manumission "was largely an urban phenomenon" (1975, p. 334). Orlando Patterson (1982), citing examples from Jamaica, South Africa, ancient Greece and Rome, Han China, and the Islamic lands, has extended Bowser's conclusion to much of the slave-owning world. In ancient Rome, voluntary manumission occurred on a massive scale.

Slave resistance also was different in cities from in the countryside. Slave revolts have been rare throughout the history of the institution, but at least in the New World they have been more characteristic of rural slaves than of urban. In the United States, running away was a much more common form of resistance than outright revolt. Even in this, however, urban-rural differences appear, and scholars such as Gerald Mullin (1972) have found that urban slaves, being more acculturated, tended to run away individually, while rural slaves tended to run away in groups.

Urban Slavery and Acculturation. The greater proximity of slaves and masters promoted acculturation to the latter's culture. We have little evidence from the ancient world that urban slaves were long shut out from the dominant culture of the masters. One reason for this undoubtedly was the enormous ethnic and national diversity of slaves in the ancient world. In classical Greece, slaves included Italians, Illyrians, Thracians, Scythians, Phrygians, Armenians, Arabs, Palestinians, Egyptians, and even Ethiopians, with an especially heavy concentration coming from Asia Minor (modern Turkey), Syria, Thrace (modern Bulgaria), and the northern coast of the Black Sea. In Rome, slaves were drawn from these groups plus Greeks, Sardinians, Spaniards, Gauls, Germans, and Carthaginians. It is generally not even possible to distinguish slave from free in ancient Roman portraits and art, causing scholars to invest heavily in name analysis to distinguish foreign-born slaves. Even in Muslim lands, where black Africans formed a racially distinctive slave population, the evidence points to rapid cultural assimilation. It is primarily in the race-based slave societies of the Americas that slave acculturation to the mores and folkways of the dominant society was retarded. Even in those societies, however, urban slaves acculturated more rapidly than their rural counterparts. In the United States, urban slaves more quickly learned standard English, Christianity, and white ways than did their counterparts in the rural Deep South.

In some cases, however, the reverse was true. Cities in the Caribbean and Brazil typically had large populations of blacks, both slave and free. They congregated in streets and squares that were relatively free of white supervision, which helped them preserve their African cultural background. When whites in Bridgetown, Barbados complained in the 1820s of being regularly "annoyed" by the sound of drums and dancing, this was a sign that they were unable to control the traditional cultural expressions of slaves and free blacks. In Havana, Salvador, and Rio de Janeiro blacks, both slave and free, forged new African-based religions, which flourished in Latin American cities more than in the countryside.

The United States provides a case in which African cultural forms survived more directly in isolated rural areas of the Deep South. Partly this was because house servants were more prevalent in urban areas than in the countryside, and the pressures on house servants to assimilate the master's culture and religion generally were greater than among rural laborers. However, in New Orleans, the famous Congo Square sponsored large slave gatherings on Sundays, whereby traditional dances and African practices were maintained.

[*See also* Europe, *article on* Ancient World; Occupational Mobility; Occupations; *and* United States, *article on* The South.]

BIBLIOGRAPHY

Bowser, Frederick P. "The Free Person of Color in Mexico and Lima, 1580–1650." In *Race and Slavery in the Western Hemisphere: Quantitative Studies,* edited by Stanley L. Engerman and Eugene D. Genovese. Princeton: Princeton University Press, 1975.

Chanana, Dev Raj. *Slavery in Ancient India, as Depicted in Pali and Sanskrit Texts.* New Delhi: People's Publishing House, 1960.

Davis, David Brion. *The Problem of Slavery in Western Culture.* Ithaca, N.Y.: Cornell University Press, 1966.

Finley, Moses I., ed. *Slavery in Classical Antiquity: Views and Controversies.* Cambridge: W. Heffer, 1960.

Goldin, Claudia. *Urban Slavery in the American South, 1820–1860.* Chicago: University of Chicago Press, 1976.

Higman, Barry W. *Slave Populations of the British Caribbean, 1807–1834.* Baltimore: Johns Hopkins University Press, 1984.

Mendelsohn, Isaac. *Slavery in the Ancient Near East.* New York and Oxford: Oxford University Press, 1949.

Mullin, Gerald. *Flight and Rebellion: Slave Resistance in Eighteenth-Century Virginia.* London: Oxford University Press, 1972.

Origo, Iris. "The Domestic Enemy: The Eastern Slaves in Tuscany in the Fourteenth and Fifteenth Centuries." *Speculum* 30 (1955): 321–366.

Patterson, Orlando. *Slavery and Social Death: A Comparative Study.* Cambridge, Mass.: Harvard University Press, 1982.

Wade, Richard. *Slavery in the Cities: The South, 1820–1860.* New York and Oxford: Oxford University Press, 1964.

Wilbur, C. Martin. *Slavery in China during the Former Han Dynasty, 206 b.c.–a.d. 25.* Chicago: Field Museum of Natural History, 1943.

—LAURENCE GLASCO

WAGE SLAVERY. A number of different labor systems have been called "wage slavery" by socialist and proto-socialist writers during the past two centuries. Karl Marx used the term rhetorically as part of his powerful critique of early capitalism in the first volume of *Capital.* To him, "wage slavery" was what happened when chattel slavery, feudalism, and other labor systems had been replaced by the capitalism of free trade:

> [T]he annihilation of the necessities of life [that now occurred, resulted in the workers'] continuous reappearance in the labour market. In the days of classical Rome, the slave was bound in chains; the wage worker is bound to his owner by invisible threads. The appearance of independence is kept up by means of the perpetual change from one wage lord to another, and by the legal fiction of the contract. (Marx, 1972, p. 540)

Nonetheless, slavery remained, in the sense both of great oppression and of external control. Under capitalism, workers were condemned to sell their labor power in return for wages with which to purchase the means of subsistence. Marx considered this a very poor bargain for the workers concerned. Because of the nature of capitalist mechanization, their wages were on a generally downward spiral. "Wage slaves" were doomed to ever-increasing immiseration until the birth of a new order.

In retrospect, Marx's interpretation is all too easy to reject because of the dramatic improvements that occurred subsequently in wages during the twentieth century in advanced capitalist countries, but it was a different matter when Marx was writing. Workers' conditions under early capitalism seemed worse in certain respects than under chattel slavery. The growing "reserve army" of unemployed workers also seemed likely to weaken employed workers' bargaining powers with capitalist bosses. Marx's hostility to early capitalism was not unique; it was paralleled by criticisms of its impact made by ethical and utopian socialists throughout the nineteenth century.

Charles Fourier lived at the close of the eighteenth century and the beginning of the nineteenth. He considered commerce of any kind to be a major cause of evil in France of his time. Society needed to be reconstructed. Merchants should become the servants, not the masters, of manufacturers and producers of wealth. People should therefore be regrouped into communities of no more than two thousand; each community, or "phalanx," would then cultivate up to five thousand acres of land. Workers would not be paid wages but would be socially recompensed in more rewarding ways. Subsequently, Marx criticized the utopian character of Fourier's writings. Nonetheless, a number of "phalanxes" inspired by Fourier were set up later at Red Bank, New Jersey, at Guise in France and, most recently, in Israel, the former Yugoslavia, and the Third World. Fourier's ideas were also to have an impact, together with those of Marx and his followers, on socialists' attitudes toward similar labor systems well into the twentieth century.

John Ruskin was representative of nineteenth-century English ethical socialism's reservations. "The immediate operation of justice in this respect," wrote Ruskin in 1862, is "to diminish the power of wealth, first in acquisition of luxury, and, secondly, in exercise of moral influence." Otherwise, slave-owners and slaves alike would be morally compromised. Ruskin went on:

> There is not yet, nor will yet for ages be, any real over-population in the world; but a local over-population, or, more accurately, a degree of population locally unmanageable under existing circumstances for want of forethought and sufficient machinery, necessarily shows itself by pressure of competition; and taking advantage of this competition by the purchaser to obtain their labor unjustly cheap, consummates at once their suffering and his own; for in this (as I believe in every other kind of slavery) the oppressor suffers at last more than the oppressed.

By the early twentieth century, English socialists were more concerned with the fate of those oppressed by the wage system than with those benefiting from it. To the "guild socialists" who flourished immediately before, during, and after World War I, political democracy seemed to offer little; the British Labor Party remained a small pressure group, and industrial workers in Britain were at the mercy of capitalist employers concentrated into even larger industrial corporations than existed in Marx's lifetime. Workers' control seemed a more worthy objective to strive for than workers' representation at Westminster. Revived guilds of craftsmen seemed more preferable paths to progress than the general strike viewed favorably elsewhere at this time. Many "guild socialists" were Marxist in sentiment; others were medievalist in imagination, many of them Anglo-Catholics seeking to revive craft associations from the precapitalist era as instruments of self-governing industry in modern times. Inevitably, when labor became short in British factories during World War I, industrialists and politicians listened to trade unionists more respectfully; and when wartime conditions of production led to friction between workers and employers, workers demanded control more insistently. However, when a surplus of labor returned to Britain after the war, employers' attitudes changed, and with the increased popularity of central planning among socialists with the rise of the Soviet Union, "guild socialism" disappeared into the history books.

Following the collapse of the Soviet Union and its satellite states with the end of the Cold War, the socialism of civil servants has suffered a fate similar to the earlier attempted regulation of wages by workers' control. *Wage slavery* is today a phrase more frequently employed by historians than by politicians, industrialists, or trade unionists. Sometimes it is used as a general description of the era following the emancipation of chattel slaves in the Americas during the nineteenth century, when contract, indentured, and forced-labor systems multiplied and capitalists used every device imaginable to frustrate the fair and unfettered operation of the free-enterprise system. Adam Smith's *Wealth of Nations* (1776) was probably right to predict that, all other things being equal, slaves would prove better workers once they were free. But all other things were not to be equal. When chattel slaves were freed from their slavery, their former masters and future employers were also freed from any lasting concern for their workers' welfare. The trickery, political manipulation, and sheer brutality manifested during the era of contract and indentured labor did not create the best environment in which an expansive and liberal capitalism might emerge in the Third World. Nor did the forced labor regimes of European colonial powers prove the happiest and most efficient stimulants to free labor and enterprise in the early twentieth century. Analytically, *wage slavery* is probably better used by historians not as a blanket term for indentured, contract, or forced labor in the Third World,

but as it was actually used at the start of the era of free trade capitalism in both the Old and New worlds: as a description of the oppressed status of newly waged workers, used by these workers themselves or by contemporary observers of a Marxian, Fourierist or Ruskinesque disposition.

[*See also* Capitalism and Slavery; *and* Marxism.]

BIBLIOGRAPHY

Gray, Alexander. *The Socialist Tradition*. London: Longmans, Green, 1946.

Marx, Karl. *Capital*. Vol. 1. Rev. ed. by Frederick Engels, 1890. Translated by Eden and Cedar Paul. London: Dent, 1972.

Ruskin, John. *Unto This Last . . .* [1862] Rpt., London: Dent, 1979.

Turner, Mary, ed. *From Chattel Slaves to Wage Slaves: The Dynamics of Wage Bargaining in the Americas*. London: Ian Currey, 1995.

Twaddle, Michael, ed. *The Wages of Slavery: From Chattel Slavery to Wage Labor in Africa, the Caribbean and England*. London: Frank Cass, 1993.

—MICHAEL TWADDLE

Illustration Credits

Alinari/Art Resource, New York, p. 195; American Antiquarian Association, Worcester, Massachusetts, p. 276; Art Resource, New York, p. 40; Barbados Museum and Historical Society, St. Ann's Garrison, St. Michael; p. 215; Bibliotheque Nationale, Paris, p. 69; Boston Public Library, pp. 52, 53; Trustees of the British Museum, p. 68 (bottom); The John Carter Brown Library at Brown University, Providence, p. 117; Carnegie Museum of Art, Pittsburgh, p. 76 ; Chicago Historical Society, p. 75; École Nationale Supérieure des Beaux-Arts, Paris, p. 373; Giraudon/Art Resource, New York, pp. 2, 20, 133, 341, 349; Library of Congress, Washington, D.C., pp. 24, 26, 33, 99, 139, 176, 177, 202, 219, 259, 324; The Library of Virginia, Richmond, p. 330; Louisiana and Special Collections, Earl K. Long Library, University of New Orleans, p. 267; Collection of the Madison County Historical Society, Oneida, New York, p. 57; Frank McGlynn, pp. 127, 220, 328, 406; The Menil Collection, Houston, p. 67 (top and bottom); Museum of Fine Arts, Boston, p. 71 (bottom); National Archives, Washington, D.C., p. 319; National Library of Australia, Canberra, pp. 206, 313; National Library of Jamaica, Kingston, p. 71 (top); National Maritime Museum, Greenwich, London, p. 11; Oberlin College Library, Oberlin, Ohio, pp. 377, 379; Onandaga Historical Association, Syracuse, New York, p. 304; The Philbrook Museum of Art, Tulsa, Oklahoma, p. 74 (top); Christopher Schmidt-Nowara, p. 16; Photographs and Prints Division, Schomburg Center for Research in Black Culture, The New York Public Library, Astor, Lenox, and Tilden Foundations, New York, pp. 47, 103, 390, 401; James Smalls, pp. 70, 201, 258, 277, 291, 316; United States Army Military History Institute, Carlisle, Pennsylvania, p. 216; United States Holocaust Memorial Museum, Washington, D.C., pp. 298, 299; Walker Art Gallery, Liverpool, p. 74 (bottom); James F. Warren, pp. 84, 85; West India Committee, London, p. 114; Wilberforce House, Hull City Museums, Art Gallery and Archives, U.K., pp. 68 (top), 72

Index

⚜

Note: Page numbers appearing in boldface type indicate a major discussion; those appearing in italics refer to illustrations.